British Cinema

British Cinema

A Critical History

Amy Sargeant

 Publishing

For Big Bro. – thanks for watching.

First published in 2005 by the
BRITISH FILM INSTITUTE
21 Stephen Street, London W1T 1LN

The British Film Institute's purpose is to champion moving image culture in all its richness and diversity across the UK, for the benefit of as wide an audience as possible, and to create and encourage debate.

Cover design: Carroll Associates/Kenneth Carroll
Cover illustration: (front) *The Man Who Fell to Earth* (Nicolas Roeg, 1976, British Lion Film Corporation; (back) *The Wicker Man* (Robin Hardy, 1974, © British Lion Film Corporation)

Stills courtesy of BFI Stills, Posters and Designs

Set by Fakenham Photosetting Limited, Fakenham, Norfolk
Printed in the UK by Cromwell Press, Trowbridge, Wiltshire

British Library Cataloguing-in-Publication Data
A catalogue record for this book is available from the British Library

ISBN 1–84457–066–5 (pbk)
ISBN 1–84457–065–7 (hbk)

Contents

Acknowledgments

This book has been longer in the writing than was originally intended. I am enormously grateful to Professor Ted Braun and Sarah Braun, Professor Christine Gledhill, Professor Lynda Nead, Professors Richard Dyer and Richard Taylor, Dr Tag Gronberg and putative Professor Charlie Gere for their support and encouragement way beyond the course of duty. Alison Butler has taught me anything I know about teaching this stuff. Special thanks are due to to Susie Painter, Margaret Deriaz, Aliki Roussin-Croney, Maisoon Rehani, Tamerlan Dzhabrailov, Reimar Volker, PC 1479 (Trinity Road, Bristol) and the paramedics for getting me through the most ghastly bits. Dr Toby Haggith – and as per above and below – of the Imperial War Museum, Dave Berry of the Welsh Film and Television Archive, Elaine Burrows (NFTVA), Jenny Hammerton (British Pathé – I think you'll find more about knitting here than in any other book on British Cinema), Ine van Dooren (South East Film and Video Archive), Frances Carlyon (University of Bristol Theatre Collection) and the John Rylands Library in Manchester all supplied me with materials. Twentieth Century Flicks is due thanks not only for its extensive back catalogue but for the tolerance of its staff towards my daily grumbles – and yes, Ben, I will buy a DVD player now! At the BFI, thanks are due to Bryony Dixon, Kathleen Dickson, (I.Gotyer) Steve Tollervey, June Macmillan, Janet Moat (Special Materials) and the underappreciated library staff. Stephen Bottomore, Tony Fletcher (Cinema Museum), Pamela Hutchinson, Jeremy Jago, Dr Mike Allen, Dr Jim Ellis and Kate Myers (Academy Productions) all allowed themselves to be cajoled into reading draft chapters; Dr Lawrence Napper, Professor Nick Cull and Sigrid Schnögl undertook the onerous task of reading the whole manuscript (thanks also to Erich and Charlotte). Where I have ignored their sound advice, sheer exhaustion is my only excuse. I am especially grateful to Andrew Lockett, who commissioned the book and put up with an extraordinary amount of bolshiness on my part, and to Sophia Contento, who saw it through to completion.

Introduction

This book is intended to provide a survey of three centuries of film production, distribution and exhibition in Britain. It is also concerned with the larger institution of cinema. It outlines the reception of films by various audiences and various critics (in the trade press, the regular press and journals) and refers to spaces of film viewing (from the fairground to the fleapit, from the dream palace to the multiplex, from home-viewing to amateur and workplace societies, to video-hire, the internet and the gallery). The book mostly covers a selection of films that were actually made and released, although the vicissitudes of intervention from government and other funding and regulatory authorities, to aid and abet this process, are also brought into the discussion.

Like most histories, this one is organised chronologically but a number of notions are reiterated across its chapters: the relationship with Europe (the movement of people, ideas and the nature of the marketplace); the relationship with America; certain themes, character types and recurrent models of society (including lodging houses, schools, prisons, hospitals, ships, city streets, villages and the country house). Equally pervasive are certain representations of the social and physical landscape of Britain itself: the town versus the countryside; the country and the coast; the metropolis; the suburbs; the highlands and islands; old industry and new money; regional and class mobility. Consequently, I am as much concerned with a shared imaginative history as with the peculiarities of British life witnessed at any particular point in time. This broader perspective informs the selection of the case studies at the end of each chapter. In chapters devoted to the First and Second World Wars, I refer to later decades in order to demonstrate that subsequent portrayals have owed much to conventions established and affirmed in the duration: as with many historical dramas, these often resort to the use of archival fictional and non-fictional footage to establish their credentials. Sometimes I have taken the liberty of stretching a decade where national or film history seems to require it (for instance, the 1930s begins with the introduction of sound in the 1920s, the 1970s begin around 1968 and 1979 leaks into the 1980s).

British cinema is no longer (in the words of Alan Lovell) 'uncharted territory'. However, I have been especially concerned to integrate the early decades of British cinema into the whole, recognising the artificiality of 'bracketing-off' its first thirty years. Few film historians of British cinema (Rachael Low, Christine Gledhill, Charles Barr and Andrew Higson are notable exceptions) have considered the silent period worthy of equal attention to its more recent past. This is a great shame. In terms of the above generic interests and in the personnel involved (directors such as Anthony Asquith, Alfred Hitchcock, Maurice Elvey, Michael Powell, Walter Forde and Noël Coward;

producers such as Herbert Wilcox and Michael Balcon; designers such as Andrew Mazzei and Edward Carrick; actors such as Gordon Harker, Ivor Novello, Raymond Massey and Betty Balfour) the distinction seems entirely arbitrary and merits reappraisal. There is much, I contend, which aligns early cinema programming with current television scheduling and variable viewing patterns; film series and serials of the teens attracted audience loyalty in the manner of previous literary precursors and radio and television successors.

I have also sought to re-examine a number of preconceptions about British cinema. With Alan Bennett, I find myself in disagreement with a stance which identifies American policy and practice as a standard for imitation and emulation. Sometimes (as the collapse of British Lion, Goldcrest and Palace Pictures amply demonstrates) such a policy has proven misplaced. Meanwhile, British acting talent (from Victor McLaglen to Samantha Morton) has proven to be one of the native industry's most successful exports to Hollywood – an achievement that merits celebration. Collaborations with Europe (as in the 1920s, 1930s, 1960s and 1990s) appear a more useful development as a means of ensuring that non-American films secure comparable admission to British screens, both small and large.

British cinema has frequently been lambasted for its reliance on other areas of cultural practice for its source material, as if this were a weakness. Indeed, this complaint is frequently voiced in Rachael Low's multi-volume *History of the British Film*, which remains invaluable to any contemporary historian, critic or enthusiast. However, this tendency is far from unique to British cinema, as a national cinema, and European and American film-makers have also chosen British material for adaptation (from the 'classics' to J. M. Barrie's *Peter Pan*, from Patricia Highsmith's *Ripley* series to Nick Hornby's *High Fidelity* and Alan Ayckbourn farces). Broadway has embraced musical versions of *The Full Monty* (1997) and *Billy Elliot* (2000); *The Ladykillers* (1955), *Alfie* (1966) and *The Italian Job* (1969) have been flattered by imitation. I am disposed to regard the integration of British cinema in a larger cultural map as one of its strengths and an enormously fruitful area for enquiry. The hybridity and eclecticism of British cinema should be deemed a virtue rather than a vice. Nor should this relationship be regarded as entirely predatory: while cinema has drawn from novels and plays and the visual arts, these in turn have taken cinema as a source for imagery and inspiration (for instance, Forkbeard's *Shooting Shakespeare*, Terry Johnson's staging of *Cleo, Camping, Emmanuelle and Dick*, stage versions of *The Third Man* and *Billy Elliot* and Matthew Bourne's choreography of *Play Without Words*). Both Evelyn Waugh and Edgar Wallace produced novels in which aspects of the British industry feature; Wallace, Arnold Bennett, Alan Bennett, J. B. Priestley, Graham Greene and Ian McEwan have written for page and screen; Coward, Terence Rattigan, Shelagh Delaney, John Osborne, Harold Pinter and David Hare have written for stage and screen; numerous British actors, directors and technicians have moved between stage, television and film, and singers and models have turned actors. In other words, I am keen to stress exchange rather than derivation. Contemporary film and television producers (and gallery installation artists) even assume a familiarity with Britain's cinematic heritage in their quotation from older texts and established genres (I am thinking of various Aardman Animation productions, Victoria Wood's Bond spoof enacted in a London Eye capsule, French and Saunders' evocation of costume dramas set in 'olden days', the *Trainspotting* [1995] Bond girls debate and Steve Coogan's mountain bike chase through Manchester in *The Parole Officer* [2001], mimicking *The Italian Job*).

There is also another form of critical segregation which I have attempted to avoid. Subjects, iconography and the careers of personnel often move between different types of film appealing to different audience taste and are shared between 'high-brow' (or art house) and 'low-brow' (or popular) production, let alone the much (and repeatedly) maligned 'middle-brow'. Michael Gough can be seen in 1950s Hammer Horror (Arthur Crabtree's *Secrets of the Black Museum*), in Ealing's *The Man in the White Suit* (1957) and in Joseph Losey's eminently respectable (and respectful) version of *The Go-Between* (1970); Tim Curry in *The Rocky Horror Show* (1975) and *The Ploughman's Lunch* (1983); Hattie Jacques in repertory in the *Carry On*s and alongside Lindsay Anderson in *The Pleasure Garden* (1952). Martin Campbell's directorial career can be traced from soft porn (*Eskimo Nell* [1974]) to a musical (*Three for All* [1974]) to television (*Edge of Darkness* [1986]) to Bond (*Goldeneye* [1995]). The great Billie Whitelaw, muse to Samuel Beckett, filmed for television in *Not I* (1977) and *Happy Days* (1979), appears in gritty film noir (*Hell is a City* [1960]) and quality adaptation (*An Unsuitable Job for a Woman* [1981]). Often I question the critical usefulness of the inherited categories and vocabulary. The once rigid 'art-house' distinction loses much of its status when the omniverous DVD or video renter has freer access to all sorts of different films.

What this book is not is a history of box-office hits. In the selection of films recommended and discussed I have been led pretty much by personal preference. However, there are films covered here which, although a popular success when first released, seem to have been critically neglected since (such as *Sunshine Susie* [1931]). There are often many other films that could serve as examples of the various themes used to organise the chapters: this, in itself, seems to prove their validity. Some very well-known films (such as *The Rat* series, *Genevieve* [1953], *Victim* and *Chariots of Fire* [1981]) have been largely by-passed because they have been dealt with adequately elsewhere. Nor am I overly concerned with defining the particularity of British cinema as a product distinct from that of other nations. I am more concerned here with interpreting and resuscitating the films themselves than with reiterating the sometimes ossifying academic debates which have accrued around them. I want to convey a sense of why – or, sometimes, why not - British audiences valued and enjoyed them (what they looked like, sounded like and felt like), of the circumstances in which they were experienced and why they continue to be worth watching now.

Chapter 1 | Turn of the Century and Tens

The job of the film maker, is to entertain as many people as possible. The questions of raising tastes and education are there too – but they are asides. Entertainment counts and it is the most difficult thing of all. You can affect an audience three ways – you can make them laugh, make them cry, and make them sit forward in their seats with excitement. You should never *degrade* them . . . We are in the show business now, and we come from the fairground and the fairground barker. The barkers may have worn checked coats and crude colours, while we are more elegant. But never forget, we are the same. It is show business – and we should make a good show.

Alexander Korda[1]

The willingness of an international film-maker and entrepreneur of the next generation, such as Korda (see Chapter 5), to embrace cinema's fairground heritage is both selective and provocative. Certainly, many of his contemporaries (producers, distributors, exhibitors, audiences and commentators) might have preferred to trace other lines of descent – for instance, from music halls, lecture halls and domestic entertainments. Certainly, elements of both 'realism' and 'tinsel' were present in early film shows, often sitting alongside one another in a single programme, in the manner which continues in much television scheduling today.[2] But, at the outset, Michael Balcon's infamous distinction (see Chapter 7) was less significant than the phenomenon of film itself. While frequently inheriting subject matter and techniques from other, older, areas of cultural practice, the very novelty of film was its first and principal attraction for audiences. As with current commercial television broadcasting, items could be sponsored by manufacturers (as in the 1906 G. H. Cricks and J. H. Martins film, *A Visit to Peak Freans Biscuit Works*) and adverts were made on film (following the example of lantern slides) for Bird's Custard, Dewar's Whisky, Ogden's Cigarettes, Lever Brothers' Sunlight Soap and Nestlé; Lever Brothers also provided lecturers and operators for charity screenings and devised various promotional tie-ins.[3] Machines which doubled as cameras and projectors (such as Birt Acres' Birtac – patented in 1898) encouraged amateur use of the new medium, these often produced in a variety of casings to suit different budgets and settings.[4] As a novelty, it was also often regarded with some scepticism by competitors and potential investors, and producers and exhibitors sought to sustain the novelty (with the introduction of new subjects and longer formats) beyond its programming as a single item in a mixed bill. As with current hybrid

Superimposition in Clarendon's *The Tempest* (Percy Stow, 1908)

'infotainment', drama-documentary and 'docusoap', it can prove difficult to categorise the products of Britain's film pioneers. Sometimes these pioneers were more interested in the apparatus than they were in the material projected, this dominating the bill as the principal attraction.

Informing: *The Tatler* and *Tit Bits*

The first public demonstration of film projection in Britain is usually dated to the showing of the French Lumière cinematograph at Regent Street Polytechnic in February 1896. But on the same day, R. W. Paul (a maker of scientific instruments) exhibited his 'Theatrograph' at Finsbury Technical College. John Barnes suggests that Paul constructed his machine following illustrations of the Edison Kinetoscope, shown at the 1895 India Exhibition at Earls Court and previously illustrated in American magazines with a wide distribution in Britain. Paul, in collaboration with the American Birt Acres, then set about manufacturing a camera in order to produce films to use in the projector; Paul also sold equipment to France. Some early British film-makers (a 'chance agglomeration', says Rachael Low, 'of adventurers, crusaders and craftsmen'[5]), such as the Brighton pioneers, James Williamson and George Albert Smith, and William Friese Greene, came to film from photography. Cecil Hepworth, the son of a photographer (who also wrote about photography), came to film from magic lantern exhibition and lecturing, working for the Warwick Trading Company (an American subsidiary) before setting up his own company;[6] the Yorkshire firm, Bamforth, produced slides, then films (notably the *Winky* series of the teens) and postcards.

Certain subjects of early single-reel, single-shot films (such as Acres' *Sea at Dover* [1895], *Rough Sea* [1900], Paul's *Breaking Waves* [1900] and Biograph's blue-tinted 1900 *Feeding the Seagulls*, showing birds swooping in the wake of a ship's stern) feature movement within the frame and movement towards or away from the camera as their focus of interest. Others, such as the 1900 Biograph film of Clifton Suspension Bridge and Avon Gorge, take a well-known fixed landmark and employ a camera pan as an additional feature. But even the earliest programmes included newsworthy items, where the subject matter attracted attention. Sporting events contributed topical variety and proved enduringly popular. Regular events in the calendar (such as Henley Regatta, the Boat Race, horse racing, fencing, golf, football matches, cricket matches – including films of W. G. Grace and Ranjitsinhji) were inserted alongside such *Tit Bits* novelties as boxing cats and kangaroos: such material could be substituted by travelling exhibitors according to particular times and places. People came to see themselves (in the numerous films of sea fronts, factory gates, city streets and spectator sports) and to see celebrities. The life of the former prime minister, William Gladstone, was recorded in *Gladstone Sketches* and his demise was memorialised in Smith's film of his funeral.

The final years of Queen Victoria's reign, notes Lytton Strachey, 'were years of apotheosis. In the dazzled imagination of her subjects Victoria soared aloft towards the regions of divinity through a nimbus of purest glory.'[7] While the Prince of Wales' horse, Persimmon, was filmed by Paul winning the blue riband at the 1896 Derby, and the film of the 1898 Derby was shown at Buckingham Palace within a few hours of its being made, Princess Maud's wedding was photographed by

Acres in a series of episodes from 'The Departure of the Bride from Marlborough House' to her 'Arrival after the Wedding' and 'Going Away'. The stage paper, *The Era*, reports that these scenes were shown to large audiences, prompting loud cheers.[8] A Royal Command Performance was given at Marlborough House and Acres duly marketed the film on condition that his projection equipment was included in the purchase of the print. Royal Command Performances of the 70mm Biograph were given for the Prince of Wales at St James's Palace and Sandringham. In 1900, the Queen was filmed on her visit to Dublin; in 1897, the Prince of Wales was filmed yachting in Nice, reviewing Yeomanry at Cheltenham and the Fire Brigade at Windsor.

In 1896, the Saxe-Coburg-Gothas allowed us into their beautiful home at Balmoral, J. and F. Downey (a Southshields subsidiary of a London firm accustomed to photographing the Queen) taking shots of carriages, children and various dogs. The event was amply illustrated and covered by the *Lady's Pictorial*: 'Her Majesty was delighted with the animated photographs . . . After her Majesty's departure, some of the Royal children came behind the screen and displayed much curiosity as to the working of the views . . .'.[9] Again, a private screening was arranged at Windsor before (with Royal endorsement) the film was distributed to the general public, together with a series of slides to be projected during the change-over of reels. Foreign royalty (Dutch, Russian, Danish) and the Pope also made early appearances, with the crowning of Queen Wilhelmina in Amsterdam being filmed and projected within forty-eight hours in London. In 1897, films of the pageantry marking the Queen's Diamond Jubilee were greeted enthusiastically. *The Optical and Magic Lantern Journal* proclaimed that, 'even in the smallest out-of-the-way villages it would be a difficult matter to find many persons who have not seen this interesting event on the screen'.[10] In Bradford, *The Daily Argus* organised a screening at midnight (to an audience of thousands) of the film made in London by R. J. Appleton and Co. earlier in the day. At the funeral of Queen Victoria in 1901, the cameras again jostled for prime position along the route of the cortège and Hepworth recalls that he was obliged to print copies of his film 'night and day' to fulfil public demand.[11] One film, fixing its frame at a bend in the road, captures the procession in the background moving left to right, snaking round to appear again in the foreground moving right to left, recording successive detachments of uniformed riders, groomed and plumed horses, carriages and gun carriages.

Such exhibitions of regal and military pomp and ceremony were spectacularly enhanced by the introduction of colour. *The Bioscope* in 1908 reports the Kinemacolor process (invented and demonstrated by Smith and the American Charles Urban), while *Kine Weekly* remembers previous experiments with coloured discs performed by Friese Greene. Smith chose a march-past of the Lancers as a subject which would display his system to best effect (scarlet uniforms similarly employed in Technicolor and Technirama for *Zulu* [Cy Endfield, 1964]).[12] But there were also concerns that the film camera might present these elevated persons in an inappropriate manner: Acres inadvertently captured the Prince scratching his head at Cardiff's Exhibition of Industry and Arts in 1896 and, in 1908, *The Bioscope* indicates 'the regulation of access' of cameras to Sandringham: 'His Majesty holds no objection to being filmed at public ceremonies but is very strict where his own private movements are concerned.'[13] 'Informal' films of the Royals, such as *The Royal Family* at *Afternoon Tea in the Garden of Clarence House* (1897), were, as Stephen Bottomore suggests, staged as a photo-opportunity;[14] the 1912–13 tour of industrial Britain and First World War films showing encounters with the King's troops were conceived as propaganda (see Chapter 3).

The Delhi Durbars of 1903 and 1911 were intended to affirm India's place as 'the most splendid appanage of the Imperial Crown' and to acclaim the King of Britain as Emperor. The Dowager Empress of Russia found the Kinemacolor film of the second event 'wonderfully interesting and very beautiful [giving] one the impression of having seen it all in reality'; in some theatres it ran for more than a year after the event.[15] The Viceroy, Lord Curzon, staged the 1903 Durbar with consummate attention to detail and little regard to economy: some commentators accused him of extravagance and a craze for display.[16] *The Tatler*, in December 1902, provided a photo-spread showing the Duke of Connaught, Lord Kitchener (Commander-in-Chief of the Indian Army) and their hosts, the Viceroy and Vicereine with pictures of the locations of the ceremony's principal events; in January 1903 it pictured the 11 foot-high elephant on which the Duke rode in the Durbar and the howdah (made of pure gold and silver) lent by the Maharajar of Benares. Paul's film of the Durbar records mounted and foot regiments of the Indian Army as they process past the dais, 209 smaller elephants and the Durbar's honoured guests (the ruling Indian princes

Mitchell and Kenyon record Manchester's Whitsuntide Catholic Procession (27 May 1904)

with their attendants). The event also included sports, music and competitions alongside the ceremonials.[17] The journal *Black and White*, in January 1903, shows a society lady in the stalls at London's Hippodrome watching the film through opera glasses, presumably attempting to identify the indistinct figures in the crowd.

More humdrum and regional pageantry was recorded in topical films of actual events in Hackney (the horse and cart parade), Coventry, Carisbrooke, St Albans, Oxford, Romsey and Bury St Edmunds; often one can see someone directing the action in front of the camera. In similar mode, Hepworth's 1903 film of Lewis Carroll's 1865 *Alice in Wonderland* (closely following Tenniel's illustrations for the original publication – and offered for sale as separate scenes and in its entirety) includes the Queen and her playing-card entourage (played by children) processing past the camera, with his wife as the white rabbit and his cutting-room assistant, Mabel Clark, as Alice.[18] Mitchell and Kenyon filmed the Manchester Catholics Whitsuntide Procession (recreated at a smaller scale for the Salford of David Lean's 1954 *Hobson's Choice*) and May Day celebrations and the annual well-dressings in Derbyshire. Films of troops departing for and arriving from service overseas ('History on Tap') provided further opportunities for local audiences to recognise themselves and their loved ones on screen (see Chapter 3). Conversely, in Rudyard Kipling's 1904 short story 'Mrs Bathurst' a group of cockney tars holed-up in South Africa discuss the fate of Vickery, who went AWOL in demented pursuit of a touring circus which showed films of 'Home and Friends' between the performing animals:

> London Bridge with the omnibuses – a troopship goin' to the war – marines on parade at Portsmouth an' the Plymouth Express arrivin' at Paddin'ton . . . it was most interestin'. I'd never seen it before. You 'eard a little dynamo like buzzin', but the pictures were the real thing – alive an' movin' . . . We saw the platform empty an' the porters standin' by. Then the engine come in, head on, an' the women in the front row jumped: she headed so straight.[19]

Vickery believed he saw the young Auckland widow, Mrs Bathurst, among the passengers alighting from the train and that she had arrived in London to search for him. There was also evidence of criminals imitating scenarios enacted in films and of others being apprehended as a consequence of being caught on camera.[20] Occasionally, the camera is an unwelcome intrusion; more often its subjects prove willing and eager to have themselves photographed and acknowledge its presence. Films of military manoeuvres were sometimes shot as actuality (as in Joseph Rosenthal's Boer War footage for Warwick and by Frederic Villiers – a newspaper photographer for the *Graphic*, the *Standard* and *Black and White* – and, reputedly, by others in the Sudan in 1898).[21] Army and navy exercises and drilling were a recurrent subject. *The Bioscope* in 1909 advertises an Empire Picture showing the work of the First Aid Nursing Yeomanry Corps, with 'the ladies under War Conditions'. Sometimes (as Stephen Bottomore and Simon Popple have observed) war films were shamelessly fabricated to satisfy an audience's appetite for stories of current interest, although the Warwick Trading Company maintained that it distributed nothing but the genuine article and warned that the showing of fakes would harm the reputation of an exhibitor.[22] Williamson's 1901 *Attack on a Chinese Mission* represents the Boxer uprising in China by means of a dramatic rescue narrative. But, as Kevin Brownlow maintains, such staged war films should not be dismissed as merely duplicitous.[23]

Early factual films match the content of newspapers and periodicals, from the mass circulation *Tit Bits* to the more exclusive *Tatler*. True stories proved as popular with viewers as with readers. The first specialised news cinema, the Daily Bioscope, opened opposite Liverpool Street station in London in 1906 (a precursor of the news cinema in Charing Cross Road in which the fugitive hides in *They Drive By Night* [1938] – see Chapter 7) while newsreels were launched with The Topical Budget in 1911 (see Chapter 4).

Educating: Travellers and Tourists

The turn of the century's World Fairs provided a site for the demonstration of apparatus and material for film-makers. In Warwick Trading Company's 1900 film of the Paris Exhibition (also documented by Hepworth), the camera, attached to the side of a boat, pans along a line of exotic national pavilions constructed on pontoons and on the river bank. 'Virtual' travel was also offered by Hales Tours (introduced to London in 1906) where, from mock railway carriages running on tracks, patrons could watch phantom ride films (photographed by a camera mounted on the front of a train) to the accompaniment of suitable sound effects. Smith, a fixture in the 1900 schedule at the Brighton Aquarium, presented slide shows of an 'Astronomical Entertainment' (*The Glories of the Heavens, or a Tour through Space*) and (inspired by Jules Verne) *Twenty Thousand Leagues Under the Sea*, concluding the bill with a selection of his own short films. H. G. Wells' 1895 *The Time Machine*, set in the year 802,701 (in which the protagonist, attempting to convince the assembled journalist, editor, psychologist and medical man of the veracity of his claim to have travelled through time, bemoans, 'If only I had thought of a Kodak!'),[24] was the inspiration for an unrealised project of R. W. Paul, 'in which animated photographs formed an essential part':

> In a room capable of accommodating some 100 people, he would arrange seats to which a slight motion could be given. He would plunge the apartment into Cimmerian darkness, and introduce a wailing wind. Although the audience actually moved but a few inches, the sensation would be of travelling through space. From time to time the journey would be combined with panoramic effects. Fantastic scenes of future ages would first be shown. Then the audience would set forth upon its homeward journey. The conductor would regretfully intimate that he had over-shot the mark, and travelled into the past – cue for another series of pictures. Mr Paul had for a long time been at work on this scheme . . .[25]

Paul's 1901 *The Countryman and the Cinematograph* refers to apocryphal accounts of earlier audiences ducking or fleeing when faced with films of oncoming trains, footage of a dancer, the train and then the country film explainer himself (spooning with a milkmaid) superimposed in the frame.

Paul produced *The Arrival of the Paris Express at Calais* (1896), in imitation of Lumière's famous *The Arrival of a Train at Ciotat* (1895). Train films were regularly inserted into a mixed programme, increasingly with the camera positioned at the side of the train to maximise a panoramic, sweeping view. Many films, locally made, captured views of tramways and streets familiar to their audiences (for instance, Mitchell and Kenyon's films of Sheffield).[26] Some of the tourist films captured the views once often used, as photographs, to decorate the interiors of railway carriages: picturesque views of Bournemouth (filmed in 1911), the Scottish Highlands (1908), the Cornish Riviera (1904). Mitchell and Kenyon photographed holidaymakers in Blackpool, subsequently projecting the films to their subjects. Cricks and Sharp combined natural history with spectacular views in their 1907 film of collectors climbing for birds' eggs at Flamborough Head. *A Holiday Trip to the Clyde Coast of Scotland* (1909), made to promote the London and North Western Railway, includes scenes at Glasgow station, the interior of a dining carriage, rural scenery and a shipyard, 'The Birthplace of Navies'. More adventurous would-be travellers were delighted by scenes of *The Great Victoria Falls* (1907), *The Alhambra, Gibraltar* (1911), *Life in Jaffa* (1905), *Native Life in Borneo* (1909), *Kashmir* (1903) and *Shanghai* (1901). *Moonlight Trip on the Nile* (1909), directed by Scott-Brown for Hepworth, used colour staining and toning (red for firelight, blue for night) to enhance its exotic appeal.

Sometimes, travelogue was combined with an informative record of a particular manufacturing or agricultural process – for instance, whaling or date-farming. These leavened a heavy diet of films recording domestic agriculture, fishing and industry, which, according to *The Bioscope* in 1909, failed to entertain a considerable percentage of the audience (suggesting that poor explanation of the material was partly to blame), although *Kine Weekly* reports in 1907 that the Bryant and Mays girls 'made strenuous efforts to locate themselves and their acquaintances' in a film of their factory. Hepworth's 1903–4 *A Day with the Hop Pickers* portrayed 'East-end coster women, plain of face but sharp of wit', with their 'dishevelled children', in the annual exodus to Kent (see Chapter 2).[27] *A Visit to the Sunlight Soap Works* (continuing Lever Brothers' patronage of film) was advertised in 1907, alongside Hepworth's film of chain-making at Sykes and Son, Cradley Heath (showing iron bars, beating, welding etc.), Gaumont's *From Forest to Fireside* (illustrating the production of *Lloyd's News* from the felling of timber in Norway to the making of paper from pulp to the setting of print etc.) and Walturdaw's *Making of a Modern Newspaper*. In 1905, LNWR sponsored (and exhibited at White City) *The Building of a British Railway*. *A Day in the Life of a Coalminer*, produced in 1910 by the Kineto Company (specialists in education and actuality films), punctuates its narrative with titles: 'The Pit Head'; 'The Coal Shaft'; 'Pay Time'; 'Light after Darkness'; 'The Belles of the Black Diamond Field' (indicating the women who push trucks, load wooden props and sort, screen and rake the coal). Part of the process (the men's work at the coalface) is staged in daylight. The film opens with a coalminer kissing his wife and children goodbye in the morning and finishes, 'Light after Darkness', with a child running from the same cottage to greet him; meanwhile, at 'A Cosy Fireside' a maid stokes a fireplace for a middle-class family enjoying the fruits of the miners' labour. *A Visit to Peak Freans Biscuit Works* similarly uses titles to announce

Biscuit making at Peak Freans (Cricks and Martin, 1906)

successive episodes in the manufacturing process, progressing from opening general views to concentrate on specific activities ('Rolling out the Dough'; 'Making Brighton Biscuits'; packing, weighing, labelling and soldering tins for export). The camera pans left to right, following the conveyor belt which feeds the biscuits into the ovens. An untoward incident ('A False Alarm of Fire') provides a dramatic interlude in the morning routine (an engine on a cart is trundled out for practice) before the workhands leave for dinner (walking towards camera, in the manner of earlier factory gate films) and the film ends with Peak Freans vans departing the factory to deliver the goods. The sponsorship of such 'actuality' films may be compared, as Rachael Low has observed, with many notable 'documentary' films of the 1930s (see Chapter 5), and of the 1950s.[28]

While film had early established itself in public lecture halls, institutes and clubs, there were also calls in the trade press for its introduction as an educational aid in schools. It would be, said a contributor to *The Bioscope* in 1908, 'the newspaper and book of tomorrow'. The journal vaunted the potential of film to portray 'the natural history, engineering, architectural, commercial and artistic achievements of the rest of the world'.[29] In 1907, an exhibition of Colonial pictures (intended for use in schools) was held at the Royal Agricultural Halls. At Warwick Trading Company, the enterprising Charles Urban had produced a popular science series since 1903. *The Unseen World*

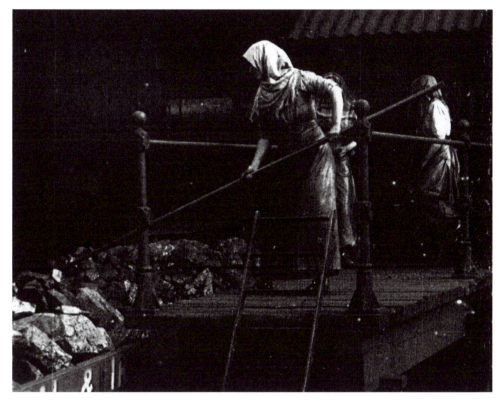

'The Belles of Black Diamond Field' in *A Day in the Life of a Coalminer* (Kineto, 1910)

used microscopic photography (previously employed in lantern slides) and time-lapse filming, in the manner of BBC TV's equally celebrated 1995 *The Life of Plants*. Frederick Talbot, in 1912, refers to films of microbes, flowers, insects and polyps. The exhibition of X-rays (Röntgen rays) had proved a brief but popular success in 1896, commented upon by Warwick Trading Company's 1897 *The X-Ray Fiend*, in which

> A pair of lovers on a seat are approached by a professor with X-Ray apparatus. *He reveals their bones*, and, having satisfied his scientific curiosity, retreats as quietly as he came, leaving the lovers to continue their spooning quite unconscious of the grotesque figures they have cut.[30]

Fascination with new-fangled science is also treated as a humorous subject in Clarendon Film Company's *A Lesson in Electricity* (1909) in which naughty boys (ubiquitous comic protagonists in the tens and teens) watch the demonstration of the hatching of an egg and the peeling of an orange; they then decide that it would be a jolly good jape to seize the apparatus and perform their own 'experiment', electrifying a pavement and causing the pedestrians to jump about disconcertingly. Finally, the students receive their comeuppance (as in *Vice Versa* [1910]): the electric current is passed through them, causing them to grimace most horribly. Gaumont's 1907 *The Magnetic Man* ('much applauded at London's Hippodrome') shows a coat of mail charged with electricity by mischievous workmen, 'everything metal which he approaches flies to him including a breakfast tray'. Hepworth provided a variant on the theme of *That Fatal Sneeze* (1907) with *The Professor's Anti-Gravitation Fluid* (1908), where the scientist himself, rather than the boys who have misappropriated his invention, is victimised by an angry mob.

Both Cecil Hepworth (in Algiers) and Nevil Maskelyne (in North Carolina) had filmed the solar eclipse of 1900, the latter film screened at the Egyptian Halls in Piccadilly; previous eclipses had been photographed. Sir George Newnes' 1898 Antarctic Expedition was also equipped with a Kinematograph camera. Some educational subjects were designed to exploit the capacity of the new medium to record time and motion, while in others film replaced still photography. Some films commented on new technology as a source of narrative amusement.

Entertaining: Trick Flicks, Cops and Robbers; Poachers and Gamekeepers; Estranged Lovers and Dead Babies

Generally, informative and educational films were interspersed in programmes constructed to make the audience 'laugh, cry and lean forward with excitement'. Films (shown at fairgrounds and else-where) employed camera tricks and devices similar to those applied by Urban to scientific subjects. Smith and Hepworth both made reversal films. Hepworth's 1900 single frame *Bathers* (apparently in imitation of a Georges Méliès precedent) shows men stripping down poolside, diving into water and then emerging from the water, feet first, ascending in a graceful arc back to the shore: 'their clothes are seen to be flying up into their hands, one by one, producing an effect which is weird and extremely comic'. Smith's *The House that Jack Built* (1900) shows a young girl building a house from toy bricks which is then demolished by her spiteful brother. A caption (possibly the first in British cinema) is interjected to announce the film's reversal, showing the blocks re-assembling them-selves. In *Vice Versa* (directed by Dave Aylott for Cricks and Martin) a conjuror entertains a house party, a naughty boy in an Eton collar then stealing his wand and effecting a number of performed reversals (achieved by stop-motion): a shoe-shine boy swaps with a businessman; a policeman and a ruffian change places in a chase; a 'masher' and a maid scrubbing a doorstep exchange roles and passing suffragettes are obliged to do the work of men, digging a hole in the ground. In Paul's *The Human Flies* (1903) the frame itself is reversed, the 'trick' again prompted by a conjuror, tossing his hat then himself into the air; people, recorded in slow motion, appear to float with parasols, som-ersault and leap from the 'ceiling', with the backing flat of the drawing room re-set upside-down.

James Williamson's famous 1901 *The Big Swallow* uses a tripartite structure, in which the camera itself is cast in the action: a man approaches and opens his mouth until it fills the frame; a camera and its operator are submerged in darkness; the man retreats from the camera, walking backwards, chewing and swallowing. Williamson's *Grandma's Reading Glass* and *As Seen Through the Telescope* (both 1900) used comic-strip close-ups (cued by a magnifying glass and a telescope and vignetted accordingly) as cut-ins between wider shots, to indicate the object of interest to a character in the film. Actual exterior footage of trains (as in the travelogue films) was sometimes cut either side of interior 'made-up' scenes (framing an action performed in a single shot with a 'before' and an 'after'), separated by black leader to intimate to the viewer the train passing into a tunnel: numerous versions of *The Kiss in the Tunnel* scenario were produced in this manner (for instance, by Smith and by Bamforth in 1899).[31] *Mary Jane's Mishap* (G. A. Smith, 1902/3), with Mrs Smith as the importunate maid, uses a vertical wipe between her ascent up the roof through the chimney and the scene of her final resting place: 'Here lies Mary Jane who lighted the fire with paraffin – rest in pieces', her ghost then rising from the grave and returning.

Stop-motion photography was used to convey sudden, 'miraculous' costume changes and to allow the substitution of actors and/or dummies in motor car accidents (as detailed in Talbot's *Motion Pictures* – see Chapter 2). Williamson's 1905 *An Interesting Story* (providing an opportunity for much expressive face pulling) presents a man so engrossed in his reading that he falls over a woman scrubbing a step, gets caught in a skipping rope, bumps into a donkey cart and is then flattened by a steam roller: two cyclists re-inflate him with their bicycle pumps before he retreats into the distance, still thoroughly absorbed in his book. In Hepworth's 1900 *The Explosion of a Motor Car*, an overloaded car self-combusts and blows its occupants into the sky; a passing police-man picks up the bodies, clothes and limbs which fall to the ground. In his 1902 *How to Stop a Motor Car*, the policeman himself (a novel twist) is dismembered, while in his *How it Feels to be Run Over* (1900) a car approaches and passes the camera, hotly pursued by another which runs over the camera: 'Oh!! Mother will be pleased' is flashed onto the screen word by word, to indi-cate the hapless victim of the assault 'seeing stars' and the heavens. *The '?' Motorist* (directed by W. R. Booth for Paul, 1906) employs superimpositions, stop-motion and animation to convey the propulsion of a car (chased by policemen) to Saturn, via the Moon, and its mutation into a horse and trap, before coming to a halt; Paul repeats the gag in *The Lady Luna(tics) Hat* (1908). Interti-tles can serve as an item of interest in their own right as well as contributing towards narrative exposition: Mitchell and Kenyon produced animated titles (for non-fiction films and for 'made-up' subjects, such as their 1903 *Diving Lucy*), the letters jumbled then sorted in the manner of *Tit Bits* anagrams and acrostic puzzles.

Williamson (like Hepworth, an experienced lecturer and lanternist) applied a number of magic lantern techniques to film. Their derivation (and other precursors of cinema, such as shadow pup-pets, dioramas, silhouettes, thaumatropes and various optical 'toys') are amply and pertinently demonstrated in *Comrades* (1986 – see Chapter 11), directed by the pre-eminent pre-cinema enthusiast and collector, Bill Douglas; a lanternist (as in *Warning Shadows* – see Chapter 4) serves as narrator.[32] *Are You There?* (Williamson, 1901) uses a curtain to split the screen between paral-lel action in two distinct places, a man on the left of frame speaking on the telephone to a woman on the right; the call is intercepted by an older man (perhaps the woman's husband, perhaps her father) while the first (perhaps her lover) unwittingly continues his conversation with nonchalant ease – and is duly thrashed for his impertinence. Both *Santa Claus* (1898) and *The Little Matchseller* (1902 – from the Hans Christian Andersen original) employed superimpositions to connotate dreams and visions. Hepworth's *Alice in Wonderland* (directed by Percy Stow) introduces the Cheshire Cat as a superimposed image in a hedge and Alice is superimposed in miniature (as she drinks a magic potion); stop-motion allows a baby to turn, instantaneously, into a piglet. Clarendon used multiple exposure to effect a flashback to the wreck (with which the original play opens) in its 1908 abridged and episodic version of Shakespeare's *The Tempest* (Stow again combining sets and location filming), with stop-motion employed to transform Ariel into a monkey (to confuse Caliban) and disappearing and reappearing (to confuse Ferdinand). This is a more imaginative and persuasive staging of the Bard than Mutoscope and Biograph's static 1899 *King John*, featuring Herbert Beerbohm Tree (but then, as James Agate waspishly noted, 'as a tragic actor Tree was a farce'): the film's four scenes were intended to promote Tree's concurrent stage production.[33] In *Rescued in Mid Air* (1906) Stow, again for Clarendon, returns to the perennial theme of a roadway collision, with a Mary Poppins-style figure, blown skywards and supported by an umbrella, eventually retrieved from a lamppost by a scientist and his wonderful flying machine. However, in spite of cinema's debt to the lantern, in its subjects and its techniques, Deac Rossell and Richard Crangle have wisely urged caution against histories that posit the lantern as merely a putative (and implicitly inferior) form of cinema, soon to be superseded by cinema proper: certainly, film and the lantern coexisted in exhibition in a number of settings and in the design of apparatus for some time to come.[34]

Frank Gray has commented on the recurrence of Fire Brigade rescue narratives in slide series and films: the 1890 series, *Bob the Fireman, or, Life in the Brigade* (consisting of twelve slides and a 1,600-word commentary), proved especially popular.[35] For instance, in Williamson's *Fire!* (1901), the action cuts briskly from a house with smoke billowing, to Hove Fire Station (with the engines and men rushing left to right), then continues with the horses galloping left to right across frame up the road, to a man in the burning building – where a fireman breaks through the window and hoses down the flames, to an exterior shot of the man being safely lifted out and carried down a ladder. Hepworth suggests that he produced numerous local permutations, 'all smoke and sparks and perspiring horses', to satisfy his clients and their audiences.[36] But the chase (and the rescue or apprehension) was a theme which traversed non-fiction and fiction, enhancing the momentum of dramatic, comic and pathetic subjects. Here, again, film action finds its precedents in a range of sources. *The Miller and the Sweep* (Smith, 1898) combines a circus or pantomime slapstick gag (revisited by Will Hay in the 1930s – see Chapter 5) – an argument between the two results in the one getting floury and the other getting sooty – with a chase joyfully enacted by men, women and children pursuing the protagonists out of the frame. The scenario of Gaumont's 1906 *The Story of a Brown Hat* or *The Missing Legacy* (directed by Alf Collins) is wittily elaborated in the 1930s, in *The Lucky Number* (Anthony Asquith, 1933) and *The Twelve Chairs* (see Chapter 5). *It's Not My Parcel* (Gaumont, 1906) and *Pimple and the Snake* (1912 – see Chapter 2) indicate, by parody, that the particular object of the chase is immaterial to the interest of the film's generic subject – in the latter a woman's feather boa is mistakenly identified and is pursued by an accumulating group of people across successive shots. Policemen (and gamekeepers) chasing robbers (and poachers) and feather boas are as often represented as the butt of humour as the upholders of decent law and order. In *That Fatal Sneeze*, directed by Lewis Fitzhamon, a boy prankster sprinkles powder on a man's bed. The man gets up, sneezing, causing pictures and shelves to fall from the walls and furniture to overturn. He leaves the house, followed by the boy, past a hardware store (where baskets are dislodged from their moorings), past Hepworth's 'Hepwix' shop front (incidental branding and advertisement!), the man's sneezes bringing down a lamppost. A sailor, the hardware merchant and a policeman join the chase, then a woman whose hat and wig are blown off (most unseemly). The man escapes his pursuers up a ladder (and out of frame) only to have it collapse beneath him. Such is the violence of his sneezing that the camera itself reels from side to side. There is a final convulsion and, in stop-motion, the man disappears in a puff of smoke.

Jack Shepherd (the notorious criminal, eventually hanged at Tyburn, celebrated in the 1903 *Tit Bits* series 'Romances of Newgate Prison') was adopted as the popular hero for Paul's 1900 film, *The Hair-Breadth Escape of Jack Shepherd.* Hepworth, followed in 1913 by British and Colonial, celebrated the career of Dick Turpin and his noble steed, Black Bess, with Samuelson creating a fictional highwayman for its *Deadwood Dick* series; a girl poses as a highwayman (see Chapter 7) in Hepworth's 1910 period romance, *In the Good Old Days*, directed by Fitzhamon, while male convicts sometimes cross-dress as women, like Kenneth Grahame's Mr Toad, to effect an escape (as in *The Convict's Escape* [1903]). William Haggar's 1905 *Charles Peace* (a subject also filmed by Frank Mottershaw for Sheffield Photo Company – 'the Sensational Leap from the Train *taken on the actual spot*') similarly returns to a historic figure (immortalised in wax at Madame Tussaud's and visited by Lupin Pooter in the Grossmiths' 1892 *The Diary of a Nobody* – see also *Pimple in 'The Whip'* [1917], Chapter 2), a professional criminal imprisoned in 1879.[37] Haggar, a travelling showman in Wales, performed in and produced films with his family, for exhibition at fairs. Haggar stages Peace's career in a series of tableaux, from his first burglary, to his murder of his lover's husband, to a dramatic rooftop chase, to another burglary, to his disguise as a parson (foiling the police), to his eventual capture, trial, escape, recapture (following a struggle in a railway carriage), identification by a witness and execution: the fairground public's continuing appetite for such ghoulish entertainment is witnessed in the fairground of Anthony Asquith's *The Lucky Number* and by wide-eyed and open-mouthed children in Lindsay Anderson's 1953 film of Margate Amusement Park, *O Dreamland* (see Chapter 8). Clarendon invokes literary precedent in *The Downfall of the Burglar's Trust*, advertised in *Kine Weekly* in 1908 as 'a hot chase ending in a cold plunge, concluding with the capture of Bill Sikes . . . a lively policeman finds the gem in Sike's coat pocket'.[38] Mottershaw's vigorous *A Daring Daylight Burglary* (1903) follows thieves and the police in pursuit, aided and abetted by an alert boy and police reinforcements, continuing the chase from the house, to rooftops, over land and water to a moving train. Haggar's *A Desperate Poaching Affray* (1903) augments gamekeepers (shot) with police and substitutes burglars for poachers, but similarly proceeds via rough and tumble and fisticuffs across land (closely passing the camera) and through water before the culprits are apprehended. Mottershaw's *Mixed Babies* (1905) – its slapstick comedy enhanced by its implicit pathetic possibilities – opens with a newspaper boy outside a shop, with customers leaving prams outside as they enter to make purchases. The boy prankster laughs as he swaps the babies. Realising the mistake, a male customer is chased by a woman, then pursued by a policeman and another boy, on a bicycle; the woman wallops the man (with his baby) then gives it to the policeman (who falls and rolls over onto it) before throwing it over a garden wall (only to have it promptly thrown back at him).

Hepworth's 1905 *Rescued by Rover* (directed by Lewin Fitzhamon) proved so successful with audiences that he wore out the negative making prints and re-made the subject three times over: it is remarkable for its sustained pace, its construction (parallel and continuity editing) and its unusual length (seven minutes – although Hepworth's drama, *Falsely Accused*, also produced in 1905, ran to fourteen minutes).[39] His wife wrote the story and appeared as the bereaved mother, with Hepworth himself as the father and the family dog (Blair) as the hero, here and in its sequels (*Rover Drives a Motor* [1908 – 'a perfect gem', exudes *Kine Weekly*, 'combining as it does a clever conception and a rare example of animal sagacity'], *A Plucky Little Girl* [1909] and *The Dog Came Back* [1909]). For the first time, he cast professional actors, Mr and Mrs Smith assuming the roles of flirtatious soldier and wicked child thief. The film is constructed as an exemplary chase narrative, but equally can be aligned alongside stories featuring intrepid pets (including horses and elephants – praised, in the manner of Landseer paintings and popular prints, as 'Dumb Sagacity') and pathetic and moral tales of misplaced babies. As in Hepworth's 1914 *The Lure of London* (see Chapter 2) and *The Portrait* (1911) – in which children are restored to their rightful guardians only years later – tippling, fecklessness and vagrancy are rendered disapprovingly, while in Warwick Trading Company's *The Page Boy and the Baby* (1907) a gypsy is found innocent of the theft of a baby hidden in a roll-top desk by (yet another) mischievous boy and in *The Miser's Lesson* (1910), directed by Bert Haldane for Hepworth, a gypsy child reforms a miser. Urban revisited the subject in 1908 with *Kidnapped by Gypsies*, setting the action in 'delightful scenery of woodland, sea and shore', to add to the narrative interest. As in Grahame's 1908 novel, *The Wind in the Willows*, the middle-class propriety of Badger (as opposed to the 'not nice' habits of the weasels, stoats and foxes which encroach upon him in the Wild Wood) is upheld by *Rescued by Rover* as a virtue. A begging gypsy woman is turned away by a woman with a baby in a carriage, outside a well-appointed suburban house. As the baby's nanny (Mabel Clark) flirts with a soldier (a theme revisited by Graphic's 1907 *The Tricky Twins* – where a policeman saves the baby), the gypsy seizes the child and takes it to her garret. The distraught nanny informs her mistress of the theft and the family dog is despatched to discover the child's whereabouts. Rover enthusiastically runs out (in one shot), down the road, towards the camera (in another shot), paddles across a river and shakes before resuming his search on the other side. Locating the hideaway by scent, Rover returns (leaping through the window) to fetch the father and the family is duly reunited.

Hepworth finds a happy ending for a similar sorry story in his 1907 *The Man Who Could Not Commit Suicide*: a young man is desperately in love with a pretty girl and declares his passion but is rejected and, becoming despondent, resolves to put an end to his life. His first attempt (attaching a tube to a gas bracket) is foiled by a dog, but, taking this as an omen, he again approaches the girl and is refused. He tries hanging (but the rope breaks) and is again refused. Finally, he climbs into a barrel, intent upon drowning, whereupon the lady relents and carries him off in her arms.

Many tales did not end so fortuitously for their protagonists, provoking tears from their audience rather than smiles. Pathos films often drew upon familiar sources, for instance, R. W. Paul's scenic portrayal of *The Poor Orphan's Last Prayer* (1902) and Harrison's 1902 *Little Jim* both illustrated well-known songs, while Walturdaw's *Jessica's First Prayer* referred to Hesba Stretton's bestseller, published by the Religious Tract Society in 1882.[40] Warwick Trading Company's 1900 *The Death of Poor Joe* (depicting the death of a child crossing-sweeper in the snow) referred to a famously contrived photograph by Oscar Rejlander, staging an incident in Charles Dickens' 1852–3 series *Bleak House*, while Clarendon's 1909 *Hard Times* invoked the Dickens novel of 1854; *Little Nell and Burglar Bill* (1903) and Clarendon's *Nancy, or the Burglar's Daughter* (1908) recall characters in *The Old Curiosity Shop* (1841) and *Oliver Twist* (1837–9). R. W. Paul's *Buy Your Own Cherries* (1904) retains the episodic structure and painterly style of the famous lantern slide sequence on which it was based: a workman spends the household income on drink and his children cower in fear of him; a clergyman persuades him to take the pledge (which he honours by by-passing a pub); in due course the children become happier and better dressed (he now brings them presents) and the house better kept and appointed.

Many of these pathetic narratives were timely releases prompting charity in the Christian season of goodwill, or served as a didactive inducement to temperance as much as entertainment – for instance, the Sheffield Photographic Company's 1906 *Lost in the Snow. A Grandchild's Devotion*, *A Child's Prayer* (in which a poor child's letter to Santa is blown up the chimney and down into the rich house next door) and Hepworth's *Little Meg and the Wonderful Lamp* (in which a rich couple save an orphan who has stolen a pantomime lantern) were released in December 1906; Hepworth's *Poverty and Compassion* (depicting a family in a garret) appeared in December 1908 and *Tempered with Mercy*, featuring a policeman who urges sympathy on a hard-hearted baker who seeks to prosecute a thieving child, was a Christmas release in 1909, along with Cricks and Martin's *The Motherless Waif*, featuring a drunkard father and another kindly policeman. In *The Little Matchseller*, a little girl scampers in the snow trying to sell her wares. She is ignored by a man in a top hat. A boy enters the frame, throwing snowballs at her then stealing her only shoe. The lamplighter ignores her – she huddles to the wall and cries. Lighting a match, she summons a vision of a fireplace (at which she attempts to warm her hands), then a table, heavily laden with annual fare, which disappears as she approaches; then a Christmas tree appears, richly decorated. An angel descends and the girl collapses before being carried upwards as a spirit (an image repeated in *The Poor Orphan's Last Prayer*). When a policeman arrives and shines his torch into the corner, he finds her body slumped on the ground.

Other unfortunate children serve to reunite estranged lovers or to confirm sibling loyalty. In the 1910 British and Colonial film *Two Little Shoes*, a man is driven to crime to provide food for his wife and child, but the infant nevertheless dies and the father is sent to prison with only a shoe by which to remember her. On release, he breaks into a house and finds the pair to the shoe and is thus reunited with his wife. Williamson's *Orphans* (advertised at Christmas 1907 as 'a story with a moral on the lines of our well-known *Stowaway* film') has the brother led astray by bad company while the sister is adopted by a lady of means; fifteen years later the boy breaks into the house of the girl's benefactor, recognises their mother's locket and determines to reform, 'With God's help and your good example'. A comparable moral ('it's never too late to mend') is served by *Nancy, or the Burglar's Daughter*. Cricks and Sharp's *A Woman's Sacrifice* (1906) affords a reconciliation of a father and mother over 'the little peacemaker's' sick-bed, whereas in Hepworth's 1907 *A Lovers' Quarrel*, a boy is despatched to return a lady's engagement ring to her fiancé, is run over by a motor car but reunites the couple in hospital before dying. *For Baby's Sake* (1908), directed by A. E. Coleby for Cricks and Martin, described as 'a pathetic picture in six scenes', is given the following entry in the catalogue:

> A lady and gentleman are talking in a drawing room, their child playing with her doll, when a friend of her husband's is announced and duly introduced to the wife and child. A telegram arrives making it necessary for the husband to go out . . . so, telling the friend he will not be long away he hurries off. The nurse in the meantime has taken the child and returns for her to say goodnight before going to bed. As soon as the nurse has departed, the gentleman, being in an amorous mood, attempts to kiss his friend's wife but she indignantly repels him and as she is struggling with him the husband returns and strikes his false friend to the floor. The husband is indignant with the friend and wife and leaves the house. Next we see the mother and child at home, the mother very sad. The child suggests writing to her 'dear daddy' and the mother humours her, hoping it will bring him back. The letter is written (copy shown) by the child, addressed and they go together to post it. The gentleman sadly looks at his wife's portrait. A footman brings the letter from the child. He cannot resist the appeal and returns hastily. A happy reconciliation takes place all due to the little peacemaker.

In *The Motherless Waif* the death of the little match-girl brings about the drunkard's reform: 'in deep remorse, the father, with hands raised to Heaven, swears never again to touch the cursed bottle and . . . dreams that his beloved wife comes and takes the child with outstretched wings up into the starry firmament'. In *Tempered with Mercy*, one sister works as a flower-girl to support the other. *Two Little Waifs* (Williamson, 1905) has a boy in a sailor suit stolen by gypsies and taken to a gypsy caravan; he befriends a little girl at the camp and they escape to his home where the father embraces the boy but rejects the girl, who is then, again, kidnapped. The father and the boy search for the girl, the father eventually saving the girl from a burning building and welcoming her into his own nice family.

Films presented as entertainment often drew their material from older narrative and pictorial subjects which audiences could readily recognise. Cinematic devices were used to invest this inherited content with new interest and to advertise cinema itself. Early film-makers frequently took to imitating one another, establishing and reinforcing generic distinctions identified by audiences and exhibitors. Different themes appear intended to appeal to different audiences.

The Catalogue; the Programme; the Playbill; the Press

Kine Weekly, the trade journal founded in 1907, reported the Mammoth Fun City at Olympia, an exhibition which brought the fun of the fairground to the centre of London. Mrs F. Collins' Kinematograph show is celebrated as 'the finest in England', elaborately ornamented and decorated with lamps to attract the punter, with a powerful organ to accompany the entertainment.[41] Other seasonal fairs (such as Nottingham's autumn Goose Fair, recorded by Mitchell and Kenyon) appeared as the subject of films, showing the attractions with which the early cinema (enticingly named 'Electric Palace', 'Wonderland' or 'Theatre of Delights') competed for the punters' trade and the size of its potential audience, including boxing booths (as seen in Hitchcock's *The Ring* [1927] – see Chapter 4) and switchback rides (at Blackpool). Other films, in a variant of the train phantom ride, conveyed the experience of being in a switchback carriage. The supreme showman, 'Edison' Thomas, promoted himself and the films he showed by exploiting a confusion of his name with that of the American inventor, Thomas Edison. Hepworth recalls:

> He plastered the whole town wherever he went (and went nearly everywhere) with tremendous posters in brilliant colours describing his wonderful shows and still more wonderful self . . . He would parade the town in person, mounted high on an open lorry, actively turning his camera on every little knot of people he passed . . . Unfortunately for their hopes the camera had no film in it . . . and if they failed to see themselves on the screen, it was just too bad. The hall was filled and they had a good show for their money, so what's the odds?[42]

George Pearson, a schoolteacher who directed his first films in the teens (see Chapters 2 and 5) recalls the boyhood experience which initiated his interest in the new medium:

> With sixpence to spend I had gone to a funny little shop in the Lambeth Walk where Pollock's gory melodramas for his Toy Theatres were sold, sheets of characters for a penny plain, twopence coloured. Fourpence went rapturously on *Alone in the Pirates' Lair*. With twopence jingling a farewell in my pocket, since the toffee-shop was near, I zig-zagged through the hurly-burly of the busy street, when presto! . . . the great adventure began. It was outside a derelict greengrocer's shop. The hawk-eyed gentleman on a fruit-crate was bewildering a sceptical crowd. In that shuttered shop there was a miracle to be seen for a penny, but only twenty-four could enter at a time, there wasn't room for more. His peroration was magnificent . . . 'You've seen pictures with people in books, all frozen stiff . . . you've never seen pictures with people coming alive, moving about like you and me. Well, go inside and see for yourself, living pictures for a penny, and then tell me I'm a liar!' One of my pennies went suddenly; I joined twenty-three other sceptics inside. Stale cabbage leaves and a smell of dry mud gave atmosphere to a scene from Hogarth. A furtive youth did things to a tin oven on iron legs, and a white sheet swung from the ceiling. We grouped round that oven and wondered. Suddenly things happened, someone turned down a gas-jet, the tin apparatus burst into a fearful clatter, and an oblong picture slapped on to the sheet and began a violent dance. After a while I discerned it was a picture of a house,

but a house on fire. Flames and smoke belched from the windows, and miracle of miracles, a fire-engine dashed in, someone mounted a fire-escape, little human figures darted about below, and then . . . Bang! . . . the show was over. Exactly one minute . . . I had been to the Cinema![43]

However, such 'gaffs' were the cause of much concern to local authorities, and under the guise of protecting the audience (and especially children) against the physical danger of fire (resulting from highly combustible film stock), crushing in inadequate escape exits and the supposed moral danger of some of the material shown (with children truanting from school to attend during the day), legislation was introduced in 1909 to regulate exhibition. Contributors to the parliamentary discussion and the trade press urged that reports of fires (in Britain and elsewhere) were much exaggerated and that the Bill proposed 'grandmotherly, and in many cases, entirely unnnecessary precautions'.[44] They also cited the equivalent potential of cinema to provide 'moral improvement' through the types of religious and temperance themes shown in church halls, Salvation Army citadels and schools (to be restricted, by the Bill, to two days per year); others questioned the advisability of county councils holding power over licences and whether films should be singled out for particular discrimination (a debate which continues). Jon Burrows suggests that the 1909 Act was partly the product of ulterior political motives (regulating gatherings of immigrant communities in the East End of London – demonised in Hepworth's 1905 *The Aliens' Invasion* and documented in Gaumont's 1911 film of the notorious *Great East End Anarchist Battle*)[45] while, on the other hand, the discretion accorded to the London County Council allowed 'subversive' imported films (notably from Soviet Russia) to be given limited screenings in the 1920s, even while they failed to secure general commercial distribution (see Chapter 4).

The trade press, not surprisingly, suggested that investment in films and in the construction (or adaptation) of premises to designated use was a sound move and broadly welcomed the stamp of respectability which government intervention bestowed. 'Let us put ourselves on record once and for all', says *The Bioscope* in 1908 (not for the first nor last time),

that the motion picture furore is not a 'fad' and will never meet the fate of business bubbles that have burst as rapidly as they have risen . . . It began with experiment, was tried out as an experiment, slowly grew like an oak, deeply rooted in the affections of the people, reaching upwards to higher levels and branching out into varied fields of interest.[46]

However, Nicholas Hiley has ably demonstrated that caution was well justified in the light of previous forms of entertainment which had promised great returns but which had proved no more than a passing novelty (he draws a specific comparison with the recent skating boom):[47] local gazettes, such as *The Manchester Programme*, convey a sense of the competition, varying from summer to winter. The shift at the end of the 1900s towards the production of longer films and self-standing programmes (dispensing with elephants and variety turns) he therefore aligns with the demands of exhibitors and distributors (now hiring rather than selling – the rate dependent on the age of the film) intent upon attracting patrons prepared to pay for novelty, comfort and for content directed, perhaps, at more elevated tastes. 'The craving on the part of exhibitors for new subjects rather than good', continues *The Bioscope*, is to be deplored; 'the efforts of manufacturers to uplift the quality of their productions will meet with the warm support of the public'.[48]

In practice, it seems, producers continued to provide novelty (if only in the form of a variation or adaptation of a familiar theme) alongside quality. Clarendon's *The Tempest*, Williamson's *Hamlet*, Gaumont's *Romeo and Juliet* ('A Magnificent Gorgeous Cinematic Representation' claiming to include more than forty London artistes in its cast), *Anthony and Cleopatra* (proclaiming its presentation 'by properly qualified actors and actresses') and *Richard III* may be indicative of a cultural shift, while also trading on a longstanding popular appetite for the pictorial depiction of Shakespeare. More opportunistically, they contributed towards and profited from a more widespread American and European Shakespeare 'boom' in 1908.[49] A similar timely release was Hepworth's *The Death of Nelson* (shown to the accompaniment of a popular song), produced for the centenary of Trafalgar. Williamson produced a Cromwellian drama, *Just in Time*, in 1907, proceeded by Clarendon's pairing of *The Cavalier's Wife* and *The Puritan Maid and the Royalist Refugee* in 1908. For Christmas 1907 Clarendon released *The Water Babies, or the Little Chimney Sweep* (from Charles Kingsley's 1863 novel) and *The Pied Piper of Hamlin* – featuring 'period costumes and real rats'. Gaumont (the French-based company) advertised a Grand Pantomime (in two versions – as with toy theatres, 'tuppence coloured, penny plain') and, for Easter 1908, produced *Salome*, *Nazareth* and *The Life of Christ*.

Films which drew upon pre-cinematic precedents, in theme, characters or performances, would seem to require little introduction or explanation to their audiences. The adventures of the cartoon cockney figure, Ally Sloper (a favourite of Bert Smallways in H. G. Wells' 1908 *The War in the Air*) was transposed to a series of three films by Williamson, the success of the original prompting *Ally Sloper's Visit to Brighton* (1898) and *Ally Sloper Batting* (1898).[50] Dickens proved a perennial favourite, both directly from the novels (themselves originally serialised) and from lantern slide series (such as the pathetic tale of Paul Dombey in his 1848 *Dombey and Son*). Smith's 1898 *The Corsican Brothers* employed double exposure to render the vision of a ghost in Dion Boucicault's sensational 1852 play, then proving a popular success on stage at the Lyceum. Other films directly recorded stage performances (such as the famous pantomime dame, Dan Leno, the music hall stars Florrie Forde, Vesta Tilley, Harry Lauder and Will Evans, and the D'Oyly Carte production of Gilbert and Sullivan's *The Mikado*, filmed in 1907 by Walturdaw and supplied with gramophone recordings) or documented music hall performers and actors as celebrities (as in *Miss Marie Lloyd* [Warwick Trading Company, 1898] and *Ellen Terry at Home* [Warwick Trading Company, 1900]).

Many films employ familiar, stock figures as the perpetrators of jokes or as the butt of humour (the largest category of fiction film production). In Gaumont's 1909 *How Percy Won the Beauty Competition*, the camera pans across the line of smiling belles; one flirts outrageously and takes a tipple from a flask; the 'ruse' is not noticed until the prize is awarded and Percy's sidekicks reveal the disguise. Women's dress and vanity are similarly aped (literally) and ridiculed in Cricks and

Martin's 1908 *Lord Algy's Beauty Show*, *The Bioscope* commentary advising us that the 'First Prize is a husband; the Second, a bull pup; the Third, a silk dress with consolation prizes of powder puffs'. The trade press was adamant that good verbal exposition, preferably written by the lecturer himself, could but enhance the experience of a film for an audience, even when it included titles. 'One of the most urgent requirements to-day is that every picture shall be introduced to the audience in a manner that will ensure the good points of a film being intelligently appreciated', urges *The Bioscope* in 1908, 'the lay mind . . . is quite incapable of seeing and comprehending the inner nature and underlying humanity which are the life and soul of to-day's greatest creations':

> The lecturer should know the picture well before he attempts to explain it to others; he should keep perfect pace with the projection machine, should quietly indicate the inner causes when the outer result is taking place; he should indulge in no stock phrases, no personal reminiscences which the picture may recall, no opaque phrases, no drawn-out windy sentences . . . Above all else, make the story bright and the explanation worthy of a beautiful picture.

Where appropriate, the lecturer's exposition could be accompanied by sound effects.[51] Elsewhere, there was discussion of accompanying music cueing an appropriate response. Concerning 'Wordless Pictorial Songs' (such as sentimental, patriotic and imperial themes) *The Bioscope* maintained that 'even the poorest hall affords a pianist who can play popular songs and his modest talents with a few song films or a number of more humble song slides are all that are required', indicating an amount of audience participation.[52]

The Bioscope suggested that, where a two-hour programme of films proved wearying for an audience, there was something wrong with the programming 'rather than with *film as such*', again resisting its augmentation by elephants and variety turns.[53] French films frequently featured alongside the home-grown product. There was much insistence upon the technical stipulation of clear photography (on the part of producers) and flickerless projection (on the part of exhibitors). It published and commented upon samples of programmes witnessed by correspondents across the country and indicated the balance of actuality, topicality, comedy, drama and pathos which might expected to be well received. The following example is given by *Kine Weekly* in 1907:

A Great Temptation
Railway Ride
His First Camera
A Grandchild's Devotion
Balloon Races at Ranelagh
How Jones Saw the Derby
Two Little Scamps
The Alhambra
Serenade

The Negro's Revenge

Clarnico Fire Brigade

The Good-Hearted Judge

The Launch of a Japanese Battleship

Ascending Mount Snowdon

Our Ice Supply

False Coiners

A Visit to Sunlight Soap Works

The Villain still Pursued Her[54]

Pathos tends to appear towards the top or bottom of the billing but never opens or closes the show, this reserved for more rousing subjects (thrilling chases, patriotic or sports fixtures). Meanwhile, audience members could drift in and out at any stage or see the programme right through from any point. Hepworth (again, in imitation of lantern slide and stage precedent) produced 'curtain' films in 1900 intended to open and close programmes of naval films, showing the furling and unfurling by bluejackets of a ship's sail from a halyard, a most excellent device 'for any series descriptive of England's might, or the lives of her Naval Heroes'.

The lecturer's description of the scenes was often supplemented by a printed programme. For instance, the Biograph's third anniversary at the Palace Theatre, Cambridge Circus, was marked with a souvenir booklet illustrated with photographs and stills from its Boer War films made by W. K.-L. Dickson, accompanied by extracts from his war diary. *The Bioscope* suggested souvenir nights and gifts of golliwogs at children's matinées to encourage trade. Filoscope flick-books (produced from a series of stills from films) were a form of early spin-off, while Nestlé and Lever Brothers subsidised reduced seat prices for filmgoers producing appropriate chocolate and soap wrappers. The programme (and the producer's catalogue) might provide a lecturer with information which was not apparent in the film itself – the content of a telegram (as in *For Baby's Sake*) or (as in *A Daring Daylight Burglary*) the fact that a telegraph has been sent ahead to inform the police that the thieves have fled by train.

Producers' catalogues and trade journals categorised films and gave synopses to enable exhibitors to order and advertise films to best effect. The longer films produced towards the end of the decade incorporated and combined themes from the earlier simpler scenarios. A successful plot, advises *Kine Weekly*, 'must arrest and sustain the audience from first to last'. Urban's 1907 *A Waif of the Sea* is advertised as a 'Pathetic Picture Story of Rescue, Unrequited Love and Magnanimous Renunciation' (with Normandy coastal scenery as an extra attraction). Clarendon's 1907 *The Soldier's Wedding* (trading on its previous success, *The Sailor's Wedding*) is advertised as 'Romantic, Exciting, Pathetic and Humorous'; *The Missionary's Daughter* as 'Thrilling, Pathetic and Romantic': the girl is seized by slavers and 'rescued from an awful death' by British Tars. Walturdaw's *The Story of a Locket* involves a 'struggle that will grip your audience' between a son who has done well in the world and the father who fell prey to drink and deserted him years previously.

In order to 'Rope them In', *The Bioscope* advocated that posters should be placed all over the town telling 'briefly and in bold type the kind of story that the film illustrates: e.g. *The Auto Heroine* – "a thrilling drama of a Motor Race"; *Lockjaw* – "a rattling good side splitter"':

> Bill matter is by far the most important item in a provincial manager's business. The majority of show-men have pictures chosen for them by a hiring house in London, but it is his own business to see that the greatest possible importance is attached to each picture in the programme . . . keep your bill matter smart.[55]

Unfortunately, the majority of the films produced in Britain in cinema's first decade have not survived and publicity material in posters, catalogues and journals are their only record. The evidence suggests that early British film-making was marked by variety and ingenuity. However, these sources are also valuable for the information conveyed about cinema as an industry and a social institution in its early years and the extent to which, from the outset, American and European films and film-making have constituted a large part of the British filmgoing experience.

Facials

Often early British producers include primitive 'facials' in their lists of films for sale and, subsequently, for hire through distributors; these, it is frequently claimed, require little explanation to the audience, the performers' contortions providing the primary and sufficient object of interest. But the urge to record fleeting shifts in expression crosses comedy, drama and 'facials' proper. Many longer films of the later tens and teens (see Chapter 2) still feature facial expression as an attraction, prompted by a narrative which calls for transitions in a single frame or cumulative changes in a sequence of intercut scenes (Florence Turner's 1914 *Daisy Doodad's Dial* is an excellent example of its use in comedy; *Lady Audley's Secret* employs the reading of letters as a 'set-piece' thespian exercise). While generally promoted as entertainment, these films also refer to a scientific interest in human and animal physiognomy (see, for instance, Graphic's 1906 *Some of Our Relations*), gesture and expression; while apparently essentially visual, these films draw upon the fascination of contemporary popular novelists (such as Marie Corelli and Arthur Conan Doyle) with traits characteristic to nationality and temperament; while recorded in movement (as in theatrical representation) they also recall the concerns of the pictorial and plastic arts (from academy paintings to much-published caricatures) over several centuries.[56]

   Pulling faces for the camera was one of the earliest and most popular forms of film entertainment, with precedent in lantern slide series such as a Fry's Chocolate advertisement: a small boy 'expresses' desperation; pacification; expectation; acclamation; (then, finally, smiling broadly) realisation 'It's Fry's'. R. W. Paul produced *The Troublesome Collar* (1902), *Funny Faces* (1904), *Spooning* (1906) (showing a couple's expressions as they kiss) and *The Fidgety Fly* (1907); Smith produced *Comic Faces* in 1898 (showing an old man drinking a glass of beer and an old woman taking snuff); Goodwin Norton, *Expressions* in 1899 and Hepworth, *Comic Grimaces* (1901–2). *A Day in* the *Life of the Bishop of St Swithin's* (1907) includes 'a delightfully amusing study of expression' in close-up, with the Bishop encountering a cartoon of himself in *The Westminster Gazette*. Meanwhile, a contributor to *Kine Weekly* in 1907 suggested that animated political cartoons be produced to match those of *Punch* and *The Westminster Gazette*, proposing Mr Balfour, Mr Lyttleton and Lord Roberts (a much filmed and photographed Commander-in-Chief in the South African campaign) as subjects and in Smith's 1901 *The Monocle* a man attempts to imitate a cartoon of Joseph Chamberlain.

Sometimes, a character is shown alone, the audience privy to their undisguised, spontaneous expression of emotion, frequently occasioned by receipt of a missive or the self-absorbed reading of a news item. In Smith's 1902 *Pa's Comments on the Morning News*, father describes in gestures the stories as he encounters them: first, he shows a long, drawn face, thumps the table, mimes a noose around his own neck, twisted around and then tugged until his mouth drops open and his tongue falls forward; he touches his tongue and points to his boiled egg to indicate 'the taste of death' in his own mouth. Looking at the next story, he shadow-boxes, indicates a black eye and a broken nose, then claps and thumps the table laughing; such is Pa's distraction that he puts his hand in his own breakfast. Mutoscope and Biograph's 1898 *The Fatal Letter* (produced by the British subsidiary of an American company) shows a single-frame close-up of a man's face as he reads of his aunt's death. Ben Nathan plays the nephew, at first respectfully flicking out his cigarette and removing his hat, then opening the letter, drawing away from it as if rejecting its contents, then crying; but he reads on . . . He then folds the letter, smiles, snaps his fingers, sings to himself and kisses the letter. Smith's 1899 *The Legacy* similarly shows a beneficiary's expressions as he reads of a death and his consequent inheritance. The catalogue describes the performance:

> Another film in which facial expression is vividly depicted. The subject of the picture is going through his correspondence when he comes to a black-edged envelope. He reads with deep concern of the death of a favourite aunt, but when turning overleaf discovers that he is the recipient of a legacy. The change from gravity to extreme joy is most amusing, the delight of the reader being quite contagious. A well-known actor was the subject for this picture.

R. W. Paul's 1902 *Facial Expressions*, again providing a minimal narrative pretext for its action, presents:

> An actor with wigs and face paint making it understood by dumb show that he is impersonating various people, imitates a sanctimonious old man reading then an old woman with wigs and a shawl. The facial expressions are exceedingly funny.

These single-frame, miniature scenarios require the performer to produce one facial contortion then another in quick succession, not only to display an expression significant of a particular emotion but also then to transform the expression as the reading or action proceeds.

Other films use more than one protagonist, reacting to one another. In R. W. Paul's *Tea: The Twins' Tea Party* (1896) ('an improved edition of the favourite *Twins' Tea Party*') two children are seen taking tea at table when a quarrel occurs over the cake. 'One of them gets smacked by the other, causing her to cry vigorously, the expression being very funny.' Smith's 1899–1900 'Two Old Sports' (played by the prominent comedians Hunter and Green) perform to each other on several occasions (requiring, notes the catalogue, no description of the action, 'the expressions of the faces telling the tale'), as do the men in *A Good Joke* (1899), in Paul's *A Naughty Story*, showing characters reacting to and sharing an item in a newspaper or magazine, and Smith's 1900 *Where Did You Get It?* (four men passing around a naughty photograph). *The Quarrelsome Couple* (1902) concerns an argument over a newspaper story. In Smith's 1900 *Scandal over the Teacups*, two spinsters gossip while drinking tea, while in *The Old Maid's Valentine* (also 1900) a spinster (Eva Bailey) performs to her feline familiar. It tells a tale of hopes raised, then dashed, then of dignity affronted. A woman of a certain age sits sewing, poker-faced, eyes downcast, her mouth tautly drawn and her chin pulled in. She turns and notices the date and sighs. A large envelope is delivered, which she receives with some surprise. She wags an index finger at the cat and taps her nose conspiratorially, smiles then excitedly clenches a little fist to her bosom and fans herself. She laughs flirtatiously as she opens the envelope but her expression turns to horror as she realises the prank. The words 'JUST LIKE YOU MAMA' frame a clownish figure of a baby. Putting her hand to her forehead, she drops the letter, shakes her head tut-tuttingly, clasps her hands primly and resumes the original expression.

Hepworth's 1905–6 *What the Curate Really Did* employs contrasting acting styles to comic effect and, as in *The Tell-Tale Telephone* (Cricks and Sharp, 1906), uses overlays to convey dual meaning. The original event (a young curate giving a little girl a ha'penny in exchange for a bunch of flowers) is performed naturalistically, whereas the proceedings successively elaborated (by Mrs Jones to Mrs Brown, by Mrs Brown to Mrs Robinson, and by Mrs Robinson to the Bishop) are enthusiastically portrayed and narrated in an increasingly histrionic manner, entailing much pulling of shocked faces and matronly flourishing of fans: an overlaid image shows the 'little girl' of the original story represented by the gossips as a young woman and the 'ha'penny' as a kiss. All is forgiven and peace restored when the little girl is introduced to the Bishop.

Notes

1. Michael Korda, *Charmed Lives: A Family Romance* (London: Allen Lane, 1980), p. 434.
2. Michael Balcon made this distinction in his appraisal of Cavalcanti's BFI-sponsored film, *Film and Reality* [1942]: 'It traces the story of film production from its earliest days, and the persistent influence of realism through newsreels, scientific films, travelogues, documentaries, etc., is traced through those periods of film making in which the film succumbed to tinsel-artificiality induced by too close an adherence to the artificialities of the stage'; see 'The British Film during the War', *The Penguin Film Review* 1, 1946, p. 69.
3. *The Bioscope*, 10 December 1908, p. 9; John Barnes also cites an advertising campaign launched by Lever Brothers and Nestlé whereby visitors to the Jubilee films were admitted at half price, on

presentation of a Nestlé Milk or Sunlight Soap wrapper: *Pioneers of the British Film: The Beginnings of the Cinema in England 1894–1901*, vol. 2 (London: Bishopsgate Press, 1983), p. 197.

4. John Barnes, *Pioneers of the British Film: The Beginnings of the Cinema in England 1894–1901*, vol. 1 [1976] (Exeter: Exeter University Press, 1998), p. 63. Amid a flurry of interest in early film among British artist film-makers in the 1990s (Sam Taylor-Wood, Mark Dickinson, Denise Webber, Steve McQueen, Jayne Parker – see Chapter 12), Steven Pippin has made cameras from household objects, including toilets and washing machines, which develop as well as expose prints; see Julian Stallabrass, *High Art Lite: British Art in the 1990s* (London: Verso, 1999), p. 166.

5. Rachael Low, *The History of the British Film*, vol. 1 [1949] (London: Routledge, 1997), p. 13.

6. See Cecil Hepworth, *Animated Photography: the ABC of the Cinematograph* (London: Hazell, Watson & Viney, 1897); for a discussion of the influence of photographic practice on Cecil Hepworth's films, see Andrew Higson, *Waving the Flag* (Oxford: Clarendon Press, 1995), pp. 54–6.

7. Lytton Strachey, *Queen Victoria* [1921] (Harmondsworth: Penguin, 1978), p. 236.

8. *The Era*, 12 September 1896, quoted in Barnes, *Pioneers of the British Film*, vol. 1, p. 76.

9. *Lady's Pictorial* supplement, 5 December, 1896, quoted in Barnes, *Pioneers of the British Film*, vol. 1, p. 213; see also George Earle Buckle (ed.), *The Letters of Queen Victoria*, vol. 3 (London: John Murray, 1932), pp. 87 and 105: 'After tea went to the Red drawing room, where so-called "animated pictures" were shown off, including groups taken in September at Balmoral. It is a very wonderful process, representing people, their movements and actions, as if they were alive.'

10. Quoted by John Barnes, *Pioneers of the British Film: The Beginnings of the Cinema in England 1894–1901*, vol. 3 (London: Bishopsgate Press, 1983), p. 8.

11. Cecil Hepworth, *Came the Dawn: Memories of a Film Pioneer* (London: Phoenix House, 1951), p. 78.

12. See *Kine Weekly*, 13 June 1907, p. 73; 'Natural Color Films', *The Bioscope*, 10 December, 1908, p. 15 and, for Acres' unsustained boasts of achieving colour already, Barnes, *Pioneers of the British Film*, vol. 2, pp. 180–1.

13. *The Bioscope*, 18 September 1908, p. 16.

14. Stephen Bottomore, '"She's just like my granny! Where's her crown?": Monarchs and Movies 1896–1916', in John Fullerton (ed.), in *Celebrating 1895: The Centenary of Cinema* (Sydney: John Libbey, 1998), p. 175.

15. Jay Leyda, *Kino* (Princeton: Princeton University Press, 1983), p. 47; Stephen Bottomore, '"An Amazing Quarter Mile of Moving Gold, Gems and Genealogy": Filming India's 1902/3 Delhi Durbar', *Historical Journal of Film, Radio and Television* vol. 15 no. 4 (1995), p. 511; see also '"Have You Seen the Gaekwar Bob?": Filming the 1911 Delhi Durbar', *Historical Journal of Film, Radio and Television* vol. 17 no. 3 (1997).

16. Nigel Nicolson, *Mary Curzon* [1977] (London: Phoenix, 1998), pp. 161–5; see also Hon. George Curzon, *Russia in Central Asia* (London: Longmans, Green and Co., 1889), p. 14.

17. Bottomore, 'An Amazing Quarter Mile', p. 499.

18. For further discussion of *Alice*, see Hepworth, *Came the Dawn*, p. 63 and Andrew Higson, 'Cecil Hepworth, *Alice in Wonderland* and the Development of Narrative Film', in Andrew Higson (ed.), *Young and Innocent? The Cinema in Britain 1896–1930* (Exeter: Exeter University Press, 2002).

19. Rudyard Kipling, 'Mrs Bathurst', *Traffics and Discoveries* [1904] (London: Macmillan, 1973), pp. 353–5.

20. See 'Fact Follows Fiction', *Kine Weekly*, 13 June 1907 and 'Too Much Realism', *The Bioscope*, 14 January 1909; also Richard Crangle, 'Secrets, Lies and Living Pictures: Motion Picture Technology and the Revelation of Truth', in André Gaudreault, Catherine Russell and Pierre Véronneau (eds), *The Cinema, A New Technology for the 20th Century* (Lausanne: Editions Payot, 2004), pp. 63–72.

21 See Stepen Bottomore, 'Frederic Villiers – War Correspondent', *Sight and Sound*, Autumn 1980,
    pp. 250–5, and 'Joseph Rosenthal: The Most Glorious Profession', *Sight and Sound*, Autumn 1983,
    pp. 260–5; also John Springhill, '"Up Guards and At Them!" British Imperialism and Popular Art,
    1880–1914', in John Mackenzie (ed.), *Imperialism and Popular Culture* (Manchester: Manchester
    University Press, 1986), pp. 58–9.

22 See Bottomore, 'Joseph Rosenthal' and Simon Popple, '"But the Khaki-Covered Camera is the *Latest*
    Thing": The Boer War Cinema and Visual Culture in Britain', in Higson, *Young and Innocent*, pp. 19–20.

23 Kevin Brownlow, *The War, the West and the Wilderness* (London: Secker and Warburg, 1979), p. 149.

24 H. G. Wells, *The Time Machine* [1895] (London: J. M. Dent, 1992), pp. 62–3.

25 *The Era*, 25 April 1896, quoted by Simon Popple, 'The Diffuse Beam: Cinema and Change', in
    Christopher Williams (ed.), *Cinema: the Beginnings and the Future* (London: University of Westminster
    Press, 1996), p. 97; see also Terry Ramsaye, *A Million and One Nights: A History of the Motion Picture*
    (London: Frank Cass, 1964), p. 154, and H. G.Wells, *The King Who Was a King* (London: Ernest Benn,
    1929), p. 10, for Wells' distant recollection of Paul's project.

26 See Ian Yearsley, 'On the Move in the Streets', in Vanessa Toulmin, Simon Popple and Patrick Russell
    (eds), *The Lost World of Mitchell and Kenyon* (London: BFI, 2004), pp. 181–90.

27 *Kine Weekly*, 13 June 1907; Low, *The History of the British Film, 1906–1914*, p. 57.

28 Rachael Low, *Film Making in 1930s Britain* (London: George Allen and Unwin).

29 *The Bioscope*, 10 December 1908, p. 9, and 11 February 1909, p. 5.

30 See Richard Crangle, 'Saturday Night at the X-Rays: the Moving Picture and "The New Photography" in
    Britain, 1896', in Fullerton, *Celebrating 1895*, pp. 138–44.

31 For a discussion of these variants on a theme, see Frank Gray's paper given at 'Location! Location!
    Location!', Nottingham British Silent Cinema Festival, 2003.

32 Much of the material collected by Bill Douglas and Peter Jewell is now held by the Bill Douglas Centre,
    University of Exeter; see also, Olive Cook, *Movement in Two Dimensions* (London: Hutchinson, 1963),
    and Stephen Herbert, *A History of Pre-Cinema* (London: Routledge, 2000).

33 James Agate, 'Charlie not their Darling', *My Theatre Talks* (London: Arthur Baker, 1930), p. 223; also
    'Plays on the Screen', *The Bioscope*, 28 January 1909, p. 33, advocated the use of film 'trailers' for stage
    productions.

34 See Deac Rossell, 'Double Think: the Cinema and Magic Lantern Culture', in Fullerton, *Celebrating 1895*,
    and Richard Crangle, 'What Do These Old Slides Mean? Or Why the Magic Lantern is Not an Important
    Part of Cinema History', in Simon Popple and Vanessa Toulmin (eds), *Visual Delights* (Trowbridge: Flicks
    Books, 2001).

35 Frank Gray, 'James Williamson's Rescue Narratives', in Higson, *Young and Innocent*, p. 33.

36 Hepworth, *Came the Dawn*, p. 59.

37 George and Weedon Grossmith, *The Diary of a Nobody* [1892] (Harmondsworth: Penguin, 1975), p. 45;
    for a discussion of the Haggar and Mottershaw versions, see David Berry, *Wales and Cinema: The First
    Hundred Years* (Cardiff: University of Wales Press, 1994), and Andrew Clay, 'True Crime? Charles Peace
    and the British Crime Film, 1895–1905', in Linda Fitzsimmons and Sarah Street (eds), *Moving
    Performance* (Trowbridge: Flicks Books, 2000), pp. 123–36.

38 *Kine Weekly*, 30 January 1908, p. 207.

39 Hepworth, *Came the Dawn*, p. 67; for an exemplary analysis of *Rover*, see Charles Barr, 'Before
    Blackmail: Silent British Cinema', in Robert Murphy (ed.), *The British Cinema Book* (London: BFI, 1997),
    pp. 7–9; for *Falsely Accused*, see also Low, *The History of the British Film, 1906–1914*, pp. 100–3.

40. For further discussion of pathos, see Ine van Dooren and Amy Sargeant, 'Dead Babies', in Popple and Toulmin (eds), *Visual Delights* (Sydney: John Libbey, 2005).

41. For further discussion of fairground exhibitors, see Vanessa Toulmin, 'Women Bioscope Proprietors Before the First World War', in Fullerton, *Celebrating 1895*.

42. Hepworth, *Came the Dawn*, p. 59; see also Vanessa Toulmin, 'The Importance of the Programme in Early Film Presentation', *KINtop* II, pp. 19–33.

43. George Pearson, *Flashback: an Autobiography of a British Film Maker* (London: George Allen and Unwin, 1957), p. 14; see also Ford Madox Brown's citation of 'twopenny gaffs in Mile End' in his vibrant account of London leisure activities in *The Soul of London: A Survey of a Modern City* (London: Alston Rivers, 1905), p. 139.

44. See *Parliamentary Debates* (Commons) 1909 III (London: HMSO, 1909), pp. 1597–8; also IX 1748 (reporting a fire in Southsea), and *Kine Weekly*, 16 January 1908, p. 161 (reporting an accident in Barnsley, in which sixteen children were crushed to death); *The Bioscope*, 8 April 1909, p. 12 re-prints the text of the Bill.

45. Jon Burrows, 'Penny Pleasure: Film Exhibition in London during the Nickelodeon Era, 1906–1914', *Film History* vol. 16 no. 1, 2004; for a synopsis of *The Aliens' Invasion*, see Low, *The History of the British Film, 1906–1914*, p. 58.

46. 'Not a Fad', *The Bioscope*, 23 October 1908, p. 11.

47. Nicholas Hiley, '"At the Picture Palace": the British Cinema Audience 1895–1920', in Fullerton, *Celebrating 1895*, pp. 97–8; see also 'Fifteen Questions about the Early Film Audience', in Daan Hertogs and Nico de Klerk (eds), *Uncharted Territory* (Amsterdam: Stichting Nederlands Filmmuseum, 1997), pp. 105–18.

48. *The Bioscope*, 23 October 1908, p. 11.

49. For the place of *The Tempest* in this cycle see Pamela Hutchinson, 'The Shakespeare Boom: 1908–1911', unpublished MA dissertation, Birkbeck College, University of London, 2003.

50. For the popularity of the original nineteenth-century cartoon see David Kunzle, *The History of the Comic Strip* (Berkeley: University of California Press, 1990), pp. 316–22; also, Stephen Bottomore, *I Want to See this Annie Mattygraph* (Pordenone: Le Giornate del Cinema Muto, 1995), pp. 32 and 65.

51. 'Explain the Pictures', *The Bioscope*, 10 December 1908, p. 5, and 'The Printed Lecture', 17 December 1908, p. 21; also, 'Auxiliary Aids to the Pictures', 7 October 1909.

52. *The Bioscope*, 10 December 1908, p. 3.

53. 'Mixed Programmes', *The Bioscope*, 17 December 1908, p. 18.

54. *Kine Weekly*, 11 July 1907.

55. 'Pictorial Advertising', *The Bioscope*, 4 February 1909, pp. 5 and 24.

56. See Amy Sargeant, 'Darwin, Duchenne, Delsarte', paper given at *Moving Performance*, Bristol, 1996, Fitzsimmons and Street, *Moving Performance*, pp. 26–43.

Chapter 2 | Teens

Mr May had come to Woodhouse not to look at Jordan's 'Empire', but at the temporary wooden structure that stood in the old Cattle Market – 'Wright's Cinematograph and Variety Theatre'. Wright's was not a superior show, like the Woodhouse Empire. Yet it was always packed with colliers and work-lasses. But unfortunately, there was no chance of Mr May's getting a finger in the Cattle Market pie. Wright's was a family affair, Mr and Mrs Wright and a son and two daughters and their husbands: a tight old lock-up family concern. Yet it was the kind of show that appealed to Mr May: pictures between the turns. The cinematograph was but an item in the programme, amidst the more thrilling incidents – to Mr May – of conjurors, popular songs, five-minute farces, performing birds, and comics. Mr May was too human to believe that a show could consist entirely of the dithering eye-ache of a film.

D. H. Lawrence[1]

Contemporary commentators, such as Harry Furniss (an occasional British producer for Thomas Edison and producer of animation films from his own celebrated cartoons), Low Warren, Frederick Talbot and the trade press, were already in the teens mapping a history which presented British cinema's decline in international markets after the glorious pioneering efforts of its early years.[2] Certainly, America had replaced France as the major producer even before the outbreak of war, a position that its late entry into the fighting (1917) enabled it to consolidate. British cinema of the teens has been criticised by subsequent historians (notably Rachael Low, taking her cue from Furniss) for its adoption of material from the stage and page (conveniently declared 'non cinematic') and for its failure to take American action and comedy films as a correct ('cinematic' and popular) model for imitation.[3] However, the turn towards drama and literature as a source for the new multi-reel productions of 1913 onwards was not novel (see Chapter 1) nor unique to Britain. The Pathé adaptation of Emil Zola's *Germinal* (Albert Cappellani, 1913), with a cast drawn from the Comédie Française, was highly praised in the British press and was recommended to British producers as an example to follow.[4] Meanwhile, American cinema also looked to British plays and novels for subjects: for instance, Vitagraph's 1912 version of Charles Dickens' *Pickwick Papers*, starring the comic actor John Bunny; Edison's 1913 version of Robertson's 1867 *Caste*; the Irish émigré Herbert Brenon's versions of J. M. Barrie's 1904 *Peter Pan* (1924) and his wartime play, *A Kiss for*

Aurèle Sydney, as Ultus, leads his gang

Cinderella (1925); Kalem's version of Dion Boucicault's 1860 melodrama *The Colleen Bawn* (filmed on location in Ireland in 1911) and D. W. Griffith's *Broken Blossoms* (1919 – see Chapter 4), taken from Thomas Burke's 1916 Limehouse short story, 'The Chink and the Child'. Many West End productions were toured in the provinces; some West End stars enjoyed a transatlantic success. Certainly, the industry sought in the films it produced and in the improved conditions of exhibition to appeal 'more and more to the cultured classes', who (insists Frederick Talbot, exaggerating his case) 'constitute its most substantial support'.[5] Picture palaces like the Woodhouse Empire – vaporised, fumigated, decked with palms and plush perfumed draperies and showing lantern slides alongside films – coexisted with the fleapits and sheds reeking of 'the beer drunk by colliers', such as Wright's Variety Theatre. The industry itself lobbied for the installation of Britain's first film censor, appointing four examiners under the directorship of G. A. Redford in 1912 (replaced by T. P. O'Connor in 1917), hoping thereby to assure its patrons of respectable and standardised entertainment. During the war, all films covering the hostilities were subject to censorship. The National Council of Public Morals, concerned primarily with its connection to juvenile crime, reported on cinema in 1917.[6] British film production in the teens was, in fact, highly diverse in scale and quality, with much action and comedy leavening the range of genres and styles on offer in a variety of venues. D. H. Lawrence, like Aldous Huxley, J. B. Priestley and Richard Hoggart thereafter (see Chapters 5 and 8), meanwhile, preferred to extol the virtues of more traditional, 'live' performances on the popular front, while some actors on the legitimate stage continued to prefer appearance before a live audience.

Stage, Page and Screen

The legitimate stage of the teens was a many splendoured thing, with much discussion of the themes of new plays, the treatment of old plays, the style of performance, the training of actors and the rival claims of actors and settings. While the letters pages of the high-brow the *New Age* (in which cinema is conspicuous by its absence) covered the debate concerning the attribution of Shakespeare's plays to the Bard or to Bacon, its theatre critic, Huntly Carter, a devotee of experimental European theatre, frequently disparaged the presentation of the plays on the stage. In November 1911 he comments on a 'hodge podge of setting, cutting and acting':

> The misuse of Shakespeare may be seen at the New Theatre, where *Romeo and Juliet* has been butchered to make a Roman holiday for Miss Nielson-Terry. In order to pad out her part, Friar John is cut, Tybalt is emaciated; while the conclusion linking the action with eternity is buried in Juliet's tomb. Besides this, the scenery is chaotic and the faithful moon, poplar trees and Italian architecture never leave Juliet. The cast is bewildering. It comprises actors of all schools – Devereaux (modern drama), Fisher White (Repertory Theatre methods), Brydone (old, very technical Shakespearean school), Louis Calvert (modern, natural Shakespearean), Berry (Benson declamatory), Ivan Berlyn (Dickens intense character) and so on.[7]

Meanwhile, the film trade press identified national differences in performance in modern comedy and drama (in which the Americans excelled – while being poor in period costume), in (superior) French and (stilted and stereotypical) Italian styles: 'But the worst by far for gesture and pantomime is the British', says *The Bioscope* in 1911; 'Our ordinary actor uses little or no gesture . . . the modern tendency is to eschew emotion'.[8] We are presented with national distinctions of theatrical style (inherited from the 18th century); alongside distinctions drawn between progressive and conservative theatre; alongside distinctions between theatre and cinema; and between cinematic genres.[9]

Ashley Dukes similarly reported Beerbohm Tree's abridged staging of Shakespeare's *Henry VIII* in 1910, duly further cut for William Barker's film of 1911: as played at His Majesty's, it was reduced to three acts and eleven scenes, ending with a pageant in dumb show, representing the coronation.[10] In a much publicised stunt, Barker subsequently destroyed copies of the film, reputedly to prevent the circulation of second-rate material which would damage the reputation of its star.[11] Sir Johnston Forbes-Robertson's (modern, natural Shakespearean) 1913 production of *Hamlet* was abridged for its simultaneous adaptation to film by Cecil Hepworth for Gaumont. The production employs its sets in a currently accepted manner: 'Whether we like it or no', remarked William Archer (ardent Ibsenite) in 1912, 'scenery has ceased to be merely a suggested background . . . the stage now aims at presenting a complete picture with the figures . . . completely in it'; 'the growth of modern drama has been accompanied and conditioned by an ever-increasing harmony between the action and its background, its scenery'.[12] In costumes and settings in the style of Charles Ricketts (heavy brocades and chain-mail; moulded plaster columns patterned after Durham Cathedral), the original Drury Lane *Hamlet* company perform, silently voicing – rather than miming – the text (explained in an accompanying programme and novelisation). The Lyceum Theatre's *Romeo and Juliet* and the Coliseum's production of Dickens' *Scrooge* were also transferred wholesale to the screen. In the manner of theatrical advertisements, Robertson and his co-star, his wife, Gertrude Elliott (as Ophelia), are posed at the outset of *Hamlet* with italic-written banners indicating key lines of text: 'There's rosemary . . . that's for remembrance' (as Ophelia proffers a bouquet). Jon Burrows has suggested that these banner subtitles refer directly to the 'immemorialisation' of the stage text by the screen.[13] Hepworth moves the action between interior settings (which reproduce props and stage devices, such as the arras behind which Polonius and the King hide, employ vast columns as stage wings to provide an off-stage space and use stage depth and blocking between foreground and background in the play within the play rather than intercutting) and exterior settings (the castle portcullis built with Lulworth Cove in the distance; its beach nearby used as a location). Hepworth also uses directional lighting to indicate the time of day in which the action is set and camera movement to indicate the appearance and disappearance of the ghost, itself rendered 'cinematically' by the superimposition of a faint, over-exposed figure. The intertitles of the film reproduce the content of the prose and the scanning of Shakespeare's verse, as character and action dictate; subsidiary characters perform 'stage business' as a background to Hamlet's speeches. The 'players' are marked by their performance in Benson declamatory mode.

Gorgeous historic pageantry in *Jane Shore* (Bert Haldane and Martin Thornton, 1915)

In sum, the Hepworth film is a rich and interesting amalgam, vaunting and reproducing the credentials of its source text and delivery while also employing techniques specific to a newer medium.

William Barker's typically gorgeous *Jane Shore* (Bert Haldane and Martin Thornton, 1915) features banquets and pageants, lavish sets, built in the studio and outside, with location shooting and vast numbers of supernumeraries in period costumes (pudding-bowl haircuts, armour and wimples), horses, pigs and other animals. Herbert Brenon, 'authentically' filming action at Chepstow Castle, and the British company, Zenith, proceeded in similar style for their *Ivanhoe* productions of 1913 (also pastiched as *Pimple's Ivanhoe* [1913]). Talbot reports that the Duke of Argyll loaned his Scottish estate for the filming of *Rob Roy* in 1911, 'volunteering suggestions in order that everything might be as correct as was humanly possible', and that Williamson's *Lady Jane Grey* included scenes shot at the Tower of London.[14] *Sixty Years a Queen* (1913), covering the life of Queen Victoria, was vast in scope and scale, and featured scenes at St Paul's Cathedral: the film reaped commensurate returns for its producer, Barker.[15] Backcloths in *Jane Shore* are painted in perspective to enhance the depth of the sets (deep staging and background action also featuring prominently at the Empire Theatre and the Mephisto Club in Barker's *Rogues of London* [1915]); exteriors are cluttered with extraneous business. Dialogue intertitles and letters reinforce the archaic setting (the action involves the rivalry of the Yorkist and Lancastrian factions under Edward IV): 'Sire, thou doest me a wrong – that lady is my affianced wife' (says Matthew Shore); 'Rise, Sweet friend, of a truth thou hast a winsome advocate' (says Edward to Lord Hastings) and (says the archbishop to Jane, accused of witchcraft and sorcery): 'You shall be hounded from street to street and woe to whomsoever offers you succour'. The blonde Jane, 'that white-faced strumpet', is melodramatically cast against a black-haired rival. Barker's sets frequently use upper galleries and stairs (in the manner of the stage) to expand and comment upon the action, while large figures, positioned foreground (in cinematic style), are sometimes used to frame the action.

Elsewhere in the *New Age*, Huntly Carter mocks the Fabian tracts presented by George Bernard Shaw as 'undramatic', and finds the new social, intimate dramas of Galsworthy, Bennett, the Manchester School (Houghton, Monkhouse and Brighouse) and Granville-Barker (*The Voysey Inheritance* [1909] dubbed 'The Viewsy Inheritance') tub-thumping but shallow.[16] In the same journal, Bertrand Russell describes the popular dramatist Arthur Wing Pinero (whose *Sweet Lavender* [1888] and *The Gay Lord Quex* [1899] were among other plays transferred to the screen) as 'an exploiter of the obvious', 'the Franz Liszt of drama'.[17] Nevertheless, all these authors commanded a following in the teens and were ripe for adaptation to film. Furthermore, when critics in the 1950s complained of 'Loamshire' productions in their own time (Loam House, Mayfair, appearing in the 1902 stage directions for J. M. Barrie's *The Admirable Crichton* and Loam Hall, England, in the opening subtitle to Lewis Gilbert's 1957 film version) they castigate their fellow 'Angry Men' of a previous generation (see Chapter 8). Galsworthy's 1914 *Justice* (filmed by Maurice Elvey in 1917, with Gerald du Maurier and Margaret Bannerman, and again in 1920) concerns a clerk who impetuously forges a cheque to steal funds from his firm in order to secure the escape of his lover from a loveless, brutal marriage, who is then imprisoned and commits suicide rather than be returned to its harsh regime while he is on bail. Hepworth's 1911 *Rachel's Sin*, equally effectively applying elements of domestic stage melodrama, features a refused lover who stands trial and goes to prison to protect a woman (Gladys Sylvani) who murders her husband in self-defence; he is released and then returns to her. Pinero's *The Second Mrs Tanqueray* (directed by Fred Paul for Ideal in 1916, with Sir George Alexander and Hilda Moore), like Oscar Wilde's 1892 *Lady Windermere's Fan* (also filmed by Ideal), Arnold Bennett's 1912 *Milestones* (filmed by Samuelson in 1916), William Somerset-Maugham's 1921 *The Circle*, George Bernard Shaw's 1894 'unpleasant play' *Mrs Warren's Profession* (first performed in 1902, with Granville-Barker) and Noël Coward's 1926 homage to the genre, *Easy Virtue* (see Chapter 4), concerns the moral judgments of one generation upon another and a different moral code prevailing between men and women. Broadwest's 1915 film of Grant Allen's 1895 notorious and scandalous novel, *The Woman Who Did*, covers similar territory, with a commonplace daughter (in spite of the hopes invested in her) rejecting her mother's 'unconventional' life. But, while Maugham, Bennett, Wilde and Shaw preach humility and mercy, Pinero (as in *The Woman Who Did* and Galsworthy's 1920 *The Skin Game* – first filmed in 1921) has Paula Tanqueray, a 'woman with a past', committing suicide before the lesson is learned.

Oscar Wilde (whose memorial in Paris is the subject of discussion in the *New Age* in 1912) was the much vaunted source of Ideal's *Lady Windermere's Fan* (Fred Paul, 1916). Ideal, a distribution company that embarked upon production in 1915, systematically promoted transferrals from the stage. The author's own moral is cited ('there is the same world for all of us . . .') in addition to the original stage production, in ornamented title cards. Mrs Erlynne (Irene Rooke, from the Gaiety Theatre – who appears also in Elvey's second adaptation of the Gaiety's *Hindle Wakes* [see Chapter 4]), in bed in Paris, opens her post (mostly unpaid bills) – then sees a picture in a magazine of her daughter, Margaret (Netta Westcott), whom she has deserted, now married to Lord Windermere (Milton Rosmer, also from the Gaiety Theatre troupe). Mrs Erlynne travels to London and, on Astoria Hotel paper, requests a meeting with her son-in-law – who, initially, is not pleased to meet her: 'You have no right to claim her – you abandoned her as a baby, for your lover, who abandoned you in turn.' But Windermere subsidises Mrs Erlynne in high style, while she is courted by Lord 'Tuppy' Lorton (Nigel Playfair) (consequently, the laughing stock of his club) who proposes to live with her in exile on the Continent. Discovering notes of payments to Mrs Erlynne, Margaret becomes suspicious but Lord Windermere urges that she forgive her mother, 'little more than a girl' when she sinned. In turn, Mrs Erlynne finds a note left by Margaret saying that she is preparing to leave with her lover: 'the same words I wrote to her father – my real punishment is tonight, is now'. While Lord Windermere warns Margaret against her, Mrs Erlynne endeavours to persuade Margaret to remain with her husband and child. Eventually, Margaret becomes aware of Mrs Erlynne's true identity and Lord Windermere assures Tuppy that the 'wonderful' woman he is marrying is really 'very good'.

Contemporary performances were transferred from both the legitimate and non-legitimate stage to the screen. Marie Lloyd appeared in *Marie Lloyd at Home and Bunkered* (1913), George Robey in *The Anti-Frivolity League* (1916) and *My Old Dutch* (directed by the American, Larry Trimble, 1915) featured the coster performer Albert Chevalier, with Florence Turner as his 'donah'. Past luminaries, meanwhile, were invoked in tributes to David Garrick (the London Film Company, Ruffell, Britannia, Hepworth and Zenith all casting eminent thespians in the role), and to Garrick's favourite, Peg Woffington in *Masks and Faces* (Fred Paul, 1917) – also in Anna Neagle's tribute performance in Wilcox's *Peg of Old Drury* (1935). Amid general enthusiasm in France for things English in the last quarter of the 18th century, David Garrick was enormously well received. Garrick, in turn, thought the French style insufficiently natural. At home, his authenticity of delivery was compared favourably with that of Quin (who appears as a character in the play and in the film *Masks and Faces*) and anecdotes abound as to his ability to convey his roles convincingly. He once criticised a French actor's rendition of a drunk, saying that his left foot was insufficiently inebriated, and it is this tale that seems to be the basis of a similar episode in Britannia's 1912 film *David Garrick*, starring Gerald Lawrence, based on Robertson's 1858 play (and, in turn, on Melesville's 1852 *Sullivan*, written for the Comédie Française).[18] These films, should, I think, be viewed in the light of a longstanding campaign to raise the standing of the acting profession in society.

Masks and Faces was made at the suggestion of J. M. Barrie, an enthusiast for film who appreciated its novelty and potential.[19] It is, on the one hand, an adaptation from Charles Reade's popular 1852 play *Masks and Faces: or, Before and Behind the Curtain* and its companion novel, *Peg Woffington*; on the other, a tacit reference to William Archer's 1888 *Masks or Faces*. Archer's essay frequently cites the Reade text and its theme of the duplicity of acting and the sincerity of actors. The film takes some lines (conveyed in intertitles) directly from Reade: 'Stage masks may cover honest faces and hearts beat true beneath a tinselled robe'; 'Yes', concludes Peg, 'sure those kind eyes and bright smiles one traces/Are not deceptive *masks* but honest *faces*'. The film introduces the play proper with a gathering of alumni of the British stage (Pinero, Barrie, Squire Bancroft, Shaw, *et al*.) discussing the project to make a film to raise funds for the Academy of Dramatic Art's building scheme. 'The "pictures" owe much to the stage. It shall repay . . .', remarks Pinero; the film, says Alexander, will prove 'a worthy memorial of the English stage of today'. The cast of the play includes Dennis Neilson-Terry as the foppish Sir Ernest Vane and Irene Vanbrugh as Peg. 'A daylight bomb-dropping expedition against the Neptune Studios at Elstree', says *The Bioscope* reporter, 'would have wiped out 50% of England's leading theatrical talent'.[20] The film, says the reviewer, will serve as a perpetual gala recording of these star performances. But whereas *The Bioscope* praises Forbes-Robertson's 'sincerity and pathos', it seems to me that he also takes his cue from Reade's description; this is to say that Forbes-Robertson (as Triplet) and Vanbrugh (as Peg imitating the doyenne Bracegirdle) act acting by demonstrating a style now outmoded. Triplet is a jack of three trades and a master of none, bidding his farewells in semaphoric mode:

> He bowed in a line from his right shoulder to his left toe, and moved off . . . He came back, exuberant with gratitude. 'I am gone!' These last words he pronounced with his right arm at an angle of 45° and his fingers pointing horizontally . . . In his day, an actor . . . delivered his message in the tone of a falling dynasty, wheeled like a soldier and retired with the left arm pointing to the sky, and the right extended behind him like a setter's tail.[21]

In other words, the film deliberately contrasts the 'over-acting' of Colly Cibber and Triplet with Peg's usual lack of ostentation.

In 1916, Hepworth filmed Pinero's 1898 play *Trelawny of the 'Wells'*, faithfully reproducing the costumes, sets and even the publicity material from the original production. He engaged his regular cast of Stewart Rome, Chrissie White and Alma Taylor in starring roles. Both play and film record the passing of a previous generation of plays and players: Pinero's florid and grandiloquent Tom Wrench is written as a caricature of Robertson; Trelawny himself is a picture of Samuel Phelps, erstwhile manager at London's Sadler's Wells. 'The heavy tragedian Telfer', says a reviewer of the film in 1916, 'is played with proper ponderous dignity';[22] Telfer, a so-called 'old, stagey, out-of-date actor', bemoans the absence of real speeches in the new play ('nothing to dig your teeth into', he says) while Arthur, the young buck, finds that parts match his own self, 'Why, Mr Wrench, some of this is almost me!'[23] Hepworth's 1912 *The Lie* uses a comparable pastiche of acting styles, but to comic effect, contrasting the dastardly Doctor Hume's devilishly arched eyebrows, his fiendish hand rubbing and claw-like hand clenching (performed by Stewart Rome), with Frank Forrester's distraught and frenzied knee-slapping (performed by Lionelle Howard): 'Let us eat, drink and be merry for tomorrow we die!', against Doris' relatively unperturbed and everyday delivery (performed by Chrissie White). This delightful little film tells the story of two rivals for the love of a girl: Doctor Hume tells the hypochondriac Frank that he has a weak heart and only one year to live and, as a consequence, Frank gives up Doris to Doctor Hume; subsequently, encountering Frank after his engagement to Doris, the doctor tells Frank that it was all a ruse, but when Frank draws a gun on him it is the doctor who collapses with a fatal heart-attack.

Maurice Elvey transferred Ada King (as the grasping Mrs Hawthorn) from the Manchester and London productions of Stanley Houghton's 1912 *Hindle Wakes* to the screen in 1918. Elvey himself acknowledged that many American films were superior in their elaborate sets and abundance of detail, but, nevertheless, 'the fact [could] not be gainsaid that the British public dearly loves real sentiment and English sentiment and English atmosphere in its pictures' (a different 'sentiment' and 'atmosphere' to that purveyed by Hepworth's *Comin' Thro' the Rye* [1916 and 1923]).[24] 'The story is strong, simple and straightforward', said *The Bioscope* of Elvey's 1918 film, 'and therefore well-adapted to silent drama. It gives ample scope to its artists and a very efficient company takes every advantage of the opportunities provided by many strong characters in situations of great dramatic effect.'[25] In 1958, as a fiftieth anniversary tribute to the opening of the Gaiety Theatre, Granada TV produced Harold Brighouse's *Dealing in Futures*, Houghton's *The Younger Generation* and Allan Monkhouse's *Mary Broome*, consciously aligning the earlier Manchester School with such contemporary plays as *Billy Liar!* and *A Taste of Honey* (see Chapter 9).

The American director and producer, Harold Shaw, literally takes to the stage for his seasonally pathetic tale of *The Two Columbines* (1914) (see Chapter 1); Pearson's 1920 *Nothing Else Matters* similarly deploys the traditional figures of Pierrot, Columbine and Harlequin in its prologue. On Christmas Eve, a theatre cleaner (Christine Rayner) unveils a spindly Christmas tree and tells her daughter of the time, years ago, when she danced the pantomime role of Columbine: a flashback shows a sumptuous set, with Columbine accompanied by Harlequin and Pantaloon; the dancer injures an ankle and is told by a doctor in the house that she will never perform in public again. While the mother tucks up her daughter in bed, another Columbine waits for her fiancé, another Harlequin, to accompany her to a dress rehearsal. The daughter hangs up her Christmas stocking and talks to her dolly. The cleaner forlornly goes to the theatre, where she is greeted by a whiskered doorkeeper (Charles Rock). Enraptured (then sad) she watches the rehearsal and sways to the music. The poor daughter imagines Santa Claus (in the manner of Smith's 1898 *Santa Claus* and Cricks' 1916 *Here We are Again* – also with Harlequin and Columbine in attendance) bringing presents (which she will not receive) and the mother contrives a way of giving her a 'proper' Christmas. She carries her to the theatre, by-passing a now tipsy doorkeeper, and in Columbine costume, painfully dances for her under the lovely 'light of other days' until her leg and her heart give up. A policeman (as in *A Kiss for Cinderella*) is called in from the snow and the other Columbine tells the daughter that mamma has gone to sleep. Finally, in superimposition, Santa and the mother appear blessing the child's union with a surrogate, theatre family.

Many of the costume adaptations of the teens draw upon stage and novel versions of similar material (as with a number of Dickens adaptations, *East Lynne*, on stage and screen and Reade's *Masks and Faces/Peg Woffington* and in his *It Is Never Too Late to Mend* [1865] – the title referring to a reformed convict and to the story's romantic interest). While Thomas Bentley (the Dickens intense character actor turned director) acknowledges Dickens directly in *The Old Curiosity Shop* (1918), *Jo, the Crossing Sweeper* (1918) and *Scrooge* (1913) refer indirectly, respectively, to *Bleak House* and *A Christmas Carol*, of which there were timely releases in 1911 and 1914. Thomas Hardy's *Far From the Madding Crowd* (originally serialised in 1873) was filmed by Larry Trimble with Florence Turner and Henry Edwards in 1915. *The Mighty Atom* (Cricks and Martin, 1911) appropriates the title of Marie Corelli's enormously popular 1896 story (in its thirtieth edition by 1912) while, in content (a son heroically following his father into war against the Arabs), it has more in common with the redemption narrative of her Boer War novel, *Boy*.

Along with the novelists Arnold Bennett and Eden Philpotts (popular in spite of carping from the *New Age*), the urbane A. E. W. Mason provided material for films. Possibly better known for his work with Korda in the 1930s (one of several British and American versions of *The Four Feathers* – first adapted in 1915, *The Drum* [1938] and his own screenplay for *Fire Over England* [1937] – see Chapter 5), Mason's 1910 *At the Villa Rose* was adapted by Sinclair Hill for Elvey in 1920 and again filmed by Leslie Hiscott in 1930 and by Walter Summers in 1939. The 1920 version appeared in a series of adaptations of the work of 'Eminent British Authors', produced by the eminently entrepreneurial Oswald Stoll, a former music hall impresario: other authors featured included Conan Doyle, H. G. Wells and Marie Corelli. Elvey transfers the action from Aix-les-Bains to the fashionable Riviera (a former haunt of Paula Tanqueray) and finds, in Terry Arundell, a delightfully 'elephantinely elfish' detective Inspector Hanaud, casting Norman Page as his foil, the amateur sleuth, Ricardo.[26] Elvey, in luridly coloured sequences, exploits the novel's references to the occult, matching Douglas Payne's *Fraudulent Spiritualism Exposed* (1913) and the uncredited *How a Spiritualist Séance was Disturbed* (1908). Glamorous costuming and exotic locations provide an additional attraction. Hanaud exposes the fiancé of the companion to a wealthy widow to be both the murderer of the widow and the source of allegations against the companion. Ricardo, meanwhile, identifies only the false trail set by the culprit. As with *Ultus*, newspaper intertitles are used to advance the story and written depositions are used in evidence. Elvey's brisk handling of his material confirms that, at their best, adaptations need not be slavishly wordy nor stagebound.

Lovers and Letters

Harold Shaw's 1914 *Trilby* again seeks to secure credentials, and to profit, from the enormous success of its literary and stage precursors. Sir Herbert Beerbohm Tree bows to his audience at the
outset, assuming a pose inherited from du Maurier and from the stage. Furthermore, Tree
suggested that a 'private' shot of himself be shown to demonstrate his transformation into the
role. George du Maurier's 1895 novel, illustrated by the author and drawing on his own experiences as an art student in Paris, led to a 'Trilby craze' in Britain (songs, sketches, costumes and
other ephemera);[27] Tree made the role of Svengali his own in his inaugural 1895 stage performance at His Majesty's, faithfully reproduced (as testified by contemporaneous photographs and
advertisements) to the screen and concurrently performed as a music hall turn. As the evil Jew, the
performance also owes something to Tree's interpretation of Shakespeare's Shylock in *The Merchant of Venice* (staged in 1913). Backcloths show the roofs of Paris and Notre Dame from the
South Bank, set against 'the comfortable English home' of Billee, who is in love with Trilby. Again,
there is a combination of stage devices (conversations overheard between doors and screens) with
a proliferation of cinematic cut-aways in close-up to (diegetic) lovers' letters, lawyers' letters, locket
pictures, telegrams, calling-cards, posters (announcing Trilby's performances) and the (non-diegetic)
spider in his web, which du Maurier intends as a metaphor for the etiolated and malevolent Svengali captivating Trilby, his 'fly' (somewhat compromised by the ample form of Beerbohm Tree).
Tree's copy of the scenario comments that 'the average cinema audience is not fond of solving
problems – nor are the average exhibitors fond of showing films that are unsatisfactory to the average audiences'.[28] Otherwise, the film faithfully reproduces du Maurier's illustrations, Trilby, the
artist's model and tone-deaf concert performer (Viva Birkett), herself appearing in characteristic
military jacket, broad-striped skirt and much fetishised bare feet.

Barker's lavish 1913 adaptation of *East Lynne* (directed by André Beaulieu) advises that it has
been adapted from Mrs Henry Wood's 'world famous novel' (1861) and that it is to be performed
by Barker's All-British Stock Company. Burke's Pansy Greers spends her Sundays in Limehouse in
bed reading *East Lynne*;[29] there had been numerous stage productions (it was a staple of provincial Repertory Theatre) and playbills showing Little Willie reaching out to the angels prior to his
demise (yet never having called Lady Isabel mother) are reproduced as a key scene of the film. A
variety of roles are distributed, from a Dickensian character part (a solicitor's clerk) to the *grand
guignol* of Levinson, to the melodramatic sufferance of the much-wronged Isabel. An American
adaptation was produced by Fox in 1916. However, unlike Hepworth's versions of popular literary
classics in the teens (notably *Comin' Thro' the Rye*), Beaulieu directs the action at a cracking pace,
cutting easily between interiors and exteriors, often blocking actors' moves on the diagonal and
directing them past the camera rather than holding them in long shot, full-figure, full-square.
Camera moves follow couples as they trail after each other around the village pond. The *mise en
scène* (walls, gates, hedges) is deployed to convey overheard conversations and to amplify opportunities missed. While *The Second Mrs Tanqueray* features letters burned, Hepworth's 1911 *Stolen
Letters* (with Gladys Sylvani) finds a goldminer returning in time to save his wife from suicide after

a jealous postman destroys his letters. *East Lynne* has the dastardly Levinson (children cower as he approaches) intercepting a letter, 'to poison Lady Isabel's mind against her husband'. The receipt of a letter from her gives Carlyle, in turn, an opportunity for acting in the declamatory mode: he clutches at his face, then at his throat, before showing the letter to his sister. 'A terrible surprise', forewarns the intertitle: 'To remain under your roof after your conduct this night would be unbearable – may heaven forgive us both'; hearing the silent cry accompanying the action, the servants rush in to see what has happened.

Turner's *East is East* (1917), also an adaptation from the stage, was directed by Henry Edwards and starred the American Florence Turner. It shares with her *Shopgirls* (1915) a contemporary setting, but depicts the East End in a more picturesque manner than is allowed by the novels of Burke and Wells. Barker, too, generally opts for a darker vision when filming life 'East of Mansion House'. Henry Edwards is cast as the lovable cloth-capped coster Bert Grummet: in the darkness of a picture palace, he declares his love for his childhood sweetheart, Victoria Vickers: 'Vicky, I finds yer orl rite – S'pose we walks aht togevver?' While Bert dreams of owning a fish shop, a Western Union cablegram arrives announcing that Henry Vickers has left £¼m to his niece Victoria, whom he last saw fifteen years ago in Stepney. Victoria and her family go hop-picking in Kent and the executors endeavour to find her. Newspaper intertitles convey the hot pursuit. Just as a telegram is being prepared, her discovery is announced: thus is Vicky transported from rags to riches and, like Eliza Doolittle (in Shaw's 1912 'romance', *Pygmalion*, filmed by Asquith in 1938), 'Victoria takes her first step Westward'. But Bert continues on his own path of hard-earned self-advancement. Having seen a newspaper announcement of dogfish surpluses, he not only secures the shop with marble-topped tables, delivery vans and subsidiary branches, but also a patent, in the style of Wells' 1909 *Tono Bungay*, for 'Grummet's Gargle'.[30] As proof of his entrepreneurial success, he shows Vicky his business stationery. Bert (now in top hat with wing collar and buttonhole) is distraught when he sees a newspaper bill advertising the engagement of the 'Hopfield heiress', then relieved when he reads that she is not to marry, after all. 'To hell with being ladylike! I'm East, I am!' asserts Vicky, wanting to be rid of 'the atmosphere of unreality' to which her inheritance has introduced her. Bert and Vicky are eventually reunited over a cup of tea at the half-timbered cottage in Kent, amid chickens and chicken-pens, where they first contemplated their ideal future: despite their social adventures and vicissitudes, 'home' with one another is best for them, after all.

The introduction of letters and other written materials into dramatic narratives is significant of film's inheritance of devices from pre-cinematic precedents, as a continuing prompt to performance and for the development of cinematic techniques, such as parallel editing. It may also suggest that these films were directed towards a literate audience, as opposed to the more general appeal of slapstick. As a visual element, written materials can convey narrative information quickly and efficiently. But increasingly, long letters and long intertitles are deemed to delay action and are discouraged.

To be Continued . . .

Series and serials, both home-produced and imported, were the most popular films of the teens. Imitating a practice established in print weeklies and quarterlies, series and serials fostered loyal and regular cinema attendance;[31] during the war, the number of visits and visitors was boosted by the urge to see the latest pictures from the front. The film of Percy Moran's Lt Daring story, *Lt Daring and the Secret Service Agents*, is advertised in *The Bioscope* in December 1911 with a telegram, to be followed by *Lt Daring and the Ship's Mascot* (1912); *Lt Daring, RN, Defeats the Middleweight Champion* (1912) and *Lt Daring, RN, Quells a Rebellion* (1912). Chrissie White and Alma Taylor first appeared for Hepworth in comedy shorts as 'the Tilly girls' – launched with the dancer Unity More in the title role as *Tilly the Tomboy* – including *Tilly's Party* (1911), *Tilly and the Smugglers* (1911), *Tilly Works for a Living* (1912), *Tilly in a Boarding House* (1912) *Tilly and the Coastguard* (1913) and further Tomboy tales. Later they graduated to more serious dramatic roles and were credited under their own names, in *Lancashire Lass* (1915), *The Outrage* (1915), a 'soft' adaptation of Pinero's 1901 *Iris* (1916), *Her Marriage Lines* (1917), *The Nature of the Beast* (1919) and *Comin' Thro' the Rye*.

Some series stars portrayed characters, or pursued careers, previously established on the popular stage in 'five minute farces'. The comedians Joe and Fred Evans, for instance, in their numerous *Pimple* films, frequently adopted identifiable music hall garb and make-up, often a loud-checked jacket, mis-matched trousers and an under-sized hat perilously perched on the back of Fred's head. The speed with which these shorts were made enabled the Evans brothers to respond to current news stories and events. In January 1914 *The Bioscope* remarked upon *Lt Pimple and the Stolen Submarine*: 'In spite of the fact that this series has been running for some considerable time at the rate of one production a week, there seems to be no end to Mr Evans' fertility of invention'; comedies, it adds, need 'to be acted with vim to be received well'.[32] *Lt Pimple's Dash for the Pole* (1914) refers to the expeditions of Scott and Shackleton, while *Pimple in 'The Whip'* (1917) refers to the stage revival of an already ancient melodrama. This and *Pimple's Uncle* (1915) – a litany of wills, letters and faked letters which are betrayed by their handwriting – simultaneously mock cinematic and stage conventions. 'The Whip' opens with the *dramatis personae* introduced to the audience (in the manner of Trilby and so forth): Lord Elpus (a s'nice man – and his fiasco, Lady Jones – some girl); Lord For Givus (s'horrible man); Lady Bird (s'awful woman). The villain of the piece is more dastardly than *East Lynne*'s Levinson (with exaggerated moustachios and rolling eyes – 'Ha! Ha! Ha', he cackles); the coquettish 'Eroine has a false snub nose and the 'Ero is, of course, Pimple himself. The cast is augmented, we are told, by jockeys, horses, rabbits, mice, chorus girls and parsons etc. (again, a reference to elaborate 'naturalistic' stagings then in favour). The slapstick is unashamedly cheaply and cheerfully executed, with additional topical and visual gags in the intertitles: 'The Whip' (a pantomime horse, as in *How*

Alma Taylor as a clerk in Hepworth's *Tilly* series

Pimple Saved the Kissing Cup [1913]) carries odds of 4¾d to 2d; when the horses are 'off' all the jockeys fall off. Charlie Peace, the famous murderer (see Chapter 1), suffers the indignity of sharing a waxwork museum with the Kaiser. In Morecambe and Wise (or Reeves and Mortimer) manner, Pimple issues instructions to the beleaguered stage hands who fail repeatedly to time the release of the horse before the arrival of another (very cardboard) train. 'Saved!' reads a redundant intertitle, at long last. In *Pimple's Part* (1916), Pimple lampoons the grandiloquent speech and gestures of declamatory actors: 'Ah Slave! Go forth and bring hither a goblet of crushed malt, a slice of pig's flesh and two sittings of ye hen boiled!' while in *Pimple's Waterloo* (1913) – a spoof of British and Colonial's 1913 *Battle of Waterloo* – and in *Pimple's Charge of the Light Brigade* (1914), Alfred, Lord Tennyson's 1864 verse is pastiched as the cavalry mistakes its course and arrives at 'The Valley of Death Inn':

> Was there a man dismayed?
> Tho' in a turning wrong they'd strayed
>   and could smell the bacon burning
> Theirs not the fat to chew
> Theirs but to go straight through
>   and find the right turning.

> 'We'll all die together' – the six hundred echoed 'NOT ARF'

> Theirs not to reason why
> Theirs but to do or die
>   and as their throats were dry
> Into the Valley of Death
>   flew the six hundred.

Pimple's Inferno (1913) is advertised as 'Pimple's – not Dante's'. In the *Pimple* films, robust humour survives from earlier comedies: suffragettes, spinsters and spooning couples appear as the butt of pranks executed by small boys (and older boys), sometimes (as in *Pimple's Complaint* and *Pimple's New Job* [both 1913]) equipped with glue pots.

George Robey's music hall stage performance as the original Pears' Baby, from John Everett Millais' 'Bubbles' (1886), is some sort of a precedent for Clarendon's *Did'ums* series (see Chapter 1). More immediately, however, the series satirises by exaggeration the fashion of dressing and grooming middle-class infant boys and girls alike as if they were would-be angels, as in *Did'ums and the Christmas Pudding* (1911). Did'ums and a donkey wreak havoc in *Did'ums and the Bathing Machine* (1911), making a spectacle of a bather whose clothes have been stolen, and the child causes mischief in a hotel by swapping room numbers in *Daddy's Did'ums on a Holiday* (1912); Did'ums embarrasses and thwarts the plans of his elders and betters in *Daddy's Little Did'ums Did It* (1910), when he stows away to Paris in an oversized hatbox and then climbs into the nuptial bed,

Aurèle Sydney shows how it's done in *Ultus and The Grey Lady* (George Pearson, 1916)

and in *Daddy's Little Did'ums and the New Baby* (1911) hides the new baby in a coalscuttle. The tradition of segregated schools and colleges provides the subject matter of much situation comedy. In Clarendon's *Love and the Varsity* (1913), the headmistress of the local finishing school, Miss Spinster, is ridiculed for failing to recognise the Varsity boys in disguise, and then for failing to prevent the elopement: with axe in hand, she arrives at the Registry Office just in time to see them wed. In *Tilly's Party*, men are found in the house after hours; in *Tilly in a Boarding House*, girls escape the supervision of their governess by dressing in men's clothes.

Other series have higher aspirations to taste and respectability. According to the director, George Pearson, *Ultus* was initiated by British Gaumont as a response to the hugely popular *Fantômas* series, produced by its French parent company.[33] *Ultus: the Man from the Dead* (1916), *Ultus and the Grey Lady* (1916), *The Button Mystery* (1917) and *The Secret of the Night* (1917) combined a rugged tale of a friendship, sealed in blood but betrayed in the Outback (as in the Klondike stories of Jack London), with supernatural mystery and suspense, detective thriller and romance. It shares with its French precedent a fascination with intrepid escape, ingenious and improvised devices and devious disguises. In *Ultus and the Grey Lady*, Aurèle Sydney (as Ultus) somewhat laboriously adopts false whiskers in front of a mirror on camera: like Conan Doyle's Sherlock Holmes (in *The Sign of the Four* [1923] – see Chapter 4), Hornung's swell cracksman Raffles and John Buchan's Richard Hannay, he resorts to disguise in order to get the better of his adversaries. The firms Kineto and Imp both produced adaptations of Robert Louis Stevenson's 1886 *Dr Jekyll and Mr Hyde* in 1913, while both Sydney and Alma Taylor (in Hepworth's 1920 *Anna the Adventuress*) appeared in dual roles in double exposure in the same film. The *Daily Mirror* in December 1913 suggested how easily disguises could be effected by showing one man variously made-up; it subsequently reported that a murder suspect had been apprehended cleverly disguised with shaved eyebrows, a shade over his right eye and wearing spectacles.[34] The *Ultus* stories were serialised in the popular magazine *Pictures and the Picturegoer* and adapted as a novel by Reginald Hodder, where Morris Morgan, aka Ultus, is described as 'a long thin, hairpin-looking man, with hooked nose and deep-set, hawk-like eyes' – in other words, identifying Sydney himself with the character.[35] The action moves between the city and country estates, recognisable landmark locations and nondescript stretches of river (where the crooks hide out), between palm-strewn high-class dinner-rooms in the West End and murky, sometimes sinister, dens in the East. In Barker's *The German Spy Peril* (Bert Haldane, 1917), our hero, refused for active service by the Medical Board, intercepts a conspiracy to tunnel under the Houses of Parliament and plant a bomb, and (following the example of Ultus) cuts the ropes with which his adversaries have tied his wrists with a broken bottle.

The heroine of *The Exploits of Three-Fingered Kate* (produced by British and Colonial in 1912) boldly operates on the windy side of the law, flaunting her mark rather than disguising it. Kate and her sister have evidently managed to sustain a life of some style by their adept organisation of crime (at the beginning of *Kate Purloins the Wedding Presents* [1912] their maid delivers a new hat to Kate) and they live in comfort in suburbia. Kate intercepts a letter entrusted to a child from which she learns that her next-door neighbour is hiring a private detective (Sheerluck) to guard gifts valued at £1,000. Her confederates 'come to receive their daily instructions' and, during the night, commence operations, removing the back of a connecting fireplace. Sheerluck's assistant poses as a butler to keep watch, but he is entirely outwitted by Kate who, with supreme bravado, sets an alarm clock to ring twenty minutes after the gang have made their getaway. Winking to camera, Kate salutes the audience, while the wedding guests discover her note: 'Compliments to Detective Sheerluck'.

Audiences were also exposed, in combined programmes of shorts and feature films, to series of 'scientific' films, either imported (as Talbot suggests, from France and Germany) or home-produced by Percy Smith (who continued, with Mary Field, to produce educational films into the 1930s). But Furniss advised against their incorporation in an evening's entertainment:

Up to the present we have had some very ingenious but eminently disagreeable 'educational films' which are all right in their proper sphere, that is, in the lecture hall or the schoolroom, but are altogether out of place sandwiched between films of a popular and entertainment nature. When one strolls to a picture palace after dinner, say, to enjoy a cigar and pictures, one hardly expects to be treated to the spectacle of cheese-maggots enlarged to the dimensions of alligators, or the progress of garden slugs, or tadpoles, or equally slimy and unbeautiful abominations, from the figurative cradle to the metaphorical grave.[36]

Nevertheless, Talbot acknowledges that in the field of 'popular science' (as opposed to the microscopic study of bacteria), 'the world's market is practically supplied by the English company, Kineto', and praises Smith's 'happy faculty of investing his subjects with quaint fascination which compels appreciation'. He details the patience with which Smith constructed the apparatus necessary to photograph the hatching of an egg (over two days) to produce one minute on screen and to record the development of a flower from seed to blossom. He also presented flies and bluebottles juggling and balancing, 'humanising' his subjects as they turned wheels and supported weights. Yet again (see Chapter 1) the programme of silent cinema merits comparison with the 'flow' of television described by Raymond Williams in the 1970s (see Chapter 10).

Talbot praises the continuing place in the programme of non-fiction features. Especially successful, at home and abroad, were films such as Ponting's record of Scott's final expedition to the South Pole in 1912 and Frank Hurley's *South* (1919). Both films are significant in their contribution to what Francis Spufford calls 'the imaginative compost' in the mentality of an age; indeed, the Antarctic expedition of 1898 had also been equipped with a film camera.[37] Ponting's film ends with pictures taken after Scott's death of the monument erected by the search party. *South* opens in militaristic terms: 'a wonderful and true story of British pluck, self-sacrifice . . . and courage'; Shackleton and Worsley are shown 'ready for the fray'. While Ernest Shackleton is depicted as the leader of the expedition, his ship, *The Endurance*, is presented as a model of team spirit (as is, one might suggest, HMS *Torrin* in *In Which We Serve* [1942] – see Chapter 6): 'all the crew help with jobs'. We are introduced to different personnel and their various scientific and naval responsibilities and the slow progress through the icy seas of the South Atlantic. The prow of *The Endurance* noses through ice four feet thick and the crew encounters the 'Castle Berg', 'a familiar landmark for nine months', thirty-two miles long and 150 feet high. A litter of pups is delivered during the freeze and seals and a whale are killed to feed the dogs. Much is made of the smallness of the ship, the boats in which the crew evacuates and the sledges with which they routinely train, set against the vast expanse of white, 'Shackleton and his men went 800 miles to South Georgia to get help'. Hurley (like Ponting) records at some length the fauna (shags, petrels, sea elephants) and their native habitat. 'South Georgia boasts more than one Charlie Chaplin', comments the film of a flock of waddling king penguins. 'The fairy-tale aspect of the ship' is shown at night (with the aid of eighteen arc lamps), 'the magical effect of frost on the rigging', set off by the intense darkness of the sky. The outcome of Shackleton's expedition (and, in contrast, Scott's demise) is hardly unknown to the audience, but we are told: 'On the fourth attempt, Shackleton succeeded in rescuing his 22 companions: all saved, all well'. Furthermore, lest we forget, we are finally reminded of the intended moral: 'A story of British heroism, valour and self-sacrifice . . . of British honour . . .

which will be remembered as long as the Empire lasts'. The film ends with a shot of a sunset, as if to recall the Empire on which the sun never sets.

In addition to the intentional narrative and character series of the teens, there are recurrent subjects (such as suffragettes) and a cycle of films which employ a particular setting (notably London) as their location. In November 1911, the *New Age* announces the launch of a new weekly feminist review, *The Freewoman*: the first issue included discussion of the definition of marriage; university degrees for women; the psychology of sex; municipal lodging houses for women; the illusion of a propagandist drama and 'the spinster'. In February 1911, a symposium on Women's Suffrage organised by the *New Age* invited contributions from the great and the good, H. G. Wells commenting that 'the militants have now become ridiculous'. Mrs Pankhurst (caricatured as 'Mrs Spankfirst') and her 'wimmin' followers are regularly lampooned by the *New Age* and the general press. The activities of actual suffragettes were documented on film: suffragettes had been involved in the making of a propaganda film in 1908, Furniss reports filming suffragettes in White-hall for Edison and Emily Davidson's death under the King's horse at the Derby was recorded in 1913.[38] However, popular entertainment on the legitimate stage and in the halls, and films made for a popular audience, tends to adopt a dismissive attitude towards women's emancipation and the suffrage question. In *How Pimple Saved the Kissing Cup*, a jockey disrupts a 'Votes for Women' meeting and accordingly receives a kicking and a beating from the suffragettes. Cricks and Martin's 1913 *Finding Your Counterpart* mocks those who would turn the world topsy-turvy, 'men in skirts and women in trousers', while in Clarendon's 1913 *Milling the Militants*, the harridan Mrs Brown dumps the children on her husband in order to demonstrate with her suffrage sisters; in his dreams, the suburban Mr Brown becomes Prime Minister, is visited by David Lloyd George, and legislates for the suppression of the suffragettes – a fitting punishment for setting fire to pillar boxes is to shame women into six weeks in trousers . . . they apparently do not take to men's work and menswear after all.[39] Sportswomen, as in *Wife: the Weaker Vessel* (1915), and academics are also the butt of humour, sometimes for ineptitude in the activity itself (women should not attempt what men do better), and sometimes, by extension, in the assumption that they must thereby somehow be, or become, less femininely attractive (men do not make passes at girls who wear glasses or cycling gear). The suffragettes responded in kind to these frequent attacks with similar jibes. For example, the eponymous hero of Gertrude Colmore's story 'George Lloyd', published in the weekly woman's suffrage newspaper, is a suffragette in disguise.

Many films of the teens share with contemporary literature a long-established vision of London as the Great Wen. H. G. Wells described the 'yeasty expansion' of the city into the suburbs and characterised 'the whole effect of industrial London and of all London east of Temple Bar and of the huge dingey immensity of London port' as 'something disproportionately large, morbidly expanded, without plan or intention, dark and sinister towards the clean, clear social assurance of the West End'.[40] For Thomas Burke, a Son of London, 'horrid things have to be told of Limehouse', a dingy place of black and yellow faces and 'lurid girls in gin-warmed bars'.[41] In 1913, *The Mystery of the £500,000 Pearl Necklace* is advertised by its scenes shot in London (prominent hotels;

a motor chase; Liptons; Trafalgar Square; a sensational escape by crane) and in Paris (the Tuileries; the Eiffel Tower; the Gare du Nord; crossing the Channel). Hepworth's 1914 contribution to the cycle, *The Lure of London*, was similarly praised for scenes enacted among the hustle and bustle of the city, with Daisy (Ivy Close) working as a Flower Girl in Piccadilly (a forerunner of Pearson's 1920s *Squibs* series – see Chapter 4). Daisy and Charlie, who believe themselves to be brother and sister, have an unhappy life with their adoptive parents, the Brooks (who, like Burke's Battling Burrows, are often the worse for drink and beat their charges). An artist encounters Daisy, dancing to an organ-grinder in an alleyway, and is attracted by her picturesque poverty and good looks; at his St Johns Wood studio he introduces her to a theatre impresario who offers her work on the stage. She signs for an Australian tour and finally is restored to her long-lost parents.

British and Colonial's *When London Sleeps* (1914), a story of 'love, jealousy and villainy', acknowledges the sensational potential of its setting with 'sad rogues' (comparable to the *Ultus* character, Lester, an ex-convict and police snout) set against 'manly and charming heroes' (such as the debonair Man from the Yard, Conway Bass, 'a man worthy of Ultus' steel'). Christine Gledhill identifies Maurice Elvey's use of landmarks (Westminster Bridge and the Houses of Parliament) as a 'selling-point' in his first film as director, *The Great Gold Robbery* (1913).[42] In Barker's *Rogues of London* (Bert Haldane, 1915), a society gentleman, Ralph Munt (Fred Paul), dupes a maid, Ruth Davies (Blanche Forsyth), into robbing from her mistress with a promise of marriage. The jewels secured, he rejects her and wishes to be rid of her. Meanwhile, Dick Hume, in the idyll of the countryside, proposes to Mary, his father's ward, and is accepted. A newspaper insert announces the hunt for Ruth but she demonstrates her fundamental goodness by selflessly assisting the police to apprehend a pickpocket. Dick returns to his lodgings in Westminster to resume his studies and befriends Ruth. Ralph encounters Dick at the Turkish baths and, as men about town, together they indulge in the pleasures of the Rat Pit, the race course, the Empire Variety Theatre, where Ruth has a job as a programme-seller, and the Mephisto Club, a flesh-pit where Munt meets and plots with the worldly Vera Verez (Maud Yates). Ruth resolves to 'save Dick from the claws of those vultures'. Dick at last admits that Ralph has been the ruin of him and is reunited with Mary. Barker made something of a speciality of London films, with *London by Night* (1913) garnering praise for its scenes on the Embankment and in the shadow of Big Ben (stretches of the Thames also covered in Ruth's attempted suicide in *Rogues of London*, by A. E. Coleby's *Mysteries of London* [1914] and reappearing in the night and fog of David Lean's *Oliver Twist* [1948]). This was, said *The Bioscope*, 'a Sims cum Shirley cum Melville type of melodrama, essentially well-adapted because of the rapid succession of scenes and sensations'.[43] Barker turned to George R. Sims himself for *The Lights of London* (Bert Haldane,1914), on which he served as both author and producer. Sims, as Low Warren confirms, was (like Dickens and Burke) as much concerned with reporting and improving the living conditions of London's poor as with exploiting it as material for fiction.[44]

The opposition between town and country (as in *East is East*) reappears in Elvey's 1914 *Her Luck in London*, in which a beautiful farmer's daughter is lured to the wickedness of the city, and in Arthur Rooke's 1920 *The Lure of Crooning Water,* in which an actress (Ivy Duke) is sent by her doctor to the country to recuperate. She seduces the farmer (Guy Newell) in whose house she is guest, only to cast him aside when he follows her back to London: he returns to his wife and family. But the actress has become as she is, it is shown, as a result of abuses suffered in the darkness of the city, and the country (especially her attachment to the farmer's bonny, healthy children) serves to redeem and restore her both spiritually and physically.

Many films, both British and imported, were presented as series and serials in the teens and became an important item in the programme. There are also self-contained films which can be placed thematically into series extending beyond the teens into British cinema's subsequent history; they can also be related to patterns of representation which are shared by cinema with other areas of British culture.

Manuals and Mantras

As Jane Bryan has observed, fan magazines of the teens served primarily to reproduce the stories of photoplays, sometimes serialised.[45] Subsequently, they reported news of Hollywood stars (Mary Pickford, Charlie Chaplin, the cowboy Tom Mix) and British aspirants: Hepworth's Gerald Ames had previous experience on the boards of the legitimate stage (but declared no consequent loss of dignity and no intention to return); Alma Taylor, when twelve, was invited to what she thought was no more than a fancy dress ball and then was told that she had appeared in a film for Hepworth; Chrissie White joined the company at eleven and was similarly celebrated (also in Valentia Steer's 1913 *The Romance of the Cinema*) for her *lack* of theatrical convention.[46] Although stars (such as Pickford and Chaplin) may be born and not made, even Chaplin, reports *The Evening News* in 1917, 'was only five years ago, just a face in the crowd'.[47] In 1919, Aurèle Sydney, a former stage actor in Australia, was said to be the highest-paid contract player in Britain, signing to Gaumont for 'approaching three figures a week' while the humble crowd super could earn as little as £1 a day;[48] *Pictures and the Picturegoer* reported British and Colonial's leading star, Elisabeth Risdon, to be earning £10 a week in 1915 and Steer notes that salaries are considerably higher in America and on the Continent.[49] Hepworth resisted the creation of 'stars' who could transfer themselves elsewhere and command a larger percentage at the expense of his profits; in other companies' productions, captions indicate where an actor is on 'loan' from his Hepworth contract.[50] Meanwhile, Sydney's career as Ultus was further promoted by souvenir postcards, tireless publicity tours and acting manuals, advertised in the press.

'Your special business as a kinema artiste is to find a way of acting in this unnatural manner so that it will appear perfectly natural when reproduced on screen,' advises Sydney in a manual of 1917 or thereabouts.[51] Opinions differ as to whether stage experience was a help or a hindrance, although the manuals often endorse rehearsal exercises reminiscent of established dramatic academies. The authors of the manuals (or, more probably, their ghost writers) are keen to stress the professionalism with which they approach their work. Steer (former editor of *The Pathé Animated*

Gazette) presents in his 1920 *Secrets of the Cinema* a list of 'dos and don'ts' apparently culled from Theda Bara; Sydney advises,

> Free your mind of the idea that the kinema business is a sort of Bohemian pleasure ground. On the contrary, it's one of the most arduous professions you could select and requires the maximum amount of ability, energy and common sense . . . In every sphere of life all of us have to make small beginnings, starting at the bottom of the ladder in order that one may acquire at every rung the essential knowledge that takes us to the top.[52]

George Edgar's *Careers for Men, Women and Children* (1911) reminds his readers that film work is likely to prove seasonal and irregular. Sydney's readers are initiated into the jargon and procedures of the trade and advised on the costumes which a super might be expected to supply.

But amateurs were undeterred and the fan, trade and general press continued to fuel their fantasies. Talbot indicates that cinematograph studios outside London often used touring theatre companies as a supply of personnel. In 1913, the International Cinematograph Exhibition at Olympia ran a contest attracting some 3,200 applicants, including many servants. Competitors were required to express various emotions (as indicated in the manuals – for instance, Stewart Rome doing Happiness, Horror, Doubt, Determination, 'some of the more common facial expressions the film actor and actress may be called upon to portray'; Violet Hopson doing Anger, Uncertainty, Mollification, Disgust, Terror) before a panel of judges, including Hepworth.[53] As a result, thirty-two of those selected secured jobs with film companies. Steer, in 1920, suggested that youth, slender build, dark eyes and blonde hair would find favour in a woman. In 1919, Ivy Close came to producers' attention following her success in the *Daily Mirror* beauty contest and, the following year, the *Daily Express* and *Pathé Pictorial* launched a Screen Beauty Competition, promising large cash prizes.[54] But all the manuals stress that good looks alone are not enough.

Nor was there any shortage of advice and instruction in other areas of production. Talbot describes the separate elements of the filming process and even reveals a number of cinema 'tricks'. The producer, Kenelm Foss, and the foremost British screenplay writer of the silent period, Eliot Stannard, contributed (alongside Chaplin, Pickford, Sydney, Hopson and Rome) to a series of manuals advertised by *Pictures and Picturegoer* in 1919. Meanwhile, as studios became inundated with solicited and unsolicited scenarios, Furniss tendered to amateurs the advice of Mr Punch regarding marriage: '"Don't" . . . Every studio employs its quota of photo-play writers – men and women who condense or "bovrilise" some well-known story, or expand some incident in real life.'[55] *The Bioscope*, in 1914, recommended that '"leaders" (or "subtitles") cannot be more than 20 words in length, and should be much shorter. Letters cannot contain more than 30 or 40 words' and *The Pictures*, in 1912, cautioned 'use subtitles or leaders sparingly – only when they are necessary to the proper understanding of the play. Make action in the pictures tell the story as nearly as possible. Never use a note or letter, unless the action absolutely demands it.'[56] Meanwhile, the American advocates of self-help, Epes Winthrop Sargent (1913) and Henry A. Phillips

(1914), suggest that 'characters, their relationships and motives', may be differentiated in the public reading of a letter or will, or in the style of the handwriting employed: kissing lovers' letters (recommends Sargent, wanly) has by now become overdone and tiresome (but see Chapter 1).[57]

At the turn of the decade, the trade journal *The Motion Picture Studio* discussed a number of complaints against colleges and courses offering industrial training by correspondence. One of the most prestigious establishments, Edward Godal's Victoria College, was advertised extensively in the press and was keen in its own publicity material to distance itself from charlatan rivals.[58] 'Are you tired of doing just the same sort of thing over and over again . . . Are you striving to escape from the monotony, the grind, the restrictions that modern business and trade conditions impose upon you?' it enquires, before enumerating the rigours of cinema:

> Technique is the scientific equipment of the actor . . . Every profession, every hobby even, has tech-
> nicalities which must be mastered. Even a 'walking part' on the ordinary stage requires training to
> be performed properly. How much more so must be the case in cinema-acting, where the camera,
> ever facing the artist, is a merciless recorder of every motion, of every shade of expression and admits
> of no repeats save to increase the already onerous cost of turning the handle.[59]

Its brochure contains satisfactory testimonials from trade journals, production companies and erst-while students. The comparative success of the Victoria seems due not only to its professional system of training (and it, too, offered courses by correspondence) but also to its procurement of places for those to whom it awarded certificates: a number of Victoria graduates gained a con-spicuous entrée with Sir George Alexander and the potted palms in *The Second Mrs Tanqueray* and alongside Milton Rosmer and Nesta Westcott in 'The Society Affair of the Season' in *Lady Win-dermere's Fan*. After the war, Godal appealed to women to train as operators, to replace the film industry's casualties. Much hope was invested in the growth of the industry, after its own war serv-ice. There was hope that, as Steer says, 'conservatism in certain quarters, which still classes the pic-ture palace on a par with the travelling circus and "penny gaff"', had been overcome.[60]

Lady Audley's Secret (Jack Denton, 1920)

Eliot Stannard's scenario from Mary Elizabeth Braddon's 1862 sensation novel opens with a por-tentous foreword, setting out the action of Ideal's film: '. . . the blind yielding to callous selfish-ness, and brooding discontent . . . then the first false deed, that must be helped out by new treacheries, new crimes, new wickedness, till the whole edifice of evil tumbles and crashes from its own inherent rottenness . . .'. Furthermore, a familiar moral is drawn at the outset: 'Oh what a tangled web we weave/When first we practise to deceive'. In the customary manner, intertitles introduce characters (and the performers), use italics for dialogue and employ different styles of handwriting in letters, telegrams and luggage labels for the protagonists alongside the distinctive print of newspaper announcements (see Chapter 4). A closing iris frequently marks the end of the story's successive episodes. As in Charles Reade's play and companion novel *It is Never Too Late to*

Mend (filmed by A. E. Martin in 1918), in the *Ultus* series, in the Yukon of *The Scapegrace* (Cricks and Martin, 1913) and in Alexander Butler's 1916 *Just a Girl* (in which an Australian heiress marries a miner in preference to an impoverished aristocrat), gold prospecting is seen as a means of securing financial, social and romantic goals. As in Mrs Gaskell's novels and Hepworth's *Stolen Letters*, the post is the means by which estranged siblings and lovers endeavour to sustain long-distance relationships.

Helen Maldon (Margaret Bannerman), the daughter of a reprobate old sea captain, determines 'at all costs to have done with shabby gentility'. Secretly, she marries George Talboys (Randolph McLeod), the only son of a rich father – who subsequently disowns him. Helen 'tastes wealth' on her honeymoon for the first time but is then disconcerted to be returned to her previous financial state when George fails to find work. He accepts an offer from a stranger (dressed in loud checks) to go gold prospecting in Australia and leaves a letter for Helen: 'Unless I can bring you back wealth and happiness you will never see me again.' Helen adopts a new life as Lucy Graham, like Isabel in *East Lynne*, as a governess. She pretends to be an orphan and packs for London, where she is employed by Sir Michael Audley, a wealthy widower: he duly falls in love with Helen/Lucy. Meanwhile, George for two years finds comfort in the book given to him by Helen on their honeymoon and believes her to be waiting for him. While Helen puts her past behind her and prepares to become Lady Audley, George strikes gold and prepares to return. Audley's nephew, Robert (Manning Haynes), is a barrister with chambers near Temple Bar, who knew George at Eton. A newspaper announces George's sale of his shares in Australia and Helen warns her father to create a diversion: he bribes his housekeeper to have her consumptive daughter buried (as she surely soon will be) as Helen Talboys. Thus, 'Lady Audley wins the first move'. But Robert bumps into George as he arrives at the railway station. He promptly faints on reading the newspaper report of Helen's death, but is then amazed to find a photograph of the new Lady Audley the exact semblance of his erstwhile wife. Robert invites George to spend time at his uncle's country estate where, unavoidably, he encounters Helen/Lucy. He insists that Sir Michael give her up: she pushes him down a well but (again, with parallels to *East Lynne* and to Clarendon's 1912 *The Gamekeeper's Revenge*) the event is overseen by an 'evil witness' (Luke the gardener) who proceeds to blackmail Lady Audley in exchange for his silence. Luke marries Phoebe, Lady Audley's maid, and is set up as a publican. Telegrams are sent and requested between duplicitous characters, to keep one another abreast of events.

Sir Michael's daughter, Alicia (Betty Farquhar), joins the chase to uncover the truth about her wicked stepmother and Robert determines to find out what Luke knows. On the other hand, Phoebe warns her mistress that, when drunk, he has been talking. 'In her desperate determination to rid herself of two enemies', Lady Audley sets light to Luke's bedroom. Robert finds a letter in Luke's belt signed by George, which testifies to his wife having tried to kill him (in a well long since dry, from which Luke has retrieved him); George says that he prefers that she believe him dead while he has gone to Cape Town. This is a letter which has never been delivered to Robert, for Luke 'wasn't going to kill the golden goose by telling'. 'So does conscience make cowards of us all', we are advised. Lady Audley seeks to resolve her predicament by taking her own life with a sleeping draught and is found dead in bed by Phoebe in the early morning: her secret must die with Robert, and Lord Audley, says the good Alicia, must never know.

All this plotting, counter-plotting and subterfuge is executed at a cracking pace and is set against sets (sometimes doubled) which convey the action in London, the Isle of Wight, Dover, France and the Audley estate. While Lady Audley is deliciously bad (rendered so by her social ambition as much as by her persistent lying and betrayal of the love of a husband whom she conveniently assumes dead), Alicia and Robert are clearly the 'good' exemplars which 'conscience' bids the audience to follow; meanwhile, Captain Maldon, Luke and Robert's charlady Mrs Maloney (an understudy for Miss Flyte in *Bleak House*) are Dickensian cameo roles, leavening the melodrama's moral tone.

Notes

1. D. H. Lawrence, *The Lost Girl* [1920] (Harmondsworth: Penguin, 1977), p. 110; see also, *Sons and Lovers* [1913] (Harmondsworth: Penguin, 2000), pp. 11 and 347: 'Next evening Paul went into the cinematograph with Clara for a few minutes before train time . . . The pictures danced and dithered.' Lawrence's antipathy towards the cinematograph is further evinced in his suggestion that it be employed in 'lethal chambers' designed to exterminate 'the sick, the halting and the maimed': see John Carey, *The Intellectuals and the Masses* (London: Faber and Faber, 1992), p. 12.
2. Low Warren, *The Film Game* (London: T. Werner Laurie, 1937); Frederick A. Talbot, *Moving Pictures: How They Are Made and Worked* (London: William Heinemann, 1912); Harry Furniss, *Our Lady Cinema* (Bristol: J. W. Arrowsmith Ltd, 1914).
3. Rachael Low, *The History of the British Film* vol. IV [1971] (London: Routledge, 1997), pp. 136 and 157.
4. '*Germinal*: A Wonderful Production by a Wonderful Firm', *The Bioscope*, 18 September 1913, p. 913.
5. Talbot, *Moving Pictures*, p. 196.
6. See Nicholas Hiley, paper given at *Moving Performance*, Bristol, 1996, and The National Council of Public Morals, *The Cinema: Its Present Position and Future Possibilities* (London: Williams and Norgate, 1917).
7. Huntly Carter, the *New Age*, 2 November 1911, p. 11.
8. 'The Cinematograph and the Actor', *The Bioscope*, 7 December 1911, p. 679; see also 2 November 1911.
9. See Denis Diderot, 'Observations sur une brochure intitulée "Garrick ou les Acteurs Anglais" . . .', in *Diderot's Writings on the Theatre*, ed. F. C. Green (Cambridge: Cambridge University Press, 1936), and for the continuation of such national and regional distinctions, Gustave Garcia, *The Actor's Art: A Practical Treatise on Stage Declamation, Public Speaking and Deportment* (London: T. Pettitt and Co., 1882), p. 31.
10. Ashley Dukes, the *New Age*, 15 September 1910, pp. 474–5.
11. See *The Bioscope*, 20 April 1911, p. 95, and for a picture of the stunt, Valentia Steer, *The Romance of the Cinema* (London: C. Arthur Pearson, 1913).
12. William Archer, *Play Making* (London: Chapman and Hall, 1912), p. 51.

13. Jon Burrows, *Legitimate Theatre: Theatre Stars in British Cinema, 1908–1918* (Exeter: Exeter University Press, 2003), p. 119; see also Emma Smith, '"Sir J. and Lady Forbes-Robertson Left for America on Saturday": Marketing the 1913 *Hamlet* for Stage and Screen', Linda Fitzsimmons and Sarah Street (eds), *Moving Performance* (Trowbridge: Flicks Books, 2000), pp. 44–68.

14. Talbot, *Moving Pictures*, pp. 158–9.

15. Low, vol. III, p. 89.

16. Huntly Carter, the *New Age*, 16 November 1911, p. 60.

17. Bertrand Russell, letter to the *New Age*, 28 March 1912.

18. For favourable comparisons of Garrick with Quin, see Frank Hedgcock, *David Garrick and his French Friends* (London: Stanley Paul and Co., 1911), p. 43; on Cibber's foppishness, Quin's 'weighty, dignified pomposity' and a comparison with Garrick and Peg Woffington, see Karl Mantzius, *A History of Theatrical Art*, vol. 5 (London: Duckworth, 1909), pp. 368, 382 and 386; see also, Henry Siddons, *Practical Illustrations of Rhetorical Gesture and Action* (London: Sherwood, Neely and Jones, 1822).

19. Barrie once staged a 'cinema supper' at which his guests were filmed, then shown the result; neither George Bernard Shaw (dressed as a cowboy in a Western burlesque) nor the Prime Minister, Herbert Asquith, were amused by the record of themselves on screen and refused permission for these films to be screened in public; see Andrew Birkin, *J. M. Barrie and the Lost Boys* (London: Constable, 1979), p. 218; his questionnaires confirmed Chaplin as the favourite of his surrogate family of 'lost' boys.

20. 'Theatrical Celebrities on the Screen: an Epoch Making British Production', *The Bioscope*, 8 March 1917, p. 994; see also '"Peg": the Wonderful Life Story of the Heroine in Masks and Faces', *Pictures and the Picturegoer*, 30 December 1916, p. 291.

21. Charles Reade, *Peg Woffington* (London: Chatto and Windus, 1852), p. 176.

22. See James Anderson Collection Box 25, BFI Special Materials; 'The stage of 1863 . . . recalled by the Pinero stage play of 1898 . . . and by the Hepworth Pinero Picture Play 1916'; also Ioulia Pipinia and Amy Sargeant, 'Performing and Being: Responses to Naturalism on Stage and Screen', paper given at Nottingham British Silent Cinema Festival, 2000.

23. *Trelawny of the 'Wells'* [1898], Act IV, *Plays by A. W. Pinero*, ed. George Rowell (Cambridge: Cambridge University Press, 1968).

24. *The Bioscope*, 9 May 1918, p. 23; regarding *Comin' Thro' the Rye*, see Andrew Higson, *Waving the Flag* (Oxford: Clarendon Press, 1995), pp. 28–73.

25. *The Bioscope*, 27 September 1917, p. 23: 'the stage play has reached some 4,000 performances and has been seen by more than three million people during the last five years, but on screen it should achieve still greater triumphs'. This first film version included location sequences at Blackpool's Pleasure Beach, the Tower Ballroom and in Llandudno.

26. *The A. E. W. Mason Omnibus* (London: Hodder and Stoughton, 1931), pp. 10 and 23; see also Amy Sargeant, *'Everyone's Doing the Riviera* because *It's So Much Nicer in Nice'*, paper given at 'Location!, Location!, Location!', Nottingham British Silent Cinema Festival, 2003.

27. Adrian Poole, 'A Short History of the Trilby', paper given at Cambridge University Edwardian Literature and Popularity symposium, 1999.

28. Bristol University Theatre Collection, Beerbohm Tree Collection Box 9.

29. Thomas Burke, 'The Sign of the Lamp', *Limehouse Nights* (London: Grant Richards Ltd, 1917); see also Jonathan Rose, *The Intellectual Life of the British Working Class* (New Haven: Yale University Press, 2001), p. 100, and, for high-brow dismissiveness, Ashley Dukes, the *New Age*, 30 June 1910, pp. 209–10.

30. See H. G. Wells, *Tono Bungay* [1909] (London: T. Fisher and Unwin Ltd, 1925), for the marketing and promotion of 'mitigated water', and Gareth Stedman Jones, 'The "Cockney" and the Nation, 1780–1988', in *Metropolis: London* (London: Routledge, 1989), pp. 273–324 for a discussion of Grummet's antecedents and descendants.

31. Martin Priestman, *Crime Fiction from Poe to the Present* (Plymouth: Northcote House, 1998).

32. *The Bioscope*, 22 January 1914, p. 357; see also Michael Hammond, '"Cultivating Pimple": Performance Traditions and the Film Comedy of Fred and Joe Evans', in Laraine Porter and Alan Burton (eds), *Pimple, Pranks and Pratfalls* (Trowbridge: Flicks Books, 2000), pp. 58–68.

33. George Pearson, *Flashback: an Autobiography of a British Film Maker* (London: George Allen and Unwin, 1957), p. 54; see also Judith McLaren, '*Ultus*: The Films from the Dead', in Laraine Porter and Alan Burton, *Crossing the Pond* (Trowbridge: Flicks Books, 2002), pp. 45–52.

34. *Daily Mirror*, 17 December 1913, p. 9, and 22 December 1913, p. 1.

35. Reginald Hodder, *Ultus: the Man from the Dead* (London: Hodder and Stoughton, 1916), p. 27.

36. Furniss, *Our Lady Cinema*, p. 40; see also Talbot, *Moving Pictures*, pp. 160, 190.

37. Francis Spufford, *I Might be Some Time: Ice and the English Imagination* (London: Faber and Faber, 1997), p. 8.

38. Furniss, *Our Lady Cinema*, p. 136.

39. See Amy Sargeant, 'Funny Peculiar and Funny Ha-Ha: Some Preliminary Observations on Men in Frocks in Early British Cinema', in Porter and Burton, *Pimple, Pranks and Pratfalls*, pp. 96–100; also Michael Chanan, *The Dream that Kicks* (London: Routledge, 1996), pp. 268–9.

40. Wells, *Tono Bungay*, pp. 131–2; see also Raymond Williams, *The Country and the City* (London: Chatto and Windus, 1973), pp. 217–21.

41. Burke, 'Beryl, the Croucher and the Rest of England' and 'The Knight-Errant' in *Limehouse Nights*; for the continuing Chinese presence in Limehouse see *Piccadilly* and *The Sign of the Four* (Chapter 4) and *Fires Were Started* (1943) (Chapter 6).

42. Christine Gledhill, *Reframing British Cinema* (London: BFI, 2004), p. 50.

43. *The Bioscope*, 2 October 1913, p. 73; for the popularity of Waterloo Bridge (especially the Surrey side) with suicides see Charles Dickens, 'Down with the Tide', *Complete Works* (London: Heron Books, 1970).

44. Warren, *The Film Game*, p. 79.

45. Jane Bryan, 'Under the Influence of the Clutching Hand: The Exploits of Elaine in Britain', in Porter and Burton, *Crossing the Pond*, pp. 53–9.

46. Valentia Steer, *Secrets of the Cinema* (London: C. Arthur Pearson, 1920), p. 78.

47. Quoted in *Victoria Cinema College and Studios* (London: The Victoria Cinema College, ca.1919), p. 17; see also Amy Sargeant, 'Manuals and Mantras: Advice to British Screen Actors', in Laura Vichi (ed.), *L'uomo visibile* (Udine: University of Udine Press, 2002), pp. 311–20.

48. Low, *The History of the British Film*, vol. IV, p. 275.

49. Steer, *The Romance of the Cinema*, pp. 43–4.

50. Cecil Hepworth, *Came the Dawn: Memories of a Film Pioneer* (London: Phoenix House, 1951), pp. 63, 81.

51. Aurèle Sydney, *How to Act for the Kinema*, vol. 7 (London: FAS Publications, ca. 1917).

52. Aurèle Sydney, *A Practical Course in Cinema Acting*, vol. 4 (London: Standard Art Book Co., 1920), p. 23.

53. Michael Sanderson, *From Irving to Olivier* (London: Athlone Press, 1984), p. 211.

54. Jenny Hammerton, 'Screen-Struck: The Lure of Hollywood for British Women in the 1920s', in Porter and Burton, *Crossing the Pond*, pp. 100–5.

55. Furniss, *Our Lady Cinema*, p. 45.

56. *The Pictures*, 17 August 1912, and *The Bioscope*, 5 February 1914, quoted by Low, vol. II, pp. 253 and 255.

57. Epes Winthrop Sargent, *Technique of the Photoplay* (New York: The Moving Picture World, 1916), p. 154.

58. See *The Motion Picture Studio*, 1920–1.

59. *Victoria Cinema College and Studios*, p. 5.

60. Steer, *The Romance of the Cinema*, p. 25.

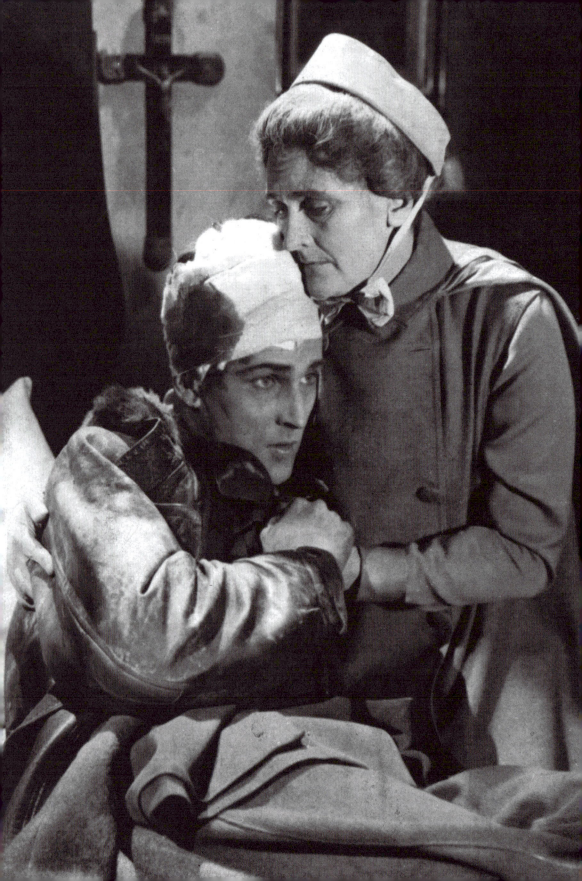

Chapter 3 | First World War

In *The Great War and Modern Memory*, Paul Fussell suggests that a reading of soldiers' letters from the front yields little more than an inventory of hand-knitted socks:[1] he turns instead to the testimony afforded by the war's poets, including Rupert Brooke, Robert Graves, Siegfried Sassoon and Wilfred Owen. Subsequent historians have garnered more from such letters and have found Fussell's account partial.[2] However, his observations are useful in as much as they cast doubt on the extent to which supposedly 'primary' documents can be relied upon as an accurate or adequate record of experience. The population at home received much of its information from newspapers (like the letters and standardised Field Service Postcards, subject to official censorship) and, eventually, from photographs and films (equally, restricted by access and practical and military exigency). But time and time again, grainy stills and footage, supposedly 'primary' materials, appear in historical representations and reconstructions of the war on the land, the sea, the air: from David Wark Griffith's 1917 *Hearts of the World*, Maurice Elvey's 1919 *Comradeship* and Adrian Brunel's 1927 *Blighty* (which includes film of the fighting and of the Armistice) to Derek Jarman's 1988 *War Requiem* (a compilation of Benjamin Britten's score with Owen's poems), documentary footage is intercut with drama to authenticate the action. Joseph Losey's 1964 *King and Country* has black and white stills merging with its figures as, indeed, the bodies of the missing merged with the mud of Flanders. Geoffrey Barkas' wartime training as a cameraman contributed to Anthony Asquith's retrospective account of the Gallipoli campaign, *Tell England* (1931), while *Oh! What a Lovely War* (Richard Attenborough, 1969) features a cameraman as a master of ceremonies and a seaside pier peep show displaying highlights of the battles, Verdun, Ypres and Vimy Ridge. In Nick Willing's 1997 *Photographing Fairies*, a photographer, convinced that he has already lost the only woman he can ever love to a better world, fearlessly records the casualties under shellfire. William Boyd's 1999 *The Trench* finds an actor cast as the Official War Photographer, Geoffrey Malins, directing action at the front for the camera, and his fictionalised history, *The New Confessions* (1987), features a director who serves his apprenticeship in a wartime film unit.[3] Joanna Bourke indicates that, even during the war itself, men envisaged the killing in terms of 'a living screen' on which the 'grey devils' dropped down in their hundreds.[4]

Edith Cavell (Sybil Thorndike) nurses a fallen airman in Herbert Wilcox's *Dawn* (1928), 'a film with a mission'

Mud, Rats, Lice, Ice

Troops marching through burned-out villages, cramped trenches, barbed wire, duckboards, mud and scarified trees constitute a pervasive image of the war in northern France. James Whale's 1930 film adaptation of R. C. Sherriff's 1926 stageplay, *Journey's End*, opens with an officer swatting flies in the dug-out with a wet sock. *The Battle of the Ancre* (1917) includes a panning shot of this 'swamp', with men 'knee deep' in 'a sea of mud', issued with rubber thigh boots to prevent frost-bite, and sleighs being used to convey the wounded. During the war, the home front and troops on leave received most of their information from newspapers, often presented under lurid and powerful banner headlines such as 'Germany Adds Blackmail to her other Graces', 'The Kaiser's Motto: Women and Children First' and 'The Mailed Fist becomes the Mauled Fist' (all from the *Daily Express* in 1918). A bulldog is shown in 1914 barking across the Channel to Germ<u>huny</u>: 'Come out, you Mongrel', reads the caption. Such xenophobic sentiments are endorsed in the film titles *Huns of the North Sea* (1914), *In the Clutches of the Hun* (1915) and *Under the German Yoke* (1915). Joanna Bourke describes how the circulation of newspapers soared:

> The *Daily Mirror* sold 850,000 copies per day in 1914; 1,580,000 in 1916. In total, more than six million copies of newspapers sold each day. At times of particular crisis even greater numbers were sold, as in the case when, at the start of the Battle of the Somme, The *Sunday Pictorial* alone sold nearly 2.5 million copies.[5]

Alongside the increasingly depressing news of minor advances abroad and disillusion at home, the *Daily Express* (under Beaverbrook's ownership from 1917) printed the lists of the dead (regiment by regiment), physical specifications and age limits for new recruits (gradually relaxed as optimum candidates proved in meagre supply), notice of conscription (from 1916), maps, 'khaki rhymes', advertisements for products which boasted their British origins and patterns for shirts for able-bodied and injured servicemen. It announced a blanket collection and the *Daily Express* Shilling League, for the relief of families of British soldiers.[6] Likewise, at the Department of Information, Beaverbrook arranged for British war charities to receive 60 per cent of the net receipts from *Hearts of the World* (D. W. Griffiths, 1918), hoping for a success equalling Griffith's *The Birth of a Nation*, widely shown in 1915.[7] Lord Haig (Commander-in-Chief on the Western Front) famously com-mended correspondents for playing up 'splendidly', while in November 1918, the *Daily Express* complained that censorship of its reports had not yet been lifted.[8]

Although actuality films had been made of previous military engagements (notably of the Boer War – see Chapter 1) the British authorities were slower to allow access to the front than others among the Allies. Lord Kitchener (Secretary of State for War) and Lords Jellicoe and Fisher (at the Admiralty) imposed an outright ban at the outbreak of war in opposition to interests expressed by the cinema industry, anxious not only at what material might be shot but also at the opportunities for interference during processing.[9] The industry was further antagonised by the imposition of taxes on entertainment and on film imports. Nevertheless, timely editions of popular film series were produced, notably *Pimple Enlists* (proceeded by *Lt Pimple's Sealed Orders*, *Lt Pimple and the Stolen Submarine* and *How Lieutenant Pimple Captured the Kaiser* [all 1914] and *Pimple Strafing the Kaiser* [1916] – see Chapter 2) and Clarendon's 1915 *How Lieutenant Rose, RN, Spiked the Enemy's Guns*, comparable to the Second World War features which recruited *Mother Riley* and *Inspector Hornleigh* (1939) (see Chapter 6). Hepworth produced film 'tags' (short propaganda films comparable to the MoI films of the Second World War) and approached the outbreak of war dramatically (with *The Outrage* and *His Country's Bidding*) and humorously (with *Simkin Gets the War Scare*), announcing these 1914 films under a huge Union Jack. While Powell's Second World War *Blimp* (1943) appropriated a character from an *Evening Standard* cartoon, Bruce Bairnsfather's 'Old Bill' from the *Bystander* magazine was imitated by a Cochran review, George Pearson's 1918 *The Better 'Ole* and Thomas Bentley's 1924 *Old Bill Through the Ages* (see Chapter 4). *With Our Territorials at the Front* (1916) shows a soldier mimicking Bill to the amusement of others. In the absence of actual footage, Pearson used re-enactment to represent the first fortnight of action in *The Great European War* (1914), intending to update it as events required. He recalled the response at its trade show on 17 August:

> The flagrant symbolism of our swift scene-flash of Britannia, rising majestically from her accustomed pose to stand erect and raise her long shining sword to the heavens, brought sudden cheers from that patriotic and emotional crowd. We knew then that the film had stood its test.[10]

The first official film, *Britain Prepared*, was assembled from stock and newly taken footage and widely released, at home and abroad, in 1915. Hilton De Witt Girdwood (working independently), followed by Malins, McDowell, Tong and others (officially sanctioned), then travelled to the front. As Nick Hiley has shown, much of the former's *With the Empire's Fighters* (1916) was faked, as a substitute for actuality material, using British soldiers dressed as Germans and staging manoeuvres which did not take place.[11] Far more successful with audiences, for its topicality and its excitement, was *The Battle of the Somme* (1916) although, here too, there were suspicions even at the time that some of the material was not genuine (doubts later validated by Roger Smither).[12]

Nevertheless, the film remains highly significant as a testimony to the appetite for news from the front and the entertainment value of information. It made something of a star of Malins himself, 'The Real Film Hero', appearing on the cover of *Pictures and Picturegoer* in January 1917, filming 'the historic meeting' of the King, President Poincaré, Sir Douglas Haig and General Joffre 'somewhere in France'. Much is made of the intrepid cinematographer, not least by Malins himself (formerly an employee of Clarendon), facing the dangers of the front then succumbing to a cold on his return to London:

> Like many a brave fellow in khaki, Mr. Malins is one of the most reticent of men. He neither seeks nor craves for publicity, and yet with his camera for companion he has risked his life countless times per week for two years and three months in order to secure film records of the greatest war. The marvel

British soldiers carry the enemy wounded to safety in *The Battle of the Somme* (1916) (Courtesy of the Imperial War Museum/IWM FLM 1660)

is that the man is still alive to tell the tale . . . Those who have seen *The Battle of the Somme* will guess what our determined photographer must have gone through to obtain such pictures. Up to that date it was the only British attack ever photographed. Whilst filming the whole of the British front from the front line trenches he was gassed three times. He had his camera smashed by bullets and his tripod cut in half by a piece of shell, and with a camera embedded in a sandbag which just peeped over a parapet he was in the act of photographing three mines going up at Hohenzollern Redoubt when a German sniper put a bullet *through his cap!* Then alone in a trench he filmed the destruction of a German blockhouse. The enemy was only 125 yards from his position, and the range of our guns was such that many shells fell short of their objective. In spite of this, however, Mr Malins photographed the bursting shells until the debris filled the trench in which he stood and forced him to retreat.[13]

The Bioscope published recommendations for the musical accompaniment to Malins' film (including motifs from familiar compositions by Edward Elgar and Ivor Novello – famously responsible for 'Keep the Home Fires Burning') and it was sometimes supported by local military bands.[14] Individual regiments are carefully identified: platoons of Bedfords, Suffolks and Royal Welsh Fusiliers,

London Scottish and East Yorkshires and dead Gordons and Devons (among others) appear in *The Battle of the Somme*; *The Battle of Arras* names, among others, the King's Liverpools and King's Own Shropshire regiments, Queenslanders, Tasmanians and a battalion from the London Stock Exchange. *The Battle of the Ancre* specifically cites an official communiqué commending the 'dash and gallantry' of the Irish regiments. For some viewers, it provided reassurance that their loved ones (obligingly waving and smiling to camera while marching or at ease in camp) were then still alive – even if since lost – for others, that their injuries were speedily tended: *The Battle of the Ancre* shows the administration of hot tea, sandwiches and gaspers to the walking wounded and invites its audience to join a rendition of 'Keep the Home Fires Burning'. For yet others, it proved a deeply moving experience, allowing the viewer to share in the sacrifice of life in an honourable cause. 'On the war-films I have seen', remarked Rebecca West in *The Return of the Soldier* (1918), 'men slip down softly from the trench parapet, and none but the grimmer philosophers would say that they had reached safety by their fall.'[15] Cameramen themselves confessed that the display of corpses and the extent of British casualties was severely restricted, although unprecedented and sub-sequently (in the Second World War) yet further resisted.[16] After the decision in 1915 not to repa-triate the dead, viewers could at least find comfort in witnessing their decent burial, recorded on film (as in *The Canadian Victory at Courcellette* [1917]), in France; official records of mass graves at the front were not screened publicly.

   The Battle of the Somme is especially concerned with delivering technical information regard-ing the weight of the new weaponry deployed and captured: 'plum puddings', 'flying pigs' and 'grandmothers' feature alongside panning shots of the damage wrought thereby. 'Big Berthas' and 'Jack Johnsons' (named after the heavyweight boxer) likewise appear, while *The Battle of the Ancre* comments on its 'tanks', flattening the enemy's wire entanglements, as something of a novelty. *The Battle of the Somme* has 'the vicious bark of Canadian 60 pounders' adding to 'the din of gunfire' and *The Battle of Arras* (1917) has Howitzers joining 'the pandemonium', while *Tell England* (conceived as a silent film, shot silent on location and post-synchronised) reproduces the distinctive and ominous whine of 'Clara'.[17] Munitions workers labouring at home may have been relieved to be told that dumps 'along the entire front . . . are receiving vast supplies'. Artillery horses – recurring in Walter Summers' 1923 *A Couple of Down and Outs* – and photo-genic regimental mascots serve as a reminder of the number of animals (including also dogs and pigeons – as witnessed by *The Better 'Ole* – and by *Pimple's Uncle* [1915], where the nephew jokes 'we can't get any milk anywhere, they've sent all the cows to the front') requisitioned for the war effort. Simultaneously, but less vehemently than similar reports in print, *The Battle of the Somme* also serves the purposes of propaganda and counter-propaganda: what the *Daily Express* dubbed 'The Progress of the Allies against the All-lies' and the 1917 Thanhouser film for the Department of Information labelled *London: British Fact and German Fiction*.[18] The German wounded are treated well ('the hungry though happy captives get a meal of good stew', announces *The Canadian Victory*) and prisoners of war (who do not cheer and wave) are escorted back to Britain.

Supporters of film as a legitimate instrument of war (not least in the trade) argued that it was even preferable to print in the numbers it could reach and that it was especially serviceable in addressing audiences in the Empire for which English was not the first language, for audiences in as yet non-combatant countries (above all, America, for which customised prints were cut and distributed) and for an illiterate audience on the home front. Arguably, film-viewing, as a group activity, served to consolidate support more effectively than the relatively isolated experience of reading a newspaper. Cinemas showed Roll of Service films (compiled from individual portrait shots of soldiers in local regiments) and collected funds for local memorials. In Britain, mobile cinemas toured areas not supplied with fixed screens while in August 1918, the *Daily Express* reported that 20 million people were visiting cinema theatres every week in the United Kingdom alone. Rachael Low suggests that 'the effect of the war on the number of attendances was probably to increase it rather than to diminish it' and that 'picture theatres in garrison towns were packed'.[19] There were military cinemas at home, while at the front, Robert Graves recalls, some colonels were sufficiently generous and enlightened to equip their camps with cinema huts; Colonel Bromhead (veteran of the Boer War campaign – see Chapter 1) showed films on the Russian Front and the YMCA organised open-air shows attended by several thousand troops.[20] Some live entertainers at the front (such as the cross-dressed concert party, Splinters, recalled also in Sinclair Hill's 1928 *Guns of Loos*) survived the war and produced acts which were filmed in peacetime.[21]

As in the Second World War, attitudes towards propaganda, produced officially and unofficially, shifted during the course of hostilities. *Blighty*, directed by Brunel (who worked for the Department of Information during the war) tracks progress by the use of recruitment posters as intertitles: Kitchener, in direct address, demanding 'We Must Have More Men' and the appeal 'If the Cap fits, You Join the Army Today'; Greene, the civilian, insisting in 1914 that 'it will all be over by Christmas'. But casualties escalated, resulting not only from direct fire from the new weaponry (the heavy guns at the front, the U-boats at sea, aircraft) but also from poor medical facilities and the condition of the trenches (trenchfoot, a hazard for men and horses alike, frequently resulted in amputation, sometimes gangrene and sometimes death). W. E. Johns (who was promoted from the trenches to train for the Royal Flying Corps in 1917) notes that parachutes were rare for pilots and that death in the air by accident, even during training, was common.[22] By 1916, the prospects of victory looked more remote. In the same year, Kitchener was drowned, Asquith (who tentatively proposed a negotiated settlement) was replaced by Lloyd George as Prime Minister, Lord Beaverbrook became head of the Department of Information and conscription was introduced for the first time in British history. At the front, 60,000 casualties were sustained in the first day of fighting on the Somme; by mid-November, the Allies had advanced five miles at the cost of 450,000 German, 200,000 French and 420,000 British lives.[23] However, as Kevin Brownlow laconically observes, no one seeing Malins' *The Battle of the Somme* 'could guess that this was the bloodiest defeat in British history', even if (like West) they were genuinely shocked at witnessing apparent deaths.[24]

'Home Thoughts from Abroad'

Unlike the Second World War, between 1914 and 1918 those serving on the various fronts abroad (more than 5 million men – 22 per cent of the male population were active participants in the military services) felt increasingly alienated from the population at home:[25] families and those who did not, could not or would not fight. Spies were sought out at home (as in *Comradeship*) and abroad (as in *The Better 'Ole* and *Mademoiselle from Armentières* [Maurice Elvey, 1926]). The *Daily Express* reserved its venom for the 'Nationalist gun-runners' in Ireland who opposed 'Sir Edward Carson's Patriotism', strikers (identified with 'the virus of Bolshevism'), shirkers and other malingerers (including Conscientious Objectors – 'small in number but formidable in devotion . . . they are honest enough in their aim but dishonest in their methods').[26] *Oh! What a Lovely War*, albeit satirically, recalls the recruitment songs which Joan Littlewood remembered from her childhood, often sung by girls in khaki or played by military bands; in 1914 Elvey produced a drama taking its name from the familiar pre-war tune *It's a Long Way to Tipperary*.[27] In 1918, it announced the Household Fuel rationing order. Reviewing *Blighty* in 1928, Iris Barry describes how 'it tells of the home life of ordinary folk during the war – it reminds us of the air-raids, dread telegrams, meat cards and saccharine tablets'.[28] But, in spite of these raids and the sound of gunfire from France (which could be heard the length and breadth of the East Coast), soldiers returning on leave often found Blighty a remote outpost. Few wanted to discuss the grimness of life in the trenches and preferred to seek solace or entertainment. Many went to see popular comedians and performers, such as George Robey and Albert Chevalier, at the Hippodrome and the Halls, to such long-running West-End shows as *Chu Chin Chow* (see Chapter 5), or to the cinema, where Chaplin continued to reign supreme.

Actuality and fiction films often show the writing and receiving of letters at the front: in Victor Saville's *Kitty* (1929), a malicious letter received by Alex St George from his mother has fateful consequences, overriding the photos and messages of love sent by Kitty herself. In *The National Film*, the aged mother of Private John Weaver (of the Cheshires) proudly reads a newspaper account of his holding a position against an enemy advance, shortly before a telegram is received announcing his death. In October 1914, the army postal service handled 650,000 letters per week and 58,000 parcels rising to 11 million letters and 875,000 parcels for the troops in 1916; letters from the front were subject to censorship, prompting Vera Brittain and her brother to resort to a code indicating an imminent attack.[29] Some (like Graves and Sassoon) were appalled by the cumulatively exaggerated reporting in the press of supposed German atrocities and by what they perceived as indifference among politicians and the business class (a common butt of newspaper cartoonists) to the mounting casualties: hence Sassoon's 1917 'A Soldier's Declaration' and his symbolic disposal of his Military Cross in the Mersey (portrayed in Gillies MacKinnon's 1997 film of Pat Barker's novel *Regeneration*). Hepworth's 1918 animated cartoon *The Leopard's Spots* returns to the theme, showing a bayoneted baby, the razing of a cathedral and a debauched German soldier with a post-war admonition: 'This man who has shelled churches, hospitals and open boats at sea – Robber, Ravisher and Murderer – and, after the war, will want to sell you his German

Teens stars Violet Hopson and Ivy Close serve the cause in *The Women's Land Army* (1917) (Courtesy of the Imperial War Museum/IWM FLM 1471)

goods – are one and the same person.' In contrast, many women were keen 'to do their bit' for the war effort, even if only by donating jam and blankets to the Harrods, Selfridges and *Daily Express* collections, despatching parcels, collecting for tanks or knitting socks and stockings for the Comfort Fund (clean dry woollens countered trenchfoot and are therefore not to be despised: 'When you win your first battle, mother will knit you a special pair of socks,' a soldier is advised in *Guns of Loos*).[30] While some 'sister Susies sewed shirts for soldiers' (as the song goes), some women, such as Vera Brittain and Winifred Holtby, served as nurses overseas, some as munitions workers, as in *A Munition Girl's Romance* (1917), or replaced men on the land or in the service and manufacturing industries at home. Woman often took over from men as cinema operators and managers. Emasculating lady barbers, a staple of early film comedy, reappear in the Clarendon Company's 1915 *Timothy Toddles*, at a training college for ladies in Flapper Town, 'to enable them to fill posts formerly held by men': sooner than return to the college, Timothy says that he is German and faces internment, before being rescued by the cook.

Gail Braybon suggests that certain occupations during the war, such as the Voluntary Aid Detachment, which recruited E. M. Delafield (see Chapter 6), the Land Army and the Civil Service, were the preserve of middle-class women.[31] Furthermore, the image of the 'angelic' and virginal nurse, 'appalling in her whiteness' (as in *Comradeship*, *Blighty* and *War Requiem*), as often a sister as a sweetheart, has become prominent in later depictions of the war, in spite of Brittain's own protestations that the image obscured the real work undertaken.[32] In 1915, Maurice Elvey filmed the evocative costume drama *Florence Nightingale*. Broadwest's unofficial propaganda film *The Women's Land Army* (1917) depicts the teens stars Ivy Close and Violet Hopson (see Chapter 2) as 'ladies of leisure' on whose hands time hangs heavily until one receives a letter from her brother at the front telling her 'to join the Land Army as soon as possible to help defeat the Hun'; Lancelot Speed conveys the same message graphically by cutting a leisured lady with her lap-dog against a munitions worker in *Britain's Effort* (1918). Ivy and Violet duly report to the National Service Department. 'Weeds, like U-boats, must be exterminated', we are told and Britannia herself, bestowing her blessing, appears alongside the brave girls working in the fields 'who help their men folk carry on'. The film shows the rural tasks undertaken ('where there's a will there's a way – experts said women couldn't do this heavy work') while *A Day in the Life of a Munition Worker* (1917) shows women working at Woolwich Arsenal and the care taken of their health and welfare. *Mrs John Bull Prepared* (1918) provides a more comprehensive catalogue of women's activities during the war and also seeks to counter male anxiety and prejudice against their engaging in labour (including film exhibition) previously regarded as the prerogative of men: in August 1914, it reminds us, 'the man in the street hardly realised . . . that women would not only have to bear the Burden of Sorrow and Separation, to Comfort, Encourage and Inspire, but would have to Undertake a Decisive Share in the Practical Conduct of the War and the Business of the Nation'. Again, mythical figures (Boadicea and 'The Spirit of British Womanhood') are invoked to drive home the film's rhetoric. A wounded brother is suitably impressed by their devotion to duty. We are shown women working in skilled and unskilled jobs on the railways, on the buses, in the police force, as ambulance drivers, and in aircraft and munitions factories (where TNT discolours their skin – but they still smile regardless). Film 'tags' were attached to newsreels and impressed upon the audience the need to 'Save Coal', to 'Buy a War Loan' or conveyed invaluable advice regarding the manufacture of suet dumplings in the absence of suet.

Towards the end of the war, films were made encouraging enrolment in women's units in the services. *The Life of a WAAC* (1918) shows a 'real' woman who is literally identified with the 'ideal' figure in a recruitment poster by being superimposed at the end. Proudly she wears the uniform, drills and parades, serves dinner to the male Army officers and performs various clerical duties. *WRNS* and *Women's Royal Air Force* (1918) show women in similar auxilliary positions (cleaning, repairing, working on the switchboard on shore and at base) while also persuading potential recruits that their life is not all work and, as with Second World War 'official' films such as *The Gentle Sex* (1943) and *Women Away from Home* (1942) (see Chapter 6), reassuring women and their families that camp life is safe and companionable.

A further official attempt to link the home and war fronts was made with *The National Film*. At the outbreak of war, the popular novelists, poets and playwrights John Buchan, Rudyard Kipling and John Galsworthy (see Chapter 2) had offered their services to Wellington House. *The National Film* (suppressed after the Armistice) employed the services of the great and the good, including the Irish-American director Herbert Brenon, the stage doyenne Ellen Terry and the writer Sir Hall Caine (whose own novels were promoted by the film adaptations of *The Christian* in 1915, *The Manxman* in 1916 and 1929, and *The Prodigal Son* in 1923). Caine introduces a speculative examination of how the Germans might have behaved had they invaded England by looking at life in occupied Chester. Nicholas Reeves says that it intended a contrast between 'German behaviour (symbolised by the sinking of the *Lusitania*) with the nobility of the Allied position (symbolised by Nurse Edith Cavell)'.[33] Gaumont's 1914 *If England were Invaded* (from William le Queux's novel *The Invasion of England*) and Shaw's pre-war *England's Menace* (1914) concerned a 'hostile power' intent upon invasion. Like Guy du Maurier's 1909 *The Englishman's Home* ('A Play by a Patriot') and Saki's 1913 *When William Came: a Story of London under the Hohenzollerns* (in which London's chattering classes soon solicitously cede their defences and in which, as in France and Belgium in 1914, notices on the street and at railway stations appear in German), *The National Film* desperately presumed to appeal to a patriotism worn thin by the duration.

Heroes and Superheroes: Anthem for Doomed Youth

Lancelot Speed's animated film, *Britain's Effort*, shows representatives of the territories of the Empire answering the call from John Bull, aroused from his slumber in 1914 by Britannia. Canada, Australia, South Africa, New Zealand and India join forces with Britain, while the Kaiser is repelled in Germany's colonies in Africa and Indonesia and yields command of the seas to the British Navy. In the Motherland, a farm worker, a landowner, a city clerk, a fisherman, a miner and a railway worker line up together and merge into one military figure. Victor Saville's post-war *Kitty* emulates the sentiment by straining to bring together representatives of various forces (a British soldier, sailor, airman and a Seikh in Kitty's mother's London tobacconist's) and showing uniformed Canadian and Australian passers-by on the street outside.

Many of the recruitment films privilege an everyman figure, such as the reactionary pater-familias Smith in *Mrs John Bull Prepared* and the eponymous Brown, the shipping clerk with a nice little home in the suburbs, who passes his Medical Board in *John Brown Joins the Army* (1918). D. W. Griffith, in *Hearts of the World*, abstracted his protagonists yet further, naming them simply 'The Boy' and 'The Girl' (a precedent followed by the credit sequences of *Blighty* and *War Requiem*). The film opens with an endorsement from Lloyd George and, after a private screening at Windsor, was approved by the King himself.[34] Erich von Stroheim represents rigid militarism (a rehearsal for Jean Renoir's *La Grande Illusion* [1937]) and Noël Coward receives his first fleeting film role. But this, as Kevin Brownlow remarks, is primarily a love story in which political argument intrudes little: a caricature of a brutal Prussian threatens the girl's chastity, The Boy resists the approaches of a local floosie (who looks far more fun than The Girl) and the American Army (for which read the Fifth Cavalry) marches into France and saves the day.[35] Like Griffith, Hepworth, for E. Temple Thurton's 1918 *Tares*, and Elvey, in his post-war *Roses of Picardy* (1927) and *Mademoiselle from Armentières* (both titles legendarily evoked in song), also reconstruct typical town and village scenes from the Western Front. Elvey used locations in the South of France for reconstructed scenes in *Comradeship* and *Roses of Picardy. Mademoiselle* was selected for screenings in France to mark the tenth anniversary of the Armistice and (in its publicity) boasted the credentials of its personnel as veterans of the war.[36] Its proceeds, as for *Comradeship*, were donated to the Red Cross. *Blighty* (with Nadia Siberskaia) and *Mademoiselle* (with Estelle Brody) both feature girls who serve at the local hostelry (complete with checked tablecloths) falling for men in khaki. In *Blighty*, the couple are secretly married and the girl holds the boy's dented helmet over her belly before bidding him farewell, simultaneously indicating his own vulnerability and the new life she needs must protect.

Robert Graves recounts the origins of a further trench myth:

> Thomas Atkins was a private soldier in the First Battalion who had served under Wellington in the Peninsular War. It is said that when, many years later, Wellington at the War Office was asked to approve a specimen form for military attestation, he had ordered it to be amended from: 'I, Private John Doe' . . . to 'I, Private Thomas Atkins'.[37]

'Tommy' is often paired with 'Fritz' in actuality film, as his companion in suffering as much as his opponent in battle; *Blighty* reinforces the protagonists' equivalence by having Robin in Heidelberg on the eve of war. A 1914 recruitment film describes *How the Army Made a Man of Tommy Jones*, while Asquith's *Tell England* returns to Tommy Atkins' precursor by naming its hero Edgar Doe. But Doe is more broadly characterised by his standing for the generation of 'gilded youth' lost in the war, which features in plays, novels and films produced in the first decade thereafter.[38] In these feature films, the everyman in the Other Ranks, the subject of wartime recruitment, is all too often subsidiary and rendered as a comic, rustic figure. Such are the northerners in Suvla Bay in *Tell England*, joshing over the daily tally of lice and prizing souvenir photos of giant cabbages, rather than of sweethearts (as in *Hearts of the World* and *Comradeship*). Bullying NCOs, as ever, provide an easy butt of humour from all sides. *The Battle of Arras* presents a major in charge of a battalion at the age of twenty-one. Graves and Sassoon (who survived) and Vera Brittain's lover and brother (who did not) provide actual models for these doomed public school heroes, exemplary in their sporting and academic prowess, all volunteering early in August 1914, their illusions of the glory of war rudely shattered by experience.

R. C. Sherriff's immensely popular *Journey's End* opened on stage in 1928, directed by James Whale, with Laurence Olivier as Stanhope, who has come straight to the front from school at eighteen; the play occupied the entire evening schedule on BBC television on Armistice Day 1937. Appropriately, Olivier reappears as The Old Soldier, wheelchair-bound and with medals pinned to his cardigan, in *War Requiem*. Sherriff also produced the screenplay for Sam Wood's 1939 version of *Goodbye Mr Chips* with Robert Donat (see Chapter 7 – and subsequently adapted for television) which, too, revisits the theme of youth maimed and sacrificed.[39] In *Tell England* and *Journey's End*, young officers (mere boys themselves) serve as surrogate fathers to frightened younger boys of the lower school: in *Journey's End*, Raleigh's sister waits for Stanhope. Robin Villiers, in *Blighty* (played by a disconcertingly fresh-faced Godfrey Winn), leaves schoolfriends in Heidelberg to enlist, like Stanhope, lying about his age to the Medical Board. These post-war accounts bitterly denounce the ancient mythology of a patriotic war (the imperative *Tell England* matches Owen's 'Old Lie') which had persuaded so many to volunteer their lives so willingly.

The front page of the *Daily Express* on 5 August 1914, over a picture of Lord Jellicoe, head of the fleet, invoked Nelson's words before the Battle of Trafalgar in 1805: 'England Expects that Every Man Shall do his Duty'. G. L. Tucker took *England Expects* as the title for his film released in August and Trafalgar Day was celebrated in October with the laying of wreaths at Nelson's Column, 'who protected this country from invasion and secured for Great Britain the Supremacy of the Seas'. The recruitment film *The Life of a WAAC* pictures Nelson, garlanded with the slogan 'England Expects . . . ', *England's Call* portrays Ralegh, Wellington, Nelson, Gordon and others, and *British Call to the Nation* (opening on Trafalgar Day) draws a parallel between Nelson and the Navy's current leaders with the dedication of flowers and verses. But the Navy was to suffer many reversals during the course of the war, notably at the Battle of Jutland (reconstructed by H. Bruce Woolfe in 1921), at the Battles of the Coronel and Falkland Islands ('a victory and a defeat as glorious as a victory', we are advised, in retrospect, in Walter Summers' film of 1927) and in numerous encounters in the Channel and the Mediterranean, before finally securing German surrender (as shown in *Our Day – German U-Boats Lying at Harwich*, 1918).

Maurice Elvey's *Nelson: The Story of England's Immortal Naval Hero* (1919) was made with the full co-operation of the Navy. Permission was given for filming in Portsmouth and in the cockpit of the *Victory* (most of the guns, we are advised in an intertitle, are those actually used at Trafalgar)

'The fateful choice – to fight or run': Christopher Cradock contemplates the image of Nelson in Walter Summers' 1927 reconstruction, *The Battles of the Coronel and Falkland Islands*

and Eliot Stannard's scenario was carefully vetted by Admiral Mark Kerr, who also provided a fore-word to the film's souvenir programme:

> It is well for us if we recall Nelson in our minds and to the minds of others at this time. It is still better if we never forget him, for he is the most shining example of patriotism in our history, as well as the most perfect embodiment of duty that the chronicles have given us. Patriotism cannot be dismissed as purely a sentiment, it is equally with duty a virtue and also a commercial asset; it is the spirit which binds the Empire together and makes it strong enough to keep its place in the world. It should be born in the home, thrive in the State, and reach its final growth in the Empire. In addition to Lord Nelson's work for the Empire, was the spirit he left in the Royal Navy, and it is to this spirit and his teachings of comradeship that we largely owe our success in the Great War that has just been concluded.[40]

At the launch of *Nelson* in 1919, the Alhambra Theatre in London greeted diplomats from the Allied Nations and representatives of the Admiralty and the American Navy with bunting, and flags signalled Nelson's message, 'England Expects', conveyed as an animated intertitle in the film itself.[41]

The film explicitly sets forth Nelson's career as inspirational and exemplary. Admiral Sir Robert Freemantle appears as himself, recounting the history of the naval fleet of the British Empire from

King Alfred to the present via the Armada and Napoleon, to a boy enrolled for Osborne Naval College; 'And to this very day, Nelson sweeps the seas', the epilogue concludes. Boadicea is shown appearing to Nelson in a vision and the film employs other images familiar from a variety of media during the war; a Teutonic gauntleted hand (the 'mailed fist' of the *Daily Express* and Pearson's *The Great European War*) stretches out to seize a globe. Emma Hamilton, accompanied by her spaniel, walks alongside Nelson, attributed with a bulldog. A composite of materials is assembled, comprising location and studio dramatised re-enactments of Nelson's life interspersed with Freemantle's reading with the boy, footage of battleships, model shots, animated diagrams, stylised mask shots (the view framed as if through a gun hatch; a heart framing the *Victory* to convey England's love of its hero), cartouches presenting Nelson in the manner of Nelson memorabilia, overlaid titles ('Will no one bring Hardy to me?' and 'Thank God I have done my duty' emanate from his own lips), inserts (a copy of Nelson's last letter to Emma) and intertitles (conveying datelines, reported speech, commentary and location: 'the position of the fleets at 1 p.m.' is inscribed as if on a schoolroom blackboard). Elvey's efforts to achieve authenticity might be set against Edison's *The Battle of Trafalgar* (1911), which prompted complaints to the British trade press for its inaccurate costuming and depiction of Nelson.[42]

In the wake of the Franco-British wartime alliance, Napoleonic France is reduced to a cipher in *Nelson*'s opening allegorical sequence. The French high command is cut against the readily identifiable figures of Pitt and Wellington (in boots and cockaded hat). Elvey devotes much space to Nelson's defence of Naples and the Neapolitan court against Imperial expansion. Nelson's superior humanity (as propaganda claimed for the British handling of German captives on the Western Front) is shown in the generosity which he extends to his enemy. Elvey has Nelson's valet confronting his master after the loss of his arm: 'You ain't never going to die, Sir,' he says, wiping a tear from his eye; 'I couldn't bear it.' Nelson is deemed a hero as much for his kindness as for his wisdom as a strategist and bravery as a warrior, 'ever in the forefront of battle'; 'Roll call after battle: Nelson's concern was always for his gallant men', and the admiral is shown visiting the wounded below deck. Nelson is seen to be a leader of men but in his affinity with the men is simultaneously one of them. Elvey effectively dramatises the comparison by showing a sailor in the cockpit expiring as victory is announced and immediately prior to Nelson himself. Furthermore, the emphasis on Nelson's humble origins and the personal odds which he overcame suggest that such heroism is a worthy ambition for anybody. At the end, one of the Osborne recruits declares, 'There will never be another hero like Nelson'; but an intertitle interjects, 'What about Jack Cornwell?' and we are shown the boy who has answered the call, who bravely manned his gun to the last in the Battle of Jutland (1916), standing between the guns on a modern battleship and directly addressing the camera.

Nurse Edith Cavell, who famously said that 'Patriotism is not enough: I must have no hatred or bitterness for anyone', was, nevertheless, after her execution in Belgium in 1914, often appropriated in exhortations to further patriotic effort. Her words, inscribed on her monument at Charing Cross, are uttered to an English chaplain and also conclude Herbert Wilcox's *Dawn* (1928). Not only was she cast to be played in *The National Film* but also appears, in a re-enactment of her death, in *Nurse and Martyr* (Percy Moran, 1915) and *Stand by the Men who have Stood by You* (E. P. Kinsella and Horace Morgan, 1918). The fate of *Dawn*, starring Sybil Thorndike as Nurse Cavell, provides an interesting example of the continuation of official censorship in film exhibition in peacetime and indicates a shift in temperament after the triumphalism and euphoria of the Armistice: the actual execution was not shown. The *Daily Mail* critic, Iris Barry, claimed that 'the horror of war and its brutalities is engendered in the mind of the spectator' and that it was 'a film with a mission – and that is anti-war':

> [It] is an attempt to record . . . a noble, deliberate and sustained gesture of humanity and heroism carried through unflinchingly in peril of death. There is evident here a desire not to entertain those who see it but to plead the cause of peace and to appeal to us by bringing home the price that war exacts in making mankind as a whole abrogate those attributes, those exalted sentiments of pity and service to which at its best it aspires.[43]

Certainly, *Dawn* depicts its characters as the victims rather than the perpetrators of war and employs 'big words' against War itself rather than against the German officers who dutifully follow orders: 'The Rulers of Europe were the puppets of Carnage – some more willing than others; but all enslaved to the system of War'; 'War makes no distinction between friends and foes – those who break its rules are broken in its merciless fingers', marking thus 'the triumph of War over humanity'. One soldier deputed to the firing squad refuses to shoulder his rifle. The high-brow journal *Close Up* (see Chapter 4), to whose contributors Barry was linked, complained in 1927 of war films then showing (including *Armageddon*, the story of Allenby's campaign in Palestine, and *The Battles of the Coronel and Falkland Islands*) which adopted the 'romantic boy-adventure book angle'; relatives of those who had died in the Coronel Battle complained at Summers' film being made at all.[44] Herbert Wilcox himself, in his memoirs, declares that he drew inspiration from Rupert Brooke and duly intended to close *Dawn* with a shot of newly turned turf and the subtitle ' . . . some corner of a foreign field . . .'.[45] Establishing shots of the prison of St Gilles in Brussels and the canal at Malines locate the action and Madame Bodart (who helped Cavell in enabling the escape of deserters and British prisoners of war – 'the most pitiful victims of the war machine') 're-enacts the role she played in the war'. However, there was disagreement between the German and Belgian authorities as to whether the film corresponded faithfully to actual events and the British government and the BBFC were concerned that this fictional treatment of recent history would cause distress to nations with which Britain was then endeavouring to consolidate peaceful relations.[46] By the end of the 1920s, some audiences in Europe were not only wearying of the war as a subject for films but were also tired of seeing the victory celebrated. Maurice Elvey's 1929 *High Treason* (see Chapter 4) optimistically portrays the popularity of pacifism.

The Return of the Soldier; 'The Lament of the Demobilised'

The *Daily Express* on 11 November 1918 featured a number of 'personalities of the Great War'. These included Haig (for the Army), Sturdee and Jellicoe (for the Navy) and Lloyd George (as political leader of Britain during the hostilities). Frances Stevenson, Lloyd George's secretary and mistress, published collections of the great man's wartime speeches in *Through Terror to Triumph* (1915) and *The Great Crusade* (1918). Elvey was appointed by Ideal to produce a hagiography of Lloyd George, matching his treatment of Nightingale and Nelson. It was intended for release in ten weekly instalments from December 1918 and to bring 'dignity to the picture palaces and lift the kinema to a level of national importance never reached before'.[47] The flattery and promotion which *The Romance of David Lloyd George* afforded its subject (promoted in pre-publicity as 'The Man Who Saved the Empire') surpassed even the visions of Arnold Bennett's war satire, *Lord Raingo*: on completion, the film was advisedly withdrawn but has since been discovered and preserved. The London University historian, Sir Sidney Low, spent seven weeks in North Wales while Norman Page (the actor cast to portray Lloyd George) reputedly observed the Prime Minister in the House of Commons to capture distinctive mannerisms. The man himself was familiar to audiences not only from newspaper photos but also from newsreels.

The film ponderously trails the boy (including shots of his birthplace, furniture from Criccieth, portraits of his parents and a reproduction of his birth certificate) to his formative scripture lessons in school: the flight of the Children of Israel is matched to reconstructed scenes of the plight of Belgian women and children in the war; the battle of David and Goliath is identified with Lloyd George's 'triumph' over the Kaiser. A masked shot of Richard Lloyd's lathe tacitly compares the uncle who nurtures the boy David with Joseph, the surrogate father of Christ. He trains as a solicitor then defeats the Conservative incumbent ('a territorial magnate') in the election at Caernarvon, duly represented by tinted shots of its castle ('the Jordan Crossed'). There is direct quotation in the intertitles (many elaborately illustrated) from his interminable speeches and re-enactment of skirmishes at Birmingham Town Hall (in 1900) and of suffragette riots (see Chapter 2). His social reforms are assiduously enumerated and dramatically documented (the People's Budget; National Insurance; the 1917 Franchise Act); with the outbreak of war, he announces that, 'We shall march . . . through terror to triumph'. As Minister of Munitions he visits an armaments factory, where girls from Girton work alongside girls from Bethnal Green and 'men from all classes'. As Secretary of State for War, he is shown (entirely spuriously) visiting trenches at the Front with Clemenceau. However, this 'Champion of Civilisation, Democracy and Peace' is also represented as a mere mortal, kissing strange babies, comforting the bereaved, dandling his own children at Downing Street, playing golf at Walton Heath and returning to his roots (silhouetted against the Welsh shoreline) for rest and recuperation. His confidence in 'the God of Righteousness' is justly rewarded as 'all manner and means of men, women and children' celebrate the victory.

Unveiling of the Ystalfera War Memorial (1922) (Courtesy of the Imperial War Museum/IWM FLM 3207)

While burial ceremonies were recorded in France, so also was the commemoration of Lutyens' provisional cenotaph in Whitehall. The language of intertitles in *The British Victory Parade in London* (1919), as always, vetted by the War Office, endeavours to convey the sense of occasion, its pomp and solemn liturgy, and to justify the victory won: 'Not least amongst the saviours were the women who marched through the bedizened streets' we are told, as they pass through Admiralty Arch; 'When Field Marshall Haig passed in lordly dignity, the welkin rang with the loud shouts of a myriad lusty voices'; 'the cohesion of the widespread parts of the empire was proved again'; 'their Majesties the King and Queen share in the utter fullness of joy'. The bereaved mourned but also, sometimes, sought to sustain contact with the loved and lost. Vera Brittain recalls the success of Oliver Lodge's occult novel *Raymond* during the war, while *Photographing Fairies* presents the efforts of Sir Arthur Conan Doyle and others to reach the dead in their afterlife in the aftermath:[48] a photographer, a war veteran accustomed to the concrete experience and evidence of death, initially dismisses the claims of the spiritualists as sham.

The Imperial War Graves Commission set about constructing memorials for the dead buried on the field of battle. Meanwhile, arrangements were made for the return of one anonymous corpse which would symbolise the sacrifice of many. Six bodies were exhumed from Ypres, Cambrai, Arras, the Somme, the Aisne and the Marne from which one coffin was selected and transported to Westminster Abbey, where it was interred in French soil. Beaverbrook's Pathé Gazette, *Home-coming of an Unknown Warrior*, records the coffin's journey and the cathartic ritual on Armistice Day 1920, in which the King, Lloyd George and the people united: the crowds in London are cut against wooden crosses in France: more than half a million people made the 'Great Pilgrimage' to the Abbey in four days. 'The white cliffs', we are told, 'never saw a more stirring scene'; we are shown 'a memorable scene almost painful in its intensity of feeling'. French ceremonies parallel the action in Britain. Pearson's *Reveille* (1924) was constructed around the idea of a two-minute silence in the film's score, to mark Armistice Day and commemorate the dead. *Land of Hope and Glory* (Harley Knoles, 1927) re-enacts the unveiling and dedication ceremony of a Celtic cross, by a village community, to the accompaniment of Edward Elgar's 'immortal song': families, survivors, invalids and their nurses participate in the occasion. The ceremony is typical of a number of events witnessed by documentary accounts.

Lloyd George's political campaign at the end of 1918 responded to demands that the effort and sacrifice of the war years should not be in vain. *Britain's Effort* concludes with a representation of the peace which the country means to secure: happy families and busy industries. The *Daily Express* boldly announced 'a new era for the working man', and carried the admonishing slogan, 'What did you do in the Great War, guvnor?'[49] However, returning soldiers and demobilised supply and dilution workers were often disappointed by their lukewarm reception: 'And no one talked heroics now', wrote Brittain, 'and we/Must just go back and start again once more'.[50] In *Land of Hope and Glory* the surviving Whiteford brothers find themselves still without work a year after demobilisation and are despatched to make careers for themselves in the Dominions. In Pat O'Connor's *A Month in the Country* (the 1987 adaptation by Simon Gray of J. L. Carr's novel), two soldiers recuperate in the Yorkshire village of Oxgodby: Moon wonders whether it is worse for them not having 'anything to show for it' – apart from Birkin's twitch and stammer and their nightmares, they both appear to have survived intact. The *Daily Express* offered free advertisements for women seeking work after the war and the *Daily Mail* launched a beauty competition for women workers. *Mrs John Bull Prepared* ends with a quotation from Lloyd George: 'the women of Britain have shown that they can share the hardships of war . . . they shall share in the triumph'. Where strikes had been organised during the war for equal pay, Lloyd George proposed oppor-tunities for women, their enfranchisement and for trades' unions. His manifesto for the 'khaki elec-tion' also vaunted better housing and wages, welfare provision and easy access to the land. On the international front, he backed free trade and a League of Nations (to free the world from the menace of war). Before 1914, housing and town planning had been discussed in the architectural press and, more generally, in symposia organised by Patrick Geddes in supplements to the *New Age*.[51] The garden suburb architect, Raymond Unwin, used film to proselytise for housing schemes and the clearance of slums, the 'homes fit for heroes' motif recurring in flashback at the begin-ning of Noël Coward's *This Happy Breed* (1944 – see Chapter 6).[52] At the end of *Mademoiselle from Armentières*, Tommy, limping from his war wound, is shown returning to his semi in the sub-urbs, to his French wife and their happy children. In *Kitty*, the suburban idyll is relocated to the riverside, with chintz, gingham and neat flower beds (and entrepreneurial zeal) very much in evidence.

Rebecca West's *The Return of the Soldier* (filmed by Alan Bridges in 1982) presents a shell-shocked officer who, in his illness, wills himself (determines his doctor) to forget the recent past and instead returns in his mind to his childhood. He thereby sees the world as a wise child, attain-ing something 'saner than sanity'.[53] His upper-class wife and cousin are jealous of his attachment to the shabby and suburban Kitty, whose affection he remembers from a shared past and from which the other women are excluded. West's vision is, however, optimistic for a future which he has dared to imagine as much as it is nostalgic for a dream. In the immediate post-war years, West, Brittain and others on the Liberal left hoped for a reconstruction of society and a transformation of international relations. The *Daily Express* found a new enemy in the Bolshevik revolutionaries of Russia and their supposed foreign agents. Within a decade, beliefs that the Great War would prove 'a War to end War' were largely shattered.

Comradeship (Maurice Elvey, 1919)

During the war it became routine to celebrate pilots as the knights errant of the skies, worthy war-riors matched in single combat on 'steeds of steel and wire'; 'Every flight is a romance, every record an epic', rhapsodised David Lloyd George, Prime Minister of the Coalition Government from 1916, 'They recall the old legends of chivalry'.[54] W. E. Johns, himself responsible for the romanticisation of pilots through his numerous *Biggles* stories, notes that then 'only politicians saw romance in it' and Joanna Bourke concludes that: 'Chivalry was evoked to stifle fears of senseless violence; inti-macy was substituted for confusing anonymity; skilfulness was imposed to dispel numbing monot-ony'.[55] However, in the aftermath these were not the only servicemen to be presented in terms which recall medieval codes of honour. *Comradeship*, directed by Maurice Elvey and strikingly pho-tographed by Paul Burger, delineates social and personal vices against which the war is justly fought and (like Chaucer's 'The Romaunt of the Rose') honours a beautiful lady of nobility who suffers patiently and whose trust in hope is rewarded.[56] The virtuous love of one man (who is pre-pared to deny himself when he believes the object of his affection is promised elsewhere) is con-trasted with the unchaste love of another. The pairing of rival suitors is a theme shared with European films of the war years and, indeed, is poignantly revisited in flashback at the first meet-ing of the English Wynne-Candy and German Kretschmar-Schuldorff in Michael Powell's Second World War film, *The Life and Death of Colonel Blimp* (see Chapter 6).

Melcombe is cast as the typical English village, the Cotswolds featuring as prominently here as they were a generation later. Half-timbered cottages flank a street 'so quiet that tortoises could meet'. But the local draper, John Armstrong (Gerald Ames), an orphan, has been stirred by the fanaticism of his uncle: at first, Armstrong opposes war against Germany, claiming that she rep-resents 'efficiency and the survival of the fittest', and that 'the most efficient side will win', although his precise political allegiances are rendered less clearly by the film than the suggestion that any sort of political agitation is suspect and un-English (it may even be that he is reading Marx). 'We want merciful efficiency', argues Betty, and intercut footage recalls the 'rape' of Belgium in 1914.

At Fanshawe Hall, the lord of the manor, Colonel Mortimer, lives with his son, Lionel Baring (Guy Newall), and his niece, Betty (Lily Elsie); the virtuous and beautiful lady of nobility is shown in her nurse's uniform, reflected in a mirror and framed within a heart-shaped mask in the film's opening titles. Lionel has received notice of mobilisation and is alarmed when he notices Armstrong's German cutter, Liebmann, with photographs of the village landmarks: indeed, Liebmann's 'cover' is significant, given competition between Germany and Britain in the cloth trade before the outbreak of war. Baring advises Armstrong to dismiss Liebmann, but Armstrong refuses, insisting that he is a good worker and denouncing talk of war. Fortunately, others in England are better prepared and a battleship is shown as Parliament meets in night sitting. His confidence is shown to be misplaced when Liebmann and accomplices leave Melcombe, leaving the shop assistant, Peggy (Peggy Carlisle, here with fluffy Mary Pickford ringlets and ribbons), expecting his child: Peggy's stepmother duly rejects her and, while Betty attempts to comfort the girl, Armstrong begins to wonder whether 'the survival of the fittest' is the most fitting moral after all. 'It's the duty of every Englishman to protect every Englishwoman', the Colonel reminds us, and a newspaper boy announces the outbreak of war.

Betty's charity prompts an offering from Armstrong's 'full heart'. He donates funds to the hospital at Fanshawe Hall and she shows him the wounded 'who have suffered in order that your business may continue'. Conscience-stricken, Armstrong enlists and promises to write to Betty, whom he confesses he has always worshipped. Other female 'angels' on the home front are shown serving in the Victoria Canteen (which features also in *Mrs John Bull Prepared*) on Ginger's leave in 'dear, delightful, dirty, foggy old Blighty'. Our knight meets his cockney squire, Ginger Dickens (played by the comic Teddy Arundell – an equivalent for Tommy Trinder in films of the Second World War), at the training camp where they exchange vows of mutual allegiance: a similar coupling appears in *Mademoiselle from Armentières* and *High Treason*. The regiment departs for France, their train passing a crowd of mothers, wives, sisters, sweethearts and friends, Betty among them, running the length of the platform (matching the departure at the docks in the recruitment film, *The Call to the Young*, 1918); Armstrong is now pleased to be in service and he and Betty promise to exchange letters. The ordeals of men in the trench ('Being bally well strafed'; 'Goin' acrost – a nasty job o' work') are cut against domestic tragedies on the home front: Peggy loses her baby, Betty comforts her, and the scene is held in midshot in an oval frame.

Returning on leave, Armstrong wonders how he once (like the trader Greene in Brunel's *Blighty*) could have thought business so important. He sees Betty with Baring and assumes him to be a rival for her affection, while Ginger saves Peggy from unwanted attentions and tells her that he would like to think that he was 'leaving someone behind' when he next goes to the front: 'And well might they pray for their loved ones', an intertitle reminds us, when they return. Silhouetted against smoke and flames (matching the end sequences of *The Battle of the Ancre*), Baring is shown throttled and stabbed by Liebmann, now serving in the German Army, but Ginger intervenes and drags him off. He tears up the photo of Peggy in Liebmann's pocket while Armstrong, finding Betty's locket on Baring, leaves it and pulls Baring aside: similar exchanged tokens sustain the affection between The Boy and The Girl in *Hearts of the World*. Armstrong gallantly resists his baser instincts and, in saving his comrade at arms, is himself blinded by an exploding shell.

The cessation of hostilities in 1918 coincides with Ginger's next leave in London. He witnesses the fireworks and other celebrations and thumbs his nose at the captured Hun guns at Buckingham Palace. Peggy, mournfully, wishes that she had told him earlier of the attachment to Liebmann while Baring tells Betty that he has discovered the locket which she intended for Armstrong. The tradesman, Armstrong, continues to prove the new nobility of his soul by bringing Peggy and Ginger together ('there is some use in a blind man, after all') and when, in return, Peggy tells him of Betty's love, he sacrifices his own interests: 'it would be unfair to tie her'. Peggy weeps and Betty resignedly waits (a watercolour pastoral scene shows the passing of the seasons).

Baring, now on crutches, and Armstrong join a Comrades' Club in Melcombe. Armstrong addresses a public meeting, its tone now very different from the 'fanaticism' of his uncle's campaigning. A woman in the audience suggests that his survival depends on a woman's help. Betty proposes marriage, the audience raises a cheer and in future months he recovers his sight and fitness: a similar miraculous transformation is effected by the love of a good woman in *Kitty*, and in *Palais de Danse* (Maurice Elvey, 1928) a child-woman (Mabel Poulton) plays the little mother to her war-wounded father. 'What a pity that the comradeship of the Army does not continue in civilian life', ponders the wounded Armstrong in his hospital bed; 'I'm afraid of peace – what's a blind helpless man to make of his life?' But, in the words of the King, quoted in the film's prologue, the moral of the story seems to be 'the hope that the comradeship of war survives into peacetime'; wartime friendships here survive and strengthen the peace. Betty is attracted by Armstrong's 'masterful intellect, in spite of their social difference', but he, in turn, is inspired by her dedication to service and humanised by her affection. Such constancy, as in *Kitty*, where a knight of ancient lineage (and also a pilot) is patiently loved and miraculously restored to health by the daughter of a shopkeeper, or in *Blighty*, where the former chauffeur returns to marry Lord Villiers' daughter, overcomes class distinction. Meanwhile, Peggy is redeemed by the pity and compassion of Betty and Ginger and Armstrong makes a friend in Ginger. These sentiments look towards the building of a better society in peacetime. However, the outright warning against agitators, 'even in peaceful England' places the film on a firm conservative footing. In the immediate aftermath of war, *Comradeship* is opportunistically reminiscent of wartime propaganda and still portrays a German character as personally dastardly and Germany as the source of unwelcome (albeit ill-defined) political ideals.

Notes

1. Paul Fussell, *The Great War and Modern Memory* (Oxford: Oxford University Press, 1975), p. 183.
2. See, for instance, 'A Turn of Speech', in Samuel Hynes, *A War Imagined* (London: Pimlico, 1990), pp. 109–19.
3. William Boyd, *The New Confessions* (Harmondsworth: Penguin, 1988), pp. 170–94.
4. Joanna Bourke, *An Intimate History of Killing* (London: Granta Books, 2000), p. 27.
5. Joanna Bourke, *Dismembering the Male* (London: Reaktion, 1999), p. 21.
6. *Daily Express*, 15 August 1914.
7. Nicholas Reeves, *Official British Film Propaganda* (London: Croom Helm and IWM, 1986), pp. 68 and 121.
8. *Daily Express*, 11 November 1918.
9. Reeves, *Official British Film Propaganda*, p. 33.
10. George Pearson, *Flashback: an Autobiography of a British Film Maker* (London: George Allen and Unwin, 1957), p. 45.
11. Nicholas Hiley, 'Hilton Dewitt Girdwood and the Origins of British Official Filming', *Historical Journal of Film, Radio and Television* vol. 13 no. 2, 1993, pp. 129–48.
12. Roger Smither, '"A Wonderful Idea of the Fighting": the Question of Fakes in *The Battle of the Somme*', *Historical Journal of Film, Radio and Television* vol. 13 no. 2, 1993, pp. 149–68.
13. 'The Real Film Hero', *Pictures and Picturegoer*, 27 January 1917, p. 376.
14. Toby Haggith, 'Reconstructing the Musical Arrangement for *The Battle of the Somme* (1916)', *Film History* vol. 14, 2002, pp. 12–13; see also Michael Williams, *Ivor Novello: Screen Idol* (London: BFI, 2003), pp. 62–7 and Hynes, *A War Imagined*, pp. 36–7.
15. Rebecca West, 'The Return of the Soldier', *The Essential Rebecca West* (Harmondsworth: Penguin, 1983), pp. 4–5; see also Siegfried Sassoon, 'Picture-Show'.
16. 'Embedding: in Bed with the Generals for the First Time?', presentation given by Toby Haggith at Sheffield International Documentary Festival 2003.
17. R. J. Minney, *'Puffin' Asquith* (London: Leslie Frewin, 1973), pp. 60–5; see also HM review, 'The War Film', *The Spectator*, 11 April 1931, p. 581: 'when we get away from the "great romance of glorious youth" aspect, *Tell England* has moments of realism which set it, as a realistic spectacle of war . . . well beyond anything yet from America'.
18. *Daily Express*, 1 October 1914.
19. *Daily Express*, 24 August 1918 and Rachael Low, *The History of the British Film*.
20. Robert Graves, *Goodbye to All That* (London: Jonathan Cape, 1929), p. 330.
21. See Amy Sargeant, 'Funny Peculiar and Funny Ha-Ha', in Laraine Porter and Alan Burton (eds), *Pimple, Pranks and Pratfalls* (Trowbridge: Flicks Books, 2000), p. 96; *The South Wales Echo*, 26 February 1927, p. 8, comments that, 'most of the Splinters group have costumes bought for them by their wives' and that 'a really effeminate chorus follow a poor female impersonator'.
22. Peter Beresford Ellis and Piers Williams, *By Jove, Biggles!: The Life of Captain W. E. Johns* (London: W. H. Allen, 1981), p. 39.
23. Rev. John Michael Stanhope Walker in Michael Moynihan (ed.), *People at War* 1914–1918 (Newton Abbot: David and Charles, 1973), p. 69.
24. Kevin Brownlow, *The War, the West and the Wilderness* (London: Secker and Warburg, 1979), p. 61; see also Hynes, *A War Imagined*, pp. 122–5.
25. Bourke, *Dismembering the Male*, p. 15.

26. *Daily Express*, 20 July 1918; in June 1918 pacifists were barred from voting for five years.
27. Joan Littlewood, *Joan's Book* (London: Macmillan, 2000), p. 676; for 'It's a Long Way to Tipperary', as sung by Florrie Forde, see Penny Summerfield, 'Patriotism and Empire', in John M. Mackenzie (ed.), *Imperialism and Popular Culture* (Manchester: Manchester University Press, 1986), pp. 40–1.
28. Iris Barry, *Daily Mail*, 6 February 1928, p. 17.
29. Bourke, *Dismembering the Male*, p. 22, and Vera Brittain, *Testament of Youth* [1933] (London: Virago, 1978).
30. Bourke, *An Intimate History of Killing*, pp. 4–5, regarding letters which seamlessly weave domestic trivia with a narrative of murder: 'you can hardly have too many [socks] in service, especially if you have much murdering to do'; for 'tank banks' see Trudi Tate, *Modernism, History and the First World War* (Manchester: Manchester University Press, 1998), pp. 126–30.
31. Gail Braybon, *Women Workers in the First World War* (London: Routledge, 1989), p. 11.
32. Brittain, *Testament of Youth*, pp. 453 and 468.
33. Reeves, *Official British Film Propaganda*, p. 127.
34. *Daily Express*, 31 August 1918.
35. Brownlow, *The War, the West and the Wilderness*, p. 152.
36. See Amy Sargeant, '*We're All Doing the Riviera* because *It's So Much Nicer in Nice*', in Laraine Porter and Alan Burton (eds), *Location, Location, Location* (Trowbridge: Flicks Books, 2004).
37. Graves, *Goodbye to All That*, p. 122; for Kipling's invention of Tommy Atkins as a literary type, see Hynes, *A War Imagined*, p. 50.
38. See Paul Rotha, *Celluloid: the Film Today* (London: Longmans, Green and Co., 1933), p. 172; for a discussion of Ernest Raymond's 1922 novel *Tell England*, 'A Great Romance of Glorious Youth', see Hynes, *A War Imagined*, pp. 332–5.
39. See James Hilton, *Goodbye, Mr Chips* [1934] (London: Hodder and Stoughton, 1951), pp. 45, 69, 89–99.
40. See Amy Sargeant, 'Do We Need Another Hero?', in Claire Monk and Amy Sargeant (eds), *British Historical Cinema* (London: Routledge, 2002), pp. 15–30.
41. Low Warren, *The Film Game* (London: T. Werner Laurie, 1937), p. 123.
42. *The Bioscope*, 9 November 1911, p. 511.
43. Iris Barry, 'Austen Chamberlain Seeking to Ban *Dawn*', *Daily Mail*, 1 March 1928, p. 11.
44. Bryher (Winifred Ellerman), *Close Up* vol. 1 issues 184, July and October 1927.
45. Herbert Wilcox, *Twenty-Five Thousand Sunsets* (London: Bodley Head, 1967), p. 27.
46. See J. C. Robertson, '*Dawn*: Edith Cavell and Anglo-German Relations', *Historical Journal of Film, Radio and Television* vol. 4 no.1, 1984, pp. 15–28.
47. David Berry and Simon Horrocks (eds), *David Lloyd George: The Movie Mystery* (Cardiff: University of Wales Press, 1998), pp. 4 and 13.
48. Graves, *Goodbye to All That*, p. 290; see also Adrian Conan Doyle, *The True Conan Doyle* (London: John Murray, 1945), pp. 18 and 22–3.
49. *Daily Express*, 2 December 1918.
50. Brittain, 'The Lament of the Demobilised' [1933], p. 467.
51. See supplement to the *New Age*, 3 November 1910, 'Symposium on Town Planning'.
52. 'Cinematograph Exhibition of Housing Schemes', *The Builder*, 30 May 1919, p. 543.
53. West, 'The Return of the Soldier', p. 48.
54. Bourke, *An Intimate History of Killing*, p. 59.

55. Ibid., p. 68; Beresford Ellis and Williams, *By Jove, Biggles!*, p. 71; H. G. Wells had similarly predicted a 'medieval fashion' of warfare in *The War in the Air* [1908] (London: T. Fisher Unwin, 1926), p. 240.

56. See 'The Romaunt of the Rose', in F. N. Robinson (ed.), *The Complete Works of Geoffrey Chaucer* (Oxford: Oxford University Press, 1976); Abel Gance's *J'accuse* (France, 1919) similarly portrays a love triangle between Jean, François and an un-aristocratic Edith.

Chapter 4 | 1920s

The Intellectuals and the Masses (Part One)

In 1924, Evelyn Waugh came down from Oxford and found himself with time on his hands. Between reading Edgar Wallace and Gertrude Stein, T. S. Eliot (whose poems he thought 'incredibly good') and Herbert Read (whose essays on art he failed to understand) he visited the Stoll cinema, the Tivoli and the Coliseum (where in 1924 he witnessed the stereoscopic 'Plastigram'); he saw the films of Charlie Chaplin (for whom, like the Film Society, he was an enthusiast, and thought him a modern genius on a par with Einstein and James Joyce) but preferred Harold Lloyd; he thought *Warning Shadows* (Germany, Arthur Robison, 1922) quite superb when he saw it at the Shaftesbury Avenue Pavilion and in 1927 he attended the first night of Fritz Lang's *Metropolis* (Germany, 1926).[1] He admired the drawings and typography of Eric Gill and, in spite of the large quantities of beer imbibed during the week and nights mis-spent at Elsa Lanchester's Charlotte Street 'Cave of Harmony', was able to rouse himself to hear Robin Knox's sermons at Westminster Cathedral. He made an amateur film, *The Scarlet Woman* ('An Ecclesiastical Melodrama'), with Lanchester and the founder of Oxford University's Cinematograph Club, Terence Greenidge, but later resented the expense and regretted the results.[2] In *Labels* and *Vile Bodies* (1930) he commented disparagingly on the advent of sound: 'In February 1929 London was lifeless and numb . . . Talking films were just being introduced and had set back by twenty years the one valid art of the century. There was not even a good murder case.'[3] *Vile Bodies* concludes with Colonel Blount inviting a film crew from 'The Wonderfilm Company of Great Britain' to make a costume drama in the grounds of Doubting Hall. Waugh's enthusiasms and prejudices were in many ways typical of a group of bohemian intellectuals associated with British film culture in the 1920s. A further defining feature was the group's antipathy towards the generality of British film production.

On Sunday, 25 October 1925, the Film Society held its first screening at the New Gallery Kinema, Regent Street, London. Founder members included Ivor Montagu and Adrian Brunel, the zoologist Julian Huxley, the notorious communist and Cambridge biochemist J. B. S. Haldane, the sculptor Frank Dobson, the graphic designer E. McKnight Kauffer, the art critics Roger Fry and Robert Herring, the socialist author H. G. Wells and polymath George Bernard Shaw, economist John Maynard Keynes, Iris Barry and the film critic of the *Evening Standard*, Walter Mycroft, the actors Ellen Terry,

Anna May Wong as exotic attraction in E. A. Dupont's *Piccadilly* (1929) – competing for attention with Alfred Junge's dynamic set

Ivor Novello and John Gielgud, the film directors George Pearson and Anthony Asquith and producers Michael Balcon and Victor Saville. The Society declared its mission, according to Brunel,

> In the belief that there are in this country a large number of people who regard cinema with the liveli-
> est interest and who would welcome the opportunity seldom afforded the general public of witnessing
> films of intrinsic merit whether old or new . . . [It] is important that films . . . should not only be shown
> under the best conditions to the most actively minded people both inside and outside the film world,
> but that they should, from time to time, be revived. This will be done. In this way, the standards of
> taste and of executive ability may be raised and a critical tradition be established. This cannot but affect
> future production, by founding a clearing-house for all films having pretensions to sincerity.[4]

The Film Society showed a wide range of material, from France (Clair's 1924 *Entr'acte*, Léger's
1924 *Ballet mécanique* and L'Herbier's 1924 *L'Inhumaine*), from Germany (Pabst's 1925 *The Joy-
less Street*, Ruttmann's 1927 *Berlin: the Symphony of a Great City* and Leni's 1924 *Waxworks*),
from Japan (Kinugasa's 1928 *Crossroads*) and the United States (von Stroheim's 1925 *Greed*),
alongside the work of its own members: the 1926–7 season included Brunel's burlesques, the
fourth season screened Montagu's 1929 *Bluebottles* (from a script by H. G. Wells); Lotte
Reininger's 1926 *The Adventures of Prince Achmed* and Len Lye's 1929 animation *Tusalava* were
both shown (see Chapter 5). Montagu battled with the censors, with the licensing authorities and
the foreign distributors, to secure screenings of material otherwise banned or unobtainable in
Britain.[5] Rachael Low, whose own critical criteria in *The History of the British Film* are largely
inherited from the Film Society agenda, declares that 'its importance can scarcely be overesti-
mated'.[6] In addition to making all these films available, the Society endeavoured to improve the
standard of debate and, as Jen Samson has noted, 'consistently drew attention to formal experiment'.[7] For this reason, Montagu was less keen to show Alexander Sanin's 1919 *Polikushka* (in the
second season) than he was to screen the great classics of the Soviet avant-garde (Eisenstein's *The
Battleship Potemkin* [1925], Pudovkin's *Storm over Asia* [1928] and Room's *Bed and Sofa* [1927]),
which he deemed revolutionary and progressive both in style and in content. Montagu's invitation
of Pudovkin and Eisenstein to address the Society, and his translation of their significant writings,
was acknowledged as a seminal influence by Hitchcock and others.[8]

Although Brunel and Montagu worked professionally in the film industry, their own 'experiments' shown to the Society are somewhat akin to Waugh's hobbying *The Scarlet Woman*. This
opens with 'found' footage of the Vatican City and includes irreverent literary quotation in its titles:
'This is a far, far deeper hurt than I have ever felt before,' says the Dean to the Prince of Wales, in
the style of Sidney Carton in Dickens' *A Tale of Two Cities*; 'To sleep, perchance to dream – aye,
there's the rub,' says Beatrice, writhing in bed, recalling Shakespeare's *Hamlet*. The burlesques
often mimic current practice rather than offering something altogether new. The 1920 Brunel and
A. A. Milne collaboration, *The Bump*, mocks the heroics of a William Brown explorer: 'I've explored
places where no white man has ever set his feet before . . . I once had all my teeth out without

gas . . .';[9] Adrian Brunel's *Crossing the Great Sagrada* (1924) (produced, we are told in the credits, by D. Spoof and E. Lastic, photographed by Lincoln and Di Kipp, 'at great personal risk'), a parody of the documentary film account of Angus Buchanan's Sahara expedition (widely shown in 1924), comprised titles, shots drawn from various existent travel films and shots of Brunel himself in his back garden in equal measure. The audience is advised that sections have been glued together in a hurry and its forgiveness is begged for any resulting mistakes: titles referring to Blackfriars and Wapping are cut against a jungle bridge and native huts; YWCA bathing belles are topless native girls censored by a BBFC certificate; the 'Great Cascara of Sagrada' (before and after crossing) is rendered by a shot of a waterfall and its reverse.

Similar films (*Travelaughs*) were made by Michael Powell and Harold Lachman, on the Côte d'Azur, 'straight' for local audiences and as 'spoofs' for export ('concerning the adventures of a party of tourists on their journey from Cannes to Mentone'): views of tourist attractions (the perfumerie at Grasse, a pottery and marionettes – as in Pearson's 1926 *The Little People*) and gorgeous panning shots of the sea and the hinterland are interspersed with comic interludes. The fat, wealthy widow, Madame Papillon (Madeleine Guitry) suffers, we are told, 'with rheumatic nerves and pneumatic curves'; Cicero Simp (Powell), the nutty naturalist, 'is still trying to find out why the butterflies'; 'Not every artist who comes here works on canvas. We found two old masters working hard on china pots' (and we are shown two old peasants drinking from tankards). There are knowing references to the movies, to elephants in film spectacles, to Mary Pickford's curls and to Rudolph Valentino in *The Sheik* and *The Son of the Sheik* (US, George Melford, 1921 and George Fitzmaurice, 1926): 'Sheik Abdul Krimp, who deserted the desert for fame in the movies. He played the snake in the Garden of Allah' (referring to the 1927 film directed by Rex Ingram, for whom Powell was then working). Maurice Elvey's 1928 *Palais de Danse* equally includes timely references to American imports and American stars (the vivacious Clara Bow and now late lamented Valentino): 'Palais de Danse – Romance by Chance – where every girl thinks she has "IT" and every boy believes he's the son of a sheikh.'

The Pathetic Gazette (1924) and *The Typical Budget* (1925) mimicked the style of newsreels.[10] *The Blunderland of Big Game* (1925) ('in which not a single wild animal appeared') referred to *The Wonderland of Big Game*, also widely shown in 1924. The humour of these Brunel burlesques drew attention to forms of construction and conjunction already widely accepted and routinely taken for granted: *Armageddon*, Bruce Woolfe's 1923 film account of Allenby's Palestine campaign, comprised re-enactments, contour maps and documentary footage drawn from the archive; Elvey's 1926 *The Flag Lieutenant* (starring Henry Edwards as an officer and gentleman who endures dishonour rather than 'rat on a friend'), his 1927 *The Flight Commander* (in which real-life *Boy's Own* hero Sir Alan Cobham appears as himself, defending ex-pats. from Chinese bandits) and his 1927 *Hindle Wakes* (of which more anon), all comprise elaborately constructed studio sets, flatly staged tableaux, location shots and actuality sequences. In *Bluebottles*, Elsa blowing a policeman's whistle summons up the constabulary and intercut footage of the infantry, the air force, the artillery and the navy. When told that she is to meet 'the promising young constable' whose life

Elsa Lanchester corners comic-strip burglars in Ivor Montagu's *Bluebottles* (1929)

she has saved, she imagines him, in intercut, superimposed frames, as Douglas Fairbanks (who appears also as a pin-up in another Montagu and Brunel short, *Daydreams* [1928]) or the French star, Adolphe Menjou, or the cowboy Tom Mix (all with policemen's helmets superimposed on their souvenir portrait shots) and not Charles Laughton (who plays the constable and who married Elsa in 1929). 'Mabel' and 'Elsa' say their goodbyes outside a cinema advertising *The Constant Nymph* (in which Mabel Poulton and Elsa Lanchester had appeared with Ivor Novello earlier in 1928). The Montagu–Brunel films suggest that a 'revolution' in form could be undertaken for fun (as advised by D. H. Lawrence) rather than in 'deadly earnestness'.

Many of the films screened by the Society were discussed in the journal *Close Up*, published in Switzerland from 1927 to 1933. Film criticism was contributed by Winifred Ellerman (Bryher), Eric Elliott, Oswell Blakeston, Norman McPherson, Robert Herring and Ernest Betts; items were also accepted from the poets Gertrude Stein and Dorothy M. Richardson. Like the journals *L'Esprit*

Nouveau, Veshch' Gegenstand Objet and *Kino i kul'tura, Close Up* aimed at a cosmopolitan audience and Jean Prevost's articles appeared in French. Reports are made upon production facilities
and procedures in studios abroad. Bryher, like Montagu, was concerned with questions of censorship (defending Pudovkin's scientific film *The Mechanics of the Brain* [1925] against the BBFC)
and of the use of film as an educational tool. Her comments on Walter Summers' 1927 *The Battles of the Coronel and Falkland Islands*, portraying the war from 'the romantic boy adventure book
angle', are echoed by Penelope Houston, writing about 1950s war films for *Sight and Sound* and
The Monthly Film Bulletin (see Chapter 8).[11] These critics delight in disparaging fandom and the
'eyewash and bunk . . . desired by the masses'.[12] Like Paul Rotha (see Chapter 5), Blakeston reviles
British directors (they 'have no more pretensions to be called film directors than they have to be
called plumbers or clothes dealers') but then reassures us that he intends no malice by his comments; 'Everyone is talking of a revival of British films', says Blakeston in 1927. 'The phrase is hardly
felicitous. Where in the history of British pictures are to be found films with the aesthetic merits of
Caligari [1919], *Warning Shadows* or *The Last Laugh* [Germany, F. W. Murnau, 1926]?'[13] The most
damning remarks are reserved for the lavish costume productions undertaken by Stoll (such as
Woolfe's 1926 *Boadicea*) and British National: snobbery about what were later to be dubbed 'heritage' pictures, it should be noted, is nothing new (see Chapter 11), although their sometimes irreverent handling of history proved eminently exportable. 'And the worst movie is seldom as indecent
as a play, except *Nell Gwynne* and one or two others . . .', says McPherson in an early editorial, of
the 1926 film directed by Wilcox as a star vehicle for Dorothy Gish:

> Then I ask you to think of Nell Gwynne, that bright and glittering specimen of culture and good breed-
> ing. Here, as accurate as the Georgian panelling our eye could not miss, we learn that the inimitable
> Nell entered State Banquets by sliding down the banisters at the moment when dessert was served,
> would jazz to where her monarch fed beside a Lady Castlemaine that none but a British censor could
> unblushingly permit and tossing herself athwart the Royal table, think of something bright and girl-
> ish, such as pulling his moustache or throwing a rotten plum at a nobleman. Now, films like this must
> be excessively harmful.[14]

However, it would be wrong to think that *Close Up* and the Film Society held the prerogative over
such debates and were the only places where experimentation was encouraged. The Shaftesbury
Avenue Pavilion followed the Society's example, recognising the kudos which 'artistic' and European productions bestowed on cinema as a whole. From 1922–8, Caroline Lejeune stalwartly
defended her corner at the *Manchester Guardian* and armed herself against accusations of 'intel-
lectualism' (see Chapter 5). She complained that such films as *Kean* (1924) (directed by Volkoff
and starring Ivan Mosjoukine), seen in a small suburban cinema in Paris, had yet to be distributed
in Britain. She ventured to suggest that British exhibitors were wary of its frequent superimpositions and vision sequences. She praised British films where praise was due but refused to hype
material which was less than meritorious. In 1927 she concluded that:

The injury which the British studios have drawn to themselves by praise of bad and inefficient work-manship is almost incalculable. In the name of patriotism they have misled the public over so many trivial British pictures that the few good ones have been sceptically received . . . There is no real appreci-ation for a fine film like *The Ring* [1927] because *The Flight Commander* and *The Glad Eye* [1927] . . . and other absurdities have used up all the superlatives we know. There is no real recognition of an Estelle Brody in an industry that counts Ivor Novello and Matheson Lang as giants of the screen. To do our kinema justice I think that all, or most of its faults are negative ones. It has not the harsh tech-nique of Italy, nor the crudeness of Russia, nor the insatiability of France nor the heaviness of Germany, nor the vulgarity of America. It simply has nothing, neither character nor courage, neither commercial success, skill nor artistic sense. It has no big men and no big ideas . . . Strip the British kinema of its essentials and you will find . . . one director, Alfred Hitchcock – who can be relied upon and two – Maurice Elvey and Walter Summers – who can be expected to provide the audiences with good things and four films, *The Ring*, *The Battles of the Coronel and Falkland Islands*, *Hindle Wakes* and *The Lodger* [1926] – which have quality enough to give them extra national fame.[15]

Lejeune's tastes were more catholic than those of the *Close Up* and *Film Society* contingents but it is their agenda that have largely informed much of the subsequent critical appraisal of British film-making in the 1920s. Their appreciation of silent film is partly grounded in aesthetic prefer-ence ('less is more' modernism), partly in an abstract social aspiration for a medium which could appeal across classes and across national boundaries: Chaplin (now American in spite of himself) was expediently invoked to endorse a general thesis. However, their disdain for 'the talkies' might also be referred to the snobbery of intellectuals towards another arriviste medium, televison, in the 1950s (see Chapter 8).

The Minor Art of Intertitling

Ivor Montagu and Adrian Brunel were required, as a matter of course, to produce English titles for the foreign films screened by the Society. In order to satisfy the censor, they sometimes cut material and occasionally introduced shots and titles which altered or qualified the original inten-tion. For instance, in Pudovkin's *Storm over Asia* (shown in the fifth season), Montagu introduced a disclaimer for the patently British uniforms and regalia of the 'White' officers of the Russian Civil War and introduced a close-up of a dollar bill to re-cast an English merchant as American. Adrian Brunel's comic short *Battling Bruisers* (1925) pastiches the non-orthogonal framing of the pho-tographers Alexander Rodchenko, Anatoli Golovnia and Edward Tisse (Eisenstein's cameraman on *Battleship Potemkin* – also shown in the fifth season), their non-continuity editing and inter-jects titles written in cod Cyrillic. Walter Summers' *The Battles of the Coronel and Falkland Islands* uses Gothic black letters over an eagle to denote the names of German vessels (*Nürnberg*, *Dres-den*, *Leipzig*), and sailors' hat bands, flagged signals, calendars, clocks, pressure gauges and wire-less reports to forward the action. In Hitchcock's *Downhill* (1927) Ivor Novello is improbably cast in a version of his own stageplay as a highly promising public schoolboy wrongly accused of a misdemeanour (but honour prevents him from peaching on a fellow); he is expelled by the school and renounced by his father, Sir Thomas Berwick (Norman McKinnell). Snaking paths illuminate the capital letters of the intertitles, some tinted, marking his descent through the social ranks. Thomas Bentley's *Old Bill Through the Ages* (1924) employs 'olde worlde' lettering and appropriate illustrations to mark the successive episodes of its pantomime-style pageantry (see Chapter 3).

In *Fox Farm* (Guy Newall, 1922), the intertitle cards are decorated with pictures of wild animals. *Laughter and Tears* (B. E. Doxatt-Pratt, 1921), a Dutch co-production, set in Paris and during the annual carnival in Venice, its 'lagoons not water but the overflowing tears of love', introduces characters with appropriate graphic illustrations: 'Mario Mari, a painter – his head filled with dreams, his pockets artistically empty'; 'Ferrando, a Futurist composer' and Pierette (Evelyn Brent), the milliner who devotedly sacrifices herself for Mario's material happiness. Mario is seduced by Sonia Countess Maltakoff (Dorothy Fane), 'patron of art and artists', but eventually returns to Pierette and to Venice where, next spring, 'cupid is crowned King of the Feast', again to the accompaniment of an illustrated intertitle.

Montagu was invited by Hitchcock to work on the editing of *The Lodger* and was responsible for the integration of McKnight Kauffer's deco-style captions. These are interesting not only for their explicitly graphic quality but also for the manner in which they consequently announce characters ('Daisy' and 'the Avenger') and segment the narrative ('Next Morning', 'One Evening', 'All Stories have an End'). The opening title shows a figure heavily muffled in hat and coat, exposed by a white chink in the dark screen . . . which then (as in Edgar Wallace's 1923 novel *The Dark Eyes of London*) closes over him as if swallowed into the thick London fog.

However, by 1926 this stark interventionist mode is the exception rather than the rule. Efforts were more usually directed towards the suppression of inserted captions and the increasing use of more plastic and pictorial material. Elvey's *Comradeship* (1919), long in advance of *Notting Hill*'s digitised climate (see Chapter 12), used a sequence of drawn pictures of a pastoral landscape which is transformed as the seasons pass and the return of the loved one is awaited. *The Last Laugh* (Murnau, 1926) was claimed to be unique as a film without titles, and, with *Vaudeville* (Germany, Dupont, 1925), was taken as a model of imitation for Asquith's *Shooting Stars* (1928);[16] a similar claim to novelty was made in the publicity for Hepworth's 1923 *Lily of the Alley*. *The Ring* (adapted from the popular stageplay by Edgar Wallace – who chaired British Lion in the 1920s) used visual material as a substitute for written exposition: an unravelling roll of tickets shows time passing and the great number of punters flocking to Jack's fight; the size of lettering and his place on the bill chart Jack's rise to the top of his profession; the snake bracelet given to the girl recurs as a (possibly Germanically heavy) leitmotif denoting Bob's seduction of her. But *Close Up* complained of Hitchcock's mannered mishandling and the number of occasions on which he resorted to diegetically integrated material, which it thought laboriously avoided a brief caption:

Well, it *is* treated visually, but then its merit ends. Mr Hitchcock's method is to depict one simple fact, that a sub-title could have got over, by a long sequence, or a number of elaborate tricks . . . the time and expense were out of proportion to the effect.[17]

At the wedding of Jack (Ian Hunter) and the girl (Lillian Hall Davies), 'Wilt thou have?' appears in an elaborately decorated font, as if drawn from the printed page of the Order of Ceremony. In Elvey's 1929 *High Treason*, siren-suited peace-maidens sing silently to italic lettering, while in *Call of the Road* (A. E. Coleby, 1920) the music and lyrics to folk songs are overlaid and intercut as a vagrant fiddler accompanies Victor McLaglen's soundless voice.

   Although Low is of the opinion that H. G. Wells' 1929 'book of the film' *The King who Was a King* was 'highly intellectual and verbal . . . [suggesting] that he had little understanding of film as visual story-telling', sometimes, I think, he tried a tad too hard. Heraldic devices are used to denote opposing national interests (as in *High Treason*) and often there are references to newspapers (type-set and formatted according to Central European custom), placards and fly-posters waft like thistledown (Wells advises that the producer study skate swimming in an aquarium in order to master this effect);[18] letters appear on the screen and then vanish as one player whispers to another. By the end of the 1920s, ticker-tape is something of a cliché and Hitchcock had long-since advised against the hackneyed use of hour-glasses and scales of justice: the prime concern of the caption artist, he declared, was that titles be boldly written, well-spaced and convey dialogue quickly and efficiently, not suspending the action. In *High Treason*, the scenic artist has (as Wells would say) 'gone large', or at least as large as meagre British budgets allowed. Attempting to emulate the example of *Metropolis* and *L'Inhumaine*, Andrew Mazzei uses an impressive array of sticky-back plastic gadgetry to locate the action in 1950: television screens, sliding doors, maps and a vast display board checking in the 25-millionth member of the Peace League.[19]

   Asquith's 1928 *Underground* and *Shooting Stars* are spartan in their use of titling. In the former, the famous Edward Johnston sans serif-lettered fascia above an actual station announces the film; similarly Dupont's *Piccadilly* (1929) carries its opening credits in the advertising slots along the lengths of three buses . . . which all arrive together. The illuminated background lights 'Cochran Review: "One Dam Thing After Another"' (exhibited in colour in Graham Wilcox's 1924 *London by Night* – 'As the first shades of night fall over London, so does the gilded West begin to sparkle with a myriad lights') locate the action and provide commentary in the night scenes of *Palais de Danse* and *Shooting Stars*. In Hitchcock's 1929 *Blackmail* (see Chapter 5) a flashing sign over Piccadilly Circus (a device re-used in *Bridget Jones's Diary* in 2001 – see Chapter 12) reminds Alice of events earlier in the evening: an advertisement for a spirit 'at the heart of a cocktail' becomes a stabbing knife. Walter Forde cuts to a flashback by spelling out the names of the fictitious Far East traders, WINSFORD & LEGARDE, across hessian-covered tea-chests on a quayside in *The Silent House* (1929). In *Underground*, a commonplace sampler which appears initially on the hall wall in the lodging house, merely as set dressing, is subsequently approached in close-up as a moral to be learned: 'Any good thing I may do or any kindness I may show let me do it now for I shall not pass this way again'. *Shooting Stars* sometimes employs diegetically integrated written material (the journalist's notebook; the film studio's call-sheet; Julian Gordon's contract; the script of the film being made and the titles of the film which Julian watches at the cinema). *Shooting Stars* labours the double meaning of its title: 'don't shoot', says Mae; 'shoot!' says the director. Sometimes titles are superimposed over the image, and the radio announcement of Andy Wilks' accident is punched up as individual words, as if on a telegram.

Some of the opposition to adaptations from literary and theatrical texts was prompted by the presumption that they would, of necessity, entail long intertitles which would retard the action and slow the pace of the film. Certainly, scenes which conveyed information and maintained momentum in short dialogue exchanges were favoured over those which regaled and detained the viewer with lengthy explanations. Sometimes titles have a specific contemporary resonance: the Sunday joint at Mrs Black's boarding house in *The Vagabond Queen* (Geza van Bolvary, 1929) knows 'more disguises than Sexton Blake', referring to the fictional detective, and Bolonia and Chicago are said to have much in common – 'here today and gun tomorrow'; 'Ah Bisto!' says the tour guide, mimicking a well-known advert for gravy browning, in Powell's *Travelaughs*. Brunel's Sagrada includes 'in-jokes' in its intertitle card logos: 'Thirst National Attraction' and 'Navy Cutts'. Ben Travers, famous in the 1920s for his Whitehall farces, produced pithy intertitles for the 1928 Robbins and Dryden adaptation of the Walter Ellis stageplay, *A Little Bit of Fluff*: Mamie Scott (Betty Balfour) is, we are told, 'an actress whose head had been turned by press agents and peroxide' and is 'celebrating the tenth anniversary of her 25th birthday'; her husband, Bertram (Syd Chaplin) has taken up the flute 'because the trombone had too many ins and outs'; a bee stings him 'in the sitting room', he says, coyly indicating his bottom. Verbal irony also occurs in Graham Cutts' *The Triumph of the Rat* (1926), where Comte Henri Mercereau (Lewis Mannering) is introduced as a man 'who kept his soul in his trouser pocket – with other small change', while his kept woman, Zelie de Chaumet (Isabel Jeans), 'had she been a man would have been a Receiving Officer – as it was, she took all she could get and asked for more'.

Arnold Bennett, eminent novelist and playwright, recognised the distinction between types of delivery and knew which he preferred.[20] In his 1913 novel *Buried Alive* and his screenplay for *Piccadilly*, Bennett economically concludes with courtroom scenes and dispenses entirely with superfluous third-person narration. At the beginning of *Piccadilly*, two women gossiping in the powder room tell us as much as we need to know about Mabel and Vic: 'Why, they're the talk of the town . . . Without him there wouldn't be a woman in the club.' In *The Lodger*, the girls in the dressing room, half-scared, half-thrilled, joke about the Avenger murders and wonder who will be his next golden-curled victim. The lodger's landlady already ominously refers to her daughter in the past tense: 'But Daisy didn't worry', before we know what has befallen her. Cutts' 1924 *The Passionate Adventure*, on the other hand, begins with lumpen, brooding contemplation of the 'human condition', drawn from its source novel: 'two forces reside in every human heart, one pure and divine and one dark and bestial. These two forces struggle over the soul of Mankind – this is life.'

Some dialogue titles are used to denote a particular accent and indicate the origins of the speaker. Pearson's 1922 *Squibs Wins the Calcutta Sweep* concludes with Ivy and the newly rich Squibs happily reunited in Paris: 'Ain't we sisters?' Meanwhile, the slang of the stable lads in Guy Newall's 1922 *Boy Woodburn* (whose allotments are called 'Sloperies' after Ally Sloper – see Chapter 1) is similarly rendered. A Londoner in Paris for the Longchamp races in *The Return of the Rat* (Graham Cutts, 1929) exclaims to his companion in the White Coffin Club: 'Cor lumme! – I ain't seen such a spread since pore Aunt Florrie died!' William Elliott's 1926 *The Cab* (a 'little drama of everyday life') finds Olive St John-Brown, the young daughter of a respectable middle-class family in Stoke Pendleton, 'a stronghold of the suburban snobbocracy', attracting the attention of a French impresario: 'Monsieur! You must not wallop ze child! She is a *genius*! – For my theatres I gif her £20 a week!' Haynes' 1926 *London Love* has the Jewish East End tailor turned film producer, Aaron Lewinsky, bemoaning the expense of daughter Sally's wedding: 'Much vaste vith confetti and vaste of good rice but all a great publicity.' In Hitchcock's 1928 film of Eden Philpott's stageplay *The Farmer's Wife* (adapted for the screen by Eliot Stannard), the curmudgeonly hung-lipped West Country yokel Churdles Ash (Gordon Harker), with meat-chop sideburns, knotted neckerchief and string garters over corduroy trews, bemoans, 'Beer drinking don't do arf the 'arm as love maken'. . .'I've seed the Master 'ave 'is eye on a woman or two of late.' *Hindle Wakes* often lifts phrases intact from Houghton's Lancashire script: 'Happen our Fanny is cleverer than we think,' says the grasping Mrs Hawthorn. 'Or summat worse,' says her husband, Chris; confronted by Sarah Hawthorn's false sanctimony, 'The ways of the Lord are mysterious and wonderful. We can't pretend to understand them. He used Mary as an instrument for His purpose,' Nat Jeffcote deflates her with, 'Happen. But if he did it seems cruel hard on Mary, like'; when, in Elvey's version, Fanny's 'boy next door' invites her to go the pictures with him, after her escapade, she replies, 'Ay, 'appen will'.[21] *Owd Bob* (Henry Edwards, 1924), a story of shepherding filmed in the Lake District, gives us 'Ye darena!', 'Dinna scold him!', 'yer ken' and 'yer mun', 'coom doon', 'shallna', 'yon' and 't'' to match the border tweeds and dry stone walling. The costume drama *Call of the Road* casts McLaglen as 'The Lamb', a Regency buck in boots and breeches and improbable side-burns, well able to use his fists to defend his honour. The character would surely be appreciated by William Hazlitt, but not the arcane language. A servant (amid much forsoothing, perchancing and travelling hither and forth) bemoans the departure of the young master from his uncle's house:

'Tis kindly, but grieve not for me; I am as a bird let free from its cage.

Most birds 'ave other birds that prey on 'em – can't I share your freedom?

'Tis glad I am to call you friend but must needs take my way alone – goodbye.

Walter Forde's *Wait and See* (1928) looks, in its visual gags and slapstick, like an American comedy from the teens, notwithstanding the final chase by train, plane and automobile. Were its titles to appear in another context, they might have been appreciated as high-brow and stylistically inventive, rather than low-brow and merely humorous. In Asquith's *A Cottage on Dartmoor* (1930), the banter of the barber shop's customers is represented by inserted footage of cricket matches, motorcycling, polo and David Lloyd George with a mower. The leather on which Joe, the barber, sharpens his razor is stretched to breaking point (as are his nerves) and a flash of red indicates the ease with which he might rid himself of his rival in love: 'Don't move or I'll cut you throat – you've tortured me enough, now it's my turn'; an upset flask and a dark smear on Joe's forehead suggest an assault which the film does not actually record. In *Wait and See* there is often a playful twist on the double meaning of words in conjunction with images and frequently these titles serve as a nudging 'aside' to the viewer. This follows, of course, in the finest traditions of pantomime and postcards. Montagu Merton (Walter Forde) is tricked by his workmates into thinking that he has inherited a fortune. He goes to the solicitors to make his claim and asks various people for directions. One man replies in French. His words appear on the screen rolled down top to bottom, individual words are registered in staccato fashion, with increasing speed. Eventually, the words are gathered into a ball which explodes and scatters the separate letters. Monty is invited to dinner with the boss and his daughter Jocelyn, where he and Eustace Mottletoe, her suitor, become embroiled in a fight over her favours. The butler enters and the words 'Dinner is Served!' appear in increasingly large-scale lettering, finally exploding as he attempts to make himself heard. Monty does not want to tell Jocelyn that there is no inheritance, but his 'excuse for postponing telling the truth was very slim', reads a title, '– she was also very pretty'.

The short film *What's Wrong with the Cinema?* (Brunel, 1925), purportedly 'produced in Three Weeks by Ellof A. Grin' for The Stupid Film Company and directed by I. Gotyer Steve with the assistance of Johnnie Walker, summarises the conventions and comedic possibilities presented by titling – it is entirely comprised of caption cards. This 'priceless production', 'A stupendous, staggering, sumptuous side-splitting spectacle in several feet, some inches and sevenpence three farthings' is, we are told, 'A Dramatic Drama drivelling with diabolical dullness' starring Rudolph Vaselino alongside Lillian Dish, Douglas Hairbanks and Harold Cellulloyd. 'This story made Oscar Wilde' and 'Arti-choke with laughter', but 'Like other great SUPER FILMS there is very little story in this PRODUCTION'. 'Wild animals' have been 'supplied by the lodging-house landlady and trained by Professor Keating' in addition to 'Performing Shrimps kindly lent by Sam Isaacs'. Motor cars have been 'supplied by Woolworths (all we could a-ford)'. The lettering is suitably augmented by pictures of whisky bottles, molluscs, automobiles and old-age pensioners. 'That Night' and 'Dawn' are scenically conveyed while clouds announce 'A Week Later', 'Another Week Later' and (yet more clouds) 'A Year Later – how time flies!' Grown-ups in the auditorium (we are advised) are permitted to hold hands but shots of topless native girls have been omitted from the programme. The film concludes, wryly, that 'NOTHING is wrong with the cinema – it's absolutely perfect'.

The contribution of intertitles to British silent cinema is, it seems to me, a neglected area of study. Not only are they worthy of consideration as an inserted visual element, but also for the audience recognition and participation which they often infer. Certainly, the incorporation of titles suggests that audiences could move easily between different viewing positions, sometimes placing themselves within a story and sometimes reading written material as external commentary.

The West End and the East

In his recent survey of 1920s British cinema, Kenton Bamford holds producers accountable for a failure to respond to popular taste and cites, as an example of their ineptitude, the preponderance of material and personnel drawn from the West End stage. He contrasts these with the American product, with which, he claims, working-class audiences could more readily identify. He praises George Pearson (the exceptional case study by which the rule is proved) for answering the reception of the first *Squibs* film with three subsequent sequels, starring Betty Balfour as his 'cockney sparrow' Piccadilly flower-seller and Hugh E. Wright as her lovable-rogue-of-a-father, loud-checked bookie Sam Hopkins.[22] The last, *Squibs' Honeymoon* (1923), related the story so far:

> Squibs, whose escapades as Flower Girl, Calcutta Sweep winner, milk vendor and MP had astonished even herself, felt that after all the simple life was best . . . So she resigned her seat in Parliament, fixed the wedding day with ex-policeman sweetheart Charlie Lee and joined her milk business with that of her old opponent, but now staunch friend, Miss Fitzbulge.

While the success of Squibs is undeniable and while British screens were undeniably dominated by American films throughout the 1920s, I find much with which to disagree in Bamford's account, both in the evidence which he presents and in the conclusions which he draws. There were films devoted to a 'smart society set', such as Saville's 1927 the *Arcadians* (adapted from a musical comedy) and 1927 *The Glad Eye* (adapted from a French farce). There were films with popular appeal which drew upon proven stage credentials such as Ivor Novello's *The Rat* (1925) (written with Constance Collier), transfering Novello (as the Apache, Pierre Boucheron) and Isabel Jeans (as the bored courtesan who determines to have him) to Cutts' 1925 film, and Elvey's 1918 (see Chapter 2) and 1927 versions of Houghton's *Hindle Wakes*. There were also films which drew upon acts and stars from music hall (Eliot Stannard devised *Squibs* from a sketch, Pearson filmed Harry Lauder in *Auld Lang Syne* [1929] and George Dewhurst made the comedy *A Sister to Assist 'Er* [1922] from a Fred Emney item). Pearson's *Nothing Else Matters*, which launched la Balfour in 1921, tells the sorry tale of a music hall family divided by shame . . . and then reunited.

However, the films which Bamford dismisses are, I think, more diverse and rewarding than he seems prepared to acknowledge, and the reasons for the British industry's supposed failure considerably more complex. While drawing upon Low's magisterial and exemplary scholarship, he seems entirely to take for granted her original premise: 'It was widely accepted at the time, and has been so ever since, that few of the films made in England during the twenties were any good.'[23]

Certainly, actors such as Milton Rosmer (in Elvey's 1921 version of H. G. Wells' novel *The Passionate Friends*), Matheson Lang and Irene Rooke (in *Hindle Wakes* and *High Treason* – see also

Chapter 2) did have established careers in the theatre; but Ivor Novello, together with Balfour the most consistent and exportable stars of British cinema in the 1920s, had appeared on stage since 1921. Certainly Noël Coward was the sensation of the West End in the mid-1920s, with his own plays and his Cochran Review, *On With the Dance*, and doubtless Gainsborough hoped to capitalise on his success with this audience when it purchased rights to *The Vortex* and *Easy Virtue*. Coward's own motive in writing *The Vortex* (inspired by the death from a cocaine overdose of Cochran Review girl Billie Carleton) was, he admitted, 'to write a good play with a whacking good part in it for myself'.[24] The part of Nicky was taken by Novello in Brunel's 1927 film (yet another Eliot Stannard adaptation). But these society dramas are far from uncritical of the society which they themselves represent. Both *Hay Fever* and *The Vortex*, and Pinero's *His House in Order* (filmed by Ayrton in 1928), are concerned with young men infatuated with actresses who are past their prime; there is tacit criticism of theatrical artifice and 'posing' and of the irregular liaisons of urbane thespian folk. Indeed, it is not at all hard to see just how Coward persuaded the Lord Chamberlain's Office that *The Vortex* was little more than a moral tract:[25] Mummy's boy Nicky Lancaster, a concert pianist, is engaged to boyishly attractive Bunty Mainwairing, who proceeds to break it off and return to erstwhile sweetheart Tom Veryan (hearty athletic type in flannels), meanwhile toy-boy to Florence (Wilette Kershaw). Nicky is driven to drugs and despair, 'his divine little gold box' or 'the little box of forgetfulness' described in the 1927 intertitle. *Easy Virtue* (filmed by Hitchcock in 1927) was written by Coward in celebration of a splendid type of woman 'with a past' whom he thought was then disappearing from the stage: divorcee Larita Whittaker (Isabel Jeans) meets John (Robin Irvine), her junior, at the tables in Cannes, but after their secret marriage finds that John's mother and prim sister are reluctant to accept her. There are the usual country pursuits of tennis and house parties, but Coward is clearly critical of the connotated 'respectable' conventions by which Larita finds herself judged. In Dupont's 1928 *Moulin Rouge*, the sophisticated 'older woman', dancer Parysia (played by Olga Chekhhova – niece of the great author Anton Chekhov, and reputedly a Russian spy), is cast against her own daughter, Margaret (Eve Gray), in competition for the love of André (Jean Bradin), Margaret's fiancé. When Parysia visits André's father, the Marquis de Rochambeau, in the hope of persuading him to approve the match, he too falls for Parysia's charms. A road accident (in spite of which Parysia's show goes on) tests André's honour and he marries Margaret. Parysia, scantily clad in tinselly finery and feathers, returns to the stage.

In 1924, the newspapers coined 'Bright Young People' to describe London's new bohemian set, all 'hectic and nervy' like Bunty and Nicky – only more so. Like the 'Angry Young Men' of the 1950s, the phenomenon was perhaps more a figure of the imagination than that of reality (see Chapter 8). Its artistic aspirations are ably caricatured in *The Cab*, with Olive's older sister (a would-be painter) posing with a cigarette holder and her older brother (a would-be poet) sporting a floppy bow-tie. Waugh and Lanchester send themselves up in *The Scarlet Woman*: 'Beatrice de Carolle, the cabaret queen, at her Bohemian flat'; 'Bills, dear me', says Borrowington, 'and cocaine, surely not . . .'. The more common and substantial 'flapper', as Lesley Hall suggests, 'emancipated but no feminist, released from chaperonage and the heavy garments of the pre-war era, madly dancing and bent on having a good time, is often seen as epitomising the twenties'.[26] Certainly, the BYP's frenetic clubbing and the flappers' dance crazes are spectacularly represented in British fiction and non-fiction film. Hitchcock's *The Ring* features leggy dancing Charleston-style; the Parisian settings of Cutts' *The Rat* and 1926 *The Sea Urchin* call for Apache gymnastics and for a fox-trot ('the Rat Step') from Novello and Dorothy St John to music provided by Novello himself while *The Triumph of the Rat* adds Isadora Duncan-style 'Greek' dancing. *Alley Cat* (Hanns Steinhoff, 1929) provides further opportunities for elaborate choreography, high-kicking and athletic back-flips. *Piccadilly* has Cyril Richard in Jack Buchanan top-hat and tails routines with Anna May Wong, skimpily dressed, as floor-show exotica. Jack Buchanan appears in person together with Annette Benson in Cutts' 1927 *Confetti*. *Palais de Danse* has fox-trots, waltzes and onesteps (not 'high-brow stuff') and *Hindle Wakes* goes downmarket and records vast numbers of holidaymakers shuffling around Blackpool's Tower Ballroom (see also *Sing As We Go* [1934], *Love on the Dole*, *A Taste of Honey* [1961] and *Bhaji on the Beach* [1993], Chapters 5, 7, 9 and 12). Robbins' *A Little Bit of Fluff* combines Balfour and the Plaza Tiller Girls while *Chu Chin Chow* (Herbert Wilcox, 1923) transfers glamorous costumes, sets and dance routines from a long-running stage production. Elvey's *High Treason* includes a peculiar halting waltz and a floor-show of girl fencers, evidently devised to register its strange and futuristic location. While the West End fetishised the new all-singing, all-dancing negro review, *The Blackbirds*, the East End (so *Piccadilly* suggests) had its own strict codes governing informal interracial pairings. *The Sign of the Four* (Elvey, 1923 – from Arthur Conan Doyle's original short story) has the arrival of 'posh' (a much-used word in the 1920s) society guests at a function at the American Embassy commented upon by lower-class spectators and the 'Limehouse Night' episode (following the example of Thomas Burke's novels and anticipating Humphrey Jennings' 1943 *Fires Were Started* – see Chapter 6) shows sailors, floosies, a Chinese organ-grinder and a negress singing and dancing in a battered straw hat.

The East End features frequently as the foil of the West. In *Squibs Wins the Calcutta Sweep*, the Hopkins' neighbours include a Pearly King and Queen; while Squibs sells flowers in Piccadilly, her brother-in-law, 'the Weasel', 'tries to earn a living' (breaking and entering) in Park Lane. *Blinkeyes* (1926), again with Betty Balfour, was described by its director as a story of London's Chinatown, 'a melodramatic mixture of lovers, crooks, dupes, dopers, pubs and palaces, calamity and courage; an unholy dish for which the leaven of strong comic relief was vitally essential'.[27] A chorus girl (Balfour) marries into the peerage, a match for the scenario of *Evergreen* (1934) (see Chapter 5) and the actual lives of Olive May (Countess of Drogheda), Gertie Millar (Countess of Dudley) and Camille Clifford (who married the Hon. Lyndhurst Henry Bruce). *London Love*, too, played its rags to riches theme as romantic comedy: Sally becomes a slave in an East End tailor's shop to supply her stepmother with drink . . . she delivers clothes to Sir James Daring in Mayfair – who helps to make her a film star. *London* (1927), directed by Wilcox as another star vehicle for Dorothy Gish, and *Lights O' London* (Calvert, 1924), a further adaption from G. R. Sims' famous Victorian melodrama (see Chapter 2), are similarly sentimental. But many depictions of the East End are altogether more dark and sinister. Steinhoff's *Alley Cat*, adapted by Joan Morgan from Anthony

Carlyle's story, and Hitchcock's *The Lodger*, adapted by Stannard from Mrs Belloc Lowndes' novel, draw, like Pabst's *Pandora's Box* (Germany, 1929) and Leni's *Waxworks*, upon the mythology of Whitechapel and Jack the Ripper. The publicity material for *Lily of the Alley* (1923 – reputedly the first British film without intertitles, and written and produced by the actor Henry Edwards) quotes Edwin Pugh to convey the atmosphere in which the action takes place, reminiscent of Dickens' *Oliver Twist*:

> Old Thames is shrouded in fog . . . there is heavy moisture in the air and a greasy dampness that . . . seems to rise from the cluttered, puddled causeway and which beslaves the giant gables with dank ooze; it covers the stones with slippery slime.

Lily (one in an apparently interminable succession of 'Broken Blossoms') is mercilessly thrashed by her drunken father, assaulted by roughs, and life becomes utterly and abjectly miserable; Edwards returns to the theme in 1925 with *A Girl of London*. In *Piccadilly*, the studio set atmosphere is heightened by colour washes (blue for the Limehouse exteriors; coral for the interior of Shosho's room – denoting what Burke calls 'the Eastern hush that hangs in the air of this quarter'), contrasting with the brightly lit and sharp flashing panorama of Piccadilly by night. In *The Sign of the*

Night and fog shroud London's East End in Maurice Elvey's 1923 *The Sign of the Four*

Four, Holmes pursues his prey by motor boat, from Richmond, Kew, Hammersmith and Putney to Barking, while Abdullah Khan negotiates the traffic eastwards, from Hyde Park Corner, to Trafalgar Square, to the Bank of England.

In *Alley Cat*, the glamorous review celebrity, Melora Miller (Margit Manstad), a 'transatlantic triumph', escorts her beau on a tourists' trip to an after-hours Chinese drinking den in the East End: yet more fiendish Chinese appear in *The Silent House*. Meanwhile, a South African millionaire is found dead in his West End residence and Jimmy Ryce (Jack Trevor), pursued by the police on suspicion of murder, finds refuge with Polly (Mabel Poulton) in the lodging house adjacent to the Red Lion tavern, run by 'Ma' (Marie Ault assuming her usual role). In the darkness of the night, Beck, the sometime sailor and smalltime crook (Clifford McLaglen), assaults Melora. Polly witnesses the scene, across tatty back fences and washing lines, and rescues her. As a reward, she is invited to the theatre and Jimmy is discovered to be the promising composer whom Melora once knew. In spite of her jealousy over their renewed acquaintance, Polly stands by Jimmy and sullies her own good name to safeguard him. In daylight, 'the 'tecs' continue their enquiries in the throng of the docks and Polly barters for a feather boa in a bustling street market. Eventually, the murderer is cornered and Jimmy resumes his previous career, taking the talented young Polly as his 'inspiration for life'.

Precisely because of this threatening, rough, underworld aspect, it is this London which fascinates and attracts the smoothly aristocratic Adrian St Clair in *The Passionate Adventure*, seeking a substitute for the perilous thrill of war (see Chapter 3). As Christine Gledhill has observed, its protagonist is allowed 'to travel forward in time geographically' by exploring the located identity of another.[28] The film alternates, announces the press book, between 'Mayfair opulence and East End poverty and the two women who provoke the conflict between the normal and abnormal in the man are products of social extremes'. Although the author of the original novel, Frank Stayton, praised the film for its respectful treatment, the character of the 'innocent' fallen girl is distinctly softened (in the book, Vickey, far from innocent in any sense, is first encountered by Adrian when picking pockets on a bus; only extraordinary chivalry allows him to resist her sexual advances).[29] *The Bioscope* duly criticised the film for its timidity and want of passion.[30] The film announced its theme as 'a social problem of the day – the marriage from which the primary instincts of mating are excluded'. The St Clairs (Clive Brook and Alice Joyce) are 'wealthy – immaculate in manners and dress – finished products of society – married – passionless – peaceful – childless – partners in a union of detached harmony, subsequently disturbed by the War'. However, the plot device of redemption achieved through a girl's self-sacrifice is all too familiar. The contrast of Vickey with Drusilla, through which the trauma is resolved, is matched by the tragic jealousies of *Piccadilly* (Valentine and the Chinese Boy, Jim, compete for Shosho; Mabel, the older woman, competes with Shosho, the Chinese girl, for Valentine).

Underground is also a story of romantic jealousy, also played out across the city. But Asquith's film employs actual locations and gives its characters more humdrum occupations: a Selfridges shop assistant (Lissa Landi), a seamstress (Norah Baring), an underground porter (Brian Aherne) and an electrician (Cecil McLagen):

The Underground of the great metropolis of the British empire, with its teeming multitudes of 'all sorts and conditions of men' contributes its share of light and shade, comedy and tragedy and all those things that go to make up what we call 'life'. So, in 'The Underground' is set our story of ordinary workaday people whose names are just Nell, Bill, Kate and Bert.

The underground participates here as protagonist as much as setting. The film opens with a 'phantom' ride into the station (see Chapter 1), with the camera positioned at the front of the train. A variety of Londoners are shown in the carriage: a soldier, a sailor, a WPC, a girl powdering her face and a man who attempts to flirt with her. Bert, the electrician, sees Nell on the tube and later discovers her at work in the department store. The Manager (the fastidious Captain Peacock type from BBC TV's *Are You Being Served?* [1973–85] and Carol Reed's *The New Lot* – see Chapter 6) looks on disapprovingly. These scenes, in the underground, the shop and later in the pub, in some ways presage the 'omnibus' films of the 1940s (see Chapter 7). Meanwhile, Nell (a common type – as in the musical comedy *The Shop Girl*, revived in 1920 with Evelyn Laye as Bessie Brent) also encounters Bill and he, too, falls for her. Kate, who shares lodgings in Kennington with Bert and has been his girlfriend, is now told that they're finished. Nell arranges to meet Bill and they take a trip on an open-topped bus to picnic in the park. By the lakeside, under a tree, they kiss and cuddle to the pipes of Pan (well, a boy in a Chelsea cap plays the harmonica for them, at any rate). Bert, jealous, exploits Kate's affection and expectations and devises a scheme to lose Bill his job and to break up the blossoming relationship. He then leaves the lodging house and deserts her. 'He did you down, same as me', she tells Bill. Kate and Bill go to the power station to confront Bert: there is a fight, the power supply is cut and an underground train jolts to a halt. Kate lies dead. A dramatic chase ensues, culminating in the underground tunnel. The power is switched back on and tension mounts. Bill and Bert make for the lifts, there is further fighting and eventually Bert is overcome. The film ends, as it began, with the train now receding into the tunnel until the screen becomes completely dark. The *Daily Express* claimed *Underground* as 'one of the most sensational films ever seen on the screen';[31] in the publicity material, Asquith was praised for the stunning crane shots in the power house and the thrilling roof-top sequences, but also for his 'wonderfully human characterisation' and 'the astounding realism of the entire production'. Rotha, on the other hand, writing in 1949, waspishly accused the film of degenerating 'into a movie of London "types"', 'instead of being a direct exposition of the spirit of an inanimate organisation' (tacitly referring to Watts' 'fine film' *Nightmail*) and accused Asquith of 'becoming lost in a Victorian conception of a lift-boy' (see Chapter 5).[32] The theatrical stylisation of the power station office (the silhouettes of massive cogs and pulleys seen through a semi-opaque screen), some of the camera angles (Kate, viewed overhead by lamplight, working late into the night) and the framing and editing seem in debt to the European 'art' films shown at the Film Society; but *Underground* was also unashamedly populist and responsive to the domestic market in its subject matter and treatment.

The representation of a divisive topography of London in films of the 1920s seems to me to follow a pattern already evinced elsewhere and which continues into succeeding decades: in this, it bears comparison with the depiction of the town and the country in films of the teens (see Chapter 2). But there is also a new enthusiasm for the city itself which the earlier films very rarely display.

Julian the Cowboy

In the parliamentary debates leading up to the Cinematograph Films Bill of 1927, it was commonly stated that 'something like 5% of films at present shown in the British Empire are of British origin'.[33] It was also claimed, somewhat spuriously, that Britain had lost a dominant position in international markets as a result of the World War, with the migration of acting, writing and technical staff to America and with American producers enabled to overcome the European competition unchallenged: in the 1920s, Clive Brook and Ronald Colman cut a dash in Hollywood as cool, aristocratic Englishmen, Victor McLaglen established himself in the war film *What Price Glory?* (Raoul Walsh, 1926) and Elinor Glyn (keenly) and William Somerset-Maugham (grudgingly) accepted work as scenographers;[34] meanwhile, Asquith served an apprenticeship prior to his directorial career in Britain and Andrew Mazzei worked in America and Europe before returning to design for Elvey. The aims of the Act were modest and essentially remedial, 'to restrict blind booking and advance booking of cinematograph films and to secure the renting and exhibition of a certain proportion of British films', of which the Act proceeded to volunteer a definition. But in the absence of such protective legislation, in the early 1920s, a number of strategies were employed by producers, distributors and exhibitors to enhance the artistic and commercial standing of British cinema abroad and, more urgently, in an attempt to redress the balance at home.

Between February and March 1924, a number of Film Weeks were launched, promoting British films nationwide. Alongside announcements of the death of Woodrow Wilson, the release of Gandhi from prison, the interment of Lenin, the disinterment of Tutankhamen, advertisements for Eastern Silks Week at Selfridges and discussion of the prospects for salmon in the Thames, newspapers endeavoured to interest their readership in British cinema. The front page of the *Daily Mail* presented a gallery of English lovelies: Isobel Elsom, Ivy Duke, Betty Balfour, Violet Hopson, Gladys Cooper, Chrissie White and Alma Taylor.[35] A cinema in King's Cross ran a competition to garner the best-expressed views on the relative merits of American and British pictures. 'Strong in the conviction of its own merit', declared the *Daily Telegraph*, 'the British film industry is appealing for the reversal of the popular verdict that it is incapable of competing successfully with some of its rivals.'

> This demonstration, rendered possible by the cordial co-operation of film producers, film renters or distributors and owners of theatres will, it is hoped, not only raise the credit of British films in popular estimation but will also convince investors and capitalists generally of the commercial possibilities linked with systematic film production, conducted on sound, business-like methods.[36]

Heralded as the most notable British films to be seen in this first week were *Bonnie Prince Charlie* (1923) (directed by Calvert and starring Novello and Cooper), Hepworth's *Comin' Thro' the Rye*

(1923) and Clift's *The Loves of Mary Queen of Scots* (1923). During filming of *Bonnie Prince Charlie*, railway companies had run special excursion trains to enable the public to watch Novello in action on Culloden Moor. 'Others that may be commended' were: a *Bill of Divorcement* (1922, directed by Clift from the play by Clemence Dane), Hepworth's *The Pipes of Pan* (1923) and *The Naked Man* (1923), Clift's *This Freedom* (1923, starring Clive Brook and Fay Compton), the Conan Doyle adaptation *Fires of Fate* (1923, directed by Terriss), *Lily of the Alley* and *Lights O' London*. 'Of the films in which Miss Betty Balfour appears it is unnecessary to speak . . . in a different category are the films in which Britain is first rank: *Crossing the Great Sagrada*, *Tree Tops* and *The Wonderland of Big Game*'.[37] Critical appreciation of British non-fiction production, it should be noted, preceded Grierson's coinage of 'documentary' in the 1930s (see Chapter 5).

The problem faced by the British industry is put precisely: 'The most formidable difficulty is the small home market.'[38] As observed by many commentators over subsequent decades, America was in the highly advantageous and enviable position of relying on the home market merely to cover costs while looking abroad for its profits (see Chapter 8). In spite of *The Daily Telegraph*'s optimistic claim to 'cordial co-operation', the respective and conflicting concerns of producers, distributors and exhibitors remained essentially the same for years to come. In November 1924, the trade press gloomily announced that no British films were in production.

Alongside this extensive press coverage, exhibitors staged promotional campaigns corresponding to the content of particular films. The London premiere of D. W. Griffith's 1919 *Broken Blossoms* was spectacularly launched with the theatre and its usherettes dressed in Chinese fashion. At the Scala, *Comin' Thro' the Rye* was accompanied by a prologue at each performance, in which Alma Taylor and other Hepworth Picture Players appeared. In Hammersmith, *Armageddon* was shown with a guard of honour of local troops who had served in Palestine, and Fay Compton appeared with children of the Royal Caledonian Schools to launch *Mary Queen of Scots* at the Marble Arch Pavilion. Not to be outdone, Angus Buchanan brought a native 4,500 miles to see himself on screen, and was photographed with him at the Palace Theatre.[39] Caroline Lejeune noted that such stunts as these, during the Film Weeks and throughout the year, threatened to eclipse the films themselves:

> [T]he film today is the least important part of a super-kinema programme . . . [there are] programme girls and commissionaires in fancy costume, exhibits from the film, copies of songs or books from which the films have been adapted, souvenirs, photographs . . . [I have seen] a monkey . . . a hooded falcon . . . white roses . . . red roses . . . and a handkerchief stall – for the tears shed when watching . . .[40]

Lejeune also itemises various competitions, in which the audience was invited to pick out named stars from among the extras or to guess a film's ending.

Shooting Stars is of interest for its depiction of studio procedures and of popular film culture in the 1920s, although it appears to reproduce the plot of Clarendon's 1913 *Behind the Scenes*, in which a cowboy film actor mistakenly fires real bullets and kills a faithless actress; in Asquith's *A Cottage on Dartmoor*, Joe invites manicurist Sally (Norah Baring), to accompany him to a 'talkie' at the Elite Cinema.[41] She accompanies another suitor, her subsequent fiancé, and Joe spies on them in the dark. Nothing of the Elite's programme is seen, but Asquith shows a variety of audience reactions and the flickering light of the screen reflected on their faces: one man sleeps and has his hat lifted for the National Anthem. In *Shooting Stars*, we see the cue sheets, property men, the studio orchestra, wardrobe staff and so forth, also the fans who plague the crew on location and a fanzine journalist who eagerly lists Mae's hobbies, habits and affectations. While the style of the film owes more to Europe (the titling, the superimpositions, the cast shadow of the fatefully swinging chandelier), the commentary relates British practice to Hollywood. It opens with Julian, the cowboy (Brian Aherne), almost thrown by his wooden horse. The comic character Andy Wilks (Donald Calthrop) is defined by his moustache, hat and umbrella, cropped trousers and tightly fitting checked jacket, and has an idiosyncratic gait reminiscent of Chaplin (whose own immense popularity with British audiences was confirmed by his 1921 tour). Rumours that Mae Fisher (Annette Benson) is intending to leave with Andy for America follow in the wake of the actual

Film fans keep up with the news in Asquith's *Shooting Stars* (1928)

departure of actors Clive Brook, Ronald Colman and Victor McLaglen. Conversely, there were actual American performers who were attracted by the opportunities in Britain. Contrary to Bamford's suggestion, these stars were not all already on the wane. Tallulah Bankhead was suitably cast for *His House in Order* and the Canadian Estelle Brody played her parts for Elvey with Clara Bow vivacity in *Hindle Wakes*, *Mademoiselle from Armentières*, *Mademoiselle Parley Voo* (1928) and *The Glad Eyes*; Mae Marsh (known hitherto for her work with D. W. Griffith); Alice Joyce appeared in *The Passionate Adventure* and Anna May Wong in *Piccadilly*. Dorothy Gish was cast by Wilcox in the costume dramas *Nell Gwynne*, *Tip Toes*, *London* and with the Douglas Fairbanks surrogate Antonio Moreno in *Madame Pompadour* (1927). Whatever *Close Up*'s reservations, *Nell Gwynne* was well received commercially and secured American distribution.

On the other side of the pond, even before the 'euro puddings' concocted by British International Pictures in the late 1920s (*Bright Eyes*, *Moulin Rouge*, *Piccadilly*), there were raids and exchanges between Britain and Europe. German and British companies, and especially the directors Elvey and Cutts, spent much of their time working for Stoll on the Côte d'Azur, known for its well-equipped studios, glamorous and varied locations and auspicious climate.[42] Coleby shot exteriors for *The Great Prince Shan* (1924) with the international superstar Sessue Hayakawa and his wife Tsuru Aoki; here, too, appropriately enough, Cutts made *Confetti* (using footage of the Nice Carnival) and Denison Clift shot *Paradise* (1928), in which Betty Balfour plays a vicar's daughter who spends the prize money from a crossword competition on a dream trip to the Riviera; she unmasks a Russian jewel thief before happily returning home with her new amour. Pearson shot exteriors for *The Little People*, a village near Mentone doubling for Italy, with sets designed by Cavalcanti (see Chapter 5). Less predictably, it was chosen as the setting for Elvey's *Slaves of Destiny* (1924, from A. E. W. Mason's *Miranda of the Balcony*) for Stoll, a ripping yarn set in London, Andalusia, Gibraltar and Morocco, and for his adaptation of *The Wandering Jew* (1923, also for Stoll), set in Jerusalem at the time of Christ, medieval Sicily and Spain. For Sinclair Hill's 1923 *The Hindu Lovesong* and *One Arabian Night* and the Malaysia of his 1926 *The Chinese Bungalow* (in which Matheson Lang has his eyes pulled sideways in the fashion of *Broken Blossoms*' Richard Barthelmess), French landscapes substituted for settings even further afield.

In France and Germany, protective measures had been initiated before the passing of the Cinematograph Act in 1927 and the quotas imposed were considerably more severe. There were fears on the part of British distributors and exhibitors that there would be a retaliatory American embargo, a fear which materialised in the late 1940s when similar legislation was introduced, without consultation. In the debates preceding the passing of the Act there was objection, in principle, to the protection of vested interests and comparisons were made with commodities: on this occasion, tobacco, coal and bananas. Why, it was asked, were British music halls not thus protected, nor American-owned department stores, such as Whiteleys and Selfridges, thus restricted?[43] Here again, there is much which presages discussion after the near collapse of the British industry following the Second World War (see Chapter 8). Some speakers observed that what constituted 'Britishness' in a film or its making was inadequately defined or potentially too generous to foreign concerns, and the exact meaning of the term 'scenario' was left open to interpret-ation.[44] Protestation from the 'high-hats' (Blakeston and Rotha) that the Act did nothing for qual-ity of production and that it would result in 'a lot of futile and rubbishy films' being forced on the public, was also predicted in the parliamentary discussion; Pearson was similarly dismayed that a glut of 'quota quickies' would do nothing for the reputation of British films abroad. The Act was, it was said, attempting to regulate demand before dealing with supply.[45]

Winifred Foley, newly arrived in London from the countryside and working in domestic serv-ice, remembers being taken to the Olympia Shoreditch, for a three-hour programme including Japanese jugglers, dancers and a screening of *Drums of Love* (US, D. W. Griffith, 1928):

> Peanut shells and sweet wrappings crackled under our feet . . . The tang of orange peel fought with
> tobacco and the warm body odour rising from the stalls and balcony . . . How drab and insignificant
> everything seemed, compared with the world of stage and screen!'[46]

She recalls the stale smell of cheap perfume in the ladies' cloakroom and the strange boys who tried to lure her into the cinema's side alley after the show. Burke has his older Mrs Dumball going to 'the "pictures" twice a week, and hot suppers afterwards at the fishbar . . . It was this dream-panorama that kept her eyes open for the bit of luck that never came.'[47] Iris Barry, who frequented cinemas on the other side of town, reported the preponderance of women in cinema audiences, outnumbering men by three to one.[48]

While (in the wake of the 1926 General Strike and introduction of Universal Suffrage in 1928) there was concern regarding hostile foreign propaganda (including the Soviet films exhibited by the Film Society and the London County Council), the Parliamentary discussion acknowledged film as a means of propagandising for Britain at home and abroad; especially, it was claimed, in the Empire, with its 'common outlook, same ideas, same ideals, common language and common litera-ture'. King Vidor's First World War epic *The Big Parade* (US, 1925) was said to be a 'great picture', but one 'in which not one single mention was made of the English army'. Female audiences were of particular concern. Chili Bouchier, frequently cast in the chorus line in 1920s cinema, signifi-cantly chews gum from beginning to end of *Palais de Danse*. The *Daily Express*, then owned by Lord Beaverbrook (extensively involved in film distribution), presented the matter succinctly:

> From beginning to end of these quota negotiations, not one word has been said about producing the
> kind of film which the British public wishes to see, but the ordinary man will be disposed to think that
> that should be the keystone of the whole discussion. The plain truth about the film situation is that
> the bulk of our picture-goers are Americanised to the extent that makes them regard a British film as
> a foreign film and an interesting but more frequently an irritating interlude in their favourite enter-
> tainment. They go to see American stars; they have been brought up on American publicity. They talk
> America, think America and dream America. We have several million people, mostly women, who, to
> all intent and purpose, are temporary American citizens.[49]

Beaverbrook's disapproval is hardly disguised. But nor is it unique. The Film Society and *Close Up* were equally wary of Americanisation. Britain's cultural and economic relations with America continued to preoccupy producers, distributors, exhibitors and critics while audiences continued to appreciate American films. Another topography – the association of America with commerce and Europe with art – was already established before the coming of sound.

Champagne (Alfred Hitchcock, 1928)

In spite of the star billing of the immensely bankable Betty Balfour and of the French actor Jean Bradin (later to be seen in *Moulin Rouge*), and of a scenario by the consummate professional Eliot Stannard, from Walter Mycroft's story, BIP's 1928 *Champagne* was not critically well received at the time of its release. Hugh Castle dismissed it as 'champagne that had been left in the rain all night' and *The Bioscope*'s appraisal was no more than tepid: 'Though the interest at times is thin, it never flags. It is a picture which may not rouse great enthusiasm, but may be depended upon to please every class of audience.'[50] In conversation with Truffaut in 1962, Hitchcock himself disparaged the film, especially its want of storyline. Truffaut provided a synopsis:

> Betty argues with her millionaire father as a result of a love affair. She leaves for France. Her father persuades her that he is ruined in order to compel her to earn her own living. She is hired by a cabaret to encourage clients to drink the self-same champagne to which her father owes his fortune. Finally, having instructed a detective to follow Betty and having never lost sight of her, the father concludes that he has gone too far and at last gives his consent to Betty's marriage to the man she loves.[51]

Between the *Squibs* series and *Champagne*, Betty had ventured into a number of roles far removed from the Piccadilly flower-girl, but had retained her popularity with a variety of audiences. While being critical in general of a system that promoted stars rather than stories, Iris Barry remained loyal to Betty: 'she simply has bags of talent and is worth seeing every single time'.[52] She appeared as the Ruritanian Princess Zonia of Bolonia (ensconced at the Coronia in Mayfair), and her unwitting double, a maid in a Bloomsbury boarding house, in *The Vagabond Queen* and as the daughter of the black sheep of a wealthy family in *The Sea Urchin*, again transformed from rags to riches. For Louis Mercanton she had filmed the society comedy *Monte Carlo* (1925) and for Marcel L'Herbier had appeared as the tragic heroine of a story of Normandy fisher folk, *Little Devil May Care* (1927). Writing for *The Studio*, Robert Herring praised L'Herbier's direction, saying that he had drawn from his star a performance which no British director had as yet managed to discover.[53]

But Balfour's rendition of the American millionaire's daughter in *Champagne* owes much to Squibs, reversing the social trajectory of *Calcutta Sweep* (where, before her win, she masquerades in 'cod' finery with a basket and feather on her head). There are plenty of visual gags at Betty's expense and any opportunity for playful stage business is exploited to the full. Betty arrives at the beginning of the film by aeroplane, with the marks of her flying goggles on a sooty face; Betty's floury hand prints are left on the boy's back as he leaves the garret; Betty's first attempts at rolling pastry and baking bread are doomed to failure; Betty is obliged to wear the oversized engagement ring on her thumb but when she and the boy argue, their lovers' tiff is frustrated and rendered comical by the swaying of the boat. At the cabaret, Betty and her father argue at the foot of the stairs, frustrating the persistent attempts of a waiter to get past them (a gag reworked by Hitchcock for *The 39 Steps* [1935]). Alongside Gordon Harker's fine character-acting as the firm but fair patriarch, well served by his blood-hound face, there are various cameo appearances for familiar types: the haughty French *doméstique*; the oleaginously smarmy, penguin-suited *maître d'* (Marcel Vibert) at the cabaret (reminiscent of the Bates cartoons in *Punch* and a reprisal of a role established in *The Sea Urchin*), rubbing his hands as he fawns to his patrons and twirling the ends of his waxed moustache; there are wild apache dancers and even wilder floosies. Betty, like Fanny in *Hindle Wakes*, likes to think of herself as a modern girl and resists her father's attempts to organise her life for her (in *Calcutta Sweep*, Sam Hopkins is less than enthusiastic about Squibs' attempts to curtail his drinking and malingering). But, in *Champagne*, her boyfriend too reminds her that she behaves high-handedly and that her money makes

'Worth seeing every single time': Betty Balfour stars as poor little rich girl attempting to keep house for her father (Gordon Harker) in Hitchcock's 1928 *Champagne*

her think that she can do just as she pleases. She reminds him that her father's money allowed her to fly halfway across the Atlantic to be with him (and, at the end, to provide an aeroplane to meet them in New York). He reminds her that her father could well afford to send a wire advising against marriage to a fortune hunter: he too has his pride. Prompted by her extravagance in Paris, he informs her that simplicity would be 'more in good taste', and, duly chided, Betty makes her mocking entry as Little Orphan Annie.

However supposedly thin the storyline, there is much to confirm Betty's character as endearing. She gives one of her gowns to a dowdily dressed assistant from the boutique and, misunderstanding orders to give a button-hole carnation to men in evening dress at the cabaret, presents the flowers to the gentlemen of the orchestra. In the film's spectacular display there is much to appeal to a female audience: Betty as aviatrice; Betty as flapper (she occupies herself in Paris with the invention of new cocktails and shimmies absent-mindedly in her chair at the cabaret); Betty as house-keeper to her father; Betty as mannequin and Betty as Betty herself are subsidiary roles which echo the subject matter of popular newspapers, newsreels and the Pathé series, *Eve's Film Review*.[54] Such material was shown in the programme at larger cinemas (such as the Stoll venues) alongside documentary shorts and animated cartoons (*Felix the Cat* or *Bonzo the Dog*). Indeed, this material frequently proved more popular with audiences than the accompanying main feature.

In an indictment of British film in 1933, *Film Weekly* commented that the stories of American films were frequently thin, but nevertheless 'clever and carefully thought-out' in their details and were consequently well received by British audiences. *Kine Weekly*'s complaint of Americanism in *Champagne* appears to reside in the 'remarkable technical details not compensating for the negligeable plot value', and in its flaunting of the lifestyle of an American heiress.[55] *Champagne* also appeared imitative in its style: Hitchcock contrives movement within the frame and slick transitions between frames in order to maintain a constant pace. At the cabaret, a static conversation between Betty and her 'mystery man' (the private detective) is dark in the foreground while an exotic dancer, fully illuminated, gyrates behind them; Hitchcock cuts from Betty's remembered image of the Cunard liner's dance hall to a framed picture in a travel agent's window; a time ellipse is staged by a cut from a white sheet filling the frame to a chequered tablecloth being shaken and laid across the table. The film opens and closes with the scene framed and viewed (literally) through the bottom of a glass. It is from these and similar mannerisms that Hitchcock seeks to distance himself in his conversation with Truffaut, I think. But the complaints of *Kine Weekly* seem to refer to a wider debate which appears in British film culture in the 1920s and resurfaces in the 1950s and 1970s (see Chapters 8 and 10). Criticisms of *Champagne* are echoed in the responses to Dupont's 'euro puddings', *Moulin Rouge* and *Piccadilly*, 'euphemistically British' and 'un-English'. British films were required to compete with the European and American product but on their own terms, by 'being British', rather than as an ersatz version of something foreign.

Notes

1. Michael Davie (ed.), *The Diaries of Evelyn Waugh* (London: Weidenfeld and Nicolson, 1976), pp. 189 and 283.

2. Selina Hastings, *Evelyn Waugh: A Biography* (London: Sinclair-Stevenson, 1994), p. 118; Waugh left Oxford £200 in debt. See also Amy Sargeant, 'Elsa Lanchester and Chaplinism', in Laraine Porter and Alan Burton (eds), *Crossing the Pond* (Trowbridge: Flicks Books, 2002), pp. 92–9.

3. Evelyn Waugh, 'A Pleasure Cruise in 1929', *When the Going was Good* (London: Duckworth, 1946), p. 13; see also *Vile Bodies* (London: Eyre Methuen, 1986), p. 91: 'They had arranged to go to a cinema together. She said, "You're much later than you said. It's so boring to be late for a talkie." He said, "Talkies are boring, anyhow."'

4. Adrian Brunel, *Nice Work* (London: Forbes Robertson Ltd, 1949), p. 112; see also George Pearson, *Flashback: an Autobiography of a British Film Maker* (London: George Allen and Unwin, 1957), p. 132, and BFI special materials, Brunel collection.

5. See Ivor Montagu, *The Political Censorship of Films* (London: Victor Gollancz, 1929), pp. 12–13, and Film Society archive, BFI special materials.

6. Rachael Low, *The History of the British Film* vol. IV [1971] (London: Routledge, 1997), p. 34.

7. Jen Samson, 'The Film Society', in Charles Barr (ed.), *All Our Yesterdays* (London: BFI, 1986), pp. 306–13.

8. François Truffaut, *Hitchcock* (London: Secker and Warburg, 1968), pp. 2 and 181; see also Graham Greene, John Russell Taylor (ed.), *The Pleasure Dome* (London: Secker and Warburg, 1972), p. 1.

9. See Richmal Crompton, 'William the Explorer', in *William – in Trouble* [1927] (London: Macmillan, 1991), and 'William – the Great Actor' [1928] (in which a play is staged in order to raise money for a cinematograph for the village), in *William the Good* [1928] (London: Macmillan, 1989).

10. See BUFVC Newsreel database for the genuine article.

11. Winifred Ellerman, 'The War from Three Angles' and 'The War from More Angles', *Close Up* vol. 1 no. 1, July 1927, pp. 16–22, and October 1927, pp. 44–8 – nevertheless, Ellerman praised the film for holding her attention; see also Amy Sargeant, '*The Battles of the Coronel and Falkland Islands*: "A Victory and a Defeat as Glorious as a Victory"', *Film and the First World War* (Vienna: Austrian Film Archive, 2005).

12. Norman McPherson, *Close Up* no. 1, July 1927, p. 15.

13. Blakeston, *Close Up* vol. 1 no. 1, July 1927, p. 17.

14. McPherson, *Close Up* vol. 1 no. 3, September 1927, p. 12; for the success of *Nell Gwynne* and *Madame Pompadour* in America see Sarah Street, *Transatlantic Crossings* (London: Continuum, 2002), pp. 22–30.

15. Caroline Lejeune, 'Cinema', *Manchester Guardian*, 8 October 1927, p. 11.

16. R. J. Minney, *'Puffin' Asquith* (London: Leslie Frewin, 1973), p. 44.

17. See Low IV, p. 237, and *Close Up* vol. 3 no. 2, August 1928.

18. Low is repeating a complaint made by Paul Rotha, *The Film Till Now* (London: Vision, 1951), p. 111, re. H. G. Wells, *The King Who Was a King* (London: Ernest Benn, 1929); see also Rebecca West (Wells' lover from 1913–23), 'Black Lamb and Grey Falcon', in *The Essential Rebecca West* (Harmondsworth: Penguin, 1983).

19. See Amy Sargeant, 'Utopia, Dystopia and Eutopia between the Wars: *The King Who Was a King* and *High Treason*', in Laraine Porter and Alan Burton (eds), *Scene-Stealing*, (Trowbridge: Flicks Books, 2003), pp. 94–101; also, Alfred Hitchcock, 'Titles – Artistic and Otherwise', *The Motion Picture Studio*, 21 July 1921.

20. Arnold Bennett, 'Writing Plays', *The Author's Craft* (London: Hodder and Stoughton, 1914), p. 69; on his writing of *Piccadilly* (completed in a fortnight), see *The Journals of Arnold Bennett* (London: Cassell and Co., 1933), pp. 260–3.

21. For further discussion of *Hindle Wakes*, see Christine Gledhill, *Reframing British Cinema* (London: BFI, 2003), pp. 72–3, and Amy Sargeant, 'Popular Modernism: the Case of *Hindle Wakes*', *Film Studies* 3, 2002, pp. 47–58.

22. Kenton Bamford, *Distorted Images: British National Identity and Film in the 1920s* (London: I. B. Tauris, 1999), pp. 31, 47, 69, 89.

23. Ibid. p. 120 (whose evaluation is made in terms of films' supposed audience address); compare Low vol. IV, pp. 157–8, whose judgments are more aesthetically framed – while arriving at the same conclusion.

24. Billie Carleton (1896–1918) died of a drugs overdose and her cocaine supplier was sent to gaol. For an account of Coward's success, see *Noël Coward: Autobiography* (London: Methuen, 1986), pp. 145–7, and Raymond Mander and Joe Mitchenson, introduction to *Noël Coward Plays: One* (London: Eyre Methuen, 1979); Coward was understudied in *The Vortex* by John Gielgud.

25. Introduction to *Noël Coward Plays: One*; Graham Cutts' 1922 *Cocaine* similarly encountered censorship difficulties and was re-titled for general distribution.

26. Lesley A. Hall, *Sex, Gender and Social Change* (Basingstoke: Macmillan, 2000), p. 99.

27. Pearson, *Flashback*, p. 143.

28. Gledhill, *Reframing British Cinema*, p. 144.

29. Frank Stayton, *The Passionate Adventure* (London: Eveleigh Nash and Grayson Ltd, 1924), p. 225.

30. '*The Passionate Adventure*', *The Bioscope*, November 1924.

31. BFI SM Nashreen Kabir Collection, publicity material for *Underground*.

32. Rotha, *The Film Till Now*, pp. 315 and 320, and Paul Rotha, *Celluloid: the Film Today* (London: Longmans, Green and Co., 1933); Rotha originally wrote the book in 1929 in the hope (in spite of all his carping) of obtaining employment in the British film industry.

33. See *Parliamentary Debates*, 203 and 204 (1927); also Ernest Lindgren, 'The Early Feature Film', in Michael Balcon, Ernest Lindgren, Forsyth Hardy and Roger Manvell, *Twenty Years of British Film 1925–45* (London: The Falcon Press, 1947), p. 13.

34. See Elinor Glyn, *Romantic Adventure* (London: Ivor Nicholson and Watson, 1936).

35. *Daily Mail*, 4 February 1924.

36. Alder Anderson, 'All-British Film Week: Bid for National Patronage', *Daily Telegraph*, 4 February 1926, p. 6.

37. Ibid.

38. *The Daily Telegraph*, 4 February 1924, p. 6, and *Parliamentary Debates,* 204.

39. *Daily Express*, 4 February 1924, p. 8, and '4,500 Miles to See a Film', *Daily Mail*, 5 February 1924, p. 5.

40. Caroline Lejeune, 'The Fairground of the Film', *Manchester Guardian*, 8 March 1924, p. 9.

41. For a further 'first hand' account of working in British studios, see Cunnyngham, BFI special materials.

42. See Amy Sargeant, '*We're All Doing the Riviera* because *It's So Much Nicer in Nice*', paper given at Nottingham British Silent Cinema Festival, 2003; for the popularity of the Riviera with British tourists see also Fred Inglis, *The Delicious History of the Holiday* (London: Routledge, 2000), p. 125.

43. *Parliamentary Debates*, 203.

44. See Margaret Dickinson and Sarah Street, *Cinema and State: the Film Industry and the British Government 1927–84* (London: BFI, 1985), p. 6.

45. *Parliamentary Debates*, 203, p. 2082, and Pearson, *Flashback*, p. 144.

46. Winifred Foley, *A Child in the Forest* (London: Ariel Books, 1986), pp. 129–30.

47. Thomas Burke, 'The Purse', *East of Mansion House* (London: Cassell, 1928), p. 217.

48. Iris Barry, *Let's Go to the Pictures* (London: Chatto and Windus, 1926), p. 59.

49. *Daily Express*, 18 March 1927, quoted in *Parliamentary Debates*, 204.

50. Hugh Castle, *Close Up*, July 1929, and *The Bioscope*, 22 August 1928, p. 929.

51. Truffaut, *Hitchcock*, p. 47.

52. Barry, *Let's Go to the Pictures*, p. 120.

53. Robert Herring, 'The Cinema', *The Studio* 96 (1928), p. 99; but Michael Powell reports that Hitch himself thought Betty, 'England's ersatz Mary Pickford', 'a piece of suburban obscenity' and 'hated the frothy story *Champagne*': Michael Powell, *A Life in Movies* (London: Heinemann, 1986), p. 185.

54. See Jenny Hammerton, *For Ladies Only?* (Hastings: The Projection Box, 2001), p. 102, and *The Daily Telegraph* and *Daily Express*, February 1924, re. Mrs Atkey, the first British woman to cross the Channel, and 'Girl Air Pilot', *Daily Mail*, 30 January 1928, p. 1, re. Honor Pitman, then fifteen.

55. *Kine Weekly*, 23 August 1928.

Chapter 5 | 1930s

Day-dreaming and Dream Palaces

In October 1935, the new Gaumont Theatre, Manchester, 'the wonder theatre of the North', was opened by the British song and dance diva Jessie Matthews and her partner (and sometime director) Sonnie Hale. Newsreel footage shows a number of Gaumont Beauty Girls, dressed in an array of national costumes, adorning the grand staircase to salute Jessie as, in a famously polished accent and clutching a bouquet as large as the page boy who presents it, she wishes the Gaumont 'a long and prosperous life'. The cinema's 2,350 seating capacity was distributed over two floors and its facilities included a café and bar. The floral decoration of the mirrored balcony was drawn from the Villa Madama in Rome. The first film to be shown was Hitchcock's adaptation of John Buchan's hugely successful 1915 thriller, *The 39 Steps*: in spite of the liberties taken with the original, even Buchan himself allegedly preferred the screen version to the book.[1]

The event is significant in a number of ways. The advent of the talkies met with an enormous expansion of cinema building (notably with the characteristic art-deco style of Oscar Deutsch's Odeon chain extending into the suburbs) and in an increasing opulence of décor (notably in the fantastic interiors produced by designers such as the immigrant Kommissarevsky – disparaged by Paul Rotha as meringue decoration).[2] Sunday opening, a contentious issue in previous and subsequent decades, became common. Children's matinées (as seen in Hitchcock's 1936 *Sabotage* – which staged a screening of Disney's *Silly Symphonies*) were introduced by the Odeon circuit in 1937 and, in response to a glut of Americana, by Rank cinemas in 1943. The 1927 Cinematograph Act proved effective in promoting the production of British films quantatively (from thirteen films in 1927 to 125 films in the year 1930–1 to 228 in the year 1937–8); and, in spite of much contemporaneous criticism from high-brows (such as Paul Rotha and Graham Greene, both involved in film commentary and film production in Britain from the 1930s onwards, and who thought it often anodyne and silly), much of the output was of a high quality and much proved popular with audiences. The industry consolidated itself around two major integrated production, distribution and exhibition concerns, Gaumont-British and British International Pictures (which became ABPC in 1933); by the end of the 1930s, Rank owned three of the largest studios and by the end of the 1940s critics frequently lodged the complaint that Rank had become over-dominant. With stars

Countess Alexandra (Marlene Dietrich) shelters behind leather-clad Fothergill (Robert Donat) in Jacques Feyder's 1937 *Knight Without Armour* such as Jessie Matthews, highly rated in fanzine polls, the domestic industry managed to identify and foster talents which could effectively compete with the best of Hollywood. Both Matthews and Robert Donat (the star of *The 39 Steps*) received lucrative offers to work in America, but both chose to forge careers, for the most part, within the British industry.[3]

While competition from the example of Hollywood still continued to loom large (and the Matthews star vehicles *Evergreen* [Victor Saville, 1934], *First a Girl* [Victor Saville, 1935] and *It's Love Again* [Victor Saville, 1936] respond to both American and European models), as Stephen Guy observes, the coming of sound did not result in Britain in the predominance of musicals as a genre over others.[4] In 1929, there were films made in both sound and silent versions, to allow for the disparate conversion of cinemas across the country (Rachael Low indicating that 400 British cinemas were wired for sound at the beginning of 1929, including most of London's West End and 685 by the end of the year; 2,523 in 1930 and 3,537 in 1931):[5] these include Saville's *Kitty* ([1929] made for sound in America – see Chapter 3), Elvey's *High Treason* ([1929] – see Chapter 4) and, most famously, Hitchcock's *Blackmail* (1929).[6] Here, sound was used to dramatic effect to indicate the trepidation of Alice White, handling a breadknife the morning after she has killed the painter, Crewe, in self-defence (the silent version accentuating the motif with glaring light on the blade); spatial depth is enhanced by the leaking of noises from the street into the Whites' shop when the door is opened and enclosure is emphasised by the insulation of the glass telephone booth in which Alice and her boyfriend, Frank Webber, the Scotland Yard detective (John Longden) discuss her alibi, but through which the glove which betrays her is clearly visible to the blackmailer, Tracy (Donald Calthrop). Wilcox made a sound version of his 1923 success *Woman to Woman* in America in 1929 and of his 1926 *Nell Gwynne* in 1934, while Basil Dean remade Adrian Brunel's 1928 *The Constant Nymph* in 1933 (from Margaret Kennedy's novel and stageplay) and Walter Forde remade Wilcox's 1923 *Chu Chin Chow* in 1934 with Anna May Wong and George Robey (from the spectacular long-running West End musical – see Chapter 3). Henry Edwards pursued his career as Lieutenant Daring and the Flag Lieutenant (see Chapters 2 and 4) into the 1930s. For a short period, British variants were made of multi-language versions (such as the English and German *The Blue Angel* [1930] – with Marlene Dietrich – and the English, French and German *Atlantic*) and other suitable subjects were proposed (such as Elvey's 1920 *At the Villa Rose*, subsequently remade in English only in 1930 and 1939), but these were slow and uneconomical to shoot. Sometimes the same source material was adapted across Europe (as in French, German and British versions of Bernhard Kellermann's 1915 novel, *The Tunnel*). Sometimes foreign films were plundered for action and location footage with English dialogue sequences interspersed (such as Anthony Asquith's 1935 *Moscow Nights*, from a French original). Many prominent performers transferred from silent to sound cinema (Betty Balfour, Ivor Novello, Anna May Wong, Brian Aherne, John Stuart), a few did not (such as *The Constant Nymph*'s Mabel Poulton and *Blackmail*'s Czech star, Anny Ondra, dubbed for sound by Joan Barry).

Although silent cinema had acknowledged regional difference in the characterisation and subtitling of films (see Chapter 4), the opportunity to record actual speech and dialect and language, sometimes *in situ*, was a recurrent feature of films of the 1930s, both features and documentaries. While Rachael Low and John Sedgwick report that the cut-glass accents of West End stage actors transposed to the screen proved an impediment to exportability to America, for others a distinctive accent was a highly marketable commodity at home.[7] Dublin's Abbey Theatre Players appeared on the London stage in 1934 in Sean O'Casey's *Within the Gates* and in film versions of *Juno and the Paycock* (Hitchcock, 1929) and J. M. Synge's *Riders to the Sea* (Brian Desmond Hurst, 1935). Emlyn Williams wrote dialogue and lent an authentic accent to the American co-production of *The Citadel* (King Vidor, 1939), the action partly set in a Welsh mining village, and in *The Last Days of Dolwyn* (1949), similarly located, he directed and starred alongside Richard Burton. Gordon Harker appeared with Gibb McLaughlin as a cockney prisoner of war in *The W-Plan* (Victor Saville, 1930), a role typical of the war films of the 1920s (see Chapter 3), as a garrulous traveller in *Rome Express* (Walter Forde, 1932) and as a cantankerous and chauvinistic 'Hackney Man' in *The Lucky Number* (Anthony Asquith, 1933). Cockney comic Max Miller appeared in a number of temperate 'quickie' adaptations of a ribald music hall act, and delivered fast patter in a cameo role in *Princess Charming* (Maurice Elvey, 1934). The music hall duo Flanagan and Allen appeared in films in their own right, including *O-Kay for Sound* (Marcel Varnel, 1937) and, taking its title from their signature tune, *Underneath the Arches* (Redd Davis, 1937) and to authenticate the London Palladium setting of the final scene in *The 39 Steps*. Will Hay combined his music hall persona with Beachcomber's 'Narkover' stories in the *Daily Express*, then with fat boy Graham Moffatt as his stooge in *Oh! Mr Porter* (Marcel Varnel, 1937) and *Ask a Policeman* (Marcel Varnel, 1939). As with Formby, there is much robust clowning about in the former with animals, a chase sequence (in which an old retainer is drenched with flour and mistaken for a ghost), another chase (in which a smuggler masquerades as a ghost) and verbal gags aplenty: Murphy gives the new station master of Buggleskelly a voucher for the pigs he keeps in his office: '. . . but they're only human, after all', says Porter (Hay) after eating one for supper; Harbottle senior in *Ask a Policeman* says that the story of the phantom hearse is 'on the tip of my tongue' – 'Well, stick your tongue out and let's have a look at it,' demands Dudfoot (Hay). Other familiar voices were drawn from the radio, such as the comedian Tommy Handley and the BBC announcer, Stuart Hibberd (possibly beloved by 'Miss Bouncer' in the popular song). In *Keep Your Seats, Please* (1936), Madame Louise gives lessons in her Chelsea apartment to would-be radio crooners (a cover, her husband suspects, for less respectable assignations), while *Ask a Policeman* opens with a spoofed radio report from Turnbottom, envied throughout the South as a village without crime, 'due to Dudfoot, head of the local police force'. Edmund Gwenn appeared as a succession of hard-nosed Northerners, in the first sound version of Houghton's 1912 *Hindle Wakes* (Saville, 1931 – with Belle Chrystal), in Galsworthy's 1920 *The Skin Game* (Hitchcock, 1931 – previously filmed by Doxat-Pratt in 1921), Harold Brighouse's 1915 *Hobson's Choice* (Thomas Bentley, 1931 – with Belle Chrystal), Winifred Holtby's 1936 *South Riding* (Victor Saville, 1938) and J. B. Priestley's *Laburnum Grove* (Carol Reed, 1936) and *The Good Companions* (Victor Saville, 1933).

Basil Dean, with Associated Talking Pictures at Ealing, established the first studios designed for sound with the express intention of employing legitimate actors in theatrical adaptations, but his greatest financial successes came with his hiring of George Formby and Gracie Fields.[8] In *Keep Your Seats, Please*, directed by Fields' husband, Monty Banks (and drawn from a Russian tall tale written by Ilya Ilf and Evgeny Petrov – subsequently filmed in Russia as *The Twelve Chairs* in 1971 and in America in 1974), Formby appeared with the comedienne, Florence Desmond, as Florrie, and Binkie Stuart as Florrie's orphaned niece (a disgustingly cutesy English-style Shirley Temple). The character actor Alistair Sim appears as a solicitor intent upon depriving George, the black sheep of the family, of the fortune bequeathed him by an eccentric relative. There is much slap-and-tickle and slapstick, interspersed with Formby renditions of the film's theme tune and 'When I'm Cleaning Windows', to ukelele accompaniment, before the simpleton George is restored to the jewels, bonds and cash which Miss Withers has buried in the seat of one of a set of dining room chairs. Asquith's equally fine *The Lucky Number* (from a story by Franz Schultz, with music by Mischa Spoliansky and sets by Vetchinsky) is structured around a similar quest: Percy Gibbs (Clifford Mollison), a former footballer (who loses a match when jilted by a girl in favour of a higher-class companion), encounters humble Winnie (Joan Wyndham) at a fairground where a game is named in his honour. Posh voices in the background comment on his conduct on the field as 'un-British'. Percy has been abroad for a year, to escape such adverse remarks, and when his wallet is stolen he has only a French lottery ticket and a picture of his lost girlfriend in his pocket. Percy, to pay his bill, endeavours to persuade a barman that the number recalls the Battle of Trafalgar . . . won by Nelson . . . a Hackney man. Beleaguered Percy tells Winnie that he's so unlucky that 'When I look up it rains' (and it does). But, assisted by Winnie, he eventually secures the funds to redeem the ticket and (more importantly) his career. Footage of greyhound racing between studio-staged scenes anticipates the atmosphere of Dearden's *The Blue Lamp* (1949) (see Chapter 7).

Formby and Fields both benefited from and promoted the sale of records and sheet-music in their cinema performances. Gracie Fields, the most popular singer of the decade (and the first star to appear on television), lent not only a recognisable accent but also, like Formby, an identifiably Lancastrian persona to the series of films made with Basil Dean:[9] *Sing As We Go* (1934), like *Hindle Wakes*, features the typical 'grand day out' in Blackpool. Priestley, in his quasi-documentary survey of Britain in 1933, characterised Fields (for whom he also wrote screenplays) as:

> not only the most popular and dominating personality of the English variety stage but also a sort of essence of Lancastrian femininity. Listen to her for a quarter of an hour and you will learn more about Lancashire women and Lancashire than you would from a dozen books. . . . All the qualities are there: shrewdness, homely simplicity, irony, fierce independence, impish delight in mocking whatever is thought to be affected and pretentious.[10]

The documentarist Basil Wright endorses this opinion in his review for *The Spectator* of *The Show Goes On* (Basil Dean, 1937), an otherwise unsatisfactory film, in which Gracie plays a mill girl: [she] really does represent a common denominator for those millions of English folk who like the humour and sentiment of the type known as homely. Her personality is not merely powerful – it represents intimacy with each audience which can arise only out of the true tradition of English music hall.[11]

The *Sunday Graphic* added: 'Gracie does enough to satisfy her fans but the film isn't likely to attract anyone else. If there is anyone else.'[12] Fields, too (before emigrating to America with her Italian husband during the war), was offered inducements from Hollywood, and Dean had no choice but to raise her fees accordingly, although in both *Sally in Our Alley* (1931) and *Sing As We Go*, she played roles which endorsed Dean's own prejudice in favour of the stage over the cinema: as Annette Kuhn observes,

> It is as if in the characters she plays, Gracie Fields the film star absolves herself from involvement in the peculiar fascination cinema held for its – and her – fans, while the pitiable figures of Florrie [in *Sally in Our Alley*] and Gladys [in *Sing As We Go*] stand as embodiments of the typical contemporary film fan.[13]

Florrie sleeps with a copy of *Film Weekly* and fanzine souvenir postcards on either side of her pillow, while in *Rome Express*, a film actress signs autographs in front of a railway station news-stand selling copies of *Film Weekly*, with her picture on the cover: the magazine features her story, 'Asta Marvell – Shop Girl to Starlet'. Furthermore, although Priestley sometimes bemoans the decline of traditional working-class entertainments, challenged by the cinema (in both *English Journey* and *The Good Companions*), he nevertheless lauds cinema as a democratising aspect of modern England; a super cinema is symptomatic of 'progress' for Osbert Lancaster in the landscape of his fictional Pelvis Bay and in the fictional Sloughborough of Basil Dearden's *The Smallest Show on Earth* (1957) (see Chapter 8).[14] Certainly, cinemagoing was a widespread activity, whether accounting for the enforced leisure of the unemployed and miserable, seeking warmth in George Orwell's *The Road to Wigan Pier* and Graham Greene's 'A Little Place off the Edgware Road' (1939), the star-struck ambitions of Seth Starkadder in Stella Gibbons' *Cold Comfort Farm*; or the trance-like submission of Olivia in Rosamund Lehmann's *The Weather in the Streets*. Some cinemagoers occupied their time shelling peas; during the glass shortage of the 1930s, some paid for their tickets with jam-jars.[15]

Twins and Duplicitous Doubles

Jessie Matthews was born above a butcher's shop in Soho, the seventh of sixteen children. According to Michael Balcon, Jessie's concern for the rest of her family (and the nervous and physical stress which accompanied her stardom) kept her in Britain.[16] Matthews' own story of transformation from humble origins to the glorious demi-monde of film society was mirrored by the plots of much of the studios' output. *Goodnight Vienna* (1932, based on a radio play) was directed and produced by Herbert Wilcox with the former Cochran revue girl, Anna Neagle (subsequently married to

Wilcox), playing opposite the immaculate song and dance man, Jack Buchanan. Viki (Neagle) is a poor flower-girl in pre-war Vienna in love with Max (Buchanan), a wealthy and elegant army captain. By the end of the war, Viki has become rich and famous as a singer while Max has been reduced to earning a living as a shop assistant. The 'story of the poor man's rise to musical fame' and its potential pitfalls had become familiar by 1937, when *Film Weekly* reviewed *Song of Freedom* (J. Elder Wills, 1936), in which Paul Robeson appears initially as a docker, Tom Zinga, overheard singing by an operatic impresario. By becoming a concert performer, he achieves his dream of travelling to Africa, where he is discovered to be the legitimate ruler of his tribe, to which he duly reinstates a British pattern of law and order. The review comments that the story and the sincere performances of Robeson and Elisabeth Welch (as his wife – and appearing in her own right as a variety turn in *Death at Broadcasting House* [Reginald Denham, 1934]) gave 'a natural unity to the transition', making the film more than simply an opportunity to display a magnificent voice.[17]

In the films directed by Victor Saville, the story establishing and linking Matthews' song and dance numbers (in which she effectively appears as herself) requires her to portray a character who, however improbably, appears to others as something other than she is. Emlyn Williams' adaptation of Benn Levy's *Evergreen*, originally staged by C. B. Cochran, opens with the farewell performance of Harriet Green (Jessie Matthews) at the Tivoli Theatre. The sets (by Alfred Junge), costumes (by Borleo) and period songs ('Daddy Wouldn't Buy Me a Bow-wow') locate the action before the war and Harriet's understudy, Maudie, is played by the silent-screen favourite, Betty Balfour, 'a part carried off with a good deal of the old racy skill', noted *The Spectator* (see Chapter 4).[18] The theatre barmaids portentously discuss her 'last appearance': 'she'll be back – they always are'. At the champagne supper held in her honour, Harriet receives an urgent message. She goes to Hackney and meets the father of her illegitimate daughter, who has been blackmailing her under threat of revealing this disreputable secret. Harriet deserts the millionaire marquis who wants to marry her and leaves her child in the care of her dresser, Hawkie. As Harriet removes her engagement ring, the lights go out at the Tivoli.

The action now moves emphatically to the present, the dialogue spattered with contemporary references: 'I don't know you from Amy Johnson,' says Thompson, the publicity man, to a new arrival at the theatre's auditions, before thinking up 'a stunt that will put Hitler in the shade' and, as in *The Good Companions*, puts pay to the competition from the cinema down the road. Hawkie recognises the new arrival (Jessie Matthews) as Harriet's daughter. While another actress complains that Thompson reports her age as thirty-five ('I'm twenty-eight' – when she is actually thirty-eight), he and the stage manager (Sonnie Hale) decide that Harriet should pretend to be her mother, returning to the boards at sixty but miraculously unmarked by the intervening years. Maudie (now the widowed Lady Shropshire, still played by an equally unmarked Betty Balfour) connives in the scam. Meanwhile, two journalists suspect that Miss Green meets the press wearing a high collar to disguise the scars of a face-lift.

Jessie Matthews paired with on-screen and off-screen partner Sonnie Hale in *First A Girl* (Victor Saville, 1935)

Although *Evergreen* originated as a stage production, Saville rendered the film as a distinctly cinematic spectacle. Andrew Higson notes the influence of Warner's *backstage* musicals, *Footlights Parade* (1933) and *Gold Diggers of 1933* (1933).[19] Charles Davy (one of Greene's predecessors at *The Spectator* and a more sympathetic critic) noted that its verve and clever production 'interpreting the interplay of characters and feeling into visual terms' compensated for its thin story. Rachael Low states that the film marked the first use of the 'extended proscenium', the choreography accommodated to the space of the screen rather than being restricted to the stage on which the action supposedly takes place (see also *The Red Shoes* [1948], Chapter 7).[20] In one sequence, 'Springtime in your Heart', Harriet turns a giant hour-glass back to 1924 (intercut with jazz and dancing in the streets), to 1914 (with robots being stamped out on a production line in the form of bullets), to 1904 (with a polka being danced to 'Here Comes the Galloping Rajah'). The film ends with a Busby Berkeley-style routine featuring revolving platforms and closing on the younger Harriet's wedding ring, in the manner also (only typically even more so) of Ken Russell's 1972 *The Boyfriend* (see Chapter 10). The choreography, sets and costumes emphasise the rise in social rank-

A big stage number from Victor Saville's 1934 musical *Evergreen*

ing of young Harriet, as she achieves fame and fortune (a neat little hat and day-dress superseded by chiffon and feathers, so that even off stage as Harriet, Jessie is on stage as Jessie) and the shift in styles from Edwardian to ultra-modern (Susie Cooper cups and Marcel Breuer chairs). Harriet (and therefore Jessie) appeals to all, young and old, across the generations. And whereas old Harriet faced the dilemma of publicly acknowledging an illegitimate child, the younger Harriet is caught in the trap of Thompson's making: at first they cannot become lovers because he is supposed to be her son; then she cannot, after all, announce herself as the daughter because this would make Thompson her brother (incest supersedes illegitimacy as a taboo). Meanwhile, the elderly Marquis of Staines admits, sentimentally, that he knew that young Harriet could not be her mother . . . but he admired her pluck and wanted her to get away with it.

Pluck and resourcefulness equally characterise Jessie's dual role in *First a Girl*, previously made in Germany by Alfred Zeisler as *Viktor und Viktoria* (1933). A seamstress (Jessie Matthews) is despatched by a dress designer, Madame Serafina (Martita Hunt), to deliver a dress to Princess Miranoff (Anna Lee) at the Savoy Hotel. She asks Madame Serafina if she can be a show-girl, modelling dance-frocks but her request is met with abruptly: 'Do what you've got to do, not what you want.' Turned away in her own humble day-clothes, Jessie finds that she is admitted by a theatre doorman when she dresses in the gown intended for the Princess. She encounters a would-be tragedian (Sonnie Hale), currently working as a female impersonator, Victor/Victoria. They are both down on their luck and commiserate together in a chop-house. He suggests that he pose as her manager and that she, as Bill, take his place at the music hall (and much slapstick involving geese and slippery puddles ensues). Bill is spotted by an impresario who proposes presenting him/her before a more refined audience. They, and the film's viewer, are promptly whisked off on a world tour of neon lights, skylines and landmarks, eventually landing at the Casino des Folies in Paris where the Princess and her bored fiancé Robert (Griffith Jones) have come to see the phenomenal Bill. Robert instinctively recognises 'him' as 'her': 'what a marvellous girl!' while Victor reminds Bill that she should 'smile like a man . . . at the Princess not the Prince'. Robert engages in a conversation with Bill, man to man, fuelled by cigars and brandies (which she does her best to avoid); but he wonders in retrospect why Bill should ask whether Robert found her attractive and he and the Princess determine to discover the truth. A farcical bedroom caper fails to provide the answer. The foursome meet up again on the Riviera (where people are often not what they seem) and Robert discovers Bill swimming. 'I'm sorry', he says (to have found out her deceit); 'He's sorry?!' she says (intimating a fear that all is lost between them). Robert gallantly insists to the Princess that Bill is, indeed, a boy but betrays his true feelings by describing the stage performance as 'adorable . . . I mean marvellous'. Bill is prepared to sacrifice the career for her love for Robert and Victor reassures Robert that there has never been anything between him and Bill: 'you have an unclean mind!' Victor appears on stage once more as Victoria, in a crude caricature of the performance by which the impresario was supposedly duped and a journalist is keen to investigate. The Princess, in turn, rewards Victor's professional ambition by agreeing to sponsor his Hamlet – 'I'll be the greatest Cleopatra the world has ever seen', he insists. The film plays with notions of propriety of gender recognition while being careful to engage the audience in the joke: Jessie in close-up winks directly to camera (she knows and Robert finally asserts – first a girl is always a girl). Nevertheless, Jessie's narrow body and her gamine face were well matched and fashionably appropriate to the part. Elisabeth Bergner, meanwhile, took the traditional travesty role of Rosalind in Shakespeare's *As You Like It* (Paul Czinner, 1936). Graham Greene (who liked girls dressed as boys) found her 'mischievously good' with Laurence Olivier, as Orlando, 'even more satisfying', in spite of the attempts of Lazare Meerson's sets and numerous sheep and fowl to upstage them: the production attracted comparison with Max Reinhardt's *A Midsummer Night's Dream* (1935).[21]

From *Evergreen* onwards, films were tailor-made for Jessie Matthews as a singing, dancing romantic comedienne and they evince a common set of themes and set-pieces. Robert Donat, on the other hand, with a background in the legitimate stage (he had toured with Benson's Shakespeare company and spent a year teaching at RADA) endeavoured to pursue a variety of roles, in the theatre and in film. After his appearance as Culpepper in Korda's *The Private Life of Henry VIII* (1933), he was persuaded to take the title role in *The Count of Monte Cristo* (1934); Donat feared that remaining in Hollywood would restrict his range (although he consistently played romantic heroes) and instead fulfilled his outstanding American contractual obligations with productions based in Britain (*The Citadel* and *Goodbye, Mr Chips*) and worked for British companies. He maintained that all his roles were equally well received by his many fans.[22] Impressed by the French silent comedy, *The Italian Straw Hat* (1927) and by the early sound film, *Sous les toits de Paris* (1933), both designed by Lazare Meerson, Korda selected René Clair (one of his numerous imports) to direct Robert Donat in *The Ghost Goes West* (1935). Following the grandiose example of *Henry*, the sets are large and lavishly detailed. Donat took the dual roles of Murdoch Glourie, an eighteenth-century Scottish noble who returns to haunt the ancestral castle, and his descendant, Donald. Donat played Donald as a shy stooge to his amorous forebear, more interested in canoodling with shepherdesses than the serious business of defending the family's honour.

By the twentieth century, the estate has fallen into debt and the castle verges on dereliction, and Donald determines to sell the Glourie estate to repay his creditors, even if this reduces him to poverty. An American businessman, Joe Martin (Eugene Pallette), is keen to make the purchase, in order to transport the edifice, stone by crumbling stone, to Sunnymede, Florida. His daughter, Peggy (Jean Parker), encounters Murdoch, whom she mistakes for Donald, is amused by his flirting and finds his costume romantic (but she is confused by Donald's subsequent denial that it was him). Murdoch accompanies the stones to their new site. The film makes gentle fun of the businessman's vulgar aspiration to apply Old World patina to his New World wealth – the castle's 'cute improvements' include a gondola ('to add a sort of European touch'), a black jazz band in kilts playing 'real Scotch music' and gadgets such as a whisky keg which plays music: Osbert Lancaster likewise mildly satirises 'solid pressed steel carefully grained and varnished', passing for 'age-old oak beams'.[23] Donald is not impressed. Joe Martin, small, chubby, cigar-chewing, battles for retail business with Bigelow (a descendant of the clan McLagen), who sees in the rumour of the ghost an opportunity for a 'stunt'. A shoot-out between rival gangsters serves to locate the action when the stones arrive in New York. Bigelow's bluff is called when the ghost (or, rather, Donald) reappears and he is required to apologise to the Glourie clan. Family honour is redeemed and Donald returns to Peggy the forfeit demanded from her by Murdoch.

Another pair of twinned roles occur in Paul Czinner's *Stolen Life* (1939). Bergner chose as co-star Michael Redgrave, as a mountaineer, Alan McKenzie, who marries one sister (Sylvia), only to discover that he should have married the other (Martina). The film includes a mock documentary sequence, reporting a successful but difficult expedition to Tibet and, with its powerful Walton scoring, celebrates the 1930s enthusiasm (of 'thick-skinned' types, says Anna in *The Weather in the Streets*) for the Tyrol and the Dolomites abroad (see also *The Constant Nymph*, *The Man Who Knew Too Much* [Hitchcock, 1934], *The Secret Agent* [1936], *Escape Me Never* [Czinner, 1935] and *The Lady Vanishes* [Hitchcock, 1938] for various uses of location shooting and back-projection) and the Pennines and the Peaks (and Cumberland in *High Hazard*, 1935) at home.[24] While Alan is away Sylvia embarks on an affair with a neighbour but is killed in a boating accident to which Martina alone is witness. Martina gives a false name to the police in order to be united with Alan on his return. He, meanwhile, has already noticed a change in tone in the letters he receives from home. Alan's dog senses the subterfuge at once; her dying father wonders why she has resigned herself to never being loved for herself. His squiffy team-mates tell Alan that Martina was always the girl for him. After much agonising (Martina, as Sylvia, is challenged by Alan with the affair) the truth will out (Martina, as Martina, is simply too irresistibly good to be thus compromised).

Abdul the Damned (Karl Grune, 1935), co-funded for British International Pictures by the Austrian producer Max Schach, is a farcical skit on the Young Turks' rebellion of 1908, featuring Fritz Kortner as the double employed by the Sultan to evade assassination. There is discussion of royal bearing as something to which one is born rather than a matter of acquisition. It also features incidental music (joyous fanfares and anthems – 'all for one and one for all') written by the temporarily exiled communist and collaborator of Bertolt Brecht, Hanns Eisler. Delightful Turkish-ish dancers appear in extravagantly choreographed and set numbers with exposed legs, midriffs and quantities of glitter, feathers and chiffon, against lavish sets 'with the atmosphere of a corrupt Turkey' designed by John Mead.[25] An old lady traveller arrives in Constantinople for the sixth time and declares (almost wistfully) 'I have never been accosted once . . . what can the Sultan do with 300 wives?' Exotic idioms are employed to humorous effect: 'the night has a million eyes' (says Ali, the chief eunuch); 'find out which eye and put it out' (orders Sultan Abdul). The dancer, Terese (Adrienne Ames), submits to the Sultan's attentions in order to secure the release of her fiancé: a very dead parrot (who has eaten the poison intended for Abdul) seems likely to thwart her plans, until the Sultan's Personal Guard refuse to march on his behalf: 'but we've better propaganda!' he insists. Eventually, the double rebels and the Sultan is deposed and agrees to go peacefully (stroking his cat, in the manner of the Bond series' Blofeld).

Early cinema had used double exposure to duplicate an actor within a single frame (for instance, in the *Ultus* series). Disguised split personalities (of the Jekyll and Hyde type) continue into the 1930s, for instance with Michael Powell's quota quickie, *Rynox* (1931). But for the most part, the novelty of the 1930s films resides in showing two characters sharing a similar voice. The doubling is identified in repetition, aurally, as much as visually, in sequence. As soon as it becomes technically possible to present an actor's performance as an organic, integrated unity (with the introduction of synchronised sound) the separation of the aural and visual elements seems to assume a peculiar narrative interest.

Mitteleuropeans

The gala performance of *Stolen Life* in January 1939 was held in aid of the Fund for Refugees and the Women's Appeal Committee for German and Austrian Women and Children, a charity with which Elisabeth Bergner was associated. While many directors and performers were invited to work in Britain in the 1930s (René Clair, Jacques Feyder, Marlene Dietrich, Paul Fresnay, Peter Lorre, Douglas Fairbanks Jr, Robert Young), partly in order to enhance the marketability of films abroad, other personnel migrated more permanently. Czinner and his wife, Bergner, moved to Britain and then to America while the actors Conrad Veidt and Anton Walbrook, the designer Alfred Junge and the cameraman Mutz Greenbaum emigrated to escape the rise of fascism in Germany.

The Hungarian Alexander Korda, who founded London Films in 1931, had previously worked in France and America and was responsible for the importation of much European talent (including his own brothers, the artist/designer Vincent and director/producer, Zoltan). The strategy sometimes met with a haughty, not to say overtly racist response in the press, Greene sneering at 'the tasteless Semitic opulence' of Korda's Denham Studio productions. His attacks on Korda and his films did not, however, prevent their later association.[26] The Gainsborough producer Michael Balcon thought his own approach to film-making timid in comparison to that of Korda; Robert Donat (Culpepper in *Henry VIII*) said of Korda: 'I think of him as three personalities. The Dreamer, planning wonders that could never happen, only in the never-never land. The Practical – yet invariably biting-off twenty-two times one hundred per cent more than he can ever chew. The World-beater.'[27] Korda was known for his flamboyance and in *The Citadel* a joke is made at his own expense: an Hungarian film producer is one of the guests at a select society dinner.

The Private Life of Henry VIII proved seminal to British cinema in the 1930s, prompting foreign investors (such as Max Schach) and the City to back film production. Korda's nephew suggests that the film was a reprise of a successful German enterprise of 1920.[28] The tone of the film is established in voiceover: Katharine of Aragon (Henry's first wife) is not to be discussed because she was respectable (and clever) and 'therefore not of interest here – he divorced her'. We move to a 'below stairs' discussion of the King's 'marrying mood', the ladies of the household unpicking initials embroidered on linen in order to replace them. Spectators at Anne Boleyn's execution then ask for her to remove her hat, 'We can't see the block'. There are rudimentary concessions to historically recorded fact: 'I have such a little neck,' says Anne (Merle Oberon). A French executioner boasts of his finesse and his English counterpart complains of his workload. 'Chop and change', joke the girls in the royal entourage. The King sets his cap at Catherine Howard (whom he shall eventually marry); Catherine, meanwhile, is courted by Culpepper and Boleyn's initials are replaced.

The new Queen, Jane Seymour, dies giving birth to Henry's heir, the weakling Edward. Prattling among the kitchen staff continues, and the King poses for his Holbein portrait. He next marries Anne of Cleves, who forestalls their consummation by dressing in a bell-tent and playing cards – and beating him: 'I play for cash.' They divorce amicably. Henry takes Catherine Howard as a wife, ominously (under the circumstances) feeling her neck; she is duly punished for her affair with Culpepper (and the same bickering couple turn up in the audience for her execution). A date, carved in relief on a building, reminds us that we are now in 1543. Henry's old friend, Anne of Cleves, reminds the King that he should marry again, but now choose someone neither clever nor ambitious, neither stupid nor young. He takes Catherine Parr, who harangues him about his diet and nags him into taking a nap: Henry's life is simultaneously ordinary and extraordinary. Charles Davy praised Korda's unsurpassed, sumptuous and brilliant production, Laughton's acting 'with gusto' and the 'racy, rabelaisian handling' of the story, with 'no attempt at period dialogue'.[29]

The extravagant scale of Korda's productions (*The Scarlet Pimpernel* [Harold Young, 1934]; *Four Feathers* [Zoltan Korda, 1939], *Fire Over England* [William K. Howard, 1937]) was well received in America, justifiably bearing comparison with Hollywood's own treatment of British historical subjects. Other British studios ventured to follow, sometimes disastrously. C. A. Lejeune (a critic whom Greene liked to mock as much as the films she praised) wrote rapturously of *Henry VIII*: 'California, here we come!'[30] Charles Laughton's performance was rewarded with an Oscar and he and his wife, Elsa Lanchester (Henry's fourth wife, Anne of Cleves), were persuaded to move to Hollywood. Korda attempted to repeat the formula in 1934 with *Catherine the Great* (Douglas Fairbanks Jr coupled with Bergner, with Flora Robson as the older Empress), and in 1936 with *Rembrandt* (again coupling Laughton with Lanchester), both films shot by Clair's cinematographer, Georges Périnal. Fairbanks was also engaged for *The Private Life of Don Juan* (1934), handsomely costumed by Oliver Messel: Korda, it was said, was cornering the personal history of European monarchs.[31]

He turned to a more recent Russian theme in 1937, with *Knight Without Armour* (taken from a novel by James Hilton, a much-adapted author, to which Donat himself had secured the rights). A silhouette of the bronze statues on the Anichkov Bridge, indicating Nevsky Prospect in old St Petersburg, backs the title sequence and the film opens with Countess Alexandra (Marlene Dietrich) and Fothergill (Donat) both at Ascot in 1913. Their paths subsequently cross in Russia, with the earnest intellectual Fothergill assuming the identity of Peter Uranov in order to infiltrate a Revolutionary Movement which plants a bomb on the route of Alexandra's wedding procession. A horse gets killed, Alexandra's veil gets torn and Peter gets sent to Siberia. Having missed the war, in 1917 Peter is liberated and re-emerges as a leather-jacketed hero of the proletariat. Meanwhile, Alexandra is having a hard time of it (relatively few costume changes here) and loses a chiffon scarf to a Bolshevik. Peter is deputed to escort her to Petrograd to face Revolutionary discipline. 'Long live Russia!' she spits, defiantly, 'I despise you – vermin!' He suggests that for her own safety she dress less conspicuously. With her face carefully framed in a peasant shawl, mistily photographed in approved Sternberg manner (and her eyebrows perfectly pencilled) Alexandra waits at Peter's side for the train – which never comes. He recites English verse to keep them awake (Rozsa's score rises to match Browning) – 'it's optimistic, like the English', she says and recites Russian verse in return – 'it's hopeless and pessimistic, like the Russians'. More confusion ensues as to who is in charge of what but, miraculously, a large selection of 1930s net and sequin evening wear is produced so that Alexandra (after a bath – censored for American exhibition) can be properly dressed for dinner: 'More's the pity,' says the maid, 'you don't know what you're missing.' 'I can't believe I'm really here safe and with friends,' says the Countess. The Russian émigré designer, Meerson, provides a well-appointed dacha with a gallery and staircase such that a sheathed Dietrich can make her entrance to maximum effect. There are more interviews with another bunch of unsavoury types in leather jackets, reduced by now to cynicism (echoes of the beleaguered functionaries in *Henry VIII* and *The Queen's Affair*): 'soldiers are soldiers – white or red, there's no difference'; but one of the commissars takes pity on them. Peter and Alexandra, disguised in army great coats and shaggy fur hats, escape into a forest which 'belongs – belonged' to her and make a modest repast of the tinned lobster and brandy which he has managed to barter in exchange for his watch.[32] Loyal retainers from the family estate refuse to denounce the Countess and a love-struck broken-down boy kills himself sooner than betray her. Temporarily separated, Peter faces death by firing squad but is, at last, reunited with Alexandra on a hospital train.

Technically, the film was enormously ambitious, the cost to Denham Studios, substituting for the vast expanse of the USSR, reputedly exceeding £300,000.[33] Donat thought Harry Stradling (who shared camera credits with Jack Cardiff and Bernard Browne) the best cameraman with whom he had ever worked, but was disconcerted to find himself sharing the billing with a star who commanded, and commandeered, more attention than he could manage. As Greene observes (taken aback to find himself thrilled by this melodramatic, adolescent, wish-fulfilling concoction of 'rescues, escapes and discarnate embraces'): 'she never acts – she lends her too beautiful body: she consents to pose: she is the marble motive for heroisms and sacrifices: as for acting . . . it goes on all round her: she leaves it to her servants'.[34] But the film is not just obsessed with Dietrich, it also (in common with Buchan) seems besotted with White Russia. *The Spectator*, meanwhile, advertised *Things I Remember* (1931), by Marie, Grand Duchess of Russia, alongside E. H. Carr's 1932 *Maxim Gorky and his Works*, coverage of the 1933 Moscow trials of suspected Vickers spies and reports on the Soviet economy.

A Russian on the home front appears in *I Lived With You* (Elvey, 1933), echoing Ronald Firbanks' 1920 sapphic Zena Zoubaroff (who causes disruption among bored society newly weds in Florence). Louche Felix (Ivor Novello – with an accent more Valley Boy than Volga) encounters Ada Wallace in the maze at Hampton Court and, posing as a prince (his mother 'was a guest of the king'), inveigles himself into the affections of the Wallace household. Felix ensconces himself on the family sofa and indulges himself in his mourning for his lost past and homeland, introducing a few 'atmospheric items' into the domestic décor: cushions, drapes, a samovar, flowers and confectionery, playing the balalaika while respectably lower middle-class Ma Wallace dusts around him. Pa Wallace is nervous of his talk of ballerinas, urging him not to speak in a *'News of the World* manner'. Felix causes general disruption in the family's affairs, diverting the attention of the grown-up daughter and setting up the father for a fling; he teaches a gathering of prim ladies to knock back vodka and spikes the tea of those who refuse it. Without conspicuous effort, the indolent guest pokes fun at his hosts' social pretensions and romantic delusions, before returning to the maze to entice their unwitting successors.

Robert Stevenson's *Tudor Rose* (1936), concerning the short reign of Lady Jane Grey, and the Wilcox/Neagle historical films *Victoria the Great* (1937) and *Sixty Glorious Years* (1938) are customarily viewed as contemporary commentary on the coronation and abdication of Edward VIII and his succession by George VI in 1936. Happily, in a Ruritanian context Wilcox is less deferential towards the monarchy (although still sympathetic) and his treatment of Central European politics is frivolous. *The Queen's Affair* (1934) bears comparison with *The Vagabond Queen* (see Chapter 4), Coward's *The Queen Was in the Parlour* (produced for the stage by Basil Dean in 1926 and filmed by Cutts for Gainsborough in 1927) and Karl Grune's *Abdul the Damned*. Drawn from a musical play, the film begins with Anna (Neagle) working as a shop assistant in New York. She is summoned to the boss' office and informed that she is the legitimate heir to the throne of Sirocca. She returns to Europe for her coronation, escorted by two courtiers. Meanwhile, a band of black-shirted anarchist republicans led by Carl (Fernand Gravvey), with the hired services of the national army, conspire to cause insurrection and depose her: 'there will be oceans of blood . . . the sea must flow with . . . lots of it . . .', he says, rapturously. The band performs a gesture which lampoons a Nazi salute (in the manner of Chaplin's 1940 *The Great Dictator*). However, the Queen escapes with her maid, who remembers her mother's flight to Chicago, under similar circumstances, and they set off for Paris. Anna says she would rather be back in America selling stockings; 'so would we all', says Marie, solidly, reminding her of her duty, and Anna is duly seen reading the Vansittart biography, *Sixty Glorious Years* (on which Wilcox was to base his own film), as if to show that she intends to take her responsibilities as a monarch in exile seriously. Meanwhile, the new regime in Sirocca is proving no more effective than its predecessor: Britain refuses to acknowledge its government as Sirocca has no football association. President Carl escapes and finds himself accompanying Anna across the border (more beautiful lakes and mountains): both are travelling incognito and, without the trappings of state, fail to recognise each other. Two palace guardsmen provide a rustic commentary on events back home: there may be different uniforms but otherwise little has changed; the republican party has split into two factions and Anna is summoned by her courtiers to return. Carl and Anna, somewhat inconveniently, have fallen in love but their mutual duplicity leaves them suspicious of motives. When the truth is discovered, Anna determines on a reconciliation. She renounces her regal finery and takes the throne with the president as her consort, thereby restoring peace to Sirocca at last. As with *Princess Charming* (which concerns the marriage of a Ruritanian princess to an elderly and impoverished ruler of a neighbouring country), taken from an Austrian original, *The Queen's Affair* 'does not ask to be taken at all seriously', Charles Davy concluding of the former that 'an attempted satire on dictators would be more effective if it were not implied that the right answer to social discontent is loyalty to a lovely Princess'.[35] Balcon, in his autobiography, regrets that European politics were not more fully addressed in the films produced in his own studio.[36]

More serious political tensions underlie *Rome Express* and *The Lady Vanishes*. Both bring together a disparate band of travellers on trans-European trains: in *Rome Express*, Zelder, an art thief (Conrad Veidt – in one of a number of roles adopted in exile as 'bad' foreigners), is accompanied by Fisher, a golfing enthusiast (Gordon Harker as 'old lag' again), a film star and her American publicist. A murder is committed and investigated during the journey, the film beginning and ending in a railway station with a variety of languages being heard amid the hustle and bustle. *The Lady Vanishes* introduces the Launder and Gilliatt characters, Caldicott and Charters (see Chapter 6), as Englishmen abroad whose main and abiding interest, for the duration, is the cricket score at home: 'Nothing but baseball!' splutters Caldicott, picking up a copy of *The Herald Tribune*. They are accompanied by a couple conducting an affair (the man, Charles, seeking to evade any complications en route), the young woman, Iris (Margaret Lockwood), insisting that she sat with Miss Froy on the train, a musician, Gilbert (Michael Redgrave), who becomes increasingly interested in Iris, and Miss Froy (Dame May Whitty), who vanishes. Caldicott and Charters speak out against pacifism ('the early Christians tried it and were fed to the lions') and a barrister, leaving the train bearing a white flag, is shot down. Miss Froy has been despatched to receive a message betraying

'Same old sausage, same old cheese, same old tea': routine boarding-house fare for Renate Muller in *Sunshine Susie* (Victor Saville, 1931)

a pact between two European countries. The message is coded as a tune, delivered to her by a Tyrolean street singer, which she passes to Gilbert for him to memorise and take to the Foreign Office. At the end, Iris casts aside Charles in favour of Gilbert, they are reunited with Miss Froy and the test match has been abandoned because of floods (even the weather in Britain is distinctly uncontinental).

The Secret Agent, based on William Somerset-Maugham's first Ashenden story, opens with a reminder of its Great War context (silhouetted figures above a trench), while employing contemporary settings and costume: Ashenden is assumed to have died in action as the story starts and worked incognito. *The 39 Steps*, based on John Buchan's 1915 novel, is transposed to the 1930s, and Russian Jewish anarchists are replaced by more topical foreign villains as a cause for concern. Hitchcock casts John Gielgud as the debonair agent Ashenden and Robert Donat as Richard Hannay; in both films, Madeleine Carroll plays a woman who sometimes helps and often hinders the hero's pursuit of his goals. In *The 39 Steps*, the casting of a strange, dark woman as the spy who initiates Hannay's mission (Buchan's 'Scudder' is the victim of the Portland Place murder) and of Carroll as 'love interest' mark a departure from the homo-social atmosphere of the original.[37] Hannay is pursued for the murder, of which he is innocent, around studio reconstructions of the Scottish Highlands. Here, the crucial code (the object of Hannay's pursuit) is carried by 'Mr Memory', a star turn at the London Palladium.

Balcon's *Sunshine Susie* (Victor Saville, 1931), with sets by Vetchinsky, shot by Mutz Greenbaum and adapted by Angus McPhail from the German film *Die Privatsekretärin* (1931), retains Renate Muller (as Susie) from the original production, alongside a British favourite, Jack Hulbert. In 1931 it won *Film Weekly*'s readers' poll for Best British Film, was a huge box-office success and ran for as long as a year in some cinemas.[38] An animated sun winks an eye and spouts the letters of the titles, to the strains of an oompah-pah band; a train arrives in Vienna and a girl (framed within a frame) leans out of a window, facing the camera. Susie, newly arrived from Germany, is too wise to be taken advantage of as a girl in a big city – 'I know just what I want from life' – and takes a taxi straight to a hotel for businesswomen. 'Same old sausage, same old cheese, same old tea', chant her fellow guests, and advise her that she'll need a 'friend' (or, better, two) in order to secure a job. Next day she persuades the porter at the Commercial Bank, Hasel (Hulbert), to arrange an interview for her with the manager. Klapper offers her a job – on certain conditions – which she disregards, leaving him standing in the rain at the proposed rendezvous. Susie instead returns to the hotel and giggles a lot. Klapper punishes her for tricking him by keeping her late at work; alone in the office, bent over her typewriter, Susie is approached by the bank's boss, whom she mistakes for a fellow clerk. Franz Arvray (Owen Nares) takes her to a biergarten where Hasel is giving a concert with his musical society – but is at pains to keep his identity a secret from her. Both agonise over their worthiness for each other, act proud, act hard to get but eventually get together, much abetted by the long-suffering Hasel: 'think of the happy ending!' he urges, in exasperation. Sections of the *mise en scène* (the typing pool working in unison, the hotel window blinds raised and lowered to announce the end of the film) are choreographed to Paul Abraham's

jaunty score; similarly, in Hitchcock's 1934 *Waltzes from Vienna*, the processes of a bakery are conducted in 3/4 time, to the strains of Strauss. Susie on several occasions breaks into song: 'Today I
Feel So Happy'. Primarily, the film provides Hulbert with a chance to display an idiosyncratic, lol-
loping, loose-limbed style of dance and a repertoire of eye-rolling grimaces, becoming increasingly
exaggerated and grotesque as the evening in the biergarten wears on. Generally, Hulbert appeared
in screen musicals with Cecily Courtneidge (as in Forde's 1934 *Jack Ahoy*), a partnership launched
as a variety act.

The presence of exile, émigré and itinerant personnel in British cinema in the 1930s is well
known, although some films (such as *Abdul the Damned* and *Sunshine Susie*) have been inexplicably overlooked. This was not a new phenomenon but it became more conspicuous and more
forcefully felt than it had been hitherto. European themes and subjects (as in the future collaborations of Powell and Pressburger) were as apparent as producers, actors, directors, technicians –
and artists in pre- and post-production.

Artists and Industry

In the manner mocked by Osbert Lancaster, *The Spectator* frequently discussed the contending
merits of the modern versus the ancient home. G. M. Boumphrey urges shops to support good
design in china, glass and textiles and encouraged his readers to recognise that modernity was not
of necessity foreign: 'How often', he asked in 1932, 'does one hear it urged against modern architecture that it is German or, still more horrible thought, Russian – at any rate, it is un-English!'[39]
He singles out Wells Coates' contribution to the decoration of the new BBC building in Portland
Place for particular praise and, in 1933, welcomes the Gorrell report on Art and Industry: 'it is at
last dawning on those elusive entities – the Powers that Be and the Man in the Street – that design
is of importance to others beyond artists and the arty – more – that good design may actually be
good business'. Herbert Read, in *Art and Industry: the Principles of Industrial Design* (1934), published paintings by Ben Nicholson (who also designed textiles) alongside taps, cutlery and Bauhaus
crockery, coffee machines and jars, and again blamed the 'middleman' for foisting bad design on
the public. Read thanks Laszlo Moholy-Nagy and declares Walter Gropius 'the inspiration and
leader of all who possess new vision in industrial art'.[40]

The message was not lost on the film industry. Michael Balcon and his head of publicity, the
Russian émigré Monja Danischewsky, report that the painters and lithographers, John Piper, Ronald
Searle, Edward Ardizzone and Edward Bawden, were appointed to design posters for Ealing films
in the 1930s and 1940s. The studio, he says, earned a reputation alongside London Transport for
its promotion of good design: Moholy-Nagy, Paul Nash and Edward Bawden worked for London
Transport also.[41] The exterior styling of the Odeon cinemas was as distinct and modern (as a stan-
dardised product) as Charles Holden's stations on the Piccadilly line. Edward McKnight Kauffer
(who had produced titlecards in the 1920s – see Chapter 4) drew posters for the railways and, with
Ben Nicholson, Edward Bawden and Rex Whistler, for Shell advertising campaigns; meanwhile,
Shell appointed the poet John Betjeman and the painter John Piper to edit its County Guides (pub-

lished from the late 1930s) and established a film unit, with the documentarist Edgar Anstey in 1933.[42] Under the aegis of Jack Beddington, publicity director for Shell Mex and BP (who was to become a significant figure in official film policy in the Second World War – see Chapter 6), the New Zealand artist, Len Lye, was assisted by Humphrey Jennings in 1936 on *The Birth of a Robot*, with a score incorporating music from Holst's *The Planets*. The film allowed Lye to pursue his interests in colour and abstract film while incorporating a mechanical figure already established as a Shell Lubricant logo: 'Modern Worlds need Modern Lubrication'. In 1935, Lye made *A Colour Box* (again using superimpositions of colours and abstract shapes) before it was acquired by Grierson for the GPO, duly introducing the words 'Cheaper Parcel Post' and the relevant postal rates. The fine artist William Coldstream followed the dour *The King's Stamp* (1935) – concerning the manufacture of the postal stamp – with the frivolous *The Fairy of the Phone* (1936) – in which a dozen female switchboard operators, in frilly white collars (like the typists in *Sunshine Susie*), sing public information advice to a score composed by Walter Leigh. While the Polish émigré architect Berthold Lubetkin was appointed to design new pavilions at London Zoo, its director, Julian Huxley (a Film Society supporter and colleague of H. G. Wells – see Chapter 4), made a series of education films publicising the work of the Zoological Society and provided the commentary for *Enough to Eat* (1936), sponsored by the Gas, Light and Coke Company. For the BBC (for which the typographer and sculptor Eric Gill was busily employed alongside the architects Coates, Maufe, McGrath, Myer and Watson-Hart), the GPO produced *BBC – Droitwich* (Harry Watt, 1934) and *BBC – The Voice of Britain* (1935), garnering support through cinematic release for a corporation which, as *The Spectator* remarked, enjoyed a privileged monopoly.[43]

Junge's sets for Balcon's *Evergreen* associated art deco with glamour and helped to popularise modern streamlining, in dress and interior décor. Korda turned to his fellow Hungarian émigré, Moholy-Nagy (who, like Gropius, came to Britain from the Bauhaus), as adviser on the adaptation of H. G. Wells' *The Shape of Things to Come* (William Cameron Menzies), made in 1936 alongside its companion piece *The Man Who Could Work Miracles* (Lothar Mendes). The former is epic in the scale of the themes it attempts to tackle (war and peace in the twentieth century and beyond), in its geography (from a studio-built 'Everytown' in England to outer space) and in its vast sets and extensive cast of extras. But Wells warned in advance against the inevitable comparisons with Fritz Lang's *Metropolis* (see Chapter 4): 'all the balderdash . . . about "robot workers" and ultra skyscrapers etc. etc. should be cleared out of your minds before you work on this film'.[44] The succeeding generations of a family serve to link the episodes. Its counterpart is less portentous, taking for its model a department store and the boarding house shared by its employees (comparable to the haberdashers of *Kipps* – filmed by Harold Shaw in 1921 and known to Wells from personal experience). George Fotheringay (who can grant wishes) is a bit frightened by his new gift: one lodger suggests he heal people, another asks for money, another a tip for a race; his boss wants him to use his powers for the firm's exclusive use, to secure a monopoly. George finds that, while he can make Ada look like Cleopatra, 'like in the movie', in tiara and pearls, he cannot make her love him. However, there is still a familiar sense of political urgency in the speeches given to Wells' protagonists. Confronting the world's Great and the Good, from past and present (bankers, politicians, teachers and preachers), George insists: 'I want my new world *now*!' But Greene found Wells' futurism increasingly outdated:

> The unreligious mind when it sets about designing a heaven for itself is apt to be trivial, portentous, sentimental. Out of the simmering, seething, teeming ideas of Mr Wells there emerges, after the reformed dresses, the underground city, the new machinery, the classless society, the television, the tiny wireless sets worn on the wrist, the endless little mechanical toys, the realization that something after all is still missing. It never ceases to come as a shock to a mind like Mr Wells's that a man can still be unhappy when he has leisure, food, comfort, and the best modern dynamos. But it comes as even more of a shock to his audience that Mr Wells can think of no less old-fashioned a way of appeasing this sense of dissatisfaction than by shooting two of his characters at the moon . . . and the film closes with a sky of stars and some hollow optimistic phrase about the infinite spaces and the endlessness of man's future progress.[45]

Kurt London's *Film Music* (1936) commented on the score provided by Arthur Bliss for *Things to Come*, noting that it was also arranged and performed successfully as a concert suite. William Walton ('England's Hindemith') is commended for *As You Like It* and *Escape Me Never* and Eugène Goossens for *The Constant Nymph*, which cuts between Lewis (Brian Aherne) conducting a concert and those who listen to it on the radio, at home. The Australian, Arthur Benjamin, is discussed for *The Man Who Knew Too Much*, where a radio broadcast of a choral concert similarly links parallel action, between foreign villains who have conspired to use the music to cover the sound of a sniper's gunfire and those (in the Albert Hall) heroically intent upon preventing the assassin from acting. London also praises his work for Korda on the costume drama, *The Scarlet Pimpernel*, and for Rank's moral tale of Yorkshire fisherfolk and technical progress, *The Turn of the Tide* (Norman Walker, 1935). The work of Walter Leigh and Benjamin Britten on documentary films is deemed exemplary

> in forming the musical elements of a film into universal representations of sound. Their film music transcends the score of musical notes and absorbs within itself the sound of real life (in a stylised form), whether it be of single voices, of choruses, or of natural noises, by turning it to music and giving it rhythm.[46]

Balcon, however, says that Britten's ideas for involving the composer at an earlier stage of production were commercially unviable.[47] Low justifiably accords Jack Ellit an equal place with Len Lye on their 1930s films for the GPO, as a compiler of material and for his own compositions: On *N or NW?* (1937) – a return to a 'teens narrative of lovers' stray letters (see Chapter 2) – handwritten credits, floating eyes and spinning pillar boxes are set against a mix of songs from Fats Waller.[48]

On both *Coalface* (Alberto Cavalcanti, 1935) and *Nightmail* (Basil Wright for the GPO, 1936) Britten worked with the poet W. H. Auden. Auden also provided verse commentary for a Gas Council film, *The Londoners* (1939), made to celebrate the fiftieth anniversary of London County Council, while Britten (again for the GPO) in 1939 arranged Rossini themes to accompany Lotte Reininger's coloured paper cut-outs of cherubs, huntsmen and fairy princesses touting *HPO* (a 'Heavenly Post Office'). Harry Watt describes in some detail the making of *Nightmail*, using a mock-up of a railway carriage in the studio (a practice employed elsewhere by Cavalcanti) and a model train to produce the 'clickety-clack' for the soundtrack, matched by the rhythm of Auden's poem.[49] This has since been reworked in Tony Harrison's commission for the GPO's shortlived descendant, Consignia (BBC TV, 2002). Britten's score was largely delivered by Jimmy Blades, who was also hired to hit the gong for Rank's title sequences, as a sound 'double' for Bombardier Billy Wells. The original *Nightmail* depicts the journey of a train from London to Scotland, cataloguing changing accents and landscapes, interspersed with precisely timed and co-ordinated operations (a bag of waiting mail is snatched from a railside gantry without any slowing of the train's relentless passing onwards and upwards). The efficiency of the system is coupled with 'personal' interest: a farmer and 'old Fred's coupon night'. Humphrey Jennings' *Spare Time* (1939) records the shift patterns of steel, cotton and coal workers in Yorkshire, Manchester and Wales and the division of their day between labour and leisure. There are whippets and pigeons; amateur dramatics and choral rehearsals; netball, football and occasional dancing; wrestling matches and fairgrounds (but, notably, not cinemas and dance halls). The film's sections are divided by black leader and it is framed by a trumpet voluntary, played by the steel mill's brass band.

While Read appears to look forward to a modern Britain (modernised by way of a European model), much of the documentary activity records a traditional Britain, even where it is innovative in presentation.

Baggy Trousered Intellectuals and Ragged Trousered Philanthropists

Evelyn Waugh (who was later to write in praise of the baggy trousers favoured by his set of the 1930s) produced, in *Scoop* (1938), a spoof of a newsreel company ('Excelsior Movie Sound') to match the 'Wonderfilm' of *Vile Bodies* (see Chapter 4); Excelsior compete with the hapless and ill-equipped print journalists of *The Daily Beast* to get to the best story first.

The fact that many of the 'documentary' or 'realist' films were produced as a form of advertising was not lost on contemporary critics. Peter Fleming wrote an appreciation of *Drifters* (1929), showing at The Academy in 1931, for *The Spectator*, noting both its plot and purpose:

> Directed by John Grierson for The Empire Marketing Board, it was conceived, primarily, as an advert for the herring industry – one of the oldest industries in these islands and conducted by a very fine body of men, predominantly Scottish. Unfortunately, just as there has been recently a flight from the Mark in Germany, so in England since the War there has been a flight from the herring . . . The result is . . . the finest advertising I've ever seen – this prosaic and even slightly comic fish has provided the

excuse for camera-work at once satisfying to the eye and emotions . . . It observes the herring's progress from the high seas to high teas and has anatomised a trade well-worth watching . . .[50]

Lejeune was similarly enthusiastic: 'The most valiant work in the industry is being done by the film publicists . . . shaping their talents to a definite propagandist purpose, selling goods through the film, selling social betterment through the film.' Graham Greene, too, noted the ability of certain examples to do more, artistically, than required by their sponsors (for instance, Basil Wright's 1935 *Song of Ceylon*), sometimes to exceed their brief politically: 'For the second time the Gas, Light and Coke Company has undertaken a work which should have been the responsibility of the Ministry of Health . . . There is no propaganda in *Enough to Eat* any more than there was in *Housing Problems*.' He favourably compared the residents of the London slums interviewed by Ruby Grierson for *Housing Problems* (Arthur Elton and Edgar Anstey, 1935) with 'the frightened ironed-out personalities with censored scripts whom the BBC present as "documentary"'.[51]

Some of the documentarists' films (such as *Nightmail*, *Song of Ceylon* and *BBC – The Voice of Britain*) were registered under the quota legislation and received cinematic release; *Nightmail* was screened for three days at the newsreel cinema on Charing Cross Road (which appears in Arthur Wood's *They Drive by Night* – see Chapter 7). However, the 1930s saw an expansion of societies both making and screening films in a variety of venues: schools, universities and workplace clubs. The first national convention of amateur cine clubs was held in 1929. Schools were much discussed as both the subject and site of screenings, with the editor of *The Spectator* providing the commentary for *Children at School* (Basil Wright, 1938). The Film Society in London continued to present foreign films (often not otherwise available, or censored), and the new British documentaries: *Drifters* was well received. While Sir Stephen Tallents (in *The Projection of England* in 1932) and John Grierson (whom Tallents appointed to the EMB and took with him to the GPO in 1934) suggested that films should show more than 'one single mile within the Empire', many amateur film-makers were already taking their cameras and projectors beyond 'London and the West End'.[52]

Grierson's professional concern to 'treat actuality creatively' has its parallels in the photographic expeditions of Humphrey Spender and Bill Brandt, the Mass Observation campaigns led by Tom Harrisson and the sociologist Charles Madge, and the reportage of George Orwell's *The Road to Wigan Pier*. Joan Littlewood (see Chapter 9), with Ewan McColl, attended Ramblers' Rights demonstrations in the 1930s and recorded local songs and 'un-ironed-out' voices for the BBC. However, as John Taylor has indicated, the subjects of their work often resented the intrusion and did not care to be patronised, however well-intentioned the documentarists' motives.[53] Among the film-makers associated with the 'documentary movement' there were differences of opinion with regard to both stylistic aims and political objectives, Grierson, the stern Calvinist, seeking primarily to inform, Paul Rotha tending rather to encourage reform of the conditions he observed. Rachael Low notes that in *Shipyard* (1935) (made for Vickers Armstrong and the Orient Shipping Line), he reminds the viewer that unemployment awaits the Barrow-in-Furness workers after the completion of the order.[54] Both Rotha and Grierson thought Flaherty over sentimental and unduly preoccupied with the exotic and archaic. *The Spectator* recognised the danger of sentiment in a film about sheep farming in the Cheviots and preferred the plotting of Evelyn Spice's *Weather Forecast* (1934), made with the co-operation of the Air Ministry, the GPO and the BBC. Indeed, the themes which were most likely to appeal, as with the makers of actuality films at the beginning of the century (see Chapter 1), were those in which a logically ordered process and outcome could readily be discerned.[55] Like Orwell, many documentarists found manual labour and hunky, grimy male bodies especially photogenic.

Non-fiction production in the 1930s did not hold the prerogative over 'real' narratives and 'real' locations beyond Grierson's square mile. In Hitchcock's treatment of Joseph Conrad's 1907 *The Secret Agent*, *Sabotage*, the foreigner, Verloc (Oscar Homolka), is intent upon disrupting orderly English life and, worse, despatches a boy with the bomb (hidden in a nitrate film tin) which is intended for Piccadilly Circus underground station on the day of the Lord Mayor's Procession. As in *Blackmail*, our man from the Yard (John Loder) protects Verloc's murderer by pre-empting her admission of guilt and the weapon of choice is a much-featured knife. Balcon's production evades the political scope of the original which, like Graham Greene's 1939 rewriting of the same material, *The Confidential Agent*, acknowledges shared interests between similar classes of workers across international boundaries.

Walter Greenwood's 1933 novel, *Love on the Dole*, was considered potentially inflammatory and was not adapted for film until 1941, 'recalling one of the darker pages of our industrial history':[56] a girl, Sal (Deborah Kerr), agrees to a loveless attachment to the local fixer, Sam Grundy (Frank Cellier), as her only means of self-preservation – she's 'sick of vermin' – and the older women of the community (a recurrent chorus) are more sympathetic to her plight than judgmental of her course of action. *Hard Steel* (Norman Walker, 1942), from Roger Dataller's 1938 novel *Steel Saraband*, is set against similar back-to-back Northern terraces, with a manager pursuing personal ambition at the expense of the safety of the workers at the steel foundry. His wife reproaches him for his tyranny, but it takes a death and the onset of war to amend his values. Management and labour swear to give the country more steel and to co-operate: 'that's the answer!' Carol Reed's *The Stars Look Down* (1939), from the 1935 novel by A. J. Cronin, carries a prologue worthy of documentary: '. . . the story of simple working folk . . . of all time . . . men who take heroism for granted as part of daily life . . . the backbone of the nation . . . in all countries and at all times'. The workers of Neptune Colliery in Tynecastle warn of the danger of flooding; the owner disagrees and a strike ensues. The trade unionist, Davy Fenwick (Michael Redgrave), studies for a scholarship, a 'caring professional' in the making (see Chapter 7): 'I'm going to educate myself in college to fight for the working men.' In *Love on the Dole*, a Welsh activist tells his fellow workers: 'I'm trying to show you what capital is!', but they josh him for his proselytising and his talk of 'a better world' ('it's all talk,' says a woman, 'and where does it get us?'). Davy's younger brother, Hughie, hopes to escape the pit by becoming a footballer; Sal's younger brother in *Love on the Dole* similarly wants to be a footballer or a boxer. His mother is refused a bone for beef tea, his

When a working-class hero was something to be: *The Stars Look Down* (Carol Reed, 1939) on Davy Fenwick
(Michael Redgrave)

father and his mates smash and loot the butcher's shop and are imprisoned. Joe Garland (Emlyn
Williams) empties the till and sets himself up as a slick, sharp-suited bookie with a string of girls at
his beck and call. Davy, disappointed in love (Jenny has married him for social advancement),
perseveres with schoolmastering and nobly turns down private tuition in the evenings in order to
work for his degree (Varsity Boys, we are reminded, have life easier). Davy's mother sniffs at Jenny's
pretensions and Jenny deserts Davy for Joe. On the eve of the team trial, Hughie is trapped underground. There are shots of the pithead (in the style of *Spare Time*), silhouetted against the sky, and
shawled women (in the style of *Man of Aran*) are statically and stoically posed, awaiting news of
their loved ones. Davy returns with his mother, ready to see that the miners are justly represented.
With a grand flourish, the film's ending looks forward to a better future, in which the miner's son
and the owner's son will stand together.

Film-making in the 1930s was often prompted by hopes of social integration and equality. This tendency has generally been identified with the documentary movement but was also narrated in the productions realised by a number of studios. Certainly, it informed the activities of many producers, directors and writers who volunteered themselves for wartime service. Cinema, meanwhile, established itself as the most popular leisure activity with commercial exhibitors continuing to programme both fiction and non-fiction (documentary and newsreel material). Television, only partially introduced in the late 1930s, was not as yet a force to be reckoned with.

Man of Aran (Robert Flaherty, 1934)

Looking back on a lifelong career in films, the producer Michael Balcon singled out the contribution of the documentary movement in Britain for particular praise.[57] Certainly, *Man of Aran* presents a very different impression of Ireland from the Buggleskelly of *Oh! Mr Porter* or from the whimsical Scotland of Victor Saville's 1937 *Storm in a Teacup*. A number of members of the documentary movement in the 1930s (such as Cavalcanti) came to work with Balcon at Ealing in the 1940s (see Chapter 7). However, he acknowledged also that his own Gainsborough picture for Gaumont British, *Man of Aran*, was commonly referred to by the studio as 'Balcon's folly'.

The Irish American director, Robert Flaherty, established his credentials with the silent documentaries *Nanook of the North* (made in 1921, under the auspices of the fur traders Revillon Frères, about an Inuit community in Canada) and *Moana* (made in 1926 in Samoa). The subject of Aran appealed as a similar story of a 'desperate environment [in which] man fights for existence . . . until he meets his master . . . the sea'. John Grierson, with whom Flaherty made *Industrial Britain* (1931), suggested that the director's romantic vision was unsympathetic to more contemporary material:

> His flair for the old crafts and the old craftsmen was superb and there will never be shooting of that kind to compare with it; but he could not simply bend the conception of those other species of craftsmanship which go with modern industry and modern organisation.

However, he defended Flaherty's right, as an artist and poet, 'to distil life over a period of time and offer only the essence of it'.[58]

'For a thousand years', an intertitle informs us, the Man of Aran has searched crevices for soil in order to cultivate a meagre supply of crops. Maggie (Maggie Dirrane) struggles with her basket of seaweed against the driving wind, bent double under the weight; lambs are reared; fish are caught; shark are hunted; boats are plugged and tarred. Tiger (Colman King), Patch (Patch Ruadh), Maggie and Mikeleen (Michael Dillane) are celebrated as archetypal figures, the product of their harsh environment. Mikeleen and Maggie are shown silhouetted against the sky, staring out to sea awaiting the return of the men, as generations of women and children have waited. Tiger is shown in close-up in three-quarters, and the viewer is given ample time to ponder every line and furrow of this 'dramatic' face; at the end of the film, the family is isolated in the centre of the screen against a big sky, disappearing into the distance. There is much that is reminiscent of J. M. Synge's description of the islands a generation earlier:

> The absence of the heavy boot of Europe has preserved to these people the agile walk of the wild animal, while the general simplicity of their lives has given them many other points of physical perfection. Their way of life has never been acted on by anything much more artificial than the nests and burrows of the creatures that live round them, and they seem, in a certain sense, to approach more nearly to the finer types of our aristocracies – who are bred artificially to a natural ideal – than to the labourer or citizen, as the wild horse resembles the thoroughbred rather than the hack or cart-horse. Tribes of the same natural development are, perhaps, frequent in half-civilised countries, but here a touch of the refinement of old societies is blended, with singular effect, among the qualities of the wild animal.[59]

Unlike Brian Desmond Hurst's adaptation of Synge's *Riders to the Sea*, which used players from Dublin's Abbey Theatre and included an introductory note regarding accents and dialect, *Man of Aran* was filmed silent and subsequently dubbed in English by its Gaelic-speaking actors; *The Brothers* (David Macdonald, 1947) and *I Know Where I'm Going* (Michael Powell, 1945 – see Chapter 7) employed Gaelic to indicate the strangeness of off-shore islands to English-speaking newcomers. John Goldman, the assistant editor despatched by Balcon to hasten work on the rushes produced on the island, wrote the intertitles. As with Powell's 1937 *The Edge of the World*, a Celtic-style font is employed in the title sequence and W. L. Williamson's musical score, with singing from Glasgow's Orpheus choir, is a composite of orchestrated folk tunes; Arthur Elton routinely selected 'Over the Hills to Skye' for his 1931 documentary about salmon fishing, *Upstream*. Sometimes, in *Man of Aran*, there is just the sound of seagulls, wind and sea (as in Harry Watts' 1937 GPO film, shot in Cornwall, *The Saving of Bill Blewitt*), sometimes the music parallels the action (for instance, when the sea is calm or when Tiger lifts and smashes rocks). As in Walker's *The Turn of the Tide* (filmed in Yorkshire) and *Man at the Gate* (1941, filmed in Cornwall), also *The Brothers* (filmed on a Scottish island), there are expansive panning shots of the sea (frequently Flaherty used a whole magazine of film on one shot), pans up and down which emphasise the sheerness of the cliff face which Mikeleen scales and from which he spots the first shark. Another shark lurks beneath treacly black water. However, Grierson maintains that while Flaherty experimented with long focus lenses, filters and stocks, he rejected shots that were appreciated solely for their artful composition and photography and praises the rhythm of the film as being 'natural' rather than imposed.

In an article for *Film Weekly*, Balcon called for more films to be made which displayed the British landscape and in a round-table discussion for *The Listener* in 1932 he announced that filming in Ireland on *Man of Aran* was under way. But he soon became alarmed by the length of time that Flaherty was taking and the vast quantities of raw stock that he commandeered. Eventually, he visited the island to see for himself what the makeshift laboratory and editing rooms were producing. The film was three years in the making, the inordinate schedule (said Flaherty) partly the result of appalling weather. Other members of the crew said that Flaherty's obsessions and his lack of discipline accounted for the delay. Harry Watt, who along with John Taylor served an apprenticeship on Aran, recalled this formative experience:

> On the board when I arrived there was a piece of paper which said: 'Shots Wanted. Seagulls and Maggie on cliff'. When I left a year later this piece of paper was still on the board, and it was all the script I ever saw . . . Flaherty was primarily a cameraman and his direction was always subsidiary to photographing a set-up. He was inclined to shoot endlessly for photographic effect with little thought of continuity and cutting.[60]

Flaherty appointed Pat Mullen, a native of Aran, as his assistant and translator, and together they set out to search for 'dramatic faces', a quality which Mullen admitted, more often than not, eluded him. Mullen also arranged for the building of turf cottages to serve as sets for the filming and accommodation for the crew. Flaherty risked the lives of his actors by filming during storms and insisted on the shark hunt although the practice had long since been abandoned. An intertitle tells us that it takes two days to extract the oil needed for lamps and we are shown the cauldron in which it is rendered. The whole community gathers on the shore when the shark is landed. Not only was this considerable portion of the film an anachronism but it also took considerable time and trouble and caused the death or injury of numerous poor basking sharks. Although we are told that 'school upon school of these monsters' migrate every year to this coast, Mullen found it hard to track them down.

The activities of Flaherty in the big house which he appropriated for himself were the matter of much local gossip (and, subsequently, of Martin McDonagh's 1996 play, *The Cripple of Inishmaan*). People were initially suspicious of a visitor they supposed to be godless, then eager to supplement their pitiful income by offering services to help with the filming. His own supply of fancy tinned food prompted amazement.

The film was vigorously promoted prior to its release in April 1934, Balcon doubtless keen to recoup its excessive costs. Mullen and the cast were brought to London, where they visited the new BBC building and met Evelyn Laye (currently starring in *Princess Charming*). The Irish Guards band played for the opening at the New Gallery Theatre, a stuffed basking shark was exhibited in the window of the Gaumont British offices in Wardour Street and a Guinness Party organised. The cast appeared in costume for the premiere (and, says Mullen, was duly applauded and cheered by its society audience) and at its release in Dublin, with Mikeleen and Tiger returning to Britain to tour regional cinemas.[61] Feature films (such as *Turn of the Tide* and *Man at the Gate*) followed Flaherty's example. But the critical reception of *Man of Aran* was mixed. Its inauthenticity was noted, both in its staged material (the shark hunt) and its language (this was, as Flann O'Brien observed, a time when the real Gaelic was very much in vogue).[62] Graham Greene thought the film 'bogus and sentimental', comparing it unfavourably with a film about peasant farmers in Friesland, similarly struggling for their existence at the edge of the land with the sea; C. A. Lejeune, for once in agreement with Greene, complained that 'The real story . . . is the fight to hold the land against eviction – women and children gathering on the cliffs with stones and missiles, the police rowing out through a storm in open boats with orders to pull the roofs from cottages.'[63] Certainly, Flaherty makes no mention of the thousands of islanders, including Pat Mullen, driven by poverty and famine to migrate across the Atlantic in the hope of an easier life. Charles Davy, reviewing the film for *The Spectator*, notes that the islanders are presented in a series of magnificent photographic studies, 'more as figures in a landscape than as human beings' and notes the omission of poteen, dancing, schooling, communication with the mainland and the keeping of cattle, while scarcely touching the indoor life in the cottages. The magazine returned to the film with the publication of Pat Mullen's book about his involvement, Derek Verschoyle commenting that it 'is not often today that one's interest in a film is extended to the circumstances in which it was made', praising the courage of its participants while deploring the dangers and disasters to which Flaherty exposed them.[64] Lorna Hay summarises the discussion which the film provoked in her report for *Picture Post* of Flaherty's return to Aran in 1949, it having too much struggle with nature and not enough class struggle; too much sea and not enough long winter evenings:

> It over stressed the primitive and the picturesque. And, of course, it had *spoilt the island*. That was the worst of all. All sorts of people would know about it and might even actually go there. No one would ever again be certain of being the only man in Belsize Park to own a *criss* or the only girl in Kensington in *pampooties*. Civilisation was setting in and all would soon be lost.

But Hay concludes that jet propulsion and peanut butter are as responsible as Flaherty for changes in island life.[65]

Man of Aran seems interesting not only in that it illustrates the limitations of Flaherty's approach (that the camera does not infallibly reveal the entire truth of that which it records) but also in the debate which it initiates about documentary procedures and practice. As Lorna Hay and Martin McDonagh indicate, hoping that a film's subject will remain unmarked by the experience, for better or for worse, may prove a misplaced aspiration also.

Notes

1. See Allen Eyles, *British Gaumont Cinemas* (London: BFI, 1996), p. 212, for the Manchester Gaumont, now demolished; C. A. Lejeune comments on Buchan's approval and audience enthusiasm for *The Schoolmasters' and Women Teachers' Chronicle*, 27 June 1935, p. 1132.
2. Paul Rotha, *Celluloid: the Film Today* (London: Longmans, Green and Co., 1933) p. 72.
3. Donat archive, John Rylands Library, Manchester, FRD/6/1/1.
4. Stephen Guy, 'Calling All Stars: Musical Films in a Musical Decade', in Jeffrey Richards (ed.), *The Unknown 1930s: an Alternative History of the British Cinema 1929–39* (London: I. B. Tauris, 1998), p. 99.
5. Rachael Low, *The History of the British Film 1929–1939* (London: George Allen and Unwin, 1985), p. 75.
6. For a further discussion of sound and silent versions, see Tom Ryall, *Blackmail* (London: BFI, 1993), and Charles Barr, '*Blackmail*: Silent and Sound', *Sight and Sound* vol. 52 no. 2, 1983.

7. Low, *History of the British Film*, p. 190; John Sedgwick, *Popular Filmgoing in the 1930s* (Exeter: Exeter University Press, 2000).

8. Dean archive, John Rylands Library, Manchester, 4/5/2.

9. Asa Briggs, *The Golden Age of Wireless* (London: Oxford University Press, 1965), p. 548; see also Simon Frith, 'Northern Soul – Gracie Fields', *Music for Pleasure: Essays in the Sociology of Pop* (New York: Routledge, 1988), pp. 67–71.

10. J. B. Priestley, *English Journey* [1933] (London: Heron Books, 1949), p. 253, re. *Look Up and Laugh* and *Sing as We Go*.

11. Basil Wright, *The Spectator*, 13 March 1937.

12. Dean archive, 4/5/12.

13. Annette Kuhn, 'Cinema Culture and Femininity in the 1930s', in Gillian Swanson and Christine Gledhill (eds), *Nationalising Femininity* (Manchester: Manchester University Press, 1996), p. 178.

14. Priestley, *English Journey*, p. 402; Osbert Lancaster, *Progress at Pelvis Bay* (London: John Murray, 1936), cover panorama.

15. George Orwell, *The Road to Wigan Pier* [1937] (Harmondsworth: Penguin, 1975), p. 72; Stella Gibbons, *Cold Comfort Farm* [1932] (Harmondsworth: Penguin, 1979), p. 188 – and see also Dodie Smith, *I Capture the Castle* [1949] and Noel Streatfield, *Ballet Shoes* [1936] for similar rags to silver screen riches narratives; Rosamund Lehmann, *The Weather in the Streets* [1936] (London: Virago, 1981), pp. 293 and 344; Annette Kuhn, 'Jam Jars and Cliffhangers', *An Everyday Magic: Cinema and Cultural Memory* (London: I. B. Tauris, 2002), pp. 39–65, and John Ellis, 'British Cinema as Performance Art: *Brief Encounter, Radio Parade of 1935* and the Circumstances of Film Exhibition', in Justine Ashby and Andrew Higson (eds), *British Cinema: Past and Present* (London: Routledge, 2000), pp. 95–109.

16. Michael Balcon, *Michael Balcon Presents . . . A Lifetime of Films* (London: Hutchinson, 1969), p. 86.

17. 'Song of Freedom', *Film Weekly*, 6 March 1937, pp. 34–5.

18. Charles Davy, *The Spectator*, 15 June 1935, p. 920.

19. Andrew Higson, *Waving the Flag* (Oxford: Clarendon Press, 1995), p. 135.

20. Charles Davy, *The Spectator*, 15 June 1935, p. 920, and Low, *The History of the British Film*, p. 136.

21. Graham Greene, (ed.) John Russell Taylor, *The Pleasure Dome* (London: Secker and Warburg, 1972), p. 98. Here, and in *Escape Me Never*, Bergner's androgyny mirrors her previous roles in German films.

22. Donat archive, FRD 1/7/5.

23. Lancaster, *Progress at Pelvis Bay*, p. 20.

24. Lehmann, *The Weather in the Streets*, p. 233; *Beyond This Open Road* (B. Vivian Braun, 1934) features walkers, swimmers, cyclists and motorcyclists.

25. Edward Carrick, *Art and Design in the British Film* (London: Dennis Dobson, 1948), p. 131.

26. Greene, *The Pleasure Dome*, pp. 135–6; he nevertheless thought the sets for *Fire Over England* (1937) 'magnificent'. Greene's charming 1955 novella *Loser Takes All* was written for Korda as a mark of their friendship.

27. Balcon, *Michael Balcon Presents . . .*, p. 94, and Donat in *The Picturegoer*, 10 March 1951, p. 8, re. *Perfect Strangers* (see Chapter 6).

28. Michael Korda, *Charmed Lives: a Family Romance* (London: Allen Lane, 1980), pp. 72–3; Siegfried Kracauer, *From Caligari to Hitler* [1947] (Princeton: Princeton University Press, 1966), p. 49.

29. Charles Davy, *The Spectator*, 27 October 1933, p. 574.

30. C. A. Lejeune, *The Observer*, 21 October 1934; see Low, *The History of the British Film*, p. 143, for details of the collapse of high-budget costume dramas attempting to emulate *Henry*'s success.

31. Charles Davy, *The Spectator*, 2 February 1934, p. 235.

32. Cecil Beaton took publicity shots of Dietrich encased in dark furs for *Vogue*; Dietrich's role owes something to such late silent films as *The Tempest* (Sam Taylor, 1928) and much to her appearance as Catherine II in Sternberg's 1934 *The Scarlet Empress*.

33. Greene, *Night and Day*, 30 September 1937, in *The Pleasure Dome*, p. 170. Denham was also ambitiously decked-out as India's north-west frontier for *The Drum* (1938), again photographed by Périnal.

34. Greene, *The Pleasure Dome*, p. 170.

35. Charles Davy, *The Spectator*, 13 July 1934, p. 51.

36. Balcon, *Michael Balcon Presents . . .*, p. 99.

37. See François Truffaut, *Hitchcock* [1966] (London: Secker and Warburg, 1968), p. 75, and introduction to John Buchan, *Greenmantle* [1916] (Oxford: Oxford University Press, 1993), p. x, re. Hitchcock's decision to film *The 39 Steps* 'a smaller subject', 'in respect for a literary masterpiece': one is left to imagine what Hitch might have made of the glacial Hilda von Einem!

38. Kuhn, 'Cinema culture and femininity', p. 180; for 'luck as the vehicle of success' in the original version see Kracauer, *From Caligari to Hitler*, p. 213.

39. G. M. Boumphrey, 'This Foreign Stuff', *The Spectator*, 9 December 1932, p. 833; F. R. S. Yorke, *The Modern House* (London: Architectural Press, 1934) presents examples from America, Germany, France, Switzerland, Norway, Hungary and Czechoslovakia.

40. Herbert Read, *Art and Industry* (London: Faber and Faber, 1934), p. 1.

41. Balcon, *Michael Balcon Presents . . .*, p. 142; see also *Thirties: British Art and Design Before the War* (London: Arts Council of Great Britain, 1979) and Monja Danischewsky, *White Russian: Red Face* (London: Victor Gollancz, 1966), p. 141.

42. David Matless, *Landscape and Englishness* (London: Reaktion, 1998), p. 64; Timothy Mowl, *Stylistic Cold Wars* (London: John Murray, 2000), p. 55.

43. See, for instance, 'The Future of the BBC', *The Spectator*, 10 January 1931, pp. 36–7.

44. H. G. Wells, *Things To Come* (London: Cresset Press, 1935), p. 13.

45. Greene, *The Pleasure Dome*, p. 55, re. *Things To Come*, and pp. 97–8 re. *The Man Who Could Work Miracles*.

46. Kurt London, *Film Music* (London: Faber and Faber, 1936); see also Muir Mathieson (an indefatigable conductor for films), 'Developments in Film Music', *Penguin Film Review* 4, 1947, p. 41, and Roger Manvell, *Film* (London: Penguin, 1944), p. 63.

47. Balcon, *Michael Balcon Presents . . .*, p. 148.

48. Low, *Documentary and Educational Films*, p. 148.

49. Harry Watt, *Don't Look at the Camera* (London: Paul Elek, 1974), p. 91.

50. Peter Fleming, *The Spectator*, 1 August 1931, p. 153; see also John Grierson, 'The Future for British Films', *The Spectator*, 14 May 1932, pp. 691–2, and J. L. Myres, 'The Film in National Life', *The Spectator*, 11 June 1932, pp. 825–6; although Grierson is often credited with coining the term 'documentary', it was already in common usage in Europe.

51. Graham Greene, *The Spectator*, 16 October 1936; *The Pleasure Dome*, p. 108.

52. Grierson, 'The Future for British Films', p. 692.

53. John Taylor, 'Documentary Raids and Rebuffs', *A Dream of England* (Manchester: Manchester University Press, 1994), pp. 152–81.

54. Low, *Documentary and Educational Films*, p. 95.

55. Charles Davy, *The Spectator*, 30 March 1934, p. 502, and 2 November 1934, p. 670.

56. See Jeffrey Richards, *Best of British* (London: I. B. Tauris, 2002), pp. 169–70.

57. Balcon, *Michael Balcon Presents . . .*, p. 130.

58. Forsyth Hardy, *Grierson on the Movies* (London: Faber and Faber, 1981), pp. 173–4.

59. J. M. Synge, *The Aran Islands* (Oxford: Oxford University Press, 1979), pp. 24–5; BFI special materials, H28.

60. Harry Watt to Michael Balcon, 10 December 1951, Balcon archive, BFI special materials, H28.

61. Pat Mullen, *Man of Aran* (London: Faber and Faber, 1934), pp. 284–5.

62. Flann O'Brien (Brian O'Nolan), *The Poor Mouth* [*An Béal Bocht*, 1941], tr. Patrick C. Power (London: Grafton Books, 1986), pp. 46–61.

63. Greene, *The Pleasure Dome*, p. 14.

64. Charles Davy, *The Spectator*, 4 May 1934, p. 697; Derek Verschoyle, *The Spectator*, 19 October 1934, p. 576.

65. Lorna Hay, 'Flaherty Returns to Aran', *Picture Post*, 10 September 1949, pp. 21–3, 45; Hay reports that many of the islanders were still there, including Mullen and Maggie.

Chapter 6 | Second World War

To be brought up in Leeds in the forties was to learn early on the quite useful lesson that life is generally something that happens elsewhere. It is true that I was around in time for the Second World War but so far as Leeds was concerned that was certainly something that happened elsewhere. From time to time the sirens went and my brother and I were wrapped in blankets and hustled out to the air-raid shelter that stood outside our suburban front door, there to await the longed-for rain of bombs. Sheffield caught it, Liverpool caught it, but Leeds, it seemed, hardly ever. 'Why should it? I live here', was my reasoning, though there was a more objective explanation. The city specialised in the manufacture of ready-made suits and the cultivation of rhubarb and, though the war aims of the German High Command were notoriously quixotic, I imagine a line had to be drawn somewhere. Thus, in the whole course of hostilities, only a handful of bombs fell on Leeds, most of which did little damage and were promptly torn apart by schoolboys, famished for shrapnel.

Alan Bennett[1]

The Second World War was experienced differently across the various fronts abroad and among the British, émigré and foreign population at home. Films produced by the forces, by official departments and units, and in the commercial sector, addressed these concerns and responded to changes in war and the course of warfare in the duration (the phoney war, mobilisation, D-Day, the Blitz, the Battle of Britain, American entry to the war and Russian enlistment with the Allies, victory in North Africa). Often films describe the war as a personal rite of passage, set against a broader canvas (as in the redemption of Vivian Kennaway in Sidney Gilliat's 1945 *The Rake's Progress* or the resuscitation of Kathy and Robert in Alexander Korda's 1945 *Perfect Strangers*). This notion is revisited, in retrospect, in more recent films such as John Boorman's autobiographical 1987 *Hope and Glory*, Michael Radford's 1983 *Another Time, Another Place*, David Leland's 1997 *Landgirls* and Michael Apted's 2001 *Enigma*. As an instrument of positive and negative propaganda, film policy responded to the needs of the state and to audience reception (extensively reported for Mass Observation); sometimes there was direct intervention from Winston Churchill, First Lord at the Admiralty from 1939 and subsequently Minister of Defence and Prime Minister of the wartime coalition government. As Philip Taylor observes:

Theo Kretschmar-Schuldorff (Anton Walbrook) interned in a POW camp in Derbyshire in *The Life and Death of Colonel Blimp* (Michael Powell, 1943)

The Second World War [a war of political ideologies between mass societies] witnessed the greatest propaganda battle in the history of warfare. For six years, all the participants employed propaganda on a scale that dwarfed all other conflicts . . . [T]he continued development of the communications revolution had, since the advent of sound cinema and radio, provided a direct link between those they governed, and between the government of one nation and the people of another. Propaganda was in this respect the alternative to diplomacy.[2]

Here and Now

As a source of both information and entertainment, across all war fronts, radio was more immediately and more broadly significant than cinema.[3] Important wartime broadcasts are repeatedly intercut in film soundtracks, as if to indicate a shared and unifying memory, and often appear in historic reconstructions to evoke a particular moment. In Noël Coward's stageplay and film *This Happy Breed* (David Lean, 1944), the Gibbonses are gathered together in Clapham in 1936 to hear of the approaching death of George V, whereas in E. M. Delafield's *Time and Tide* serial 'The Provincial Lady in Wartime', on 3 September 1939, the wireless is placed on the pulpit in the village church.[4] In *Men of the Lightship* (David MacDonald, 1940), the radio continues to broadcast even when the crew has taken to the lifeboat; in *Millions Like Us* (Frank Launder/Sidney Gilliat, 1943) and *Listen to Britain* (Humphrey Jennings, 1942) the mobilised women listen to 'Workers' Playtime' while rhythmically performing their duties on the factory assembly line and in *Desert Victory* (Roy Boulting, 1942) women armament workers cheer: 'That'll show 'em . . . there's plenty more where that came from' when British and Forces Radio announces Rommel's full retreat. *49th Parallel* (Michael Powell, 1941), the only feature film made during the war with Ministry of Information backing, contrasts the 'truth' of Canadian radio reports with the 'lies' perpetrated in Germany. The documentarist Humphrey Jennings shows a number of different radio sets in *A Diary for Timothy* (1945), broadcasting news, music and the anthems of the Allied Nations to homes and a convalescent home, while in *A Matter of Life and Death* (Michael Powell, 1946), radio coverage of cricket matches (in Britain) and of dance music (in America) is used 'in evidence' presented before a celestial grand jury. *Listen to Britain* honours the BBC, 'sending truth on its journey round the world', features a concert in the National Gallery (with the Queen in the audience) and intercuts Flanagan and Allen on stage and on the airwaves with broadcasts in different languages 'with special best wishes to those serving abroad on land, sea and air and in the merchant navy'. 'There's That Man Again', says Tiny (John Mills) in *The Way to the Stars* (Anthony Asquith, 1945) at the sound of a siren, quoting comedian Tommy Handley's famous catchphrase from the radio show, ITMA (*It's That Man Again*); the cellist, Beatrice Harrison, repeats her radio performance, playing to a nightingale in Asquith's 1943 *The Demi-Paradise*. Knitting mothers and their families in blacked-out houses throughout Britain, in crofts, cottages, parlours and salons, are shown huddled around Bakelite boxes eagerly or anxiously awaiting news of their nearest and dearest overseas.

While many writers and film-makers were keen to volunteer their services at the outbreak of war, they sometimes found the MoI strangely reluctant to enlist them and the corridors and offices of London University's Senate House (requisitioned as its headquarters – hence its appropriation as the hub of propaganda in Michael Radford's adaptation of Orwell's *1984* [see Chapter 11]) proved hard to fathom. Delafield's Provincial Lady, up in town from the country, spent months in a canteen under the Adelphi, awaiting notice of her Important War Work ('What is the MoI for if it doesn't *tell* one much?'); Evelyn Waugh's Basil Seal, with a past matching that of Vivian Kennaway, finds the MoI in *Put Out More Flags* (1942) full of amateurs and incompetents, not knowing what to do;[5] George Orwell himself was hired to write directives in an expedient argot ominously reflected in newspeak and made broadcasts to the nation for the BBC. Much of the information subsequently supplied by the Ministry was hardly likely to be warmly received, even if rendered more palatable by the humour of Richard Massingham in such shorts as *The Five Inch Bather* (1942). Harry Watt, employed with the GPO Film Unit in the 1930s (see Chapter 5), describes how he and others seized the initiative in the apparent absence of official direction:

[It was] then that Cavalcanti, magnificent old Cav, the alien, whom some Blimps always suspected, took the law into his own hands and sent us all into the streets to film anything we saw that was new and different. Cavalcanti realised that history was being made all around us and a tremendous opportunity to record it for posterity was being lost, so six small units went out with all our film stock and filmed the extraordinary scenes of a nation amateurishly preparing its capital for a new kind of war. We filmed the frantic sandbag filling, new balloons rising up in the oddest places, endless drilling in parks, new auxilliary policemen – I remember I got a chap in plus-fours and a monocle directing traffic at Piccadilly Circus – anything that was different from the normal peacetime way of life.[6]

The First Days (1939) was bought from the GPO and distributed by Pathé, in anticipation of audience interest. People go to church on the first Sunday in September, or take to the countryside on bikes. The declaration of war is heard on the radio in a café, at home, in church or over a loudspeaker in the street. Barrage balloons are sent up, sirens go off and, good humouredly, Londoners descend to the shelters (where there is yet more knitting) with the streets swamped by an almost absolute darkness: for the first time since Cromwell, the theatre lights are dimmed in the West End, while in the East End, nothing can stifle the cockney voice of London. Pets are labelled and evacuated and the National Gallery's paintings are safely removed to slate mines in Wales. The sound of London – 'London Calling' – continues to be transmitted around the world. Made prior to American entry to the war (but in the hope of enlisting support), *London Can Take It* (GPO, 1940) is introduced and narrated by the London correspondent for the journal *Collier's Weekly*, Quentin Reynolds; meanwhile, American female readers were greatly impressed by Jan Struther's Mrs Miniver column in *The Times*, subsequently filmed with Greer Garson as its resourceful heroine (William Wyler, 1942).[7] The blackness of night, as in Jennings' *Fires Were Started* (US, Crown, 1943), is only briefly interrupted by flashes of searchlight and smoke. The Queen is shown surveying the damage to the streets (a cat is saved from the rubble) and the film ends with a shot of the shattered Gothic tracery of the Houses of Parliament. However, its central theme is the heroism and indomitable spirit of ordinary people, who, like 'great fighters, get up from the floor when they are knocked down', 'repudiating Goebbels' claim that British morale is diminished'.

The commercial sector was quicker and keener in its response. Balcon, endorsing widespread criticism of the MoI, told Beddington (head of the film unit from 1940 to 1946 and formerly Director of Publicity for Shell [see Chapter 5]) that 'the primary function of the Films Division is to get films made and not to make them';[8] the documentarist, Paul Rotha, and Mass Observation's Tom Harrisson, urged that account should be taken of the impact of information films on their intended audiences.[9] Sidney Bernstein, who held extensive commercial interests in British cinema and had previously collaborated with Ivor Montagu in the Film Society (see Chapter 4), was appointed as special adviser to the MoI's film division. Adrian Brunel (see Chapter 4) duly directed *Food for Thought* (1940) (a film instructing viewers about nutrition) and *Salvage with a Smile* (1940) (advising against the waste of scrap paper, metal and bones) for Ealing.

Established pre-war successes were enrolled for wartime service in both short and feature film production. The popular comedian, Will Hay, appeared in *The Goose Steps Out* (Will Hay/Basil Dearden, 1942), while *Let George Do It* (Marcel Varnel, 1940) was an Ealing vehicle for George Formby (see Chapter 5). Tommy Trinder was cast in Ealing's *The Foreman Went* to *France* (Charles Frend, 1942), scripted by J. B. Priestley from the real-life story of a Welsh foreman snatching vital machinery from the Germans during the withdrawal in 1940 to Dunkirk: in his BBC *Postscript* broadcasts, Priestley described Dunkirk (characterised by the role played by the good ship *Gracie Fields* – see Chapter 5) as a typically British, or rather English, epic.[10] Trinder also appeared in *The Bells Go Down* (Basil Dearden, 1943), in the recruitment film *Laugh it Off* (John Baxter, 1940) and, to promote the Ministry of Food's new restaurants, *Eating Out with Tommy Trinder* (Strand, 1941).The familiar 1930s double-act, Arthur Lucan and Kitty McShane, appeared in *Old Mother Riley Joins Up* (P. Maclean Rogers, 1939), Naunton Wayne and Basil Radford (Caldicott and Charters from Hitchcock's 1938 *The Lady Vanishes* [see Chapter 5]) reappear in *Night Train to Munich* (Carol Reed, 1940) and *Millions Like Us*, while Gordon Harker and Alastair Sim, in a series drawn from a radio original, teamed up for *Inspector Hornleigh Goes To It* (Walter Forde, 1941). Hornleigh initially thinks that he has been seconded to investigate a fifth column, only to find, to his chagrin (and with no disparagement of actual GPO staff), that he is to make enquiries into the theft of stocks and provisions. His sidekick, Sergeant Bingham, is urged to remember the wartime mantra, 'Dangerous Talk Costs Lives' ('Have you been talking in your sleep?' asks Hornleigh), and not to trust all the pretty faces by which he has been all too readily seduced ('She's totally innocent,' asserts Bingham of Daisy Johnson; 'What, after an afternoon with you in a punt?' queries Hornleigh).

During the war, or in its immediate aftermath, personalities engaged in forces' entertainment (either in regular service, or as part of Basil Dean's Entertainments National Service Association, or in public service broadcasting) moved between stage, radio and screen: 'Aren't we going to have an ENSA concert?' jokes Parsons (Hugh Burden) when his company find themselves in a godforsaken Mediterranean café in *The Way Ahead* (Carol Reed, 1944). Jack Warner contributed to Workers' Playtime before establishing himself in film and television (see Chapter 7). Joyce Grenfell translated her ENSA experiences, entertaining and maintaining morale among Allied troops abroad, into a sketch for a Noël Coward revue in 1945, which also produced a gymslip role, revived for Miss Gossage in *The Happiest Days of Your Life* (Frank Launder, 1950) and the unrequited policewoman, Ruby Gates, in three of Launder and Gilliatt's *St Trinians* series (1954–7). The Goons (prisoner of war slang for German guards – see, for instance, Guy Hamilton's 1954 *The Colditz Story*) appeared collectively on BBC radio and then separately on screen from the 1950s onwards (see Chapter 8). Walter Forde directed ITMA's team in *It's That Man Again* (1942) and Bud Flanagan appeared in *Dreaming* (John Baxter, 1944), entertaining the masses and outwitting a fascist conspiracy.

However, even though the early commercial films were broadly quite well received at the time of release, they caused embarrassment among critics as the war wore on. Dilys Powell, in 1947, recalls the 'complacency' of Korda's *The Lion Has Wings* (Michael Powell/Brian Desmond Hurst/Adrian Brunel, 1939), showing 'with a naïveté which makes one shudder today, a German air-attack on London frustrated by the height of a balloon barrage'.[11] *Pimpernel Smith* (1941), starring and directed by Leslie Howard (who was tragically killed in an aircrash in 1943), traded on his own success in Korda's 1934 *The Scarlet Pimpernel* (directed by Harold Young); David Niven appeared in Powell and Pressburger's version of the Baroness Orczy original in 1950. Howard's film is presented as fantasy – 'but based on the exploits of courageous men who have, and are, risking their lives . . . champions of freedom against Nazism'. In Berlin in 1939, a Jewish research scientist (who displays a picture of Marx in his laboratory) is mysteriously smuggled to safety and his friend, the writer Kozlowsky, is suspected of complicity in the escape. Meanwhile, in Cambridge, Horatio Smith (Howard), an academic archaeologist, concerns himself with the dust accumulating on a statue of Aphrodite in the Museum of Antiquities. He joshes with the attendant – he is no Visigoth (that is, an ascendant of the Hun) intent upon the desecration of beauty. Smith then enlists a group of students, among them an American, on an expedition to 'Romantic Germany'. Smith convincingly masquerades as the archetypal absent-minded professor at a society reception, hosted by his brother George, a diplomat: here he encounters Kozlowsky's daughter, Ludmilla (Mary Morris), who is working as a double agent. The Nazis are played as buffoons, failing to appreciate the British sense of humour ('their secret weapon') and are consistently outwitted by Smith's guises and disguises. The students pose as a party of journalists (allowed to examine conditions in a concentration camp) in order to free Kozlowsky. Against a rousing and rising score, Smith recites from Rupert Brookes' 'Home Thoughts from Abroad'. Cornered at a railway station near the border, on the eve of the invasion of Poland, Smith is confronted by General von Graum (Francis L. Sullivan). Smith speaks portentously (in encroaching close-up) of 'the wilderness of misery and hatred' for which the Nazis are accountable; as von Graum bends to pick up a dropped shard (no proof of Aryan civilisation whatsoever, says Smith), Smith disappears into the darkness and only his voice remains: 'Don't worry – I shall be back – we shall all be back.'

Howard is similarly cast by Powell and Pressburger as Philip Armstrong Scott, the aesthete explorer in *49th Parallel* (MoI and Rank). When the Nazi fugitives first encounter him, he is sitting in a boat, on a lake, fishing: 'A nuisance, the war,' he muses, mildly; 'in the Rockies the war seems so remote'. Kommandant Hirth (Eric Portman) disapproves of Scott's tastes, finding Thomas Mann and the copies of Matisse and Picasso with which he travels (and his research of native Americans) degenerate. Scott, on the other hand, finds nothing superior in Goebbels' tribal leadership and the repeated declamation of Hitler. The Kommandant accuses him of being a coward for not retaliating with violence: he retains his equanimity when his pictures and papers are destroyed – 'you're behaving like spiteful little schoolboys' – and receives a shot in the leg to ensure that no bullets are left to cause further harm. 'You can't expect me to go after an armed Nazi without getting hurt a bit,' he says, suggesting the unfairness of the match, meanwhile giving one of Hirth's men a hefty thump. The action of *49th Parallel* is located across the border between Canada and the United States, with a score by Ralph Vaughan Williams which contributes (as with Charles Frend's 1948 *Scott of the Antarctic*) to a sense of a vast, open frontier. Although production began prior to American entry to the war, it is an American, Andy Brock (Raymond Massey), who returns Hirth to the Allies as a prisoner: Brock tacitly sides with 'the dirty little democracies' which Hirth despises.

Then and There

The plight of small countries far away, of which Britain knew little at the outbreak of war, was increasingly brought to public attention as the hostilities continued. *Picture Post* recorded the activities of actual refugees in London while *Dangerous Moonlight* (Brian Desmond Hurst, 1941) cast Austrian émigré Anton Walbrook as the gushingly romantic lead, a Polish pianist fleeing to America in 1939 and then coming to Britain to join the RAF during the Battle of Britain.[12] Joyce Grenfell, friend and onetime professional partner to Richard Addinsell, the composer of its score, describes its effect on audiences:

> '[T]he Warsaw Concerto' from *Dangerous Moonlight* was famous and had become a favourite with troops and especially the RAF. It is romantic music with clear, strong tunes. The theme was played by concert pianists, dance-band pianists and by ear on lamentable canteen uprights through the length and breadth of Britain, and was continually broadcast. I heard it in every form and, like the rest of the listening public, I whistled it, hummed it and loved it.[13]

Paul Soskin's 1942 *The Day Will Dawn* and *Men of Norway* (March of Time, 1942) were made as a tribute to the Norwegian Resistance, while Belgium's struggle against occupation was honoured in Asquith's *Uncensored* (1942) and in *Against the Wind* (Charles Crichton, 1948). George King's 1942 *Tomorrow We Live* was made with the co-operation of the Free French, while the French Resistance was commemorated by Hitchcock (for the MoI). *School for Danger* (made by the RAF Film Unit in 1947) reported, in the security of peacetime, the wartime underground activities in France of two British agents; *Carve Her Name With Pride* (Lewis Gilbert, 1958) honoured the service in France of agent Violette Szabo (see Chapter 8). *One of Our Aircraft is Missing* (Michael Powell/Emeric Pressburger, 1942) finds supporters of Dutch Resistance tuning in to the BBC and Pat Jackson's 1944 *Western Approaches* (shot in Technicolor by Jack Cardiff for the Crown Film Unit), reproducing an encounter between the Royal Navy and a German U-boat, was made with the co-operation of the Royal Netherlands Navy. In *The Gentle Sex* (directed by the Hungarian émigré, Leslie Howard, 1943), a Czech girl in the ATS reminds the others that she knows what it is to be free whereas they do not and do not know what the war really means: 'the French cheer British bombs'; 'You don't know the filth of the Gestapo – the misery'. In John Baxter's 1941 *Let the People Sing* (from a J. B. Priestley script), Alistair Sim played a Czech refugee. Meanwhile, in *The New Lot* (Army Kinematograph Service, 1943), a military training film trailing *The Way Ahead*, a Czech soldier, separated from his wife and children, urges five raw recruits to remember 1938 (when Neville Chamberlain pursued a policy of appeasement with Hitler): 'we are all together . . . millions of us'. Exteriors shot in Wales doubled for Yugoslavia in *Undercover* (directed by the Russian émigré, Sergei Nolbandov, 1943) and, at the suggestion of Humphrey Jennings, the Crown Film Unit travelled to Cymgiedd in the Swansea Valley to honour the Czech village of Lidice, which 'lit in the Fascist darkness a lamp that shall never be put out'. Jennings' *The Silent Village* (1943) restages events of June 1942 (the assassination of Heydrich and the subsequent Nazi reprisals) as if they had occurred in Wales. The Morristown Male Voice Choir, singing or humming, provided much of the film's diegetic and non-diegetic soundtrack. *Picture Post* described the procedure:

> Before he could compose a script, the miners had already taken charge and the film was evolving itself. The Unit's cameramen, assistant directors and electricians arrived for their four months' stay at the village and looked for a hotel . . . instead the miners gave them hospitality in their homes and so the unique situation arose that the men making the film formed part of the life they were recording . . . To such an extent did the Welsh miners identify themselves with the Czechs that in the film they decided to use their own names. Williams, miner, Evans, miners' agent and Powell, grocer, are all there taking parts in the film that they live in reality.[14]

Like Czech children, the children of Cymgiedd receive lessons in their own language (though some in the village might remember English suppression of the native tongue) and watch Disney cartoons when their lessons are done; men play cards in the pub and a woman prepares for her wedding (much in the manner of *Spare Time* [1939]). A state of emergency is declared with the Nazi invasion (a loudhailer mounted on a car mechanically, anonymously, barks out instructions): anyone sheltering Jews or Bolsheviks will be destroyed. Secret assignations are made in the mountains. Resistance supporters sabotage the mine and the 'Deputy Reich Protector' is assassinated. Court martials are held and sentences passed while the radio reports the continuation of the Reich. But in front and back parlours and shops, the people remain impassive and indomitable. Defiantly, the singing continues as the men are lined up against the cemetery wall and summarily executed. But the name of the village cannot be washed away – the name of the community is not obliterated

Pastor Niemöller (Wilfred Lawson) confronts Nazi authority (Bernard Miles and Marius Goring) in *Pastor Hall* (Roy Boulting, 1940)

but immortalised – it lives in the hearts and minds of miners the world over – and the river carries with it the traces of the people's lives.

Before the Blitz, films set in the present were made which drew a distinction between 'good' and 'bad' Germans. In both *49th Parallel* and *Pastor Hall* (Roy Boulting, 1940) their goodness is conveyed by their Christian faith, contrasted with the heretical idolatry of Nazism. In the latter, children in a typical Bavarian village (the buildings are half-timbered and the skirts are floral and dirndl) are taught devotion to the Führer once the Nazis assume authority. In the former, in Canada, Hirth and his men encounter an egalitarian Hutterite community – their leader Peter (Anton Walbrook) sits among them undistinguished and unsaluted. A girl, Anna (Glynis Johns), has lost her mother after the ship in which she was fleeing to Britain was torpedoed and her father, too, has been killed by the Nazis. Peter tells Hirth that he should feel ashamed to call himself German: 'we are not your brothers'; 'our children are free to grow up as children without being forced into uniforms'. Hirth responds by quoting Bismarck (discipline and order should overcome emotion) and by asserting the supremacy of the Nordic race. One of the fugitives wants to join the community but is court-martialled and sentenced to death before Hirth and the others resume their journey.

Pastor Hall, a dramatisation of the persecution of Pastor Niemöller, was submitted by the Boultings for official approval in July 1939, but was refused permission to go into production until the outbreak of war.[15] The kindly village priest, Friedrich Hall (Wilfred Lawson), refuses to inform on his parishioners to the local officer, Fritz (Marius Goring), and continues to denounce Nazism from the pulpit. An elderly Jewish couple are evicted and their shop is destroyed. Lena, a young girl, returns from a youth training camp having been raped by a boy who is the nephew of a statesman (and who will therefore not be prosecuted): knowing that she will not survive her pregnancy and that an abortion would be considered a crime against the state, Lena takes her own life. Hall is imprisoned for his resistance but one stormtrooper, Heinrich (Bernard Miles), recognising the Pastor and recalling his past kindness, helps him to escape. The party has meanwhile installed its own priest in the village. However, Hall returns to the church again and addresses the people one last time, speaking to them of righteousness – 'the voice *will* be heard' – before walking calmly and alone (as the music rises) to his certain death.

While some films refer to the current war being fought by other nations, other films are concerned with past wars in which Britain has achieved victory. In the past there were good Germans too. Sometimes the past is invoked in order to render the present as distinct and modern (I am thinking here of the Chelsea pensioners intermittently bemoaning the demise of the Gloucesters [the 'Dogs'] in *The Way Ahead*, or the older generation of Coward's *This Happy Breed* and *In Which We Serve* [1942]). The distinction appears most emphatically in *The Life and Death of Colonel Blimp* (Michael Powell, 1943), although, as in *Pastor Hall* and *This Happy Breed* (which opens with Frank Gibbons [Robert Newton] returning to his wife, Ethel [Celia Johnson], demobbed after the Great War), we are reminded that even old soldiers and armchair soldiers were once young.

Colonel Blimp, as Angus Calder observes, was a common figure of fun, especially for the *Daily Mirror*, the specific pre-war derivation for the Powell and Pressburger film being the David Low cartoons which appeared in the *Evening Standard* from 1934;[16] Captain Waggett of the Home Guard (Basil Radford) in *Whisky Galore!* (Alexander Mackendrick, 1948), based on an actual incident, is another example of the type.[17] During the war, Ralph Richardson played Blimp in radio broadcasts to America. Powell's General Clive Wynne-Candy (Roger Livesey), in 1943 a grand old man in retirement, trains men for service: he is sufficiently regarded and established to find himself on the front cover of *Picture Post* but a broadcast recorded for the BBC is deemed ill-timed and inexpedient with the accession of Pétain (the collaborator) to the premiership in France, and is duly replaced by one of J. B. Priestley's 'Postscripts'. However, he is outwitted by an impudent young officer, Lieutenant 'Spud' Wilson (James McKechnie), the boyfriend of Wynne-Candy's ATS driver Angela 'Johnny' Cotton (Deborah Kerr), who refuses to play by the rules of his war game ('War begins at midnight!' he splutters in his bath). Spud replies that in this war the enemy has invalidated the old rules, and that Wynne-Candy's professional code, 'clean fighting and honest soldiering', has been dishonoured (he cites Pearl Harbor as an instance); what is now required is initiative and, if needs be, subterfuge. When Spud mocks Wynne-Candy's walrus moustache, the film flashes back to a younger Wynne-Candy in the same London club (even then with its older members), disclosing how he came to acquire this memento of his own youthful bravura and disobedience. During the Boer War, Wynne-Candy (already awarded a Victoria Cross) defies the advice of his superiors and goes to Berlin to counter German propaganda against the British in South Africa. Here he meets a spirited English governess, Edith Hunter (Deborah Kerr), and, at a public gathering, insults a German official. Lots are drawn to decide who will confront Wynne-Candy in a duel, to restore German honour. While Edith waits in the snow in a carriage, Wynne-Candy and Oberleutnant Theo Kretschmar-Schuldorff (Anton Walbrook) face each other with sabres. Wynne-Candy receives the scar which his prodigious moustache disguises, but, during his convalescence, befriends Theo and sacrifices his love for Edith in his favour. Meanwhile, Edith continues to assert that German reporting of the war is false. Again, in Flanders during the Great War, Wynne-Candy claims that German and British methods of conducting warfare are different, but his personal affection for Theo is sustained, enquiring for news of him from officers in the same regiment. His batman, Murdoch (John Laurie), remains in his service after the war.

Wynne-Candy discovers a young nurse, Barbara (Deborah Kerr, again), whom he later marries, and tracks Theo to a prisoner of war camp in Derbyshire: but Theo, in defeat, will not now see him. 'How odd they are, how queer', says Barbara, of the Germans; 'writing beautiful music and poetry then suddenly bombing undefended ships and butchering children'. Back at home, Theo at first thinks that anti-militarism in Britain provides the raft which will allow for rearmament, but subsequently finds himself at odds with the Germany of Hitler: his Nazi children reject him and fail to attend Edith's funeral. He seeks solace in England and Clive's friendship (Barbara, too, has died, but not in a foreign country, Wynne-Candy insists, imperiously, but in Jamaica). Wynne-Candy offers Theo sanctuary as an enemy alien. In an air-raid, his house is destroyed and Murdoch is killed (in this war, there is no sanctuary). A water tank is constructed in its place and Wynne-Candy, sentimentally, pathetically even, ponders a leaf floating on its surface: 'Now here's the lake and I still have not changed'. The end titles of the film reiterate the archaic tapestry of its opening, while the march tune of the British Grenadiers (to which Wynne-Candy salutes) gives way to a dance band, the popular music of the masses in a Britain which looks more (it is suggested) to the new world of democratic America than to the old world and old hierarchies and dominions of Europe. Churchill, however, thought that the film, while still in production, was likely to prove 'detrimental to the morale of the army' and, as Jeffrey Richards has described, attempted to intervene in its release. But by the end of 1942, the war had turned in Britain's favour, and *Blimp* was well rewarded at the box office.[18]

Selznick's evocative Civil War epic, *Gone With the Wind* (Victor Fleming, 1939), with British actors Leslie Howard and Vivien Leigh, proved the most consistent box-office success of the war, playing continuously.[19] It rocketed Leigh (hired out by Korda to Selznick) to stardom. Nelson and Trafalgar was, reputedly, suggested to Korda by Winston Churchill himself as a subject and so satisfied was he with the result (*That Hamilton Woman*, 1941) that he kept a copy of the film in his bunker and took it with him on expeditions abroad.[20] 'As before and since in her history', wrote

Churchill, 'the Royal Navy alone seemed to stand between the island and national destruction.'[21] Nelson, costumed by Cecil Beaton, appeared also in Carol Reed's 1942 *The Young Mr Pitt* (the story of the Prime Minister who despatched him to his final, fatal battle and remained in office at the cost of his own health). Both Pitt and Nelson figured in propaganda campaigns throughout the war.[22] Robert Donat (as Pitt) appeared also in celebratory radio broadcasts, delivering speeches from the film. *Picture Post* found obvious the parallels between Pitt and Churchill, 'as England's men of destiny in hours of national danger'.[23] Korda (like Rattigan thereafter) appreciated the story as a conflict between Nelson's domestic life and his career as a naval hero, casting Leigh and her partner Laurence Olivier as the romantic couple. The story is told in flashback by Emma Hamilton, now destitute, Nelson's 'bequest to the nation' long forgotten. The successive injuries sustained and honours garnered mark his progress: 'they told us of your victories but not of the price you paid', she says. Olivier is painstakingly photographed with shadows masking the supposedly blind eye. Much is made of the contrast between Nelson's dowdy estranged wife and his vivacious, glamorous mistress, publicity emphasising the number and extravagance of Leigh's costumes. While Horatio is bold in his conduct of military strategy, Emma, equally regardless of correct social form and convention, determines to stand by him. 'I know that I must not come back,' he confides, passionately, 'and that nothing in this world will keep me away.' Snooty Lady Nelson thinks her a common adventuress and finds Emma's mother merely vulgar (a stock character role for Sarah Allgood). Korda employs devices standard to historical films of the period, intercutting engravings as establishing shots, framing shots with reference to familiar paintings (and allowing ample exposure of Olivier's manly chest), subtitling key dates and directly quoting from reported speech. Flags signal 'England Expects'. The lush, surging orchestral score incorporates strains from the National Anthem as Nelson nears his death. The Young Mr Pitt appoints various grooms, hawkers and boot-blacks to comment on the action (in the manner of the kitchen hands in Korda's 1933 *The Private Life of Henry VIII* [see Chapter 5]). Both films, it should be noted, are advisedly careful of Allies' sensibilities, distinguishing between Napoleon (the tyrant), the excesses of the Revolutionary mob and French moderates with whom Britain can do business.

Laurence Olivier returned to the screen to direct and star in Two Cities' *Henry V* (1944), largely filmed in Ireland. This was pageantry on a grand scale, matched on the streets of London in 1942 by Basil Dean's *Cathedral Steps* performed at St Paul's (with Martita Hunt, Eric Portman, Sybil Thorndike, Edith Evans, Marius Goring [as Henry V], Dennis Noble [singing 'Drake's Drum'] and Leslie Howard [reciting Nelson's prayer before Trafalgar]) and shadowed in the modest amateur theatricals recorded by *Picture Post*, in *The Way to the Stars* and *The Demi-Paradise*.[24] Noël Coward's 1947 stageplay, *Peace in Our Time,* reiterates the potency of such figures as Nelson and Shakespeare in the nation's mythology.[25] Olivier's film opens with a dedication to the commandos and airborne troops of Great Britain, before capturing a wind-blown scrap of paper announcing a performance at Shakespeare's Globe Theatre in 1600, with London presented in overview as a model. A prologue, performed on the theatre's stage (in which Henry is reminded of his duty to defend his European territories), gives way to studio-staged exteriors ('eke out our performance with your mind', urges the chorus in voiceover). 'No King of England, if not a King of France!' is here, in the wake of German occupation, a slogan of deliverance. William Walton's score incorporates a 'Song of the Auvergne' as background to the film's stylised French settings. The King's performance, incognito, as 'Henry le Roy' and his rendition, as King and Commander, of the Saint Crispin speech on the morning of battle (the English archers facing extraordinary odds) serve as a reminder of similar unequal victories, at sea, at the River Plate in December 1939 and, in the air, in the Battle of Britain of August 1940.

The Many and the Few

Depictions of the total war frequently resort to typical metaphors of the struggle at home and abroad. *This Happy Breed* opens and closes with an aerial shot of London terraces, establishing one house selected among its neighbours: 'there are worse things than being ordinary', Frank lectures his uppity daughter, Queenie (Kay Walsh).[26] While the documentarists took to the streets, many feature film productions favoured the lanes and pastures of an idyllic countryside, endorsing the *Picture Post* series 'What We Are Fighting For'.[27] In *Spy for a Day* (Mario Zampi), scripted by Emeric Pressburger (and in production September 1939), we are presented with a biscuit-tin picture of thatched cottages, orchards and oasthouses under the film's credits. A montage of images of armies parading, newspaper headlines and posters, and subsequent archival footage, refer the viewer back to the major events of 1914, when Sam Gates (the comedian Duggie Wakefield), a Yorkshire farmer's lad, finds himself cast as the idiot in an Essex village, rejected for military service (he's C3).With only his pet goat, George, for company (who makes brisk work of the fake roses and ivy around the villagers' doors), Sam harbours secret intentions on the village postmistress, Martha Clowes (Paddy Browne), to whom he has not yet dared to propose ('In the last ten years, I haven't got it out'). Everything is about to change. A German plane lands in the cabbage field and the pilot, mistaking Sam for the agent Paul Juperts (in the familiar manner of 1930s doppelgängers), kidnaps him and lifts him to occupied France: in a similar cabbage patch episode in Boorman's *Hope and Glory*, middle-aged women pillage the grounded parachute for scraps of silk while the eldest daughter is more interested in the pilot himself, while in Michael Frayn's novel *Spies* (2002) a fallen pilot is tragically misidentified and in *The Landgirls* he fails to survive the crash. Sam protests his innocence and the inferiority of Germany: 'If your Fatherland's got no beer and no tea what's the point of defending it?' Taken to the trenches, Sam then encounters a German, Oskar (George Hayes), who is pretty much his equal (if not his likeness): they discuss the quality of soil for crops and so forth. Oskar cannot shoot Sam. Then the British capture Sam (mistaking him for Juperts and admiring his fiendishly persuasive mastery of a Yorkshire dialect), and hold him captive in a country house previously requisitioned by the Germans. Brought before a firing squad, Sam continues to protest. His story is checked and confirmed by Martha, while the village supply committee is concerned that he will betray its various scams and misdemeanours to a higher authority. Meanwhile (somewhere in France), Sam strives to remember the overheard name of Juperts' hide-out (it is the name of a cow at home). Sam is delivered back safely to the village (to the same cabbage patch) by Captain Bradshaw, where he is now greeted as *Mr* Gates and accepted by Martha. To the tune of 'Pack up your Troubles', he accepts Bradshaw's invitation to return to the war as his batman.

In spite of its apparently frivolous and fanciful treatment of the last war, *Spy for a Day* employs imagery and themes which are common to the more earnest endeavours of film producers between 1939 and 1945. These traverse Balcon's critical opposition of 'realism' (of which he approved) and 'tinsel' (of which he was dismissive) (see Chapter 1). Similarly, in spite of the magnificent, monumental bombast of *A Matter of Life and Death*, very superior technicolour tinsel, there is much in common thematically with standard film production of the duration. In Asquith's evocatively titled *The Demi-Paradise* (written and produced by the Russian émigré, Anatole de Grunewald), the archetypal English village, its annual round of pageants, fêtes and festivals and the fixtures of its high street, remains unchanged over the year in which its Russian guest, Ivan Kuznetsov (Laurence Olivier – brushing up an accent previously rehearsed in *Moscow Nights* [1935] – see Chapter 5), is absent – although he finds notices directing him towards the night shelters, the butcher, the bridge players, Miss Fentmore (Margaret Rutherford), selling daisy badges for charity (elsewhere described by Kenneth Tynan as monstrously vital, 'the soul of Cleopatra . . . trapped in the corporate shape of an entire lacrosse team'), are permanently in place.[28] For Ivan's host, Runalow (Felix Aylmer), such rural pastimes are as important in life as his work as a captain of industry. The village is favourably compared by Ivan with his first impressions of rainy London, where a humourless landlady mispronounces his name while pronouncing her house to be respectable ('We don't allow any goings-on') and her cooking to be plain ('None of your fancy stuff'). Dilys Powell, film critic of *The Sunday Times*, appreciated the affectionate irony and wit of this formulaic representation of English life (affectively repeated for the family reunion of Harold French's 1943 *Dear Octopus*) while *Picture Post* was more cautious in its recommendation:

> [it is] intended as propaganda for an international get-together . . . based on the idea that the Russians and the British have a similar sense of humour. For ourselves, if a typical musical comedy is regarded as the test of the British sense of humour, we should prefer the Russians to be different. However, it provides a wealth of escapist beauty and capable character actors.[29]

A comparable village, complete with pond, thatch, codgers and landgirls (and another token Russian), appears in *Tawny Pipit* (Charles Saunders and Bernard Miles, 1944), also viewed by Powell as mild satire, where the England for which the war is being fought welcomes foreigners (like the pipits) who cannot help being foreign and have chosen England as their home. Although a Cotswold location replaces the studio set of *The Demi-Paradise*, and Colonel Barrington (Bernard Miles) is here the local patriarch, the theme is the same. A cricket match provides the village ritual and a band of anti-social ornithologists intent upon the theft of the pipits' nest is cast as a crypto-fifth column. In *A Matter of Life and Death*, Reeves, the local general practitioner (Roger Livesey), replaces the lord of the manor as the figure who benignly oversees the activities of a half-timbered village, and amateur theatricals (involving stationed American GIs in a performance of *A Midsummer Night's Dream*) substitute for the pageant; in *Waterloo Road* (Sidney Gilliatt, 1945), Livesey performs the same function for a village within the city.

However, in *Went the Day Well* (1942), directed for Balcon by Alberto Cavalcanti (who moved to Ealing from documentaries in 1940), the pastoral idyll is invoked only to be subverted. As in Saki's *When William Came* (1913) (which warned against German invasion before the First World War), Jenning's *The Silent Village*, Coward's *Peace in Our Time* (which envisaged the scenario after Britain's loss of the Battle of Britain) and Kevin Brownlow's and Andrew Mollo's *It Happened Here* (1963) (see Chapter 8), which imagined collaboration and resistance in an occupied Britain, retrospectively, after the Second, *Went the Day Well* describes events which did not happen but which might have. Based on a Graham Greene short story, the film opens and closes with a rustic directly addressing the audience in peacetime, as if at some unspecified, misty, future date, recalling Whitsun weekend in 1942 when German troops planned to invade Britain. Again, a Cotswold village is emblematic of the nation and soldiers from the Gloucestershire Regiment augment the cast. A sailor, Tom (Frank Lawton), engaged to Peggy, two landgirls, Peggy and Ivy (Elizabeth Allan and Thora Third), the postmistress (Muriel George) and Mrs Fraser and the vicar's daughter, Nora, at the manor (Marie Lohr and Valerie Taylor), along with the local poacher and a rapscallion cockney, George (Harry Fowler), show themselves alert to the signs that Major Hammond and his men, newly arrived in the village, are not all that they seem to be: Ivy (from Stockport) is suspicious when a soldier claims to know Manchester but thinks of Piccadilly as London; a bar of German Schokolade is found in Hammond's bag and telegrams are written using continental numerals. Ingeniously, the women of the village endeavour to pass messages to the outside world. Mrs Fraser is scornful of suggestions of treachery and the presence of a fifth column but her confidence is shown to be misplaced. The German invaders are shown to be brutal (they threaten the children and shoot the vicar in the middle of Tom's and Peggy's wedding) but, worse, are duplicitous: Mrs Fraser is nearer the truth than she realises when she fears what it would be like 'never knowing who was working for the enemy'. Eventually, the wounded George informs the Home Guard at a neighbouring village. Wilsford (Leslie Banks), the local squire, whom the villagers have appointed as their spokesman, proves to be the traitor in their midst. His wounded arm, which excuses him from war service, is sham. Poignantly, he stands with Hammond in front of the church memorial to the dead of the Great War, discussing the planned invasion. Mrs Fraser sacrifices herself for the sake of the children, while Nora, who has previously been attracted to Wilsford, discovers him unbolting the manor's barricaded windows and shoots him dead.

Went the Day Well depicts a supposedly typical and timeless rural community in order to urge vigilance on the home front. However, with Peggy, Ivy and the evacuee George (what Delafield's Provincial Lady's daughter calls 'a little evacument'), it also indicates shifts in population brought about during the course of the war.[30] Films which locate their action in the midst of battle (rather than on the home front) have their equivalent model communities and range of characters. *Men of the Lightship*, produced by Cavalcanti, was made with the co-operation of officers and men of the Royal Navy and Trinity House and recounts an event of 29 January 1940. Newspaper headlines are overlaid on the opening fog. Until then, spits the commentator, for three centuries, even during the wars with France, lightships and lighthouses had been considered international. The unprecedented horror of the Nazis (which 'we can – we must stop') is shown to be brutal ('planes continue to pepper the sea with fire even when the ship has been bombed') and inhuman. There is much stress on the cameraderie of the men and of the men as individuals: the lifeboat is rowed in one continuous movement; their exhausted faces are shown in individual close-up. One man sews while another plays hymns on an accordion; one man is about to be married while another is concerned for the whereabouts of the ship's mascot (the tortoise, Lightning) even when they disembark. Rank's *In Which We Serve*, based on Lord Mountbatten's ship, starred, was written and co-directed (with David Lean) by Noël Coward. The roles of the noble paternalistic guardian and his dutiful wife are assumed by Captain and Alex Kinross (Coward and Celia Johnson): he takes the blame on himself when a frightened raw recruit to the ship deserts his post; she speaks movingly of the *Torrin* as the undisputed and implacable rival in their marriage, of whom she is both proud and fond. Coward suggests that there was initial official opposition to the idea of filming the story, as it represented a naval defeat rather than a victory.[31] But it proved enormously successful at the box office (the most popular British film of the war years) and a critical achievement for Coward (the premiere, given in aid of Naval Charities, 'resulted in ecstatic reviews'). 'Altogether, the finest piece of work to come out of the British studios for a long time past', concluded one young male Mass Observation respondent.[32] When President Roosevelt's wife visited Buckingham Palace in October 1942, *In Which We Serve* was selected for a private after-dinner screening, with Churchill in attendance.[33]

Although the film declares itself to be the story of a ship – the destroyer *HMS Torrin* – the community which it incorporates extends beyond the crew at sea. Jack Cardiff's photography in *Western Approaches* makes dramatic use of the open sea as the boat's location but also lingers on the faces of individual crew members (portrayed by non-professional actors); *San Demetrio, London* (Charles Frend, 1943) identifies different character traits which together pull the crew through to safety. *In Which We Serve* is told as a series of flashbacks, with captain and crew remembering significant events in their shared and personal pasts, beginning with the ship's construction and her ceremonial launch and salute. Sometimes, a single motif (the singing of a hymn to raise morale, or of popular songs such as Flanagan and Allen's 'Run Rabbit Run', which recurs to locate the wartime action of Pressburger's 1956 *The Battle of the River Plate*) can prompt a variety of reminiscences (Christmas on board and Christmas on leave). They remember the stretches of boredom (writing letters home), the battle itself and remember receiving news of births and deaths on the home front also. There is gentle ribbing on shore between the Army and the Navy and black humour on board: 'Remember Nelson?' says Hardy (appropriately); 'Yeah, and look what happened to him,' quips Shorty Blake (Mills). Some men have served with Kinross on previous expeditions – Hardy (Bernard Miles), Blake, Adams – and remember his motto ('a very happy and a very efficient ship'). These memories are privileged, but as Kinross bids farewell to the crew at the end,

The last of *H.M.S. Torrin*: Kinross (Noël Coward) attempts to keep bodies and souls afloat in *In Which We Serve* (Noël Coward, 1942)

he does so indiscriminately, as if any selection of men would provide a similar sample. Finally, alone in the dock, Kinross departs in silence, as if, without the crew, there is nothing.

After the victories of Montgomery, Auchinleck and Alexander at El Alamein in 1942 ('the battlefield of giants', as J. Lee Thompson's 1958 *Ice Cold in Alex* informs us), Churchill (as recorded in *Desert Victory*) announced that 'the fame of the Desert Army has spread throughout the world'; after the Battle of Britain, Churchill famously addressed the nation: 'Never in the field of human conflict was so much owed by so many to so few.' Post-war films often celebrated pilots as unique individuals (as in Kenneth More's portrayal of Douglas Bader in *Reach for the Sky* [Lewis Gilbert, 1956]), while elsewhere (as in Kenneth More's stage performance in Terence Rattigan's *The Deep Blue Sea* [1952]), the pilot becomes pathetically isolated once the war is over.[34] The mythical status of the doomed pilot is resurrected in Ken Russell's casting of Robert Powell (appearing elsewhere as Christ) in 1975, as father to Tommy, born on VE Day 1945 (see Chapter 10). During the war, films made in, with, or by the RAF sought to represent the collaboration between different members of a flying crew (as in *Journey Together* [John Boulting, 1945]), between ground crew and flight crew (as in *The First of the Few* [Leslie Howard, 1942] or the MoI's 1940 *Story of an Air Communiqué*), between the RAF and the other services (with the WAAF and the Navy in *Coastal Command* [1942] and with the USAF in *Way to the Stars*). In *The First of the Few*, told in flashback, Station Commander Geoff Crisp (David Niven) urges a bunch of young pilots to remember R. J. Mitchell (Leslie Howard), 'the wizard' who dreamed and perfected the Spitfire, at the cost of his own life. Crisp, the dashing ace of the First War, is the ideal companion to Mitchell in the years of development and a fearless competitor at international tournaments: in 1927, Bertorelli (a cameo appearance by Filippo del Giudice, the boss of production company Two Cities) is obliged to concede a defeat for fascist Italy. Royce is subsequently an equal partner in the design of a new engine. But Mitchell appreciates the larger significance of his work when he sees the Hitler Youth marching in Germany in 1931 and witnesses the increasing preparations for war: while British public opinion opposes rearmament and the government preaches appeasement, Mitchell receives funds from private sponsors. Like Barnes Wallis, inventor of the bouncing bomb (Michael Redgrave in *The Dam Busters* [Michael Anderson, 1955]), Mitchell is portrayed as an artist and idealist, whose vision lesser mortals are all too often slow to grasp. At the close of *The First of the Few*, Churchill's portentous address accompanies the flight of planes, in formation, into the sunset.

Many of the films covering the war in the air feature spectacular aerial photography and flamboyant acrobatics ('victory rolls'), which serve as stunning publicity for a service already, in 1939, widely regarded (and self-regarding) as an élite corps.[35] Delafield's Society Deb, amid an 'Outbreak of Knitting', knits exclusively in airforce blue.[36] *Journey Together*, like *One of Our Aircraft is Missing* and the army film *The Way Ahead*, stresses the individual unit of operation as a representative team on which the effectiveness of the whole service depends and acknowledges individual particular skills (Wilton's mathematical brain in the former, the language skills of a former travel agent in the latter) as jointly contributing to the unit's success as a team. *The Way Ahead* (in the manner of BBC television's *Dad's Army* [see Chapter 10], complete with John Laurie as perennial token Scot) ends with the men in individual close-up, marching through smoke with fixed bayonets towards the camera. Both *Journey Together* and *The Way Ahead* (and *Desert Victory*) detail the rigours and procedures of training, which produce a competent airman or soldier. The Airforce and the Army are shown to be managed by caring professionals, concerned for the welfare of their men and their dependants (for instance, in *Journey Together* it is feared that Wilton [Richard Attenborough] is 'the old story of a disappointed pilot' who thinks navigation a sissy job; in *The Way Ahead* Parsons is given a war emergency grant and allowed furlough in order to return home to his pregnant wife who is being bullied for HP payments: 'You're not alone against anyone – Germans or furniture shops – that's one good thing about the Army,' Perry [David Niven] reassures him). In *Ice Cold in Alex* (made with the co-operation of the Royal Army Service Corps in Libya), the military insignia is conspicuously shown in close-up when Sergeant Tom Pugh (Harry Andrews) places his arm on a shoulder to comfort nurse Diane Murdoch (Sylvia Syms). While Wilton hopes to be married after the war and his training officer has to get back from the middle of the Channel to be married on Thursday, Toddie (Rosamund John), in *The Way to the Stars*, persuades Tiny to propose to Iris (Renee Asherson), in spite of his fears that he will leave her a widow.

Viewed generically, the airforce films are also marked by a particular style of banter and slang and by particular character traits (of which the taciturn stoicism of Bob Trubshaw [Robert Coote] in *A Matter of Life and Death* – 'bad luck, old boy' – set against a caricature of Gallic expostulation, is generally representative). In *Way to the Stars*, the Americans' swaggering brashness is set against English understatement – 'devilish poor show' – to their mutual amusement. 'It's such an anachronism,' says Hester in *The Deep Blue Sea*; 'as dated as gad zooks and odds my life.'[37] The sparse interiors of huts, with wicker chairs, dartboard, cigarette packets and a few items of personal memorabilia, seem standard and readily recognisable. But in *The Way to the Stars* (like *Journey Together*, scripted by Rattigan, himself a former air gunner and wireless operator) this typical scene is surveyed mournfully, the camera casually passing over the dereliction left by a departed crew before the film proceeds to invest the debris with specific history and significance. A girlie pin-up reappears alongside David Archdale's lucky lighter (which he has left behind in the hut on the night his plane explodes); we discover how Archdale (Michael Redgrave) came by the German sign (a peacetime trophy) above his bed and how the phone number of a girl at the hotel in the nearby village (David's future wife, Toddie) comes to be written on the hut wall.

Although *Journey Together* strives for equality, asserting that all members of the flight crew are equally valuable (and it is the navigator who ultimately saves the day), the pilots of these films seem thrice blessed: not only do they enjoy their wartime status but also, in general, are seen to be drawn from a socially privileged and élite fraternity. Stefan Radetsky, in *Dangerous Moonlight*, is a concert pianist and composer who volunteers as a pilot; Archdale is a poet (and Redgrave recites lines written by the actual poet-pilot, Squadron Leader John Pudney: 'Do not despair/For Johnny head-in-air'); in *Journey Together*, Aynsworth (Jack Watling) has interrupted his studies at Cambridge, while in *A Matter of Life and Death*, Peter Carter (David Niven) is the son of a Great War flying ace (killed in 1917), an Oxford man who is himself a poet and who recites Andrew Marvell to the operator, June (Kim Hunter), as his plane goes down.[38] Nevertheless, he is, he insists, 'Conservative by nature, Labour by experience'. The mythical figure of poet-pilot has since been resuscitated in ITV's *Foyle's War* (2003).

Winning the Peace

During the war there were enormous movements of population in Britain. Angus Calder says that 'from the outbreak of war to the end of 1945 some sixty million changes of address took place among a civilian population of about 38 million'.[39] Some of these were evacuated children (such as George in *Went the Day Well*, Mrs Hemmings' brood in *Perfect Strangers* and the ghastly and precocious Connollies in *Put Out More Flags*), some people voluntarily sought the relative safety of the countryside (such as the fearsome Mrs Winterton and her brow-beaten daughter in *The Way to the Stars*), some were women temporarily employed on farms (such as the Landgirls of Rotha's 1942 *Land Girl* or the girls in *Tawny Pipit*). Many women found themselves displaced as a consequence of Ernest Bevin's directive: 'Mr Bevin needs another million women, you know,' Celia is advised in *Millions Like Us* (subtitled '. . . and Millions like you'). As Antonia Lant, Christine Gledhill and Gillian Swanson have observed, films concerned with the mobilisation (*The Gentle Sex*, *Millions Like Us*, *Perfect Strangers*) work to present the experience as positive, allowing women to fulfil unrealised potential, but also to provide reassurance that they will have the support of a surrogate family for the duration.[40] Celia is supported by Gwen when she hears of the death of her new husband in an air-raid in *Millions Like Us*; in *Perfect Strangers*, Dizzie (Glynis Johns) is loyal to her fiancé 'not seen since Singapore'; in *Waterloo Road*, Tilly remains exemplarily true to Jim (John Mills) in spite of the evident attractions of spiv Ted (Stewart Granger, more than a bit gorgeous in a white vest). Sometimes it is clear that jobs have been undertaken temporarily, easing fears that women will take work hitherto regarded as the preserve of men, at other times it is suggested that women will be prompted to continue in their new careers: for instance, Joan (Barbara Waring), in *The Gentle Sex*, decides to stay in the Army.

Personally, the experience is generally life-enhancing: the sheltered Betty (Joan Greenwood) in *The Gentle Sex* acquires confidence and learns to fend for herself and for others, while Joan becomes less blunt and more sociable; Kathy (Deborah Kerr) and Robert (Robert Donat) in *Perfect Strangers* are individually reinvigorated by their service in the Navy (Kerr demonstrating that 'beauty is duty' and Donat working backwards from the older to the younger Chips [see Chapter 7]) and their marriage resuscitated; in *Millions Like Us* the snobbish Jennifer (Anne Crawford), who likes to give the impression that she is something 'better' than a waitress, is rumbled by the foreman, Charlie Forbes (Eric Portman), who says he is prepared to marry her in spite of her shortcomings – and she responds in kind ('I'm turning you down without even asking you,' he teases). *The Gentle Sex*, *Millions Like Us* and *Journey Together* depict wartime encounters across class and region which may not have occurred so intimately nor so easily otherwise. But they also suggest that the consensus the war has produced, the nation's expedient shared ideals, needs must be extended into peacetime; indeed, that the sacrifices of war will be justified only if the nation itself is reconstructed. After Celia (Patricia Roc) has received news of the death of young Fred (Gordon Jackson), Jennifer and Charlie muse on the future: 'Are we going to slide back after the war?' Leslie Howard, as narrator of *The Gentle Sex*, addresses a male audience by concluding 'Let's give in at last and admit that the world will be better because women are helping to shape it.' Emotionally and physically fitter, at the end of *Perfect Strangers*, Kathy and Robert return to the attic flat by which their pre-war life was stifled and confined. Their horizons have been extended beyond the routine escape to Clacton and their ambitions speak for a new society as much as for themselves as a newly restored couple: 'the strongest thing in the world is grass' says Elena (Anne Todd), a nurse who has lost her explorer husband in Burma, but who tells Robert that nothing excited him more than the streets of the City. Kathy sits on the window sill and surveys the remains of London, the light now flooding in where before there was darkness: 'Well, we'll just have to build again – what

Jennifer (Anne Crawford) meets her match (Eric Portman) in a munitions factory in *Millions Like Us* (Frank Launder/Sidney Gilliat, 1943)

does it matter? – we're young,' they agree as the camera zooms to a bomb site beyond, promising future development and improvement rather than dwelling upon the devastation of the recent past.

Millions Like Us opens with an on-screen definition of an orange, acknowledging that its audience might not have seen one for so long that it could require a reminder. Wartime privations and rationing continued into the 1950s, Alan Bennett's *A Private Function* (Malcolm Mowbray, 1984) narrating the secret fattening of a pig in readiness for the celebration by Yorkshire worthies of Princess Elizabeth's marriage to Prince Philip in 1947. However, throughout the hostilities, *Picture Post* provided a platform for the discussion of a new Britain in peacetime and supported a Labour Party agenda which secured its decisive victory in the General Election of 1945. Contributions on health, education, working women, cities and the countryside were invited from Julian Huxley, Cecil Joad, J. B. Priestley, the architect Maxwell Fry and the general reader. Planning was to be a key component in its future achievement: 'A Plan for Britain' is announced in January 1941 over a picture of naked toddlers on a playground slide; in January 1942 a baby in a tub is dubbed 'The

Heir of Britain's Inheritance'. Town planning is welcomed in 1946 with the LCC's announcement of new housing for 'The Doomed East End' and in 1949 with a report on slum clearance.[41] The Beveridge Report of March 1943 is greeted as 'the most famous in British Social History' and in July 1948 *Picture Post* portentously proclaims 'The End of a Long Struggle':

> Years of education and agitation are crowned by the introduction of a national social security scheme which embraces both duke and dustman. The 'Panel' and the 'Poor Law' go. In their place the new scheme provides the principle and machinery by which all people are concerned together in ending poverty and insecurity.[42]

Such is the background, then, to a number of films portraying urban communities in Britain in the second half of the decade. Ealing's *Passport to Pimlico* (Henry Cornelius, 1948) opens with the residents (a fishmonger, a hardware merchant, a dressmaker, a policeman, a bookie) going about their everyday business in the midst of an extraordinary heatwave. Children play amid bombed-out ruins, Arthur Pemberton (Stanley Holloway) proposing a scheme for a community playground and pool on the site with councillors discussing its sale to developers. 'Les Norman and his Bethnal Green bambinos' are heard on the radio. Much of the film's humour is highly contemporary.

A toast to the future: *A Diary for Timothy* (Humphrey Jennings, 1945)

'Forget that Cripps Feeling', reads a poster, referring to the austere wartime minister, Sir Stafford Cripps; the 'evacuated' Burgundian children see newsreels at the cinema which intercut actual footage of mass demonstrations at Trafalgar Square, bomb sites and Churchill arriving at Downing Street with 'faked' interviews with the Burgundians. An unexploded bomb is set off accidentally and a document is discovered in the rubble which proves that the area still falls under the jurisdiction of Burgundia, outside British law and customs. On hearing this news from the professor (Margaret Rutherford), the residents celebrate in the local pub, tearing up their ration books and identity papers. Meanwhile, the men from the ministry argue about whose responsibility the Burgundians become – whether they are to be classified as aliens or undesirable aliens. The rest of Britain supports the 'plucky little Burgundians'' bid for independence and resistance to bureaucracy (echoed in the rural landscape of *Whisky Galore!*). Eventually, order is restored when the bank loans its treasure to Britain – and even the weather returns to normal.

E. M. Forster's commentary to *A Diary for Timothy* (spoken by Michael Redgrave) addresses a baby born a year before the war's end, suggesting (like Jennings' 1951 *A Family Portrait* – see Chapter 8) a larger community beyond the security of his Oxford home: Alan, the farmer; Bill, the engine-driver; a pilot wounded in war, sharing Timothy's cottage hospital; miners wounded and unemployed in peacetime ('though that shouldn't be . . .'). He is reminded that, in spite of the dangers of war, to be born in Holland, Poland or a Liverpool slum would be yet less comfortable. *A Diary for Timothy* (like *Picture Post* and *Millions Like Us*) employs the iconic shot of St Paul's dome intact among the smoke and flames to evoke the Blitz: the narrator hopes that Timothy 'will never have to hear that sound' as an air-raid siren looms.[43] A companion for Timothy appears at the end of *Waterloo Road* with Doctor Montgomery (Roger Livesey), the film's occasional narrator, intoning over Jim's and Tilly's baby: 'We'll need good citizens when this is all over – millions and millions . . . Why did they allow it? . . . But you must admit, taking it all in all, they didn't do a bad job . . . Well, Jim, you've got the future – it's all yours.'

Frieda (Basil Dearden, 1947), a variant, says Terry Lovell, on the 'public service' film, suggests that international brotherhood may prove harder to forge than is hoped for Timothy and Jim, and returns to the early war theme of 'good' and 'bad' Germans.[44] In March 1945, Frieda (Mai Zetterling) is married in Cracow to the RAF officer, Robert Dawson (David Farrar), who then takes her home: 'There's nothing to be frightened of in England, where I come from' (he reassures her). But Denfield, like the settings for *The Demi-Paradise* and *Dear Octopus* ('an ordinary town like any other', with the family house just off the square), proves less than welcoming to Robert's new German wife. Judy (Glynis John), the widow of Robert's 'lucky' brother Alan, shot down in the same raid over Cologne in which Frieda's parents were killed, is torn in her affections (she 'was always going to marry one of us' and sees 'Alan in everything Robert does'). Meanwhile, Eleanor (Flora Robson), Robert's aunt, stands by prejudices inculcated in wartime (Robert's father was killed in the First World War), thinking that the marriage will count against the family in the forthcoming election and refusing to exempt Frieda from culpability for the war and its atrocities. 'It isn't wicked to hate Germans,' protests younger brother, Tony, to Edith, the housekeeper; 'it says so in the papers. I think she's beastly.' Fighting her own battle against loss and desire, Judy asserts 'I think she's sweet' and takes Frieda under her wing. When Tony has a cut knee, Frieda offers to help ('I'm a nurse . . . in any country') and the family is reminded that she helped Robert to escape. Asked about the concentration camps, she admits knowledge: 'Some of us were inside them'. The arrival of Frieda's brother proves a further test: while he presents her with a swastika, she maintains that 'Heine, Goethe, Schiller, Beethoven, Brahms' represent *her* Germany, insisting that she and Richard are two separate people. Moreover, Poznan (their birthplace) has been alternately German and Polish, according to succeeding post-war treaties. Frieda is driven to a melodramatic gesture to take her own life ('a sure way out for all of us', determines Eleanor, grimly). But Robert and Judy, in saving Frieda, realise that to treat someone as less than human is to become less human oneself. 'We've changed,' concludes Edith.

The Third Man (Carol Reed, 1949)

The Second World War did not end with VE Day on 8 May 1945. Fighting continued in the Far East until VJ Day on 14 August 1945 and in Europe the victorious military powers turned their attention to policing the occupied countries and repatriating (sometimes forcibly) people displaced during the conflict, since, as the film's duffel-coated Colonel Calloway (Trevor Howard) comments, laconically, 'the business started', in 1939.[45]

The Third Man, directed by Carol Reed and co-produced by Reed and David Selznick (whose interventions Reed wisely ignored), has opening titles laid over the strings and sound-hole of a zither, an almost abstract image presaging the sequences produced by Saul Bass for Hitchcock in the 1950s and 1960s. The Anton Karas score pervades the film, endorsing both its location (a Mitteleuropean Vienna) and its mood: the famous Harry Lime (Orson Welles) theme is woven into an almost continuous warp. This is reinforced for modern audiences by the often oblique framing and cast shadows of Robert Krasker's monochrome cinematography (matching the night sequences of *Odd Man Out* [1947] – see Chapter 7) and by references (backwards) to Fritz Lang's tell-tale children and a balloon-seller in *M* (Germany, 1931) and (forwards) to the spiral staircases and sewers of the Cracow of Resistance fighters in Andrej Wajda's *A Generation* (Poland, 1954). Exceptionally, the chase sequence below ground, in the sewers of the city, replaces music with the echoes of running feet, clattering against cobbles and the amplified sound of voices, dogs' barking and gunfire.

Calloway, as anonymous commentator, casually, conversationally, recounts his own war story, introducing the action. He tells us that Vienna (smashed and dreary, 'bombed about a bit') is divided into four zones (Russian, British, French and American) with an international area at its centre, delineated by the Ringstrasse, 'with its heavy public buildings and prancing statuary'. The montage of images of street racketeers dealing from suitcases in watches, fakes (including German gin and diluted penicillin), would be familiar to readers of *Picture Post* in the immediate aftermath of war, as would be the profiteering of Lime and the plight of his ex-lover, Anna Schmidt (Alida Valli – well received in Britain for her roles in Italian neo-realist films),[46] a Czechoslovakian citizen holding forged identity papers over whom Russia now claims authority. Some (like the punctilious Doctor Winkel [Erich Ponto]) appear to dine well while his compatriots struggle for survival; even Baron Kurtz (Ernst Deutsch) is 'reduced' to playing the violin at a nightclub. Anna (possibly duplicitously) acts in period costume in Viennese light comedies while her own persona is entirely tragic: she can summon only one laugh for Harry's adoring friend, there is no capacity for more.

Holly Martins (Joseph Cotton), an American author of pulp fiction (you can pick it up and leave it, says Calloway's sidekick, Sergeant Paine [Bernard Lee]), arrives in Vienna at the invitation of an erstwhile friend, Harry Lime: *The Third Man* reunites and recollects something of the nostalgic, sentimental spirit of *Citizen Kane* (Orson Welles, 1941). Martins, in the manner of Richard Hannay in John Buchan's *The 39 Steps* (Alfred Hitchcock, 1935 [see Chapter 5]) is, in sub-plot, invited by Crabbin, the representative of an organisation akin to the British Council, to speak about The Novel, in the interests of cultural re-education, to an anglophile audience. The episode emphasises a distinction between a low-brow (but exportable) American culture and the European high-brow: one Austrian devotee asks Martins about the work of (the émigré) James Joyce. The smooth-talking Romanian, Popescu (Siegfried Breuer), who has previously flaunted his dubious material status by giving Anna cigarettes ('keep the packet') and standing her and Holly double whiskies at

Anna (Alida Valli) anxiously receives a call in post-war Vienna in Carol Reed's 1949 *The Third Man*

the Casanova Club, asks questions which refer to the plot proper: will Martins' next book (*The Third Man*) merge fact with fiction (dangerously, Popescu cautions), a tacit warning against Martins' further interference in the case of Lime.

Martins, supposedly, arrives just as Lime is being buried after a tragic street accident. Two men carried the body to the ambulance, insist Lime's accomplices, Popescu, Kurtz and the accessory, Doctor Winkler, while Lime's house porter, Koch, insists that another man, a third, was there too. The porter is subsequently exterminated but Martins is suspected of his murder: in an atmosphere of mutual suspicion, where past and future allegiances are in a state of flux and negotiation and everyone needs must live for present survival, the conspicuous foreigner becomes readily identifiable as suspect: 'Everyone ought to go careful in a city like Vienna,' advises Popescu. Martins' alienation and incomprehension is stressed by the use of German dialogue in the film, translated for him by Anna and Calloway. Calloway, in turn, insists on his Englishness and corrects Martins when he incorrectly identifies him as Irish (as in Callaghan).

Anna's continuing love for Lime, in spite of the revelation of his treachery and crimes against humanity (as in Elizabeth Bowen's 1949 *The Heat of the Day*, in which Stella, the protagonist, discovers her wartime lover to have been a traitor to his country) – 'What difference does it make, the more you know about someone?' insists Anna. 'I wish he was dead – then he'd be safe from all of you' – is challenged by Martins, who has been persuaded by Calloway of Lime's guilt and has been disillusioned in his belief in friendship. For Anna, the betrayal of love is a greater crime: she shrugs off the coat which Martins offers to keep her warm on her compromised journey to sanctuary and she does not acknowledge his presence in the long tracking shot, amid falling leaves, which concludes the journey (and the film) from Lime's 'second' and conclusive funeral. Holly entirely fails to replace Harry in her affections, although she obsessively refers to Holly as Harry and even advises Holly to 'find himself a girl'. Graham Greene, author of the screenplay for *The Third Man* (his first story written specifically as a film), acknowledged that the film's ending was suggested by Reed and that it improves upon his original scenario:

> One of the few major disputes between Carol Reed and myself concerned the ending, and he was proved triumphantly right. I held the view that an entertainment of this kind was too light an affair to carry the weight of an unhappy ending. Reed on his side felt that my ending – indeterminate as it was, with no words spoken, Holly joining the girl in silence and walking away with her from the cemetery where her lover Harry was buried – would strike the audience who had just seen Harry's death and burial as unpleasantly cynical. I was only half convinced: I was afraid few people would wait in their seats during the girl's long walk from the graveside towards Holly, and the others would leave the cinema under the impression that the ending was still going to be as conventional as my suggested ending of boy joining girl.[47]

Lime is betrayed by a cat, whose affections he has readily acquired, rather than by any other character in the film. Anna's pet kitten runs to his feet while he is hidden in a doorway and the soundtrack immediately cues identification. Lime arranges to meet Holly at the ferris wheel at the fun-fair; while cautiously covering his tracks, Lime endeavours to present an apology to Martins, suggesting that his own entrepreneurial activities are no more than the private equivalent of a public, socialist Five Year Plan. There is a mock grandiose heroism in his argument (in lines contributed by Welles himself): amid war and pillaging, death and destruction, the Borgias produced the Italian Renaissance and Michelangelo, while the Swiss (he says), for all their democracy and pacificity, have contributed no more to the history of civilisation than the cuckoo clock. Similarly, Harry has perpetrated the grand scam and secured the girl while Holly, the hack-writer, is portrayed as a lone loser.

Although critics after the war valorised the representation of the war itself as key to the revival of British cinema, Christine Gledhill indicates that, thematically, distinctions between films may be more difficult to sustain: both melodrama and films directly addressing the war concern questions of 'the empty shell marriage, the brief romantic idyll, the pain of parting and betrayed friendships'. 'As modes of imagination', she pertinently observes, 'documentary, melodrama and romance guarantee nothing in themselves'. *The Third Man*, set against the documented racketeering and politicking of post-war Vienna, employs melodramatic stylisation to effect these ubiquitous war themes.[48]

Notes

1. Alan Bennett, *Telling Tales* (London: BBC Worldwide, 2001), p. 26.
2. Philip M. Taylor, *Munitions of the Mind* (Wellingborough: Patrick Stephens, 1990), p. 188.
3. See Asa Briggs, especially 'Attack by Radio', *The History of Broadcasting in the United Kingdom*, vol. III (London: Oxford University Press, 1970), pp. 221–35.
4. E. M. Delafield, 'The Provincial Lady in Wartime', *The Provincial Lady* (London: Macmillan, 1947), p. 379.
5. Delafield, *The Provincial Lady*, p. 463; Evelyn Waugh, *Put Out More Flags* [1942] (London: Chapman and Hall, 1959).
6. Harry Watt, *Don't Look at the Camera* (London: Paul Elek, 1974), p. 128; Clive Coultass suggests that Watt exaggerates the significance of their intervention: 'The Ministry of Information and Documentary Film, 1939–45', *IWM Review*, 1989, pp. 103–11.
7. See Ysenda Maxtone Graham, *The Real Mrs Miniver* (London: John Murray, 2001), p. 104 (for donations to Lord Baldwin's Appeal Fund for Refugees) and for discrepancies between image conveyed in *The Times* column and its author.
8. James Chapman, *The British at War: Cinema, State and Propaganda 1939–1945* (London: I. B. Tauris, 1998), p. 124; see also Michael Balcon, *Michael Balcon Presents . . . A Lifetime of Films* (London: Hutchinson, 1969), p. 13.
9. Jeffrey Richards and Dorothy Sheridan (eds), *Mass Observation at the Movies* (London: Routledge and Kegan Paul, 1987), pp. 209–16.
10. J. B. Priestley, broadcast, May 1940.
11. Dilys Powell, *Films Since 1939* (London: for The British Council by Longmans, Green and Co., 1947), p. 11; see also Richards and Sheridan, *Mass Observation at the Movies*, pp. 302–30, for contemporaneous audience and critical responses, and Chapman, *The British at War*, p. 180.

12. *Picture Post*, October 1941: 'The French in London', with a Soho pub their unofficial HQ; 27 December 1941 and 15 January 1944 for Norwegians in London; see also Graham Greene, *The Ministry of Fear* [1943] (Harmondsworth: Penguin, 1985).

13. Joyce Grenfell, *Joyce Grenfell Requests the Pleasure* (London: Macmillan, 1976), p. 167; *The Time of My Life* (London: Hodder and Stoughton, 1989), p. 169.

14. *Picture Post*, 3 July 1943, pp. 16–18.

15. James Chapman, 'Why We Fight: *Pastor Hall* and *Thunder Rock*', in Alan Burton, Tim O'Sullivan and Paul Wells (eds), *The Family Way: The Boulting Brothers and British Film Culture* (Trowbridge: Flicks Books, 2000), pp. 82–3.

16. Angus Calder, *The People's War: Britain 1939–1945* (London: Pimlico, 1992), pp. 122 and 288.

17. Ibid., p. 56; see p. 111 for a story from 1940 as the 'real' background to *Tawny Pipit*.

18. Anthony Aldgate and Jeffrey Richards, *Best of British* (London: I. B. Tauris, 2002), p. 90; Richards and Sheridan, *Mass Observation at the Movies*, p. 220; see also James Chapman, '*The Life and Death of Colonel Blimp* Reconsidered', *Historical Journal of Film, Radio and Television* vol. 15 no. 1, 1995, pp. 19–54.

19. Richards and Sheridan, *Mass Observation at the Movies*, p. 15; ITV's 2003 *Foyle's War* dutifully included a trip to a cinema showing *Gone With the Wind*.

20. Michael Korda, *Charmed Lives: a Family Romance* (London: Allen Lane, 1980), p. 150.

21. Winston Churchill, *A History of the English-Speaking Peoples*, vol. III (London: Cassell, 1957), p. 242.

22. See Amy Sargeant, 'Do We Need Another Hero?', in Claire Monk and Amy Sargeant (eds), *British Historical Cinema* (London: Routledge, 2002).

23. See Robert Donat cuttings books, John Rylands Library, for March 1946, and *Picture Post*, 8 November 1941, pp. 12–13, and 2 July 1943.

24. Basil Dean, *Mind's Eye* (London: Hutchinson, 1973), p. 281.

25. Noël Coward, *Peace in Our Time* (London: Heinemann, 1947), Act II Sc. 1; 'the Demi-Paradise' refers to John of Gaunt's speech in Shakespeare's *King Richard II*, Act II Sc. 1.

26. See Andrew Higson, *Waving the Flag* (Oxford: Clarendon, 1995), p. 253, for a discussion of Queenie's reluctance to be 'ordinary'.

27. See J. B. Priestley, 'A Tribute to Britain', *Picture Post*, 28 April 1945, pp. 14–17, and 19 May 1945.

28. John Lahr (ed.), *The Diaries of Kenneth Tynan* (London: Bloomsbury, 2002), p. 12.

29. Powell, *Films Since 1939*, pp. 30–1, and *Picture Post*, 20 February 1943, pp. 20–1.

30. Delafield, *The Provincial Lady*, p. 375.

31. Noël Coward, 'Future Indefinite', *Noël Coward: Autobiography* (London: Methuen, 1986), pp. 421–35.

32. Richards and Sheridan, *Mass Observation at the Movies*, p. 223.

33. Calder, *The People's War*, p. 304.

34. For this shift to the individual in post-war films, see Christine Geraghty, *British Cinema in the Fifties* (London: Routledge, 2000).

35. See Toby Haggith, '*Journey Together*', in Burton, O'Sullivan and Wells, *The Family Way*, pp. 109–21.

36. Delafield, *The Provincial Lady*, p. 492.

37. 'The Deep Blue Sea', in *The Collected Plays of Terence Rattigan*, vol. II (London: Hamish Hamilton, 1953), Act II.

38. For 'the Royal Advertising Force' and the original poet/pilot see Calder, *The People's War*, pp. 458 and 521; for Niven's unsuccessful attempts to enlist with the RAF (at twenty-nine) and his successful casting (at thirty-five) in *A Matter of Life and Death*, see David Niven, *The Moon's a Balloon: Reminiscences by David Niven* (London: Hamish Hamilton, 1979).

39. See Calder, *The People's War*, pp. 315–17, and Antonia Lant, *Blackout: Reinventing Women for Wartime British Cinema* (Princeton: Princeton University Press, 1991), p. 5.

40. See Christine Gledhill and Gillian Swanson, 'Gender and Sexuality in Second World War Films', in Geoffrey Hurd (ed.), *National Fictions: World War Two in British Films and Television* (London: BFI, 1984), pp. 56–62, and Lant, *Blackout*, p. 76.

41. *Picture Post*, 'How to Get the Houses: the Outline of a Plan', 14 July 1945, pp. 16–17; 31 January 1946, pp. 11–16 (re. the Gorbals); 'The LCC Announces an Imaginative Plan', 9 March 1946, pp. 8–11; 'Why not Use our Bomb Sites Like This?', 16 November 1946, pp. 26–9; 'Housing: London Shows How', 22 January 1949, pp. 7–9.

42. 'The End of a Long Struggle', *Picture Post*, 3 July 1948, pp. 24–5.

43. See 'History Under Fire', in John Taylor, *A Dream of England* (Manchester: Manchester University Press, 1994), and 'Morning after the Blitz', *Picture Post*, 3 May 1941.

44. Terry Lovell, '*Frieda*', in Hurd, *National Fictions*, p. 31.

45. 'Vienna: City of the Frozen Smile' and 'The Black Market: Europe's Scandal', *Picture Post* 19 January 1946, pp. 8–11, and 16 March 1946, pp. 10–13; see also Graham Greene, *The Third Man* [1950] (Harmondsworth: Penguin, 1977).

46. 'Makers of the World's Best Films', *Picture Post*, 27 March 1948, pp. 10–14, and Roger Manvell, '*Paisa*: How it Struck Our Contemporaries', *Penguin Film Review* 9, 1949, pp. 53–61.

47. Graham Greene, *Ways of Escape* (Harmondsworth: Penguin, 1981), p. 97; see also *The Tenth Man* (which he claims to have forgotten at the time of working on the filmscript for Reed) (Harmondsworth: Penguin, 1986). Peter Ustinov (who played the proprietor of the godforsaken Mediterranean café in *The Way Ahead*) endorses Greene's fond memories of working with Reed: 'Carol was a captain who behaved as though the war was a superb invention of Evelyn Waugh. He had a tendency to daydream (most engaging and blissfully unmilitary) and a mind tremulous with tender mischief': *Dear Me* (London: Heinemann, 1977), p. 116.

48. Christine Gledhill, 'An Abundance of Understatement: Documentary, Melodrama and Romance', in Christine Gledhill and Gillian Swanson (eds), *Nationalising Femininity* (Manchester: Manchester University Press, 1996), pp. 217–23; for a categorisation of production (instructional; propaganda; escapist) see Michael Balcon, 'The British Film During the War', *Penguin Film Review* 1, 1946.

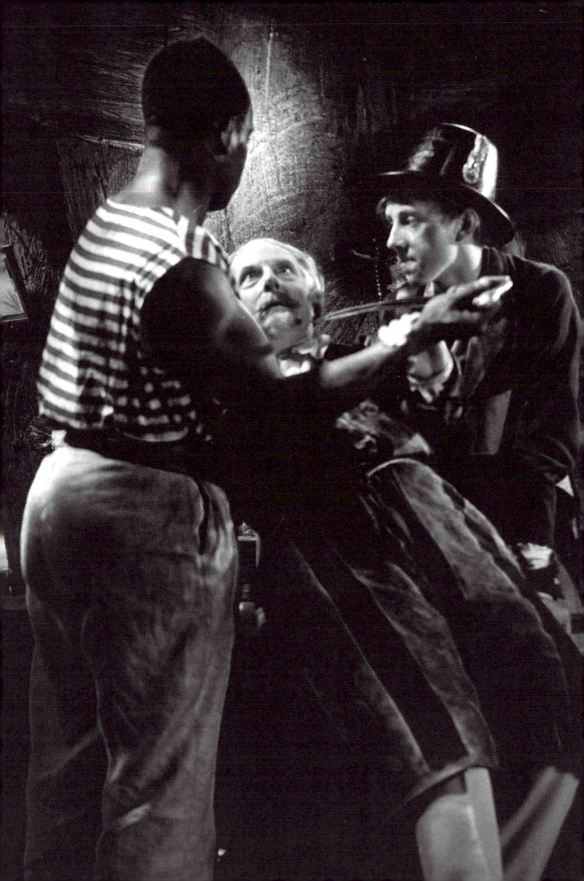

Chapter 7 | 1940s

Picture Post, the popular weekly modelled after the American magazine, *Life*, was launched by Edward Hulton and Stefan Lorant (later joined by editor Tom Hopkinson) in 1938.[1] It simultaneously addressed escapist fantasy, mundane practicality and hope for the future. After its demise, many of its personnel went to work in television (see Chapter 8). Between its articles on the war on the home front (for instance, Surbiton Women's Home Defence), on planning (sometimes contributed by Gropius' disciple, Maxwell Fry), on health (often from Julian Huxley) and on leisure (often from J. B. Priestley), there is much discussion of cinema and film and reporting of film stars' private lives (Laurence Olivier, soon to join the Fleet Air Arm, and Vivien Leigh, newly married, are pictured at home together in 1941).[2] While lavish picture spreads cover Cecil Beaton's dresses for Sally Gray in *Dangerous Moonlight* (1941) (see Chapter 6), Tamara Lee (Rank starlet) posed in Edwardian-style outfits as 'The Gibson Girl', Deborah Kerr (then working on *The Life and Death of Colonel Blimp*) showed off 'new utility wear for women' in 1942 and Susan Shaw (in 1947 to be seen in *Double Pursuit*) modelled a hand-knitted jumper which used fewer coupons than its shop-bought equivalent. During the war, readers were advised on the making of necklaces from silver sugar tongs, varying collars and buttons to evade rationing, knitting Fair Isles from scraps and improvising swimsuits from dusters. Patricia Roc, in 1946, endorsed cosmetics ('My! She must use Miner's Make-Up'), Margaret Lockwood (in 1948, appearing as Nell Gwynne) announced 'Drene leaves my hair shining with Glamour' and Michèle Morgan (in 1948, appearing in *The Fallen Idol*) advertised Lux toilet soap. Even during the war, film stars were employed to remind women that 'beauty was duty'. Such tie-ins and promotions served to encourage the identification of female audiences with their favourite stars, and with the heroines they portrayed.

Rural Romps

The wind was a torrent of darkness among the gusty trees,
The moon was a ghastly galleon tossed upon cloudy seas,
The road was a ribbon of moonlight, over the purple moor,
And the highwayman came riding

Mesty (W. Robert Adams) and Jack (Hughie Green) tackle Don Rebeira in Carol Reed's costume romp, *Midshipman Easy* (1935)

Riding – riding –
The highwayman came riding, up to the old inn-door.

He'd a French cocked-hat on his forehead, a bunch of lace at his chin,
A coat of the claret velvet, and breeches of brown doe-skin;
They fitted with never a wrinkle: his boots were up to the thigh!
And he rode with a jewelled twinkle,
His pistol butts a-twinkle,
His rapier hilt a-twinkle, under the jewelled sky.[3]

The protagonists of costume films of the 1940s enjoy a history (or, rather, a mythology) which long predates cinema: pirates, highwaymen, bandits and other intrepid felons feature large. While Graham Greene was often disparaging of 'lightweight' historical fiction, its adaptation and its audience (Roedean and Cheltenham public schoolgirls, he presumes), Alison Light and Pam Cook have subsequently explained how such stories appealed to women, constrained by their actual, everyday lives, seeking action and adventure through escapist fantasy.[4] *Midshipman Easy* (1935), adapted from Captain Marryatt's 1836 novel, found Greene and Lejeune in agreement, recommending the film to children and its director, Carol Reed, for future honours: Reed's war and postwar record justified their enthusiasm. With interiors designed by Edward Carrick, it also displayed vast expanses of open sea. Comparing the film to the 1934 American version of Robert Louis Stevenson's *Treasure Island*, Lejeune was delighted to discover that Easy (Hughie Green – later better known as an ITV compère) brought out the boy in her: 'it is extraordinary to find an English picture that moves with such a pace from adventure to adventure, that suffers from so few inhibitions and flings out its extravagances so generously'.[5] Jack Easy, the son of an eighteenth-century country gentleman of philosophical bent (who preaches 'the equality of men'), is invited by Captain Wilson (Roger Livesey) to join the HM sloop *Harpy*. He soon makes his mark defending the black cook, Mesty (W. Robert Adams), and a smaller boy, Gascoigne, against the bullying of others. However, his zeal and idealism are soon matched by the naval discipline exercised by the heavily tattooed Boatswain Biggs: exchanges between the officers and the sailors are conducted (often humorously) in the style of Reed's wartime films (see Chapter 6), while the ship's mascot monkey continues to scratch, disregardingly. Easy leads an assault on a Spanish galleon, seizes 14,000 doubloons and encounters the precociously flirtatious Donna Agnes Rebeira (Margaret Lockwood) and her wealthy parents, en route for Palermo. Their paths cross again when Easy, Mesty and Gascoigne save the family from the notorious Sicilian bandit, Don Silvio, and again when he saves Don Silvio from the wreckage of a convicts' ship. Mesty fights Silvio at the edge of a cliff, allowing the swooning Easy to believe that his own was the victory: he thereby casts the film's entire scenario as make-believe.

Pink String and Sealing Wax (Robert Hamer, 1945) employs Victorian playbill lettering for its titles to locate its action, while *Fanny By Gaslight* (Anthony Asquith, 1943) uses street vendors' songs. While *Midshipman Easy* indicates its literary and historical source at its opening with the unrolling of a scroll and an engraved title, Rank's *Great Expectations* (David Lean, 1946) begins with the pages of Dickens' novel, adopts its first-person narration and sometimes uses direct quotation. But for the critic Richard Winnington, the exemplary quality of the production was not dependent on a much venerated original text:

> The costume [by Motley] and the sets show what can be done with the English scene. No pains and expense have been spared. But the point is that all this pain and cost is in the celluloid itself, and a lot more. Unlike any other British costume film, the clothes are lived in by the persons who wear them. The houses and streets have an air of being warmed by inhabitation.[6]

On a wind-blown marsh (designed for the studio by John Bryan and photographed by Guy Green), the young Pip (Anthony Wager) meets the escaped convict, the fearsome Magwitch (Finlay Currie).[7] Amid swirling mists (where even cows assume sinister shapes), the boy delivers a pie, brandy and a file stolen from his lowly guardians, the Gargeries (Bernard Miles and Freda Jackson) to the convict. A year later, he is taken to Satis House, kept as a shrine by the awesomely grand Miss Havisham (Martita Hunt) to the memory of a wedding which never took place: in the gloom, a stopped clock marks the fateful hour at which she was jilted; cobwebs hang over the banqueting table and the cake has been gnawed 'by sharper teeth than of mice'. Pip also meets a girl, the 'proud, pretty and insulting' Estella, 'brought up to have no sentiment', through whom Miss Havisham endeavours 'to reek revenge on all the male sex'. Estella little knows that she is the adopted daughter of Magwitch. The older Pip (John Mills) goes, 'with expectation', to work in London and shares rooms with Herbert Pocket (Alec Guinness – transferring the buoyancy of his stage delivery to the screen), where he receives gifts of money from an unknown source. But, he tells us, 'in trying to become a gentleman, I had succeeded in becoming a snob'. He supposes his benefactor to be Miss Havisham (but 'Who am I that I should be kind?' she tersely reminds him). Slamming the door on her, Pip dislodges a log from the fire and the dessicated old lady is swallowed in flames. When, finally, Pip and Estella re-meet at Satis, he tears down the dusty drapes to let in the sun: 'Let's start again – together!' he cries, and they rush away from the house. As Brian McFarlane has observed:

> The orphan boy who eventually succeeds to a more prosperous future was perhaps an apt hero for post-World War II Britain; . . . it does not seem fanciful to see the tearing down of the rotten drapes to let the light into the gloom of Satis House . . . as a metaphoric letting in of light on British life at large after the rigours of the war years. In its scrutiny of class structure, in the significance of Satis House as the symbol of an ossified attitude to wealth and class, of a structure that *needs* dismantling, *Great Expectations* may be seen as very much a product of its time and place.[8]

Similarly, *Pink String and Sealing Wax*, for all its studio-built period paraphernalia, warns against the preservation of Victorian values and urges tolerance towards the ambition and vision of a younger generation. Edward Sutton, the Brighton pharmacist and stern paterfamilias, instructs his wife not to behave too kindly towards their servants; she, in turn, advises him that by being as harsh as his own father he will turn his children against him. In Lean's 1954 adaptation of Harold Brighouse's 1916 *Hobson's Choice*, the wilful eldest daughter, Maggie Hobson (Brenda de Banzie), teaches boot-maker Willie Mossop (Mills), the son of a workhouse brat, to write on his slate 'There is always room at the top' – and how to take over her father's business.

Largely studio-bound, with sets designed by Tom Morahan, *Jamaica Inn* (Alfred Hitchcock, 1939 – reissued 1944 and 1948) opens with a shot of crashing waves and a declaration that, in the early 19th century, Cornwall was a lawless corner of England in which gangs planned wrecks. J. B. Priestley and Sidney Gilliatt share credits for the script, from Daphne du Maurier's 1936 novel. Mary Yellan (Maureen O'Hara) arrives from Ireland to stay with her Aunt Patience at the Inn. The local squire, the dissolute Humphrey Pengallan (Charles Laughton, swaggering here and in *Hobson's Choice* in what Lejeune classifies as his 'roguery-poguery' manner), soon decides that he will add Mary to his store of beautiful possessions, but Mary is more attracted to the youngest of her uncle's band of smugglers, James Trahearne (Robert Newton). She helps him to escape when the others set about punishing him for treachery, then fearlessly and feistily defies all their attempts to imprison her, in turn, for her betrayal. Her bodice gets ripped. Just as her aunt (and then her uncle) are about to tell her the name of the smugglers' leader they are shot and Mary is kidnapped. Trahearne declares himself an officer of the law who has been sent to investigate the Cornish wreckings and, with the help of the militia, arrests the band and snatches Mary to safety.

Popular myth suggests precedents for the characters of the novel and film *The Wicked Lady* (1945) also: for instance, the well-known ladies' man Captain James Hind (seized and executed for treason in 1652) or Captain Philip Stafford (who downed a pint of wine on his way to the gibbet).[9] In a gesture towards historical context, Caro and Kit Laxby meet on the frozen Thames of 1694 (see also *Orlando* [1992], Chapter 12). The deliciously bad Barbara (Margaret Lockwood) sets out to steal the fiancé of her cousin Caro (Patricia Roc) who, wearisomely good to the last, surrenders him to her. Caro even offers her the use of her gown, but Barbara says that she would not even be buried in it, let alone be wed. 'Pretty is too tame a word for her,' snaps the dowager aunt (Martita Hunt); 'cats have green eyes – I don't like cats'. Barbara soon tires of life with Ralph (Griffith Jones) and the Buckinghamshire country set, wanting 'to live in a fashionable world and to be admired'. She loses her mother's brooch (from which she has previously promised never to be parted) to Ralph's urbane sister in a game of cards but then determines to seize it back in the guise of a notorious highwayman. Captain Jackson himself (James Mason) is annoyed to find his territory encroached by another man, exhilarated to discover his rival to be a woman: 'Do you always take women by the throat?' gasps Barbara; 'No, I just take them,' he replies, thereafter scoring a trail of wenches and doxies. Barbara has less scruple in the conduct of her new-found diversion than does her professional accomplice, shooting dead the driver of a bullion coach. She makes a show of contrition by donning sober dresses and collars but then poisons the old family retainer, a Puritan, who has found out her secret. Jackson is caught and convicted, but cut down from the gibbet by his admirers at the last minute. He recognises the heraldic crest on Barbara's carriage at the hanging and pursues her to exact revenge: 'it will be a new experience to take you against your will'. Barbara, meanwhile, deprives Caro of a second suitor. But her feigning is ultimately her undoing and Caro is reunited with Ralph, just as the viewer is rudely returned from the delights of a fictitious past to stark, present realities.

In *Dead of Night* (Cavalcanti, Dearden and Hamer, 1945) and *The Man in Grey* (the most popular film at the British box office of 1943), objects from the past have a sinister impact upon the lives of characters in the present. In the former, a chinoiserie framed mirror bought by Joan Cortland (Googie Withers) as a wedding present for her husband (Ralph Michael) threatens to separate the couple, whereas in *The Man in Grey* the auction of the furniture and effects at a house sale bring together a RAF officer and Lady Clarissa, the last of the Rohans, while serving to introduce a flashback sequence in which the objects' history is narrated. In *Fanny By Gaslight*, a brooch which Fanny is given as a child reappears throughout the story. In *Dead of Night*, Sally (Sally Ann Howes) tells how she once came across a boy in Victorian costume, crying in a nursery, at a fancy-dress ball in a country house rumoured to be haunted, and Joan recounts the story of the mirror to the assembled guests by way of response. Peter saw 'something odd' in the mirror, the reflection of a room with a four-poster bed with dark red silk hangings and an open fire rather than the modern apartment in which it had been hung. Joan stands with him and tells him to force himself to recognise their own image, but when she goes away for the weekend, leaving Peter alone, the sensation becomes worse. When she returns he speaks to her in the voice of Etherington, who had been confined to his bed after an accident, and, believing his wife to have taken a lover, strangled her before cutting his own throat before the mirror. The object's spell is only broken when, at the final moment, Joan too sees the room and smashes the glass.

In *The Man in Grey*, a trinket box bought at the sale is located at a school for young ladies in Regency Bath where Miss Patchett (Martita Hunt) is headmistress. Hesther (Margaret Lockwood) gives the box to Clarissa (Phyllis Calvert) as a present. Hesther wickedly elopes with the ensign who has been courting Clarissa but Clarissa leaves the school in protest at Hesther's expulsion. In London she meets the man in grey, the notorious Lord Rohan (James Mason – whom Caroline Lejeune thought 'dark and masterful') who determines to marry her in spite of her 'grizzly girlish innocence' simply in order to secure an heir.[10] The rich, we are reminded, are fortunate but may not be happy. A fortune-teller predicts that Clarissa will find herself married to one man while loving another. Hesther schemes her way into the Rohan household, where the master recognises her as a kindred wild spirit and takes her as his mistress. Clarissa's true love, Swinton Rokeby (Stewart Granger – whom Lejeune thought 'scrumptious'), like Ralph in *The Wicked Lady* and Hapwood in *Fanny By Gaslight*, is portrayed as a more benevolent soul, who informs her of his intention to return to Jamaica to tame the rebellious slaves while his own blackamoor, Toby, is told to take care of Clarissa in his absence. For Rokeby, Rohan is 'just a well-bred scoundrel' and for Hapwood, Manderstoke (James Mason, again) is 'a drunken bully'. But as in *The Wicked Lady*, Hesther surpasses her partner's expectations in her cruelty.

Both James Mason and Stewart Granger moved to Hollywood after the war. Discussing his British films with *Picture Post* in 1947, Mason appears to endorse the critics' prejudices, reiterating James Agate's evaluation of *The Man in Grey* as 'Bosh and Tosh' and finding *The Wicked Lady* (a 'shoddy' 'Gainsborough horror', according to the *Penguin Film Review*'s Richard Winnington) an 'extremely vulgar' screen version of an excellent story, complaining also of its historic inauthenticity (in its 'detail and any genuine sense of period'). He found the Boultings (for whom he had appeared in 1942 in *Thunder Rock*) 'over portentous', 'striving possibly too hard for "good" cinema' and cited *Odd Man Out* (Carol Reed, 1947) as his 'one completely satisfactory film', praising (as did Dilys Powell) Carol Reed's direction of actors.[11] Roger Manvell, in his definition in the *Penguin Film Review* of 'the low, the middle and high film', says that *Odd Man Out* 'could hardly be bettered as a prestige film'.[12] Mason admits himself to have been amazed by the overwhelming success of *The Seventh Veil* (Compton Bennett, 1945), for which he gave credit to Sydney and Muriel Box, as authors of the screenplay. But it seems worth noting that the subjects and roles tackled by Reed and Mason (and Granger and Googie Withers) fall either side of Balcon's division between 'Realism and Tinsel', and across Manvell's schematic demarcation.[13] This suggests that certain personnel were sufficiently versatile to turn their hand to whatever came their way (or whatever a studio offered), and, perhaps, that such categories should always be regarded as provisional and be handled with caution. Furthermore, 'Real' themes are often addressed even when characters are dressed in seemingly 'Tinselly' apparel. John Ellis notes that, in the 1940s, 'documentary versus extravagant entertainment defines the difference between quality and prestige films for most of the critics'. Both Gainsborough's low-budget *The Wicked Lady* and Rank's midfield *Brief Encounter* (David Lean, 1945) may readily be construed as melodrama, but critics generally disparaged the former while esteeming the latter as a film which could advertise British quality production and compete effectively in the home and export market.

> The critics themselves recognised the originality of their project and the idea of the 'quality film' they were constituting. They saw it as different from traditional 'art cinema'. Crucially, 'the quality film' was something that they passionately hoped the wide public would come to recognise and appreciate. They hoped to change the nature of mass cinema in Britain.[14]

Suburban Wives

In the history of British cinema, suburbs figure not in tragedy, but in melodrama and farce. Frequently, an idea of suburban life is invoked rather than an actual setting: indeed, a suburb's lack of specific identity is all too often presumed to be its single defining feature. Michael Anderson's 1953 *Will Any Gentleman?* is a prime example of this type: Henry Stirling (George Cole) is a bowler-hatted Pooterish bank clerk (like Holland in *The Lavender Hill Mob* [1951]), a Rotarian who daily packs his sandwiches and travels to his job in town. Under hypnosis, he loses his inhibitions, takes the day off to go to the races, takes to hard drink in the afternoon and takes up with the maid, Beryl (Joan Sims); his wife, meanwhile, returns to her mother. In spite of the vaunted comforts and convenience of its regulated lifestyle, the suburb can readily betoken unfulfilled or unspoken desire and an unsettling sense of betwixt and between, as much psychological as geographical. 'Slums may well be breeding-grounds of crime', opines Cyril Connolly airily in 1944, 'but middle class suburbs are incubators of apathy and delirium.'[15] Of interest here is this sometimes settled, sometimes unsettled suburban mentality and attitude, wherever the action of the given film takes place.

29 Acacia Avenue (Henry Cass, 1945), adapted by Muriel and Sydney Box from a stageplay, opens with a disclaimer denoting the presumed familiarity of its subject: 'any resemblance to people you know is quite unavoidable'. Shirley, the maid (Meg Jenkins), helps lower middle-class Mr and Mrs Robinson (veterans Gordon Harker and Betty Balfour on good form) with their packing for a Mediterranean cruise – their first holiday abroad. Mr Robinson duly swaps his pinstripes and bowler for a double-breasted, brass-buttoned blazer and bags. While 'mother' cautiously wonders whether their usual Bognor excursion would not be preferable, Mr Robinson affects confidence: 'Foreigners always understand English if you speak loudly enough' (but subsequently admits his own apprehension). Mrs Robinson wonders whether he wouldn't like a more intelligent and younger companion – but is flattered to hear that he finds her want of youth and intelligence 'restful'. More cosmopolitan neighbours (precursors of the Leadbetters from BBC TV's The Good Life) advise against Athens – no golf courses. Meanwhile, son Peter (Tommy Hanley) is detained from his appointment with girlfriend Pepper ('hot' Dinah Sheridan) at the tennis club by glamorous, upper-class Fay (Carla Lehmann) and her yet more glamorous motor. Daughter Joan (Jill Evans) announces her engagement and her disinclination to accompany her parents; Peter approves the match (the fiancé, Michael, drives a green MG) and will not take her place (there are novel and exotic distractions enough at home). Inspite of the jibes at the Robinsons' expense, Michael's upper middle-class snobbery (inherited old silver is preferred to newly bought silver-plate cutlery) and Fay's upper-class lax morals (she's married) are ultimately held to be less appealing than the apparently settled suburban comforts of Bognor, begonias, bakelite mugs (even for claret), erratic clocks and errant dogs.

Clem Morgan (Trevor Howard) in They Made Me a Fugitive (Alberto Cavalcanti, 1947) is convicted for a murder he did not commit and is imprisoned. He escapes and heads for London, making his way through woods and then breaking into a house. A woman offers him clothes, food and a bath – and requests a favour in return. Asked if he has ever killed a man, Clem replies that he once used a beer bottle against a German in the war. The glazed-eyed, sozzled wife, wants rid of her inebriated husband. Clem refuses the gun she offers and leaves, only for her to shoot the husband repeatedly herself. Clem's justifiable act, the injustice of the accusations against him and the purpose with which he pursues his journey, endangering himself, is set against the mutually destructive stagnant life of the suburban couple.

Guilty pleasures: Laura (Celia Johnson) takes afternoon tea with Dr Alec Harvey (Trevor Howard) in *Brief Encounter* (David Lean, 1945)

At the beginning of Rank's production of Noël Coward's *Brief Encounter*, Laura (Celia Johnson) says that she was perfectly happy as a suburban wife to Fred and mother to Bobby and Margaret before her calm contentment was disrupted by her chance meeting with Alec Harvey (Trevor Howard) at Milford Junction. Johnson affectively repeats her quietly pained performance in *Dear Octopus* (1943) (see Chapter 6), bruised but not battered from an affair. Already, she is mourning for what might have been between them and 'for all the places I've always longed to go' (Venice, a cruise, a tropical island). 'For a few stolen minutes each week,' commented Caroline Lejeune,

> over the thin cups of tea from the urn and the prosaic Bath bun, they escape into a world of enchantment that would probably never have been theirs had they met earlier, when each was free: when neither had contracted responsibilities that were heavy enough to escape from.[16]

Habitually, her trips to town entail a visit to Boots library, to the shops, sometimes to the pictures and to the Kardomah for lunch; she regularly meets Dolly Messiter (Everley Gregg), who unwittingly jokes about telling Fred about Alec (as if the truth of the situation is unimaginable for her). Staff and regular travellers exchange the usual banter in the tearoom, oblivious of Laura's inner turmoil. Alec thinks her sane, uncomplicated and awfully nice – 'it sounds a little dull', she replies; nor, she says, is she brave enough to throw herself under a train when the chance arrives. Laura realises that Alec won't tell his wife about her – 'and the first awful feeling of danger' sweeps over her. Laura is restrained by her sense of guilt (she perceives Bobby's minor accident as a punishment for her pleasure) and, repeatedly, she urges herself to be sensible. Even when Laura silently wishes that Dolly, 'chattering away nineteen to the dozen', were dead, she instantly corrects herself. Both Laura and Alec realise that their love for each other is desperate and both are hampered by their sense that an affair is 'sordid' (they resort to deceit only reluctantly) and that the 'price is too high' (possibly for themselves, possibly for those whom they love besides each other). 'Alec behaved with such perfect politeness – no one could have guessed what he was really feeling,' remembers Laura in voiceover, when Dolly stumbles upon their 'last few precious moments': Alec has accepted a job in South Africa. Laura both knows he has gone for ever (leaving with the merest touch on her shoulder) and, listening for the guard's whistle, wants him not to be gone at all. With Laura, the audience waits for sounds to appear and for train smoke to clear in the hope that Alec will emerge. Fred, on the other hand, represents stability but not passion nor excitement (he asks her to lower the volume when Laura's 'theme', the Rachmaninov concerto which dominates the soundtrack, is playing on the radio). Ultimately, he is grateful to her for returning to him from 'the long way away' of the dream (or memory) which the film has presented. Lejeune, who thought *Brief Encounter* 'one of the most emotionally honest and deeply satisfying films that have ever been made in this country' (while suspecting that it would not prove generally popular), was not alone in her praise. E. Arnot Robertson, writing for the *Penguin Film Review*, contrasted familiar 'cute' and adolescent female characters with 'certain glorious exceptions like *Brief Encounter*, blessedly adult, truthful and contemporary'.[17] Richard Dyer suggests why, and why, perhaps, for particular audiences, it is still worth watching *Brief Encounter* now, beyond the 'cups of tea, banal conversation and guilt', for 'the pressure of emotion' which it enacts and constructs:

> On the one hand, their – and especially Laura's – holding back from going with their longing for one another is not just conventionality or inhibition, but also a sense of affection and loyalty to others, a desire not to hurt anyone . . . Such restraint is not the absence of feeling. Indeed, there can be no concept of restraint without an acknowledgement of feeling – restraint must keep something emotional in check . . . The very familiarity of this for some people is a pleasure because it confirms part of how we experience our affective lives.[18]

If I am in the mood for crying, Celia Johnson can still reduce me to tears – although even more so when she's talking about boats in *In Which We Serve* than when she's talking to herself about Alec in *Brief Encounter*. For the most part, I think, I cry on her behalf but know that seeing her spending more time with David Niven (in the former) or Trevor Howard (in the latter) would afford no consolation. Indeed, I never think for a moment that she should, nor that this would necessarily console her either: Alec (no pirate or highwayman) is, after all, not so very different from Fred. I cry because her dreams are so little rather than unrealised, as confined as the suburban life to which she returns from her temporary reverie.

Frustrated or stifled desire and guilty secrets resurface in Carol Reed's *The Fallen Idol*, adapted by Graham Greene from his own short story. Philip (Bobby Henrey) sees more of the kindly gentleman's gentleman Baines (Ralph Richardson) than he does of his own father, an Ambassador; Baines delights him with stories of his adventures in Africa, and trips to the zoo with Baines' 'niece', Julie (Michèle Morgan), where Phil is especially interested in the snakes. Baines and Julie plan to elope together. The housekeeper, the narrow-minded and vicious Mrs Baines, refuses her husband a divorce but intends to punish him for his affair with Julie; she kills Phil's pet snake. Baines and Mrs Baines argue and Mrs Baines has a fatal fall. Conversations are overheard and assumptions are made on Phil's behalf as to what he can and cannot understand. Caught in the grown-ups' games of secrets, lies and bribes (even a tart with a heart in the police station remarks that she knows Phil's daddy) Phil doesn't know what to say for the best and the more he changes his story the more the police disbelieve him, then refuse to listen. Julie, speaking to him in French, pleads with him to tell the truth. The final return of Phil's mother serves to remind us of her absence. Throughout, Reed not only elicits fine performances from his actors but also uses the architecture of the Kensington Embassy to dramatic effect. At night, Baines, Julie and Phil play hide and seek between shrouded furniture and Phil at first mistakes Mrs Baines for a ghost; a tipped balcony window remains in the back of shot as a crucial clue which is not revealed; a paper arrow (a message for Mrs Baines) is caught in foliage, then released and slowly circles the grand marble hallway before being kicked and finally picked up by a policeman; 'Treacherous stuff this marble,' complains the char (Dandy Nichols) pointedly, 'I wouldn't have it in my house at any price.'

In *Blithe Spirit* (David Lean, 1945) and *Miranda* (Ken Annakin, 1947), the disruption of contented, stable coupledom is presented as farce; both feature Margaret Rutherford conspicuously failing to restore order. As Madame Arcati in *Blithe Spirit* (produced by Noël Coward from his own stageplay), she plays a brisk, pragmatic Englishwoman who believes in spirits: she arrives late for her first séance at the suburban home of Charles Condomine (Rex Harrison) and his American wife, Ruth (Kay Hammond), because she has had a presentiment of a puncture in her bicycle tyre and has returned home for a repair kit (but there is no puncture). Charles is a celebrated thriller-writer researching for a book about a homicidal medium but both he and Ruth are initially sceptical. Arcati summons the ghost of Elvira (Joyce Carey), his first wife (who appears shrouded in green ectoplasm and is visible only to Charles). Elvira then refuses to depart. Ruth mistakes Charles' conversation with Elvira to be addressed to her and she takes umbrage. At full throttle, she drives off towards Budleigh Salterton. There is an accident . . . and she returns as a ghost. Hectored by both wives, Charles again resorts to Arcati's spells, but to no avail. Tampering with the occult results in the threesome being trapped together for ever, obliged to pursue an involuntary, irregular, bohemian ménage in spite of themselves.

As Nurse Carey in *Miranda*, yet another stage adaptation, Rutherford plays a brisk, pragmatic Englishwoman who believes in mermaids. Dr Paul Marten (Griffith Jones) returns to London from a fishing trip in Cornwall with Miranda Truella (Glynis Johns), a girl who loves men and who finds that her tail 'provides an element of surprise'. Mermen, she comments, are little-eyed and flat-nosed – 'very unattractive – that's why we're almost extinct'. Paul and the nurse endeavour to keep Miranda's identity a secret but his sophisticated wife, Claire (Googie Withers), cannot but note her various eccentricities (she sleeps in the bath, does not bother with knickers and devours the couple's pet goldfish). Paul's friend Nigel, a painter, falls for Miranda, supposing her an invalid; Isabel, Nigel's wife, temporarily falls out of love with him and Truella falls for Charles, Paul's chauf-feur. Claire asks Charles about Truella's legs: 'I've always behaved like a gentleman,' he insists; 'you'd be surprised at some gentlemen,' replies Claire. Isabel and Nigel make it up, Nigel promis-ing that he will turn his portrait of Miranda into a sunset. Miranda and Paul argue: 'You've hated me ever since I set tail in this house' and all three men return the love tokens she has given them. Miranda makes her way to the embankment and, in the manner customary to disappointed lovers, throws herself into the Thames (see Chapter 2). The following spring, she delivers a baby boy in the warmer waters of Majorca. Miranda, concludes *Picture Post*, 'breaks up happy couples, eats whelks and oysters and has a whale of a time'.[19]

Inner-city Mayhem

Many of the 1940s films narrating crime and violence in the city attempt to reassure their audience that trouble lies in the past or is under control. Meanwhile, Basil Wright's 1946 documentary, *Children on Trial*, portrayed their contemporary context. The introductory titles to *Brighton Rock* (John Boulting, 1947), adapted from Graham Greene's 1938 novel and 1943 stageplay, claim that this is 'now a large jolly seaside town' and that the gangs which caused unrest between the wars 'are happily no more'. *Odd Man Out* never explicitly names the IRA but adopts a similar prologue. Ealing's *The Blue Lamp* (Basil Dearden, 1949), scripted by wartime policeman T. E. B. Clarke and dedicated to the police force, speaks of the rise in broken homes and youth delinquency, but shows the perpetrators of crime being brought to justice with the co-operation of the community. *London Belongs to Me* (Sidney Gilliat, 1948), set with Britain on the brink of war, begins (after an aerial shot of the Thames) and finishes with an anonymous narrator describing the terrace in Dul-cimer Street, Kennington, in which Percy Boon (Richard Attenborough) shares his lodgings with his widowed mother, Connie Coke (Ivy St Helier) (a Soho club cloakroom attendant), Doris Josser (Susan Shaw) and her retired parents, and their collective landlady;[20] Alastair Sim makes an appear-ance as a charlatan medium, Henry Squales. When Percy (led astray by professional crooks) is responsible for the accidental death of a funfair cashier, the household campaign on his behalf. 'They certainly are fine houses', concludes the narrator, 'the whole length of the terrace'. Bessie Hyams (Jane Hylton), in *It Always Rains on Sunday* (Robert Hamer, 1947), in spite of the scepticism of her dodgy brother, Lou (John Slater), devotes herself to a local club which tries to keep young people out of crime and resists the suggestion that she and their father move to more salubrious surroundings. These films are often shot on actual locations: *Odd Man Out* includes a tram ride on the Falls Road; *The Blue Lamp* features car chases through Paddington, Notting Hill and White City; *It Always Rains on Sunday* repeatedly establishes the action in Bethnal Green, a railway slicing the skyline horizontally across the facing rows of terraces, a stunted church spire beyond; *Brighton Rock* documents streets and garish seaside entertainments. They also necessarily record war damage and refer to wartime experiences (in *Obsession* [Edward Dmytryk, 1948], the doctor picks his way through the derelict remains to his hide-out, sites appropriated by children at play in *Hue and Cry* [Charles Crichton, 1947], *Passport to Pimlico* [1948] [see Chapter 6] and *The Blue Lamp*). In both *Odd Man Out* and *It Always Rains on Sunday*, men on the run take refuge in shelters originally constructed against air-raids.

However, stylistically these films seem to refer back to the 1930s, both to trench-coated American B-movies and to such British quota derivatives as *They Drive By Night* (Arthur Woods, 1938). Night and rain (as opposed to the night and fog of 1920s representations of the East End) is a dominant and recurrent visual motif, while the narrative schema of underworld hierarchies, wrong accusations set right, wrong-headed intellectuals and common-sense 'judies' who stand by their men (right or wrong) in spite of everything, are firmly established. In *They Drive By Night*, Shorty (Emlyn Williams as a Londoner) is released from prison and meets the brother of a convicted murdered who is about to take 'the nine o'clock walk'. Allen's brother says that he did not mean to kill the girl and Shorty's response is a portent of his own fate. The flowers he buys from a street stall and the jaunty grinding organ in the background are painfully at odds with circumstances. Returning to his girlfriend's lodgings he finds Alice strangled in bed and realises that he will be the prime suspect. At night, he goes into the newsreel cinema on Charing Cross Road (where stories of murderers heighten his anxiety) and, on leaving, a newspaper stand announces that the Yard's hunt for him has begun. On his way North, Shorty encounters Molly (Anna Konstam), a Palais de Danse escort who believes in his innocence and helps him to throw off the police and then to hide. Former cronies prove less supportive, for fear of their own safety. Typical newspaper headlines punctuate the chase: 'Police find Glamour Girl in Car'. Eventually Shorty is cleared when he traps the culprit (he is prepared to give himself up in order to ensure an investigation – 'the police aren't stupid') and he and Molly are at the prison at nine o'clock to witness his just punishment. The film remains worth seeing for its dingy atmosphere and evocative incidental encounters, despite its simplistic psychological analysis and confident affirmation of legal process.

In Jules Dassin's 1950 *Night and the City*, an American spiv and hustler, Harry Fabian (Richard Widmark), is on the run from his creditors after yet another failed scam. 'All my life I've wanted to be somebody . . . a mister with a future,' Harry complains to his long-suffering girlfriend, Mary, who meekly thinks 'his ideas always have so much imagination'. Other crooks, older and wiser, are happy to continue with small-scale operations (black-market nylons and forgery). Meanwhile, housemate Adam (Hugh Marlowe) thinks that Mary deserves better and Harry shares his favours with Helen (Googie Withers, as eminently watchable as ever) the kept wife and partner of a Soho racketeer (the overblown Francis L. Sullivan over-playing monumentally). Helen wants to go into business for herself and enlists Harry as her dodgy accomplice. The film features the attractions of Piccadilly Circus, the docks and St Paul's (by night), double-decker buses, Tower Bridge and Trafalgar Square (by day) and well-honed and oiled torsos displayed in Graeco-Roman wrestling bouts. The seedy atmosphere of the underworld's alleyways and backrooms is heavily delineated by low-angle lighting and the intrusive shadows cast by screens and stairs. The increasingly desperate and maniacal Harry conducts himself dishonourably among his fellow thieves and is made to answer for it; Mary is finally rewarded for her devotion by being united with Adam.

Odd Man Out, photographed by Robert Krasker, cinematographer on *The Third Man* (1949) and *Brief Encounter*, opens in the manner of *London Belongs to Me* and *Night and the City* with an aerial shot locating its action. In style and in its scenario, *Odd Man Out* is comparable to the studio-constructed Dublin of *The Informer* (Arthur Robison, 1929), photographed by Werner Brandes. Dilys Powell, writing for *Picture Post*, commended the film's 'extraordinary sense of the city – women coming home from shopping, children playing under street lamps, men in the pub –

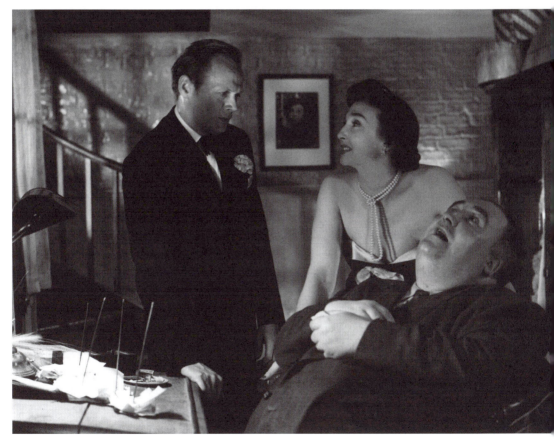

Small-time crook Harry Fabian (Richard Widmark) and Helen (Googie Withers) plan their next move over the body of her husband (Francis L. Sullivan) in Jules Dassin's sleazy *Night and the City* (1950)

conscious of a fugitive in its midst'.[21] However, while indicating its setting as Belfast the film is evasive about the identity of the organisation to which Jonnie McQueen (James Mason) belongs, preferring to represent the theme as 'the conflict in people's hearts when they become involved . . . rather than between the government and an illegal organisation'.[22] Already with a sentence in prison behind him (and accused by others that the experience has 'softened' him), Jonnie leads a raid on a bank to raise funds, but he is injured and a bystander killed. In spite of the advertised reward, family and friends (and total strangers – such as the two ex-ARP English nurses 'new to this town') shelter him as the police chase closes in, with Dennis (Robert Beatty) wearing a bandage on his arm to act as a decoy; to the local boys, 'Jonnie McQueen' is something of an urban folk hero. But charity is, for Jonnie, not entirely selfless: 'everyone wants a slice of him'. While Father Tom wants to hear his confession and comfort his soul (but will then give him up), Jonnie's lover Kathleen Sullivan (Kathleen Ryan) says that she is prepared to kill him herself and take herself with him, out of pity, and wonders about the value, in hard cash, of the priest's faith. The Constabulary Inspector, meanwhile, says that in his profession, 'there is no good or bad . . . just the innocent or guilty', and continues to do 'his duty'. Chiming clocks persistently reinforce the growing sense of urgency, as Kathleen is told to deliver Jonnie by 11 p.m. A local publican, Finsey (William Hartnell), hides him until closing time, when, with the night rain yielding to snow, he is taken in by a painter (Robert Newton – whose indulgent hamming here slackens the pace). A doctor, personally lapsed but nevertheless still professionally unconcerned by Jonnie's political affiliations, dresses his wounds ('patching him up for his execution'). At last, at the docks, Jonnie is faced with his means of escape.

An ex-lover provides sanctuary for another man on the run in *It Always Rains on Sunday*. Tommy Swann (John McCallum) escapes from Dartmoor and returns to the East End; even before his name is disclosed, Rose (Googie Withers), the barmaid at the Compasses, wishes him 'jolly good luck'. Tommy gave an engagement ring to a younger, blonder Rose before going North 'on business', but was arrested in Manchester on a smash and grab raid. Rose has meanwhile married into drudgery with the dull (but decent) George (Edward Chapman) and has a young son and two nubile step-daughters, Doris (Patricia Plunkett) and Vi (Susan Shaw), themselves now looking for excitement (even if it means affairs with a married man – not his first, says his wife – and creeping home late at night through the bedroom window). Bessie Hyams, a family friend, advises Doris to stick with her sensible boyfriend and sensibly at her job as a typist at the local gasworks, rather than indulge her dreams of a career in the West End. Rose feeds Tommy, gives him money from the housekeeping and their affair is rekindled, but when she offers him their engagement ring he fails to remember that it was his gift, thereby destroying not only Rose's present thrill but also her memory of a more joyous past: the film's score, not her face, conveys her sadness and loss. Shown in flashback in a mirror, Rose's first meeting with Tommy is (as Charles Barr observes) already 'at two removes'.[23] A squabble with Vi further reminds her of her ageing, Vi cattily calling her 'a fat old cow'. Nevertheless, she continues to cover for Tommy – 'all she can do is help him to get to a place where she'll never see him again'. While Tommy observes that George is some fifteen years her senior, Rose flatly tells Tommy that he has come ten years too late: 'You may say and think now that you want to see me but you won't'. But, with Tommy gone, Rose tries to take her own life. The police corner him in a railway yard (amid more night and rain) and George, by Rose's bedside, kindly says that they could not get along without her. The locked-shot of a street introduces and closes the film, a potent image of East End kith and kinship.

They Made Me a Fugitive uses studio reconstruction (designed by Andrew Mazzei) of comparable settings: pubs, clubs, roadside cafés and boarding houses. As with *They Drive By Night*, diegetic sound serves simultaneously as commentary: 'what if tomorrow brings only sorrow . . . who cares, I love you', is sung as Sally the chorus girl (Sally Gray) thinks of Clem in prison. An East End undertakers, Valhalla (with RIP written on its roof ridge), provides the cover for the black-market activities of Narcy (Griffith Jones) and Morgan ('what you might call free enterprise . . . a poor man's Fortnum and Mason'). Spivs of the type of Narcy and Ted Purvis in *Waterloo Road* (1945) (and subsequently Sergeant Walker in BBC TV's *Dad's Army*) became a cliché, with A. L. Vargas complaining in the *Penguin Film Review* that they had 'been thrust down our throats till we wince at the mere mention of the word' and Catherine de la Roche commenting of *They Made Me a Fugitive* that 'no idea was given of what induces men to become spivs or what might provide a counter-attraction for them'.[24] There is much in the dialogue and repartee which locates the action specifically in the post-war period: ex-RAF Clem (Trevor Howard) says that he 'went on doing what the country put me in uniform to do after they'd taken it back' but that 'the only man I killed was a sentry covered with swastikas'; 'he's never looked back since he joined the Oxford group', joshes Rockcliffe (Ballard Berkeley), the police inspector with Narcy's Limehouse gang; 'This is the last time Morgan runs his fingers through *my* permanent wave,' quips Cora (Rene Ray), the gangster's moll, in the manner of an advertisement; 'Arthur who? . . . Arthermometer . . . this must be the Third Programme,' they banter on. The black humour and eccentricity, the gangland slang, nicknames and catchphrases, the preening Narcy (Griffith Jones) (by name and by nature) and the concern to distinguish professional villains of various orders ('I may be a crook but not that sort of a crook,' insists Clem) from mere amateur-ers (says Narcy, repeatedly) carry forward into lighter weight genre films from *The Ladykillers* – filmed in King's Cross (Alexander Mackendrick, 1955) to *Lock, Stock and Two Smoking Barrels* and *Snatch* (Guy Ritchie, 1998 and 2000). The post-war disaffection, especially among men ('What he needs is another war,' says Ellen [Eve Ashley] of Clem), survives for at least a decade (for instance, in *The League of Gentlemen* [Basil Dearden, 1960] – see Chapter 8).

Ealing's *Hue and Cry* is more broadly comic, although the outwitting of criminals by small boys and their escape through a man-hole cover are also recalled by *The League of Gentlemen*. Jack Warner (who established his kindly BBC TV *Dixon of Dock Green* persona with *The Blue Lamp*, *It Always Rains on Sunday* and *The Ladykillers*)[25] for once plays on the wrong side of the law – but only just. With its thumping soundtrack and stark photography of the docks at Shadwell, *Hue and Cry* is something of a quaint and, admittedly, dated transatlantic spoof (like Alan Parker's 1976 *Bugsy Malone*) in style, with its cast shadows and the silhouette of a cat, Otto, on the stairs; it draws its story from *Emil und die Detektive* (Gerhard Lamprecht, 1931). *Picture Post* interviewed

Ida (Hermione Baddeley), 'the good-natured barmaid turned sleuth', is on the case with Prewitt (Harcourt Williams), the corrupt solicitor, in *Brighton Rock* (John Boulting, 1947)

Frank Richards, the author of the *Gem* and *Magnet* school stories, who for thirty years wrote about the boys of Greyfriars and St Jim's – and although happy to be photographed in dressing gown and skull cap surrounded by boys, he appears to be the model for Alastair Sim's camp pastiche in *Hue and Cry* (who while speaking grandiosely of 'my public' also confides that he loathes 'adventurous-minded boys').[26] As with the more serious-minded noir films of the 1940s, there is ample footage documenting, for instance, Covent Garden market, football fields and ice-cream stands (the usual haunts of boys). Joe (Harry Fowler), the leader of the gang, works as a market porter as a cover for his CID assignment (he says). Comic-style cut-ins are used to reiterate the film's references (at one time intended to be called *The Trump*), while the boys crack a code which they have first identified as a number plate in the self-same comic (and seen being read on a train). Selwyn Pike (the comic-book hero), Nicky the nark and the emphatically tattooed Jack become real for them. When the boys suspect Miss Davis, at the newspaper, of 'redirecting' comic stories they capture her while asking for a contribution towards the church choir outing and then subject her to the most devilish means of torture – not feathers, not water, not a penknife but a solitary white mouse. Matching the film's opening (a boys' choir rendition of 'Oh, for the Wings of a Dove', at which the comic is confiscated) the film ends after a set-piece chase sequence, with the same aria rendered by boys with walloping black eyes.

The juvenile Tom Riley (Dirk Bogarde) in *The Blue Lamp* is one of the youngsters for whom the old crooks and snouts have no time – especially once he has killed the local bobby. As the disturbing baby-faced gangster Pinkie, in *Brighton Rock*, *Picture Post* judged Richard Attenborough a real triumph, in an 'evening of unusual excitement' on stage:

> *Brighton Rock* on paper is a work so sordid, so dusty with decay and smelling of evil as to be untranslatable in completely human terms. Its characters are despicable – almost to a man or woman. And you can't lay all the blame on their environment . . .[27]

Greene, himself, complained that the film adaptation lost the social outrage which he had intended in the novel while accepting the dramatic necessity of its changed ending (Rose [Carol Marsh], Pinkie's expedient child bride, is allowed to believe in his continued affection beyond the grave).[28] Certainly the film conveys the pace which critics witnessed in the theatre. Hermione Baddeley as Ida ('the good-natured barmaid turned sleuth'), caught inadvertently between the old guard and the young pretender, accompanied Attenborough from stage to screen. Exaggeratedly raucous, cackling Ida (who never forgets a face) places her faith in dead Fred's betting tips and the chancing upon letters in a newspaper (a ouija board in the novel), common sense (outwitting the drunkenly off-guard lawyer, Prewitt [Harcourt Williams]) and gut instinct (Fred looked 'ever so queer'), whereas Pinkie's Catholicism tells him he is fated to damnation already (he and Rose *know* that they are evil) and his nervousness (the constant twitching and playing of a cat's cradle) belies his adolescent bravura. While Ida poses as Rose's mum in the hope of saving her from danger, Pinkie (to whom Greene persistently refers as 'virginally boyish') recoils from the sound of a baby crying and Rose pitifully confesses to Dallow (William Hartnell) (who finally turns against the boy) that she wishes that she were even so much as Pinkie's friend.

Prewitt, a corrupt professional, has become progressively disillusioned in the course of a twenty-five-year marriage to a woman he no longer loves and considers his social inferior (he says); the solicitor in *London Belongs to Me* is interested only in the amount of money which the Jossers can raise for Percy's defence. However, in *They Drive By Night*, a one-time schoolmaster is identified as potentially suspect by his reading of Havelock Ellis and secret stash of nudie magazines and female paraphernalia (in addition to his confidence that he can 'manage' a perfect crime). Also, as played by Ernest Thesiger, he is identifiable as the well-meaning (but wrong-minded) Mr Maydig in *The Man Who Could Work Miracles* (1936) (see Chapter 5) and the certainly deranged scientist Dr Praetorius in James Whale's 1935 American production of *The Bride of Frankenstein*. Robert Newton, it can fairly be said, carries a similar weight of baggage to many of his roles and is often most convincing when a character requires that he should swagger at several sheets to the wind (as Lukey in *Odd Man Out* and Bill Sikes in *Oliver Twist* [1948]). In

Obsession, directed by Edward Dmytryk in exile from America and scored by the Italian composer Nino Rota, Newton, as the psychiatric doctor Clive Reardon, manages an altogether lower-key delivery. While Greene drew partly on actual events for *Brighton Rock*, *Obsession* (based on a novel) anticipates the notorious Haig acid-bath murders of 1949.[29] Here the criminal is outwitted by a white toy poodle called Monty (doubtless named after the victorious general at the second battle of Alamein) and a nameless moggy – but even more so by the overweening arrogance with which he assumes his own logic to be impregnable and pre-eminent. 'All murderers are amateurs', Detective Superintendent Finsbury (Naunton Wayne) obligingly corrects him; 'The only professionals are those who try to catch the murderers . . . perhaps you hadn't thought of that.' Reardon maintains a strict routine of visits between home, club, consultancy and garage. He nonchalantly assures his captive that there is nothing personal in his proposed elimination – it is merely his misfortune to be 'the next one' in his wife's succession of lovers. He assumes that power resides entirely in his own hands and ineffable planning, that short of suggesting a better mix of Martini to him, his captive will leave no impression. In his club, Reardon calmly sits through discussions of British economic dependence on America and of a certain American missing in London. However, by engaging his captive in conversation he acquires a turn of phrase which sets Finsbury on his tail.

Caring Professionals

Vivian Kenaway (Rex Harrison), in Sidney Gilliat's 1945 *The Rake's Progress*, is a 1930s playboy, a man of yesterday, until his life is given meaning by the outbreak of war. His family's attempt to exercise privilege in order to secure him a comfortable position in business come to nothing and those who have worked their way into management through the ranks resent the imposition. Meanwhile, there are many instances of professionals who have achieved success through application, disappointment and sacrifice (as in *The Stars Look Down* – see Chapter 5); but integrity, dedication and ambition are also matters for debate and few professionals survive untested.

In *Waterloo Road* (1945) (see Chapter 6) the doctor to the local community serves as occasional commentator and as protagonist. At the end of the film, he reveals that the efforts of Ted to avoid conscription have been wasted; his professional code obliges him to confess that a medical test would have proved him unfit for service and that the dodgy certificate for which he has paid over the odds is, in fact, valid. He advises him to 'stay off wine, women and song'. Alec Harvey, in *Brief Encounter*, shares his sense of vocation and idealism with Laura – he wants to serve his Yorkshire community by pursuing research into pneumoconiosis and preventative medicine, improving the living conditions and hygiene of the workers (subjects, incidentally, much discussed by *Picture Post* in advance of the Beveridge Report and the setting up of the National Health Service). His enthusiasm reminds Laura 'of a little boy'. *The Citadel* (1939), adapted from the 1937 novel by A. J. Cronin (even better known for subsequent BBC radio and television adaptations of *Dr Finlay's Casebook*), cast Robert Donat as the initially eager young Scottish doctor, Andrew Manson, despatched to a similar mining town in Wales: on arrival, row upon row of terraces (built as sets) confront him through the lashing night rain. Dr Denny (Ralph Richardson), care-worn and driven to drink, tells him that the typhus bug seeps into the houses from the main sewer. For the greater good, Denny and Manson resort to unprofessional means, demolishing the sewer to ensure its replacement. Manson marries the local schoolmistress, Christine (Rosalind Russell), who shares his hopes – but they encounter resistance both from established bureaucrats and from the miners themselves (accustomed to receiving pink medicine and leave from work as the only available cure). Manson resigns and sets up in private practice in London, where he acquires a moustache, a wing collar and a brass plaque . . . and a number of wealthy colleagues and even wealthier clients, who like to be pampered. But his conscience continues to prick him. Denny (now busy in the East End) asks him to join his new clinic: Christine (in a marked departure from the Cronin original – possibly to indulge the American sponsors' taste for 'happy endings') rejoices at Andrew's return to worthy causes.

Donat again assumed the role of a middle-class professional as the popular long-serving public schoolmaster in Sam Wood's 1939 adaptation (again, with lavishly constructed sets) of James Hilton's 1934 novel *Goodbye Mr Chips*. An embittered example of the type is delivered by Michael Redgrave as Crocker-Harris (the finest classics scholar the school has ever known) in Asquith's 1951 *The Browning Version* (where a crabby and unpopular master, 'Himmler of the lower fifth', is touched by the small gesture of an undistinguished boy). Professionalism (the pursuit of justice), tempered by self-sacrifice and a sense of rightness, is represented by Donat's Sir Robert Morton, QC, in another film version of a Rattigan stageplay, *The Winslow Boy* (Asquith, 1948); Asquith returned to a similar theme in 1954 with *Carrington VC*. Meanwhile, public schoolmasters and mistresses are played for laughs in *The Happiest Days of Your Life* (1950), where confusion seems to thwart the personal ambitions of the Headmaster of Nutbourne College (Alastair Sim) for promotion until the ever brisk and pragmatic Margaret Rutherford (as the Headmistress of St Swithin's, instructed to share Nutbourne's premises) takes command and (eventually) saves the day.[30] There are topical verbal and visual references to the nationalisation of the railways, *The Third Man*, *Oliver Twist* and *The Wooden Horse* (Jack Lee, 1950). The formula was repeated in the Launder and Gilliat *St Trinians* series, with George Cole playing a comedy spiv.

Sometimes, professional potential (as a social, rather than a personal good) is seen to be marred and compromised by individual circumstance. In *The Small Back Room* (Powell and Pressburger, 1948), from a novel by Nigel Balchin, a young scientist, Sammy Rice (David Farrar), is engaged on important wartime research. But the pain and shame of a crippled foot oppress him with a sense of failure. *Picture Post* commended Hein Heckroth's sets and the film's hallucination sequence, literally transforming 'the small back room into a little vision of a dipsomaniac's hell'.[31] When a friend is blown up trying to dismantle a new type of German booby-trap, Rice takes it to pieces successfully and regains his self-esteem. Personal neurosis and physical damage poses a danger to an industrial chemist, Jim Ackland (John Mills), in *The October Man* (Roy Baker, 1947): a bus accident (again, set against night and rain) results in the death of a small girl and Ackland blames himself, triggering a tendency towards suicide. Ackland is set up as the prime suspect for the murder of a fellow lodger in his suburban London lodging house but Jenny (Joan Greenwood), the sister of a colleague at work, believes in his innocence and saves him from himself. Staring over the railway lines, Ackland clutches a hankie knotted into rabbit ears (as he had for the child on the bus): 'I didn't give in . . .', he cries to Jenny, 'I didn't give in.'

Refusal to surrender is elevated to national tragedy in Mills' leading role in *Scott of the Antarctic* (Charles Frend, 1948). Not only is the British attempt at the Pole set in competition with Roald Amundsen's Norwegian bid, against Scott's better judgment ('I'm not going to race,' he says, stressing the 'real work' and importance of a scientific expedition), but also it is shown to embrace the efforts and aspirations of those at home: South Hampstead High School collects subscriptions for a husky. While Amundsen suggests that dogs can be eaten (if it comes to it), the English look upon their dogs as friends and, whatever the consequences, take ponies and motor sledges for transport. On the one hand, Scott's selection of his company for the final stages ('Scientists and a soldier – what better companions could a man have?') is accepted stoically; on the other, the notion of 'the team' is marked by clear recognition of rank and the conduct of military drilling. Ultimately, Scott's failure (so near and yet so far) is redeemed by his appeal to God and his hope (had they succeeded) for every Englishman – the account of Scott's recovered diary. The score, from Ralph Vaughan Williams, makes great use (as the *Penguin Film Review* and Balcon noted) of its silences: a requiem for all those lost in a noble cause.[32]

Overweening professional ambition is itself represented as neurosis in *The Red Shoes* (Powell and Pressburger, 1948) and *The Seventh Veil*, where one character is used as the object of another's success; in *Dead of Night*, a film framed by the visit of an architect to a country property, a tool of trade (a ventriloquist's dummy) assumes control over its increasingly deranged and jealous master (Michael Redgrave). Powell and Pressburger based *The Red Shoes'* Lermontov (Anton Walbrook) on Sergei Diaghilev, whose Ballets Russes company was for a long time based in the South of France (to which Powell returned for filming – see Chapter 4) and, at vast expense and frequent inconvenience, secured the services of Robert Helpmann and Ninette de Valois (a pupil of Diaghilev).[33] The 'stage' numbers are, however, designed (by Alfred Junge) and gloriously choreographed for the screen, photographed by Jack Cardiff (like *A Matter of Life and Death*) in celebratory post-war Technicolor enhancing the sense of the dancer's rapture in performance. These remain the most effective and memorable sequences. Vicky Page (Moira Shearer) witnesses the resignation of one prima ballerina (for the sake of her marriage) and is then caught between her attachment to the composer, Julian Craster (Marius Goring), and her career: Lermontov tells her that 'a dancer who relies on uncertain human love will never be a great dancer'; 'great simplicity can be achieved only by the great agony of the body and spirit'. He wants 'to make something big out of something little' – out of Vicky – and she in turn thinks him 'a gifted, cruel monster'. While Lermontov refers to the company as his 'family' he is jealous of Julian – their 'adolescent' love is not a luxury he will allow, he says, and he dismisses Julian, purportedly for producing a second-rate score. When the company performs *The Red Shoes* as a tribute to Vicky, her place is taken by a single spotlight, as if indicating the emptiness in Lermontov which he has never acknowledged; the magic red shoes (the natural gift of an artist) have been both a blessing (as in the Hans Christian Andersen fairytale) and a curse.

In *The Seventh Veil* (which withstands re-viewing less well), a girl pianist, Francesca Cunningham (Ann Todd), is the object of her guardian's ambition. Nicholas (James Mason) opposes her engagement to Peter (Hugh McDermott), an American, who plays music for enjoyment rather than as a career; Nicholas does not care for such 'suburban shop-girl trash'. Repeatedly, Nicholas tells Francesca to take care of her hands (her most precious possession) and, when she is injured in a car accident, her fixation on her hands delays recovery. A flashback explains the caning they received at school, on the eve of a scholarship examination. While Nicholas insists that he has spent ten years 'making' Francesca, when Francesca escapes to be with the painter, Maxwell Layden (Albert Lieven), he, too, endeavours to speak for her and control her actions; Dr Larson (Herbert Lom) also presumes to speak on her behalf, through his professional diagnosis of her condition. Eventually, Francesca (now looking radiant) is invited to choose for herself which man she loves, trusts and cannot be without. Success and happiness apart from their pernicious interference is never presented as an option.

Joan Webster (Wendy Hiller) in *I Know Where I'm Going!* (Powell and Pressburger, 1945) is presented as a determined girl who has always known what she wanted: the film's credits are incorporated into the action, as if Joan herself is in a rush to get launched. At twenty-five she tells her father (George Carney) (a bank manager), in business-like manner, that she is going to be married to one of the wealthiest men in England. Her father muses that Sir Robert Bellinger (Norman Shelley) must be about his own age. Indeed, in her dreams she imagines marrying Consolidated Chemical Industries itself and the train wheels' clattering reminds her of her father's promise to put money into her account. She fondly conjures up visions of tartan-covered hills as the train speeds north. But in the Highlands, Joan, unaccustomed to having her plans thwarted, finds that she will have to wait for the time and the tide to cross to the island where she is to marry Bellinger. Meanwhile, she encounters the Laird Torquil Kiloran (Roger Livesey), at home on leave from the Navy, and his friends, Catriona (Pamela Brown) and a retired colonel (who keeps falcons in his baronial hall). The isle works its magic, Joan is charmed by Torquil and her 'town' values are challenged: 'Why should you think your lives so important and not ours?' says the boatman; 'Money isn't everything,' says Catriona when Joan suggests that she could sell her house to raise funds. However, the critic Catherine de la Roche noted the contradictions of *I Know Where I'm Going!*: 'money, it implies, is not a thing to covet, but the beautiful life that a goodish amount of it can buy is. Perhaps the film did at least indicate *what* to go for!' She complained that even apparently 'realist' films (those dealing with 'modern characters and ideas in modern idiom') developed their subjects

in vacuo, detached from the wider issues of the day; nor were they meant to be anything else . . . if the particular can be a valid basis from which to proceed towards the general, evasion cannot serve as a foundation for anything save confusion.[34]

Indeed, with its masquerading prince and romantic references to spells, curses and hauntings it may better be regarded as a modern fairytale.

Fame Is the Spur (Roy Boulting, 1947) charts the social progress of a particular individual, Hamer Radshaw (Michael Redgrave), against a general history of political events of the twentieth century: the campaign for votes for women, industrial unrest and the hunger marches of the 1920s and 1930s. It closes with Radshaw's failure to draw an ancient sabre from its scabbard – it has not been drawn for so long that, his manservant advises him, it has rusted. As Jeffrey Richards has noted, the sabre is a recurrent motif, inherited from the film's source novel, originally seized by Radshaw's ancestor at the Peterloo Riots in Manchester in 1819.[35] Its rusting signifies the dulling of Radshaw's original steel and his preparedness to compromise his principles as he gains worldly wealth and status: 'Keep it bright, dear,' he's advised when he has the decorative sheath made for it. His wife, Lady Anne (Rosamund John), meanwhile helps to organise his election to a seat previously in the pocket of the local landowner, and supports women's suffrage while Radshaw opposes it – she is imprisoned and her death is hastened by the force-feeding she suffers. Anne accuses him of watching himself from the outside and behaving accordingly, but he insists that he still has integrity: 'I was born poor . . . and my life is still dedicated to the service of the poor in spite of my changed circumstances.' His childhood friend is imprisoned during the Great War as a Conscientious Objector, while Radshaw opportunistically seizes a chance to promote Labour's interests. Hannaway (Bernard Miles), a businessman who has risen from the same Manchester slum, still sees Radshaw as a boy holding a rat. The South Wales miners inform him that the war is not of their making and send him home. By 1935, posters of Sir Hamer are being defaced and the audience to his speeches find him merely pathetic.

While the election of a Labour government in 1945 and the social reforms which it initiated augured well for a new meritocracy (and for which *Picture Post* had consistently argued in the duration), *Fame Is the Spur* warned that those who rose through the social hierarchy as a consequence of professional achievement should yet remain loyal to their origins and to the ideals by which they had attained promotion.

Kind Hearts and Coronets (Robert Hamer, 1949)

George Perry dubs 1949 the 'annus mirabilis' for Ealing, with *Whisky Galore, Passport to Pimlico* and *Kind Hearts and Coronets*, together with the less successful *A Run for Your Money* (Charles Frend, 1949) and the earlier *Hue and Cry* proving a pattern for the comedies of the 1950s.[36] Michael Balcon says that these were known, in America, as 'Guinness' films and he is featured in multiple guises in *Kind Hearts and Coronets, Barnacle Bill* (Charles Frend, 1957) and as the Comte Jacques de Gue and his hapless English double in Hamer's direction of du Maurier's *The Scapegoat* (1958). Guinness himself, however, modestly preferred to think of himself as a character actor rather than a star.[37]

In its period setting and in its style of humour, *Kind Hearts and Coronets* seems at first glance more atypical than characteristic of the Ealing product. Although costume dramas were popular in the 1940s, on page and stage, sometimes subsequently adapted for the screen (such as Carol Brahms' 1949 *Trottie Trice* and the story of the Victorian arsenic murderess Madeleine Smith, staged in 1944 and filmed by Lean in 1949), these were more generally produced at Gainsborough and Two Cities. *Saraband for Dead Lovers* (1948) (Stewart Granger in customary breeches and ruffles, but for the first time at Ealing, in colour), *Pink String and Sealing Wax* (portraying the short life of another great poisoner) and part of *Dead of Night* are among the few exceptions. *Kind Hearts and Coronets* was drawn from Roy Horniman's novel, *Israel Rank*; Perry suggests that the source was not explicitly mentioned for fear of upsetting the film's distributor.[38]

Discussing Clive Donner's 1964 *Nothing But the Best* for *The Listener*, Gerald Kaufman cited *Kind Hearts and Coronets* as an exemplary 'Comedy of Bad Manners':

> The comedy of manners is a cinematic genre fraught with extreme hazards. The comedy of bad manners is beset with even more formidable artistic hurdles. If the regrettable behaviour of deplorable protagonists is to elicit amused acceptance rather than natural distaste, the artificiality of the proceedings must be emphasised by a pervasive atmosphere of heartless elegance. Not surprisingly, this is rarely achieved.[39]

Both films plot the rise of their protagonist through the social hierarchy, by means generally foul and occasionally fortuitous. Although, for Ealing, there is the usual gentle mockery of official protocol and deferral to status (the executioner, wondering about correct forms of address, looks forward to his retirement after the hanging of a duke with a silken rope and can never content himself with hemp thereafter), there is sharper criticism of class snobbery and hypocrisy, aligning the film with contemporaneous pressures for a more open and democratic society. This also lends the film some of its continuing appeal, both to British and foreign audiences. As Edith d'Ascoyne (Valerie Hobson) reminds her future husband, 'Kind Hearts are more than coronets/And simple faith than Norman blood'. It relies for much of its effect on what is understood, rather than what is said (understatement, evasion and irony), and for the style, rather than the content, of its delivery, divided between the telling and the showing of events.

The opening titles are framed paper-doily style, setting the tone for what is to come. Louis d'Ascoyne Mazzini (Dennis Price), incarcerated on the eve of his execution, narrates the sequence of circumstances which have brought him thus far. His story is told in flashback, in a measured, even manner, in an accent which suggests that he is, indeed, 'to the manor born'. Louis has been ostracised by the d'Ascoynes on account of his mother's elopement, so it is alleged, with 'an Italian organ-grinder', of whom he is the sole offspring. She has been obliged to leave the ancestral castle and set up home in the suburbs. Her plans for him to go to Trinity, followed by the diplomatic service or a profession, are thwarted by their humble situation, so, while she rolls pastry, he goes to work as a general assistant in a draper's shop. Mama assures Louis that he is entitled to inherit the dukedom of Chalfont but when she is fatally injured in an accident her family refuses her (a mere widow from Tooting) a place in the vault and she is instead interred in a 'hideous suburban cemetery'. Louis, the 'penniless boy from Clapham', vows vengeance on the family which has spurned his mother for marrying for love (while marrying beneath her) and humiliated him (by obliging him to live beneath his station). Twelve people then stand between him and the dukedom.

Louis progresses to a shop in the West End. He frequently meets the wily and feline Sibella (Joan Greenwood), a friend since childhood. She rejects his proposal of marriage in favour of Lionel who, while certainly tedious ('He has the most extraordinary capacity for middle age in a man of twenty-four'), is yet more certainly, she says, destined to be rich. Louis also encounters his first d'Ascoyne victim, Ascoyne d'Ascoyne, who seals his own fate by having Louis dismissed from the shop for impertinence. Convinced that, the member of 'an inferior race', he can travel unrecognised, Louis follows Ascoyne and a girlfriend to Minehead, swiftly despatching the former and simultaneously, he consoles himself, saving the latter from 'a fate *worse* than death' during the course of their weekend.

Guinness, in the role of Ascoyne's father, is more kindly disposed towards the dispossessed Louis and offers him a job in the family bank. He again meets with Sibella, who encourages his advances (while intimating that merely kissing is not the full extent of caddish behaviour to which she might surrender), yet insists that she will marry Lionel. Sure enough – 'revenge is best eaten cold' – Louis conquers Sibella before the wedding and then embarks on an equally mismatched coupling with the priggish widow of Henry d'Ascoyne (Alec Guinness), an amateur photographer and secret tippler who blows himself up in his dark room. 'Needless to say', recounts the memoir, Louis was too late to save him. Revenge is yet chillier when Lionel is obliged to approach the bank for a loan. Although Louis is curt with him, he accedes if not only to ensure that Sibella's increasingly extravagant tastes in dress and accommodation are maintained at the husband's expense rather than that of the lover.

The d'Ascoynes (all played by Guinness) continue to fall, each hoisted by their own individual petard, sometimes ably assisted by Louis' intervention:[40] while Ascoyne falls foul of his weekend philandering and Henry of the chemicals associated with his dark habits and hobbies, an obstinate admiral fails to acknowledge a fatal error of judgment and a Blimpish general is the casualty of an all-too-realistic restaging of a battle in the confines of his club. A suffragette's campaigning (see Chapter 2) is no more than hot air and Ethelred, the last to go, is caught in one of his own mantraps on a hunting excursion, where he is shot by Louis as the just reward for his 'intolerable pride'. Meanwhile, Louis is promoted at the bank and the affair with Sibella is conveniently conducted in his new rooms in St James's. He now finds her suburban (the ultimate dismissal) in comparison to the dignity and bearing of Edith (who continues to postpone marriage to Louis, for the sake of propriety). He admits, in voiceover, that he *admires* dear Edith when with Sibella but *wants* the captivating Sibella when with Edith. Edith discerns in Louis 'a man of principle' (although not of the principle she imagines) while Louis, more cynically, tells Sibella that their affair is 'only wrong if people find out about it'. Awaiting the arrival of Sibella, he is keen to be rid of Edith, notwithstanding her acceptance of his proposal. Sibella recognises Edith's scent in the apartment and passes her on the stairs, immediately preparing her own strategy.

Sibella proves herself more than a match for him, and the undoing of his own 'intolerable pride'. Lionel now bankrupt, Sibella endeavours to blackmail Louis. In her finest hat and gown so far she feigns tears to inform him that Lionel is aware of the affair and that he intends to start divorce proceedings. This, says Louis, is 'very unsophisticated of him', but thinks that he was innocently cuckolded and suspects Sibella of bluffing.

After the murder of Ethelred and the sudden death of the banker, Louis finally succeeds to the dukedom. But, again, he is outwitted by Sibella. Lionel dead, Louis is accused of a murder for which he is not responsible and in court, the widow, magnificent in black, tearfully and decorously refers to her 'terms of intimacy' with the defendant by whom she was then so shamefully discarded. Even the defence counsel is affected by Sibella's performance. With the pronouncement of the verdict, Edith covers her face (but dutifully marries Louis in prison) while Sibella is triumphant – for she has the power not only to save Louis, she surmises, but to save him for herself. At the end, Louis' fate is doubly uncertain. He would prefer Sibella (were there not Edith) or Edith (were there not Sibella) – a perennial conundrum; having arrogantly courted celebrity by writing his memoirs (which a reporter from *Tit Bits* is eager to receive), temporarily reprieved, these same memoirs might then be the death of him. Furthermore, the split between what is shown and what is told invites us not to take Louis entirely at his own word; his condescending form of address to his audience, 'Yes, Sibella was pretty enough . . .', assumes complicity but prompts criticism. Of all the d'Ascoynes, he is the most fearfully in thrall to social status and the most intolerably proud. As Harry Hopwood insists in *Fanny By Gaslight*, 'in less than a hundred years' there will be no class distinctions, and it is his snobbish sister, Kate, who is put in her place at the end. This period piece, one might hope, far from encouraging escapism into the past, suggests that an old order should be relegated once and for all.

Notes

1. See tenth year celebration, *Picture Post*, 18 September 1948.
2. *Picture Post*, 5 April 1941.
3. Alfred Noyes (1880–1958), *The Highwayman*; see also Bruce Duncan, *Lovers, Parricides and Highwaymen* (New York: Camden House, 1999), p. 3 for the origins of such dramatic figures in the 18th century.
4. See Graham Greene, book review, *The Spectator*, 7 April 1933, p. 508, and *The Pleasure Dome* (London: Secker and Warburg, 1972), p. 135; also *Penguin Film Review* 1, 1946, re. 'school girl love'; Alison Light, *Forever England: Femininity, Literature and Conservatism between the Wars* (London: Routledge, 1991), pp. 156–60, and Pam Cook, *Fashioning the Nation* (London: BFI, 1996), p. 59, are better disposed towards the material and their 'supposed' audiences.
5. C. A. Lejeune in *The Observer*, Basil Dean archive 4/5/9; see also Greene, *The Pleasure Dome*, pp. 42 and 91.
6. Richard Winnington, 'Critical Survey', *Penguin Film Review* 2, pp. 18–19.
7. For Bryan's drawings for the set, see Edward Carrick, *Art and Design in the British Film* (London: Dennis Dobson, 1948).

8. Brian McFarlane, *Novel to Film* (Oxford: Oxford University Press, 1996), p. 111; see also Regina Barecca, 'David Lean's *Great Expectations*', in John Glavin (ed.), *Dickens on Screen* (Cambridge: Cambridge University Press, 2003), pp. 39–44, for Lean's divergence from the original text.

9. Captain Charles Johnson, *Lives and Exploits of English Highwaymen, Pirates and Robbers* (London: Henry G. Bohn, 1842), pp. 54 and 67.

10. Caroline Lejeune, *Chestnuts in her Lap* (London: Phoenix House, 1947), p. 119.

11. See 'James Mason Talks about his Films', *Picture Post*, 1 February 1947, pp. 14–17, and Dilys Powell, 'Carol Reed – Director of Acting', *Picture Post*, 9 October 1948, pp. 23–5.

12. Roger Manvell, 'Critical Survey', *Penguin Film Review* 3, p. 11.

13. See Michael Balcon, 'The British Film during the War', *Penguin Film Review* 1, 1946, p. 69.

14. John Ellis, 'The Quality Film Adventure: British Critics and the Cinema 1942–1948', in Andrew Higson (ed.), *Dissolving Views: Key Writings on British Cinema* (London: Cassell, 1996), p. 69; Ellis discusses the humanist assumptions, aesthetic criteria and understanding of the industry which prompted the critics' appraisals.

15. Cyril Connolly, 'Ecce Gubernator', *The Unquiet Grave* [1944] (Harmondsworth: Penguin, 1984), p. 57; Connolly is echoing a prejudice as old as the suburbs themselves – for an earlier instance of sniffing at the suburbs 'as a place of dreary lives', see Ford Madox Brown, *The Soul of London* (London: Alston Rivers, 1905), p. xv.

16. Caroline Lejeune, 'No Cups Outside', *Chestnuts*, p. 162.

17. E. Arnot Robertson, 'Women and the Film', *Penguin Film Review* 3, p. 32; for a discussion of *Brief Encounter* as a 'fanciful' representation of wartime Britain, see Antonia Lant's comments on its décor in *Blackout: Reinventing Women for Wartime British Cinema* (Princeton: Princeton University Press, 1991).

18. Richard Dyer, *Brief Encounter* (London: BFI, 1993), pp. 66–7; Dyer makes an argument for the film appealing especially to a gay sensibility while rooting it also in white middle-class culture.

19. 'A Mermaid has Tail Trouble', *Picture Post*, 4 October 1947, pp. 19–21.

20. Percy, significantly, is shown reading horror comics (successors to *Gem* and *Magnet*), a portent of anxieties more forcibly expressed in Britain in the 1950s; see Martin Barker, *Comics: Ideology, Power and the Critics* (Manchester: Manchester University Press, 1989), pp. 9 and 14.

21. Powell, 'Carol Reed'.

22. See Catherine de la Roche, 'The Mask of Realism', *Penguin Film Review* 7, 1948, p. 41, and 'No Demand for Criticism?', *Penguin Film Review* 9, 1949, p. 92.

23. Charles Barr, *Ealing Studios* [1977] (London: Studio Vista, 1993), p. 68.

24. de la Roche, 'The Mask of Realism', p. 37; see also A. L. Vargas, 'British Films and their Audience', *Penguin Film Review* 8, 1949, p. 73, complaining re. spivs thrust down the audience's throat.

25. George Perry, *Forever Ealing* (London: Pavilion Books, 1981), p. 102.

26. 'Frank Richards', *Picture Post*, 11 May 1946, pp. 19–21; see also George Orwell, 'Boys' Weeklies' [1940], *The Collected Essays, Journalism and Letters*, vol. I (Harmondsworth: Penguin, 1970).

27. 'Brighton Rock: an English Gangster Play', *Picture Post*, 20 March 1943, pp. 18–19; see also David Hughes, 'The Spivs', in Michael Sissons and Philip French (eds), *Age of Austerity* (London: Hodder and Stoughton, 1963), pp. 81–100.

28. See Graham Greene, *Brighton Rock* [1938] (Harmondsworth: Penguin, 1983*)* and *Ways of Escape* (Harmondsworth: Penguin, 1981), pp. 58–62; see also *Kiss and Kill* (Brighton: Royal Pavilion, 2002).

29. Greene, *Ways of Escape*, p. 61.

30. See Sue Harper and Vincent Porter, *British Cinema of the 1950s: The Decline of Deference* (Oxford: Oxford University Press, 2003), p. 258, regarding the unruliness of the subsequent St Trinians series.

31. 'An Essay in Neurosis', *Picture Post*, 24 July 1948, p. 18.

32. Balcon, *Michael Balcon Presents . . . A Lifetime of Films* (London: Hutchinson, 1969), p. 147.

33. Michael Powell, *A Life in Movies* (London: Heinemann, 1986), p. 395; see also pp. 614–31.

34. de la Roche, 'The Mask of Realism', p. 41.

35. Anthony Aldgate and Jeffrey Richards, *Best of British* (London: I. B. Tauris, 2002), p. 99; see also Brian McFarlane, 'Fame is the Spur: an Honourable Failure', in Alan Burton, Tim O'Sullivan and Paul Wells (eds), *The Family Way: The Boulting Brothers and British Film Culture* (Trowbridge: Flicks Books, 2000).

36. Perry, *Forever Ealing*, p. 111.

37. Balcon, *Michael Balcon Presents . . .*, pp. 165–6, and Alec Guinness, *My Name Escapes Me* (Harmondsworth: Penguin, 1997), p. 71.

38. Perry, *Forever Ealing*, p. 121.

39. Gerald Kaufman, 'Comedy of Bad Manners', *The Listener*, 19 March 1964, p. 471.

40. For an able discussion of Guinness' transformations, see Ken Tynan, *Alec Guinness* (London: Barrie and Rockliff, 1961), pp. 11–12.

On the poster:

DI 30 DÉCEMBRE
à l'aube
TES SAVANTES

ENS !

...onnce des me-
...ue j'ai prises
...e à la popu-
...délai expirant
...944, pour dé-
... de l'attentat
...bre, rue Cham-
...une bombe ex-
...ession à coups
...a été victime,
... dans la nuit du
...944, un officier
...ce de Santé.
...e sans qu'aucun
...obtenu, le Mili-
...n France prendra

...E REPRÉSAILLES
...GOUREUSES

Le Commandant du Grand-Paris
Signé : SCHAUMBURG
Generalleutnant

...NÉR...

Chapter 8 | 1950s

In Basil Dearden's 1957 *The Smallest Show on Earth*, an impoverished young author, Matt Spencer (Bill Travers), hears that he has inherited a cinema from his uncle. Fondly, he and his wife, Jean (Virginia McKenna), imagine spending the proceeds on exotic foreign travels. However, the Sloughborough Bijou demolishes his dream: confronted with competition from both the Grand down the road and from television, the old fleapit is struggling to survive. Hardcastle (Francis De Wolff), the Grand's hard-bitten owner, wants to buy the Bijou for £750 to use the site as a car park but is encouraged to up his offer by reports of its intention to install CinemaScope and stereo sound. A buxom ice-cream-seller is hired to promote trade. Meanwhile, the three retainers who have operated the cinema since its silent days are prepared to accept payments in kind from its loyal patrons (a more private arrangement pertains between the staff themselves). 'What about Entertainment Tax?' Matt asks the cashier, Mrs Ferzackerlee (Margaret Rutherford); 'I can hardly send one third of a chicken to the Chancellor of the Exchequer', she retorts. Eventually, the Bijou is rendered profitable, Matt sells to Hardcastle for £10,000 and sends a postcard to Old Tom (Bernard Miles) from Samarkand. With gentle humour, Dearden celebrates the comforts and beauty of age and smallness, and comments upon the changed circumstances facing British producers, distributors and exhibitors in the 1950s.

A Prognosis and a Prospectus

Following the rehabilitation of the industry in the 1940s, the post-war period saw an increase in government intervention. As in the 1920s, action was taken not simply on commercial grounds but because there was a feeling that British screens should not be filled exclusively by imported (and, more especially, by American) films. In 1947, without adequate consultation with the industry, the Labour government endeavoured to reduce the earnings of foreign films in Britain by imposing a duty of 75 per cent. This prohibitive level resulted in an embargo and British producers were urged into hurriedly made films to attempt to satisfy the exhibitors. Under pressure from Washington, the duty was subsequently repealed and a backlog of American films flooded the market.[1] In 1950, imports exceeded 70 per cent.

Undercover assignment: Jean (Paul Massie) in *Orders to Kill* (Anthony Asquith, 1958)

The National Film Finance Corporation was founded in 1949, originally as a temporary measure, in response to this crisis, and especially to save Alexander Korda's distribution company, British Lion. The following year, the Eady Levy was instated to direct a proportion of exhibitors' receipts back into production.[2] In 1951, the patrician chairman of the NFFC, Lord Reith (former director of the BBC – see Chapter 5), reported to Harold Wilson, future prime minister and then President of the Board of Trade. Yet his clear statement of account would seem to hold true for more than the immediate situation and the consequent proposals now seem typically short term and small scale (the impending collapse of British Lion is again reported in 1954). As in the 1920s, distributors and exhibitors resented any suggestion that they should 'subsidise' the home-grown product when the alternative was potentially more attractive to audiences and potentially a more lucrative venture. Producers, meanwhile, argued that many other imported goods were subject to customs duties, that many other countries protected their own film industry and that the British case should not be regarded as an example of unequalled inefficiency:[3]

> The provision of money for film production is bound to be speculative . . . unless difficult arrangements are made between producers, distributors and exhibitors so that producers get more than they do today; this over and above any assistance or alleviation which may come in other ways . . . 1) the cost of a first feature is high and there is no return for a while; 2) even if a film is a box-office success, it is some months before the costs are recovered; 3) public taste is chancey and unpredictable.[4]

The NFFC recognised that regular finance for production was hard to secure if risks were concentrated on single films and it therefore advocated a spread such that losses could be set off against profits. It proposed the setting up of three holding and management companies, one under the auspices of Rank at Pinewood, the other with Associated British Pathé at Elstree. Group Three was located at Southall (later Beaconsfield), under the supervision of Michael Balcon and John Lawrie, with the express remit to foster new talent, including documentary projects. Eight feature films were contemplated for the first year. John Grierson, the first operational manager at Group Three, initially cited Harry Watt (whose credentials were already long since established – see Chapter 5), fellow documentarist Philip Leacock, Lindsay Anderson and Alexander Mackendrick as names to watch for the future. Edgar Anstey, like Watt a veteran of the documentary movement of the 1930s, reviewed the 1952 releases *Time Gentlemen Please!* (Lewis Gilbert), *You're Only Young Twice* (Terry Bishop) and *The Brave Don't Cry* (Philip Leacock) for *Sight and Sound*:

> The intention of [Group Three] was to divert a modest part of the British Film Production Fund into experience for technicians untried in that field. . . . Many people had expected that John Grierson and John Baxter would provide us with documentary realism in the Italian manner. Instead . . . Group Three has done something equally difficult and in the long run of more value to the industry. They have faced the need cheaply to produce British entertainment which would amuse the regular cinemagoer. Equally important is the existence of a group of film-makers, a school, already strong enough to be sufficiently identified by such a humble label.[5]

However, hopes that the Exchequer could look to increased cinema attendances over the decade to boost the revenue from duties proved ill-founded. A number of explanations have been offered for the decline (alternative forms of leisure attracting significant sections of the potential market) of which the growth in home-viewing seems one of the most obvious. The televising of the Coronation in 1953 provided a particular impetus to the purchase of sets (20.5 million people, 56 per cent of the adult population, watched the proceedings on television);[6] in 1954 licences were granted to commercial companies and in 1955 the *Daily Film Renter* reported that 'the BBC estimates that the television audience rose [in the last quarter of 1954] from 8,400,000 to 11,000,000. During the evening hours it is estimated that 41.5% of the television public are using their sets.'[7] By 1959, television reception had reached virtually the whole country.

Responses to the challenge presented by the small screen were varied. Major players, as in the 1980s and 1990s (see Chapters 11 and 12), diversified their holdings to protect their interests: Lord Rank announced in 1959 that profits from non-cinematic interests could soon exceed those from cinema.[8] As with radio previously, some television exchanged personnel, performers and productions with film: Ted Willis' television material was adapted for the screen (as with *Woman in a Dressing Gown* [1957] and *The Young and* the *Guilty* [1958]) but he also scripted the *Huggetts* and wrote George Dixon from *The Blue Lamp* (see Chapter 7) into *Dixon of Dock Green* (serialised on television from 1954). As in America, which saw a boom in colourful and musical extravaganza, flaunting cinema's capacity to exceed television, some British producers turned to spectacular *mise en scène*, epic proportions and large picture format: the war films *Bridge on the River Kwai* (David Lean, 1957) and *Cockleshell Heroes* (José Ferrer, 1955), the costume dramas *The Adventures of Quentin Durward* (Richard Thorpe, 1955) and *The Dark Avenger* (Henry Levin, 1955), the luscious locations of *Action of the Tiger* (Terence Young, 1957) and Jack Lee Thompson's 1956 remake of the J. B. Priestley musical *The Good Companions* (see Chapter 5) were all shot in CinemaScope. Val Guest's 1957 *Expresso Bongo* was shot in DyaliScope. Powell and Pressburger used Paramount's Vista Vision (a widescreen system which did not require exhibitors to invest in new projection facilities) for their 1956 war films, *The Battle of the River Plate* and *Ill Met by Moonlight*.

Others recognised the cinema as a venue in which material could be shown that was deemed unsuitable for domestic television transmission or to exploit such potential suggested by a television original: both *The Quatermass Experiment* (directed for Hammer by Val Guest, 1955), based on the BBC science fiction series, and *Quatermass II* (Val Guest, 1957) were released under the 'X' certificate introduced in 1951. It allowed for the release of such seminally controversial material as *Peeping Tom* (Michael Powell, 1960), in which the audience itself is made complicit in the action. Mark Lewis (Karl Böhm) is the son of a scientist (played in simulated home movies by Powell himself) who specialised in the study of fear in children and who used Mark as the subject of his experiments. He now works as a focus puller in a film studio. He lets out rooms in his house to lodgers, but the rooms are still wired for sound as they were in his father's day. Mark knows that he is suffering from a madness, not simply scoptophilia (as a psychiatrist blithely supposes); relentlessly he records his crimes and the police investigation. 'I'm making a documentary,' he explains. Helen (Anna Massey), a children's librarian who fantasises about a 'magic camera' (and who innocently suggests that Mark's own camera has grown into an 'extra limb'), is set against the models in sheer nylon negligées and scarred Soho prostitutes whom Mark generally selects as victims; to Viv (Moira Shearer), the stand-in at the studio, he says 'I've waited a long time for this and so have you.' Helen's blind mother (Maxine Audley), meanwhile, has sensed that he is troubled and, moreover, dangerous to her daughter. Mark's victims not only experience fear but witness their own fear at the point of death. The film audience's fear is displaced to Helen's horrified reaction as she watches Mark's film. The voice of Professor Lewis at the end: 'Don't be a silly boy – there's nothing to be afraid of,' is far from reassuring.

Advertisements for the X-rated *Look Back in Anger* (Tony Richardson, 1959) showed Mary Ure and Claire Bloom in bed (but not together). Directors and producers recognised the procedure of film classification as something positive rather than as an infringement of 'personal' freedom, whatever the genre of film. There was general praise for John Trevelyan, chairman of the BBFC from 1958, for his endorsement of serious material: 'there is practically no adult subject which could not be considered for the "X" certificate if treated with sincerity and restraint'; of the critically and popularly well received *Room at the Top* (Jack Clayton, 1959), he remarked: 'there was

X-rating for Tony Richardson's 1959 *Look Back in Anger*

no nudity or simulated copulation but there was rather more frankness about sexual relations in the dialogue than people had been used to'.[9]

Television was deemed in some quarters to share a similar agenda or to be setting an example, even to place directors in an enviable position: much independent documentary work was reliant on institutional or corporate sponsorship, as it had been in the 1930s (see Chapter 5). A number of journalists from the seminal and popular *Picture Post* (see Chapter 7) moved, after its closure, to the BBC *Tonight* programme. *Sight and Sound* in 1957 devoted articles to Associated Rediffusion's 'actuality' broadcasting, including *Fan Fever*. 'If the television documentarists see themselves as captives of their own techniques, they are also prepared to admit their particular freedoms', writes Penelope Houston:

> Because television needs material and has broken down a good many of the preconceived ideas about audience tastes in entertainment, it can allow film-makers this freedom of choice . . . Set Associated Rediffusion's watching millions against the total potential audience of about 12,000 for the first three Free Cinema programmes at the NFT and a significant point emerges. Television documentary has found and is holding its mass public. Free Cinema, covering the same sort of subject – people at work and off duty – is a minority movement, not through choice but through necessity. There is nothing more essentially esoteric about *Momma Don't Allow* or *Every Day Except Christmas* than about *Tramps* or *Fan Fever* or *Members' Mail Service*. Television profitably shows what Commercial cinema continues to regard as a dangerous risk.[10]

Houston urges that cinema regard the challenge of television as a stimulus.

The Aftermyth of War

Examining the output of British studios in the 1950s, one is immediately struck by the number of war films produced. The preponderance of the genre itself became the butt of criticism in some quarters. In 1955, 'one's general impression of the year is of a great deal of domestic comedy and wartime reconstruction'; writing in 1958, Penelope Houston comments: 'With the unceasing flood of war films still pouring from the studios . . . it is becoming increasingly difficult for the artist who wants to adapt the conventions of the war picture to make some statement of their own.'[11] Similarly, she complains at Lean's privileging of the epic elements in *Bridge on the River Kwai* over the irony intended in the source material.[12] Gavin Lambert had previously vilified *A Matter of Life and Death* (1946) (see Chapter 6): 'hokum with serious or metaphysical pretensions is one of the most disagreeable aspects of cinema . . . a very arid and pretentious work'.[13] Lindsay Anderson acknowledged the popularity of such films but condemned their apparent endorsement of an established class structure and their escapism from current and future problems: 'Back here, chasing the Graf Spee again in *The Battle of the River Plate*, tapping our feet to the march of *The Dam Busters*, we can believe that our issues are simple ones – it's *Great* Britain again!'[14] But such tendentious polemicising disguises the range of films actually produced and the serious and complex questions which could be broached within a popular form. Also, it would be a mistake to suggest that there was an appetite for nothing more than obvious or partisan heroics (given the reception, discussed above, of *The Third Man*). Certainly, there are films which celebrate the triumphs of actual individuals or of the few: *The Dam Busters* (Michael Anderson, 1955) with its monumental Eric Coates score and *Reach for the Sky* (Lewis Gilbert, 1956) stand as a memorial to Barnes Wallis and Douglas Bader; more quirkily, *I Was Monty's Double* (John Guillermin, 1958), casting John Mills as a major subsequently promoted to brigadier, reports the promotion of a bit-part actor in the Pays Corps to a role in British Intelligence.[15]

Odette Churchill was played by Anna Neagle in *Odette* (Herbert Wilcox, 1950) and served as adviser on *Carve her Name with Pride* (Lewis Gilbert, 1958), with Virginia McKenna playing the secret agent, Violette Szabo, sent on a mission to occupied France: the film employed the poem devised by Leo Marks to enable her to remember codes as a romantic link with the husband lost at El Alamein. Here, as in *Secret People* and *Orders to Kill* (Anthony Asquith, 1958), stress is laid on the heroism of ordinary folk in wartime. *The Wooden Horse* (Jack Lee, 1950) and *The Colditz Story* (Guy Hamilton, 1954) record the escape of British officers from Nazi POW camps. It is these films which have been so readily satirised, from Peter Cook to Blackadder, as the aftermyth of war. Nevertheless, this particular dead (let alone wooden) horse continued to be flogged in such throwbacks as Attenborough's 1977 star-studded epic *A Bridge Too Far*, which substitutes personal loyalty in the ranks for misplaced duty to incompetent leadership. Indeed, Anderson's complaints of the potential of such films to mythologise individuals and events (as with the peacetime heroism of Frend's *Scott of the Antarctic*, or Roy Baker's *A Night to Remember* [1958]) is echoed in current debates around the distortion of historical evidence in the American remake of *Colditz*. However, many war films and other films of the 1950s genuinely engage with questions of war and its aftermath.

The Cruel Sea (Charles Frend, 1953), says Andy Medhurst, is the closest British cinema came to an anti-war statement.[16] I tend to disagree, but more because of the lack of rigour with which the term is employed in general than as a comment on the intentions or outcome of this particular film. Undeniably, it proved that films which explored the nature of war could be made as well as those which nostalgically revisited 'Our Finest Hour'. There are certain familiar elements: the gathering together of men in service from different areas of civilian life; the loyalty of a junior officer, Lockhardt (Donald Sinden), a former journalist, to a senior officer and to their ship at the expense of personal advancement; the contrasting of the 'good' woman (not for the last time, Virginia McKenna is cast as posh totty in uniform – 'a commissioned lovely in ops. . . . a prize Wren') who motivates survival and the warrior's homecoming against the 'bad' woman (Morrell, the society barrister, gives up the ghost upon recalling his wife's infidelity). Balcon claimed that the original story by Nicholas Monsarrat and the casting of McKenna, Sinden, then both virtually unknown, and Jack Hawkins (as Captain Ericson) would prove a success with British and American audiences: 'The story's the thing, character and content . . . star names, in the long run, are only valuable as a substitute for other qualities.'[17] Hawkins was duly voted most popular actor in the

Picturegoer Annual Awards for 1953 (and the film remained the favourite of Rob Flemming's dad in Nick Hornby's 1995 novel, *High Fidelity*). 'The Enemy' hardly ever appears and its absence, until late in the mission and the film, is remarked upon by Ericson himself: 'Number One, this is quite a moment,' he says; 'They don't look very different from us, do they?' says Lockhardt. The claustrophobia of the boat is relieved by periods of home leave. Ericson is shown capable of uncertainty, fallibility and regret in the face of impossible decisions (as for John Mills' ambulance officer, Anson, in J. Lee Thompson's 1958 *Ice Cold in Alex*): he orders a torpedo attack, thinking that German submarines are in the area and that other British ships are endangered, but when British men in the water are killed he is accused on his own ship of murder. There is a sense of isolation on the part of the crew and of their not being sure of the larger picture. Bob Tallow (Bruce Seton) returns home to find his widowed sister dead in a bomb attack, Jim Watts (Liam Redmond), the chief engineer, thereby losing the woman he hoped to marry. But stoical comments on the nature of war (that it is brutal, wasteful and sometimes nonsensical, 'We've just got to do these things and say our prayers at the end!' remonstrates the captain) do not, to my mind, constitute an argument against war per se and are frequently scripted elsewhere for sentimental heroes who serve most selflessly.

From a pragmatic perspective, war film scenarios often allowed for co-productions or for the casting of foreign stars enhancing the appeal of British films abroad. Columbia's *Bridge on the River Kwai* (filmed in Sri Lanka) billed together the internationally marketable Alec Guinness, Jack Hawkins and Sessue Hayakawa (see Chapter 4). *Ice Cold in Alex* cast the peripatetic Anthony Quayle as a South African German agent who is reprieved for good conduct; British Lion's *Orders to Kill* cast French heart-throb Paul Massie alongside Hollywood doyenne Lillian Gish as Gene's mother and the character actor, James Robertson Justice, as the ex-Navy Commander. Boston 1944: a distinguished American pilot, taught fluent French as an infant by his mother's maid, is despatched to England to acquire the tricks of a different and more devious trade. Gene (now Jean) is to eliminate an agent of the French Resistance who is thought to be betraying his compatriots to the Nazi occupying forces. In many ways, this is a personal 'war as rite of passage' film, but which also comments on the particular techniques required by supposedly 'modern' warfare: '[Don't] encourage him to enjoy himself quite so much,' says Mac (Eddie Albert) to the Commander, 'killing a man is not a game'; 'As we grow more civilised so does our way of killing. . . . I've got to stop civilised men thinking about it . . . otherwise they might not do it,' replies the Commander to Mac. Hitherto John has simply dropped bombs from the sky; strangulation with the thumbs or coshing someone is a tedious and messy business. Lafitte (Leslie French), the target of John's mission, unwittingly befriends his potential assassin, showing him small kindnesses and displaying his 'humanity' in his caring for the family pet. But 'Goebbels is a wonderful father,' sardonically remarks Léonie (Irene Worth), the Resistance contact, when Jean expresses his doubts: 'You still believe the best of people . . . war hasn't corrupted you yet.' Jean dutifully carries out his orders, only to discover later that the evidence against Lafitte was fabricated. Léonie, who has already lost a son in the war, is now tortured and shot. Mack decides to lie to John and to tell him of the great service he has performed, of the great number of lives he has saved. But he has grown worldly-wise and appreciates his own betrayal. On VE Day, he returns to France and tells Madame Lafitte and her daughter of the unsung Resistance hero, unknown even in his own family.

The post-war period saw not only a recognition of those compromises required of individuals' morality and humanity alongside the celebration of their supremacy in time of war; there were also films which acknowledged the difficulties of adjustment to civilian life after the excitement afforded by military service. A comparison may be made, it seems to me, with Cutts' 1924 *The Passionate Adventure* (see Chapter 4): in both cases men are seen to require some substitute in everyday life before reconciling themselves to mundane banalities. Adrian St Clair seeks solace in the criminal underworld of the East End; *The League of Gentleman* (Basil Dearden, 1960) has Colonel Hyde (Jack Hawkins), Major Race (Nigel Patrick), Lieutenant Lexy (Richard Attenborough) and Quarter-master Mycroft (Roger Livesey) planning to sustain the bonds of male camaraderie and the dangerous thrill of the war game left behind by planning a bank raid. 'As a regular soldier I served my country well and was suitably rewarded, after twenty-five years, by being made redundant,' says Hyde. It's a pity, he says, that all their training at the taxpayer's expense should go to waste. The script is peppered with mock military procedures, jargon and slang, and Major Rupert Rutland-Smith (Terence Alexander) continues to sport his service moustache: 'I'm your husband, not your bloody batman,' he tells his errant wife; 'The war's been over a long time, nothing's rationed now, there's plenty to go round,' she replies. 'I had a bloody good war,' he says: 'Perhaps you'd better find another one,' she ripostes. 'I've nothing against heroes,' says Hyde, 'except that they usually crook it for other people', but at the end he pulls rank and, in spite of protestations that 'this isn't *Beau Geste*', orders Race to make his escape without him. However, this time the gesture proves futile and the league is outwitted by an eight-year-old boy and a novice police constable.

Throughout the 1950s, and especially following the founding of CND in 1958, there were also films which alluded directly or indirectly or speculated further on the prospects of 'civilised killing'. In *Carry on Nurse* (Gerald Thomas, 1959) a hospital patient (Kenneth Williams) informs the ward that he is studying nuclear physics; he informs his neighbour (a boxer) that boxing is savage – 'But no more so than nuclear physics,' the boxer pertinently and promptly replies. The Boulting Brothers' *Seven Days to Noon* (1950) has a nuclear scientist threatening to blow up London unless all atomic research ceases within a week. Mario Zampi returned to the mistaken identity theme of his 1939 *Spy for a Day* (see Chapter 6) with his Cold War comedy, *Top Secret* (1952), casting George Cole as a guileless sanitary engineer who is caught with secret plans from an atomic research plant. Halas and Batchelor produced an animated adaptation of George Orwell's critique of Stalinism, *Animal Farm* (1954), while his *1984* was made for film (Michael Anderson, 1956) and for television (also 1954, adapted by the author of *Quatermass*, Nigel Kneale). Kevin Brownlow and Andrew Mollo (following the example of Saki's *William* [1913] – see Chapter 3) contemplated the outcome of German occupation of Britain in their BFI-funded film (submitted 1958, completed 1963) *It Happened Here*, attempting 'to present a realistic picture of war, particularly of partisan warfare, showing both its futility and its inevitability'.[18] Jews, communists, partisans, anarchists and freemasons are incarcerated or shot. A newsreel, 'Mirror on the World', shows Londoners paying tribute to National Socialism and a newspaper, *The Fascist*, reports the Party's triumphs. Unconsolingly, among the British, there are both collaborators and those who resist the occupation.

Military service did not end on VE Day, not only in that war continued on other fronts but also in that obligatory National Service in Britain lasted into the 1950s. In *The Entertainer* (Osborne's 1957 play, adapted and filmed in 1960), a tired (and often emotional) music hall performer, Archie Rice (Laurence Olivier), ekes out a living in Morecambe, his reputation now lost to comedians with television appearances to their name drawing the crowd. While his father, Billy (Roger Livesey), sings songs in a Working Men's Club in praise of the British Navy, his son, Sergeant Michael Rice (Albert Finney), is taken prisoner in Suez (locating the action in 1956): Archie's act mocks Churchill's victory sign. Archie pathetically seeks reassurance by bedding Tina (Shirley Anne Field), an impressionable young girl, in his caravan, hoping that her father will stump up the cash to support his modest ambitions for a face-saving show at the Winter Gardens. Billy, meanwhile, disapproves of Archie's mercenary philandering. Jimmy Porter, in *Look Back in Anger*, has, as a child, watched his father's lingering death after the war in Spain. War as the experience of succeeding generations is also acknowledged in the homely banter of *The Huggetts Abroad* (1949): 'I drove one in the war,' says Jim (Jimmy Hanley) indignantly, inspecting the truck which will transport the family; 'I drove one in the war before yours,' pa Huggett reminds him.

Among conscripts, the reactions to the hierarchical organisation, antiquated procedures and nonsensical rituals often provoked similar reactions. *Carry on Sergeant* (Gerald Thomas, 1958), as a response to National Service training, might be compared with Arnold Wesker's semi-autobiographical play *Chips with Everything* (1962). The men in both companies are divided by class and education; in both there is the assumption that the sons of officers should aspire to follow their fathers, yet they don't. Both contain their awkward squad and both are commanded by officers who remind the servicemen of the purpose of the training: 'You think that we are at peace. Not true. We are never at peace . . . We are simply the men who must be prepared . . . That is why you are here to learn obedience and discipline.' But whereas the *Carry On* men at the last are obedient and disciplined to the letter, in Wesker the outcome is bleak. Furthermore, I think it worth drawing attention to the presence of the war in films which do not obviously fall into the broader genre: for instance, in *Room at the Top* (set in 1947, published in 1957 and filmed by Jack Clayton in 1959), children still play in the bombed-out ruins of Northern terraces, yet to be replaced by the blocks suggested by the planners to Mr Brown; Joe Lampton (Laurence Harvey) shares his ration book with his landlady. More importantly, Joe's supposed self-advancement (by which he is thoroughly disillusioned by *Life at the Top* [see Chapter 9]) is partly driven by the superiority asserted by the ex-pilot Jack Wales (John Westbrook). Two years after the war, Wales continues to address Lampton as 'Sergeant'; Wales has a distinguished service record and the medals to prove it; Wales escaped imprisonment while Lampton was content to sit out the war in a camp (although, as the scenario of *The Colditz Story*, *Kwai* and the opening titles of *The Wooden Horse* remind us, 'it was the constant hope of every prisoner of war – if not his duty – to escape'). In *Town on Trial* (John Guillermin,

1957), John Mills plays Police Superintendent Halleran, who has spent ten years working his way up through the ranks. He endeavours to investigate a murder, questioning the reputation of a Wing Commander – but the war record to which the community pays deference proves to be sham. Increasingly, in the 1950s, respect for authority has to be earned rather than presumed.

The Intellectuals and the Masses (Again): Hoggartry and Huggettry

Anderson's disdain for the British war film was part of a larger critical project pursued primarily in the journal *Sequence* (1946–1952), subsequently in articles in *Sight and Sound* and, by example, in the work directed in the 1950s and thereafter. Alan Lovell has identified a number of ways in which the Free Cinema programme as a whole differed from the position outlined in the earlier journal.[19] But a consistent strand, in Anderson's own part in these endeavours, is his attachment to positions and paradigms drawn from literature and literary criticism.

Even the term 'Free Cinema', in spite of the looseness and variability of its application, seems to invoke a late nineteenth-century movement in European theatre, similarly promoting the individual author, decrying the intervention of censorship, representing the life of ordinary people in authentic locations. Like the theatrical precedent, the Free Cinema programme included homegrown and imported product and a range of content (from documentary to drama and something in between). The very first issue of *Sequence* appropriates Virginia Woolf's famous attack on the 'middle-brow' as the enemy of genuine culture (see Chapter 4). The *Sight and Sound* questionnaire following Anderson's famous 'Stand Up! Stand Up!' (which itself quotes from John Osborne's 1956 *Look Back in Anger*) invites responses from such leading literary luminaries as Kingsley Amis, Iris Murdoch, Ken Tynan, John Wain, Colin Wilson and Osborne. Following the publication of *The Uses of Literacy* in 1957, Richard Hoggart was invited to review Reisz's *We Are the Lambeth Boys* (1959). Although there are infuriating lapses in the rigour with which Anderson conducts his own arguments, much inconsistency and a reluctance to define precisely what might be understood politically by his vaunted 'committed criticism', he is none the less intent upon raising the standard (and tone) of seriousness with which film is discussed. 'It is a matter of fact' for him, not of opinion, 'that cinema is an art' and he decries the prevalence of British anti-intellectualism and amateurism in production and commentary. For Anderson, cinema is a potent cultural and propagandistic force.

The existence of contemporaneous groupings in literature prompted critics to nominate a parallel in film. In 1956, following the opening of *Look Back in Anger*, George Fearon, press officer at the Royal Court, inadvertently coined the term 'Angry Young Man'. Joan Littlewood, meanwhile, complained that the Court was too soft-centred, 'very middle-class and proper', and reports the Irish playwright Brendan Behan's remark that Osborne was 'about as angry as Mrs Dale' (by then, played for the radio by Jessie Matthews – see Chapter 5).[20] But the term rapidly gained currency:

> What is modern society angry about? It seemed that no-one could exorcise the whole invention. The inertia, defeatism and conformist suspicion of the despairing years of life in Britain since 1945 seemed to have been injected into some previously armoured nerve.[21]

In spite of attacks elsewhere on the BBC as a bastion of the establishment, the movement proper consisted of a number of poets and novelists included in the 1952–3 radio programmes *New Soundings* and *First Reading* (edited by John Wain). Similarly, the commercial success of *Look Back in Anger* on stage benefited enormously from the televising of an extract; funding for the 1959 film version (directed by Tony Richardson, formerly collaborator with Karel Reisz on *Momma Don't Allow* [1956]) was secured by the involvement of Richard Burton, already an established star (and really too old to play Porter), while the film of Osborne's *The Entertainer* was carried by the leading light of the English stage, Laurence Olivier. Other participants of Free Cinema worked differently and with different results and were not necessarily in agreement as to any collective objectives among themselves.[22] In 1957 the publisher Tom Maschler opportunistically compiled *Declaration*, inviting contributions from Doris Lessing, Wain, Osborne, Tynan, Anderson, Wilson, and others:

> A number of young and widely opposed writers have burst upon the scene and are striving to change many of the values which have held good in recent years . . . This volume aims at helping the public to understand what is happening while it is actually happening – at uncovering a certain pattern taking shape in Britain today.[23]

Polemic and debate seemed the purpose of the exercise rather than consolidation. Dilys Powell, film critic at *The Observer*, wryly observed that a new establishment had simply been substituted for the old.[24]

The approach of a number of the British films screened from 1956 to 1959 in the Free Cinema programme at the new NFT not only drew their material from contemporary life but can also readily be aligned with a recognisable contemporary critique of society. Raymond Williams' *Culture and Society* (1958) outlines a position from which 'committed' critics might gain focus in an age of public education and mass literacy, but warns against an academic defensive retreat into minority élitism. Richard Hoggart warns against undue sentimentality in his survey of the decline of traditional forms of entertainment and expression and is careful not to consign 'popular' taste to the working classes alone. Although he says little about film specifically, his comments on pulp fiction seem equally applicable to such products as *The Devil Girl From Mars* (David Macdonald, 1954) and *Fire Maidens from Outer Space* (Cy Roth, 1956) and the 'flimsy nylon' trivia of fanzines such as *Picturegoer*:

> [The] lowest level . . . is illustrated in sales here of American or American type serial books of comics, where for page after page big-thighed and big-bosomed girls from Mars step out of their space machines and gangsters' molls scream away in high-powered sedans. Anyone who sees something of servicemen's reading of . . . American and English comics . . . knows something of all this . . . the process continues, for a substantial number of adolescents especially; the passive visual taking-on of bad mass art geared to a very low mental age.[25]

One cannot help but feel reminded of Orwell's railing against the vulgarity of Donald McGill post-cards in the 1930s.[26] In *Sapphire* (Basil Dearden, 1959), sheer nylons and a frothy diaphanous baby-doll nightie erupt from a locked drawer, accompanied by a sleazy soundtrack, crudely denot-ing the 'dark' life of a murder victim (a half-caste girl who is passing for 'white'). But Hoggart blames 'the popularisers with their great new machines for persuasion' rather than the consumers themselves. Anderson's portrayal of commercialised leisure in *O Dreamland* (1953) is similarly criti-cal of the phenomenon, 'a scathing and wordless commentary on modern popular culture', says a programme note, 'everything is ugly . . . a drearily tawdry, aimlessly hungry world . . .', says Gavin Lambert, but the film seems as ill-disposed towards the participants themselves.[27] Arthur Machin in Lindsay Anderson's *This Sporting Life* (1963) is a reader of the type of pulp fiction of which Hog-gart so stalwartly disapproves. Osborne's *The Entertainer* was researched in the few surviving London music halls, 'not yet quite defeated by grey, front-parlour television'.[28] Lorenza Mazzetti's *Together* (1953), dedicated to the people of the East End, records children's games and songs (a motif employed also in Tony Richardson's *A Taste of Honey* [see Chapter 9], a twangy pub piano alongside the jukebox and various forms of dance in a pre-Conran Butler's Wharf. *Momma Don't Allow*, familiarly privileging jazz as an authentically modern form of expression, is announced as 'a candid camera excursion to . . . Wood Green . . . An informed piece of urban folklore.' *Every Day Except Christmas* (1957) records the nocturnal life of the people who work and play in Covent Garden market, a way of life soon to disappear: although, as John Hill remarks, the voices of those to whom the film is dedicated are strangely absent, Alun Owen's accented narration contrasts tellingly with the received pronunciation of the radio excerpts in the backing track.[29] But Hoggart's review of *We Are the Lambeth Boys* identifies a directorial position with which he finds himself slightly at odds:

> Free Cinema is immensely tougher, more honest and sensitive and more intelligent than commercial cinema and we are all grateful for that . . . it has dispelled a lot of suffocating fog of phoney senti-ment and false observation. But it still has the vaguely 'poetic' blur of sensitive commitment and social concern around its edges . . . it will only stand out clear and sharp, committed and concerned in the right way, when it faces the better and more demanding (and more exciting) problems of the imagination.[30]

Together, although filmed in actual locations, is more drama than documentary. Paul Rotha found in 1958 that it was increasingly difficult to draw such distinctions. To my mind, John Fletcher's soundtrack is the most interesting (and experimental) of all the Free Cinema projects. The film con-cerns a couple of deaf-mutes who work together and share lodgings with a family. The two men are perpetually taunted by the local children, who draw skinny and fatty caricatures on the walls and pavements, pull faces or skip after them in Pied-Piper fashion. The camera records their games of marbles and of tig on roller skates. Sometimes the soundtrack captures location sound: the hubbub of the market, 'Knees Up Mother Brown' on a fairground organ and on the pub piano, jazzy dance music on the jukebox and the cry 'Time Gentlemen, Please!', the children's clapping rhymes 'Michael Finnegan' and 'Eenie Meenie Miney Mo'; there are the sounds of the dock machinery, tug hooters, barges and trains, the exaggerated clatter of cutlery on plates. But there are also more abstract motifs, the melancholic strain of a cello and a flute as the thin man (Michael Andrews) and the fat man (the painter, sculptor, contributor to the Festival of Britain and designer of *Declaration*'s cover, Eduardo Paolozzi) converse with one another. In the pub, an old man talks at the thin man, gesturing emphatically in his face: the soundtrack remains silent; when he finds himself there alone, a young woman worse the wear for drink, sits beside him, they stroke hands and then return to the lodgings. The thin man gazes at the older daughter of the family longingly but makes no further sign while the younger daughter looks across the table at the fat man nervously. Theirs is a desolate life, isolated from a community which misunderstands them and doomed when they are separated.

'The small personal voice': Lorenza Mazzetti films London's East End in *Together* (1953)

For Anderson, the ability of film to address actual material 'poetically' was that which he most valued in the work of the preceding generation of British documentarists, especially in Humphrey Jennings (see Chapter 6). Grierson, meanwhile, was found to 'appeal primarily to the sociologist or educationalist and only incidentally to the student of cinema'.[31] But Anderson employs similar terms in his praise of *The Quiet Man* (1952) and *The Sun Shines Bright* (1953) and of Ford's work generally (in 'People We Like' and 'People of Talent'), in spite of the production structure in which he operated: 'the result is a successful amalgam of subtlety and knock-about popular entertainment and poetry extraordinary in an age culturally corrupt and divided as our own'.[32] For Anderson, this quality rendered the work personal, authentic and distinct.

What Doris Lessing called 'the small personal voice' was to be found also in European, Japanese and Indian cinema. For sure, bringing these films to the awareness of a broader audience was one of the most positive contributions in the 1950s of the NFT programmes and the journals. A self-conscious parallel was sometimes drawn with the efforts of *Close-Up* in the 1920s and 1930s (see Chapter 4). Walter Lassally, cameraman on *Momma Don't Allow*, *Together* and *Every Day Except Christmas*, acknowledges the part played 'in bringing intelligent and artistic [continental] films to the notice of the British public' but wonders 'what percentage of Britain's cinemagoers attends this kind of show and what influence have these endeavours had on a mass audience outside the specialised circles?'[33] Furthermore, while *Sequence* and *Sight and Sound* celebrate Italian neo-realism (as had *Picture Post* in the late 1940s), little is said of Italian popular cinema and when Visconti and Rossellini are led elsewhere by a 'personal' sense of direction (or ambition) the response is lukewarm.[34] 'You don't get *that* in *Sight and Sound*,' says a camera assistant to Mark Lewis, passing him a glamour shot of a busty brunette. The Italian and French systems of funding films are contrasted favourably with the conditions under which British would-be film-makers laboured. Anderson and Reisz, like Truffaut, Godard and Rivette, moved between film criticism and direction. Superficially, there seem to be similarities between *Sight and Sound*'s elevation of auteurism into a critical tenet. Certainly they hold in common esteem *Sciuscià* (Vittorio de Sica, 1946), *La Terra trema* (Luchino Visconti, 1948) and *Paisà* (Roberto Rossellini, 1946) as exemplars for their own work. 'The significant movement today', reports Anderson from Cannes in 1956, 'is away from the spurious inflation and theatricalisation that has so far tended to characterise the use of new techniques, further and further *into* reality.'[35] But French film criticism has yet, in the 1950s, to become the model for serious film comment in Britain. Blindly but typically accusing others of his own faults, Anderson launches himself at the *Cahiers* contingent:

[In France] you have a magazine like *Cahiers du Cinéma*, terribly erratic and over-personal in its criticism which has been enraging us all for the last five years. But the great compensation is that its writers make films, that three or four of its critics are now making films independently. And this means that they have a kind of vitality which is perhaps finally more important than critical balance.[36]

But, equally, it seems to me, they hold in common disdain the standard product of British studios, 'nothing worth even adverse criticism'. A single issue of *Cahiers* (January 1959) gives reviews of *A Horse's Mouth* (Ronald Neame, 1958), adapted from Joyce Cary's superlative novel and featuring Alec Guinness and paintings by the 'angry man' of the art world, John Bratby: 'an ambitious subject . . . treated and played according to the formulae of English comedy'; *Carve Her Name With Pride*: 'the unsuccessful battles of the Resistance matched with the unproductive manner of English cinema'; *The Vicious Circle* (Gerald Thomas, 1957), declared puerile in its resolution of a very complicated plot; and *The Tommy Steele Story* (Gerard Bryant, 1957), the autobiography of the nineteen-year-old English celebrity, 'mental age: nine'. Truffaut's notorious, and repeatedly cited, indictment of British cinema is far from merely personal.[37]

Attacks on the industry in *Sequence* and *Sight and Sound* did not pass unheeded. Balcon was driven by factual errors and disparaging references to 'Huggettry' (named after the Ken Annakin series of the 1940s, starring Jack Warner and launching a nylon-clad Diana Dors) and *The Blue Lamp* (also starring Jack Warner) to seek legal advice.[38] Indeed, as a key figure in the institutions which funded much experimental activity, at Group Three and at the BFI, including Ken Russell's youthful and exquisite 1958 *Amelia and the Angel* and some of Free Cinema's output, he surely had a right to feel aggrieved. *Chance of a Lifetime*, directed by Bernard Miles and featuring Hattie Jacques (who appeared also as a plump fairy alongside Anderson's agonising artist, Michael-Angelico – 'is this one more *real* . . .?' – in James Broughton's 1952 *The Pleasure Garden*, but is now better known for the *Carry On*s and her television series with Eric Sykes), was one of only three films of 1950 which Anderson found worth promoting. Balcon thought the judgment 'arrant nonsense'.[39] Furthermore, critical and popular reception of the Ealing fare in foreign festivals was to prove that British films were not to be so easily dismissed. While *Every Day Except Christmas* and *Together* could be rewarded at Venice and Cannes, then so could Guinness and *The Lavender Hill Mob* (Charles Crichton) show on art-house circuits abroad and seem exotic.[40] *The Ladykillers* was rewarded with a British Oscar for its screenplay; *The Lavender Hill Mob* with the Venice screenplay prize and an Academy Award. The Americans, at least, concluded Richard Roud, 'like British films British'.[41]

The Free Cinema and British New Wave directors prided themselves on their atmospheric use of actual locations: the Locarno Dance Hall, Yorkshire countryside and blood, sweat and mud of the rugby scrum in Anderson's 1963 adaptation of David Storey's 1960 novel *This Sporting Life* (with Richard Harris, at his brutish, inarticulate best, alongside Rachel Roberts as the embittered widow with whom he lodges); the Nottingham factory, fairground and countryside of Karel Reisz's 1960 (commercially successful) adaptation of Alan Sillitoe's 1958 novel, *Saturday Night and Sunday Morning* (with Albert Finney and, again, Rachel Roberts). However, this was not the prerogative of ostensibly 'alternative' cinema. *Tiger Bay* (J. Lee Thompson, 1959) recorded Cardiff docks and the countryside of South Wales; Hammer's well-paced thriller *Hell is a City* (Val Guest, 1960) opens with an acknowledgment of the co-operation of the Manchester Police Force and the city and its surroundings feature large in the proceedings. Inspector Harry Martineau (Stanley Baker) puts his job before his home life, his junior Devery (Geoffrey Frederick) reminding him that it is a misfortune to be a loner. Martineau blames his frustrated wife for not having children but also for caring too much for the opinions of others: he remains unswayed by other women's attempts at seduction. A local gang gets involved in a theft which inadvertently leads to the murder, on the eve of the Doncaster races, of a young woman – a bookie's assistant (her body is dumped on the windswept moors) – and the American, Don Starling (John Crawford), who has upped the stakes, is revealed to be a convict who has escaped by murdering his warder. Billie Whitelaw (always a boon) appears as the bookie's wife, formerly Starling's lover – to whom he turns as a port in the storm. The screams of Devery's dumb girlfriend (transposed to the film's soundtrack) betray Starling's final hide-out. The police bargain with the local 'petty' criminals in order to secure information and an arrest, nail-bitingly effected over the edge of a parapet.

As in the 1930s, a tendency towards certain themes and settings is shared across fiction and non-fiction production and between commercial and non-commercial releases.

Meanwhile, Down Among the Alligators . . .

From the outset, the magazine *Movie* assumed the dismissive stance of *Cahiers du Cinéma* towards the generality of British films. It inherits from *Sequence* the emphasis on 'art' and the 'personal' testament:

> The British cinema is dead as before. Perhaps it was never alive. Our films have improved, if at all, only in their intentions. We are still unable to find evidence of artistic sensibilities in working order. There is as much genuine personality in *Room at the Top*, method in *A Kind of Loving* and style in *A Taste of Honey* as there is wit in *An Alligator Named Daisy*, *Above Us the Waves* and *Ramsbottom Rides Again*.[42]

There seems little regard here for the sensibilities or preferences of home and foreign audiences nor of the testing conditions under which the industry functioned. Instead, like its French progenitor, it valorised the work of a select group of American directors. Of course, American films continued to command popular appeal, frequently presenting their audiences with the very images of a consumer culture against which Hoggart and others had railed. American studios continued to offer an attractive prospect to British actors and directors, as Basil Dean had observed in the 1930s; Michael Anderson left for the States after *The Dam Busters*; Alexander Mackendrick followed *Whisky Galore!* (1948), *The Ladykillers*, *The Man in the White Suit* (1951) and *The Maggie* (1954) with the American noir classic *The Sweet Smell of Success* (1957). Tony Richardson left after *Momma Don't Allow*, *We Are the Lambeth Boys*, *Look Back in Anger* and *The Entertainer*, directing *Sanctuary* (1960) before returning to make *A Taste of Honey*. The popular press covered the activities of American stars extensively but remained loyal to those whom it continued to regard as its own, proud that Britain could produce star material: hence it gives Diana Dors the full 'star' treatment, relating not just the films but her lavish lifestyle (and consequent problems with the Revenue). But sometimes it reports with some satisfaction that everything was not so very wonderful the other side of the pond. Thus, in 1954 *Picturegoer* covers Dianne Foster's departure for Hollywood but also Mara Lane's return and Deborah Kerr's 'Seven Lean Years'; Audrey Hepburn ('the face of the decade') continues to be celebrated as British in spite of her defection after only a few fleeting appearances (in *The Lavender Hill Mob* and, more substantially, as a dancer in *Secret People*).[43] In *Expresso Bongo*, Dixie (Yoland Donlan) is a celebrity attempting to resuscitate her career with a TV show in Britain after a stint in America. Although *Picturegoer* bemoans the slowness of the British industry in 'building' stars, it acknowledges the success of its character players and seems somewhat pleased by the discomfort of its own stars in the American system. Diana Dors reconstructed herself as a de-glamourised 'serious' actress in the prison dramas *The Weak and the Wicked* (Jack Lee Thompson, 1953) and (in response to the trial and execution of Ruth Ellis – see Chapter 11) the X-rated *Yield to the Night* (Jack Lee Thompson, 1956). Dirk Bogarde, the leading British male star of the 1950s, announces to the *Picturegoer* interviewer:

> I am an actor first, a film star much later. I would rather play the right part in a little black and white picture on a perfectly ordinary screen with a good script and a brilliant director than hare across the Atlantic to wander about a cinemascope screen trying to hold my own with entire armies of ancient Egypt.[44]

Bogarde's Sidney Carton in T. E. B. Clarke's adaptation of Charles Dickens' *A Tale of Two Cities* (Ralph Thomas, 1958) was not a 'far, far better thing' than he had done before, but he does look very dashing in a frock coat. Arguably, Bogarde found his 'brilliant director' in Joseph Losey, with *The Servant* (1963), *The Sleeping Tiger* (1954), *King and Country* (1964) and *Accident* (1967) (see Chapter 9), then in Visconti with *The Damned* (1969) and *Death in Venice* (1971), and in Resnais with *Providence* (1977) (see Chapter 10). Certainly, the internationally respected actors Laurence Olivier and Richard Burton did not share *Movie*'s sweeping condemnation of all things British in undertaking films of Osborne's stage hits *Look Back in Anger* and *The Entertainer.*

As with the advent of television, responses of British cinema in the 1950s to the perennial challenge of Hollywood were varied. Some films attempted to imitate American genres and styles, some employed foreign stars and other personnel to extend their marketability. Thus *Joe Macbeth* (Ken Hughes, 1955) adopted the guise of an artfully constructed gangster movie. While Jill Adams was promoted as a British 'Marilyn Monroe', the genuine article appeared in Terence Rattigan's adaptation of his own *The Sleeping Prince*, *The Prince and the Showgirl* (Laurence Olivier, 1957), Olivier resuscitating the Ruritanian accents rehearsed in the 1930s and 1940s (see Chapters 5 and 6). Sophia Loren appeared in *The Key* (Carol Reed, 1958) and, in numerous Pierre Balmain ensembles, in *The Millionairess* (Anthony Asquith, 1960), which also provided a cameo role for Italian neo-realist director, Vittorio de Sica, as an artisan running a pasta workshop which Epifania (Loren) attempts to reorganise for efficiency. 'The intelligent capitalist need never lose!' she advises him.

'You're not a man, you're an Englishman!' she hotly informs the dour family lawyer (Alastair Sim). A kittenish (but mousey) Brigitte Bardot, as a shipping heiress masquerading as a ship's chanteuse, attempts to catch Dirk Bogarde (and a European audience) in *Doctor at Sea* (Ralph Thomas, 1955). Simone Signoret poignantly portrayed the sophisticated and mature woman with whom adventurer Joe Lampton becomes involved in *Room at the Top*, only admitting his love to himself after her tragic death: by casting the Alice of Braine's novel as French, as Christine Geraghty and Alexander Walker have noted, the adulteress was not only rendered foreign but also, effectively, classless. Both she and Joe become 'outsiders'. In *The Truth about Women* (Muriel Box, 1957), a pre-Joe Lampton Laurence Harvey gallivants his way via a Parisienne (Eva Gabor) and an American (Lisa Gaston) to discover a 'good' woman in a nurse (Mai Zetterling) – whom he loses. Bette Davis played in *Scapegoat* (Robert Hamer, 1958), Lauren Bacall in *Northwest Frontier* (Jack Lee Thompson, 1959). Katharine Hepburn was cast in 1951 with Humphrey Bogart in *The African Queen* (an American co-production directed by John Huston) and in David Lean's return to *Brief Encounter* themes, *Summer Madness* (1955) (see Chapter 7).

But there was ambivalence towards America and its products. 'No ones's complained before – are they Americans?' says a fellow guest at a dilapidated hotel of Alan (John Gregson) and his wife, Wendy (Dinah Sheridan), when they rudely arrive on the first leg of the Brighton Rally, shared with his other love, a veteran car, in *Genevieve* (Henry Cornelius, 1953) (Rob Flemming's mum's favourite in Nick Hornby's *High Fidelity* – and the unanticipated box-office hit of the year). *The Love Lottery*, later thought by Balcon to be one of the worst films with which he had ever been associated, was directed by Charles Crichton in 1953.[45] It cast David Niven as a star who tires of his fan following and offers himself as a prize. The film was heralded by some reviewers as an attempt at revitalisation, while at the same time it was mildly critical of the model it sought to emulate. Margaret Hinxman announced:

> It's happened! Ealing has discovered glamour. The studio that makes a screen virtue out of being British and homely has suddenly turned the tables and become cosmopolitan and dazzling . . . the new comedy is a deliberate detour away from the kind of humour and drama that won for its small British studio the proud motto 'The Ealing Tradition' . . . Five years ago, when most British studios thought that the best way to out-Hollywood Hollywood was to imitate it slavishly, Ealing's pursuit of 'realism' seemed thoroughly logical. Ealing did a big thing for British films after the war. It looked to its own back yard for its stories when the rest of the studios looked anywhere but . . . When Ealing hit a success, such as *The Cruel Sea*, it did so resoundingly. But of late . . . there's been a dribble of films . . . behind them . . . a kind of virtuous dowdiness about the treatment of far from dowdy plots. A feeling, perhaps, that anything lush or lavish or dazzling isn't quite respectable.[46]

Other producers found that the distinctiveness of British films, either in presentation or content, was precisely that which ensured their appeal. Even *Cahiers du Cinéma* recognised the quality of its actors (more especially when they left for Hollywood, it added, tartly); even *Sight and Sound* 'liked' Alec Guinness and Joan Greenwood.[47] In America, as Richard Roud observed, Alec Guinness could guarantee an art-house audience, he seemed the epitome of the 'character player' described by *Picturegoer* who never rose (or descended) to stardom. Wormold (a vacuum cleaner salesman) in Carol Reed's adaptation of Graham Greene's *Our Man in Havana* (1959) has some of the qualities of Sidney Stratton in Mackendrick's *The Man in the White Suit*, both eccentric misfits caught up in a political superstructure beyond their control. Stratton's affable, vulnerable dottiness prompts protection from both Daphne (Joan Greenwood), the boss's daughter, and Bertha (Vida Hope), the union activist; one of the workers gives Stratton his own coat as the suit disintegrates. The obsessive Stratton is of a piece with Holland, driven by years of thankless toil and subordination to plan the bank raid in *The Lavender Hill Mob*; but, as he rehearses in the factory wash-room a speech that he will not give ('I'm not being fired: I'm resigning'), Stratton is not a distant relation either of the crazed and dastardly professor in *The Ladykillers* (complete with stage eye-liner and very false teeth). These films may not be 'lush or lavish or dazzling' but nor are they slavishly in 'pursuit of "realism"'. 'Unimpaired by any timid concession to plausibility,' wrote Penelope Houston, '[*The Ladykillers*] is a consistently ruthless comic fantasy.'[48]

Charles Barr has noted that *The Man in the White Suit* was made in the same year that a manufacturers' cartel opposed the production of long-life light bulbs; it was also the year in which Courtaulds' American rival, Du Pont, introduced a synthetic fibre, Dacron, that promised to make ironing obsolete: 'What do you think happened to the razor blade that never gets blunt and the car that runs on water with a pinch of something?' the shop steward asks Stratton.[49] It also seems worth referring it back to the development and distribution of new materials during the war (such as fibre-glass, parachute silk and GI nylons) and to such forthcoming 1960s attractions as Bri-nylon and the drip-dry shirt: 'Clothes to last a lifetime!' declares a *Picture Post* article in 1947. More specifically, Roger MacDougall's scenario invokes the display of the beneficent potential of technology in the 1951 Festival of Britain and recently witnessed (and feared) destructive applications of 'pure' science to political ends: the processing of Stratton's wonder fibre involves 'radio-active thorium'; 'to break the fibre', says Daphne, 'you'd have to split the molecule'. Michael Corland (Michael Gough) (a typical 'in joke' referring to textile producers and Ealing Chairman Stephen Courtauld) is an etiolated young fogey who runs a mill in competition with Birnley's. While he knows little of technical processes and muses airily about 'design and style, combining the strength and simplicity of the old English hand-loom weavers with the colour and fire of the Flemish and Provençale', Stratton spouts the newspeak of science and process: 'polymerisation . . . heavy hydrogen . . . amino acid residues . . . long chain carbohydrate molecules containing ionic groups . . .'. The diminutive Daphne, hands thrust deep into the pockets of her Burberry mackintosh, tells her father that he doesn't understand and is too pig-headed to find out. Meanwhile, the industrial baron, Sir John Kierlaw (Ernest Thesiger), makes the long trek in his chauffeur-driven Rolls Royce, past an illuminated sign, 'To the North'. 'It'll knock the bottom out of everything,' says Corland. 'What about the sheep farmers, the cotton growers, the traders, the middlemen?' 'Stick to the point,' snaps Sir John, 'what about us?'

The film is well stocked with a range of typical figures: a matronly, no-nonsense nurse; a thin secretary in sensible plaid skirt, cardigan and buttoned-up blouse; Nutzen, the sinister glintingly bespectacled foreign butler (doubtless intent upon industrial espionage); the decrepit and asthmatic Dickensian Sir John, swamped by his Astrakhan collar and the Birnleys' upholstery. There are catchphrases drawn from common currency and from other media, such as 'Workers' Playtime'; 'Okay, Ducks – room for one more inside!' says one of the factory girls to Sir John as he is squashed ignominiously into the back of a car. There are also various stock sequences, such as Stratton and Wilson in steel helmets bunkered in the research lab behind sand-bags; the Birnleys' 'Loamshire' residence (Landseer prints, leather-covered wing chairs, mantle clocks) affords plenty of opportunities for farcical slapstick involving doors, loose carpets and china vases; the final night-time chase through the mill town's cobbled streets is aided and abetted by an obliging infant with pig tails and a baker whose uniform is mistaken for Stratton's suit. There are stylish performances, from Daphne, lifting herself in her chair and preening felinely as she is told that she is 'a very attractive girl' by Birnley's henchman, and from the manager himself when he addresses the shop floor in the oleaginous tones of a politician: '. . . you will see that our bone of contention is non-existent. Capital and Labour are hand in hand in this. Once again, as so often in the past, each needs the hand of the other.' All these elements together might amount to what the po-faced *Cahiers* critics received as formulaic British comedy. But there's more, if one bothers to heed the film's social commentary. Birnley assumes the scientist to be on the side of capital: when Stratton asks for the lab to be closed (for the sake of safety) Birnley assumes that he has in mind the need for secrecy (to his own advantage over his competitors) and chortles contentedly. Bertha remains personally loyal to Sidney throughout, teaching him the ropes (insisting that he takes the workers' hard-won tea-break) and offering him her post office savings. 'Sid's the one taking all the chances,' she says, 'it's Birnley's pocket he's lining otherwise he wouldn't have pushed him into it.' Once it becomes clear how many people's livelihoods would be placed at risk by the indestructible fibre, she wonders what side he is on. Sidney is on his own side, and seeks academic laurels for himself and Wilson by publication of the results in a scientific journal, but even he himself has a moment of doubt when Mrs Wilson, his kindly landlady, accosts him as the chase closes in: 'Why can't you scientists leave things alone? What about my bit of washing when there's no more washing to do?' Daphne remains loyal to her white 'knight in shining armour'. He has, she proclaims, 'won the battle against shabbiness and dirt . . . the whole world's going to bless you!' For her, Sidney's invention means progress and she welcomes it idealistically. She admires him even more when he fails to succumb to Sir John's 'bad' woman ploy and, like Rapunzel, helps him to escape from her locked tower so that the story will be told to the newspapers. Bertha and Daphne do not share in the final laughter at Sidney's misfortune. They alone appreciate the shattered dream and that the innocent knight has been sorely blooded in battle. Ultimately, leaving the town suitcase in hand, he is an isolated man.

While I would contend that *The Man in the White Suit* does contain pertinent social comment, it is not what Anderson intends by the advocated turn 'further *into* reality'. Certainly, it is more sympathetic in its representation of unionised labour than its stablemate at Ealing, *The Titfield Thunderbolt* (Charles Crichton, 1953), concerning the nationalisation of the railways, the Boultings' comedy *I'm Alright Jack* (1959) or Guy Green's earnestly reactionary (and ultimately mawkish) *The Angry Silence* (1960). However, again, it would be wrong to assume that the themes of Free Cinema's self-proclaimed 'nonconformist' productions were remotely distant from those of the entirety of commercial cinema. *We Are the Lambeth Boys* records the opinions and activities of girls and boys 'at work and off duty', adopting the same wholesome attitude towards youth clubs ('there should be more of them') as *Some People* (Clive Donner, 1962). *Teddy Boy* records similar locations to those photographed by Walter Lassally for *Beat Girl* (Edmond T. Greville, 1960). Britain produced its own version of Rebels without Causes, boldly, as in *Violent Playground* (Basil Dearden, 1958), and, rather feebly, as in *Town on Trial* and *My Teenage Daughter* (Herbert Wilcox, 1956). It seems worth emphasising that the turn 'further *into* reality' in subject matter, presentation and procedures was not unappreciated in populist reportage. In the same year that Margaret Hinxman gushed in *Picturegoer* over *The Love Lottery*, she reviewed *The Maggie*, the story of a puffer boat, filmed by Mackendrick on the Crinan Canal and in Islay:

> [It] is not the all heather land peopled by shaggy types eating oatmeal and haggis, dancing eightsome reels between tumblers of whisky and blows on bagpipes . . . Every now and again the real Scotland does appear through the celluloid mist. In *Whisky Galore!* . . . Ealing sent a unit to Barra [and set up] a temporary studio in the village hall. The players absorbed the character and atmosphere of the people. *Whisky Galore!* took more money at the Scottish box offices than any other film about the country . . . [R]emember Group Three's *Laxdale Hall* (1953), filmed partly near Applecross in the far North West, with Scottish actors using their native accents? [*Floodtide*, 1949 and] *The Brave Don't Cry* (1952), the story of the Ayrshire pit disaster, rang true too . . .[50]

As was observed as long ago as Free Theatre, 'realism' can only ever be a comparative term of evaluation and criticism. Films which attempted to tackle contentious and contemporary issues seriously need to be compared with those which treated them otherwise. Certain areas of the country received large numbers of immigrants from the West Indies from the early 1950s onwards. There were race riots in the 1950s in Notting Hill and Nottingham (as there were in the 1980s in Notting Hill, Tottenham, Toxteth and Bristol – see Chapter 11) but few films even acknowledged the Afro-Caribbean presence let alone the interracial relations. Exceptions such as *Sapphire* need to be set against more mainstream fare such as the *Carry On*s or the *Doctor* series. In *Look Back in Anger*, Kapoor is resented by the other stall-holders for undercutting their prices: 'They're all the same,' says a shopper, but Jimmy says that he should fight them. In *Tiger Bay*, the black community celebrates a wedding with dancing in the streets. But in *Doctor in the House* (Ralph Thomas, 1954) – the top box-office film of 1954 – people of colour are no more than a background as fellow medical students of the ingénu Sparrow (Dirk Bogarde), Grimsdyke (Kenneth More) and Benskin (Donald Sinden). A West Indian nurse is cast for the purposes of a racist joke. The 'No Irish Gentlemen' notice at Sparrow's first lodgings is a gen-uine sign of the times and there is a very *Fast Show* breathy sales assistant who fits Sparrow with his first stethoscope in John Bell and Croydon. Sadly, James Robertson Justice as the con-sultant Sir Laurence Spratt, informing a patient that his illness is 'nothing to do with him', is not a thing of the past at all.

The *Doctor* and *Carry On* films of the 1950s seem to be typical of a national cinema in that their humour often relies on particular linguistic devices and on the recognition of situations, types and stereotypes circulated in other areas of popular culture. Popular, of course, as Hoggart is keen to stress, does not equate with populace. Many films and film series of the 1950s drew upon other media and furthered the careers of performers who had become well known through wartime radio and launched television careers for others. Group Three made a bid for *Quatermass* and con-templated making a film version of *The Goon Show*; meanwhile Michael Bentine made a few vir-tually forgotten films and Peter Sellers became extremely famous in a string of comic roles including the ancient projectionist in *The Smallest Show on Earth*, the humourless union leader Fred Kite in *I'm Alright Jack*, in multiple roles in *The Mouse that Roared* (Jack Arnold, 1959) and a Brummie vicar in *Heavens Above* (John Boulting, 1963); in *The Millionairess* he played an Indian doctor, unimpressed by Epifania's money (or her outfits) and (in voiceover) the father to whom she owes her fortune. He also delivered an unforgettable pastiche of Laurence Olivier's performance in Shakespeare's *Richard III* (Laurence Olivier, 1955) to the lyrics of The Beatles 'It's Been a Hard Day's Night' (see Chapter 9). A film version was similarly made of the radio series *Life with the Lyons* (Val Guest, 1953) and *The Navy Lark* (Gordon Parry, 1959). Frankie Howerd and Hattie Jacques moved between television, Ealing and the *Carry On*s.

While cinema audiences declined in competition with newer forms of entertainment and media, film also sought to capitalise on their popularity. Cliff Richard variously attempted to exploit or efface his star persona in the roles he took on; *Beat Girl* featured Adam Faith; Frankie Vaughan tried harder to be taken seriously in Herbert Wilcox's 1957 tale of Liverpool gangland, *These Dan-gerous Years*; Tommy Steele appeared as himself. *Expresso Bongo* was a more diluted version of the More and Mankowitz stageplay than the authors had intended. It took some songs from the original and added choreography by Ken Macmillan. Serving primarily as a vehicle for Cliff Richard (as the unknown talent, Bongo Herbert), his performance is, nevertheless, flatter than his card-board cut-out which opens the title sequence. The story returns to the Jewish East End milieu of Mankowitz's wittily surreal short film *The Bespoke Overcoat* (Jack Clayton, 1955), while taking the viewer uptown to the strip clubs of Soho where Maisie (Sylvia Syms) works in a non-stop revue and waits for Jonny Jackson (Laurence Harvey) – a would-be impresario – to devote his undivided atten-tion to her. Bert is 'his stake in the future of British showbiz'; 'he'll be the idol of teenagers every-where'. 'Why,' he boasts to Bert's mum and dad, 'you'll even see [him] on television . . . the hot cod's eye which watches every home in Britain.' Leon's diner in Compton Street becomes the Tom-Tom Club (decked out with plastic palm trees), the subject of a Saturday night documentary, 'Cos-morama', introduced by the BBC's Gilbert Harding. A panel of worthies discuss Bert's 'symptoms'

Jonny Jackson (Laurence Harvey) shows Maisie (Sylvia Syms) a bit of backroom attention in Soho in *Expresso Bongo* (Val Guest, 1957)

(or, rather, his art) while Jonny (less worthily) proclaims him a symbol for modern youth. 'I'm just something he sells,' drones Bert; 'for me, music is a drug.'

More latte than espresso, *Bongo* still manages to convey a fable concerning the commercial exploitation of culture which is revisited in succeeding decades: with The Beatles in the 1960s, with Derek Jarman's *Jubilee* (1978) (see Chapter 12) and with Julien Temple's misconceived and ersatz 1986 rendition of Colin MacInnes' 1959 novel, *Absolute Beginners* (lurid but less colourful than *Bongo*'s monochrome – with race riots conveyed in the manner of the Robert Wise/Jerome Robbins adaptation of Leonard Bernstein's *West Side Story* [US, 1961]). Moreover, the fascination with the East End working class of television pundits, Cynthia the society deb (Susan Hampshire) and her gormless boyfriend ('Say something in cockney – apples and pears and things') remains with us yet.

Blind Date (Joseph Losey, 1959)

In 1950, *Sequence* reported the enquiry undertaken by the House Un-American Activities Committee and deplored the absence of coverage of the trials in the British press as a whole. In 1952,

Sight and Sound reported the listing of Joseph Losey and Ben Barzman as communist sympathisers.[51] Losey and Barzman duly took up residence in Britain. Other HUAC exiles (together with Lindsay Anderson) found employment on ITV's *Robin Hood*, retrospectively interpreted in Michael Eaton's *Fellow Traveller* (Philip Saville, 1989) as a parallel allegory of the struggle of a hero of the people against persecution: 'Even our bloody mythology's being colonised by yanks,' complains a Scottish disarmament activist. Losey made *The Sleeping Tiger* with Dirk Bogarde in 1954, made *Time Without Pity* with Barzman in 1957 and directed *The Gypsy and the Gentleman* for Rank in 1958. Meanwhile, on the strength of his directorial work in the States, *Cahiers du Cinéma* lauded Losey as an 'auteur' in the making.

The scenario for *Blind Date*, based on Leigh Howard's novel *Chance Meeting*, was prepared by Barzman and directed by Losey over a matter of weeks in 1959. Jan van Rooyen (Hardy Kruger, previously seen as a German pilot in Roy Baker's 1957 *The One that Got Away*), a young Dutch painter, has been having an affair with an older woman he believes to be called Jacqueline Cousteau (Micheline Presle). She makes an appointment to meet him at 5.30 – he arrives, then three policemen arrive immediately afterwards, summoned by a call from the flat. A woman's body is found in the bedroom, murdered, it is said, at 5.30. This woman is the real Jacqueline Cousteau, the mistress of Sir Howard Fenton. Jan protests his innocence. Certainly, there are in this film devices which seemingly function as trademarks of the oeuvre as a whole: thematically, the instigation of a plot by an outsider; stylistically, cast shadows used to frame actors and action; mirrors used scenographically and expressively; shots composed with graphic clarity and deliberation. Stanley Baker (previously cast as policemen in *Hell is a City* and *Violent Playground*) reappears in Losey's *The Criminal* (1960) and *Accident* and the art director is Losey's longstanding collaborator, Richard Macdonald. His *mise en scène*, announces the *Cahiers* review of *Blind Date*, is his method, he restores to the camera its original purpose as a probing instrument of scientific record.[52] There are also surface aspects of the film which mark it as something of a harbinger for the London films of the 1960s, sometimes similarly made by foreign visitors (notably Michelangelo Antonioni and Roman Polanski – see Chapter 9). The Clive Mews location recalls Jean Varley's flat in Braine's novel *Life at the Top*, Suzette's Bayswater flatlette in Colin MacInnes' *Absolute Beginners* and the photographer's studio in *Blow-Up* (1966). The lothario Julian Ormerod, in Amis' 1960 novel *Take a Girl Like You*, vainly asks the lovely Jenny Bunn whether there is any chance of her becoming 'the maisonette type'. An iconic double-decker bus passes firstly Parliament Square and lastly the Embankment; Richard Rodney Bennett's prominent score prompts comment (the first policeman says that it's jazz, 'But is it good jazz?' presses Morgan). It has sometimes been suggested, even by Losey himself, that he and other exiles enjoyed a privileged view of British institutions. In *Blind Date*, the Assistant Commissioner attempts to wield power bestowed on him by rank and social affiliation over his subordinate Morgan (Baker), the Welsh Detective Inspector. Sir Howard and Sir Brian (Robert Flemyng) are 'old school chums', and there may even be a suggestion, which recurs in many subsequent police films and television serials of the 1970s and 1980s, of masonic allegiance overriding public duty. *Blind Date* can indeed be viewed as an example within a particular genre as much as an idiosyncratically authored tour de force.

Ealing's *Man in a White Suit* and the Boultings' *I'm Alright Jack* deal to a greater or lesser extent with issues of labour relations, but the workplace situation of the comedy is recognisably similar. However, more than a decade seems to separate the social milieu of Dearden's *The Blue Lamp* from that of Losey's *Blind Date*. In place of Jack Warner's affability, Dixon's loyalty to his fellow officers and the deference of the community he serves, Stanley Baker makes no secret of the animosity and grudging mutual respect between the rough-edged Morgan (the hard cop) and the urbane pathologist. 'Oh, I'm no gentleman,' he informs Jan bitterly; Jan meanwhile enquires of the junior officers (the soft cops), presuming them to be his allies in the interrogation, whether it is usual or permissible for Morgan to behave as he does. A junior officer (Gordon Jackson, prior to television fame below stairs) regrets that young people no longer want to join the force. Morgan attacks Jan's romantic naiveté, his failure to read the evidence of Jacqueline Cousteau's surroundings (the 'facts' which Christopher Challis' camera records) and the Irishman's report of her entertaining gentleman callers. This is not just any typically baroque Losey interior, nor is it simply, as Morgan informs us, a real tart's boudoir:

> The idea was that it was a place that had been converted or redecorated three times so that there were three generations of taste and kind of person represented. If you peeled off one skin there was another skin and then another. Eventually the murder is solved through the discovery of a layer which hadn't immediately been evident, namely certain small art objects, in particular a painting that was obviously much too expensive to have been bought by the woman who occupied the place. It was the key to her other lover . . .[53]

The dark, over-upholstered, fussily decorated interior, spotlit by table lamps and the open fire, contrasts strongly with the flashbacks to Jan's white and spartan rooflit garret. Handed a wad of money by Jan, Morgan needs no more than guess at its value: £500 is a 'round sum for a pay-off', he says. But Morgan has become wise through more than the experience afforded by his job: 'It's a question of background . . . my father was a chauffeur.' 'You get to smell the difference between a giver and a taker,' he tells Jan, doubting that the woman whom he thinks of as Jacqueline would give away anything at all. Sir Brian initially appeals to Morgan to protect Howard Fenton's good name for the sake of a brilliant career as a fine public servant, in order to safeguard delicate international negotiations; later he resorts to intimidation: 'Your sort goes to the top or doesn't go at all,' but Morgan snubs his impertinence. Morgan, like Jan, is not so readily corrupted.

At first Jan fails to understand that the flat to which he has been invited is not that of the 'Jacqueline' with whom he has been having an affair; urged by Morgan to draw back the sheet and confront the dead body, Jan recoils and retches, later saying that he did not see the woman's face at all. But Jan is also duped by the Fentons, Lady Fenton has been duped by her husband (he was intending to leave her for the 'other' Jacqueline) and Lady Fenton has even mistaken herself: 'What are you afraid might happen?' asks Jan at the beginning of the affair, proudly refusing to prostitute himself by accepting her money; 'What I didn't plan was that I might love you – damn you,' she says at the end.

Both Jacquelines (the show-girl and the lady) are French. On the one hand, one might compare the casting of Micheline Presle to that of Simone Signoret in *Room at the Top* and *Term of Trial* (Peter Glenville, 1962), as some form of expedient.[54] But it seems to me that the Jacquelines are to be understood here as very different from one another . . . but then not so different (the lady, after all, is no better than a whore). The present Lady Fenton is middle-aged and sophisticated, expensively fashionable and elegantly, fastidiously coiffured. 'But ice can burn too,' she tells Jan. 'Violence is not the sole property of the poor.' She condescends to Jan; when he reveals a bare shoulder she seems to be preying on his very youth and innocence. This Jacqueline arranges everything, pays him off, says that it is the sons of butchers who are gifted with the talent to become painters, while Jan says that painting is a job of work like many others. But this Jacqueline is familiar with a Parisian scene of galleries and dealers, of which the ingenuous Jan, the would-be artist, as yet knows nothing. The accents and delivery of speech in *Blind Date* are deliberately set against each other: Morgan's bluff Welsh manner, interspersed with cynical sniffs at Jan's sentimentality, and Jan's disbelieving outbursts are contrasted with her ladyship's cool reserve: told by Morgan that the murdered girl was her husband's mistress she hardly falters: '. . . of course I knew . . . what woman wouldn't . . . it happens in the best of families'.

Notes

1. Lecture by Harold French, 7 February 1955, BFI/MEB/H94.
2. Margaret Dickinson and Sarah Street, *Cinema and State: the Film Industry and the Government 1927–84* (London: BFI, 1985), pp. 225–6.
3. BFI/MEB/G117.
4. BFI/MEB/G105.
5. See 'Project for a Production Series of Story Documentaries', 8 June 1950, BFI/MEB/G105 and H/10; Grierson soon proved himself intractable and ineffectual as executive producer and the hoped for projects were not forthcoming; *Sight and Sound*, October–December 1952, pp. 78–9. *The Brave Don't Cry* cast John Gregson alongside Fulton Mackay (later of *Porridge* fame) and players from Glasgow's Citizens' Theatre.
6. Arthur Marwick, *British Society Since 1945* (Harmondsworth: Penguin, 2003), p. 105.
7. *Daily Film Renter*, 25 January 1955, p. 1.
8. Cited by John Hill, *Sex, Class and Realism* (London: BFI, 1986), p. 39.
9. Cited by Anthony Aldgate, *Censorship and the Permissive Society* (Oxford: Clarendon Press, 1995), pp. 33 and 39; Bryan Forbes, Jack Clayton and Joseph Losey (in spite of cuts to *Blind Date*) commend Trevelyan's leniency. On the controversy surrounding Peeping Tom, see Adam Lowenstein, 'Under the Skin Horrors', in Justine Ashby and Andrew Higson (eds), *British Cinema: Past and Present* (London: Routledge, 2000).
10. Elkan Allan, 'Scripting Actuality Television', and Penelope Houston, 'Captive or Free', *Sight and Sound*, Winter 1957/8, pp. 116–21; see also 'Hollywood in the Age of Television', *Sight and Sound*, Spring 1957.

Detective Inspector Morgan (Stanley Baker) circles an innocent victim (Hardy Kruger) in Joseph Losey's 1959 *Blind Date*

11. *Sight and Sound*, Winter 1955/6, p. 114, and reviews of *Orders to Kill* and *The Young Lions*, *Sight and Sound*, Spring 1958, p. 248.

12. *Monthly Film Bulletin*, November 1957, pp. 134–5.

13. *Sequence*, 1947, p. 11.

14. Lindsay Anderson, 'Get out and Push!', in Tom Maschler (ed.), *Declaration* (London: MacGibbon and Kee, 1957), p. 160.

15. Ken Tynan noted John Mills' ability to cross ranks: 'Idea: A history of World War II based on movies about it. E.g. Start with map of the world and place pins as if indicating principal wartime activities. John Mills reaches beach at Dunkirk just as John Mills goes down with submarine in *We Dive at Dawn*. Kirk Douglas is blowing up heavy-water installations in Norway as Burt Lancaster prevents Impressionist paintings from leaving occupied France. Burt Lancaster fucks Deborah Kerr on eve of Pearl Harbor in *From Here to Eternity*. John Wayne is also nearby in *Harm's Way*. Attenborough snivels in *In Which We Serve* while crashing to his death in *The Way to the Stars* – etc. etc. (getting the films right, which I haven't). You would find, I suspect, that in one war picture or another, John Mills played every rank, commissioned and non-commissioned, in all the fighting services. It would be nice to intercut sequences so that Captain Mills, after accepting a salute from Corporal Mills, went off to report to Colonel Mills . . .'; see John Lahr (ed.), *The Diaries of Kenneth Tynan* (London: Bloomsbury, 2001), 16 January 1971.

16. Andy Medhurst, '1950s War Films', in Geoff Hurd (ed.), *National Fictions: World War Two in British Films and Television* (London: BFI, 1984), p. 36.

17. 'The Cruel Sea', 7 November 1952, BFI/MEB/H22.

18. BFI/MEB/I251 Pc17; see also *Sight and Sound*, Summer 1958.

19. Alan Lovell and Jim Hillier, *Studies in Documentary* (New York: Viking, 1972), pp. 150–6.

20. *Sight and Sound*, Spring 1957; 'Stand Up! Stand Up!' appeared in the Autumn 1956 issue; see also Joan Littlewood, *Joan's Book* (Basingstoke: Macmillan, 2000), p. 538.

21. John Osborne, *Almost a Gentleman*, vol. II (London: Faber and Faber: 1991), p. 21; see also Harry Ritchie, *Success Stories* (London: Faber and Faber, 1988), p. 26.

22. See, for instance, *Sight and Sound*, Winter 1958/9, letter from Denis Horne on his film with Lorenza Mazzetti, *Teddy Boys*, denying the existence of a movement for which Anderson had declared himself spokesman.

23. Maschler, *Declaration*, introduction.

24. But for Dilys Powell's appreciation of *Room at the Top*, see Aldgate, p. 93.

25. Raymond Williams, *Culture and Society 1780–1850* [1958] (London: Penguin, 1982), pp. 250–5; Richard Hoggart, *The Uses of Literacy* [1957] (London: Chatto and Windus, 1967), p. 166, and 1961 introduction to D. H. Lawrence, *Lady Chatterley's Lover*, re. 'The Corpse Wore Nylon'.

26. George Orwell, 'The Art of Donald McGill', *Collected Essays* (London: Secker and Warburg, 1968), pp. 167–78.

27. Programme for MOMA screening, 10 December 1957 BFI/MEB/1173 and *Sight and Sound*, Spring 1956.

28. Osborne, *Almost a Gentleman*, p. 35; Osborne denies any debt to Brecht (a critical judgment which continues to be asserted) in favour of his knowledge of the English music hall tradition.

29. Hill, *Sex, Class and Realism*, p. 133.

30. Richard Hoggart, 'We Are the Lambeth Boys', *Sight and Sound*, Summer/Autumn 1959, pp. 164–5.

31. *Sequence*, December 1946; 'Only Connect: Some Aspects of the Work of Humphrey Jennings', *Sight and Sound*, April–June 1954.

32. *Sight and Sound*, July–September 1952, p. 26, and October–December 1953, p. 88.

33. Walter Lassally, 'The Cynical Audience', *Sight and Sound*, Summer 1956, p. 12.

34. See *Sight and Sound*, Winter 1957/8, and *Cahiers du Cinéma I: the 1950s* (London: Routledge, 1985), p. 36.

35. 'Panorama at Cannes', *Sight and Sound*, Summer 1956, p. 17; see also *Cahiers du Cinéma* criticism of French super productions.

36. *Sight and Sound*, Autumn 1958, p. 275; see also Spring 1956, p. 217.

37. *Cahiers du Cinéma* 91, January 1959, and François Truffaut, *Hitchcock* [1966] (London: Secker and Warburg, 1968), p. 100: 'What I'm trying to get at – and I'm not sure I'm right about this and it's hard to define just what it is – is that there's something about England that's anti-cinematic . . . Well, to put it quite bluntly, isn't there a certain incompatibility between the terms 'cinema' and 'Britain'. This may sound far-fetched, but I get the feeling that there are national characteristics – among them, the English countryside, the subdued way of life, the stolid routine – that are anti-dramatic in a sense. The weather itself is anti-cinematic.' Osborne comments on the journal's 'arid academic body-building' but finds Truffaut less guilty than others in 'Reel Enthusiasm' [1989], *Damn You, England* (London: Faber and Faber, 1994), pp. 156–8.

38. BFI/MEB/H58; see also *Sight and Sound*, April 1950.

39. BFI/MEB/H58; the two other films were the Boultings' *Seven Days to Noon* and the documentary *The Undefeated* (1950).

40. To the surprise of the director of the Venice Festival, who had tried to exclude *The Lavender Hill Mob* from the competition, it was duly awarded with the screenplay prize. Balcon was indignant and resented the interference: 'Venice is not conferring any favours on the British film industry in allowing us to compete there . . . there is no long tradition of a successful film industry in Italy . . . it's true that a few international films have been made since the liberation but by and large they have no greater claim to distinction in Britain than we have . . . there should be no inferiority complex about better British pictures'; 'As to Italian judgement, our most successful picture in Italy in recent years is *Saraband for Dead Lovers*, probably one of the biggest failures, both commercially and artistically I have ever been connected with.' See BFI/MEB/H4 and H10. Balcon acknowledges that 'foreignness' can itself render a film attractive to some audiences.

41. Richard Roud, 'Britain in America', *Sight and Sound*, Autumn 1956.

42. *Movie*, vol. 1, 1963; see also 'Alligators and Old Lace', re. two maiden ladies sharing Chertsey cottage with two perfectly mannered alligators and a crocodile, *Picture Post*, 10 January 1948, pp. 19–21.

43. See *Picturegoer*, 2 January 1954 and 27 November 1954.

44. *Picturegoer*, 13 February 1954, p. 9.

45. BFI/MEB/H94, 14 December 1955.

46. Margaret Hinxman, 'Ealing Goes in for Glamour', *Picturegoer*, 16 January 1954.

47. 'People of Talent', *Sight and Sound*, Spring 1956, p. 191.

48. *Sight and Sound*, Winter 1955/6, p. 149.

49. Charles Barr, *Ealing Studios* [1977] (London: Studio Vista, 1993), p. 137; Susannah Handley, *Nylon* (Baltimore: Johns Hopkins University Press, 1999), p. 57.

50. *Picturegoer*, 20 March 1954; *Laxdale Hall* (1952) was directed by John Eldridge.

51. See *Sequence*, Summer 1950, p. 1, and *Sight and Sound*, October–December 1952, p. 53.

52. Jean Douchet, 'Un art de laboratoire', *Cahiers du Cinéma* no. 117, 1961, p. 47.

53. Michel Ciment, *Conversations with Losey* (London: Methuen, 1985), p. 168.

54. See Alexander Walker, *Hollywood, England: the British Film Industry in the Sixties* [1974] (London: Harrap, 1986), p. 47, and Christine Geraghty, *British Cinema in the Fifties* (London: Routledge, 2000), pp. 109–10.

Chapter 9 | 1960s

Vivian Nicholson's memories of her upbringing in Castleford match the familiar monochrome 'regional and proletarian' realism of *A Kind of Loving* (John Schlesinger, 1962), *Saturday Night and Sunday Morning* (Karel Reisz, 1960), *A Taste of Honey* (Tony Richardson, 1961), *Room at the Top* (Jack Clayton, 1959) and *Life at the Top* (Ted Kotcheff, 1965):

> . . . the houses were all alike, two up and two down, council property with no bath, no hot water, black-lead fire grates and right narrow steps. Our house was really hemmed in with five kids and me mother and father.[1]

However, thanks to a massive pools win (£152,319) in 1960, Viv and her husband Keith managed to fulfil the material aspirations of a generation and a decade. Entertained in a London hotel for the prize-giving, they experienced luxury and decided that they preferred it to the grimy North. Much celebrated, reported and photographed, Viv, flamboyant, young and attractive, obligingly posed for Littlewoods at the pithead in a crochet mini-dress and knee-high boots before her departure for Malta and the high life: fast cars, race-horses, a bungalow, different clothes for every occasion. *The People* duly rewarded her for her story. Her rags-to-riches transformation, the immediate gratification and subsequent crash of the dream (with Keith's accidental death and her bankruptcy) describe a trajectory exceptional in its excess but typical of unchecked consumerism. By luck, talent or cunning, the young could have more money and more fun than their parents had ever imagined possible, even if (unlike Viv's parents, too poor even to live on credit) this generation surrendered itself, literally or metaphorically, to the hire purchase slogan: Live Now; Pay Later.

Go to Work on an Egg

While the future novelist, Fay Weldon, cut her teeth on slogans in an agency, many future British feature film-makers (working in Britain and America) were serving an apprenticeship in advertising: Hugh Hudson; David Puttnam; Alan Parker for Cinzano; Ridley Scott for Hovis; Adrian Lyne and Don Boyd (see Chapters 10 and 11). Many films of the decade make use of slogans or of imagery familiar from contemporary ads, but frequently the reference is ironic or at least ambivalent. Dandy

Spymaster Major Dalby (Nigel Green) keeping an eye on the 'shrewd little cockney' Harry Palmer (Michael Caine) in Sidney J. Furie's 1965 *The Ipcress File*

Nichols (from 1965, best known as BBC TV's *Till Death Us Do Part*'s 'silly old moo') plays the land-lady, Mrs Bowles, a 'succulent old washbag' in Harold Pinter's adaptation of his stageplay, *The Birthday Party* (William Friedkin, 1968). She asks husband Petey (Moultrie Kelsall) whether the corn-flakes she serves up to him every morning are nice – 'They're horrible,' he replies – 'They're refresh-ing . . . it says so,' she insists, citing Kelloggs' own claim. In *Every Home Should Have One* (Jim Clark, 1970 – produced by BBC TV *That Was The Week That Was*'s Ned Sherrin) Teddy Brown, an advertising assistant (Marty Feldman), is deputed to find a 'sexier' image for McLaughlin's 'Frozen Porridge for Bonnie Bairns' and (amid much reference to 1960s television programming and debate) arrives at Goldilocks (aka his Swedish au pair) and the three bears; Teddy brushes his teeth with a 'halo of hygiene' ringing his head and an animated figure singing the 'Alka Vita' jingle. 'Wipe it on, Windolene, wipe it off, window clean', sings Tony in *The Knack . . . and How to Get It* (Richard Lester, 1965). One of a series of articles in *The Listener* devoted to exploring current cul-tural mythology addresses itself to 'The Advertising Man':

> One opinion (critical) holds that he seduces the minds of children with false and meretricious values, undermines the editorial freedom of the press and entices innocent housewives to spend more and more money on things they need less and less . . . Another (approving) sees the advertising man as the gallant upholder of free competition, a man of the future dedicated to raising the general stan-dard of consumption and increasing the satisfaction of consumers. [Accordingly], advertising plays a key role in stimulating demand and triggering economic growth.[2]

In *Bedazzled* (Stanley Donen, 1967), Peter Cook and Dudley More reprise their stage and television partnership with not only Pete (as the devil) but also Dud, as a latter-day Dr Faustus, Stanley Moon: 'I thought up the seven deadly sins in an afternoon,' bemoans Beelzebub, the Prince of Darkness (aka George Spiggott); 'the only thing I've come up with recently is advertising'. 'You painted a beautiful dream . . .,' whines Moon, the disappointed Wimpy Bar chef; 'You should never believe ads,' he's advised in return.

In *The Loneliness of the Long Distance Runner* (Tony Richardson, 1962), white exploding stars, in the manner of TV ads, appear between episodes in different shops as Colin's mum goes on her spending spree with the insurance money received after his dad's death: 'How cheap things are when you can pay cash,' says her friend as they settle on a new television set. *The Knack* invokes advertising in its script, in emblazoned lettering across the screen and in the costuming and chor-eography of its characters. Nancy (Rita Tushingham), the country mouse newly arrived in London, is both fascinated and unimpressed by Tolan's modish bravura: 'Mr Smarty . . . in your narrow slacks,' she jibes (just before fainting at his sleek Chelsea booted-feet); as Tolan (Ray Brooks) and Colin (a prototype for Michael Crawford's later television persona, Frank Spencer) comically chase through London's alleyways, fashion models are posed in the empty windows of derelict buildings (as if for a magazine photo-spread) and the boys, too, hold poses for the camera, in the 'gritty' style promoted by the trend-setting photographers John Cowan and Terence Donovan.[3] Like

Smashing Time (Desmond Davis, 1967) – also with Rita Tushingham – *The Knack* presents its mod-ishness in ironic mode, as if the moment has passed as soon as it has arrived.

Darling (John Schlesinger, 1965) and *Nothing But the Best* (Clive Donner, 1964), both scripted by Frederick Raphael, are especially cynical about the 1960s growth industries of advertising and property development and both feature narrator-protagonists who use surface appearance for per-sonal advancement. *Darling* opens with a signature tune by John Dankworth (a frequent collabor-ator on films of the 1960s) and a poster announcing the publication of Diana's story in the fictitious magazine *Ideal Woman* pasted over pictures of African children. 'Terribly Chelsea I thought I was,' at twenty, Diana (Julie Christie) – a modern Becky Sharp – recollects to television presenter Robert (Dirk Bogarde). Diana and Robert begin an affair ('but there was nothing delib-erate about it . . . the thought of breaking up someone's family was repellent to me', she insists), Diana leaving her less successful husband, Tony Bridges (Trevor Bowen), and Robert deserting his wife and children. The film persistently sets her own description of herself to the off-screen inter-viewer at odds with her appearance in events on screen: she says that she was never 'the jealous type' while criticising Robert for spending time away and being afraid that he'll leave. But more than this (as in the opening sequence) the film suggests the shallowness of the society which allows Diana to rise: dowagers dripping jewellery stuff down canapés at a charity draw in aid of World Hunger, and the chairman speaks of malnutrition and the 'brotherhood of man' amid black boys decked out as eighteenth-century flunkeys. Diana's accent becomes increasingly affected as she climbs the social ladder and, somewhat vaingloriously, refers to the succession of men in her life helping with her 'career', aborting a child lest it interfere but walking out of an audition (along-side *Z-Cars* extras) for an acting role. While insisting that she did not want anyone to get hurt, she moves in with Miles (Laurence Harvey), the advertising man, and lies to Robert: 'Your idea of fidelity is having only one man in bed!' he says. She boasts of a film trip to Italy which turns out to be no more than an advert for 'Cupid chocolates with fairytale centres', then, pitching for the son of an Italian prince, lands the elderly father instead – then complains of boredom when he leaves her to her own devices in the family palazzo. I find it impossible to sympathise with Diana (it seems to me she is less exploited than exploiter and deserves what she gets), although Raphael's snobbery towards the jobs through which she chooses to promote herself seems somewhat sim-plistic and complacent: Southgate, the author, and Tony, the struggling playwright, serve as an example of 'genuine' artistic integrity, while Diana is spoiled, selfish and unscrupulous. Robert Murphy, on the other hand, is won over by Darling and finds Robert's rejection of her 'petulant, almost sadistic'.[4]

Julie Christie proved a highly effective advertisement for British film and an eclectic range of British styling.[5] She variously appeared as the casually confident and glamorous Liz in *Billy Liar!* (with Billy's fiancée, Barbara [Helen Fraser], frumpily mumsy in contrast), as the screwed-up, poor little rich girl *Petulia* (Richard Lester, 1968), obsessively pursuing Dr Archie Bollen (George C. Scott) (whom even her looks and money cannot buy), in widescreen in David Lean's 1965 *Dr Zhivago* (with Rita Tushingham and Tom Courtenay in subsidiary roles) and as Bathsheba Everdene

opposite Alan Bates' Gabriel Oak and Terence Stamp's Sergeant Troy in *Far from the Madding Crowd* (John Schlesinger, 1967 – its Wessex weather and landscape gloriously photographed by Nicolas Roeg). As Raphael Samuel observes:

> Stamp's performance as Sergeant Troy . . . seems to have been as influential on male fashion as Christie's Bathsheba . . . making the scarlet tunic and tight pantaloons of a gay hussar a kind of alternative lifestyle uniform.

> Laura Ashley, who opened her first boutique in 1968, projected the milkmaid look as a kind of alternative national dress; while Christie's ravishing performance as Bathsheba . . . turned broderie anglaise into the latest thing.[6]

Both Liz and Petulia appear posed in stills as if to remind the films' audience of her model 'It' girl status. *Fahrenheit 451* (François Truffaut, 1965 – photographed by Roeg and scored by Bernard Herrmann), starring Christie in dual roles, and *The Collector* (William Wyler, 1965), starring 'the world's most beautiful man', Terence Stamp (a moniker secured by his appearance in Peter Ustinov's 1962 adaptation of Herman Melville's *Billy Budd* – and recalled in his casting as a transvestite in Stephan Elliott's *Adventures of Priscilla, Queen of the Desert* [Australia, 1994]), also investigate *Darling*'s opposition of commercial entertainment and cultural heritage. Although Robert Murphy claims that the premise of Ray Bradbury's futuristic novel (which takes its title from the temperature at which paper burns) and Truffaut's adaptation are 'highly improbable', events in European history of the last century (let alone the more recent past – as acknowledged by Michael Moore's polemical *Fahrenheit 9:11* [US, 2004]) sadly would appear to prove him wrong.[7] Linda (Julie Christie) spends her days in a bungalow, a ticky-tacky box, just like all the others, watching interactive television or alleviating the boredom with uppers and downers while her husband, Montag (Oskar Werner), works as a fireman, 'We burn books to ashes then burn the ashes'. Books are considered dangerous because they disturb people and make them anti-social. But Montag has met someone on a train, a probationary teacher, Clarisse (Julie Christie), who asks whether it is true that firemen once put out fires in houses, and whether he ever reads a book before setting it alight. Montag has almost forgotten how to; his Captain (Cyril Cusack) suggests that, for the sake of promotion, he should increase his dosage of sport. Montag draws closer to Clarisse and reads 'to catch up with the remembrance of the past', but is betrayed by Linda. A woman in an older house chooses to die with her secret library (including copies of *Cahiers du Cinéma* and an autobiography of Charlie Chaplin) and Montag seizes back his own book and joins Clarisse in a commune in the woods where people memorise the pages they read in order to pass them on to generations to come.

Liz (Julie Christie), back in Bradford, ponders ads for holidays abroad in *Billy Liar!* (John Schlesinger, 1963)

In *The Collector*, adapted from John Fowles' 1963 novel, a nondescript clerk, Freddie (Terence Stamp), has few friends at work and is mocked for his hobby – lepidoptery. One day, his aunt (Mona Washbourne), much to his embarrassment arrives at the bank and tells him that he has won £71,000 on the football pools. He lays elaborate plans to abduct a girl (Samantha Eggar), remembered from when she was at the local grammar school, whom he then regularly followed and whom he now stalks as an art student in London. She is locked into a vaulted, Gothic cellar, like a fairytale princess, under a deserted house in the country. But nothing can win her to him: pathetically he hopes that she may come to love him. She finds him vulgar, ignorant of books and paintings, suburban, soulless for all his material affluence, merely a 'Caliban' to her Miranda. But Miranda, in desperation, offers her body to him, thinking that by so doing she may buy her freedom. Having idealised her as an acquisition, he finds the gesture gross and common. For all her guile, like a butterfly, she withers away in the trap, and Freddie determines next time to aim lower – perhaps a nurse – 'someone I could teach'.

Jimmy Bates (Alan Brewster) in *Nothing But the Best* is the counterpart of *Darling*'s Diana, likewise intent upon self-advancement socially and materially, and the film is similarly topical in its references, with E-type Jaguars (driven by A-type ladies), exploitative property agents profiteering from redevelopment schemes, Radio Luxembourg, comparisons with John Osborne and a token appearance for critic and television pundit Bernard Levin in the crush bar of a theatre: 'Positively the worst play I've seen since Tuesday,' he says, on Thursday night. Jimmy models his dress and habits on those of Charles (Denholm Elliott), a delinquent aristocrat who takes up residence in Jimmy's rented room. But, like many other characters, Charlie is cast off on Jimmy's ascent to power and fortune: '. . . sooner or later he will have to go', runs the much-repeated refrain, in voiceover. Similarly, like Michael Caine's Alfie, he is dismissive of women he considers beneath his dignity: 'I can cope with this kind of chick with my eyes shut . . . sooner or later she will have to go' (the chick in question subsequently arriving pregnant at Jimmy's wedding). Like fellow adventurer Joe Lampton (in *Room at the Top* and *Life at the Top*) Jimmy determines to marry the boss' daughter, Anne (the singer Millicent Martin, from the satirical revue *That Was The Week That Was*, here in a non-singing role). In *Georgy Girl* (Silvio Narizzano, 1966) it is Georgina (Lynn Redgrave) who marries her parents' boss, bringing with her the baby daughter of Jos (Alan Bates) and supercool Meredith (Charlotte Rampling), who promptly takes off with a new boyfriend. Like the ambitious journalist in *The Ploughman's Lunch* (Richard Eyre, 1983) (see Chapter 11), Jimmy is ashamed of his parents (his father was a docker: 'What, import and export?' suggests Anne, when he says that he put things onto boats and took them off), pretends that they are dead and despatches them to Australia before the wedding. Like *Darling*'s Diana, his accent becomes increasingly posh. However, the upstart is not allowed to benefit from his crimes and misdemeanours. The pub sign 'The Young Pretender' bodes ill and, at the very end of the film, a crane hook is lowered into frame, like a noose, behind Jimmy's head. But, as with *Darling*, the social climber is doubly at fault for seeking to join a society which is itself sham and shallow: the crowd at the (wrong) hunt ball; Charles' cronies at his club (one of whom [Willie Rushton, another television satire stalwart] cannot quite work out just exactly where he and Jimmy have met before . . . but is sure that they must have); a partygoer who offers herself to him as a tombola prize. 'It's a horrible world,' he tells us cynically, 'you have to trick your way to the top.'

The Birth of the Cool

Liz in *Billy Liar!* is attractive not only because she is played by Julie Christie and (unlike Babs) does not dress like her mother, but because she seems 'cultured' (unlike Rita) and has travelled not only to London but to Europe. She seems more liberated and experienced than the girls who have stayed at home (even Rita, cast as the local tart), 'She's been abroad and suits herself', and it is she who initiates her coupling with Billy (Tom Courtenay). Seemingly, Billy is safer in his fantasy Ambrosian life (imagining himself as a Member of Parliament, pilot or soldier) but can never actually escape the clutches of his employer Mr Shadrack (Leonard Rossiter) and his family obligations and never manages to get beyond Bradford railway station. Vic Brown (Alan Bates) in *A Kind of Loving*, co-scripted from Stan Barstow's 1960 novel (like Billy) by Keith Waterhouse, thinks of going abroad, 'I want to get out of this town and have a look around'; he marries Ingrid (named after Bergman) (June Ritchie) when she falls pregnant but the stifling company of his mother-in-law (a splendidly vituperative Thora Hird) drives him away before he reconsiders and settles. *The Listener* found comparable 'disenchantment, hopeful idealism and getting what fun there is to be found where they live' for BBC TV's 1964–6 *The Likely Lads* (adumbrated in the title of its sequel, *Whatever Happened to the Likely Lads*, 1973–4), adding that the series (also set in the Northeast) conveyed 'the truth and sadness' underlying its comedy.[8]

Jonathan Miller, working as a producer of BBC TV Arts programmes in the 1960s, perpetuated the notion of the North of England as less 'advanced' in his discussion of his 1970 adaptation of Kingsley Amis' 1960 *Take a Girl* (in which Jenny Bunn 'progresses bravely into a slough of Southern lechery'):

> There must be a lot of girls like Jenny, especially in the North. It's not prudishness or fear that makes them hang on to their virginity. It's more a core of integrity, with their bodies wound round it like coils, like an armature.[9]

But London's supposed permissiveness is also represented as a phenomenon characteristic of the young: *The Knack* uses mock vox-pop sound-bites from affronted elderly interviewees (often as unselfconscious innuendo) advocating conscription, blaming teachers and the National Health, wondering what the country is coming to with 'girls' legs up all down the road' – one is reminded of Philip Larkin's claim that sex was discovered in 1963.[10] Veteran film producer Michael Balcon complained that the 'Swinging London' films failed to mirror the wider nation and were the product of sensationalist reporting by foreign journalists;[11] Michael Caine, celebrated with the Rolling Stones' Mick Jagger, David Hockney and others in Peter Whitehead's 1967 *Tonite Let's All Make Love in London*, claimed that 'Swinging London was the same 200 people in the King's Road trying to have it off with each other.' Even among films themselves there is ambivalence about the material and social rewards which a 'soft' metropolitan life seem to promise, the North, even in decline, continuing to be portrayed as somehow more genuine and real.

In Albert Finney's 1967 film of Shelagh Delaney's *Charlie Bubbles* (its eponymous hero played by Finney, and a figure for his own discontent) a millionaire author returns to his roots – 'You just do your writing now or are you still working?' says an old friend of his father (now a hotel waiter), who played cards when they were sitting out the Depression together. Charlie has apparently gained a world but lost his soul – a young son is growing up quite happily without him and his estranged wife (Billie Whitelaw) remains unimpressed by his success. Similar autobiographical concerns surface in Alan Sillitoe's 1984 novel *Down from the Hill*, in which a Midlands boy makes good as a television scriptwriter and returns to his roots, remembering the years when Britain was recovering from the war. In Harold Pinter's *The Pumpkin Eater* (Jack Clayton, 1964) an author, Jake Armitage (Peter Finch), like Pinter himself, achieves wealth and success as a film scriptwriter but becomes increasingly estranged from his wife and children, endeavouring to repair the damage with a return to the country idyll of a simpler past life together. Michael Marler (Nicol Williams) in Jack Gold's *The Reckoning* (1970) has acquired a well-heeled wife, a well-appointed house in Virginia Water, a Rolls Royce with a personalised number plate and a prominent position in British industry (he's 'an aggressive bastard' says his passenger). In London, a moving camera follows him from lift to office, conveying the thrusting urgency with which he manages his (and everyone else's) affairs. But *The Reckoning* offers a cautionary response to similar mogul figures in *The Power Game* (ATV, 1965–9) and *The Troubleshooters* (BBC, 1966–72). Told that his father in Liverpool (whom he has not seen for five years) is seriously ill, he drives back to the family's terrace home. Again, there is a significant shift in accent with the homecoming and the pacing of the photography, covering derelict wasteland, playgrounds and the docks, is slower. His father dies and he offers to pay for the funeral ('the best'). Meanwhile, he spends the night with the doctor's receptionist (Rachel Roberts – a reprise of her role in *Saturday Night and Sunday Morning*), whose comforting warmth and spontaneity is set against Marler's wife's game-playing: Rosemary (Anne Bell) and Marler argue and fight, she calls him 'a drunken Irish peasant' but it's obvious that a bit of rough is why and for what she married him.

Certainly, many of the films of the 1960s are the work of visiting directors, attracted by a much publicised and promoted London scene in music, art, architecture, industrial design, fashion and photography (as showcased in the international Expo '69 and regularly on BBC TV on *Tomorrow's World* [1965–]) and supported by co-production funding from abroad: in *Carry On Screaming* (Gerald Thomas, 1966), dummies' bottoms topically and patriotically sport labels announcing 'Made in England'. In *The Killing of Sister George* (1968) (concerning lesbian jealousy and the 'killing-off' of a television soapstar, memorably portrayed by Beryl Reid – 'not all girls are raving lesbians' – 'That is a misfortune I'm perfectly well aware of') American director Robert Aldrich neatly brings together a distinctive black cab, a red double-decker bus and an up-to-the-minute open-topped white sportscar in a London traffic incident. *The Knack* was awarded the Grand Prix at Cannes and François Truffaut overcame his previous dismissiveness of British cinema to make *Fahrenheit 451*: 'There's no one in England to beat these new French directors,' says a character in *Darling*. His visibility in British films secured Stamp's casting as the enigmatic stranger in Pier Paolo Pasolini's *Teorema* (Italy, 1968). In *Cul-de-Sac* (1966) Roman Polanski introduced London socialites as weekend visitors to a lonely Northumbrian island ('Is that from Carnaby Street?' asks Jackie [Jacqueline Bisset]) and in *Repulsion* (1965) cast Catherine Deneuve (sometime wife to David Bailey) as a French girl incarcerating herself in an apartment to escape the unwelcome presence and intrusive advances of other people. Here, the city is far from a fun place, the pavements, the buildings, even the walls which once protected her from the outside eventually threatening to over-power her: 'It takes a foreigner to show us London . . . [in] its Pole's-eye view of South Kensing-ton the familiar is made just that fraction unfamiliar and strange,' observed James Price; 'Polanski has always been sensitive to the mood of foreign cities in a worrying sort of way. His report on London, *Repulsion*, brought out the violence in a district where Francis Bacon lives – and South Kensington has never been the same for me since,' commented Eric Rhode.[12]

Alexander Walker reports that Michelangelo Antonioni initiated a questionnaire into current modes and mores before embarking upon his own London film *Blow-Up* (1966), scripted by

Archetypally cool: Thomas (David Hemmings) calls the shots in Michelangelo Antonioni's 1966 *Blow-Up*

Edward Bond and produced by Carlo Ponti for MGM, returning in the 1970s to make part of *The Passenger* (1975).[13] The result, as Walker observes, is something of an amalgam of Swinging London clichés, already somewhat critical of the image peddled by the media. The plot loosely follows Julio Cortazar's short story, concerning a photographer, Thomas (David Hemmings), employing John Cowan's studio and drawing upon Brian Duffy, Terence Donovan and David Bailey, working-class lads whose talents put them at the top of their profession, ousting respected 'society' photographers (Snowden, Lichfield, Cecil Beaton) of a more respectable society (Bailey's 1965 *Pin-Up Box* included the East End gangsters the Kray twins, along with his agent David Puttnam, pop idols and top models). The supermodel Verushka appears in *Blow-Up* as herself (as does Jean Shrimpton – sometime girlfriend to Terence Stamp – in Peter Watkins' 1967 *Privilege*) while two wannabe teenagers in short shifts, bright tights and kitten-heel pumps pester Thomas for photos which might launch them (but never get around to having them taken and opportunistically opt for sex instead). The film is largely concerned with the authenticity of images: Thomas appears first leaving an East End doss-house where he has spent the night documenting its residents, turns a corner and climbs into his car. Thomas persuades himself that his camera is accidental witness to an event which a woman (Vanessa Redgrave) prefers to be kept secret, whereas the wife (Sarah Miles) of his friend, Bill, says that the enlargements remind her of one of his paintings (equally subject to interpretation and equally ambiguous): 'they don't mean anything when I do them – they're just a mess – but afterwards I find something to hang onto . . . it adds up – like finding a clue in a detective story'. Antonioni pointedly constructs a pastiche of topical and conventional motifs: red telephone boxes; black cabs; a guardsman in a bearskin; an antiques shop selling junk and Victoriana whose owner wants to sell up and head off for Nepal (. . . or Morocco) and which Thomas wants to buy (poofters with white poodles are a sure sign that the area is ripe for gentrification, he says). Thomas has a studio and pad in a West End mews (complete with David Hicks-style interior) and, like Charlie Bubbles, owns a Rolls Royce. 'Happening' types in pan-stick make-up drive around the Smithsons' 1962–4 Economist building in St James's, get involved in a demonstration about something or other (it's of no consequence) and, at a Yardbirds' performance, the audience scrambles for a wrecked guitar thrown into its midst. But there is little sense of London as a real place, rather it serves merely as a site of entertainment and potential exploitation for Thomas and his agents: 'I've gone off London this week,' he tells Ron, 'it doesn't do anything for me'; Verushka, hallucinating at Ron's party, insists she's in Paris, as she's told him.

Losey, resident in Britain since the 1950s, cast Antonioni's muse Monica Vitti in his 1966 *Modesty Blaise*. Like Roger Vadim's 1967 *Barbarella*, this took a comic strip (Peter O'Donnell's *Modesty* concurrently appearing in London's *Evening Standard*) as its immediate source and, in the manner of Roy Lichtenstein's fashionable pop-art paintings, includes the original character in shots of Willie's apartment. Modesty is imprisoned in an op-art wallpapered dungeon (echoes here of Bridget Riley). In the manner of the preceding Bond movies (*Dr No* [Terence Young, 1962], *From Russia with Love* [Young, 1963]), Britain's special secret agent is paired with a beautiful accomplice (Terence Stamp again) and, like Emma Peel (Diana Rigg) of TV's *The Avengers* (1961–9), this sexy action-chick is more than a match for her pinstriped Whitehall employers. Gabriel Fothergill (Dirk Bogarde) and Mrs Fothergill (Rosella Falk) correspond to Ian Fleming's SMERSH General and his maniacal Corporal, Rosa Klebb: Gabriel is exquisitely sensitive about food, grooming and etiquette while dominatrix Claudia revels in gladiatorial encounters with their captives. The film mimics the Bond films' fascination with ingenious gadgetry (such as Gauloise cigarette packets timed to eject red and yellow smoke after ten minutes) and Vitti is costumed with heightened care and attention, often flouting continuity, let alone probability (it takes her a full hour to dress for breakfast). Cyril Connolly noted the camp qualities in Fleming's original novels and it soon became a routine observation of the films' exaggerated, travestied characters: 'the James Bond thrillers are camp, in film form anyway', concluded *The Listener*, 'because you are not meant to take them seriously'.[14] Richard Clements' 1968 spy-spoof *Otley* cast Tom Courtenay as a 'fumbling, thieving Portobello Road drop-out' accidentally recruited as a spy; 'Once more,' noted Eric Rhode in *The Listener*, 'the inhabitants of London appear to be made up of either smarties or hippies' (a 'now exhausted Illyria').[15] In *Modesty Blaise*, the whole film is flagrantly played, staged and constructed as camp: 'every possible ingenuity is employed to beguile the eye', wrote Gerald Kaufman, with relish, 'its ephemeral absurdities charm the spectator . . . even [enhancing] recollection of this captivatingly silly film'.[16]

Modesty Blaise, made for 20th Century-Fox, like many larger budget productions of the 1960s, benefited from American backing; sometimes they were shot wholly in the States (for instance, *Petulia*) and sometimes in part (for instance, *The Collector*). Many were directed by Americans (Wyler, Lester, Zinnemann, Furie). Indeed, Alexander Walker claims that American funding peaked at 95 per cent in 1968.[17] The early 1960s films, *Saturday Night and Sunday Morning* and *The Loneliness of the Long Distance Runner* were well received in America and won recognition for Finney and Courtenay (regarded by both as something of a mixed blessing).[18] Support for Woodfall Films' adaptation of *Look Back in Anger* and *The Entertainer* was encouraged by the participation of Richard Burton and Laurence Olivier although John Osborne claimed that he felt compromised by the need to accommodate American interests. United Artists profited enormously from its investment in Richardson's and Osborne's 'holiday film' *Tom Jones* (1963), casting fellow Royal Court doyen George Devine as Squire Allworthy and Finney as Tom.[19] Further American funding of costume films followed, with Fred Zinnemann's 1966 *A Man for All Seasons* and David Lean's 1962 *Lawrence of Arabia*, both with screenplays by Robert Bolt, and giving Paul Scofield and Peter O'Toole definitive roles as Thomas More and T. E. Lawrence respectively. *Tom Jones* employs period sets and costumes, and Osborne's screenplay translates many devices from Henry Fielding's 1749 original. These include the author's frequent intervention in the narrative, transferred to voiceover; its episodic structure, introduced as intertitles; and self-conscious formal stylisation, conveyed in Finney's interaction with the camera – for example, when he decorously covers the lens with a tricorn hat to hide Mrs Water's ample bobbing bosom. The famously fleshy (and potentially incestuous) banquet, at which Tom and Mrs Waters eye each other across the table while tearing at chicken thighs and pears, takes its lead from Fielding's description of the seduction as a military assault. But Tom is very readily perceived as a distinctly modern character, an opportunistic adventurer questioning the circumstances of his birth which may or may not entitle him to great wealth and the hand of his inamorata, Sophie Western (Susannah York), but equally positing distinguished parentage as an arbitrary or dubious qualification for wealth and good fortune. Stylistically and narratively, there is much in *Tom Jones* which bears comparison with *Alfie* (1966) and *Nothing But the Best*.

Bolshie Northerners and Shrewd Little Cockneys

The internationally produced *Casino Royale* (John Huston/Ken Hughes/Val Guest/Robert Parrish/Joe McGrath/Richard Talmadge, 1967) cast David Niven as James Bond, amid an array of star turns, from Orson Welles to Woody Allen. This marked a departure in tone from the previous and subsequent casting by production executives Saltzman and Broccoli of Sean Connery as the British spy. An hirsute son of the estate replaced a suave laird of the manor, Connery's Celtic accent betokening a character slightly at odds with the establishment he serves, like Len Deighton's Palmer, a slightly rougher diamond (but still one who knew a diamond when he saw one – and, as in *You Only Live Twice* [Lewis Gilbert, 1967], the Bond who took a First in Oriental Languages at Cambridge also knows the correct temperature at which to serve saki). Willie Garvin in *Modesty Blaise* is reminded that he is 'lower class'. For some of us, it is this which renders Connery the real McCoy and Roger Moore (the former knitting-pattern model who succeeded him in Guy Hamilton's 1973 *Live and Let Die*) no more than a synthetic Terylene substitute. Whereas Jimmy Brewster in *Nothing But the Best* and Diana in *Darling* sought to change themselves in order to be accepted by 'higher society', other characters confronted the established order or made a fashionable virtue of their difference. In *Morgan: A Suitable Case for Treatment* (Karel Reisz, 1966), refusenik East End boy Morgan (David Warner) competes in slapstick exchanges with the suave art-dealer, Napier (Robert Stephens), for the affection and attention of spoiled little rich girl Leoni (Vanessa Redgrave): 'You're marrying Leoni for money,' Napier insists; 'She wanted me for insecurity,' counters Morgan, 'she loves me – it's my turn.'

Ringo Starr calls a policeman outside the BBC's Lime Grove studios in *A Hard Day's Night* (directed by the American, Richard Lester, in 1964) 'a Southerner', intending this as a term of abuse. The film both endorses and undercuts the Beatles myth and the myth-making apparatus which has brought them fame and fortune. It acts as a vehicle for well-known songs ('Can't Buy Me Love', 'She Loves Me', 'I Wanna be Your Man'), dramatically enhancing a sense of the final set as a 'live' event. It plays upon the band members' advertised personae (John Lennon, larking in the bath, is certainly quirky if not surreal): 'How did you find America?' – 'Turn left after Greenland'; 'What would you call that haircut?' – 'Arthur'; 'Are you a mod or a rocker?' – 'a mocker'; 'What do you call that collar?' – 'a collar', quips John, mimicking familiar encounters with television interviewers enunciating their questions in RP English. 'Ringo's fussy about his drums – they loom large in his legend.' Much is made of the Fab Four's youthful exuberance and supposed rebelliousness: 'Give us a kiss' (says John), 'Up the workers' (says Paul) to a commuting businessman; 'I fought the war for your sort', he protests' – 'Bet you're sorry you won . . . after all, you own the train,' they retort. Wilfred Bramble (Steptoe's 'dirty old man' in the Ray Galton and Alan Simpson BBC TV *Steptoe and Son*) is cast as Paul's surrogate grandfather. While Paul tries to pull a pair of schoolgirls (but is thwarted by grandad), 'Susan' is hired as 'resident teenager' by a publicity agent – 'she's a trend-setter'. 'The new thing is to be right wing and care a lot,' he advises . . . but not for three weeks yet. The advertising men prefer a commodified 'phoney' Liverpool to the real Woolton of Lennon's childhood. The film (as David Griffiths observed in *The Listener* of the television documentaries and interviews) peddles 'the ludicrous belief that the lads have been completely unchanged by their fame. The Beatles are not so superhuman.'[20]

In *The Loneliness of the Long Distance Runner* the borstal to which Colin Smith (Tom Courtenay) is sent aims to produce model, compliant citizens. Various supposed 'experts' offer explanations for his delinquency: 'I got caught because I didn't run fast enough,' retorts Smith, simply. While television pundits discuss 'the challenge of posterity' and the new benefits offered by 'the Great Elizabethan Age', Smith insists that he cannot see the point of slaving his guts out so that the bosses get the profit. When the governor selects him to run against the public school, Ranelagh, Smith ostentatiously throws the match in favour of Gunthorpe (James Fox), sacrificing potential favours in order to demonstrate that he still knows 'what side he's on': 'let them think I'm house-trained . . . they're happy enough to put a noose around your neck'. In the same way that he refuses to accept money from his mother or her new boyfriend, Smith salvages his pride at the expense of material comfort.

Losey's *The Servant* (1963) was scripted by Pinter (who makes a cameo appearance) with music from Dankworth and Cleo Laine. James Fox appears as Tony, an upper-class twat recently returned from Africa: the beneficiary of colonialism, he now contemplates development prospects in Brazil ('the new frontier'). Barratt (Dirk Bogarde as a Mancunian) is appointed as his 'gentleman's gentleman' to see to the running of his Kensington house. Barratt soon runs rings around his master, introducing his partner (Sarah Miles) into the house as his sister, although when discovered together in Tony's bed, Tony is rendered doubly powerless. The destructive force of this cuckoo in the 'marital' nest is matched by Maggie Smith's Philpot, the lodger who becomes Jake's first lover in *The Pumpkin Eater*. Barratt meets his match in Tony's fiancée, Susan (Wendy Craig). She maintains that a servant should know his place and whereas Tony recalls the camaraderie of the army, she lets it be known that, for her, Barratt is an inferior being to be ordered about at will and bluntly states her position: 'The truth is I don't give a tinker's gob what you think'; 'Do you use a deodorant? Do you go well with the colour scheme?' Losey poses Susan's aristocratic parents in the manner of a Gainsborough portrait, their estate stretching into the far distance in the background. Although Tony maintains at the outset that 'the thought of some old woman running about the place telling me what to do rather put me off', Barratt increasingly falls into role as alternately nagging and flirtatious wife, on whom Tony becomes dependent and with whom he ingratiates himself in order to keep him. His triumph is calculated and destructive, but ultimately, as narrowly confined as the house which holds them: domestic fittings feature characteristically and prominently, often obliquely, in what Julian Barnes calls 'caressing shots of banisters and stair-cases', sometimes reflected in distorting convex mirrors.[21] They reappear in Matthew Bourne's 2002 ballet homage to *The Servant* (conscripting *Look Back in Anger*'s Jimmy Porter for good measure), *Play Without Words*. Tony's empire declines into token decadence and debauchery.

The mutual fascination of West and East London has been a recurrent theme in British cinema (see Chapters 4 and 12). Jack Wild's Artful Dodger in Carol Reed's adaptation of Lionel Bart's musical *Oliver!* (1968) (in turn drawn from Dickens and Gustave Doré's engravings of London's rook-eries) indicates that, as a character type, chirpy cockneys have pre-cinematic antecedents. David Hemmings in *Blow-Up*, Terence Stamp in *Poor Cow* (Ken Loach, 1967) and Michael Caine in *Alfie*, *The Ipcress File* (Sidney J. Furie, 1965) and *The Italian Job* (Peter Collinson, 1969) are certainly emblematic of trendy cockney personae of the 1960s but, socially and culturally, sometimes there is more at stake, I think, than fashion.

In *The Italian Job* (scripted by BBC TV's *Z-Cars*' Troy Kennedy-Martin), as in *The Loneliness of the Long Distance Runner*, a public institution stands as something of a social metaphor: Evelyn Waugh once noted the ease with which ex-public schoolboys adapted to the rigours of prison dis-cipline.[22] But whereas Colin refuses to play the game dictated by the bureaucrats, Bridger, *Mr* Bridger, the veteran con (by the end of 1969, *Sir* Noël Coward) commandeers the system by play-ing the game more effectively. 'Perhaps we can help one another', the borstal psychiatrist suggests to Colin, unctuously; the prison functions only at Bridger's behest and the favours he enjoys in return are considerable – perhaps prematurely, he graciously acknowledges the applause of the inmates on pulling off 'the job' and sits down to a lobster banquet. Bridger complains that the governor (John le Mesurier, with the mild demeanour of BBC TV's *Dad's Army*'s Sergeant Wilson) is symptomatic of 'the country's laziness'. Bridger's cell, from which he tracks the balance of pay-ment figures and masterminds his campaign to overpower the combined forces of the American and Italian mafia, is decorated with patriotic regalia, and he requires that everyone stand for the National Anthem. The film is something of a showcase for British industrial design (red, white and blue Mini Coopers – hardly the fastest getaway car but 'ambassadors' for Britain and three times winners at the Monte Carlo rally – drive through the arcades of Turin and symbolically lay claim to the test-track roof of the Fiat factory, while an E-type Jaguar and an Aston Martin get wasted in the mountains). The gang's cover is to travel as football supporters (England once won the World Cup and the film's theme tune, 'The Self-Preservation Society', was significantly adopted on the terraces in Kyoto in 2002). The membership of Caine's gang (including 'Camp' Freddie, and Benny Hill, robustly clowning as a computer boffin with a penchant for well-upholstered matrons) and the slapstick into which their preparations descend ('You're only supposed to blow the bloody doors off,' says Caine as a van goes up in smoke) are reminiscent of Ealing (and a precursor for Guy Ritchie in the 1990s and John Duigan's 2001 *The Parole Officer*) (see Chapters 7 and 12).

Footage from *Poor Cow* was appropriated in 1999 as background material to Terence Stamp's character in *The Limey* (US, Steven Soderbergh), where he is cast as an ex-gangster who travels to America to avenge his daughter's death. The central concern of the source film is the struggle of

Joy (Carol White, previously cast as Cathy in Loach's TV 1966 docu-drama *Cathy Come Home*) to support herself and her son while first her husband, Tom, and then his friend and her lover, Dave (Stamp), are sent to prison on exaggerated charges. Joy and a friend take up modelling in an attempt to make ends meet, only to be told by Tom, when he returns, that the house is disgusting and that he does not intend to mind their child. 'Life with Dave', confides Joy, recollecting their holiday in the Welsh countryside, 'was just a series of treats.' Loach represents Dave and Tom as unfairly treated (they are chancers rather than professional crooks) but does not romanticise them as criminals. His sympathies are with Joy (one of many put-upon women in his films) and her son as the victims of a corrupt and iniquitous system: 'The Flying Squad's all bent . . . like the housing list . . . like everything,' protests Tom.

'Michael Caine *is* Alfie!' announced the posters in 1966 as yet another cocky cockney Jack-the-lad strutted his stuff through a series of picaresque adventures. Direct to camera, Alfie Elkins counsels his audience on the most productive means of seduction: 'with married women, make them laugh and you're halfway there; with single women, make them laugh and it's all you'll get'; 'it don't do to get attached to nobody' . . . 'she or it – they're all birds'. Siphoning petrol, he tells us that he's 'had a fiddle' on every job he's done. As with *Darling*, it seems to me, the commentary provided by the protagonist serves to interrogate rather than endorse the action. As Cher sings at the end (over black and white stills, possibly suggesting that it all might be over for him already), 'What's it all about, Alfie?' Charles Shyer's 'effortless' retelling of the tale (US, 2004) removes the sting. Certainly the original Alfie's bravura is misplaced and there is little to celebrate. When he is presented with the child resulting from his affair with Gilda (Julia Foster), he is amazed to hear the nurse describe him as his 'son' – 'My what?' – he's disconcerted that she wants to keep it, although she has previously mentioned adoption – 'Once you've got a kid in your life, it's not your own,' but concedes 'We all need a proper father, and a proper mother, come to that – there's just not enough to go around.' But he fails in his paternal responsibilities, even in his dreams. Fortunately for Gilda, gentle Humphrey (Graham Stark) shows more of an interest in her and baby Malcolm. Meanwhile Alfie visits a doctor (Eleanor Bron, another 1960s television fixture making regular appearances at Peter Cook's Greek Street Establishment Club) who informs him that his lungs are diseased. VD being the only issue which might concern or check Alfie's gallivanting, he says that he can't be infected – 'he hasn't been with anyone'. He's undeterred by the attachments of women to other men – he tells Annie (Jane Asher) that Frank is already married, before setting up with her himself ('It's a bit limited,' he confides; 'it's scrubbed up nice and not bad at the other . . . a bit on the shy side but that makes a change these days'), meanwhile making a conquest of Lily (Vivian Merchant), the wife of a fellow patient at the chest clinic – if only destructively, to prove his doubts as to their fidelity. Lily falls pregnant and undergoes a gruesome (and illegal) abortion, to dispose of Alfie's child. As in *The Pumpkin Eater*, men presume to make decisions over women's bodies which some women (as in *The L-Shaped Room* [Bryan Forbes, 1962] and Margaret Drabble's 1965 novel *The Millstone* – 'ordinary babies aren't much of a status symbol, but illegitimate ones are just about the last word')[23] manage to resist. He leaves her alone in agony – 'I know it don't look very nice – but what does when you get up close to it?' Alfie determines to settle down with Ruby (Shelley Winters), a 'knowing' older woman, but finds that she has played him at his own game and tells him so in no uncertain terms – finding her new toy-boy in her bed, Alfie protests 'What's he got that I haven't?' – 'He's younger than you are – get it?' she replies. At the end, Alfie encounters the same girl, Siddie (Millicent Martin), with whom we saw him at the beginning, accompanied by the same scruffy mongrel (a figure for Alfie himself, after all, more Barry Lyndon than Tom Jones). His adventures have brought him full circle and he has learned nothing in the process: 'What have I got out of it? . . . ain't got me peace of mind – what's it all about? Know what I mean?' As Kenneth Tynan remarked of Stanley Kubrick's 1975 film rendition of Lyndon (with former upper-crust Mary Quant model, Marisa Berenson, as the ram-rod aristocratic partner in Lyndon's marriage of convenience):

> The indictment is the more devastating for being totally implicit. And Ryan O'Neal as Barry, the Irish outsider who tries to con his way into wealth and title, never makes the character into the usual charming rogue of costume epics (e.g. *Tom Jones*): we are invited to pity him not because he is a sexy and sympathetic swashbuckler but because he is a (rather thick) human being, quite unaware of his own pathos . . . A piece of instruction comes quietly, but indelibly, across: if you wished to breach the privileged citadel of the eighteenth-century ruling class, the only way to attempt it was by chicanery, fraud, bribery or double dealing. And the attempt would fail.[24]

Indeed, in spite of the 1960s' much-vaunted reputation for social change, the attempt more often failed than succeeded in 1960s films.

Young Turks

In *Accident* (Joseph Losey, 1967), adapted by Harold Pinter from Nicholas Moseley's novel, an Oxford professor, Stephen (Dirk Bogarde), falls for the glamorous charms of a new student, Anna (Jacqueline Sassard), an Austrian Princess, and her intellectual and sensitive boyfriend, William (Michael York). Stephen and his pregnant wife, Rosalind (Vivien Merchant), politely invite the couple for Sunday lunch (and a tense supper) in the country. But Anna proves susceptible to the more brutal and boorish assault of Charlie (Stanley Baker), a fellow academic and TV pundit, while William is the unwitting sacrificial lamb. Charlie is 'more successful than me because he appears on television' (says Stephen); 'He talks on architecture, astrology, anthropology, sociology . . . and sex . . . he suits the medium,' says Rosalind. Pinter himself plays an Oxford graduate who has become a television producer.

While a number of new universities were founded in the 1960s (including the Open University – which was to make ample use of broadcasting) some graduates from older universities were also keen to find more valid purposes for television than indiscriminate self-promotion. They also proved less squeamish (and perhaps snobbish) than Anderson and others of the *Sequence* fraternity (see Chapter 8). While, said *The Listener*, 'the *Observer*-reading liberal-humanist audience' was still inclined to distrust the 'telly', others recognised the potential of the medium to address a broad public and engaged seriously with television as contributors and critics.[25] The academic Raymond Williams (see Chapter 10) and the novelist Anthony Burgess both published reviews in *The Listener* in the 1960s; Richard Hoggart (see Chapter 8) reviewed Marshall McLuhan's seminal 1964 *Understanding Media*, which introduced the slogan 'The Medium is the Message', the idea of the 'global village' and the distinction between 'hot' media (the press and film) and 'cool' (the telephone and television).[26] Jonathan Miller moved from television satire to become producer of the BBC TV series *Monitor* (1965) (for which Dudley Moore wrote a theme tune and where Ken Russell directed a number of short films on arts subjects, also directing for *Sunday Night*). Mike Hodges, later to direct *Get Carter* (1971) and *Croupier* (1998) (see Chapters 10 and 12), worked for the Granada current affairs series *World in Action* (1963–98) and Michael Apted, later to direct *Stardust* (1974), *The World Is Not Enough* (1999) and *Enigma* (2001), directed television documentaries (notably the continuing series, *Seven-Up*). John Schlesinger graduated to film from BBC's current affairs programme *Tonight* (1957–65). Denis Potter (whose *Brimstone and Treacle* was filmed in 1982) and Alan Plater wrote their first television plays in the 1960s; Andrew Davies (scriptwriter with Helen Fielding in 2001 for *Bridget Jones's Diary*) produced his first television adaptations; Joe Orton, 'the Oscar Wilde of Welfare State gentility' (murdered by his lover, Kenneth Halliwell, in 1967), produced a screenplay for The Beatles (rejected) and his only television plays in the 1960s.[27] Philip Saville, later to direct *The Fruit Machine* (1988) (see Chapter 11), adapted Sartre's *Huis Clos* and novelist Kingsley Amis adapted Webster's *The Duchess of Malfi* in a 'pop' version for ITV. Keith Waterhouse (for *First Night*) moved between small and large screen, while Harold Pinter (for Associated Rediffusion with *The Lover* [1977] and for BBC TV with *The Caretaker* – also filmed by Clive Donner in 1963) and Samuel Beckett, with *Eh, Joe?* (1973) (written specifically for television), moved between stage and screen. Joe Orton (probably unchallenged in his own ambition to be 'the most perfectly developed of modern playwrights if nothing else') was treated 'televisually' by the Galton and Simpson adaptation of his 1966 play *Loot* (Silvio Narizzano, 1970 – with Dick Emery) and more successfully (not least by the casting of Beryl Reid) in Douglas Hickox's 1969 film version of *Entertaining Mr Sloane* (1964). Themes were shared across film and television, with Granada's 1964 *The Other Man* (concerning a Nazi invasion of England) matching *It Happened Here* (1963) (see Chapter 8), a similarly speculative historical fabrication. Caryl Brahms' *The Long Garden Party* (TV, 1964), a combination of songs, 'brilliant animation and witty montage', seemed to Burgess 'to represent an art-form uniquely televisual', evoking the Edwardian Age in a manner comparable to the Georgian context of Littlewood's *Oh! What a Lovely War* (1969).

Tony Garnett, the producer of Jeremy Sandford's seminal drama-documentary *Cathy Come Home*, summarises the enthusiasm of a post-war generation of university-educated playwrights and directors for television as a political instrument and for the technical possibilities afforded by new equipment:

> [O]ur greatest strength was our ignorance. We didn't understand or know about the BBC machinery, so we didn't know about the rules.

Much of this was made possible by the realisation that 16mm filming was quite adequate for TV transmission, was flexible, was not much more costly than studio VTR and meant ACTT minimum crewing.

The whole logic of the scripts we were getting was forcing us to use film and to shoot outside the studios on location. We were interested in social forces and the fabric of people's lives and the kind of conflicts that go on particularly at places of work, where people spend quite a lot of their lives.[28]

Television was appreciated as a medium which fostered experimentation (as in the 'vox-pop' direct to camera address of Bonnie Prince Charlie's footsoldiers in Peter Watkins' *Culloden* for BBC TV [1964]), as an appropriate means for political intervention (as in Peter Watkins' ill-fated *The War Game* [1966], vitiated by its removal to theatrical distribution) and, pre-video-recording, as a singular 'event' (as for *Festival*'s production of Bertolt Brecht's *Mahagonny* and *Cathy Come Home*).[29]

Whereas *Billy Liar!*'s Bradford and *A Taste of Honey*'s Salford are readily recognised from shots of identifiable landmarks, in Loach's second feature film, *Kes* (1969), adapted from Barry Hines' novel, Barnsley is less distinguished. Although the pithead overshadows Billy Caspar's life (he says

Billy (David Bradley) coaches his kestrel in *Kes* (Ken Loach, 1969)

that 'he wouldn't be seen dead' following his older brother Jud [Freddie Fletcher] into the mines) and it is clearly visible from the windows of his house, the skies and open fields surrounding the town find Billy (David Bradley) in his element. Simple scoring (a single recorder; strings and a harp) augment Chris Menges' atmospheric photography. Billy's own mother tells her new boyfriend that she thinks him 'a hopeless case', and at school he is told he is 'a waste of space'; he is bullied by the headmaster, indiscriminately and routinely, and by the PT teacher (Brian Glover) for allowing goals into the net – Loach presenting the fateful scoreline in a running, television-style subtitle. There is little support for Billy in his neighbourhood – the shopkeeper for whom he delivers newspapers comments that his estate has a reputation for thieving and Billy agrees: 'We'll steal your breath if you're not looking.' As a matter of course, Billy (no angel) steals milk, steals books (when he cannot get admission to the library) and, ill-advisedly, steals a racing bet (an alternative hope of escape) from his brute of a brother. But a farmer and an English teacher (Z-Cars' Colin Welland) encourage his enthusiasm and interest in wildlife – he has had birds and a fox cub in the past but the kestrel 'is the best', he insists, 'and she's not a pet – she's wild'. The previously taciturn Billy waxes garrulous when describing the training, feeding and keeping of his bird. Jud's casual destruction of Billy's happiness points more generally to the unnecessary waste of life in unforgiving circumstances.

The social significance of such items in the television schedules as The Wednesday Play (1964–70), the satirical revues TW3 (1962–3), The ABC of Britain (1964) and Not So Much a Programme More a Way of Life (1964–5), and such comedy series as The Likely Lads, Steptoe and Son and Till Death Do Us Part, has been subsequently much celebrated and revisited, not least by television itself. Kenneth Adam, BBC's director of TV, faced criticism from staff and viewers accustomed to more traditional fare:

> There never was a Golden Age of broadcasting. If you read the romantic reminiscences of some of my elders and ex-colleagues it is very easy to imagine that in, for example, the 1930s, in Broadcasting House London there was a small circle of loved, fond faces, and its programmes a perpetual ceilidh of safe and familiar songs and stories.[30]

Anticipating Jeremy Isaacs' declared policy at Channel Four in the 1980s, Adam continues: 'I consciously reject the temptation to suit the common denominator of taste all the time; so I expect to disappoint all my viewers some of the time.' Some viewers (as now for BBC digital channels) found themselves disqualified from disappointment by the limited reach of BBC 2; colour television (introduced in the 1960s) was yet to become the norm.

The late, great Joan Littlewood, who had worked on 'unsafe' BBC radio programmes in the 1930s, continued to ruffle feathers, helping Shelagh Delaney to make A Taste of Honey presentable (and marketable in the West End), adapting Shakespeare's Henry IV for television in 1964, staging Oh! What a Lovely War with her Theatre Workshop at Stratford's Theatre Royal (produced by Brian Duffy and directed for film by Richard Attenborough for Paramount in 1969) and directing the 1962 adaptation of Stephen Lewis' stageplay Sparrows Can't Sing. Littlewood's Playbarn provided the cast for *Bronco Bullfrog* (Barney Platt-Mills, 1969), in which bored teenagers bemoan the absence of things to do and places to go (especially for sex) in their East End neighbourhood, while their respective parents (apparently forgetting their own teenage travails) complain of each others' shortcomings. Anthony Burgess reports that, in a discussion between Bernard Levin and Peter Hall on television's *Encounter*, 'the name of Joan Littlewood was invoked, and the mere mention of that grinning, dedicated often muddle-headed iconoclast was enough to breathe life into a session that was inexplicably torpid'.[31]

While, for Drabble's characters, an illegitimate baby may bestow status, for Helen (Dora Bryan) in Richardson's *A Taste of Honey* it is something to be avoided: 'Why can't you learn from my mistakes? It takes half a lifetime to learn from your own,' she advises her gawky schoolgirl daughter, Jo (Rita Tushingham). When brassy Helen busies herself with a new fancy-man (who is buying a bungalow with bay windows and crazy paving for them all to share) Jo, meanwhile, befriends a black sailor and (like her mother) 'gets pregnant the first time'. Walter Lassally's monochrome location photography (of canals, streets, bridges, the Blackpool amusements) aligns *A Taste of Honey* stylistically in the New Wave canon. But Jo (unlike Billy, Vic and Arthur, her fellow protagonists in the companion Northern films) makes a successful bid for independence, getting a job in a shoe shop and setting up house with gay art student Geoff (Murray Melvin), likewise regarded as something of an oddity. Other girls think that odd-looking Jo is 'bad on purpose', but Jo knows that she is special. 'You'll be back to your usual self very soon,' says Geoff, comfortingly; 'My usual self is a very unusual self – extraordinary – and don't you forget that, Geoffrey Ingham!' she retorts. She determines to keep the child, aware that it could be black and fearing that (like her own father) it might be 'simple'. Geoff, apparently more eager to mother than Jo, even offers to 'father' the child himself, but dejectedly leaves when Helen peremptorily decides to resume her own parental responsibilities.

Sparrows Can't Sing brings Murray Melvin and Roy Kinnear from the original stage production, ably transposing and extending John Bury's simple setting to actual East End locations. According to Marshall McLuhan, the film's cockney slang was subtitled for distribution in America (Danny Boyle's *Trainspotting* [1995] and Loach's *Sweet Sixteen* [2002] subsequently being received with comparable incomprehension).[32] Harold H. Corbett (better known as television's Steptoe Jr but a Theatre Workshop regular) appears as a greengrocer stall-holder while three girls (including Yootha Joyce) provide something akin to a chorus. Maggie (Barbara Windsor) sings Lionel Bart's theme tune. As in Drabble's 1963 novel *A Summer Birdcage*, *Nothing But the Best*, *Life at the Top*, *Charlie Bubbles* and *Billy Liar!*, inner-city redevelopment is much in evidence. With Maggie's man Charlie (James Booth) in prison, Maggie has moved in with bus driver Bert (George Sewell), leaving the terraced family home for a new housing block: as in *Bronco*, residents of the flats are thought 'stuck-up'. The film mocks the caretaker's over-assiduous and precious enforcement of council regulations and his attention to the residents' comings and goings. Charlie's sister, Nell (Barbara Ferris), and friend, Chunky (Griffith Davies), ask where Maggie and Bert live, and the answer is delivered in quick-fire patter:

Caretaker: Well, you see that flat up there with the Venetian blinds up, what are down?

    – when the blinds are up and the lights are out, they're out

    – when the blinds are down and the lights are on, they're in

    Course, if the blinds are down and the lights out [sniggers] they might be out.

Chunky: Might just be a blind . . .

The film, as if bringing together the cast for a curtain call, ends in the local pub with the neighbours gathered for a drink, a dance and a song.

Children and Flower Children

While the Children's Film Fund had been set up in the 1950s to produce films and other material specifically intended for young audiences, a number of films directed at adult audiences in the 1960s featured child protagonists. They are variously portrayed as angels and demons, mawkishly innocent or disturbingly malicious. Sometimes they provide a commentary on adult behaviour, presenting a model of adult society in miniature, sometimes they pose a threat to adult authority or precociously outgrow their elders (as in *The Prime of Miss Jean Brodie* [Ronald Neame, 1968] and *The Village of the Damned* [Wolf Rilla, 1960] – adapted from John Wyndham's 1957 novel, *The Midwich Cuckoos*). The obfuscation and evasiveness of grown-ups faced with awkward questions (about God in *Whistle Down the Wind* [Bryan Forbes, 1961] and about 'spooning' in *The Go-Between* [Joseph Losey, 1970]) is matched by the conspiracy of children to keep and withhold secrets from grown-ups (in *Whistle Down the Wind*, *The Innocents* [Jack Clayton, 1961] and *Our Mother's House* [Jack Clayton, 1967]).

In *Tiger Bay* (1959), the man on the run, Bronislaw Konchinsky (Horst Bucholz), seems as much of an innocent as the young tomboy, Gillie (Hayley Mills), who becomes his accomplice. In *Whistle Down the Wind*, Hayley Mills plays Nan Bostock, in a Keith Waterhouse/Willis Hall adaptation of Mary Hayley Bell's novel (1961). Alan Bates plays 'The Derby Murderer' on the run (a match for *Great Expectations'* Magwitch [see Chapter 7], monochrome location shots of the Pennines substituting for studio reconstruction of dunes and estuaries) whom the impressionable children mistake for the reincarnation of Jesus. Charlie (Alan Barnes), in the customary manner of vicious little boys, insists that he's 'just a fella', while equally not wanting to be left out of his sisters' game. It's a bit like not wanting to tell about the litter of kittens they have saved from the lake: 'What have you got under your coat?' demands Farmer Bostock; 'My pullie,' asserts Charlie, honestly and duplicitously. But Charlie's betrayal of the secret outside of the family eventually leads to the fugitive's capture and their own disillusionment.

Dickens (with his teeth drawn) reappears in Carol Reed's 1968 adaptation of Lionel Bart's 1960 stage musical *Oliver!*, filmed for Columbia in Panavision70 and Technicolor and advertised for its premiere in Leicester Square with 'tri-vision' hoardings on Shaftesbury Avenue and Piccadilly Circus: in *Bronco Bullfrog*, Irene and Derek take a fancy trip 'up the West End', intending to see the film, but cannot afford the price of the tickets.[33] In spite of the opening contextual engravings, and the donation of takings to the NSPCC, this was more Christmas Panto than pungent social criticism. Fondly remembered by Bridget Jones (in Helen Fielding's 1999 novel *The Edge of Reason*)[34] the film's spin-off merchandising included an LP of the soundtrack (selling 100,000 copies in a fortnight), a book, sheet-music, amateur theatricals and board games. Mark Lester, a golden-haired plumptious Oliver Twist (looking like he'd never missed a meal in his life), reached out his bowl on the record sleeve. Ex-*Goon* comic Harry Secombe (see Chapter 6) was cast as Mr Bumble, the beadle, the *Carry Ons*' Hattie Jacques as the wife over whom the law (famously 'an ass') presumed he held sway; the comic actor Leonard Rossiter (not for the first or last time) was cast as the undertaker, Sowerberry, with Kenneth Cranham as his assistant. Oliver Reed showed an unfaked scar (and the bulldog, Bullseye, was equally bashed about a bit) and swaggered as convincingly as Robert Newton had (for David Lean), as Bill Sikes; Ron Moody as Fagin was more Anthony Newley than Alec Guinness (notwithstanding the competition of the extraordinary and gruesome prosthetic nose of the 1948 version [see Chapter 7]): here, Fagin's Jewishness is underscored by Klezmer strains in Bart's soundtrack. Jack Wild, as the Artful Dodger, in top hat and tail coat, something of a miniature dandy, proved himself a sparrow (sparra?) who *could* sing. Dance routines are staged in the manner of Light Entertainment on Saturday night television. While Dickens spared his reader (and himself on stage) nothing in 'The Death of Nancy' (again, more explicitly represented by Lean), *Oliver!* plays to the matinée stalls, conveying her murder in shadows and noises off. One might argue, albeit tortuously, that Dickens' concern for the welfare of his children in *Oliver Twist* (1837–9) is matched by adults' concerns about Britain's youth (perhaps prematurely propelled into adulthood) more than a century later.

Whereas Oliver is restored to the bosom of his respectable, charitable (and wealthy) family, acknowledging the privileges which birth and bloodlines bestow, in Losey's costume venture, *The Go-Between*, class and youthful insecurity alienate Leo (Dominic Guard) from his patrons, the Maudsleys, when he is invited to stay with schoolfriend, Marcus, at their Norfolk estate. Indeed, the older Leo (Michael Redgrave), a public servant, is still at the beck and call of Marian (Julie Christie). Pinter's screenplay adopts the retrospective distance of L. P. Hartley's 1953 original ('the past is another country'). Procedurally, Losey employed costumes not merely as period dressings but as a key indicator of Leo's social disadvantage: the cast dressed in costume throughout shooting, exacerbating Leo's discomfort in his smart tweeds as the hot summer wore on.[35] He really *can't* wear his school cap for cricket, 'club or county or England is the decent thing', Marcus informs him. Marian determines to have Leo fitted for more suitable apparel, ostensibly as a present but using the trip to town as an excuse to meet with her lover, her fiancé's tenant farmer, Ted Burgess (Alan Bates). A bicycle is a similar compromised gift, intended to abet their postman, a young 'Mercury', in his role as their messenger. Leo is infatuated with Marian's womanliness (and she knows it), fascinated by Ted's physical prowess and manliness (but doesn't quite know why) and seduced by the different, easy aristocratic manliness ('such command and elegance') of war-scarred Trimingham (Edward Fox): Leo cannot call him 'Mister', because he's a Viscount, but he can call him Trimingham or Hugh. Leo says that he can be called Leo. Ill at ease with everyone, talked over in the assumption that he does not understand but nevertheless understanding something that he is not supposed to, Leo is nevertheless courted for the services he can be relied upon to perform dutifully, adoringly, on behalf of others and is thus caught in the household's deceits: he cannot gain the affection or admiration of one (when catching Ted out at the cricket match) without, unwittingly, losing elsewhere. To protect Leo's innocence, Lady Maudsley covers young Leo's face; to disguise her social disgrace (perhaps), Marian hides Ted. But old Leo finds Marian still in denial, still presuming that she can despatch him on one last 'errand of love'.

Miss Jean Brodie (in an adaptation from a stage version of Muriel Spark's 1961 novel), in spite of her very worst endeavours, fails to rule the lives of her self-selected charges, like a potter 'shaping-up' (she says) the 'crème de la crème' of Marcia Blaine's Edinburgh Academy. Miss Brodie (Maggie Smith) romances her pupils (her *Mädchen* in uniform) with stories of her lover, Hugh, 'who fell like an autumn leaf' on Flanders field. Sandy and Jenny (distinguished members of the Brodie 'set'), practising the tango together in grey wool dresses and knee socks, ponder whether Jean and Hugh did 'it' before he fell and whether they had clothes on: 'Taking clothes off is so rude!' However, Miss Brodie plays shy of the physical ardour of the art master, Teddy Lloyd (Robert Stephens), and presumes to disdain the modest (and admittedly dull and passionless) proposals of Mr Lowther (Gordon Jackson). Both duly turn their attentions elsewhere, Teddy to Sandy (who sees through Miss Brodie and usurps the role ordained for Jenny) and Mr Lowther to Miss Lockhardt (who prefers golf to Giotto and il Duce). Mary, fired by Miss Brodie's fervour, follows her brother to the Spanish Civil War and is killed (on the Republican side). Eventually, the girls whom she has conscripted as disciples against Marcia Blaine's philistines turn against her: 'I didn't betray you, I put a stop to you,' says 'dependable' Sandy; 'Why must you always strike attitudes?' Brodie has persuaded herself that she gave up Teddy for her girls; Teddy tells her that she's a frustrated spinster 'taking it out in dangerous causes'. The neatly ordered framed 'album' shots of the film's opening and closing sequences belie the havoc meanwhile wrought by the school's errant teacher and disobliging pupils.

In Julian Cloag's novel *Our Mother's House*, filmed in 1967, seven children try to keep the death of their mother a secret so that they are not separated and put in an orphanage. The eldest daughter plays Wendy (from *Peter Pan* – see Chapter 2) while the youngest child (Mark Lester) is the last to know of his mother's death. A negotiated equilibrium is disrupted by the interference of authority figures (teachers and estate agents) and by a ne'er-do-well stranger and adventurer who (more echoes of *Peter Pan*) introduces himself as Charlie Hook (Dirk Bogarde). The children construct a tabernacle to their mother and invent rituals to commune with her spirit. In his adaptation of Henry James' *The Turn of the Screw* (1898), Clayton also conveyed the receptiveness of children to a ghostly 'other' world. *The Innocents* (shot in CinemaScope), noted *The Listener*, 'brilliantly exploits' its location (casting Sheffield Park, Sussex, as Bly Hall) with battlements and tall Gothic windows looming over the lake under brooding, thunderous, misty, monochrome skies.[36] At the end, the slightest breath of wind catches the boy's forehead, as if the spirit passes from him.

Home Counties schoolboys
Jack (Tom Chapin) and Ralph
(James Aubrey) turn a tropical
island into an outpost of
Empire in *Lord of the Flies*
(Peter Brook, 1963)

The house itself participates in the action, sharing its secrets with the two orphaned children, the too, too charming Miles (Martin Stephens) and Flora (Pamela Franklin), occasionally intimating something with a noise or a flash of light, just as Miles and Flora can communicate with the slightest glance and whisper. Clayton loses the sense of distance from the narrative conveyed in the original by the introduction of the account left by the impressionable Miss Gibbons (Deborah Kerr) of her time as a novice governess by another character – but foreshadows her implicit guilt, and fears of the corruption wrought by Peter Quint and Miss Jessel on two 'innocent' young souls, with an agonising title sequence.

Unman, Wittering and Zigo (John MacKenzie, 1971) depicts exceptionally nasty small boys wreaking vengeance on a novice public schoolmaster (David Hemmings) and his young wife. Peter Brook (a theatre director known in the 1960s and 1970s for 'pop' stagings of the classics) presented nastiness as exemplarily ordinary in the extraordinary circumstances of William Golding's 1954 *Lord of the Flies* (1963). The title sequence of the film is carried by grainy, monochrome stills of a school, its classrooms and its boy choristers. Suddenly thrown from an aeroplane to the coast of an exotic island, these 'Home Counties' boys attempt to organise themselves into some semblance of the society to which they are accustomed: power is divided and disputed between strong Jack (Tom Chapin) (the hunter and adventurer) and sensible Ralph (James Aubrey) (the politician and administrator – his dad is in the Navy). Plump, asthmatic and bespectacled 'Piggy' (Hugh Edwards) says he should prefer to be known by his proper name (which no one can remember) and his sound opinion is generally ignored. Piggy is deputed by the big'uns to 'mother' the littl'uns. Choirboys in fancy hats and long gowns, singing Britten's *Kyrie*, seem peculiarly out of place – but no more so than the habits and rituals of the British in the outposts of Empire. Jack endorses the metaphor: 'We've got to have rules and obey them. After all, we're not savages. We're English; and the English are best at everything.' Absurdities of the colonial experience are made even more explicit in Nicolas Roeg's 1970 *Walkabout* (named after the induction ritual whereby Aboriginal boys attain manhood): two English schoolchildren (Jenny Agutter and Lucien John), attired in felt hats and blazers, are marooned in the Australian desert when their father commits suicide, and only an Aborigine (David Gumpilil) can save them. While the girl sets out their picnic (complete with china chicken) a radio broadcast advises that one should behave 'nonchalantly' when unsure which is the fish knife in a table setting. What Jack, in *Lord of the Flies*, calls 'hunting' others call 'taking'. While a conch shell is arbitrarily invested with authority, permitting a speaker to hold the floor (somewhat akin to the talismanic power of an orb and sceptre), this model society soon manages to frighten itself with imaginary demons, to demonise the other side of the island (obscurely rendered in crashes and flashes of thunder and lightning) and to divide itself between rival factions ('We're strong, we hunt,' says Jack; 'Bollocks to the rules'). Jack's tribe takes hostages (the twins, SAMNERIC) and trophies (including Piggy's glasses) and fights over the fire which ultimately could save them all. Simon, the epileptic visionary, is mistaken for a demon, persecuted and killed (and while Ralph prefers to call it an accident, this is not what Piggy says – it's murder). When they finally encounter a naval officer on the beach, their foreheads smeared (some with blood), half-naked and dishevelled, one of the littl'uns has lost his tongue: the boys have become already the 'savages' over whom they presume superiority.

In Stephen Daldry's *Eight* (1998), freckly young Jonathan announces that his dead dad, who grew up in the 1960s, 'was a flower person . . . I think he grew from a seed'. This is sentimental and anachronistic nostalgia. The precocious child (Laraine Wickens) who organises the bohemian West London household kept by Turner (Mick Jagger) in *Performance* (Donald Cammell and Nicolas Roeg, 1971) is already jaded:[37] she recalls 'old rubber lips' 'when he was well famous . . . when I was a nipper he was a chart buster', suggesting that the revivifying effect of 1960s popular culture is already exhausted and nothing more than an over-flogged commodity. An East End gangster, Chas (James Fox), leaves his latest one-night stand with a discussion over breakfast cereals and the effect of television violence on children ('ketchup all over the screen'). He speaks, it transpires, from experience, being no stranger to the real thing. But Chas is an arch performer, fastidiously stage-managing his toilet, clothes, accessories and décor and choreographing his professional 'act' with Jacobean panache and splendour. Equally, Cammell and Roeg stylishly arrange raw bodies in the manner of Francis Bacon paintings, provide highly stylised dialogue and cut fast across action (and between Jagger in hippy mode and Jagger primped and groomed, performing as Chas' demon). However, Chas (like Turner) is deemed out of date and out of order by his fellow crooks (cast, like Jagger, to correspond with actual celebrated contemporaries) and escapes their vengeance by taking Turner's spare basement room. 'It's in the basement,' he's told by Pherber (Anita Pallenberg – girlfriend of the Rolling Stones' Keith Richards), several over the eight or over the ounce and overlooking the milk bottles on the doorstep. Chas, who laddishly likes 'a bit of a cavort', is initiated into Turner's habits and his ménage, sharing Pherber with his host and Lucy (Michele Breton) who encourage him to question the 'normal' notions in which he has previously found security. Pherber, who seems to get a lot of enjoyment from pummelling her own bottom, asserts the androgynous appeal of taut flesh and muscle. While Chas thinks his flatmates 'freaks', they, in turn, are content to retain 'it' as a guineapig, as their own object of experiment and amusement. This continues for some time, with Miss Gibbs sensibly administering breakfast and cups of tea meanwhile. Eventually, Chas is discovered and is driven to another safe haven in a white Rolls Royce, complementing the black Rolls Royce of the film's opening. Yet again, 1960s glamour seems doomed to fade as soon as it has blossomed.

The Ipcress File (Sidney J. Furie, 1965)

In Len Deighton's hugely popular spy novels *The Ipcress File* (1962) and *Funeral in Berlin* (1966) the protagonist manages to retain his cover: 'Now, my name isn't Harry, but in this business it's hard to remember whether it had ever had been.'[38] The film versions, directed by Sidney J. Furie (1965) and Guy Hamilton (1966), adopt Deighton's locations (the Soho of Italian delis, Wimpy Bars and strip joints) and the protagonist's character (his cultivated, stylish taste in clothes, food, music and women). He'd rather spend the weekend away with his new girlfriend than have it spoiled by an assignment. Deighton, like John Le Carré, details the tedium of routine bureaucratic procedures and provides a cast of backroom boys and girls as a counterweight to the glamorous thrills of spy wars. 'You'll need a TX 82 and CC 1 authority,' mocks Pat Keighley when Palmer requests police reinforcements; T108 turns out to be a particular park bench at which Palmer and Dalby meet. There is the usual jostling for position between ministries and their functionaries and between sup- posedly allied political interests.

Michael Caine plays Sergeant Harry Palmer as Alfie: he is impertinent, insolent and insubordi- nate (as described by Major Dalby [Nigel Green]) and 'a shrewd little cockney' to boot (as described by Colonel Ross [Guy Doleman]). But as his personal dossier suggests, 'a trickster, perhaps with criminal tendencies . . .' might sometimes be useful. Caine (born Maurice Joseph Micklewhite) returned to this 'upstart' role in Joseph L. Mankiewicz's *Sleuth* (1972), an adaptation of Anthony Shaffer's 1970 stageplay. Here he appeared as Milo Tindle, a London hairdresser and son of an Italian watchmaker, Tindolini, who emigrated in the hope of becoming English, opposite Laurence Olivier as Andrew Wyke, an aristocrat who regards the writing of detective fiction as a suitable 'rec- reation of noble minds'. He assumes that he will easily be rid of Tindle in an immaculately con- ceived murder. Wyke invites him to his country estate and leads him through an elaborate game in which Tindle is obliged to perform as unthinkingly as one of the antique automata which occupy the house. He informs Wyke that he intends to marry his lover, Wyke's wife. Wyke parades his ancestry and class, attempting to humiliate Milo. But 'we're all on first names, now', Milo corrects him (and proves he's superior by executing the perfect crime). To the great amusement of Wyke's captive toys, Tindle has the last laugh.

The opening scoring to *The Ipcress File*, reminiscent of Karas' zither theme for *The Third Man* (see Chapter 6), suggests that Palmer's adversaries are to be found beyond the Iron Curtain. *The Quiller Memorandum*, scripted by Harold Pinter (Michael Anderson, 1966), locates its action in Berlin with Alec Guinness rehearsing his role as Le Carré's George Smiley in BBC TV adaptations of the 1970s and 1980s (see Chapter 11). Penkovsky, a former KGB spy, defected in 1960 and a boom in spy fiction followed shortly thereafter (with Le Carré publishing *The Spy Who Came in from the Cold* in 1963 [filmed in 1965], *The Looking-Glass War* in 1965 [filmed in 1969] and *A Small Town in Germany* in 1968). In *From Russia with Love*, a cipher de-coding machine is offered by Tatiana Romanova (a Klebb protégé) to British Secret Service: she has a body 'that knows what it can be for' and Bond intimates that 'he'd like to de-code her'. All, however, is not what it seems and Palmer (and the viewer of *The Ipcress File*) is often unsure who and what is to be trusted. Sequences are ordered and even individual shots are composed to delay and obscure the revelation of the film's plot. The pre-title sequence relates the kidnapping of one man (the British boffin, Dr Radcliffe [Aubrey Richards]) and the murder of another, deftly performed as a train is about to leave. Replacing the murdered man and retrieving Radcliffe is to be Palmer's mission. He is shown surveillance film of the suspects, Housemartin (Oliver MacGreevy) and Blue Jay (Frank Gatliff), whom he duly discovers in Kensington. Believing that Radcliffe is being held at a disused factory, Palmer organises an onslaught. But his plan goes awry. Ten minutes behind schedule, his rein- forcements arrive and a Land Rover rams the factory doors. 'If he'd been here I'd be a hero,' Palmer quips to Dalby; 'But he wasn't and you're not,' says Dalby in return. Another man, who appears to be following Palmer, is subsequently shot when Radcliffe is handed over and Dalby informs Palmer that he was an American agent. 'The CIA should have told us,' Dalby tells Ross: he should not have been on their patch. At Radcliffe's first attempt at public speaking after his release (he suffers amnesia and cannot continue) Palmer is tailed by a black man, conspicuous in an otherwise white audience. Palmer, he says, is being checked by the Americans and will be killed if he's not proven clean. Jock (Gordon Jackson), Palmer's sidekick driving Palmer's car, is then shot by mistake (thinks Palmer).

Palmer searches the factory. He finds that the stove is still warm and discovers a piece of tape bearing the word IPCRESS: 'Induction of Psycho-neuroses by Conditioned Reflex under Stress'. Ross requests a copy of the tape (threatening to reveal Palmer's criminal record if he fails to comply). When the IPCRESS file is stolen from Palmer's office he presumes Ross culpable and informs Dalby, who tells him to lose himself. Palmer is abducted and told that he is in Albania. He is to be subjected to the conditioning (which caused Radcliffe's lost memory) as a result of which he will confess to stealing the file himself. But Palmer survives the treatment and escapes. 'Albania' proves to be no more than an elaborate stage set (convincingly supplied by the Bond designer, Ken Adam), complete with Cyrillic graphics and appropriately uniformed guards, constructed under the Austin's Wharf factory.[39]

Deighton's concern with Pavlovian conditioning, like that of Anthony Burgess' sub-Russk *A Clockwork Orange* (also published in 1962 – see Chapter 10), can be compared with John Frankenheimer's post-Korea *The Manchurian Candidate* (US, 1962) – which features an American prisoner of war brainwashed by his captors – and, perhaps, Don Siegel's *Invasion of the Bodysnatchers* (US, 1956) – which features a community passively surrendering consciousness to 'alien' forces. George Orwell suggested the existence of conditioning in Russia in *1984* (see Chapter 11) and, after the death of Stalin in 1953, such practices became more widely known. William Sargent's *Battle of the Mind*, published in Britain in 1957, outlined a number of brainwashing techniques employed by religious and political factions: 'one set of behavioural patterns in man can be temporarily replaced by another that altogether contradicts it; not by persuasive indoctrination alone but also by imposing intolerable strains on a normally functioning brain'.[40] Such 'strains' are graphically registered in Furie's film by Palmer's incarceration, sleep deprivation, his freezing and starving, succeeded by sequences of spoken mantras, hypnosis and disorientating flashing lights. Palmer insistently repeats his own name and inflicts pain upon himself in order to retain control. Ultimately, his loyalty to himself is all that remains and his superiors make no attempt to reassure him with patriotic or ideological platitudes: 'I could have been killed or sent completely mad,' he protests to Ross; 'That's what you're paid for,' Ross concludes, bluntly.

Notes

1. Vivian Nicholson and Stephen Smith, *Spend, Spend, Spend* (London: Jonathan Cape, 1977), p. 9; see also Gerald Kaufman re. 'regional and proletarian realism', *The Listener*, 18 June 1964, p. 997.

2. See Jeremy Tunstall, 'The Advertising Man', *The Listener*, 12 March 1964, p. 421, and Raymond Williams reviewing *The Persuaders*, 30 January 1969, p. 155; see also 'The Gang Myth', 14 April 1966.

3. See Penny Martin, 'English-style Photography?', in Christopher Breward, Becky Conekin, Caroline Cox (eds), *The Englishness of English Dress* (Oxford: Berg, 2002), pp. 173–87.

4. Robert Murphy, *Sixties British Cinema* (London: BFI, 1992), p. 124.

5. See Christine Geraghty, 'Women and 60s British Cinema: The Development of the "Darling" Girl', in Robert Murphy (ed.), *The British Cinema Book* (London: BFI, 2001), pp. 101–8.

6. Raphael Samuel, *Theatres of Memory* (London: Verso, 1994), pp. 96 and 321.

7. Murphy, *Sixties British Cinema*, p. 179; contrast Gerald Kaufman, *The Listener*, 15 December 1966, p. 898, 'just – physically possible'.

8. *The Listener*, 27 February 1969, pp. 270–1; Leon Hunt, *British Low Culture: from Safari Suits to Sexploitation* (London: Routledge, 1998), p. 20.

9. Jonathan Miller interviewed by Ted Simon, *The Observer*, 5 April 1970, p. 28; see also Lesley A. Hall, *Sex, Gender and Social Change* (Basingstoke: Macmillan, 2000), p. 173, quoting the Gorer Report, 1969: 'Despite . . . all the emphasis on the "permissive society", "swinging London" etc. . . . England still appears to be a very chaste society'; see also J. D. S. Haworth, 'Documentary', *The Listener*, 27 January 1966, p. 147.

10. Philip Larkin, 'Annus Mirabilis' [1967], *Collected Poems* (London: Marvell Press, 1988), p. 167:

    Sexual intercourse began
    In nineteen sixty-three
    (Which was rather late for me) –
    Between the end of the *Chatterley* ban
    And the Beatles' first LP.

11. Michael Balcon, *Michael Balcon Presents . . . A Lifetime of Films* (London: Hutchinson, 1969), p. 138.

12. James Price, 'Laugh-machine and Fright-machine', *The Listener*, 24 June 1965, p. 933, and Eric Rhode (re. *Rosemary's Baby*), 'Films', *The Listener*, 30 January 1969, p. 156.

13. Alexander Walker, *Hollywood, England: the British Film Industry in the Sixties* [1974] (London: Harrap, 1986), p. 320.

14. Cyril Connolly, 'Bond Strikes Camp', *The Selected Works of Cyril Connolly*, vol. 2 (London: Picador, 2002); 'Camp', *The Listener*, 20 October 1966, pp. 572–3.

15. Eric Rhode, 'Drownings', *The Listener*, 29 May 1969, p. 767.

16. Gerald Kaufman, 'Acting for the Camera', *The Listener*.

17. Walker, *Hollywood, England*, p. 451.

18. Tom Courtenay, *Dear Tom: Letters from Home* (London: Black Swan, 2001), p. 349.

19. See John Osborne, *Damn You, England* (London: Faber and Faber, 1999), p. 110, and Walter Lassally, *Itinerant Cameraman* (London: John Murray, 1987), pp. 74–80.

20. David Griffiths, 'Light Entertainment', *The Listener*, 27 August 1964, p. 319; see also Bob Neaverson, *The Beatles Movies* (London: Cassell, 1997).

21. Julian Barnes, *Before She Met Me* (London: Picador, 1986), p. 78.

22. Evelyn Waugh, *Decline and Fall* [1928] (Harmondsworth: Penguin, 1980), p. 188.

23. Margaret Drabble, *The Millstone* [1965] (Harmondsworth: Penguin, 1968), p. 75; in the 1960s, illegitimate babies were even featured in BBC Radio 4's *The Archers*.

24. John Lahr (ed.), *The Diaries of Kenneth Tynan* (London: Bloomsbury, 2001), pp. 300–1.

25. *The Listener*, 30 January 1964, p. 209.

26. Marshall McLuhan, 'The Medium is the Message', *Understanding Media* [1964] (New York: McGraw-Hill, 1968), pp. 7–21; see also Richard Hoggart's review, *The Listener*, 3 December 1964, pp. 895–6. Woody Allen's *Annie Hall* (1977) wittily presents McLuhan's response to misunderstandings of his thesis!

27. John Lahr (ed.), *The Orton Diaries* (London: Methuen: 1987), p. 12, quoting Ronald Bryden in *The Observer*, 1966.

28. Roger Hudson, 'Television in Britain: Description and Dissent', *Theatre Quarterly* vol. 2 no. 6, 1972, pp. 18–25; see also Alan Rosenthal, *The New Documentary in Action* (Berkeley and Los Angeles: University of California Press, 1977), pp. 165–75.

29. See letters to *The Guardian,* September 1980, and Peter Watkins, 'Dying to Know', *Guardian Weekend*, 6 December 1980, pp. 9–10; Lahr *The Diaries of Kenneth Tynan*, pp. 339–40; *The Listener*, 17 February 1966, p. 255.

30. See Sir Hugh Greene, 'The BBC's Duty to Society – I', *The Listener*, 17 June 1965, pp. 889–90, and Kenneth Adam, 'The BBC's Duty to Society – II', *The Listener*, 24 June 1965, pp. 925–6.

31. Anthony Burgess, 'The Arts', *The Listener*, 17 September 1964, p. 441, and 12 November 1964, p. 775.

32. McLuhan, *Understanding Media*, p. 309.

33. See Lionel Bart papers, Bristol University Theatre Collection.

34. Helen Fielding, *Bridget Jones: The Edge of Reason* (London: Picador, 1999), p. 393: '[Richard] was just wearing an ordinary suit which was nice – not all dressed up in some insane morning suit-style outfit as if one of the extras from the film *Oliver* singing "Who Will Buy this Wonderful Morning?" and doing a high-kicking formation dance.'

35. Michel Ciment, *Conversations with Losey* (London: Methuen, 1985), p. 303.

36. Laurence Kitchen, 'Landscape and Figures in the Cinema', *The Listener*, 3 September 1964, p. 351.

37. For difficulties during production, cuts required by the American producers and delays to the release of *Performance* see Walker, *Hollywood, England*, p. 411, and Colin MacCabe, *Performance* (London: BFI, 1998), pp. 58–9.

38. Len Deighton, *The Ipcress File* [1962] (London: Jonathan Cape, 1977), p. 34.

39. See catalogue to The Serpentine Ken Adam exhibition.

40. William Sargent, *Battle for the Mind* [1957] (London: Pan Books, 1959), p. 30.

Chapter 10 | 1970s

John Fowles' 1977 novel *Daniel Martin* is written, in part, in the conventional manner of a screenplay, suggesting camera shots and significant details through which the protagonist imagines an idyllic childhood in Devon. The first-person narrative describes the disillusionment of a British playwright in Hollywood who wrote his first 'big' script in 1954, when, in spite of the 'sacred monsters' in production, he most enjoyed the experience for its being totally non-English and for its lack of past or future: 'the safest dream'. Daniel is initially dismissive of and impatient with British film production,

> a bad idea in the first place, done on the cheap from top to bottom, based on the legitimate assumption that the great British cinema-going public had no taste and the illegitimate one that only water divided the UK from the US.

But, as he contemplates his return from voluntary exile, Daniel eventually determines that, as an English writer, his increasing discomfort with the Hollywood system is intrinsic to the medium itself (possibly reflecting upon Fowles' own unhappy adaptation to film of his 1966 novel *The Magus* [Guy Green, 1968]):

> The film cannot be the medium of a culture all of whose surface appearances mislead, and which has made such a psychological art of escaping present, or camera, reality. For us English the camera, a public eye, invites performance, lying. We make abundant use of these appearances in our comedy, in our humour; socially and politically; but for our private reality we go elsewhere, and above all to words. Since we are so careful only to reveal our true selves in private, the 'private' form of the real text must serve us better than the publicity of the seen spectacle. Furthermore, the printed text allows an escape for its perpetrator. It is only the spoor, the trace of an animal that has passed and is now somewhere else in the forest; and even then, given the nature of language, a trace left far more in the reader's mind (another forest) than outside it, as in the true externally apprehended arts like painting and music. . . . [Cinema and television] sap and leach the native power away; insidiously impose their own conformities, their angles, their limits of vision; deny the existence of what they cannot capture.

Latin Lovers: *Sebastiane* (Derek Jarman/Paul Humfress, 1976)

As with all frequently repeated experience, the effect is paradigmatic, affecting by analogy much beyond the immediately seen – indeed, all spheres of life where a free and independent imagination matters.[1]

The 1970s saw the continuing imitation of American genres (of science fiction in *Alien* [Ridley Scott, 1979], of westerns in *Eagle's Wing* [Anthony Harvey, 1978] and, perhaps, with gangsters in *Get Carter* [Mike Hodges, 1971] and *The Long Good Friday* [John McKenzie, 1979]). There was also an exchange of personnel (with Jack Clayton [*The Great Gatsby*, 1974], and John Schlesinger [*Midnight Cowboy*, 1969] directing stateside before returning for *Sunday Bloody Sunday* [1971]), while Sam Peckinpah directed *Straw Dogs* (1971), Kubrick directed *A Clockwork Orange* (1971) and *Barry Lyndon* (1975 – see Chapter 9). Harvey Keitel (in *Eagle's Wing* and *Bad Timing* [Nicolas Roeg, 1980]), Ryan O'Neal (in *Barry Lyndon*), Ann-Margret and Jack Nicholson (in *Tommy* [Ken Russell, 1975]) and Susan Sarandon (in *The Rocky Horror Show* [Jim Sharman, 1975]) appeared in British productions, with the Canadian actor Donald Sutherland was cast opposite Julie Christie in *Don't Look Now* (Nicolas Roeg, 1973). However, the structure of the British industry was hit hard by the withdrawal of American funding (Alexander Walker says that it fell from £31.2 million in 1969 to £17.5 million in 1970) and by the removal of state subsidies (aggravated by the British stock market collapse of 1973).[2] Yet again, the British industry was obliged to re-examine its relationship with its neighbour across the water, with the Hollywood system and the American product, and to re-position itself internationally.

Shlock and Dross

The fictional Daniel Martin was not alone in disparaging the taste of British audiences. Leon Hunt has subsequently written with relish of the decade which 'taste forgot', noting the 'permissive populism' of soft porn products such as the *Confessions of . . .* series (starring Robin Askwith) and *Come Play with Me* (George Harrison Marks, 1977) (the fate of its star, Mary Millington, providing less cause for celebration), and the impressive box-office receipts of *Till Death Us Do Part* (Norman Cohen, 1968), *Please, Sir!*, *On the Buses* and *Mutiny on the Buses*, *Up Pompeii* and *Up the Chastity Belt*, *Rising Damp*, *Dad's Army* (transferred also to radio) and the Steptoe films; David McGillivray notes the longevity of the stage comedy *No Sex Please – We're British* (1971–87) and the typically unstimulating 'woeful lack of eroticism' displayed by its filmic counterparts.[3] Fiona Richmond (vicar's daughter, ex-Bunny girl at the London Playboy club launched in 1966 and *Playboy* columnist) displayed her talents in a number of sex comedies. Michael Winner's violent collaborations with Charles Bronson were frequently the butt of criticism within the industry (in spite of their returning their costs several times over) and Winner himself facilely ascribed the hostile reception to jealousy. 'If you want art,' he told Joseph Losey, 'buy a Picasso.'[4] Losey, writing for *The Observer* in 1973, commended Kubrick's ownership of equipment and control of distribution, while slating an industry 'basically about the exploitation of bad taste':

at the moment it consists of a bunch of hard-minded, socially irresponsible businessmen desperately trying to exploit what cinema real estate has not been sold off as property developments or super-markets or warehouses . . . British films no longer have, or strive for, a national identity. It's been gobbled up by Hollywood or television.[5]

The Observer complained of Lew Grade's dumbing-down of television and Ken Tynan of the dumbing-down of the West End by Grade's brother, the theatre owner Bernard Delfont, and of the National Theatre by Peter Hall;[6] Dennis Potter, meanwhile (writing for *The Observer*), continued to promote television as the nation's theatre.[7] However, Ken Russell's *The Devils* (1971) (with sets by Derek Jarman), Kubrick's *A Clockwork Orange* and Losey's *The Go-Between* (1970) (critically rewarded at Cannes – see Chapter 9) were listed in Britain's top twenty box-office films for 1972 alongside *Steptoe and Son* and *Mutiny on the Buses*.

Certainly, there was little added value in many of the television spin-offs, some quickly exhaust-ing a storyline better suited to a half-hour slot in the schedule. *The Intelligence Men* (Robert Asher, 1965) and *That Riviera Touch* (Cliff Owen, 1966) had formulaically cast BBC TV's Eric Morecambe (appreciated by Ken Tynan as a superstar) and Ernie Wise in standard plots and locations;[8] recent examples of a similarly misplaced strategy include *Kevin and Perry Go Large* (Ed Bye, 1999), *Stella Street* (Peter Richardson, 1997), both from television series, the Bond spoof *Johnny English* (Peter Howitt, 2002), generated by a series of Barclaycard ads starring Rowan Atkinson, and *Fat Slags* (Ed Bye, 2003) from a cartoon in the comic *Viz*. Leonard Rossiter (of whom one can never have enough) appears in a feature-length *Rising Damp* (Joe McGrath, 1980). *Steptoe and Son Ride Again* (Peter Sykes, 1973) casts Wilfred Brambell and Harry H. Corbett, uses the familiar studio set (complete with recognisable stuffed bear), sees the old horse, Hercules, put out to grass and takes us (literally) to the dogs by way of topical references (as in the *Carry On* series) to Seventh Day Adventists, North Sea Gas, transplant surgeon Christian Barnard and David Lean's 1970 *Ryan's Daughter*. *Up Pompeii* remains as studio-bound as its television precursor, retaining Cassandra the sooth-sayer, relying heavily on Frankie Howerd's strengths in knowing and direct delivery of monologue as the Roman slave, Lurcio, appearing finally as holiday tour guide.[9] Often jokes assume audience familiarity with more respectful treatments of ancient history: there would be little point in Cassandra being per-petually ignored unless one knew that Pompeii was due to fall. As Nick Cull has observed of the his-torical *Carry Ons*, visual and verbal gags are employed to ape the claims to authenticity of 'quality' period reconstruction.[10] Again, there are topical (and anachronistic) references in the costuming and make-up, sets and dialogue (bingo, fishfingers, inflation, Green Shield stamps and hippy Christians), intertextual references (to Shakespeare 'lend me your feet', tabloids, Orson Welles' *Othello* [US, 1951] and to television adverts), visual and verbal ribaldry (stiffs and cucumbers, queers and eunuchs, jiggling breasts and unspoken rhymes for 'ripple') and jokes and puns in names and catch-phrases (Nausea, Procurio, Voluptua, Bilious, and 'there's no decorum in the forum'). Lurcio's self-conscious asides to his audience refer the piece back to Shakespeare's fools, music hall and pantomime and forward to the 'alternative strategies' advocated by *Pompeii*'s self-

Frankie Howerd, as Lurcio, the Roman slave, floors a champion wrestler and keeps the crowd amused in the large-screen version of *Up Pompeii* (Bob Kellett, 1971)

congratulatory avant-garde contemporaries: Howerd often gestures to or addresses the camera ('you'll see more later') and comments on the short length of the film's intermission prior to the collapse of a tackily constructed model of the city. The humour of *Monty Python and the Holy Grail* (Terry Gilliam/Terry Jones, 1974) and *Monty Python's Life of Brian* (Terry Jones, 1979) (drawing their cast from the seminal BBC TV series [1969–74]) similarly relies on the irreverent handling of historical knowledge, played 'straight' by medieval scholar Jones for BBC Radio and TV in 2002 and 2004.

The *Carry On* series continued in a similar vein of low-brow humour, with *Carry On Girls* (Gerald Thomas, 1973) referring (like the television *Pompeii*) to beauty contests and their sabotaging by feminist demonstrators: Andrew Logan responded by launching the higher camp Alternative Miss World series.[11] While Michael Reeves' *Witchfinder General* (1968) cast Steptoe senior (Wilfred Brambell) as a seventeenth-century Suffolk yokel (with an accent as improbable as that of Vincent Price's witchfinder, Matthew Hopkins), Steptoe junior (Harry H. Corbett) played the Victorian detective, Sergeant Bung, in *Carry On Screaming* (Gerald Thomas, 1966), to the accompaniment of BBC TV's *Z-Cars* theme. *Carry On Emmanuelle* (Gerald Thomas, 1978) (referring to

Just Jaeckin's 1974 soft-core commercial success, *Emmanuelle* – similarly the occasion for feminist activity) cast Kenneth Williams as a timid British diplomat with a sexually insatiable, voluptuous French wife; this last gasp of the series also tries to raise a laugh from a man (looking good, as 1970s advertising maintained, in Terylene) successfully turning a Guardsman's head where the ambassador's wife's strenuous attempts have failed; *That's Carry On* (Gerald Thomas, 1977) attempted to re-cycle material from the previous twenty years. Norman Cohen's 1975 *Confessions of a Pop Performer* likewise spoofs a familiar precedent, with regular boy-next-door Robin Askwith as a surrogate for Mick Jagger in *Performance* (1971) (see Chapter 9).

Possibly higher-class, certainly more expensive dross (but still in questionable taste) was performed at Pinewood by Keith Moon (of The Who) as a nun praying for a crashed spitfire with Ringo Starr (of The Beatles) dressed as Frank Zappa alongside Zappa himself in *200 Motels* (Frank Zappa, 1971), reported as the first rock opera filmed in Britain.[12] Ken Russell, not to be out-done, followed with *Tommy* (based on the rock opera by The Who's Pete Townsend and starring The Who's Roger Daltrey – promoting sales of the associated record release and tour), dismissed by Peter Gidal as 'putrescence'.[13] Jim Sharman filmed Richard O'Brien's adaptation of his own musical extravaganza, *The Rocky Horror Picture Show* – the 1975 film promoting, in turn, the show's long stage career and cult following. 'Something to offend everyone,' concluded John Walker in *The Observer*, 'but beneath its apparent polymorphous perversities it is as innocent as Sandy Wilson's *The Boyfriend*' (filmed by Ken Russell in 1971 with dancer Christopher Gable and 1960s supermodel Twiggy – fashion's 'Girl of the Year' in 1966).[14] Both *Tommy* and *Rocky Horror* refer to cinematic icons, myths and stereotypes, *Tommy* to Marilyn Monroe and RAF fighter pilots (the father of the blind, deaf and dumb child born on VE day); *The Rocky Horror Show* to Samuel Beckett's stageplay *Not I* (filmed for BBC TV with Billie Whitelaw in 1977), to Gothic horror settings (as in Terence Fisher's 1957 *The Curse of Frankenstein*, 1968 *The Devil Rides Out* and Prospero's crumbling mansion in Derek Jarman's 1979 *The Tempest*), white clapper-boarded middle America, the sinking of the Titanic, James Whale's *The Bride of Frankenstein* (US, 1935), RKO's *King Kong* (US, Merian C. Cooper/Ernest B. Schoedsack, 1933) ('Whatever happened to Fay Wray?' enquires the chorus) and Kubrick's *Dr Strangelove* (1963). *The Rocky Horror Show* announces itself as science fiction, a 'late night double feature show'. Like *Up Pompeii*, it puns with names and lyrics: Richard O'Brien – who began his career as a stunt rider on *Carry On Cowboy* (Gerald Thomas, 1965) – appears as Riff-Raff (a lugubrious handyman) and Tim Curry, suitably corseted and suspendered, as Frank-n-Furter ('Just a sweet transvestite from transsexual Transylvania'); 'Wise up Janet Weiss,' suggests Frank, 'Don't get hot and flustered . . . use a bit of mustard' – 'You're a hot dog, Frank-n-Furter,' quips Janet in return. Like *Up Pompeii*, *Tommy* spoofs television advertisements, throwing the boy's mother (Ann-Margret) into orgasmic rapture amid the chocolate and baked beans which gush from her screen. Small-town America is represented in *Rocky Horror* by Janet Weiss (Susan Sarandon – in white undies and half-slip) and untattooed Brad Majors (Barry Bostwick – in white Y-fronts), while Rocky (a credit to Frank's genius) is bleached blonde, fantastically honed and toned and barely clad in gold trunks and boxing boots. An expert (Charles Gray) functions as the narrator customary to science fiction.

Both films cast rock and pop performers, in *Rocky Horror*: Meatloaf; in *Tommy*, Eric Clapton commenting on the idolisation of Marilyn ('She's got the power to heal – you never fear . . . one word from her lips and the deaf can hear'); Elton John on stage eulogising the new idol, Tommy, the pinball wizard; and Keith Moon is cast in various guises as Uncle Ernie (with whom it is possibly *not* safe to leave a child), who drinks raw eggs in Newcastle Brown, a flasher and rubber fetishist who sings 'You won't scream and shout while I fiddle about . . . fiddle about'. Like Russell's *The Boyfriend* (and BBC TV's *Top of the Pops*), *Rocky Horror* uses split screening to add to the cinematic spectacle and flashes forward in response to the lyric 'It's astounding – time is fleeting – doing the timewarp.'

Amid its own balloons and bunting, flags and whistles, *Tommy*, however incoherently, attempts to offer a critique of that which it presents: Tommy's wicked stepfather (Oliver Reed), his mother (Ann-Margret) and her lover (Jack Nicholson as a lascivious quack physician who promises to cure her son) are all seen to profit from his freakish celebrity – and Tommy duly ritualistically purges her by stripping her of her ill-gotten jewels and dunking her in the sea. Tommy's followers (an impressionable vicar's daughter and the Hell's Angels incredibly inspired to lay down their arms) are shown to be gullible. However, for a film which copiously refers beyond its limits, it is hard to forget that the film itself benefits from and contributes to the following of The Who, and ultimately seems confused and self-contradictory.

Hunt suggests that, in spite of the decline in horror production after the 'boom' of the 1950s and 1960s, horror and sex were the second and third largest categories of British films released in the 1970s, but notes also the difficulty of allocating films which may cross genres.[15] He has reappraised the low-budget productions intended largely for the domestic market but finds Robin Hardy's 1974 *The Wicker Man* 'overrated' in comparison to other horror classics such as *Dracula* (Terence Fisher, 1958), *The Devil Rides Out* and *Witchfinder General* (which might count, equally, as costume drama).[16] However, there seem reasons enough for *The Wicker Man* being well received by a variety of audiences at the time of its release, for its acquiring a cult following subsequently, and then providing material for a sketch in BBC TV's 2003 *Little Britain* and (at time of writing) for film sequels. A group of Scottish islanders, under the tutelage of its laird, has set itself beyond the pale of the law and conventions of the mainland, holding instead to pagan beliefs and customs, and Sergeant Howie (Edward Woodward – then known as ITV's *Callan* [1967–72]) is despatched to investigate the disappearance of a young girl. But the local community, even the girl's mother, obstructs the enquiry. In *Straw Dogs*, a timid American mathematician, David Sumner (Dustin Hoffman), defends his liberal principles (law and private property) against hostile Cornish villagers, intent upon terrorising the wife he has stolen from them (Susan George) and lynching the local simpleton, in retaliation for the disappearance of a girl who has ill-advisedly seduced him. In *The Wicker Man*, the daughter, Willow (model Britt Ekland), of the local innkeeper (Lindsay Kemp – performance artist, choreographer for Derek Jarman and adviser to David Bowie), the schoolteacher, Miss Rose (an Ekland lookalike), who educates her pupils in the primeval derivation of such superficially quaint practices as maypole dancing and the making of corn dollies, and the local librarian (Hammer regular Ingrid Pitt as an equally Nordic but unnnatural blonde earth mother) challenge Howie's determination to stay chaste for his fiancée back at home. Miss Rose informs him calmly that Christianity is no more than one possible religion, which places as much faith in resurrection as the islanders reserve for reincarnation. Yet Howie (like Sumner) equally insists on scientific rationality, telling Lord Summerskill (another Hammer stalwart, Christopher Lee – ominously inverting his benign aristocratic role as Nicholas, Duke de Richelieu, in *The Devil Rides Out*) that it is not natural that fruits should grow on this soil. While Lord Summerskill, in hippy floral caftan, yellow polo-neck and wig leads the community in the libations to the sea and fertility rituals which (they believe) will guarantee the extraordinary return of crops for yet another year, Howie reminds him that he is the subject of a Christian country: his own fate is defended by fear as much as by conviction, to the very end, when he himself becomes the unwitting sacrifice of their rites.

In addition to the spectacular pleasures which these films provide, they also provide, however unresolved, some sort of contemporary commentary. Neither the remote wilds of the countryside nor a far-flung island can supply an idyllic retreat; while *The Wicker Man* shares with other films an association of islands with the supernatural, here it proves malevolent and obstructs the achievement of righteous goals – and even their righteousness is questioned.

Dissatisfaction and Dissent

'The catchphrase of the 1960s was the Affluent Society,' commented *The Observer* in March 1973; 'it is now of the Violent Society', citing events in Northern Ireland and recent industrial disputes.[17] '*Fuck* all this dead babies about love, understanding, compassion,' says the despicable Marvell in Martin Amis' futuristic 1975 novel, *Dead Babies*.[18] *Sunday Bloody Sunday* (its title evoking and anticipating Irish History) was directed by Schlesinger on his return from America. It seems to both recognise the new freedoms of the 1960s and to indicate some sense, already, of more sombre times to come. Only the children find a love affair between two men 'funny'. At the end of Ken Russell's 1969 version of D. H. Lawrence's novel *Women in Love* (published in 1920), Ursula (Jennie Linden) insists to Rupert (Alan Bates) that her love alone should be enough for him, but Rupert believes in two kinds of love and continues to cleave to his past erotic friendship with Gerald (Oliver Reed) – or at least something other that a claustrophobic marriage. While, in *Sunday Bloody Sunday*, a doctor, Daniel Hirsch (Peter Finch) and Bob (Murray Head) discuss the possibility of living in America, radio and newspaper headlines report TUC meetings, the unemployment figures and 'Call Girls Out on Strike'. Alex (Glenda Jackson – a recent Oscar winner for her role as Gudrun in *Women in Love* and to appear opposite TV's Doctor Kildare [Richard Chamberlain] in Russell's 1971 *The Music Lovers*) shares Bob and brings him to babysit for friends' children over the weekend covered by the film's synopsis: they precociously smoke pot (they know where their parents hide it), ask Bob whether he is bourgeois and comment on the progress of the lovers' relationship. 'Has he walked out on you? – Guess that's why you're in a bad mood,' says Lucy (six going on sixteen) to Alex. For Alex and for Daniel there is a sense of growing dissatisfaction with the ménage, and both want more, even if it means doing without the self-centred Bob. Alex takes a new older lover

Precocious children are minded by Alex (Glenda Jackson) and Bob (Murray Head) in *Sunday Bloody Sunday* (John Schlesinger, 1971)

(but is not pleased by Bob's approval of her independence – she wants him to match her own possessiveness), resigns her job, ponders her own childhood and perhaps indicates her want of a family of her own in minding her friends' children. Both Alex and Daniel return to old certainties (Alex to her parents who have 'worked at' marriage, says her mother, Daniel to the Orthodox rituals of the faith in which he was raised). For both, Bob is a disappointment of their ideals but he cannot be turned into what they want him to be; but nor do they admit jealousy of each other: 'If you look back on this – which you won't – you'll think it has something to do with Daniel – but it hasn't,' insists Alex; 'All this making do . . . sometimes nothing just has to be better than just anything.' Ken Tynan noted 'the gloomy ruefulness with which the hero and heroine squander their affection and regard on a cool and uncaring erotic object' as symptomatic of the times.[19] As with Le Carré's 1971 novel *The Naïve and Sentimental Lover*, there is a sense of personal freedom producing as much frustration and anxiety as the old social constraints. In Malcolm Bradbury's 1975 novel *The History Man* (serialised for BBC TV in 1981) the academic couple, the Kirks, find that in spite of their pretensions to being modern, 'passionate, liberated, consciousness-conscious people [the Kirkness]', an 'open' marriage is not entirely mutually satisfying. George Melly commented in

The Observer in 1973 on the mounting wave of disillusion and the defection of certain admired figures:

> Mick Jagger, the most surly, uncompromising scourge of the straight world, had suddenly changed sides. Not only did he marry but chose to celebrate this conformist act in flamboyant affluence in the South of France. Simultaneously, he emerged as one of that international cast of 'beautiful' people . . . he became, for some months, a dirty word.[20]

Lindsay Anderson's *If . . .* (1968) took a public school (and the ethos of Rudyard Kipling's 1895 poem) as its model for a critique of society at large but the reasons for the pupils' dissent are less well defined. Travis (Malcolm McDowell), and others, are told several times that their hair is too long and he has a poster of Che Guevara in his study. There is the usual indictment of fagging, estranged masters and the suggestion of estranged parents; homosexual flirtation is condemned as 'adolescent'. The film is divided between black and white sequences and colour and is broken into episodes: significantly enough, in 'Ritual and Romance', the Girl (Christine Noonan) remains nameless, unlike the Boys (Wallis, Travis and Knightly). Although the film finally casts the boys and girl as 'Crusaders', the purpose of their retaliatory violence is more demonstrative than effective of specific ends. Figures of authority, such as the Headmaster (*Dad's Army*'s Arthur Lowe) and General Denson (old boy and national hero – Hugh Thomas), are readily lampooned. With the second instalment of his Travis trilogy (*O Lucky Man!* [1973]), Anderson looked to the picaresque record of William Thackeray's 1845 *Vanity Fair*, 'a novel without a hero', endeavouring, Anderson said, to convey thereby the absurdity of ordinary experience:[21] Mick Travis, 'Confessions of a Commercial Traveller', courtesy of Joseph Andrews and Tom Jones – see Chapter 9. Again, the film employs monochrome (in faked silent footage for the opening 'Once Upon a Time' sequence, like Teddy Brown's 'dream' sequences in *Every Home Should Have One* – and in Sally Potter's 1983 *Gold Diggers*), white on black lettering indicating its sections (West, North, South, East End) and in disruptive black leader. Arthur Lowe reappears (in various guises), as does Noonan and *A Clockwork Orange*'s Warren Clarke (also several times over). Songs (a supposedly Brechtian touch) commenting on the action are provided by Alan Price, duly appearing with The Animals as a character in the film. Helen Mirren is routinely cast as socialite *Cosmo* girl, the daughter of a business magnate. BBC TV *Till Death Us Do Part*'s Dandy Nichols joins the ensemble alongside Sir Ralph Richardson and Anderson himself (self-reflexively, possibly self-regardingly, as a character in the prologue and as a director casting McDowell). Everything encountered by the film is rendered indiscriminately and messily absurd, from the magic gold suit which projects the hero to new situations (a sideways glance at Vladimir Propp's study of folklore, perhaps), to Working Men's Club strippers, to the ghastliness of inter-species transplantation and experimentation (a portent here of the dystopian scenario of Danny Boyle's 2002 *28 Days Later*), to the mock flagellation enjoyed by supposedly venerable High Court judges before, reluctantly, passing grim sentence on hapless convicts. Finally, Anderson tacitly indicts the absurdity of his own position: 'Revolution is the opium of the intellectuals', but exempts himself from answering the charge.

Kubrick's *A Clockwork Orange* presents and withstands more sustained criticism. It presciently imitates the sculptures of Allen Jones (a concurrent subject of debate in *Spare Rib*) together with the archaic and Russian transcription (and Anglo-Saxon word order) of Anthony Burgess' 1962 source novel:[22] one superpower of the 1970s is used to 'defamiliarise' the pervasive influence of another, in the (again, Brechtian) manner indicated by David Lodge in *The State of the Language* (1990). In 1978, *The Observer* presented hippies and skinheads as the modern equivalents of 'Cavaliers and Roundheads'.[23] While referring to streetfighting in Brighton between rival gangs in 1964, Frank Roddam's 1979 *Quadrophenia* (produced by and promoting The Who – who had been 'Talkin' about our own Generation' back in 1964) acquired and sustained into the 1980s a cult following for its 'mod' styling. In spite of its non-specific, futuristic setting (actually shot in carefully selected locations in the concrete wastelands of the South Bank and South London housing estates) there was much in *A Clockwork Orange* in the costuming of Alex (Malcolm McDowell) and his 'droogs' to suggest the subject as contemporary: braces, cut-off narrow trousers, Doctor Marten or combat boots. Certainly, they and McDowell with one eye ringed with false lashes (a feature of the poster campaign) soon became objects of imitation and Kubrick withdrew the film from distribution in Britain when he was accused of promoting the violence and debasement which he observed and the film portrayed. This public reaction seems to be an instance, at second remove, of the 'moral panic' which Stuart Hall and others identified in their 1978 intervention in the discussion of mugging as a new or particular phenomenon.[24] Kubrick employs the cinematic style of *The Confessions of . . .* series (a speeded-up coupling with two girls Alex has met at Kensington market) and a synthesised version of Beethoven's 9th Symphony; a slow-motion brawl is choreographed to Rossini's Thieving Magpie Overture and a rape scene played out to the droogs' rendition of 'I'm Singin' in the Rain'. But Kubrick presents Alex's punishment in prison and supposed psychiatric cure in hospital as equally violent and insidious, the bureaucrats endeavouring to coerce and enlist him to their own ends as a passive citizen. His parents, meanwhile, give his room at home to a lodger. In order to secure his release, Alex masquerades, while continuing to confide to the audience in voiceover and imagine his retribution on his captors.

Archer (Mick Ford), in Alan Clarke's 1979 *Scum* (like Colin in *The Loneliness of the Long Distance Runner* – see Chapter 9), is a borstal boy who refuses to 'eat shit' even if it means a longer sentence: 'They're not having me, the bastards . . . I want to get through in my own little way causing as much trouble to the screws as possible.' He is an old hand by the time that Carlin (Ray Winstone), Davis (Julian Firth) and Angel (Alrick Riley) arrive. He reminds a screw that the length of his chain denotes length of service and that he has become as institutionalised as his charges – he, in turn, does not care to be reminded of his loss of dignity. As with the public school model of *If . . .*, the masters are happy however order is maintained, and turn a blind eye to instances of gang rape, racism and bullying. However, the individualist Archer joins forces with the gang leader, Carlin, when Davis commits suicide in custody. A riot ensues, but the borstal inspector can do no more than dismiss the incident as 'an unfortunate, most regrettable accident'. *Scum*'s writer, Ray

Minton, contributed to *Scrubbers* (Mai Zetterling, 1982), relocating some of its incidents (but with less purpose) to a girls' remand home.

Jubilee (Derek Jarman, 1978) caustically focuses on specific circumstances (the decline of civil liberties in the late 1970s and the commercial exploitation of punk resistance), ominously regarded by the figure of Elizabeth I (Jenny Runacre) as 'the shadow of this time', where progress has taken the place of history – 'like pornography, better than the real thing', quips Borgia. 'God Bless the Queen and Her Fascist Regime', yelled the Sex Pistols (in a song banned by BBC Radio for Elizabeth II's Jubilee year in 1977 – thereby enhancing the band's glamour). Julien Temple further nailed the punk coffin in his 1979 *The Great Rock 'n' Roll Swindle* (with the participation of manager Malcolm McLaren, Sid Vicious and Johnny Rotten from The Sex Pistols) while *Rude Boy* (Jack Hazan/ David Mingay, 1980) featured The Clash with Joe Strummer (cast also by Jim Jarmusch in *Mystery Train* [US, 1989]). Runacre reappears in *Jubilee* as Bod, an artist, while Borgia Ginz (Jack Birkett – of the Lindsay Kemp Company) – a possible alter ego for McLaren – is the impresario who owns the names: 'I bought them all. BBC . . . ITV . . . I rearrange the alphabet . . . As long as the music is loud enough we won't hear the world falling apart,' he says, eventually turning his entrepreneurial attentions to car parks. Mohican-styled punk muse Jordan (assistant at Vivienne Westwood's and McLaren's King's Road shop, Sex) appears as Amyl (sometimes in the guise of Britannia) with punk popster Toyah as Mad (Bod's permanent flatmates). New Romantic (in waiting) Adam Ant as Kid, the occasional sex-object of the two brothers (Karl Johnson and 1981 *Chariots of Fire*'s Ian Charleson – see Chapter 11) complete the household. The boys are shot dead in each other's arms and the police set about the Kid with a broken bottle. The girls respond to their thuggery by slicing open a policeman's stomach. Elizabeth strides the white cliffs of Dover with the philosopher John Dee (*Rocky Horror*'s Richard O'Brien) and Amyl concludes that Dorset is the only safe place left.

Ridley Scott's *Alien* suggests that outer space may not prove any safer: 'In Space No one Can Hear you Scream'. Set in an indeterminate future, women and men work alongside one another with Ripley (Sigourney Weaver) often assuming command; the crew (of mixed nationality, race and age) dresses in a low-tech combination of uniform and mufti and is accompanied by a mascot, the cat, Jones. The film is as much concerned with the social dynamics of the crew as with displaying the spectacular gadgetry of the ship; it uses speed and suspense to shock the audience rather than elaborate simulation of its 'monster'. On a distant planet, they discover a strange life form, against which Mother (the ship's computer) warns them but which the scientist, Ash (Ian Holm), determines to investigate. The creature reproduces itself, mutating into various shapes, growing digits and a whip-like tail with which it proceeds to throttle Cain (John Hurt – who has hatched the embryo from his stomach), then acquiring teeth and tentacles. Acid seeps from the creature and burns through the ship's deck: 'a wonderful defence mechanism – don't kill it', urges Ash. While Jones proves better equipped to sense the continued presence of the unwanted stowaway, Ash voices a (literally) inhumane admiration for its purity as 'a perfect organism', without 'delusions of morality', without 'remorse'. The crew devises various devices and strategies with which to stalk the creature. Ultimately alone, Ripley manages to harpoon it and destroys the ship. She takes refuge with Jones in a cocoon-like capsule and heads home through the wilderness.

Schools, ships and prisons in the 1970s resume their habitual role as models of society. But the present and future they depict for us is mostly disorderly, bleak and pessimistic.

Alternative Strategies

'It took someone from outside Britain', comments Stephen Dwoskin, 'to make a politically meaningful film about Britain.'[25] Jean-Luc Godard was one of a number of European film-makers working in Britain, making *One Plus One* (1968) with the Rolling Stones, while Michelangelo Antonioni (see Chapter 9) returned in 1975 to make *The Passenger* (with Jenny Runacre, Steven Berkoff and a script by Peter Wollen) and Pier Paolo Pasolini enlisted non-professional talent – artist/musician David Buckler (alongside Jenny Runacre) for *The Canterbury Tales* (1971). While Dirk Bogarde was cast by Luchino Visconti, in *Death in Venice* (1971), with Charlotte Rampling, by Liliana Cavani, in *Night Porter* (1973), and, with John Gielgud, by Alain Resnais in *Providence* (1977), Franco Zeffirelli cast Kenneth Cranham and Alec Guinness in *Brother Sun, Sister Moon* (1972). Meanwhile, BBC 2 regularly transmitted classic and contemporary European films. Lavish commercial productions (such as *The Three Musketeers* [Richard Lester, 1973 – with Michael York, Oliver Reed, Frank Finlay, Simon Ward, Roy Kinnear, Spike Milligan – from BBC Radio's *The Goon Show*, Rodney Bewes – from BBC TV's *The Likely Lads*, Christopher Lee and Charlton Heston as the original Cardinal Richelieu], *Murder on the Orient Express* [Sidney Lumet, 1974 – with Albert Finney, Jacqueline Bisset, Sean Connery, John Gielgud, Wendy Hiller, Vanessa Redgrave, Rachel Roberts and Michael York] and *Death on the Nile* [John Guillermin, 1978 – with Peter Ustinov, Jane Birkin, David Niven and Maggie Smith]) called upon international star-strewn casts and foreign financing, but smaller-scale independent productions similarly looked abroad: both Chris Petit's German-style road movie *Radio On* (1979) and German-located *Chinese Boxes* (1984) were partly German-funded.

Godard's *British Sounds* (1969) was made for London Weekend TV (but banned), a companion piece in its commentary and construction to *Le Gai Savoir* (1968 – made for French television but not transmitted). It provides a timely diagnosis of 'the English disease – slow growth and bad industrial relations'. *Akenfield* (Peter Hall, 1975), adapted from Ronald Blythe's 1969 novel, was released and shown on television on the same night (a portent of collaborations in the 1980s).[26] Beautifully photographed in natural light by Ivan Strasburg, with music by Michael Tippett, improvised and played by non-professionals, worthy (but dull), it at least served as a reminder that rural Britain was as much a victim of the economic crisis as the cities. *British Sounds* combines slogans and graphics with repetition (a naked woman, 'the exploited of the exploited', tirelessly walking up and down stairs) and a characteristic long tracking shot down the Ford assembly line at Dagenham. There are interviews with employers (who talk of saboteurs) and workers (who talk of 'a better capitalist government than a capitalist government') and a child reading lessons in the history of British trade unionism and rebellion (from the Levellers, via Tolpuddle to Bloody Sunday in

Hyde Park in 1888). There is railing against immigration and 'long-haired sex perverts'. Self-evident truths', we are told, 'belong to bourgeois ideology'.

This mantra of the decade was commonly revisited by film-makers determined to discover alternative means of producing, exhibiting and distributing films and by commentators who saw theory as an essential tool in achieving these ends. The debate was heated and (in retrospect) frequently appears arcane. Some artists made films which were shown in galleries and clubs (many recently programmed for exhibition at Tate Britain), some art graduates made films released in art-house cinemas, some graduated to feature film production and mainstream distribution. Stephen Dwoskin and Peter Gidal (both associated with the London Film-makers' Co-operative, founded in 1966 – which supported screenings in galleries and clubs) both damn the efforts of the BFI's Experimental Film Fund to foster independent production, although Dwoskin does allow its funding of Bill Douglas (*My Childhood* [1972], *My Ain Folk* [1973], *My Way Home* [1978] – an intensely personal narrative) as an exception. Jarman, in turn, commented ruefully on the activities of the Co-Op:[27] '[Its] film-makers were involved in the destructuring of film; to one who had stumbled on film like a panacea this seemed a rather negative pursuit – like calling water H_2O.'[28]

Much blood was spent, in the discussion of 'correct' means and forms, over the question of history, historical prerogative and its representation. *The Observer*, in the 1970s, produced major editorial series ('The British and the Sea', 'The Making of the British', 'The Triumph of the British', 'The New British' and 'Black Britons'), promoted major historical series and films (such as *Young Winston* [Richard Attenborough, 1972 – with Simon Ward], *Anne of the Thousand Days* [Charles Jarrott, 1969] and *Mary, Queen of Scots* [Charles Jarrott, 1971]) and costume adaptations of historical fiction (such as Anthony Trollope's 1864/80 *The Pallisers* and the BBC, ITV and Bryan Forbes' 1970 film versions of E. Nesbit's 1906 *The Railway Children* – a world of smockery, sailor suiting, tinkly pianos and roses around the door). In *Screen* (the BFI's Journal of the Society for Education in Film and Television), contributors wrangled over the Ken Loach and Tony Garnett 1975 conventionally ordered and narrated BBC TV series, *Days of Hope* and *The Big Flame* (BBC TV, 1969), concerning the history of the Liverpool Docks.[29] Meanwhile, Sally Potter's *Thriller* (1979) retold the 1896 opera *La Bohème* from a feminist perspective ('What if I had been the subject rather than the object of the text?') and confronted 'bad-girl' Musette with 'good-girl' Mimi, her self-sacrifying opposite (fulfilling male 'desires to be heroes'), employing music from Giacomo Puccini's opera alongside Bernard Herrmann's screeching violins from Hitchcock's *Psycho* (1960). *Amy* (Peter Wollen and Laura Mulvey, 1980) (in the manner of Godard and of Bertolt Brecht's 1930 *The Flight Over the Ocean* [Der Flug der Lingberghs] – discussed by *Screen* in 1979 – although this is not acknowledged as its source) combines maps, newspaper headlines, the memoirs of Amy Johnson and fellow aviatrice Amelia Earhart, period reconstruction, bold typography (in the style of John Berger's 1972 *Ways of Seeing*), backing music from the 1930s and from Poly Styrene and X-Ray Spex and interviews with contemporary schoolgirls ('. . . you don't have to be famous . . .').

The Song of the Shirt (directed by Susan Clayton and Jonathan Curling at the Royal College of Art for Film and History Project, 1979) invokes Thomas Hood's 1843 poem in its title and names

Stitch stitch stitch: *The Song of the Shirt* (Susan Clayton/Jonathan Curling, 1979)

its first section after Adam Smith's 1776 treatise, *The Wealth of Nations*. This part contrasts the conditions of labour of women employed in dressmaking with the marketing of the products of their labour in period fashion plates and magazines:

'Oh, Men, with Sisters dear!
Oh, Men with Mothers and Wives!
It is not linen you're wearing out,
But human creatures' lives!
Stitch stitch stitch
In poverty, hunger and dirt,
Sewing at once a double thread,
A Shroud as well as a Shirt.

The second section (again stylised in its assembly of stills, reading and music, and reminding us of its fabrication by posing two women as viewers of a television screen) compares the situation in Spitalfields in the 1970s with the formation of unions a century earlier, cutting between figures in costume and in contemporary dress; enlargements of letters and portraits are used as back projection. Screens within screens multiply insistently in the third section, with a man reading a newspaper in a railway carriage inserted in a later frame surrounded by further printed material: here the thesis is extended to an international context. *The Song of the Shirt* addresses various issues concerning the historical condition of women and divisions between women accorded by class, issues much covered by Germaine Greer's *The Female Eunuch* (1970) and by the 1970s review *Spare Rib*; but it is also conspicuously preoccupied with presenting its essay on gender and class in a manner which obliges the viewer to acknowledge the construction of its evidence.[30]

I like *The Three Musketeers: The Queen's Diamonds*. Unlike *The Song of the Shirt*, its handling of history is fanciful rather than analytical, taking its lead from Alexander Dumas' salacious, sensational (and sensationally successful) 1844 novel. Like the historical *Carry Ons*, it is self-consciously a confection rather than a deconstruction. But it equally offers an alternative (on wet Sunday afternoons) to the more dignified and 'respectful' adaptations serialised on BBC 1 in my childhood. One might suggest that it constitutes 'post-heritage' (a term coined by Claire Monk) prior to the advent of heritage film proper in the 1980s. While *Elizabeth* (1998) (see Chapter 12) presented Christopher Ecclestone's bare bottom and French cross-dressing in the English court, *The Three Musketeers* gave us Raquel Welch (36–26–36, 5'5" and 8½ stone, records *The Observer*, photographing her in a white crochet wedding dress) and swordsmen disguised as French nuns.[31] More flourish and dash than lash, the film features as much verbal fencing and slapstick (in the manner of Lupino Lane) as it does elegantly choreographed athletic swashbuckling (in the manner of Douglas Fairbanks and Errol Flynn): d'Artagnan (Michael York) fails to scale the climbing ivy to Milady's chamber – and limply apologises. Recalling series of the teens (and the Bonds), the end of the film announces its sequel, *The Four Musketeers: The Revenge of Milady* (Richard Lester, 1974). As in the *Carry Ons* (and a century of Donald McGill postcards), there are boob jokes aplenty and a spindly Spike Milligan (as an innkeeper) rattles at the prospect of twice weekly sex with his wife (the voluptuous and younger Welch). The humble and innocent mother's boy, d'Artagnan, has his father's sword, a precious relic, hacked in half at the outset of his adventures. He is pursued by adventurous ladies and courtesans in lace bodices, but Milady traps her foot in a coal scuttle (Morecambe and Wise and Shirley Bassey come to mind) as she presses him to her bosom. There are gestural nods in the direction of historical verisimilitude, in scripting, settings (large-patterned wallpaper being fashionably styled in the 1970s by David Hicks *et al.*), 'costume frippery and what-not', instruments of torture (which rattle the innkeeper yet further) and a Real Tennis match between Aramis and Porthos. While the film does not intend to be taken seriously and is not in the best possible taste, the formal devices it employs deserve discussion alongside the presumed merits of other concurrent and subsequent representations of history.

Derek Jarman and Peter Greenaway (like Bill Douglas) both made short films in the 1970s before moving to feature-length production. *Dear Phone* (1977), *Water Wrackets* (1975) and the BFI-funded *A Walk through H* (1978) are indicative of Greenaway's later obsessions with lists and classification (sometimes apparently arbitrary or merely coincidental) and his fondness for typography: *Dear Phone* has something of the quirky quality of a game of Chinese Whispers, narrated in English with eclectic snatches of French and Italian, the street sounds of sirens, traffic and church bells backing locked-off shots of empty telephone boxes in various recognisable and anonymous locations. Typewritten and handwritten letters appear over-written and with crossings-out, rubbed-out and smudged in black, red or blue; many of the film's 'characters' (from Harold Constance to Hirohito Condottieri to Henry Clementi to Howard Contenti to Harold Contents – a telephone operator who goes deaf and resigns) share a wife or ex-wife called Zelda who phones her husband at 10.30 precisely to remind him to call.

Derek Jarman experimented with Super 8 (including his film accompaniment to Marianne Faithfull's 1979 *Broken English* – revisited in his 1987 *The Last of England*); he also presented an interpretation of Shakespeare's *The Tempest* (produced by Don Boyd), with its gloriously theatrical, apposite anachronisms (such as Elizabeth Welch, emblazoned in gold like a rising sun, reviving her performance of *Stormy Weather* – a precursor to Jimmy Summerville's finale in Sally Potter's *Orlando* [1992]) and *Sebastiane* (1976), with its startlingly correct use of Latin, masks (and a masque) in the manner of Aristophanes and music by Roxy Music's Brian Eno. The Roman soldier, Sebastian (Leonardo Treviglio), for centuries the subject of academy paintings which have elicited erotic responses from viewers, is here portrayed as the object of homoerotic fear and desire – the final sequence is played in slow motion, against the sound of the wind.[32] Jarman's historical setting facilitates a separation of homophobia from Christian morality: while firmly identifying Sebastian with the torments of Christ (a leopard-skinned figure mirrors the temptations in the desert; Sebastian's death and Justin's crowning with thorns invoke the crucifixion), the boorish Maximus (Neil Kennedy), 'a crude bugger', boasts of the orgies in which he has participated, where nothing was left to the imagination ('In those days men were men' – he will screw the first whore he finds when he gets back to civilisation – 'Men are good for a quick one but I can't wait for Rome and a real woman . . . men are worse than a Greek') and labels Sebastian a Christian faggot. Maximus can but mock his marvellous beauty and godly dancing. The uniformed centurion, Severus (Barney James), looks lustfully at his naked soldiers as they shave, scour and bathe, but his advances are rejected by Sebastian. Sebastian, it is suggested, is made to suffer for the affront which he poses to Roman authority by refusing to be subject to the centurion's will. Severus destroys Sebastian in order to rid himself of that which he fears in himself. Maximus, meanwhile, subjugates the half-dead Justin by forcing him to fire at the object of his adoration and affection.

Personnel at *Screen*, the Journal of the Society for Education in Film and Television, (some attached to the BFI) broadly welcomed the inclusion of film and television studies in the school and university curriculum, and of film and video as an option in arts school training, but there were differences of opinion as to which film texts (avant-garde or mainstream) and what theory should be appropriated. While Peter Gidal (a tutor at the Royal College of Art in the 1970s) complained of *Screen*'s 'retrograde' reading of Brecht – which certainly lacked his humour, and was often merely gestural – and lambasted Godard for authoritarianism in his films, certain *Screen* contributors endeavoured to bully its readers into pseudo-scientific (psychoanalytic and structuralist) equally authoritarian analyses of material.[33] Not for the first nor last time, other contributors questioned whose interests the BFI was serving. In 1976, a number of prominent film academics resigned in protest, complaining that *Screen* was unnecessarily obscure (when not obtuse) and inaccessible; had no serious interest in educational matters; and that 'The politico-cultural analysis that has

increasingly come to underpin [its] whole theoretical effort is intellectually unsound and unproductive.'[34] Meanwhile, interesting things were happening in British commercial cinema, even if its
formal innovations were not applied to the political and theoretical agenda pursued by *Screen* (and
thereby questioning, perhaps, the formalist presumptions of much of its polemicising).

Hugh Brody's BFI-funded *Nineteen Nineteen* (1984) restores psychoanalysis to its historical origins, featuring as protagonists supposed patients of Freud, confidentially voiced off screen (as if
talking were curing) by Frank Finlay. *Bad Timing* (Nicolas Roeg, 1980, distributed by Rank) casts an
American disciple of Freud, Dr Alex Linden (Art Garfunkel, of pop duo Simon and Garfunkel), as a
research psychoanalyst who works at the Freud Museum and teaches at the University in Vienna.
It opens (with a theme from Tom Waits) by panning across paintings in an art gallery by Gustav
Klimt and Egon Schiele (recalling the Vienna Secession) to a view through a window of the contemporary city. Brody's film is concerned with the historical account of the city (a Jewish patient
emigrates to America to escape persecution under Nazi occupation) while Roeg is concerned with
its sensitive geographical and political position, bordering Czechoslovakia (Central Europe but, in
1980, facing East, towards Russia, rather than West). Zither music recalls the location of Carol
Reed's *The Third Man* (1949) (see Chapter 6). The lake at the end of the film could be East European (to the theme from Pachelbel's Canon), could be West Coast American . . . it could be just a
lake. Meanwhile, Billie Holliday sings, 'The same old story – it's as old as the stars above' – just a
boy and a girl in love.

Bad Timing is much concerned with voyeurism (in which the film's audience, wittingly or unwittingly, is equally implicated), evidence and the telling of truth (visually or verbally). It also seemingly
endorses certain Freudian preconceptions of sexuality while demonising a practitioner of Freudian
theory: quite apart from its impressive technical accomplishment, it is, therefore, a very interesting
film. Alex himself aligns the child witness of Freud's primal scene with the systematised spying
authorised by the political regime of Joseph Stalin: as an Austrian student in his class pertinently
reminds him, he could as well show pictures of himself . . . or anyone. Alex appears to confirm her
observation and his own diagnosis of 'the usual voyeur' as 'a guilt-ridden conservative'. Alex works
undercover (his own lie) for NATO, investigating and vetting political files (including those of Milena
and Stefan). The Czech, Stefan Vognic (Denholm Elliott), loves his wife Milena (Theresa Russell –
who sounds American and, by implication, politically 'safe') sufficiently to allow her to leave him
for Vienna, where she instigates an affair with Alex – although he later admits his jealousy to Alex
directly. Alex harps on about Stefan being thirty years her senior – 'You mean you're not?' she says,
intending his conservatism (as a Freudian, Alex might be supposed to have an answer to this perfectly reasonable observation). The film cuts between past events (Milena and her dead brother,
she says, at a lake in California, witnessed by photographs, and film flashbacks to Milena with
Stefan, with Alex, with other men) and her near death (a desperate suicide attempt in which Alex
is implicated – potentially, morally, a murder) and her eventual chance encounter with Alex at a
hotel in New York. Here, again, the audience too is required to interpret the filmic events and the
evidence presented. Alex's authoritarian attempts to investigate, order and control Milena (through

a knowledge of a past about which she has sometimes lied – 'I wish you'd understand me less and love me more . . . and stop defining,' she protests in an unsent letter) are cut with the investigation of Inspector Netusil (Harvey Keitel) into the circumstances of her near death and their own battle of wills – Alex presuming himself, wrongly, his intellectual superior, and the superior of Czech officialdom (his enquiries into divorce regulations are perfunctorily dismissed). Milena frequently changes her appearance (dress and hair – and her bedsheets) as an indication of her own instability, and of her wanting Alex to love her for what she is (and what she gives now rather than what she has been and what Alex demands of her). 'Who are You?', sing The Who on the backing track. Netusil wills Alex's confession (he persistently evades questioning but bodily betrays himself) as forcibly as Alex wills Milena to confess her attachment to other men – both purport to rely on empirical evidence but both want it confirmed by admission of 'guilt' and, ultimately, believe what they want to believe, compelled by other desires (Alex, perhaps by truth, by power and sexual possessiveness – even in the ambulance, he buttons-up Milena's blouse to stop the paramedic from gazing; Netusil by truth, morality and, perhaps, by a sexual interest akin to voyeurism – he wants Alex to tell about the rape, pointedly designated ravishment – the law, he confesses, does not interest him). Both are professionally overwrought by notions of normality while being fascinated by something else. Netusil acknowledges that taking advantage of someone you love is hiding hatred – coming closer to the truth than Alex is prepared to allow. *Bad Timing*, as a title, refers both, specifically, to the arrival on the scene of Stefan (who avowedly is bothered about Milena for her own sake), pre-empting a potential confession from Alex, and, more generally, to the historic and political circumstances in which the characters find themselves.

Don't Look Now, an adaptation of Daphne du Maurier's 1970 short story, like *Bad Timing*, often uses details and colours to link abrupt shifts between different times and places: brooches are significantly shown in close-up in both films, while door handles and cracked marble flooring are foregrounded in *Don't Look Now*. Purple is Milena's characteristic colour, while a saturated red recurs in *Don't Look Now* in a child's mac, an ambulance blanket, a scarf, boots and a handbag, a church candle, red on a washing line, ink spilt on a slide (a foreboding of blood) and in flash frame. The colour traverses the two landscapes of the film (the lush England of home and school and the misty grey of Venice) and penetrates the mental map of John (Donald Sutherland) and his wife, Laura (Julie Christie), who, at the beginning of the film, lose their young daughter in an accident: Christine drowns in their pond. The couple travel to Venice, where John is employed in rescuing old buildings from the ravages of floods and tides (*The Observer* reported 'Venice in Peril' – its walls crumbling, its lagoon polluted – in 1971 and 1973). Venice (as in Italo Calvino's novel *Invisible Cities*) is portrayed as a labyrinthine city of 'twisting alleyways and sudden squares', dead-ends and too many bridges too similar to one another; as for the tourist couple in Paul Schrader's 1990 *The Comfort of Strangers*, likewise intent upon 'the tasks of tourism the ancient city imposed', it is a romantic and erotic, exotic yet sinister place, in which it is all too easy to lose one's way.[35] But for the elderly English spinsters who attach themselves to Laura and John, the city is more readily navigable: Wendy (Clelia Matania) says it is a city preserved in aspic, with too many shadows, whereas her blind sister and constant companion, Heather (Hilary Mason), deems the city safe, finding her way around by listening to the changing sound of the water. John Milton (the blind poet) loved this city, she says. At first, it seems that Laura is experiencing more difficulty in bearing the guilt and pain of Christine's death, seeking solace in the blind sister's 'second' sight: 'She's trying to get in touch with us, maybe to forgive.' Meanwhile, John apologises, pragmatically, that his wife is ill and insists, bluntly, that Christine is dead – dead – dead. However, Heather recognises John's resistance as his own presentiment of what is to come, 'a curse as well as a gift', and that Christine is attempting to warn rather than console them – a warning which he dreads yet refuses to heed.

The provisional designation 'alternative' indicates a site of exhibition as often as it describes style and content. Roeg's films, commercially distributed, were as stylistically and narratively inventive, with as much purpose, as many art-house films of the decade.

Tarnished Stars and Rough Diamonds

Other films of the 1970s used recognisable and significant locations in Britain itself in the portrayal of unnatural death, its investigation and its revenge: *Gumshoe* (Stephen Frears, 1971) – to be followed by Chris Bernard's 1985 *Letter to Brezhnev* and Philip Saville's 1988 *Fruit Machine* (see Chapter 11) – was set in Liverpool; *Get Carter* – to be followed by Mike Figgis' 1987 *Stormy Monday* and BBC TV's 1997 *Our Friends in the North* (see Chapter 11) – was set in Newcastle; *The Long Good Friday* – to be followed by *Empire State* (Ron Peck, 1987) – was set in London's Docklands, ripe for redevelopment or wasted, as in Jarman's 1987 *The Last of England*. The Cambridgeshire landscape of P. D. James' 1972 *An Unsuitable Job for a Woman* was transposed to Suffolk (as impressively shot as *Akenfield*) for Chris Petit's 1981 adaptation (subsequently remade in 1998), while his *Radio On* stopped off in Bristol.

While two *Sweeney* films (fags, slags, blags and Jags), second-rate spin-offs from the ITV series (David Wickes, 1976; Tom Clegg, 1978), featured policemen operating on the windy side of the law, 1970s television (notably G. F. Newman's 1978 BBC TV *Law and Order*) and film were often concerned with coppers (and other public servants – such as town councillors and town planners) who are thoroughly bent. Margaret Drabble covers similar territory (the strikes and black-outs of the Winter of Discontent, mercenary architects and property developers in cahoots with corrupt officialdom) in her 1977 novel *The Ice Age*. *Get Carter* was reputedly based on the story of an actual gangland killing, while Amber Films worked on its own turf to investigate the record of Poulson and the actual *T. Dan Smith* (1987). *The Long Good Friday* (produced by Handmade Films and initially intended for television) sets its metropolitan action against a shooting in rural Ireland and the activities of the IRA in the capital; meanwhile gangster Harold Shand (Bob Hoskins) endeavours to launder his profits from 'regular' crime (drugs, extortion, violence) by investing in property in collaboration with an American entrepreneur: 'Americans really think they've arrived in England if the upper classes treat them like shit,' he advises his posh moll, Victoria (Helen Mirren); 'play up the Benenden bit'. Jaguars, a Rolls Royce and a motor boat are further proof of his status. One of Harold's gang, Colin (Paul Freeman), is lured in a gay pick-up at a swimming pool to his death;

A calling of the clan: gangsters get strung up on meat hooks in John MacKenzie's 1979 *The Long Good Friday*

Harold's pubs and clubs are then attacked by Irish insurgents. Terrorism 'is special branch – it ain't normal villainy', says Harold's 'pet' policeman, Parkie (with whose help Harold has reigned over his manor peaceably for the past ten years – 'everyone keeping to his own patch'); 'if they're Irish – it's a different game . . . different rules . . .'. 'It's outrageous,' observes Harold, of an attack on his own parents, 'you don't go crucifying someone outside a church on Good Friday.' In a vain attempt to reinstate the old rules, in a set-piece sequence, Harold rounds up his old enemies and hangs them upside down in an abattoir to elicit their support. In spite of Harold's care of his family and 'family' ('the corporation') he is betrayed: he knew that Colin fancied soldiers but being driven to Belfast in a Limehouse mini-cab was taking it a bit far (but it is Jeff [Derek Thompson] who turns him over). At the end, Harold presumes, as he is driven from the Savoy, that he and Victoria have escaped, separately but safely – but a glance over the seat from his driver (whom he and the audience identify as one of the IRA assassins) leaves his fate uncertain.

Both *The Long Good Friday* and *Get Carter* owe some of their continuing popularity to their distinctive scoring, their laconic, drily comic dialogue and their visual pace and style. BBC TV's 2004 gangster saga *The Long Firm* was trailed to the accompaniment of Roy Budd's *Get Carter* theme tune. *Loaded* nominated *Get Carter* 'British pulp noir at its finest' and, in 1996, serialised the film as a cartoon (further virtualising – sad but true – Carter's 'virtual' telephone sex with Britt Ekland as another attraction) (see Chapter 12).[36] While Harold Shand insists to his American backer that British is better ('a sleeping partner's one thing – but not a coma') and that henceforth he'll do business with Krauts, he equally pronounces (as the motor boat surges under Tower Bridge) his pride in being a Londoner. Outer regions of the kingdom are deemed less ruly: Jack Carter (Michael Caine) is warned by his London colleagues against 'going up North'. Suspicions are immediately confirmed when he orders a pint of bitter in a straight glass and pub regulars look askance. The sound of fog horns, mist and back-to-backs confirm the shift of location. But Jack is honouring family duty, visiting relatives: 'That's nice,' says Eric Paice (Ian Hendry), at the races; 'It would be if they were still living,' replies Jack. Combining sex, violence and slapstick humour, drum majorettes strike up outside a Tyneside B&B as Carter opens the landlady's blouse to reveal her purple undies. He proceeds to judge and mete out justice to those implicated in the death of his brother, Frank, and the use of Frank's daughter, Doreen, in porn films – although he is equally accustomed to being the wrong side of the law himself and apparently takes pleasure in violence: 'You're a big man but you're in bad shape – with me it's a fulltime job so behave yourself'; when Margaret, Frank's mistress, tells him that she likes 'a gentleman', Jack retorts that she likes a gentleman 'once a week' (and, duly, straddling her, suffocates her then drowns her); delivering two smoking barrels into another man's guts, he welcomes the prospect of 'Strawberry Fields'. An equally 'suitable' fate for Eric is to force him to drink a full bottle of whisky, repeating his own treatment of Frank. By the same token, Jack's own fate is fair, both in the sense that he has already accomplished all he set out to achieve and that the retribution is equal. On a deserted beach, Jack carries his rifle on his shoulder and laughs contentedly; an anonymous hit-man takes aim, fires, then calmly packs up his gun and walks away.

Blood rites resurface (ironically) in *Gumshoe*, where a would-be private eye, Eddie Ginley (Albert Finney) (an on-duty bingo-caller, off-duty in trenchcoat and soft hat), informs us in Chandler-style voiceover that his 'best girl ran off with his brother'. With a score credited to Andrew Lloyd-Webber and Tim Rice (but owing more, along with its graphics, to Hollywood B-movies), its snappy exchanges ('The day I give you a present, pigs might fly' – 'That's what I mean: thanks for the flying pig') and corny one-liners ('He's not mean – he's just got short arms and deep pockets') there is much which presages Dennis Potter's more elaborately structured 1986 BBC TV *The Singing Detective* (remade US, Keith Gordon, 2003). In *An Unsuitable Job for a Woman*, produced by sometime director Don Boyd, private investigator Cordelia Gray (Pippa Guard) inherits an obligation to a client from her professional partner – as the film opens, she finds him, wrists slashed, sprawled over his desk with a 'suicide note' left for her on a tape recorder. Elizabeth Leaming (Billie Whitelaw), personal assistant to magnate Sir Ronald Callender (Paul Freeman) (business, politics, finance, 'I'm surprised you haven't heard of him,' she says, brusquely), has instigated enquiries into the death of Callender's son, Mark (Dominic Guard) – an apparent suicide. While Elizabeth assumes that it will be easy for young Cordelia to befriend Mark's friends ('to find out why'), Miss Markland (Elizabeth Spriggs), an elderly neighbour, soon establishes age difference as an obstacle: 'I don't like your generation, Miss Gray . . . the men I was brought up with weren't like that'; she says that Mark dropped out of college and his family obligations, 'but at least he directed violence against himself'. Miss Markland refers to the local children as 'pests' but they were friends to Mark and instinctively take care of Cordelia – they are significantly younger than P. D. James intended. Callender senior (who sent Mark away to school – perhaps to make a boy of him) remarks that it's difficult to tell girls and boys apart nowadays. Cordelia takes up residence in Mark's country cottage, wears his clothes, finds his passport and medical records, imagines his hanging body and asks the police for the belt with which he was hanged. Elizabeth (for her own reasons) thinks Cordelia unsuitable for the job while Callender (for his own) finds her very acceptable and promptly beds her. But Cordelia remains unconvinced by the evidence at the scene of the crime (and the police interpretation thereof) and eventually discovers that Elizabeth tampered with the body before reporting the death: Elizabeth, too, has her doubts. Meanwhile, it is feared that Cordelia is better at her job than anticipated and attempts are made to dispose of her in an uncovered well (Mark's belt saves her). Callender (in the night and rain) mistakes Cordelia for Mark. Cordelia's allegiance shifts from her boss, to her colleague (then lover) Callender, to Mark (an alter ego), to Elizabeth (as a woman), who finally shoots Callender to avenge his son's murder. *An Unsuitable Job for a Woman*, an adaptation from a novel by a highly revered and popular novelist, seems to me to be an undervalued film.[37] Yet within the compass of a fairly standard investigative formula it manages to invoke many questions addressed by the supposedly 'alternative' cinema of the 1970s; Billie Whitelaw (an underrated talent) crosses from stage, to 'art-house' television to mainstream film (as in *Gumshoe*); it anticipates much of the agenda of television drama of the 1980s and 1990s.

The Man Who Fell to Earth (Nicolas Roeg, 1976)

It's on Amerika's tortured brow
Mickey Mouse has grown up a cow
Now the workers have struck for fame
'Cause Lennon's on sale again
See the mice in their million hordes
From Ibeza to the Norfolk Broads
Rule Brittania is out of bounds
To my mother, my dog and clowns
But the film is a saddening bore
'Cause I wrote it ten times before
It's about to be writ again
As I ask you to focus on
Sailors fighting in the dance hall
Oh man! Look at these cavemen go
It's the freakiest show
Take a look at the Lawman
Beating up the wrong guy
Oh man! Wonder if he'll ever know
He's in the best selling show
Is there life on Mars?

David Bowie, *Hunky Dory*, 1971

In 1985, Julian Petley wrote of the 'failure of the critics to get to grips with the truly mythic Presentations of Self by Bowie in *The Man Who Fell to Earth* and Jagger in *Performance*, neither of which were "great performances" in the British theatrical tradition, but, rather, more "Hollywoodian" explorations and invocations of star personae'.[38] This tends to endorse what Nicolas Roeg himself said of his direction of Art Garfunkel, Mick Jagger and David Bowie when he was interviewed for *The Face* in 1983: '[They are] all interesting men. I wanted to look at acting another way. Acting schools have turned out too many competent people and competence means that inspiration can get lost. . . . I think rock stars see their performance a different way.'[39] Adam Faith, Ringo Starr, Keith Moon and David Essex likewise appeared in *Godspell* (David Greene, 1973), *That'll Be the Day* (Claude Whatham, 1973) and *Stardust* (Michael Apted, 1974), Sting in *Quadrophenia* and *Radio On* (with a soundtrack from Lena Lovich, Ian Dury and Bowie's rendition in German of *Heroes*), Toyah in *Quadrophenia* and Jarman's *Jubilee* and *The Tempest*. The Beatles' George Harrison moved into production with his funding of Handmade Films. David Bowie has frequently repositioned himself in culture – variously as rock star, patron of the arts and actor (in

Newton (David Bowie) discusses patents with his lawyer (Buck Henry) in Nicolas Roeg's 1976 *The Man Who Fell to Earth*

Alan Clarke's BBC TV 1982 adaptation of Brecht's *Baal* and in Oshima's 1982 adaptation of Laurens van der Post's *Merry Christmas Mr Lawrence*, as well as for Roeg) – but as a musician in the 1970s most often changed his stage persona. While his first appearance in *The Man Who Fell*, descending a slope from his spaceship wearing a duffel coat, once an item of naval uniform issue (as in *In Which We Serve* and *The Cruel Sea*), then a marker of political resistance (as in *Look Back in Anger*), is reminiscent of the anaemic, hippy Bowie of *Hunky Dory* (1971); he later adopts the trilby and suit of 1970s retro art-deco *Diamond Dogs* (1974) and appears in an androgenous silver body-stocking and make-up reminiscent of *Ziggy Stardust and the Spiders from Mars* (1972). In tacit reference to these shifts of role, Alan Yentob's 1975 BBC television documentary presented Bowie as 'cracked actor'.

Like much science fiction, *The Man Who Fell* deploys a yet to be realised or impossible scenario as a critique of past and present society and, like many of Roeg's protagonists, Bowie is cast as an outsider: his arrival at Honeyville and his first encounter with garish, trash culture are echoed by Gary Oldman in *Track 29* (Nicolas Roeg, 1988), with Mary Lou (Candy Clark) a close (but down-market) relation to the later Linda Henry (Teresa Russell). *Demon Seed* (1977) (directed by Donald Cammell, Roeg's collaborator on *Performance* – see Chapter 9) is similarly concerned with copying, patenting and the exploitation of resources. Initially, Bowie gives his name as Newton, invoking a genius of pure science and precursor of the Enlightenment. Asked if he is Lithuanian, he later produces a passport which identifies him as an Englishman, although no Thomas Sussex can be traced by the corporate authorities. Ultimately, he is not only, quite literally (as Mary Lou reminds him), an alien but also a non-person.

The narrative is picked up in voiceover by Nathan Bryce (Rip Torn), a self-confessed 'clichéd disillusioned scientist', who, in a distant past (it is suggested), once dared, like Icarus, to dream of flying too close to the sun . . . and wishes that he could dream again. Separated from his wife, he vainly seeks solace and excitement in a succession of one-night stands with college girls the age of his daughter. Inspired by Newton's invention of a self-developing camera, Bryce offers his services as a researcher but insists at the outset that these will be withdrawn if the company intends to manufacture a weapon. First we hear Holst's Mars theme from his *Planets* suite (a harbinger of war), later replaced by Venus (the bringer of peace) and Newton reassures Bryce that he need not be suspicious. However, it is Bryce who betrays their trust, discovering Newton's secret identity by means of a X-ray camera (which registers the alien's innards as a blank), selling him to a new master, Mr Peters (and thereby becoming a fallen man in the biblical sense). Mary Lou, the hotel maid who insists that she truly loves Tommy for himself and not for his money, is terrified when he reveals himself in his true form. She tries to bind him in a domestic and parochial claustrophobia of cookies and clapper-board churches. But she, too, ultimately finds her price and her man in Nathan. Even the chauffeur, Arthur, transfers his allegiance. Newton is denied the opportunity to return to his wife and family – a one-way journey would be unprecedented – and his planet is denied the water which he had been despatched to procure. When Oliver Farnsworth, the lawyer (Buck Henry), surveys Newton's proposed innovations, he tells him that he has nine basic patents

– a $300 million deal – and that he can take Eastman-Kodak, Dupont and RCA . . . 'for starters'. World Enterprises soon becomes a multi-media corporation. Newton's ambitions are seemingly more honourable: his research interest is energy – 'transference of energy' – and the conservation of fuel which may prove the key if he is ever to return home. But Newton having appointed Farnsworth as his sole go-between with the outside world means that, with Farnsworth out of the way, Newton can be held hostage in perpetuity.

The film itself is reluctant to celebrate the technology which, says Bryce, has 'over-stimulated' World Enterprises. Space travel is figured as a departure prompted by a sense of necessity rather than enterprise: this fallen man is as lonely as Bowie's Major Tom and misses his wife as much as Elton John's Rocket Man. 'His super-frail appearance', noted Alexander Walker, 'contrasted strikingly with his super-power status.'[40] Little is made of the potential for screen spectacle in such devices as the quasi-holographic image of Newton's family, which materialises when he holds a section of film up to the sunlight, nor the polaroid roll of film which one of the girls on campus unravels in Bryce's bed. Newton's spaceship is more primitive hut than Wonderful Flying Machine, with fragile Tiger Moth wings and wearing its rockwool warm side (in the manner of Tennyson's *Hiawatha*) outside.

Newton remains unimpressed by progress American-style. Sitting in front of a bank of television screens (newsreports which never mention his planet, cartoons, natural history programmes, reruns of Reed's *The Third Man* and Ustinov's *Billy Budd* – the full gamut of Raymond Williams' 1973 *Television: Technology and Cultural Form*) he observes that the strange thing is that 'it shows but doesn't tell'. For all the anxiety prompted by the sight of Newton's bizarre bodily appearance and oozing bodily functions, there is much which is represented as equally freakish (but nevertheless taken for granted) in the habits of modern America: Mary Lou's false nails and eyelashes match his lenses and hair. Sometimes his universe seems entirely similar. When Mary Lou asks him about his children, he says: 'They're like children – exactly like children.'

But Newton, it seems, has fallen from a different zone of time as well as space. While Peters, Bryce and Mary Lou grow old and grey around him, he remains in limbo; travelling with Mary Lou through the American countryside to find the spot where he landed, he urges Arthur not to drive so fast and sees the field populated by America's first settlers. Newton tells Bryce that there have always been visitors. Indeed, there is much of the Corporation's treatment of Newton which recalls the fate of American natives, those who preceded the settlers, his health and spirit wrecked by hard liquor to which his alien body had not been accustomed; unable to accept Newton's difference, surgeons fuse lenses to his eyeballs to make him look the same and, now that he cannot escape, hold him captive as an experimental specimen in an artificial zoo-like enclosure, an indoors which imitates an outdoors. 'Tommy's suffered enough,' pines Mary Lou, 'he's going to die like an animal.' She protests that he has failed to understand American protocol because he is essentially simple.

Conversely, *The Man Who Fell* offers a commentary on American expansion into the outer world, into other territories considered alien: having exploited certain resources (Newton's intellectual property) it then deprives them of others (the water which would have saved his family from an agonising death in the desert). Mary Lou fails to connect this alien being with the god whom she simply believes 'has got to be out there somewhere'. Mr Peters, meanwhile, is busy determining a social ecology: 'This is modern America and we're going to keep it that way'. Newton himself concludes that his own planet would probably have behaved likewise. Sadly, this contemporary morality play proffers no readily recognisable Heavenly City as its safe and final destination.

Notes

1. John Fowles, *Daniel Martin* (London: Jonathan Cape, 1977), pp. 306–7; compare Satyajit Ray's comments, quoted in Charles Barr's introduction to *All Our Yesterdays* (London: BFI, 1986), p. 9.
2. Alexander Walker, *National Heroes: British Cinema in the Seventies and Eighties* (London: Harrap, 1985), p. 115.
3. Leon Hunt, *British Low Culture: from Safari Suits to Sexploitation* (London: Routledge, 1998), p. 26; David McGillivray, *Doing Rude Things* (London: Sun Tavern Fields, 1992), pp. 15 and 67.
4. Des Wilson, 'The Brutal World of Michael Winner', *The Observer*, 27 July 1974, pp. 35–41.
5. 'Joseph Losey on What's Wrong with British Films', *The Observer*, 23 September 1973, p. 60.
6. 'Britain's showbiz Mr Big', *The Observer*, 9 December 1973, p. 43, and John Lahr (ed.), *The Diaries of Kenneth Tynan* (London: Bloomsbury, 2001), p. 128.
7. *The Observer*, 27 April 1975, p. 22.
8. Ken Tynan, 'Eric Morecambe – Superstar', *The Observer*, 9 September 1973, pp. 20–3.
9. For commentary on stand-up comics on television, see Raymond Williams, 'A New Way of Seeing', *The Listener*, 2 January 1969, p. 27.
10. Nick Cull, 'Camping on the Borders: History, Identity and Britishness in the *Carry On* Costume Parodies, 1963–74', in Claire Monk and Amy Sargeant (eds), *British Historical Cinema* (London: Routledge, 2002), pp. 92–109.
11. Derek Jarman, *Dancing Ledge* (London: Quartet Books, 1984).
12. *The Observer*, 28 March 1971, p. 6.
13. Peter Gidal, 'Film as Film', in David Curtis and Deke Dusinberre, *A Perspective on English Avant-Garde Film* (London: The Arts Council, 1978), p. 22; Alexander Walker, on the other hand, rates Russell's films the best of the decade.
14. John Walker, 'Something to offend everyone', *The Observer*, 27 July 1975, pp. 30–3; see also Meriel McCooey, 'You too can be a Fred Astaire', *The Sunday Times Magazine*, 16 April 1972, p. 44, on the revival of tap dancing.
15. Hunt, *British Low Culture*, p. 142.
16. Ibid., p. 146.
17. *The Observer*, 4 March 1973, p. 34.
18. Martin Amis, *Dead Babies* [1975] (Harmondsworth: Penguin: 2000), p. 56.
19. Lahr, *The Diaries of Kenneth Tynan*, p. 54.
20. George Melly, 'How Pop has Changed', *The Observer*, 7 October 1973, p. 24.
21. 'A Modern Vanity Fair', *The Observer*, 29 April 1973, pp. 30–3.
22. See Laura Mulvey, 'You Don't Know What is Happening Do You, Mr Jones?' [1973], in Marsha Rowe (ed.), *Spare Rib Reader* (Harmondsworth: Penguin, 1982), pp. 48–57; for American reception of *A Clockwork Orange* see Janet Staiger, *Perverse Spectators* (New York: New York University Press, 2000), pp. 93–111.

23. 'Cavaliers and Roundheads', *The Observer*, 22 February 1970, p. 24.

24. Stuart Hall, Charles Critcher, Tony Jefferson, John Clarke and Brian Roberts, *Policing the Crisis: Mugging, the State and Law and Order* (London: Macmillan, 1978), p. 16.

25. Stephen Dwoskin, *Film Is . . .* (London: Peter Owen, 1975), p. 73.

26. *The Observer*, 26 January 1975.

27. Dwoskin, *Film Is . . .*, p. 68.

28. Jarman, *Dancing Ledge*, p. 128.

29. See Raymond Williams, 'A Lecture on Realism', *Screen* vol. 18 no. 1, Spring 1977, pp. 61–74, and Colin McArthur and Colin MacCabe in Tony Bennett *et al* (eds), *Popular Television and Film* (London: BFI, 1981).

30. See Jules Holledge, 'The Lost Theatre' [1977], in Rowe, *Spare Rib Reader*, pp. 277–83, and Lis Rhodes, 'Whose History?' [1979], in Michael O'Pray, *Avant-Garde Film* (Luton: John Libbey, 1996), pp. 193–7.

31. *The Observer*, 20 December 1970, pp. 24–5; while Welch chose 'new clinging knitwear for Spring' other actresses (Helen Mirren and Julie Christie) also turned models, with Charlotte Rampling pledging not to buy wild animal furs and skins; model Marisa Berenson turned actor for Visconti and Kubrick; Britt Ekland endorsed 3M products.

32. See, for instance, Giorgio Vasari on Antonio Pollaiuolo's *Saint Sebastian*, now in the National Gallery, as a portrait of Gino di Ludovico Capponi, in *Lives of the Artists*, vol. II [1568] (London: Dent, 1963), p. 81.

33. See Colin MacCabe, 'Realism and the Cinema: Notes on Some Brechtian Theses', *Screen* vol. 15 no. 2, Summer 1974, pp. 7–27; Stuart Hood, 'Brecht on Radio', *Screen* vol. 20 no. 3/4, 1979, pp. 16–23, and Peter Gidal's letter to the editor, *Screen* vol. 17 no. 2, Summer 1976, pp. 131–2.

34. See Edward Buscombe, Christine Gledhill, Alan Lovell, Christopher Williams, 'Why We Have Resigned from the Board of *Screen*', *Screen* vol. 17 no. 2, Summer 1976, pp. 106–16.

35. See Ian McEwan, *The Comfort of Strangers* [1981] (London: Vintage, 1997).

36. See Mike Hodges discussion of *Get Carter* and Robert Murphy, 'A Revenger's Tragedy', in Steve Chibnall and Robert Murphy (eds), *British Crime Cinema* (London: Routledge, 1999), pp. 121–3; Steve Chibnall, *Get Carter* (London: I. B. Tauris, 2003), p. 100.

37. Iain Sinclair suggests that Chris Petit's vision of the film was much compromised by intervention from its producers and that P. D. James (for whom Sinclair shows little reverence) regarded the result as more Petit's film than hers; see *Lights Out for the Territory* (London: Granta, 1997); see also Geoffrey Nowell-Smith, 'Radio On', *Screen* vol. 20 no. 3/4, Winter 1979, pp. 29–39.

38. Julian Petley, 'Reaching for the Stars', in Martin Auty and Nick Roddick (eds), *British Cinema Now* (London: BFI, 1985), p. 115.

39. Neil Norman interview with Roeg, *The Face*, June 1983, p. 60.

40. See Alexander Walker, *National Heroes*, p. 138; John Walker, *The Once and Future Film* (London: Methuen, 1985), p. 97, and Tom Moylan, *Scraps of the Untainted Sky* (Boulder: Westview Press, 2000), p. 4.

Chapter 11 | 1980s

Boxed Sets

The 1980s were self-consciously preoccupied with literary and visual style and presentation across a range of contemporary cultural and political activity. 'Britain may have led the world into the industrial revolution,' Matthew Fox (Frank Finlay) informs the journalist James Penfield (Jonathan Pryce) in Richard Eyre's 1983 *The Ploughman's Lunch*; 'We now lead in TV commercials . . . The Ploughman's Lunch – traditional English fare – in fact the product of a '60s advertising campaign designed to get more people to eat in pubs . . . a complete fabrication of the past.' Bob Hoskins (aka George) of Neil Jordan's 1986 *Mona Lisa* is released from seven years in clink to realise that life in London has changed in his absence: tea comes in bags (Earl Grey or Lapsang, whereas he wants just 'leaves'), spaghetti has become ornamental, male waiters and porn shop assistants sport pony tails. The Sunday supplements were enhanced and expanded to accommodate a growing number of self-appointed style gurus (and advertisements for consumer products); there was a proliferation of magazines aimed at a younger market, often carrying relatively little advertising: *The Face* ('The World's Best Dressed Magazine'), founded in 1980 by Nick Logan, formerly of *NME* and teen mag *Smash Hits*, to cover music, fashion, film and events; *i-D* devoted editions to a variety of issues and articles to a number of media, including Celluloi-D. *The Face* carried items from Julie Birchall (on all and everything), Tony Parsons, Robert Elms (on music and style), Jon Savage and Peter York (official chronicler of the Sloane Ranger).[1] British film contributed to a heightened awareness of co-ordinated design but also, in some instances (most vociferously in the case of 'heritage' cinema), became the butt of criticism, even in the style mags themselves, for prioritising style over content: Tony Scott's *The Hunger* (US, 1983) was accused of exhibiting 'too much fashion, not enough fear' and Mo Trix, commenting on the Imperial revival as 'All the Raj', complained of David Lean's racism (being more pro-English than Forster's original novel) and his lack of concern with the offence which he caused during the making of *A Passage to India* (1984).[2]

Substantial raids and exchanges between film and other media continued and intensified. Richard Eyre (with *Ploughman's Lunch*) and David Hare (with *Strapless* [1988]) moved from stage to screen as director and writer; Hare both wrote and directed *Wetherby* (1985) and *Paris by Night* (1988). Trevor Nunn directed David Edgar's script for *Lady Jane* (1985), concerning the short reign

Charlotte Rampling as Iron Lady in David Hare's 1988 *Paris by Night* and political shenanigans of Lady Jane Grey and the English court (previously covered by Gains-borough's *Tudor Rose* – see Chapter 5). Julian Mitchell developed the screenplay for *Another Country* (Marek Kanievska, 1984), from his own stageplay, while *Insignificance* (from Terry Johnson's stageplay) was filmed by Nicolas Roeg in 1985. Harold Pinter adapted the elaborate self-reflexivity of John Fowles' 1969 novel *The French Lieutenant's Woman* (Karel Reisz, 1981) to a more tedious film-within-a-film format, matching the theme of middle-class infidelity in his own stageplay and filmplay *Betrayal* (David Jones, 1982) – with Jeremy Irons pretty much duplicating the same self-tortured role. Pinter also provided the screenplay for John Irvin's 1985 film of Russell Hoban's novel, *Turtle Diary* (concerning characters, constrained by circumstance, who organise the release of cumbersome creatures into the freedom of the ocean and thereby find themselves). Willy Russell adapted his own *Educating Rita* (Lewis Gilbert, 1983) for the screen – concerning a young woman whose horizons are broadened by studying at university and who, in finding herself, in return, teaches her tutor the importance of a decent haircut – Julie Walters playing Rita in both versions. Russell's *Shirley Valentine* (Lewis Gilbert, 1989) transferred with Pauline Collins as a middle-aged woman who rediscovers her sunnier, younger self through travel.

Sting, then lead singer with The Police, took the role of the incubus/angel figure Martin Taylor in Dennis Potter's *Brimstone and Treacle* (Richard Loncraine, 1982) and returned to his roots in the Newcastle-based *Stormy Monday* (Mike Figgis, 1987); Roger Daltrey followed his appearance in *Tommy* (see Chapter 10) by starring with Adam Faith as celebrity con *McVicar* (Tom Clegg, 1980); Phil Collins followed suit with his misconceived casting in *Buster* (David Green, 1988). Fine Young Cannibals' gorgeous Roland Gift made his screen debut in *Sammy and Rosie Get Laid* (Stephen Frears, 1987) progressing to *Scandal* (Michael Caton-Jones, 1988), while David Bowie furthered his acting career with *Absolute Beginners* (1986), *The Hunger* and *Merry Christmas Mr Lawrence*, also starring and scored by Japanese idol Ryuichi Sakomoto (Nagisa Oshima, 1982). He also provided the theme music for the award-winning animation (a growth area in the 1980s) from Raymond Briggs' book *When the Wind Blows* (1986): OAP James Bloggs (voiced by John Mills) and house-proud wife Hilda (voiced by Peggy Ashcroft) find that Second World War rhetoric and spirit (and memories of Monty) alongside the Government's advisory leaflets *Protect and Survive* and *The Householder's Guide to Survival* provide insufficient defence against a nuclear attack from the East ('Funny to think that the Russkies were on our side in the War,' comments James). Conversely, Stuart Goddard, who had appeared as the grubby sex-object in Jarman's 1978 *Jubilee* (see Chapter 10), launched himself in New Romantic ruffles and spangles as teenage heart-throb Adam Ant (although for parents of teenagers, the name evoked a 1960s television series). Alex Cox presented the decline and fall of the Sex Pistol's Sid Vicious, while answering accusations of historical inaccuracy by saying that *Sid and Nancy* (1986) was intended as no more than a love story. Furthermore, ex-Beatle George Harrison crossed over as executive producer at Handmade Films (*Mona Lisa* and *Withnail and I* [Bruce Robinson, 1986]) and Richard Branson extended his Virgin empire with his backing of *1984* (Michael Radford, 1984), a vehicle for the promotion of RCA recording artists, The Eurythmics; thereafter he quickly acquired cold feet and moved into video distribution.

Indeed, watching *1984* at home (as has increasingly become common practice since the explosion of video recorder sales in Britain in the 1980s – confounding Raymond Williams' predictions), fronted by The Eurythmics' promo video (as seen on TV), one is even more aware of these products as pre-packaged, boxed sets.

Between film and television there were the usual dealings in present and future genres, and in personnel in front of and behind the camera. Granada Television matched the lavishness of big screen production with its period dramas *Brideshead Revisited* (1981) and *The Jewel in the Crown* (1984), while Ben Cross followed his starring role in *Chariots of Fire* (Hugh Hudson, 1981) with *The Citadel* (BBC TV, 1983) and *The Far Pavilions* (Goldcrest for ITV, 1984); ex-advertising man Hugh Hudson was hired by the Labour Party to make its promo video for the 1987 General Election and by British Airways. The BBC continued to produce its standard fare of quality adaptations from the classics alongside social commentary, in the form of Alan Bleasdale's *Boys from the Blackstuff* (Philip Saville, BBC TV 1982) and *Threads* (1984 – envisaging the consequences of a nuclear attack on Sheffield), and Troy Kennedy Martin's seminal series *Edge of Darkness* (Martin Campbell, 1986). Joanne Whalley-Kilmer, the Gaia activist in *Edge of Darkness*, appeared in the BBC's *The Singing Detective* (1986) and the Bleasdale film *No Surrender* (Peter Smith, 1985); *Dance with a Stranger* (Mike Newell, 1984) provided her with a rehearsal role for her star billing as Christine Keeler in *Scandal*. Tom Bell performed sterling service in Granada Television's series *Holmes and Watson*, appearing also in sinister guise in Granada Films' adaptation of Angela Carter's *The Magic Toyshop* (David Wheatley, 1986) and in *Wish You Were Here* (David Leland, 1987). Ex-Python Michael Palin appeared with Maggie Smith in Alan Bennett's *A Private Function* (Malcolm Mowbray, 1984), among a similar parade of English eccentrics in *The Missionary* (Richard Loncraine, 1981), again with Maggie Smith, and in *Time Bandits* (Terry Gilliam, 1981), while John Cleese delivered a role somewhere between his 'Prince Philip' (for the Sheriff of Nottingham) in *Time Bandits* and television's Basil Fawlty (even repeating his car-beating on a public phone box) for the manic school headmaster Brian Stimpson in *Clockwise* (Christopher Morahan, 1985). The formula was repeated for the uptight solicitor Archie Leach (an amusingly incongruous reference to Cary Grant) in *A Fish Called Wanda*, a 1988 reprise for Charles Crichton, erstwhile director of *An Alligator Named Daisy* (1955) (see Chapter 8), Cleese playing alongside Palin and Americans on the make (Kevin Kline with Jamie Lee Curtis, as the lover masquerading as his sister, improbably seduced by Archie's fluency in Russian). Tim Roth was launched into films, including *A World Apart* (Chris Menges, 1987), by his appearance as the articulate skinhead, Trevor, in Central TV's *Made in Britain* (Alan Clarke, 1983), one of the finest and most memorable 'films' of the decade, scripted by David Leland and shot by Chris Menges. Zenith's *The Hit* (Stephen Frears, 1984) cast Roth as Myron, the rookie, alongside Braddick (John Hurt), the seasoned gangster, despatched to retrieve Parker (Terence Stamp) who has grassed to the police and escaped to sanctuary in Spain: philosophically, Parker accepts that some time the past will catch up with him – his power resides in his ability to foresee and control the situation once that time arrives. Margi Clarke's role as Teresa in *Letter to Brezhnev* (Chris Bernard, 1985) seemingly established her credentials as an after-the-watershed agony aunt on Channel Four: 'I've had my knickers pulled off me by more married men than you've had hot dinners,' she says reassuringly to her best friend Elaine, 'I've got a degree in men'; 'Be strong and see it through,' she advises, convinced that the Foreign Office has concocted a wife for Peter in the hope of preventing Elaine from going to Russia to be with him.

A new crop of alternative comedians moved from stand-up (often at London's Comedy Store) to performing and writing for television and film – following the trajectory of their music hall pre-cursors (see Chapter 5). The trend continued into the 1990s with Lee Evans' casting in a dark and quirky variant of the familial secrets and lies theme, *Funny Bones* (Peter Chelsom, 1995). Often this work took the form of pastiche (as in The Comic Strip's Channel Four 1982 *Five Go Mad in Dorset* and 1983 *Five Go Mad on Mescalin* – spoofing Enid Blyton's children's stories and Gerald Landau's 1957 serial, *Five on a Treasure Island* – and Dick Clement's 1983 *Bullshot Crummond* (compared by *The Face* to a Glen Baxter cartoon – spoofing Sapper McNeile's Bulldog Drummond). Frequently it had a satirical, political edge (as in The Comic Strip's BBC TV 1990 *GLC: the Carnage Continues*, and its feature films *Supergrass* [Peter Richardson, 1985] and *Eat the Rich* [Peter Richardson, 1987]): this was a time when even Ben Elton was political. Robbie Coltrane moved from comedy (in his contributions as Thomas in the sometimes surreal *Mona Lisa* and dragging-up as Annabelle, the Liverpool nightclub queen, in Philip Saville's *The Fruit Machine* and in Jonathan Lynn's 1990 *Nuns on the Run*) to straight roles (the dubious status of the customs officer in *Chinese Boxes* and the inscrutable Scipione Borghese in Jarman's 1986 *Caravaggio* predicating the flawed police psy-chologist, Fitz, in Channel Four's *Cracker* series of the 1990s).

Consequently, there is much which aligns the 1980s with British cinema before and since, in spite of there being much talk at the time of a distinct renaissance in film production. The trum-peting of British film and the initiatives of British Film Year in 1985 bear some comparison with the British Film Weeks of the 1920s (see Chapter 4). Colin Welland's air-punching at the Oscars cere-mony in 1982, following the success of *Chariots of Fire*, seemed to single out Hollywood as key competitor (as has film policy, apparently, in the new millennium). The significance of the new sym-biosis between television and film, however, may have lain rather in British cinema's ability to address its home audience adequately than selling an acceptable package to the outside world. The example set by Channel Four was soon followed by Granada, Central, and the BBC, films often resourced from an amalgam of interests: Mike Newell's 1988 *Soursweet*, for instance, was backed by state funds (through British Screen) together with Zenith (Central) and FilmFour; *The Kitchen Toto* (Harry Hook, 1987) attracted funding from Cannon, British Screen and FilmFour International. *Fellow Traveller* (1989) was co-funded by the BBC and the BFI, while *Melancholia* (Andi Engel, 1989) attracted backing from Germany, with Channel Four and the BFI. As Lola Young has observed, the remit of the new Channel Four (launched in 1982) to cater for 'minorities' proved crucial to aspirant black film-makers and Channel Four provided funding for such features as Hanif Kureishi's *My Beautiful Laundrette* (Stephen Frears, 1985) and Horace Ove's *Playing Away* (1986).[3] There was some criticism that films made under these terms and destined for television tended to 'think small', although they may have thereby reached a wider audience than has since become the case with 'pay for view' channels. Certainly, the investment in film was not sufficient to guarantee British film quality of production, new security, nor a safe share of the world market. Media commentators warned against complacency. Interviewing David Puttnam, producer of *Chariots of Fire* (and subsequently *The Killing Fields* [Roland Joffe, 1984] and *The Mission* [Roland Joffe, 1986], prior to his inglorious departure States-side), Neil Norman reported for *The Face* in January 1983:

> Channel Four cannot bear the burden of indigenous film-making alone. A substantial shake-up in government arts financing and other media institutions like the BBC is needed to consolidate creativity. The marketing, distribution and exhibition of the home product needs to be considered and changed quickly if we are to sustain what Puttnam called 'a moment of vigour without parallel in the film industry's chequered seventy-year history.' [4]

Big History and Personal Pasts

Karen (Suzanna Hamilton), in *Wetherby*, tells schoolteacher Jean Travers (Vanessa Redgrave) of her trip to the cinema with John (a violent stranger) to see 'the film about the Indian': 'Afterwards he couldn't stop talking. He thought this, he thought that. The philosophy of non-violence and so on. And I really didn't think anything. Except obviously the film was very long.' What seemed most extraordinary about Richard Attenborough's *Gandhi* (1982) was that it had been made at all. It drew a tour de force performance from Ben Kingsley, recording the life of the Mahatma from his studies in London, his practice as a barrister in South Africa, the struggle for Indian Independence and the War of Partition, to his eventual assassination in 1948. By any reckoning, these are significant events in British colonial history which bear upon the constituency of contemporary Britain and are internationally important given that skirmishes and atrocities between India and Pakistan continued into the 1980s; Prime Minister Indira Gandhi was assassinated by Sikhs in 1984. Epic in scale, stupendously spectacular in its management of crowds and effects, luscious in its cinematography, the history which it actually delivered nevertheless seemed somewhat simplified and curiously outmoded. It was as if Welland's caricature college dons (John Gielgud and Lindsay Anderson) in *Chariots of Fire* had swapped their gowns for uniforms. The very notion of the heroic biopic, even when devoted to the quiet heroism of Gandhi, seemed to have had its day. Jean Travers voices the fashionable rhetoric of historical and literary studies with her class (even if only to dismiss it): 'Is Shakespeare worth reading although it's only about kings?'

Robert Bolt's screenplay for *The Mission* tacitly imports lessons from history into the present, while again foregrounding the role of a particular individual, Rodrigo Mendoza (Robert De Niro), in a personal story of conversion, sacrifice and salvation. Gloriously photographed by Chris Menges, the location (the rainforest bordering Argentina, Paraguay and Brazil) is as much a subject as a background of the film. Mendoza, having killed his brother in a fit of jealousy over a woman (Cherie Lunghi), opts for an arduous penance by joining the Jesuit brothers, led by Father Gabriel (Jeremy Irons), who have established themselves among the Guarini Indians. Where previous missionaries have failed (in the prologue, one martyr, tied to a cross, is sent over a waterfall),

Gabriel, confronted by spears, persuades the natives of his spiritual purpose by sitting down and playing the recorder.[5] While the Jesuits preach Christianity, teach the Indians Old World cultural practice and introduce modern methods of farming on a 'fair trade' basis, Spain and Portugal seek to exploit the territory for commercial gain and enslave the population, not least as conscripts to their armies. In 1758, the Papacy sends its emissary (Ray Macanally) – the film's intermittent narrator – to investigate. He determines that the Mission of San Carlos should be vacated and bartered in the interests of maintaining French, Spanish and Portuguese state support for the Catholic Church in Europe; the Guarini chief informs him that he, too, is a king and that his concerns merit equal consideration. The Jesuits (an order, not a democracy, we are reminded) are divided in their response. Mendoza and Brother John (Liam Neeson) want to renounce their vows and take up arms against the European soldiers, who are initially reluctant to fire upon and raze familiar emblems of religious authority. Leaving his post for a moment to save a single child, Mendoza is shot down; Gabriel leads his community in passive resistance – and slaughter ensues. In spite of – or perhaps because of – its political contradictions (the Indians are encouraged to demonstrate their 'civilisation' and consequent right to freedom by a display of European ceremony) and its queasy sentimentality, the subject matter of *The Mission* continues to deserve attention; in 1987 it was rewarded with a Palme d'Or at Cannes.

For the most part, British cinema's engagement with the past in the 1980s was less concerned with the lives of national leaders than with history 'from underneath'. Its representation of the past tended to be more intimate, often dealing with the past of living memory, either offering an individual perspective as an antidote to or alongside Big History (such as Boorman's *Hope and Glory*, Michael Radford's 1983 *Another Time, Another Place* or Mowbray's *A Private Function*, in which the home front variously survives and thrives in the Second World War and its aftermath) or suggesting the complexities of individual allegiances in a given political scenario. *Ascendancy* (Edward Bennett, 1982) has a sister bereaved after the First World War (played by singer Julie Covington) caught in the sectarian divide in Ireland in 1920. The television drama *Staying On* (Granada, 1980) (narrating the return of a retired couple, played by Celia Johnson and Trevor Howard, from Africa) and Mary McMurray's *The Assam Garden* (1985) (in which a widow of the Raj [Deborah Kerr] is shaken from her indulgence in a false nostalgia through the friendship of an Indian neighbour [Madhur Jaffrey]) are narrower in focus but are interesting in their non-celebratory treatment of Empire. *The Kitchen Toto* is set against the 1950 Mau-Mau rebellion in Kenya (resulting in the deaths, we are informed, of eighty Europeans and 14,000 Kenyans). It opens with a Christian black priest urging his congregation to renounce the Kikuyu tribal oath which calls on them to massacre the whites. Following his assassination by rebels, his son Mwangi (Edwin Mahinda) is offered a job in the household of a British police chief, John Graham (Bob Peck). But the rebels force him to swear allegiance to their cause. While Graham's wife (Phyllis Logan) affects superiority towards the natives as a mark of her own inferior status in the colonial hierarchy (initially imitated in the imperiousness and false bravura of their noxious young son, Edward [Ronald Pirie]), Graham protects Mwangi as an act of simple kindness. While the boy suffers at the hands of whites (especially a brutal Afrikaaner), he also witnesses black on black violence and encounters Kikuyu and non-Kikuyu blacks employed in the colonial police force. Edward's forced assumption of manhood (as he attempts to protect his mother and baby sibling) has tragic consequences. Meanwhile, Graham's own personal loyalties and responsibilities are questioned when he embarks on an affair. This overlooked and relatively small film manages to incorporate more 'psychological pressure' (as Graham advises his wife) than the entirety of *Gandhi*. It also, I think, begs the question why the generality of film-makers in the 1980s (and subsequent critics) have neglected to consider areas other than India and other ranks in their discussion of the 'otherness' of Britain's ex-colonies.

Another Time, Another Place, set in 1944 in a small community in the north of Scotland, presents the seasonal rotation of crops and labour and the perennial hardships of subsistence farming: Jane (Phyllis Logan) and Dougall (Tom Watson) welcome the additional income they receive for taking on three Italian POWs. 'There are other times and other places . . . even the Italians have bikes,' Jane tells Dougall, imagining how the money might be spent. As in Bill Douglas' *My Childhood* (see Chapter 10), where a young friendless boy is befriended by a German POW – equally thought an oddball by his compatriots – for Jane, the arrival of the exotic foreigners opens other prospects and she dares to dream. One of their lodgers, Luigi, is attracted to her and while she at first refuses his desperate attempts to make love to her, equally desperate for a physical and sexual closeness she has not experienced with Dougall, she eventually gives way. Had they met at another time and under different circumstances, life might have been different for them both.[6] Meanwhile, a neighbour, Jesse, receives news of the death of her husband at Montecasino. Another neighbour, Else, is raped in the woods and she accuses Luigi although she admits to Jane that 'all Italians look the same to me'. Risking her marriage and her place in the community, Jane tells the police that Luigi cannot be guilty because he was with her, not realising that, rather than providing an alibi at her own expense, she seals his fate regardless: any association with a civilian female (in time of war) amounts to a military offence. Distraught, she turns for support to Jesse, who acknowledges her tragedy. *Another Time, Another Place* bears comparison with older films located against the unforgiving landscapes of the Highlands and Islands, such as Powell's 1937 *The Edge of the World* (see Chapter 5). But it also speaks simply to unspoken desires and longings for a life less ordinary and other than it is.

The Killing Fields (photographed by Chris Menges) represented Cambodia under the Khmer Rouge from the perspective of Dith Pran, a former aide to an American journalist – while privileging the American's attempts to trace him after his disappearance and ending mawkishly with John Lennon's 'Imagine'. *A World Apart* opens with thirteen-year-old Molly (Jodhi May) in a flamenco class in Johannesburg, a peculiarly apt image for the strangeness of colonial culture; in *The Kitchen Toto*, furnishings and prints of English landscapes recall a distant homeland. Molly's parents – based on Joe Slovo and Ruth First (Jeroen Krabbé and Barbara Hershey) – are both activists against apartheid and, as the struggle intensifies, are accordingly ostracised by their suburban neighbours. Molly, as a child, resents their involvement at the expense of her own emotional needs, preferring to keep her friends and the 'normal' life to which she is accustomed. When Diane, her mother, is

A World Apart (Chris Menges, 1987): Molly (Jodhi May) joins her mother (Barbara Hershey) in a demonstration for justice in South Africa

reimprisoned and attempts suicide, it seems to Molly that she is deserting her own daughter. While the whites live apart from the blacks, often in wilful ignorance or denial of the violence perpetrated in their name (a party hostess can blithely refer to 'people starving out there' in the garden, in spite of the actual starvation beyond the walls), Molly, of necessity, survives apart from her parents.

Often the protagonists of these smaller histories bear an identifiable similarity to persons alive or dead and are meticulous in their reconstruction or evocation of a particular period: Lynda (Emily Lloyd) – modelled on Britain's favourite madam, Cynthia Payne – was photographed for the poster accompanying *Wish You Were Here* sitting on the balustrade of a seaside promenade in the manner of Bert Hardy's 1951 *Picture Post* shot of 'Two Girls at Blackpool'; Joanne Whalley-Kilmer was posed to match Lewis Morley's 1963 photo-portrait of Keeler for the poster to *Scandal*; in *Prick Up Your Ears* (1987), Orton and Halliwell (see Chapter 9) are seen together with the television broadcast of the 1953 Coronation, while Peter Yates' 1983 *The Dresser* opens with a radio broadcast announcing the Royal Couple visiting wartime bombsites and a reduction in the meat ration. Danny the drug dealer in *Withnail and I* locates the action very precisely: 'We are sixty days from the enda this decade . . . We're about to witness the world's biggest hangover, and there's fuck all Harold Wilson can do about it.' However, *Wish You Were Here* is far from straightforwardly nostalgic in its depiction of the past, and for Lynda, the South Coast is no holiday, it's home: an isolated, bedraggled clown performs wanly and wearily under grey skies. Lynda is 'Locked in a Dream' (the title song) that things could be otherwise. This provincial town is repressed and complacently narrow-minded. While Lynda's father dispenses Durex from his barber's shop, her own curiosity is considered wayward and reprehensible. While Betty Grable's legs are exhibited on a colossal hoarding above the picture palace, it is insisted that she keep her own legs demurely covered; she gets to be the boys' favourite at the bus depot by revealing her knickers and stocking tops to them, but in the ensuing disruption, she is the one who loses her job. She proves more than a match for the harassed psychiatrist (a gem of a cameo from Heathcote Williams), assigned to effect a talking cure for her dysfunctional behaviour. She has received little information about sex from her family, and the films which she sees equally fail to enlighten. Keen to be initiated, Lynda beds Dave (Jesse Birdsall) – and bluntly states her dissatisfaction with the result. Her brashness is an anarchic affront to the polite pretentiousness, the ghastly good taste of the 'la-di-da' chintzy te room – but the looks and applause from the other waitresses and the lady pianist suggest that she is not alone in spirit; another girl on a bike with hitched-up skirts passes her on the promenade, suggesting that she will be succeeded. Her father accuses her of being a slut for becoming pregnant but says nothing of the shared responsibility of fellow-mason Terry (Tom Bell). Lynda refuses to be shamed by them and triumphantly flaunts her baby . . . although her old self is now irretrievably lost (and there is a brief flashback to how she was).

In *Distant Voices, Still Lives* (Terence Davies, 1988), a family history is recounted through an itinerary of christenings, weddings and funerals, its characters posed as a series of photographs in an album. Christopher Hobbs' set overscales the wet, black cobbles of the terraced street, as if envisaged in a childhood memory. The action is underscored by the communal entertainments which serve as an idealised alternative commentary to the family's actual stark existence: the sentimental dreams conveyed by Hollywood (the favourite diversion of the boy, Tony [Dean Williams]) and in the popular songs which the women perform in the pub. Tom (Pete Postlethwaite) rules his family by fear, casting his shadow over the lives of his wife and children (indeed, a clear contrast is drawn in the colour of the film differentiating the time before and after his death). 'Taking a Chance on Love' is played as Mum says that she married Tom because he was nice and a good dancer and continues as we see him beating her.

For all their period fittings, these films are not confined thematically to a particular date in the past. Sometimes they bear specific contemporary significance. It was difficult to watch *Scandal* on its release without recalling Monica Coghlan (like Keeler, vilified for naming names) and Jeffrey Archer in court in 1987; *Absolute Beginners* suitably, but briefly, called upon the personal services of Mandy Rice-Davies herself. The stalwart loyalty of one Tory wife (Mrs John Profumo) recalled that of others (Mrs Cecil Parkinson and the 'fragrant' Mrs Jeffrey Archer).[7] *Dance With a Stranger* perfectly captured, commented Chris Peachment in *Time Out* of the dingily-lit flat puce walls of the club at which Ellis works, 'the seedy mood of repression, so characteristic of austerity Britain in the '50s'.[8] 'Caustically scripted' (said Colin Booth in *The Face*) by Shelagh Delaney, the frustrations of Ruth Ellis (Miranda Richardson) were equally reminiscent of Jo's mum in *A Taste of*

Honey, torn between a lover, David Blakeley (Rupert Everett) (who wants mothering), and a child (who needs to be loved) (see Chapter 9).[9] *Dance With a Stranger* ends with Ellis reading aloud her confessional letter to Blakeley's own mother, declaring her love and forgiveness, deliberately pointing to each word in turn with an immaculately varnished scarlet fingernail; Ruth Ellis (in 1955, the last woman to be hanged in Britain – see Chapter 8) can readily be fitted to the model of doubly transgressive 'demon' murderess identified by Viv Chadder.[10] The cult following enjoyed by *Withnail and I* (and this is a boy thing, I reckon) seems to reside in its portrayal of a particular moment in a friendship rather than any definite time or place – and its frenetic homophobia. Withnail (Richard E. Grant) and Marwood (Paul McGann) may 'retreat' to the Lake District but it could as well be anywhere rural and distant from luvvies' London. While Withnail closes the film with 'the best rendition of *Hamlet* the world will ever see', it is his younger friend and partner in degeneracy (mixing double gins with cider, lighter fuel with antifreeze; driving a Jaguar down the motorway with a headlight missing; driving while incapacitatedly inebriated; shocking the locals in a Penrith teashop – a companion to *Wish You Were Here*'s Bournemouth – and never, ever washing up) who gets the lead part in the play, gets a decent haircut and (by implication) gets himself a life which no longer leaves room for Withnail.

A number of these smaller histories draw a larger lesson by depicting particular institutional structures as models of the nation and then describe the conduct of such institutions as formative of aspects of national character. Trevor Griffiths' *Country* (directed by Richard Eyre, BBC TV, 1981) begins with Eton boys performing a house game. The presence of an immutable school uniform suggests that it has always been thus and that it will be thus, from generation to generation, 'from your father to your son and your son's son, even until the end of the school'. Celliers (Bowie) is coupled with Yanoi (Sakomoto) in *Merry Christmas Mr Lawrence*: the Japanese officer feels guilt for not being among those executed in Tokyo in 1936; the officer in the British Army 'embraced the war with relief', seeking redemption for his betrayal of his little brother to a ritualistic humiliation at their public school in South Africa. Stephen Ward (John Hurt) in *Scandal* compares his scapegoating in the Profumo affair to the treatment meted out by his schoolmasters: 'Someone had to take a beating, Ward – it just happened to be you.' In *Another Country*, Tommy Judd (Colin Firth), the Bolshevik, compares Eton with prison ('hard labour in the saltmines of prep and public school'), as Evelyn Waugh had before him: 'Anyone who has been to an English public school will always feel comparatively at home in prison' (see Chapter 9).

Another Country presents its narrative in flashback, as if told by Guy Bennett (Rupert Everett) to a female American journalist visiting him in Moscow in 1983. Mitchell implicitly (where Alan Bennett explicitly, in *An Englishman Abroad* [BBC TV 1983]) recalls Guy Burgess' treason and defection.[11] But, says Guy Bennett, in spite of the vow they sing to their country (and the other country they have heard of long ago), 'You have no idea what life in the '30s was like – treason to whom; loyalty to what.' Burgess, similarly, invoking E. M. Forster, declares a loyalty to friends rather than to country and Guy Bennett (like Burgess), finally, admits to the journalist that it is the cricket which he misses most. There is the suggestion that Bennett's flamboyance, his ostentatious 'total indis-

cretion' as to his homosexuality, for which he and other boys (to the point of suicide) are perse-
cuted at school, can serve as a cover for his future covert political activities. 'The last laugh would
be revenge,' he says, while imagining the day when he'll be Ambassador in Paris, almost as a matter
of course. We keep the whole thing going although it's wrong, says Judd (Colin Firth), 'but we
daren't accept the logical consequence and think of anything better'. He complains that the school
is producing compliant Empire rulers rather than Empire builders and defends Stalin's efforts to construct the new USSR. Judd, 'the salt of the earth', says Bennett, is killed in the Spanish Civil War.

In many ways, school life is a routine rehearsal for pre-ordained adult roles. Accordingly, boys
rarely address one another by their Christian names. Barclay (Michael Jenn), appealing to Judd 'as
a friend', has all the makings of a politician. The boys' first loyalty is to their house and the authority they respect is that of the prefects and the gods rather than the masters (to whom they feel
superior by class). Judd (whose girlfriend is a cinema usherette) aristocratically despises the businessmen on whose behalf the last world war was fought; another boy says that his father refuses
to have Harrovians in his firm. Wharton (Adrian Ross-Magenty) and the younger boys (some so
young that they talk to their pet dogs in their sleep) fag for their seniors on the understanding that
they, too, will one day have their own fags; Wharton effectively serves as batman to Fowler
(Tristan Oliver) as Sergeant Major of the OTC. One boy in the battalion is addressed as the son of

A violent stranger disrupts the small-town cosiness and complacency of Marcia (Judi Dench) and Jean
(Vanessa Redgrave) in *Wetherby* (David Hare, 1985)

his father while Bennett insults his mother's new husband, affronts the event, the hierarchy and all it stands for by presenting himself on parade ill-kempt and entirely unprepared: he's 'a disgrace to the house and the whole school'. 'I'm hopeless with Brasso,' he jibes, 'I can only get a really good shine on my nails.'

Wetherby: Violent Strangers similarly employs flashbacks to make connections (and, sometimes, to question the connectedness) between personal pasts and the present. Jean (Vanessa Redgrave) remembers her younger self (played by Redgrave's daughter, Joely Richardson) with Jim (Robert Hines), the man she loved but never married. Jim's father says that education would be a waste for a married woman, who ought to be kept at home, but when Jim is sent to Malaya, Jean escapes to university. She confesses to friends that she couldn't talk to him, 'I can't say what I feel'. Meanwhile Jim, the flying ace, dies 'pointlessly' and ignominiously in an opium den. A generation later, Jean informs a schoolgirl, Susie (Stephanie Noblett), that education is valuable for its own sake (it 'orders thoughts') even if it fails to secure employment, but when Susie runs away to London with her boyfriend, regardless, Jean applauds her for finding her own form of escape. Jean and DCI Langdon (Stuart Wilson) – a practical man – struggle to find meaning for the single, apparently senseless violent act which threatens to disrupt her present self-contained equilibrium (around which the film is structured) and her settled, cosy, small-town life of work, dinner parties, jumble sales and tombolas. They investigate the past of the stranger, the much-educated John Morgan (Tim McInnerny) and his attachment to Karen, Langdon in turn defines himself by his relationship to a girlfriend, Chrissie (Penny Downie), who leaves him. For Jean and her chattering, educated, friends, Karen is indefinable because of her 'lack of curiosity' and inarticulate inactivity: 'I never do anything, I never say anything,' she admits, frustratedly. Susie asks whether Jean thinks people without education 'inferior'; clearly Karen and Chrissie think that they have been judged and found wanting. Karen would prefer to be allowed to be, without people perpetually pestering and 'digging into her'. Marcia (Judi Dench), the librarian, suggests that men's obsession with such women is prompted precisely by their vacuity (perhaps assigned the significance of an enigma to be resolved, perhaps as a blank ready to bear the imprint of another). The evident interest of her husband, Stanley (Ian Holm), in the new barmaid suggests that to be young and pretty (a different sort of meaning) may be sufficient. Stanley (a lawyer) seems to question the disciplined 'ordering of thoughts' required by his profession ('I kept my thoughts under cloches. But now they grow wild') and the personal security afforded by a relationship ('If you're frightened of loneliness, never get married'). Jean can but suggest that, unlike the stranger, we just 'keep trying' as our only uncertain hope of discovering some 'point' to it all:

> John : I only know goodness and anger and revenge and evil and desire . . . these seem to me far better words than neurosis and psychology and paranoia. These old words . . . these good old words have a sort of conviction which all this modern apparatus of language now lacks. . . . We bury these words, these simple feelings, we bury them deep. And all the building over that constitutes this century will not wish these feelings away.

Roger: Well, I mean, you'd have to say what you mean by that.

John: Would I?

Roger: Define your terms.

John: They don't need defining. If you can't feel them you might as well be dead.

Jean herself remembers a time when it was enough (as an alibi for her meetings with Jim) to say that *The Third Man* (see Chapter 6) was a 'good' film. While John's speech may signify precisely what he then felt, the other dinner guests are embarrassed by his directness and seemingly fail to connect it with subsequent events. For a film which questions the adequacy of language to effect contact and connect and communicate affectively (across time, between individuals), *Wetherby* is intensely wordy and preoccupied with the need to 'define terms'. As John says, 'the apparatus of language' (in the sense of both its overwrought literally literary style and its complex non-linear editing) swamps whatever conviction (or content) *Wetherby* may carry.

Present Nostalgias and Future Dystopias

The heritage cycle of the 1980s was defined as much by particular aspects of *mise en scène* (locations, costuming, casting) and cinematography (long shots, slow pans, lush lighting) as by its reliance on a respectable canon of literary source material.[12] Forster (certainly on the English A-level syllabus in the early 1980s, although, mercifully, I managed to avoid him) was a popular option, with *A Room with a View* (1985) and *Maurice* (1987) both produced by Ismail Merchant and directed by James Ivory. More especially, the cycle was associated by critics, generally disparagingly, with the activities of the Heritage industry, promoting (it was said) a bogus and commodified image of the past which bore little relation to the lives of the majority of British people or their ancestors; heritage was politically (and historically) incorrect.[13] Certainly, the poster campaign accompanying the launch of English Heritage (a state-funded body) in 1984 portrayed a village scene more reminiscent of *Trumpton* (BBC Children's TV puppet show) than anywhere currently or ever existing anywhere in the country. Critics of the Heritage industry also often complained at its complicity in the expansion of the service sector at the expense of traditional industry, museums about mining replacing working mines. Critics of the heritage film (and there were disproportionately many, given the quantity of other films which merited discussion) frequently presumed to speak on behalf of the populace while dismissing the appeal of actual films for a broadly popular audience at home and abroad. Indeed, Claire Monk urges that 'the heritage film' should more properly be regarded as a critical construct than as a genre.[14]

There was much here that recalled 'high-brow' concerns regarding popular taste of the 1930s and 1950s (see Chapters 5 and 8). While Hoggart fetishised nylon as his particular object of distaste, his successors seemed to suggest, somewhat nervously, that the mental faculties of a film's audience could be addled by an undue display of cotton lawn frills, furbelows and white flannel. It seems perfectly possible to enjoy that type of film without becoming degenerately nostalgic or politically reactionary (as Ken Tynan once suggested, one can be a Cavalier in dress while a

Roundhead in politics).[15] And while this view invested frocks and furniture with an unseemly power to distort a conception of what the past was 'actually' like (historical materialists presumed to have a firmer grasp on this slippery issue than anyone else), it often undervalued the place of props and performances – apart from their period features – in the fabrication of distinct characters (the very stuff of the social narratives with which many of the adaptations from literary fictions were concerned). Thus, in *A Room with a View*, the pompous Cecil Vyse (Daniel Day Lewis) is pressed and primped in his dress and affected (in his clipped diction and the manner in which he carries his monocle and cigarette) and affects to despise the suburban comforts of Lucy's middle-class family home (to make this absolutely clear, he looks down his nose); the lower-class George (Julian Sands), for whom Lucy (Helena Bonham-Carter) leaves Cecil, is conspicuously un-ironed out, while Lucy herself evidently would prefer to be less chaperoned and less buttoned-up in her bodice than is obliged by social convention. Among left-wing commentators, Raphael Samuel was a rare and welcome exception, acknowledging that heritage sites and films (and retro-chic) constituted a valid and even revisionist appropriation and interpretation of history proper and the literary canon: 'Heritage . . . so far from being a stationary state, is continuously shedding its old character and metamorphosing into something else.'[16]

In *Maurice*, class and sexuality are very much at issue between suburban Maurice Hall (James Wilby) – sent down but destined for the stock market – and upper-class crush Clive Durham (Hugh Grant) who, after college, trains for the bar. Durham's mother accepts homosexuality merely as a juvenile and touristic, aesthetic pleasure – to be pursued in Greece. But Durham finds the physical and emotional attachment between Maurice and rough-trade Alec Scudder (Rupert Graves), a servant on the family estate, 'grotesque'. Various professional attempts are made to cure men of their nature – in which women are proposed and proposed to as accessories. While Alec is, apparently, liberated by class and free to initiate the relationship with Maurice, Maurice appears to enjoy an economic freedom to escape abroad – before determining to stay and thereby liberate himself of other constraints. The period setting of *Maurice* (in which the name of Oscar Wilde is cursorily invoked) explains some of the repressed actions of its protagonists. However, a comparable configuration of concerns reappears in the contemporarily located *My Beautiful Laundrette*.

Set against the expansion of the City, the overheating of the stock market and the sale of shares in public utilities ('Tell Sid' – ran the British Gas campaign slogan), encouraging everyone to be a shareholder, the decision of Sands Films to adapt Dickens' 1857 novel *Little Dorrit* (Christine Edzard, 1987) and Dostoevsky's 1868 *The Fool* (Christine Edzard, 1990) was extremely timely. Nevertheless, these productions were mounted with an obsessive attention to period detail. To me, it seemed ridiculous to suggest (as it was) that Alec Guinness (who had previously blithely appeared in Bisto browning and dhoti as Professor Godbole for *A Passage to India*) required authentically hand-sewn button-holes as a prompt for his performance as Dorrit, the father of the Marshalsea. The result was over fussy and (as Samuel noted) generally too bright, apart from the candlelit interiors (following the precedent of *Barry Lyndon*) which were often irritatingly dim.[17] The film's narrative, underlining the insignificance of the very, very little Amy to many around her, followed Part

One (already long), 'Nobody's Fault' – Dickens' provisional title – with a retelling and recutting of episodes to construct the story from Amy Dorrit's perspective. 'It's everybody's fault,' she decides. One reason for Dickens' standing as a perennial favourite for adaptation is his ability to provide numerous roles for British character actors. *Little Dorrit* does not disappoint, with a cockneyfied Michael Elphick as Merdle 'the spirit of the age' (says his mannered wife, played by Eleanor Bron), a capitalist who falls foul of his reckless commercial ventures, Derek Jacobi as the hapless Arthur Clennam (an innocent among rogues – as in *The Fool*) and Roshan Seth as the rent collector, Pancks, 'paid to squeeze' – because it pays to do so. Miriam Margolyes gushes as Arthur's former fiancée Flora Casby, who loves him in spite of his indifference. Joan Greenwood is vicious as Arthur's widowed, invalid mother, while the comic Max Wall is far from funny as Jeremiah Flintwich, the old retainer, awaiting his chance for vengeance. This rich pudding is heavily inter-larded with visual metaphors: the drowning then burning of account books and bonds. The impor-tunate father of the Marshalsea (the debtors' prison) inherits the estate he was rumoured to hold, but too late to save his life, and Amy seems to be thrown by her newly won riches beyond the catch of a bankrupted Arthur.

In the 1950s, the NFFC had rejected a proposal to film a play concerning the Tolpuddle Mar-tyrs. Bill Douglas' 1986 *Comrades* addressed the same subject, in the wake of Thatcher's confron-tation with the unions, suppression of secondary picketing and especially the crushing defeat of the miners' union in the strike of 1984. *Comrades* resorts to popular imagery (kaleidoscopes, shadow puppets, slides, fairground shows, photographs and phantasmagoria) and oral history to present a past in which our narrator, in various guises (a lanternist, showman, silhouette cutter), is fortuitously omnipresent as witness to events. Michael Clark is enlisted to dance a tidy sailor's horn-pipe at a village wedding, a performance duly repeated by Aborigines in Botany Bay. This is a long film, tracing the travails of the Dorset Six (one of whom takes the place of his brother – in solidarity he counts himself 'one of them') from Britain to Australia and back again. A map is unfurled as our heroes cross the oceans; storms and shipwrecks, with lightning, Captain Pugwash-style, accom-pany the journey home, relating this tale 'even to generations yet unborn'.

Jarman turns to painting, rather than to literature, as the source for *Caravaggio*. He poses the prostitute (Tilda Swinton) – as Mary Magdalene – and the boxer (Sean Bean) in imitation of iden-tifiable pictures and the painter's known practice. Conversely, 'I painted myself as Bacchus', Caravaggio (Nigel Terry) declares, 'and took on his fate.' Studio sets (contributed by Christopher Hobbs), chiaroscuro lighting, colour washes and choreography (often emphatically symmetrical) contrive to produce pictorial scenes. The natural physiognomy of Caravaggio's actor/models, along-side pewter, earthenware, vegetables and straw, is set against this artifice. But Jarman is equally concerned with painting as a physical activity – the same knife which creates paint from pigment and body and which 'smears out wounds' on the canvas becomes a weapon against human flesh and blood. Anachronistically and eclectically, Jarman places an art critic with a typewriter in a bath reminiscent of David's 1793 *The Death of Marat* (the critic writes of 'ignorance and deprav-ity . . . a sad reflection of our times'), introduces a jazz soundtrack and attributes the state's

functionaries with pocket calculators. Ultimately, the artist, once the whore to his talents and protégé of a Cardinal (Michael Gough), is presented as a Christ-like figure, a human sacrifice to the
interests of the papacy: Scipione is prepared to turn a blind eye to his sodomy, so long as the riff-
raff are restored to the Church. Meanwhile, Peter Greenaway deliberately exaggerated the flamboyance of the 'period' costumes for *The Draughtsman's Contract* (1982) and lifted images from
Jean Cocteau (*Beauty and the Beast*, France, 1946) and from Alain Resnais (*Last Year in Marien-
bad*, France 1961 – photographed, like *The Draughtsman* and *The Cook, the Thief* [1989], by
Sacha Vierney).

Terry Gilliam's *Brazil* (1985) presents an absurd and incoherent conglomerate of second-hand
imagery (drawn from a cinematic repertoire – notably Lang's *Metropolis*, Buster Keaton and
Kubrick's *A Clockwork Orange* [see Chapter 10]) to present a dystopian view of society. While individuals are overwhelmed by bureaucracy, the infrastructure collapses: private operators (Robert De
Niro) and Central Services (Bob Hoskins) compete over contracts but mutually fail to maintain
domestic plumbing systems. The weather (as in Martin Amis' 1989 novel *London Fields*) is weird.
The sharply colourful and indulgent world of those who have (Sam's mother wears an oversized

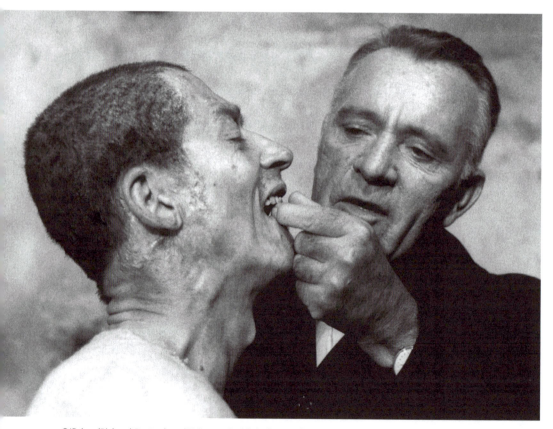

O'Brien (Richard Burton) and Winston Smith (John Hurt), ominously paired in *1984* (Michael Radford, 1984)

imitation Schiaparelli leopard-skin shoe-hat and a recent face-lift) is set against the disintegrating, grey shabbiness of those who have not. Apparatchik Sam Lowery (Jonathan Pryce) imagines himself as an angelic white knight, an Icarus figure, who will rise above dull conformity, but it is Jill (Kim Greist). the injured, bandaged, punkster girlfriend from the wrong side of town who eventually saves the day. As a brash gesture, Gilliam throws in a 'brainwashing' episode, in which Sam is questioned by an inquisitor/torturer.

1984's fine playing of a similar scene is considerably more ominous with O'Brien (Richard Burton) alternately cosseting and persecuting Winston Smith (John Hurt). Disconcertingly, the tiled interior is ambiguous: it may be a prison cell, it may be a clinic. 'You're mentally deranged . . . you have a defective memory,' O'Brien informs Smith. George Orwell's novel was written in 1948 and was understood, in Russia, as an indictment of the Soviet state under Stalin (the contracted acronyms INGSOC and ARTSEM clearly draw a similar parallel in the film).[18] 'We shall lift you clear out of history,' says O'Brien to Smith – he will not remain as a memory nor as a name in a register. Radford's film judiciously recalls a period setting (while intending the present or the future – Orwell's present future) with props invoking the atmosphere of Churchill's cabinet war rooms and Charles Holden's Senate House (the centre of MoI operations in the Second World War) providing a frequent backdrop. Here, the greyness of Smith's contemporary city is set against the colour of an idealised rural landscape and retreat in Smith's imagination – he is under arrest and investigation as a 'thought criminal' betrayed by an apparently kindly neighbour (Cyril Cusack) and condemned by a child. This is a stark and, in the history of communist regimes, a potent figure: the testimony of a child (susceptible to 'correct' indoctrination) is paradoxically privileged as 'innocent' and impartial. While *Brazil* prioritises autonomy of action, *1984* more effectively conveys an autocratic threat to individual freedom and autonomy of thought.

A Zed and Two Noughts (1985) looks and sounds like a Greenaway film of the 1980s, photographed and scored by regular collaborators Sacha Vierney and Michael Nyman. The Zoo of the title is announced in blue neon against a dark background. Like Angus Wilson's 1961 futuristic novel *The Old Men at the Zoo*, Greenaway models a dystopian view of society. Wilson presents a society rigidly divided and categorised by forms of material, physical and intellectual handicap, by which individuals are accorded or denied political authority. As in his 1989 *Dante* (for Channel Four) Greenaway ponders the portrayal of relations between animals and man in ancient myths (Leda mates with a swan; a centaur is half man, half horse), the anthropomorphism of nursery rhymes ('The Teddy Bears' Picnic') and the alternative scientific chronology provided by Darwin, 'a good story teller'. Names of human characters recall the naming of animals after humans who have recorded them: Alba Bewick (Andrea Ferreol) is paired with the white swan which causes a fatal car crash at the film's opening (the animals get their retaliation in first). Greenaway pursues his usual obsession with classification by way of Alba's children (she intends to name them serially, in alphabetical order) while the zoo director whimsically collects animals which are black and/or white: dalmatian dogs, zebras, swans, flamingoes, rhinos. Oswald (Brian Deacon) and Oliver (Eric Deacon), ex-Siamese twins forcibly separated (their symmetry destroyed), choose to be sewn into a suit

Men at the Zoo: Peter Greenaway's 1985 *A Zed and Two Noughts*

which will reunite them in death ('to free themselves from art and medicine' – once they would have been exhibited in a circus, they say – now society is more 'civilised' and displays such curiosities in hospitals and zoos). Oswald and Oliver are fascinated by the primitive sexuality of hermaphrodite snails while Alba declares that she has become pregnant by them both ('What's a few sperm between brothers?') and that she can reproduce by sitting on eggs. Alba experiments with her own symmetry (as an aesthetic and ontological issue – 'How much of your own body can you lose and still recognise yourself?') by having a leg amputated and replacing it with a prosthetic which will outlive her. While Greenaway poses intellectual questions (largely apolitical) about human identity, there is something profoundly misanthropic in his subjection of characters to various forms of mutilation; but, visually, there is also something strangely poignant in the final recoupling of the twins.

Clashing with the Double Duchess

The decade's political landscape was dominated by the figure of Margaret Thatcher. However, as John Hill has noted, in spite of her leading her party through a series of General Election victories, the Conservatives never commanded an outright majority of the poll.[19] On the cultural front, there was widespread hostility towards their domestic and international policies, fuelled, not least, by the withdrawal of subsidies and tax breaks: for instance, the Eady Levy (see Chapter 8) was abolished in 1983 and film was left to compete in a supposedly open (if not entirely free) market. In 'New Amsterdam' (1980) and 'Tramp the Dirt Down' (1989), ('When England was the whore of the world/ Margaret was her madam') Elvis Costello attacked Thatcher personally, matching Steve Bell's cartoons in *The Guardian* and Fluck and Law's increasingly crazed puppets for Central TV's *Spitting Image*; 'Let Him Dangle' (1989), like Peter Medak's *Let Him Have It* (1991), recalled the 1953 example of teenager Derek Bentley in response to Thatcher's advocacy of 'Victorian' deterrents and punishments for crime; in 'Shipbuilding' (1983) and 'Last Boat Leaving' (1989) – along with Billy Bragg's 1985 'Between the Wars' – he cited the decline of mining and heavy industry in the Midlands and the North – the subject also of Alan Clarke's excellent television adaptation of Jim Cartwright's stageplay *Road* (BBC TV, 1987) and the sub-plot of *Stormy Monday*. Birmingham band UB40, in its name and in its lyrics ('I am the one in ten'), narrated the rise in youth unemployment (the theme also of Ken Loach's 1981 Sheffield film *Looks and Smiles*). Jarman matches the 'Anthem for Doomed Youth' in *War Requiem* (1988) (see Chapter 3) with a similar lament in the present dystopia of *The Last of England* (1987). Rock Againt Racism enlisted the support of a number of musicians in response to the racial tensions exhibited in riots in London, Bristol, Birmingham and Liverpool (and the perception of police aggression and antagonism) alongside Kureishi's oblique treatment (in *Sammy and Rosie Get Laid*) and John Akomfrah's documentary *Handsworth Songs* (1986). Akomfrah pointedly mixes a distorted version of Parry's anthem 'Jerusalem' (invoked in *Another Country* and closing *Chariots of Fire*) with a reggae beat. The Clash (led by diplomat's son, Joe Strummer) turned its attention to global politics with its 1982 album *Combat Rock* (notably in 'Overpowered by Funk – don't you love our Western Ways?' and 'Rock the Casbah') while the Boomtown Rats' Bob Geldof resorted to direct action with his organisation of the 'Feed the World' single for Christmas 1984 and the Live Aid concerts in 1985.

However, many 'state of the nation' films and TV dramas of the 1980s suggested that true power in the country resided less with the elected representatives of the new radical Right (a party of grammar school boys and, as Tory MP Julian Critchley quipped, of 'estate agents') and their functionaries (the police, the army) and more with a host of reactionary and faceless mandarins, old and aristocratic 'estate owners', for whom Thatcher herself was but an expedient instrument: such, for instance, is the agenda of BBC TV's *A Very British Coup* (1988), *Defence of the Realm* (David Drury, 1985) – partly concerned with the nuclear defence programme – and Loach's *Hidden Agenda* (1991), covering the existence of an undeclared 'Shoot to Kill' policy in Northern Ireland and the subsequently obstructed Stalker Enquiry (providing material also for ITV's drama-documentary *Shoot to Kill* [1990]). The transmission of the Thames TV current affairs item *Death on the Rock* (1988), enquiring into events surrounding the killing of IRA activists in Gibraltar by the SAS, was temporarily banned.[20]

The Argentian writer, Jorge Luis Borges, memorably characterised the Malvinas/Falklands skirmish of 1982 as 'two bald men in a bar fighting over a comb'. Historically, the Falkland Islands had been important to British trade as a coaling station (see Chapter 3); in the future, territorial claims promise a stake in the mineral resources of Antarctica. At the outbreak of war with Argentina, luxury cruisers were hurriedly prepared for active service; in the aftermath, they were cheaply sent abroad rather than providing Britain's beleaguered shipyards with much-needed contracts. While *Handsworth Songs* recognisably employs archival footage of Thatcher's speeches, Ian McEwan's screenplay for *The Ploughman's Lunch* opportunistically augments material from the Conservative Party's Brighton conference following the islands' recapture: the spirit of the South Atlantic is said to represent the best of 'Our People'. Meanwhile, the radio journalist James Penfield (juggling Princess Diana and Irish matters with pandas) pursues his private research into Britain's imperial past by way of the 1950s. His hopes of cultural self-promotion through publication are dashed by his prospective publisher, intent upon a popular (and American) audience – but James is willing to compromise. Ashamed of his own working-class parentage (he lies), James pursues Susie (Charlie Dore), a television producer, partly as a means of obtaining access to her mother, the academic 'goddess' Anne Barrington; both are featured as celebrities in *Vogue* (echoes here of Losey's *Accident* – see Chapter 9). But Susie has apparently lost even her mother's vestigial socialism: the Andrzej Wajda film at which she meets James 'went on too long'. A fellow academic (Bill Patterson) advises James that Suez was, politically, an affair of the heart, not of economics; James' newspaper friend Jeremy (Tim Curry) with whom he shares silly cocktails at £11 a round, crudely and cynically advises him that the way into Susie's pants is through Anne ('up the Suez Canal'). Jeremy, trumping James by birth, in careers, at squash and in bed, should know – he's been there already.

McEwan's screenplay for *Soursweet* updates the plot of Timothy Mo's 1982 novel from the early 1960s – where Lily Chen's sister learns about England from *Crossroads* and *Dixon of Dock Green* on television – to the 1980s. Like the 1980s BBC television series *The Chinese Detective*, *Soursweet* deploys the usual stereotypes of Triads, Kung Fu and catering, casting the martial arts star Soon-Tek Oh (from the Bond film *The Man with the Golden Gun* [Guy Hamilton, 1974] and J. Lee Thompson's 1987 *Death Wish 4*) as gang leader Red Cudgel. The London listings magazine *Time Out* summarised the action of this substantially inactive film as 'bloody stuff with cleavers and shot guns'.[21] Chinese customs are perpetuated by Chen (Danny Dun) and Lily (Sylvia Chang) in Britain: Lily teaches her son to kick box, as her own father taught her back home in Hong Kong; when Chen's mother dies, never having seen her grandson, Chen suggests bringing his father to live with them – 'Just because the English can't look after their own old people it doesn't mean that we can't.' Lily grows vegetables, sets up a roadside takeaway and serves jam tart and custard to the local OAPs. She wants the family to become economically self-sufficient while wanting Man Kee to attend school in Soho, to advance his prospects. For Chen, the established Chinese community promises help (the Friendship Association respects his wishes to restore his father's honour) then threatens and exacts revenge (when he fails to settle an old debt, Lily's business is destroyed).

My Beautiful Laundrette, like the New Wave films of the early 1960s, portrays a younger generation at odds with the political and social ambitions of its parents and forming new allegiances across conventional barriers of race, class and gender. It was equally appreciated and denigrated as the 'typical' Channel Four film, both in the small scale of its budget and in its subject matter. Omar (Gordon Warnecke) is a young Pakistani set up in business by his uncle (Saeed Jaffrey). While Omar's father (Roshan Seth) is a socialist and former journalist who wants his son to go to college 'so that he can see clearly what is being done and to who in this country', the uncles (sometimes legally, sometimes not) fully embrace the enterprise economy promoted by Mrs Thatcher. The 1984 Olympic 'Anthem for the Common People' is used somewhat ironically as the laundrette is declared open. Omar enlists the help of an old schoolfriend, Johnny (Daniel Day Lewis), who has, in the past, marched with the National Front and whose white friends resent his working for Omar. Tania (Rita Wolf), Omar's cousin, tells her father's mistress, Rachael (Shirley Ann Field, of *Saturday Night and Sunday Morning* – see Chapter 9), that she disapproves of women who live off men: Rachael replies that this is a difference between them of age and class but reminds Tania that she is hardly independent herself. At the end of the film, Tania leaves the family to make her own way and asks Johnny if he'd like to come with her. But Johnny is more interested in Omar and the film abounds with cheeky references to their sexual relationship (to which Omar's family remains oblivious, continuing to attempt to arrange a more 'suitable' marriage on his behalf): Omar is never really out. Meanwhile, in *Mona Lisa*, short, chubby, middle-aged white George (some hope) falls in love with Simone (Cathy Tyson), a prostitute ('a tall thin black tart') – 'but still a fucking lady', remarks George, with unwitting obviousness – who is already in love with another girl. 'Two many Ts', advises his friend, Thomas, generously. *Laundrette*'s coy evasiveness and *Mona Lisa*'s pillory of George for the sake of 'a couple of dykes' would now seem quaint (on the one hand) and (on the other) sadly fascinated were it not for the context of Thatcher's opposition to single-sex relationships in general and specifically in relation to Clause 28 (forbidding the endorsement of homosexual relationships by local authorities).

'Does Mike Leigh really love to hate people?' pertinently enquired *The Face*.[22] The only character whom Leigh presents as consistently likeable in *High Hopes* (1987) is Shirley (Ruth Sheen) who works as a gardener. Occasionally, her partner Cyril, who works as a courier (Phil Davies, lurking behind a woolly jumper and an even woollier beard), and his pensioner mother, Mrs Bender (Edna Doré), are shown some sympathy. The couple keeps a cactus called Thatcher – 'because it's a pain in the arse' – and readily take in a stranger for the night in their King's Cross Peabody flat. But, strangely, the world of *Mona Lisa* is not rendered visible from their balcony. A favourite expedition for Cyril is a trip to the Marx memorial in Highgate cemetery (and Shirley comes too). The yuppies, new gentry, who occupy the house next door to Mrs Bender (Rupert and Laetitia Boothe-Brain – David Bamber and Lesley Manville) are reluctant to behave in a neighbourly fashion when Mrs Bender locks herself out (they suggest that she find a phone box, they're concerned about losing their opera tickets) and there is little love lost between Cyril and his sister Valerie, mocked by Leigh, in tediously familiar manner, for her suburban aspirations towards grandeur – the décor is 'noisy' (says Cyril) of the excessively loud wallpaper and brass fruit ornaments. The coffee table chess pieces are arranged in the wrong order; the hats (in imitation of Laetitia) preposterous; Chivas Regal is mispronounced – Valerie reprising the social gaffs of Leigh's earlier, equally snobbish (and invertedly snobbish) 1977 BBC television drama, *Abigail's Party*. Laetitia, meanwhile, in Sloane Ranger style, wonders about Mrs Bender's original features, caring more for her property than her person. Valerie's husband, Martin ('the jerk in the Merc', 'the wanker in the tanker'), fails to give Valerie a baby – she hysterically adopts an Afghan hound as a surrogate – and he takes a mistress. 'You've got to speculate to accumulate,' Martin advises Cyril, gratuitously and routinely. 'You aren't as stupid as you look,' Martin flatters Shirley; 'Shame I can't say the same about you,' she ripostes. 'Ever done any modelling?' he continues; 'No, but I've done a bit of yodelling,' she says, promptly putting pay to his clumsy attempts at seduction. Mrs Bender, after an unhappy birthday, is taken back to King's Cross. Looking out at the railway lines, all she wishes is to go to Margate.

Gut resentment of the newly rich resurfaces in Peter Greenaway's *The Cook, the Thief, his Wife and her Lover*. The boorish Spica (Michael Gambon) and his acolytes are dressed and posed in imitation of a vast backdrop, showing the burghers of Amsterdam. These City 'barrow-boys' – a theme to which James Dearden returns in his 1999 biopic *Rogue Trader* – are no more than gangsters (an ersatz comparison). His restaurant, an appropriate image of 1980s style and conspicuous consumption, is set against the library and old, cultural capital of Michael (Alan Howard) whom Spica's trophy wife, Georgina (Helen Mirren – dressed by Jean Paul Gaultier), takes as her lover. Spica crudely boasts ownership of Georgina – 'You're not allowed to fiddle with yourself – that's my property.' The film is punctuated by the presentation of elaborate, exotic menus and long tracking shots, repeatedly left to right, following the progress from the kitchen (colour-washed green) to the table (predominantly red). But Spica fails to appreciate the artistry of his French chef (Richard Bohringer) – Greenaway snobbishly casts Spica as a vulgar philistine, who mistakes hollandaise sauce for custard and eats with his fingers; he requests mushy peas and his mother asks for Chianti in rafia-covered bottles. Spica says that he thinks that the Ethiopians like starving: 'it keeps them slim and graceful'. Meanwhile, dogs prowl in the car park, sniffing the rotting meat in container trucks and (perhaps) something rotten in the state of Britain.

Stormy Monday and *Paris by Night* more directly represent characters who personify aspects of Margaret Thatcher's radical right credo. The mayor of Newcastle (Alison Steadman) speaks of the inspiration which American initiative affords 'this once great nation'; European politician, Clara Page (Charlotte Rampling), despises sloppiness and speaks of people 'spongeing off the state . . . people get soft – I hate that softness. If you do something you must live with the consequences.' Birmingham-born Clara is the model new Conservative. She is certainly a steely, if not an Iron Lady – and there is something disturbingly askew in her eyes. Her MP husband, Gerald (Michael Gambon), now disgusts her ('drink and cowardice in equal part – the dreary mixture') and her professional career is prioritised over her son, whom she leaves in the care of her sister. While old Tory Adam (Robert Hardy) offers Clara promotion in the Party, he also, covertly, contrives her downfall. An historian who devotes his spare time to recording his family's past, he ensures its future by producing seven children – and keeps his wife at home. However, Clara's own past catches up with her and she, too, is forced to face the consequences. Ultimately, she is not welcome in the political Gentlemen's Club. *Paris by Night* voices (and comes close to endorsing) much-worn prejudices against the ambitions of women to secure public office: women pay an unequal price, and are unduly criticised, in their pursuit of equal power. Inadvertently, it also foreshadows the ungracious 'closing of the ranks' in the Conservative Party which accompanied the fall from power of Britain's first woman prime minister.

For Clara's in-laws in Paris, being Jewish means knowing history: 'we're just guests'. Critical preoccupation with the 1980s 'state of the nation film' has inclined towards the neglect of a number of films which boldly addressed a broader political landscape. In spite of the well-documented procedural difficulties experienced by writer Trevor Griffith and director Ken Loach, these differences do not mar the effectiveness of *Fatherland* (1986) (again, admirably photographed by Chris Menges).[23] Again, an ambiguous personal past is located in a familiar map of Big History. Klaus Dittermann (Gerulf Pannach) is an East German singer-songwriter who faces imprisonment for his criticisms of the state. His mother, a teacher, reprimands him for prioritising personal issues and urges him not to forget his duty as a socialist. Rather than plead guilty, he accepts exile in the West. Like *Hidden Agenda*, *Fatherland* opens with the flurry of a press conference: his 'defection' has news value and he is valued as a commodity by his new recording company. Lucy (Christine Rose), the agent, suggests a publicity shot of Klaus by the Berlin wall: 'I don't think so,' says Klaus. He refuses to accept the terms of the proffered contract. Meanwhile, his movements and phone calls are trailed as they were in the East; Lucy persistently asks whether he has contacted his father, Jakob, a celebrated musician who adopted an alias and 'disappeared' in Britain in 1972 (Lucy can exploit this connection but also, perhaps, has other non-commercial interests at heart). A French journalist, whose family served with the Dutch Resistance in the War, has her own reasons for tracing Dittermann senior and accompanies Klaus to Cambridge. While the son thinks that the socialist state has betrayed the ideals of true socialism, the father cites the betrayal of the partisans in the Spanish Civil War. A package of mutilated photographs and letters (as in Loach's 1995 *Land and Freedom*) leads to the discovery of a secret past and an alternative history. Klaus is confronted with three laws: 1) that the innocent think there is a choice and stop at nothing; 2) that any life is better than no life; 3) that, eventually it's all one – life is nothing. Klaus loses his illusions about the father he barely knew but equally accepts (as he has always known) that the freedoms of the West are seductive but illusory.

In *Melancholia*, the past of David Keller (Jeroen Krabbé) catches up with him while he is working as a critic for a glossy art magazine. But David is disaffected: 'work is no more than a job . . . it keeps you off the street and booze . . . every day is one day less – this is the one great comfort you're granted'. Cynically, he remembers 1968, 'when Joseph Beuys was going to save the world'. Over five weeks, his life is irreversibly altered: he arrives at 'the big gesture', automatically stating the antithesis, 'of course, there's no such thing'. An ex-girlfriend (Susannah York), now married to a banker, urges him to finish the novel he has started – it's not brave to be a critic, she informs him, because he feeds upon other people's work, not his own – and offers him her house in Tuscany in which to write in seclusion. 'Do a short, serious book,' his boss advises, 'not a bestseller.'

Meanwhile, he receives a phone call from a political activist, Manfred (Ulrich Wildgruber), a Hamburg lawyer who reminds him of his previous affiliations and instructs him to assassinate Vargas, a Chilean torturer, who is due to attend a reception in London. David plans meticulously, stalks his prey and prepares his getaway. Manfred then tells David that Vargas will prove more useful alive than dead – he will expose evidence of American involvement in the death squads of San Salvador. But after meeting Sara (Jane Gurnett), the widow of one of Vargas' victims (and a victim herself), David determines to proceed with his plan. Efficiently the mission is accomplished and he travels to Italy, by way of Hamburg. Already isolated from the world ('I no longer want to be with people') and unable to face the truth about himself (Manfred insists that his usefulness to the group was dependent on his father's money), David opts for self-imprisonment. As a political thriller, the film is stylish and intriguing. Psychologically, it is more a testimony to 1960s existential angst and anomie than the melancholia anatomised by Robert Burton or figuring in Albrecht Dürer's (much featured) print.

John Hill observes that many films of the 1980s (from the splenetic parable of Lindsay Anderson's 1982 *Britannia Hospital* and the poetic allegory of *The Last of England*, to the grounded actuality of *The Ploughman's Lunch* and *Defence of the Realm*) were 'better at diagnosing contemporary ills than identifying a position from which opposition . . . might be mounted'.[24] Indeed, where there is resistance (as in the demonstration of the women at Greenham Common in *The Ploughman's Lunch*) it is frequently shown as ineffective. However, as he rightly concludes, these films, in their very presentation of helplessness (of which *Melancholia*'s futile 'big gesture' is a desperate example), express a widely felt sense of political impotence. It may be, as Jean Travers suggests in *Wetherby*, that the best one could do was to simply not lose hope and 'keep trying'.

Rita, Sue and Bob Too (Alan Clarke; FilmFour International in Association with British Screen, 1986)

Rita (Siobhan Finneran) and Sue (Michelle Holmes) are schoolgirls who live on a rundown housing estate in Yorkshire: there's 'never owt to do where we live', says Sue. Bob's wife Michelle (Leslie Sharp) – a less hysterical version of the working-class made-good suburban wife in *High Hopes* – has gone off sex and he looks elsewhere. Sue and Rita (the babysitters) willingly share him, although Bob (George Costigan) denies this when Michelle confronts him. Michelle's friend, Mavis, reports him and Michelle leaves him together with as many possessions as she can pack into a taxi, leaving Bob holding the baby. Rita tells Sue that she's pregnant by Bob, but Bob suggests that he and Sue can still get together regardless. 'I'm not going to do the dirty on Rita,' she says, and afraid that she has lost her best friend, wishes her 'all the luck in the world'. She then goes out with Aslan (Kulvindar Ghir), the Pakistani boy she's met at the taxi firm where she works after school. Fed up with her dad, Sue leaves home and moves in with Aslan and his sister, but can't stand it. Rita loses the baby. 'We can have others,' says Bob; 'He'd love for me to be bound up all the time,' comments Rita. 'Just think of all the family allowance we'd get', says Bob, sardonically, but Rita points out that she'd be doing all the work.

Sue returns to Aslan's house but he's seen Bob giving her a lift home from hospital, accuses her of continuing the affair and becomes possessive. Rita (equally suspicious) calls round to see Sue, and Aslan then hits her, later protesting that it was an accident. Rita gives him a well-placed kick and the two girls leave together. However much Aslan tries to persuade Sue to return, she'd prefer to stay with Rita. At his suggestion of an overdose, the girls collapse in a fit of giggles. Rita and Sue will share a bed and he'll have to curl up in the dog basket (if needs be, he'll even have to acquire the dog first). Told that he'll have to attend to his own tea (and finding the oven empty), Bob decides to go upstairs for a bath. Sue and Rita decide to stay together, sharing Bob, but stay with him on their own terms.

Various reasons might be advanced for the critical neglect of Alan Clarke as a director compared to, say, Ken Loach or Mike Leigh. Sadly, Alan Clarke died in 1990. All three have moved between television and film, with Ken Loach progressing from his seminal 1960s drama-documentary *Cathy Come Home* to *Kes* (see Chapter 9) and *Looks and Smiles* and *Fatherland* in the 1980s; Mike Leigh made *Abigail's Party* and *Nuts in May* (1976) for television, and also *Meantime* (1983) alongside his feature film *High Hopes*. However, the bulk of Clarke's work was commissioned and scheduled for television transmission, with *Rita, Sue and Bob Too* standing among rare exceptions.

Three's not a crowd for *Rita, Sue and Bob Too* (Alan Clarke, 1986)

Both *Made in Britain* and *Rita, Sue and Bob Too* are concerned with social tensions prominent in the decade but present no single simple political standpoint nor solution. Sue says that she thinks that her dad (Willie Ross) is 'a bit of a twat'; her mother (Maureen Long) that he hasn't 'done a day's work' in his life and that he's 'done nowt and been nowt'. But Sue's mum agrees with Sue that there's little point in going to work for £27.30 per week on a training scheme. Trevor, in *Made in Britain*, finds TDA and sniffing Evostik a more entertaining prospect than supermarket jobs at 50p an hour and refuses to be complicit with the system: 'We're not talking about honesty, we're talking about sticking to the rules,' he states, in 'a spectacular dead end of resistance'. Clarke attacks racism with humour: 'I can't help being a Paki,' bemoans Aslan to Sue's father; 'Yes you can,' he counters drunkenly. 'Anything you care about?' asks Peter, the evangelical manager at the Assessment Centre, endeavouring to cajole Trevor into signing a contract and to enlist him onto 'the project'. 'If I told you you'd confiscate it,' he spits back; 'You lock up anything that frightens you.' The housing estate of Rita and Sue, with its boarded-up windows and burned-out cars on bricks, is contrasted with the executive home, complete with double garage, stone-cladding and well-hosed turf, of Bob the builder and his affected wife. John Hill remarks that 1980s films were often set in the 'new' estates promised by 1960s planning and ambivalently showcased in New Wave films (*The Fruit Machine* even refers explicitly to *Saturday Night and Sunday Morning* [see Chapter 9] as an idealised personal past); *Vroom* (Beeban Kidron, 1988) opens with locked-frame monochrome shots of streets and a canal.[25] Unfortunately, the lack of investment in the same estate and 'never owt to do' was witnessed in *A State Affair* (2000), on a return trip by director Max Stafford Clark, as yet more bleak: heroin was described by interviewees as 'heaven on a piece of foil'.[26]

Like David Leland's *Personal Services* (directed by ex-Python Terry Jones, 1987) and *Wish You Were Here*, *Rita, Sue and Bob Too* responds to the pious exhortations of Margaret Thatcher, Victoria Gillick and others for a return to family values: Rita and Sue conspicuously engage in safe sex (for the most part) but are happy to share an affair with a married man; it may be that they are both under the legal age of consent.[27] The 2001 Channel Four screening of *Rita, Sue and Bob Too* was trailed as 'Thatcher's Britain with its knickers down'. Throughout the 1980s there were attacks from the Thatcher government on aspects of what it construed as sexual 'permissiveness', although its incantations were rarely coherent or programmatically consistent. While sex education was often cited as encouraging promiscuity ('we were only ever shown diagrams of male and female parts', says Rita), teenage pregnancy (hitherto often blamed upon ignorance) was similarly condemned. Some ministers, while declaring a return to family values as the only defence against moral decay, thought so highly of family life, it was said, that they kept two.[28] Much to the delight of Cynthia Payne (aka Christine Painter), her brothel was raided during the filming of *Personal Services*: 'The place for sex is in the home,' says Christine's Wing Commander (Alec McGowan); 'Here guests relaxed with a bridge roll and a gin and tonic before going with the lady of their choice, thus undermining the fabric of our society.' Both Leland and Frears attack a symptomatic parochial small-mindedness: 'He can't have learned those things in Leicester,' Alan Bennett has Joe Orton's brother say in *Prick Up Your Ears*.

Like many productions for the small and big screen, Alan Clarke sometimes adapted work originally presented on stage. Central Television took Steven Daldry's *Rat in the Skull* (1987) (and with it Gary Oldman) from the Royal Court. *Wish You Were Here* was originally written for television and a stage version opened in 1987. As in previous decades, the complaint was frequently made that transfers from television and stage to big screen remained small and boxed-in (for instance, *Time Out* said of Potter's *Brimstone and Treacle* that it suffered from 'stagebounditis').[29] In contrast, Clarke's work in television and film has always been remarkably cinematic in its *mise en scène* and choreography. His adaptations have interpreted material for a particular medium rather than straightforwardly transposed it; Leslie Sharp's long monologue, as the long-suffering Louise in *Road*, is delivered to camera as she walks the back alleys of the terraces and is as obsessive and passionate as Tim Roth's striding in Doc Marten 24s along roads and tunnels, casting off garments as he goes, and his pacing around the classroom in the Assessment Centre, as the swastika-bearing Trevor in *Made in Britain*.[30]

Rita, Sue and Bob Too was adapted from Andrea Dunbar's play, first staged at the Royal Court. It, too, uses Clarke's signature steadicam shot, as the girls go on an 'improving' school trip to local heritage site, Haworth Parsonage ('Can you imagine trying to have a jump with that on?' says Rita, contemplating one of the Brontë sisters' dresses); the girls stride out in bare legs and pointy-toed pumps, baggy tops billowing and arms swinging. But Clarke seems also to refer consciously to another familiar repertoire of shots: Sue and Aslan look out over 'their town' and Rita, Sue and Bob walk through cow pats, with the town in the distance, before returning to the discomfort of the reclining seats in Bob's motor. Jim Cartwright's screenplay for *Vroom* repeatedly calls for characters to run up a path through a field, then stop and turn to look back. But unlike the condescending (albeit well-intentioned) solemnity of its New Wave precursors, *Rita, Sue and Bob, Too* is gratifyingly playful and parodic and seemingly enjoys, rather than disparages, the popular culture of its protagonists: Rita and Sue bounce on Bob's leather sofas to the accompaniment of Madness' 'Welcome to the House of Fun', bop around the living room to the Bananarama video to 'It's More than Physical' on television, drive to the moors with Bob with '. . . sexy boy, sexy boy . . .' on the cassette player and conga together to Black Lace 'We're having a Gang-Bang (we're having a ball)'. The worldly wise Rita and Sue act the innocents when Bob hands over a rubber johnny, Rita snapping it between thumb and forefinger; the fellow residents of the housing estate, looking on from their balconies, urge on Sue and Rita as they give Michelle what for: 'It's better than Match of the Day, this!' The film ends with a held shot (reminiscent of 1970s' *Confessions of . . .* and *Carry Ons*) of Bob's bottom, mid-air, as he leaps onto the union jack duvet under which Rita and Sue await him: 'You took your fucking time, didn't you?' Similarly, Leland's *Wish You Were Here* and *Personal Services* boldly perform a number of routine gags, from a man stepping on a rake to a pantomime dame; *Wish You Were Here* comments ironically on the bonhomie of the seaside postcard just as *Made in Britain* invokes the ill-founded optimism of 1960s advertising slogans. But the potential critical force of the Leland films is, I think, compromised and vitiated by Christine's self-doubt (she does, after all, as the Detective Constable Timms suggests, 'ache for something straight') and by the cosy representation of her girls dispensing charity to her clients, a motley collection of mildly eccentric misfits. Rita and Sue, on the other hand, defiantly and confidently suit themselves.

Notes

1. On the content of *The Face* see Simon Frith's 'The Art of Posing', in *Music for Pleasure: Essays in the Sociology of Pop* (New York: Routledge, 1988), p. 178: 'The *i-D* staff go into the streets and use passersby as their dummies, snapping them as fashion plates, documenting their details . . . the argument is that we are what we dress ourselves up to be and that everyone is dressed up to be something. But the sociological implication is different: despite *i-D*'s selective tastes, the magazine mostly turns up people not inventing ways to express themselves, but making do with what they can get.'

2. Neil Norman interview, *The Face*, June 1983, p. 60; Mo Trix, 'All the Raj', *The Face*, April 1985, p. 71; see also (especially re. *Jewel in the Crown*) Richard Dyer, 'There's Nothing I can do! Nothing!', *White* (London: Routledge, 1997), pp. 184–206, and Neil Sinyard (re. *A Passage to India*) in Erica Sheen and Robert Giddings (eds), *The Classic Novel* (Manchester: Manchester University Press, 2000).

3. Lola Young, *Fear of the Dark* (London: Routledge, 1996), pp. 162–3; see also Manthia Diawara, 'Power and Territory: the Emergence of Black British Film Collectives', in Lester Friedman (ed.), *Fires Were Started: British Cinema and Thatcherism* (Minneapolis: University of Minnesota Press, 1993).

4. Neil Norman, *The Face*, January 1983, p. 30; by the 1980s Britain had the highest per capita videocassette recorder ownership, whereas Raymond Williams (no slouch) had predicted in *Television: Technology and Cultural Form* [1974] (Hanover: Wesleyan University Press, 1992), pp. 139–40, that 'videotape equipment will be marketed as a domestic sideline (though for very well-off people)'.

5. 'Gabriel's theme' from Ennio Morricone's score continues to be a popular item in Classic Gold Radio charts; the documentary *We Are the Indians* (Philip Cox and Valeria Mapelman, 2004) returns to the Guarini communities who took part in the filming.

6. For further discussion of *Another Time, Another Place* and *Scandal* see Amy Sargeant, 'The Content and the Form', in Claire Monk and Amy Sargeant (eds), *British Historical Cinema* (London: Routledge: 2002), pp. 199–216.

7. Beatrix Campbell, *The Iron Ladies: Why do Women Vote Tory?* (London: Virago, 1987), pp. 267–8, and Jeffrey Richards and Anthony Aldgate, 'Remembrance of Times Past', *Best of British* (London: I. B. Tauris, 2002), pp. 219–33.

8. Chris Peachment, in Tom Milne (ed.), *The Time Out Film Guide* (London: Penguin, 1989), p. 135.

9. Colin Booth, *The Face*, January 1985, p. 71.

10. Viv Chadder, 'The Higher Heel: Women and the Post-war British Crime Film', in Steve Chibnall and Robert Murphy (eds), *British Crime Cinema* (London: Routledge, 1999), pp. 71–3.

11. Regarding 'the great spy boom', see Alan Bennett, *Objects of Affection* (London: BBC, 1984), p. 218.

12. See Andrew Higson, 'Representing the National Past: Nostalgia and Pastiche in the Heritage Film', in Friedman, *Fires Were Started*.

13. See, especially, Robert Hewison, *The Heritage Industry* (London: Methuen, 1987), and John Corner and Sylvia Harvey, 'Mediating Tradition and Modernity: the Heritage/Enterprise Couplet', in John Corner and Sylvia Harvey (eds), *Enterprise and Heritage: Crosscurrents of National Culture* (London: Routledge, 1991).

14. Claire Monk, 'The British Heritage-Film Debate Re-visited', in Monk and Sargeant, *British Historical Cinema*, p. 177.

15. John Lahr (ed.), *The Diaries of Kenneth Tynan* (London: Bloomsbury, 2001), p. 144.

16. Raphael Samuel, *Theatres of Memory* (London: Verso, 1994), p. 303.

17. Samuel, 'Docklands Dickens' and 'Who Calls So Loud?', ibid. pp. 401–25; regarding Dickens' citation of the collapse of banks and financiers in *Little Dorrit* see also Hye-Joon Yoon, *Physiognomy of Capital in Charles Dickens* (San Francisco: International Scholars Publications, 1998), p. 223.

18. See Paul Chilton 'Newspeak: It's the Real Thing', in Crispin Aubrey and Paul Chilton (eds), *Nineteen Eighty-four in 1984: Autonomy, Control and Communication* (London: Comedia, 1983), pp. 33–44, and Linda Ruth Williams, 'Dream Girls and Mechanic Panic' , in I. Q. Hunter (ed.), *British Science Fiction Cinema* (London: Routledge, 1999).

19. John Hill, *British Cinema in the 1980s* (Oxford: Clarendon Press, 1999), p. 14.

20. See *Windlesham Rampton Report* (London: Faber and Faber, 1989) regarding the ban and subsequent enquiry.

21. Brian Case, in Milne (ed.), p. 555.

22. *The Face*, December 1983, p. 18.

23. See John Tulloch, *Television Drama* (London: Routledge, 1990), p. 161: 'Where . . . Loach was interested in "being", Griffiths was Concerned with Fiction, Construction, Reflexivity and Genre'; also Stuart Laing, 'Ken Loach: Histories and Contexts', in George McKnight (ed.), *Ken Loach: Agent of Challenge and Defiance* (Trowbridge: Flicks Books, 1997), p. 24.

24. Hill, *British Cinema in the 1980s*, p. 147.

25. Ibid., pp. 169–70.

26. *A State Affair* was broadcast alongside a production of *Rita, Sue and Bob Too* for BBC Radio 3 in 2000.

27. Hill, *British Cinema in the 1980s*, pp. 184–5.

28. Campbell, *The Iron Ladies*, pp. 272–5.

29. Frances Lass, in Milne (ed.), p. 77.

30. See 'Who's Spoiling Life?', in Richard Kelly (ed.), *Alan Clarke* (London: Faber and Faber, 1998), pp. 183–91, and Jim Cartwright, *Road* (London: Methuen, 1986), Act Two.

Chapter 12 | 1990s and the New Millennium

Julian Barnes' 1998 novel, *England, England,* describes a fictitious project to build a theme park simulacrum of the realm on the Isle of Wight. Market research is undertaken in twenty-five countries to ascertain the characteristics, virtues or quintessences which the word 'England' suggests. The list thereby produced includes: 'the royal family; the houses of parliament; homosexuality; shopping; the west end; perfidy; Manchester United Football Club; the BBC and classic serials; half-timbering; emotional frigidity; Oxford/Cambridge and bad underwear'.[1] On the one hand, Barnes is harking back to an idea mooted by J. B. Priestley in his *English Journey* (see Chapter 5); on the other, he is very much on message with the Blairite vision of a newly commodified 'cool Britannia' outlined in 1997 in Mark Leonard's Demos Report Britain™ and the Design Council's *Created in Britain*. Among the bodies responsible for spending public money on the projection of this rebranding, Leonard cites the Foreign Office, the DTI, the British Council, the Invest in Britain Bureau, the BTA and the BBC. The British Council responded in 2000 with a poorly advertised and pedestrian selection of screenings for three seasons in Paris. Chris Smith, Minister of Culture, Media and Sport 1997–2001, urged that 'New Creative Britain' be promoted as a place of innovation as much as of tradition and encouraged the trend for location tourism as a spin-off from television and film production. £17 million was given to competing Regional Film Commissions to further such activities. The Isle of Man was duly displayed in *The Tichborne Claimant* (David Yates, 1998), *Me Without You* (Sandra Goldbacher, 2001), *The Lawless Heart* (Tom Hunsinger/Neil Hunter, 2001) and, substituting for Ireland, in *Waking Ned* (Ireland/UK/France, Kirk Jones, 1998); the Merseyside Film Commission supported *Butterfly Kiss* (Michael Winterbottom, 1996) and *Under the Skin* (Carine Adler, 1997); the East Midlands Media Initiative invested in Shane Meadows' 2002 *Once Upon a Time in the Midlands* and Damien O'Donnell's 2002 *Heartlands*. Granada Television, based in Manchester, backed Michael Winterbottom's tribute to the city's club scene in the 1980s, *Twenty Four Hour Party People* (2002). Amber Films continued its longstanding commitment to record the lives of people in the Northeast. Alongside this apparent parochialisation of enterprise, national funds were made newly available from 1997 through the Lottery (for a larger number of films which did not receive distribution and a smaller number which did – including *Shooting Fish* [Stefan Schwartz, 1997], *Solomon and Gaenor* [Paul Morrison, 1999] and *This Year's Love* [David Kane, 1999]) and

A king as dictator: Ian McKellen in *Richard III* (Richard Loncraine, 1995)

through the Film Council from 2000 (including the Film Council/National Lottery-funded *The Revenger's Tragedy* [Alex Cox, 2002] and the Film Council/BBC-funded *Sylvia* [Christine Jeffs, 2003]). Arts Council funding (prior to its being subsumed by the Film Council) supported BBC 2's *Dance on Film* then, more surprisingly, *Plunkett & Macleane* (Jake Scott, 1999). Some film-makers (Ken Loach and Peter Greenaway) continued to look to Europe for co-funding, while others cast bankable European co-stars; some titles (notably the Richard Curtis series) attracted American backing.

FilmFour, a pioneer of television investment in film in the 1980s, ceased distribution in 2002, while the satellite company BSkyB contributed towards the production of *Beautiful People* (Jasmin Dizdar, 1999) and *My Kingdom* (Don Boyd, 2001). The BBC, meanwhile, still partially financed by the general public through the licence fee, answered the government's declared agenda by funding both the costume drama *Mrs Brown* (John Madden, 1997) and contemporary subjects presented by established directors (such as Stephen Frears' 2003 *Dirty Pretty Things* and Michael Winterbottom's 2002 *In This World*) and by newcomers (such as Lynne Ramsay's 1999 *Ratcatcher*, Pawel Pawlikowski's 2000 *Last Resort* and Dominic Anciano's 1999 *Love, Honour and Obey*).

Old Wine in New Bottles

Familiar themes, genres and cycles were sustained and resuscitated in British cinema of the 1990s. As biopics, the lives of artists found favour, either entirely invented – as in *Life and Death on Long Island* (Richard Kwietniowski, 1996) – or with varying degrees of factual accuracy: Isaac Julien addressed the life of writer Frantz Fanon (Colin Salmon) (in *Black Skin White Mask*, 1996), while Julien Temple covered punk band the Sex Pistols (see Chapter 10) in *The Filth and the Fury* (2000), and French film-maker Jean Vigo (in *Vigo*, 1998). Bill Conden cast Ian McKellen as British émigré Hollywood film-maker James Whale in *Gods and Monsters* (1998) (see Chapter 10). *Wilde* (Brian Gilbert, 1998) was quickly pursued by adaptations of *The Importance of Being Ernest* (1991) and *An Ideal Husband* (Oliver Parker, 1999). *Nora* (Pat Murphy, 2000) was concerned with James Joyce (Ewan McGregor) while *Tom and Viv* (Brian Gilbert, 1993) was concerned with the private life of poet, T. S. Eliot (Willem Dafoe) and his first wife (Miranda Richardson). *Backbeat* (Ian Softley, 1993) was concerned with the fifth Beatle while *Hilary and Jackie* (Anand Tucker, 1998) was a much contested account of the life and loves of the cellist, Jacqueline du Pré.[2] *Love is the Devil* ([John Maybury, 1998], concerning the painter Francis Bacon [Derek Jacobi]), *Sylvia* (concerning the lives of Poet Laureate Ted Hughes [Daniel Craig] and Sylvia Plath [Gwyneth Paltrow]), Stephen Hopkins' 2004 *The Life and Death of Peter Sellers* and Michael Winterbottom's forthcoming BBC film of the mis-spent Margate youth of artist Tracey Emin provide further evidence of this trend.[3] Kevin MacDonald's BAFTA-winning BBC drama-documentary *Touching the Void* (2003) – partly funded by the Film Council – spectacularly portrayed the 1985 Andes expedition of climbers Joe Simpson and Simon Yates; free screenings were held in 2004 to celebrate ten years of the National Lottery. Former documentarist Peter Webber (following the highly successful 2001 exhibition at the National Gallery) filmed Tracy Chevalier's fictional account of Vermeer, *Girl with a Pearl Earring* (2003). *Carrington* (Christopher Hampton, 1995) drew its events from the diary of the artist, Dora

(Emma Thompson), as much as Michael Holroyd's credited biography. The longstanding mutual affection of Carrington and Lytton Strachey (Jonathan Pryce) (see Chapter 1) sustains them both against a succession of other relationships, affairs and crushes. Pryce relishes his delivery of Strachey's most quotable quotes (asked, when he refuses to enlist for the First World War, what he would do should a German soldier attempt to rape his sister, he says that he 'should try to come between them') but, unlike many of Strachey's contemporaries, he provides more than an easy caricature.[4] The unconsummated love of Strachey and Carrington is presented tenderly and compassionately rather than as an example of upper-class bohemian English eccentricity. In *Iris* (Richard Eyre, 2001), based on the biography of John Bayley (Hugh Bonneville/Jim Broadbent) of his wife, Iris Murdoch (Kate Winslet/Judi Dench), the author's distancing from the world as a result of Alzheimer's is simplistically conflated with the interior life of a person who inhabits the alternative world of the novels and essays she creates. The sentimentality of this interpretation is countered by Murdoch's consultant, who, dispensing with metaphors, informs Bayley that there is no room for hope and that, sooner or later, the disease will get the better of its subject.

Jane Austen proved popular in film and as a classic serialisation on television, with *Jane Austen's Emma* (ITV, 1996), *Pride and Prejudice* (BBC TV, 1995), *Sense and Sensibility* (Ang Lee, 1996) and, twice removed, *Bridget Jones's Diary*. Christopher Hobbs dressed locations stripped to the brickwork to back an adaptation of *Mansfield Park* (Patricia Rozema, 1999) which rendered explicit the source of the Bertram family's wealth.[5] Dickens, the perennial favourite, appeared in BBC TV's *Great Expectations* (1999), *Our Mutual Friend* (BBC TV, 1998), *Bleak House* (BBC TV 1985 and Radio 4) and *Oliver Twist* (Roman Polanski, forthcoming). These productions were matched by tie-in editions of the novels, touring exhibitions and such associated publications as *The Making of 'Jane Austen's Emma'* and *The Making of 'Pride and Prejudice'*. Henry James proved popular at home and abroad with *The Portrait of a Lady* (Jane Campion, 1996) and, slightly advanced in its period setting, *The Wings of the Dove* (Ian Softley, 1998). Previously updated by Alan Plater, the BBC again revamped and reserialised Chaucer's *Canterbury Tales* in 2003. Following the example of numerous productions on stage of Shakespeare, Channel Four's *Othello* (an adaptation by the indefatigable Andrew Davies) contemporised its action in the Metropolitan Police Force and its *Twelfth Night* (starring *Bend It Like Beckham*'s Parminder Nagra) deployed surveillance cameras for the text's overheard conversations. Richard Loncraine's 1995 *Richard III*, with Ian McKellen as a disturbingly sexy hump-backed king – he sucks a ring from his finger before proposing to his future wife over the corpse of her dead husband – impressively translated the action and Richard's dictatorial ambitions to the canvas of 1930s Europe (with references in costuming and set dressings to Hitler, Stalin, Mussolini and Franco . . . as well as Britain). *My Kingdom* shifted *King Lear* to contemporary Liverpool; Kenneth Branagh's 1989 *Henry V* found Derek Jacobi, as the chorus, striding Kate Adie style atop the cliffs of Dover and his 1999 *Love's Labour's Lost* was staged as a 1930s musical. This (in the wake of Baz Luhrmann's 1996 *Romeo + Juliet*) combined evocative typography, fake archival monochrome footage ('Navarre's Cinetone News', on the eve of war) and a newspaper (*The Globe*) announcing the death of the king and the fall of France, with the high colour and stylisation of the Hollywood studios, and an overture incorporating the classic themes 'The Way You Look Tonight' and 'There's No Business like Show Business'. The action is backed by the setting of Korda's 1938 *A Yank in Oxford* (the Radcliffe Camera appears often): in this version, the hapless lovers are finally reunited with the liberation of France in 1945. Similarly, Marlowe's *Edward II* (performed also in a version by the Royal Ballet) was presented with customary stylised and anachronistic flourishes by Derek Jarman in 1991 (again, deftly designed by Christopher Hobbs). In 2001, Christine Edzard spinned Shakespeare's *A Midsummer Night's Dream* by drawing her cast from schools in south-east London.

Sally Potter's *Orlando* (1992) drew its temporal shifts from its source novel, written by Virginia Woolf for and about Vita Sackville-West in 1928. Quentin Crisp happily assumed a travesty role previously assigned to Mikhail Romm by Eisenstein (in his 1944/46 *Ivan the Terrible*) as Elizabeth I; Tilda Swinton has the androgynous good looks of a Nicholas Hilliard miniature (he is indubitably He at the outset – 'in spite of the fashion of the age'), latterly of a modern woman of the 1920s in corduroy jodhpurs and motorbike leathers (negotiating 1990s traffic), by way of paniers and crinolines in between: most memorably, running through a hardy clipped yew maze, she/he turns the corner from the 18th into the 19th century, where she encounters the embodiment of the New World, Shelmerdine (Billy Zane). Popster Jimmy Somerville appears as a castrato entertaining Elizabeth's courtiers in a punt and as an angel appearing to the female Orlando and her daughter in the present: 'I am coming . . . I am coming . . . not a woman nor a man'. Ned Sherrin, radio and former television pundit, appears as a waspish conversationalist in high society in the 1750s. Heathcote Williams (with Swinton, formerly a favourite of Jarman) appears as an impecunious poet leeching off Orlando's aristocratic patronage (in 1650) and as a Docklands-based publisher, potentially profiting from Orlando's labours to record her past (in 1990). Orlando's looks to camera follow the address to the reader of Woolf's novel, in which typography and style equally indicate temporal shifts. The film's cinematography and composition translate Woolf's observations on a changing climate. As Knole (the family house which, as a woman, she could not inherit) was for Vita, so is Orlando's home at the core of the 400-year fantasy, surviving her changed gender and various occupations. Ultimately, the house is opened to the public as a stately home and Orlando visits it with her daughter. The film celebrates the fantasy of inhabiting the right body at the right time at the right place – Orlando sails the high seas on a galleon; finds himself in London at the time of the Great Frost; serves as Charles II's Ambassador in Constantinople; witnesses the verbal exchanges of Addison, Dryden and Pope – while always returning to the same place, nostalgically looking backwards and optimistically being modern.

Shekhar Kapur's 1998 *Elizabeth* was similarly eclectic in its stylistic references (bloody French costume dramas such as *La Reine Margot* [France, Patrice Chereau, 1994], brooding battlements in *Gamlet* [USSR, Grigori Kozintsev, 1964], thriller-style lighting and camerawork) and likewise looked beyond the British stage and screen for its cast, employing TV presenter Angus Deayton and ex-footballer Eric Cantona alongside the Australian actress Cate Blanchett and the French actress (and ex-BBC trolley dolly) Fanny Ardant. Shekhar Kapur had previously directed *The Bandit Queen* (India,

1994). Such trends in the styling and marketing of British history were identified by Claire Monk as a marker of the 'post-heritage' film, differentiating the product from its 1980s precursors.[6] Meanwhile, *Plunkett & Macleane* cast *Trainspotting*'s (1995) bad boys Jonny Lee Miller and Robert Carlyle as highwaymen, opening supposedly in 1748 in Knightsbridge but with a soundtrack, costuming and set design which blatantly deviated from the declared date and locale. Sadly, in Liv Tyler's performance as pouting love interest, there was nothing so much as wayward, offering nothing of the delights of its 1945 precursor, *The Wicked Lady* (see Chapter 7). However, it seems to me equally valid to refer these manoeuvres to internationally funded and cast costume romps from the 1960s and 1970s – I'm thinking especially of Dick Lester's 1974 *The Three Musketeers*, which featured the model turned actress Raquel Welch, the comedian Spike Milligan, Hammer stalwart Christopher Lee and Richard Chamberlain (aka television's *Doctor Kildare*) alongside the British screen's 'young premier', Michael York, and 'old ham', Oliver Reed (see Chapter 10).

I Capture the Castle (directed for the screen by Tim Fywell, 2003) was adapted from a novel nostalgically written by Dodie Smith while exiled in Hollywood for the duration of the Second World War, and bears the stamp of such 1930s commentaries on the fascinating peculiarities and virtues of distinctly British and American life as *The Ghost Goes West* (see Chapter 5): as in Stella Gibbons' *Cold Comfort Farm* (filmed for television in 1995 by John Schlesinger), the local swain makes good in movies. Likewise, *Gosford Park* (2002), jointly funded by the Film Council and the American Film Institute, charged the American independent director Robert Altman with a story and largely British cast comparable to the Agatha Christie adaptations of the 1970s, *Murder on the Orient Express* (Sidney Lumet, 1974) and *Death on the Nile* (John Guillermin, 1978). Maggie Smith is magnificently and imperturbably the same as ever. The social hierarchy of the Old World country house (where a maid can be dismissed for speaking out of turn) is contrasted with New World social egality (where a millionaire film producer, the guest of the house, can offer a lift to the disgraced maid). Rigidly ordered regularity disguises personal hypocrisy, betrayal and deceit, while duplicity on the part of an American 'spy' masquerading as a Scot is soon discovered. Certainly, *Gosford Park* and *The Remains of the Day* (the 1993 adaptation by 'heritage' team Merchant–Ivory of Kazuo Ishiguro's award-winning historical novel) are less cosy representations of the country house institution than is provided by the ITV *Upstairs Downstairs* (1971–5) model – but, like recent 'reality', life-swapping television programmes, still trade upon its pervasive attractions as a dramatic subject and setting.

In Philip Haas' 1995 *Angels and Insects*, an adaptation of A. S. Byatt's historical novella *Morpho Eugenia*, a Darwinist comparison is drawn between the social organisation of the house and the study of ants (housed in a similar neo-Gothic, pinnacled container) which the governess and her charges undertake. *The Tichborne Claimant*, recorded by Arnold Bennett in *Buried Alive* as an actual event (see Chapter 4), was promoted in 1998 as 'a new Ealing comedy'. But alongside Rozema's *Mansfield Park* and BBC TV's 1998 adaptation of Philippa Gregory's *A Respectable Trade*, it acknowledged Britain's trading in slaves and a history of black servitude. Andrew Bogle (John Kani), an African in England in 1895, has served the English aristocracy all his life. The story of his dismissal and his attempts to claim justice for himself are told in flashback: in Australia, he encounters a willing pretender (Robert Pugh) to the Tichborne title and coaches him accordingly; so thorough are his efforts that 'Roger' (in reality, one Arthur Orton) tragically convinces himself of his claim to the inheritance. The judge (John Gielgud) at the subsequent trial recognises the threat which the case poses to respect for ties of blood, while the prosecution lawyer (Stephen Fry) admits without a qualm that he could have as easily swung the case in their favour. But, by posing aristocracy as merely a performance (as the judge acknowledges), the whole basis of society's deference is thrown into question. Bogle concludes, 'the older and sicker the beast' (intending the aristocracy thereby), 'the more savage he becomes'.

Writing in 1999, Robert Murphy drew a tacit comparison between Mick Hodges' 1971 *Get Carter* and the characters and structure of Jacobean drama.[7] The parallels were rendered explicit in Mike Figgis' *Hotel* (2002) (which narrated the frustration by Italian mafiosi of a bizarre attempt to make a Dogma film of Webster's 1612 *The Duchess of Malfi*) and in Alex Cox's bold transposition of *The Revenger's Tragedy* to Liverpool in 2011. However, against this dystopian vision, Cox's interpretation of the 1607 Thomas Middleton/Cyril Torneur text remained stubbornly and clumsily literal (swords are swords, a meteor is a meteor). *Get Carter* and other cult crime films of the 1970s were more conspicuously revisited in the gangster cycle of the 1990s. Simultaneously, these films were much vaunted by a crop of new lads' mags (*Loaded*, *Maxim*, *FHM*, the revamped *GQ* and the shortlived *Jack* and the late-comers *Nuts* and *Zoo*) as 'sadistically captivating and cinematically stylish', 'British pulp noir at its finest';[8] 'The Self-Preservation Society's anthem from *The Italian Job* (1969) (see Chapter 9) was taken up by English football supporters in Japan during the 2002 World Cup and it prompted a homage, F. Gary Gray's *The Italian Job* (US, 2003); its ending was also invoked in the first series cliff-hanger of Channel Four's 2004 *The Green Wing*.

Ex-footballer Vinnie Jones was cast by Guy Ritchie in *Lock, Stock and Two Smoking Barrels* (1998) and *Snatch* (2000) as the hard man, Big Chris (who protectively, repeatedly urges his son, Little Chris, to put on his seat belt). Jones doubled the trouble presented by Caine as Carter by crossing a pair of antique shotguns over his shoulders (a pose and persona duly reproduced for a Bacardi ad campaign). The quirky deadpan philosophising of *Snatch*'s milk-drinking Turkish (Jason Statham) has subsequently been appropriated by TV ads for Kit Kat Cubes. *Gangster No. 1* (Paul McGuigan, 2000) cast Malcolm McDowell as the 'ultra-violent' gangster of the title (as in BBC TV's 1997 *Our Friends in the North*), as if he were an older version of Alex in *A Clockwork Orange* (see Chapter 10). Steven Soderbergh's *The Limey* (US, 1999) used footage from Ken Loach's 1967 *Poor Cow* (see Chapter 9) to establish the past of an ex-con (Terence Stamp) seeking vengeance for his daughter. Sting and Phil Daniels (a miraculous survival), from Franc Roddam's 1979 *Quadrophenia*, reappear in, respectively, *Lock, Stock* (co-produced by Sting's wife, Trudie Styler) and BBC TV's 2004 *The Long Firm* and *Goodbye, Charlie Bright* (Nick Love, 2001). In the latter, Daniels plays a disaffected, maladjusted Falklands War veteran alongside BBC TV's *East-Enders* star Paul Nicholls, while also appearing in the 1990s in pop promos for the band Blur. *The Krays* (Peter Medak, 1990), meanwhile, glamourises Ronnie and Reggie (as did David Bailey's photographs in their prime time) by the casting of Spandau Ballet's Kemp twins (Martin later moving to *EastEnders*).[9] All these films (like Roeg's and Cammell's *Performance*) feature the 'fastidious narcissism' which Andrew Spicer finds characteristic of the genre, with Martin Kemp later appearing camel-coated in ads for Burton Menswear and Marc Warren, 'the new Malcolm McDowell' (from ITV's *The Vice* and BBC TV's 2004 *Hustle*), appearing in features for Austin Reed Tailoring.[10]

The idiosyncratic banter of the gangster cycle owes something to Quentin Tarantino's 1992 *Reservoir Dogs* (with Britain's own Tim Roth as Mr Pink) and 1994 *Pulp Fiction* (again, with Tim Roth); also (at its best) to Pinter's *The Birthday Party* (1968) (see Chapter 9) and Steven Berkoff's plays, *Greek* (1980) and *East* (1975). Significantly, both *Mojo* (Jez Butterworth, 1997) and *Gangster No. 1* first appeared on stage. An exemplary case is provided by Jonathan Glazer's 2001 *Sexy Beast* – which, in turn, appears indebted to Stephen Frears' sadly neglected 1984 *The Hit*. Ray Winstone (again, a *Quadrophenia* survivor) plays Gary Dove, an ex-gangster, now settled to a life of domestic and conjugal bliss in an isolated villa on what *EastEnders* in the 1990s dubbed Spain's 'Costa del Crime'.[11] When Don Logan (Ben Kingsley) is despatched to enlist him for one last job, Gary is determined to resist but knows that refusal is not an advisable option if he wants to save himself and Deedee (Amanda Redman). Don goads Gary: far from the bonhomie of *Lock, Stock* and *Snatch*, here there is little trust among thieves, just fear. Gary battles to overcome his own demons, to bury them and start again. Much of the Ritchie films owe less to the 1970s, I would suggest (where are the bent coppers of *The Long Good Friday* [1979], BBC TV's 1978 *Law and Order* or even Antonia Bird's 1997 *Face*?), than to such Ealing comedies as *The Lavender Hill Mob* (1951) (which presents a worn-down bank clerk to match Ritchie's disaffected middlemen) and *The Ladykillers* (1955) (which, like *Snatch*, portrays malevolent pets, slapstick and caricatured gangsters wiping out one another) (see Chapter 8). The novelty of the Ritchie films lay rather in their presentation and packaging (again, due somewhat to Tarantino), with stylish cinematography and editing of eclectic sound and image tracks.

Old Mates

The romantic comedies *Four Weddings and a Funeral* (1994) and *Notting Hill* (1999) (both written by television graduate Richard Curtis) featured a group of old friends, some settled in coupledom, some agonising over their own future and intent upon settling. With an eye to the export market, both featured Barnes' 'stately homes' and, respectively, the American stars Andi MacDowell and Julia Roberts alongside the eminently exportable Hugh Grant (who was also cast in America in *Nine Months* [1995], *Two Weeks Notice* [2002] and elsewhere). American directors Paul and Chris Weitz came to Britain to make *About a Boy* (2002), taken from Nick Hornby's 'lad lit' novel and featuring a soundtrack by Badly Drawn Boy. Here, and in *Bridget Jones's Diary* (UK/France/US, 2001), an attempt was made to to shift Grant's persona away from his usual bumbling and blustering delivery towards something (ever so slightly) more confidently raffish. *Bridget Jones's Diary*, adapted with Richard Curtis and Andrew Davies from Helen Fielding's 1995–7 newspaper column (and 'chick lit' novel), directed by Sharon Maguire (Shazza of Fielding's original) similarly centres on the relationship of Bridget and her parents and a surrogate family of friends (Tom [James Callis], Shazza [Sally Phillips] and Jude [Shirley Henderson]), plus her would-be/won't-be relationships with Daniel Cleaver (Hugh Grant) and Mark Darcy (Colin Firth): Chardonnay-fuelled conversations concern the travails of couples and alternately bemoan and celebrate singletons. The confidences entrusted to the diary are translated in the film to voiceover and handwritten over titles; on a good day, Bridget's tally of alcohol and tobacco consumption is displayed large scale over Piccadilly Circus. The film also features the 'stately home' and the 'bad underwear' identified by Barnes.

Not only did these films present a group of friends as protagonists, they also employed variations of a standard cast and crew. *Peter's Friends* (1992) appeared to be particularly self-regarding in the matching of its personnel to its narrative, with Kenneth Branagh directing ex-wife Emma Thompson and ex-mother-in-law Phylida Law alongside fellow ex-Cambridge Footlights pal Stephen Fry.[12]

Unsettled couples appear in Gwyneth Paltrow's roles in the nifty but derivative either/or tale, *Sliding Doors* (US/UK, 1998) – a directorial debut for actor Peter Howitt – and multiply in *This Year's Love* (with funding from the National Lottery and the Scottish Arts Council) – with writer David Kane directing his own screenplay. London's landmark waterways appear in the western reaches

Danny (Douglas Henshall) marks the opening of a new chapter in David Kane's 1999 *This Year's Love*

of the Thames (in the former) and at Camden Lock (in the latter). Both indicate anti-corporate, small-scale entrepreneurialism (unconvincingly successful in the former, convincingly unsustained in the latter) as a feature of Blair's Britain. The title sequence of *This Year's Love* wryly refers both to the supposed permanence of an attachment declared by a tattoo and to the business launched by Danny (Douglas Henshall). Danny and Hannah (Catherine McCormack) commit to one another but immediately separate when he learns that she has slept with their best man only two nights before. Hannah seeks solace with artist Cameron (Dougray Scott): 'She's only flirting with you 'cause she's full of self-loathing,' says her mate, Denise; 'That's fine by me,' concludes unkempt Cameron. Meanwhile, Danny is refused his place on their honeymoon flight to Jamaica (because he's very, very drunk) and offers the tickets to Mary, a cleaner at the airport and would-be singer (Kathy Burke) – whom he invites for a drink. At Camden Market, middle-class boho Sophie, ex-Roedean and single mother (Jennifer Ehle) meets gauche comic artist William (Ian Hart) and Cameron finds Hannah, whom he invites to pose for him. William finds it difficult to satisfy Sophie ('Dominate me,' she tells him; 'Alright then, what do you want me to do?' he pleads, before reminding her that it 'takes two to have crap sex'). A year later, Mary winds up with Cameron, Sophie gets together with Danny and Hannah has a fling with Alice (Emily Woof) in preference to William. Sophie demonstrates she's a fuckwit and a hypocrite (as Danny says, she doesn't know where she belongs), while Mary informs Cameron that he's a fuckwit for continuing to try to pick up 'lonely hearts' from ads in the paper. A year later still, William winds up temporarily with Mary (before finally losing his marbles), Sophie winds up with Cameron (before settling for Tarquin, whom she has met at her aromatherapy class), Hannah finally manages to make her appointment with Danny and Cameron continues to look up newspaper columns.

Mates falling in and falling out proved a successful recipe for film-makers. *Shallow Grave* (Danny Boyle, 1995) and *Trainspotting* (Danny Boyle's adaptation of Irvine Walsh's 1994 novel), both set in Edinburgh, have flatmates and old mates disputing the division of spoils come by chance. The protagonists of the former (Kerry Fox, Christopher Ecclestone, Ewan McGregor) are young professionals; at the beginning of the latter (generally set against high rises rather than Morningside), Renton (Ewan McGregor) declares a preference for heroin over anything else that a consumer society has to offer, 'It wipes out worrying about anything else.' Spud (Ewen Bremner) duly interviews for jobs (in order to claim dole) but thereby risks getting employed (which would interfere with his habit): 'earning' the cash to support this is, after all, a full-time occupation in itself. Renton and Sick Boy occupy themselves with Sean Connery impersonations and discussions of the relative merits of Bond girls (*Dr No*'s 1962 Ursula Andress, in gold bikini, is voted best: 'Are you looking for shells?' – 'No, I'm just looking'). The visual and aural pace of the film's opening, in both its scoring and punchy voiceover, attempts to convey something of the pleasure of the drug, 'otherwise we wouldn't do it', but Renton admits that 'we would have injected vitamin C if only they'd made it illegal'. Renton also observes that his mother is an addict, too, but her chosen substance is more socially acceptable, while the ex-con Begbie (Robert Carlyle) 'doesn't do drugs, he does people'. Tommy (Kevin McKidd) has the 'weakness' (says Renton) of never lying, cheating or taking drugs, yet turns to heroin for support after splitting from his girlfriend. Renton meets perky schoolgirl Diane (Kelly MacDonald) who urges him to stay clean: Renton constrains himself ('but there's final hits and final hits . . .'). Heightened toning flattens backgrounds to a patchwork of colours and surreal sequences denote Renton's near fatal collapse (the sides of the frame close in as he sinks into unconsciousness) and his subsequent painful withdrawal (worst of all, he encounters ITV's Dale Winton in his nightmares). The 'reformed' Renton, newly arrived in London, is not so very different from the yuppies of *Shallow Grave*: he takes a job as an estate agent (the lying comes easily to him). 'There's no such thing as society,' recites Renton in Thatcherite mode, 'and if there was, I'd certainly have nothing to do with it.'[13] Sickboy (Johnnie Lee Miller) has, meanwhile, reinvented himself as a pimp and a pusher. Stopping over in London, one of his first moves is to sell Renton's rented telly. The mates determine on a scam with a guaranteed return – 'Just for a moment it felt really great like we were all in it together,' observes Renton, in retrospect, but not like the £16,000 he would secure if he absconded with the total. Begbie wrecks his chance of a cut by picking a fight in a pub and Sickboy, Renton decides, would have ripped off the others first had he thought of it. Renton leaves a share for Spud: 'but let's face it, I betrayed my mates'. Disconcertingly, Renton cynically concludes that henceforth he is going to be just like his audience. Matching (but inverting) the opening sequence he opts for the job, the family, the mortgage and legitimately bar-coded consumer goods.

Betrayal between friends is coincidental to *Morvern Callar* (Lynne Ramsay, 2002). When Lanna (Kathleen McDermot) tells her best friend, Morvern (Samantha Morton), that she has fucked her husband – guiltily presuming that this might account for his disappearance – Morvern responds flatly, telling her he is dead. But her news is received indifferently, Lanna babbles on regardless. His suicide has served as a catalyst, prompting Morvern to leave her job packing shelves in a supermarket. She dismembers and buries the body in the wilds then uses the money which he has left for his funeral to book a package holiday in Spain for herself and Lanna. She sends his novel to a publisher under her own name, then, on the strength of the contract she receives, suggests that they continue their travels – again, Lanna's supposed 'betrayal' does not constitute a threat to their friendship (as for the girls in Alan Clarke's *Rita, Sue and Bob Too* – see Chapter 11): comfortably they play together with pastry and sprawl on the sofa with their jeans unzipped (this is a girl thing). But Lanna declines Morvern's offer – she wants to stay where she is, with people she knows, in a familiar place: 'it's the same crap everywhere', she reminds Morvern; she wonders 'what planet' Morvern is on. Meanwhile, the film itself, visually and aurally, carefully invites and withdraws its audience to and from Morvern's world. The pre-title credits appear in offset lower case white lettering on black, intercut with the pulsating lights of a Christmas tree, intermittently revealing the still bodies of James with Morvern huddled beside him; the film closes with the sound of the compilation tape bequeathed to Morvern shifting from a fully incorporated backing track to the action to a more distant perspective, tinnily leaking from her Walkman.

Newquay was a popular holiday destination in the 1990s. Ryanair, the new budget airline, flew there, courses at nearby universities were established in surf and beach management and its boho style, its babes and its beefcake, were covered in magazine fashion spreads.[14] *Blue Juice* (Carl Prechezer for Channel Four Films, 1995) follows a common narrative pattern and invokes the physical and spiritual regenerative potential of the countryside. It reunites a number of friends who have previously drifted apart, again recasting actors commonly seen in similar roles: Heathcote Williams appears as Shane, the local master craftsman cum shaman, and Jenny Agutter (of *The Railway Children* – see Chapter 10) appears in Terry's drug-induced vision as Guinevere. *Blue Juice* also offers the novel spectacle of Catherine Zeta Jones, as Chloë, failing to arouse her man, JC (Sean Pertwee). JC is concerned that he is approaching thirty and there still remain waves to surf (especially the infamous 'boneyard') and places to go; Chloë wants to raise the money to buy the lease on the local café, to save it from developers. Uninvited outsiders, such as the mercenary London journalist (Keith Allen – a stock role in *Shallow Grave*, *Trainspotting* and *Twenty Four Hour Party People*), are generally not welcome. Dean (Ewan McGregor) admits that he has pretty much wasted his life thus far, that neither he nor any one else shows him any respect, proving his point by selling dodgy drugs to the locals and being punched up in return; he sells the story of the 'boneyard' to the journalist, requiring JC to perform in spite of his anxieties. Josh (Steven Mackintosh), on the other hand, is mighty pleased with himself and his job ('don't go treating me like a superstar – it's no big deal') and expects the DJ, Junior Sands, to be similarly impressed – she isn't, especially as Josh has appropriated material produced by her father. Although the Aquashack is sold, Shane finds another shed for Chloë; Terry and his girlfriend go off on a world trip; Dean learns to produce surfboards; Josh and Junior produce a record of Ossie Sands (with a techno mix to pay the bills) and JC and Chloë finally manage to produce a baby. Unfortunately, the principal attraction of the north Cornish Coast (the sea) appears rarely and Pertwee's stunt double sees very little action.

Older old mates (and a familiar veteran ensemble – Sir Michael Caine, Sir Tom Courtenay, Bob Hoskins, David Hemmings – with Dame Helen Mirren and the ubiquitous Ray Winstone) reunite in Fred Schepisi's 2001 adaptation of Graham Swift's 1996 Booker prize-winner *Last Orders*. As in *East is East* (see Chapter 2) and in *Nil by Mouth* (1997) (where Billy remembers hop-picking with his nan), Londoners fondly recall their seasonal escapades in the countryside. The title is doubly significant, of the pub in which the friends have for decades habitually met as drinking buddies and of their gathering to honour the will of Jack Dodds (Caine). Together they travel to scatter his ashes over the sea at Margate. As revealed in flashback, their shared past is a story of both betrayal and loyalty – and for his adoptive son, Vince (Winstone), and estranged, disabled daughter in care, the countryside is the origin of 'all that went wrong' rather than a delightful retreat.

Actor Keith Allen returned to his roots to appear in brother Kevin's *Twin Town* (1997), from a screenplay co-written by Paul Durden, allowing him a cameo role as a contentedly stoned vagrant. *Maxim* touted the film's delivery of 'Anarchy, Laughs and Stupidity'. Hackneyed jokes about sheepshagging and rugby are told by a London drug dealer up in Swansea for the day to a straight-faced pliant cop, local boy Greyo (Dorien Thomas) and his thoroughly bent sidekick, incomer Terry (Dougray Scott). The Lewis twins (Rhys Ifans and Llyr Evans) spend their time stealing cars, sniffing their dad's Airfix and swapping magic mushrooms for Diazapans (washed down with cider) with the old-age pensioners. Their sister Adie (Rachel Scorgie), meanwhile, works in the local executive health spa (*not* a massage parlour, Mrs Lewis insists) and services Greyo while disdainfully rejecting Terry (after all, she says, she's only the receptionist). As with *Snatch*, there is slapstick involving pets – which turns nasty when the Lewis caravan goes up in smoke. The twins take their revenge, according their father the burial at sea which he had always favoured and despatching the arsonist with him. His friends in the choir assemble on Mumbles Pier to salute him. Swansea – 'an ugly, lovely town', quotes Greyo, 'a pretty shitty city (which at least rhymes)', retorts Terry – appears magnificent at the end, managing to recoup the humour previously exacted at its expense.[15]

Peter (Adrian Dunbar) and Jude (Miranda Richardson) are bound by an 'old faith' rather than by mere friendship in Neil Jordan's *The Crying Game* (1992). Defaulters risk retribution and Fergus (Stephen Rea) cannot be allowed to resign when he decides that he has had enough. 'You're never out,' Jude informs him, 'and nor is the black chick,' she threatens. The film opens with Jude acting duplicitously as bait to trap a British soldier in Northern Ireland. Jody (Forest Whitaker) is held hostage to bargain for the release of an IRA prisoner in Castlereagh. During his captivity, Jody befriends Fergus, a welcome change from the racism to which he has become accustomed, and Jody tells him about his lover, the 'black chick' Dil (Jaye Davidson), waiting for him in London. Jody respects Fergus as a fellow soldier ('It's in their nature to do what they do,' they admit, resignedly) but whereas 'We do a tour of duty and we finish' (says Jody), Fergus and the others are never finished; 'It depends what you believe in,' replies Fergus. Fergus bungles the order to assassinate Jody,

Dil (Jaye Davidson) thinks that Fergus (Stephen Rea) 'knows' in Neil Jordan's 1992 *The Crying Game*

who makes a run for it and is mown down by a British Army Saracen tank, on its way to the hide-out. Fergus honours his promise to locate Dil: both have assumed identities. Furthermore, when Fergus falls for Dil himself, it is suggested that Dil may be a surrogate for Jody in his affections and that he ultimately serves time on Dil's behalf partly as recompense for his own guilt. Dil is, perhaps, more open and less duplicitous than Fergus, who initially withholds his account of Jody's death ('I thought you knew,' Dil says to Fergus, masquerading as Jimmy). There is no escape for Fergus in London, and Jude delivers 'the tools of the trade', ordering him to shoot a legitimate target, a judge (possibly duplicitously) visiting a high-class knocking shop. But Dil prevents Fergus from meeting his assignation and, instead, uses the supplied 'tool' to wreak revenge on Jude. There is poetic justice here, reinforced by the opening, closing and theme music: Percy Sledge's 'When a Man loves a Woman', the country classic 'Stand By Your Man' (sung by a man) and Boy George's 'The Crying Game'. Sadly, the critical reception of *The Crying Game* failed to ensure the security of its production company, Palace Pictures, responsible also for *A World Apart* (see Chapter 11). Both films engaged exceptionally well with conflicts between personal and political affiliation.

Unhappy Families

At the turn of the millennium, each troubled family was unhappy after its own fashion, and happy families no longer seemed alike. However, broadly speaking, whereas in the 1950s dissident children were presented as the cause of domestic unrest, the subsequent generation found the parents a frequent cause for concern. Sometimes their actions are blamed in turn on the circumstances of their own upbringing (as in *Nil by Mouth*), sometimes they remain unexplained (as in *The War Zone* [1999]). Often children, at home or away, are seen to assume a parenting role within their own family.

Bhaji on the Beach (Gurinder Chadha, 1993) presented a contemporary image of thwarted love, divided by culture as much as by race (insists one of Hasida's numerous Indian-born aunties when she becomes pregnant by Oliver, whose father came from Jamaica). *Solomon and Gaenor* (National Lottery-funded through the Arts Councils of England and Wales) and Beebon Kidron's 1997 *Amy Foster* (adapted from Joseph Conrad's novel) provide costume versions of the same perennial theme of star-crossed young lovers. The former followed the example of Welsh-language broadcasting and cast Ioan Gruffudd (from ITV's *Hornblower* [2002]) as Solomon with Maureen Lipman (BT's Beattie) as his mother and David Horovitz as his father. While the Jewish characters speak Yiddish among themselves, Ilona Sekacz's score combines klesmer strains and instrumentation with a traditional Welsh harp. Solomon initially lies about his background to Gaenor and keeps their romance a secret from his own family. When Gaenor becomes pregnant she is denounced by the chapel minister and the local community, while her boorish, uneducated brothers set upon Solomon and accuse Jews in general of profiting from the strikes in the docks and the mines: Solomon, they notice, has soft hands. The family business is wrecked and looted and Solomon sent to Cardiff where he can be supervised and trained for a profession. Solomon's mother disowns Gaenor's unborn child and tells her to forget her son. But he chooses to die with Gaenor rather than to live without her.

In *Amy Foster*, too, love is prompted by chance and fated to fall foul of prejudice and ignorance. Janko (Vincent Perez) is the sole survivor of a shipwreck on the Cornish coast. Unable to understand him, the villagers at first take him for an idiot, then as a gypsy, then as an epileptic. 'Why still the hating?' he asks Dr Kennedy (Ian McKellen); 'You come from far away,' Kennedy explains, to which Janko replies, 'Everyone comes from somewhere.' But Amy (Rachel Weisz) takes care of him – she, too, is ostracised and taunted as a witch for her 'oddness' and has, in turn, resorted to keep silent to safeguard her isolation for herself. Amy's own mother, Mary (Zoë Wanamaker), warns her against forming a 'foolish' attachment to Janko: the reason for the family's rejection of her, it transpires, is her mother's own fear and sense of guilt, Amy's natural father being the father of Isaac (Tom Bell), the man whom Mary married. 'Bad you were conceived and bad you're made,' spits Mary. When Amy at last resorts to them for help, she and her baby are turned away as 'a gypsy woman selling curses'. The story is shown in flashback, narrated by the doctor (himself an 'incomer' from Scotland). He and the Swaffers (Joss Ackland with Kathy Bates as his sister) have been the only local residents to consistently support the couple and their child. But, as Dr Kennedy tends Miss Swaffer's injured leg, she reminds him that he too has not been free from prejudice, harbouring a grudge against simple Amy for her self-willed silence and judging her for failing to save the life of his favourite, the exotic Janko. The weather and the landscape are frequently shown as harsh: large dark skies looming over granite cliffs and surging waves. Only Amy's sanctuary in the caves is bathed in golden, warm light. The settings are sparse, the cottages low-ceilinged, the costuming unvaried, monotonous and dour. After the shipwreck, a few splashes of red cloth accentuate the scene. *Amy Foster* and *Solomon and Gaenor* offer appropriately unglamorous views of the past, in which life is often nasty and short and frequently brutish.

Contemporary brutishness was more often located against an urban background. In *Bhaji on the Beach*, Jinder has fled to a Birmingham women's refuge from the husband who has beaten her, and can agree to return only on condition that he leave his job and family. She finds temporary escape (to the strains of Cliff Richard's *Summer Holiday* theme [Peter Yates/Herbert Ross, 1963]) in a daytrip to Blackpool. After their appearances in British film and television in the 1980s, Tim Roth (most conspicuously with Quentin Tarantino's *Reservoir Dogs* and *Pulp Fiction*) and Gary Oldman (with Francis Ford Coppola's *Bram Stoker's Dracula* [1992]) were cast in independent and studio productions in America; *Loaded* 'Super Lad' Oldman also scored (idiomatically at least) with European audiences in Luc Besson's 1994 *Léon*. Both returned to Britain to launch themselves as directors and both chose to cast Ray Winstone (who, similarly, had previously worked with Alan Clarke). In *Nil by Mouth* (Gary Oldman, 1997 – with a cameo appearance from the director), he plays Ray, the grown-up bad boy of *Scum* (1979) and *Quadrophenia* (see Chapter 10), while to his wife, Val (Kathy Burke), he very occasionally reveals the lovable roguishness of *Sexy Beast* and *Fanny and Elvis* (Kay Mellor, 1999). Similarly, in *Once Upon a Time in the Midlands*, Robert Carlyle manages to combine the maniacal violence of Begbie (in *Trainspotting*) with the attractions of Gaz (in Peter Cattaneo's 1997 *The Full Monty*) and Steve and George (in Ken Loach's 1991 *Riff-Raff* and 1997 *Carla's Song*): his estranged wife (Shirley Henderson) has to decide between living with him and living without him.

Ray's wife in *Nil by Mouth* is equally much abused. His own father has not loved him (he pines to a friend that he never got a kiss or a cuddle from him – 'It's as if the word "dad" itself was enough . . . and it ain't') but he complains that he does not see his own son from a previous marriage. Ray beats Val, even though she is pregnant with his child and their daughter is there as witness. Sadly, when Ray later desperately pronounces his love for Val and scratches 'My Baby' above the empty cot (having just wrecked the flat they share), she is not there to hear it; even when he says it to her directly, Val finds it hard to believe from the evidence of his behaviour. Ray is more often seen with the lads in the local pub or out clubbing in the West End (boozing, smoking, snorting, leching), while Billy (whose father is in prison for a stabbing) fuels his own drug habits by thieving from his nearest and dearest – including Ray and Val. Val, in spite of the advice and appeals of her mother (Edna Doré) refuses to report the beatings to the police ('Yes – and then it's my turn'), pretending that the bruises are the result of an accident, and, finally, stands by her man. All this would seem very routine were it not for the force of the performances from Burke and Winstone (a pairing tepidly repeated in *Love, Honour and Obey*), which seem to reinvest the mythology of pathetic/heroic shit-putting-up-with and put-upon working-class women (see Terence Davies, Chapter 11).

Yet again, in Ken Loach's *Sweet Sixteen* (2002), a woman loves a man in spite of her own and others' (possibly better) instincts and in spite of the well-intentioned efforts of others to intervene to break a tragic cycle of abuse. The daughters of families, rather than wives, are at the receiving end of various forms of abuse in *The War Zone*, *Stella Does Tricks* (Coky Giedroyc, 1996), *The Magdalene Sisters* (UK/Ireland, Peter Mullan, 2002) and *Felicia's Journey* (Atom Egoyan, 1999). In Lynne Ramsay's 1997 short film *Gasman*, 'daddy's little girl' discovers that she shares her father with the daughter of a different mummy. The eponymous Stella (Kelly Macdonald) runs away from her aunt and her father (Ewan Stewart), whose own ambition has been to build a career for himself in London, only to find herself adopted by a surrogate father, Mr Peters (the James Bolam of the ITV Shipman docu-drama rather than the BBC *Likely Lads*), who becomes the pimp for whom she turns 'tricks': 'You're the nice man who took me in,' she says, dutifully. For Stella (like the King's Cross girls in *Mona Lisa* – see Chapter 11) the city is not only not paved with gold but even fails to deliver the little she asks of life. Stella then tries to escape Mr Peters by earning a living by other means – she takes a job on a flower stall – but falls in with Eddie (Hans Matheson) who steals from her in order to support his drug habit. However, Mr Peters is not prepared to release his hold on Stella and continues to use her for his own gain. For Stella there seems to be no escape: a weekend in Glasgow plagues her with real and imagined accusations (although she does manage to pull off her best trick ever against her father). Returning to London, Eddie, too, betrays her trust and sells her to settle a debt. The film's pessimistic, fatalistic conclusion is rendered all the more grim by the acknowledgment of real-life stories used in its making.

Atom Egoyan's stylish *Felicia's Journey* first finds Felicia (Elaine Cassidy) looking back to the small Irish port she is leaving. 'The simple faith . . . only the heart of the child' (sung on the soundtrack) refers both to the 1950s time capsule inhabited by her would-be guardian Mr Hilditch (Bob Hoskins), displayed in the title sequence, and to her own situation. The reason for her

Atom Egoyan's short and long cuts of *Felicia's Journey* (1999) find girls confiding in cars in substitute fathers: Mr Hilditch (Bob Hoskins) hears out Felicia (Elaine Cassidy)

journey to Birmingham (denoted in time and space by Spaghetti Junction and the soon-to-be demolished Bullring) is revealed in intermittent flashbacks. She is trying to locate her boyfriend, Johnnie Lysett, who has enlisted in the British Army; her father, meanwhile, has told her that Irish boys belong in Ireland and that people in their family have been executed in their fight against the British – something not to be forgotten. When she becomes pregnant she is culpable as a traitor and a whore, he says. Johnnie's mother is equally hostile to their attachment. Felicia encounters catering manager Mr Hilditch (superficially unthreatening in his Morris Minor) by chance . . . and subsequently less by chance than by his design. Flashbacks to her past are matched by garish reconstructions of his childhood, as the chubby son coerced as assistant to his glamorous and continental TV chef mother, Gala (Arsinee Khanjian): equally trapped and repressed, it is her commodified life which he still emulates, continuing to prepare family meals for himself alone in the house in which he lived as a boy. He buys clothes and shampoo to give the impression of a woman about the house when he invites Felicia to stay, giving the excuse that 'Mrs' Hilditch is ill in hospital and then ordering flowers for 'Mrs' Hilditch's supposed funeral. Sadly, Felicia comes near to meeting Johnnie, but Mr Hilditch is more concerned that they be kept apart. Sadly, Felicia is not the first girl he has 'befriended' in his profound loneliness, but, 'woebegone and bedraggled', 'she was different from the rest'. He urges her to lose her baby, projecting the unhappiness of his own childhood upon her. As Felicia awaits her abortion, Ireland appears as a strikingly green and promised land. When the lyric 'only the heart of a child' recurs at the close, it seems to refer as much to Hilditch as to Felicia herself.

The Magdalene Sisters, set in the 1960s, ends with a more fortuitous escape across the Irish Sea for Bernadette (Nora-Jane Noone). It opens with a pre-title sequence, conducted without dialogue, which serves to seal the fate of Margaret (Anne Marie Duff). At a wedding ceilidh, she is raped by her cousin, Kevin (Sean McDonagh). Nods pass between the men and she is pointed out to a priest without a break in proceedings: another priest, meanwhile, ardently sings folk lyrics which celebrate the fecundity of Ireland's women and its countryside. The next morning Margaret is taken to work at the Sisters' laundry and it is four years before her brothers (who have allowed her to go in the first instance) come to retrieve her. Another girl, Rose (Dorothy Duffy), has her child and her name taken from her; while she slaves in the laundry she is ritually humiliated, abused by a priest, Father Fitzroy, denied access to her son and her Saint Christopher (her one vestige of hope) is stolen from her. Bernadette, who defiantly favours pragmatism over prayers, plans an escape but is captured and punished. Katie (Britta Smith) has worked in the laundry for forty years and can no longer adjust to life outside. Even Margaret, standing at the garden gate, contemplating the fields beyond, is not able to seize the moment for herself when it is proffered – perhaps all men are now deemed untrustworthy – and instead stays to expose Father Fitzroy. Una (Mary Murray) runs away only to be returned, beaten and battered, by her father (Peter Mullan): she no longer has a home to go to and is received into the order. The girls sleep in the attic under a beam inscribed 'God is just'. But no compassion (certainly not the charity of Christ to the original Magdalene) is shown by Sister Bridget (a fearsomely vicious performance from Geraldine McEwan), who mercilessly disciplines the girls in her charge, harbouring no doubt of their guilt and the justness of her calling. Perversely, Bridget reserves a display of gushing sentiment for the Ingrid Bergmann film which inspired her life's devotion; new washing machines receive a benediction by which the poor girls' labour has never been blessed. As with *Stella Does Tricks*, *The Magdalene Sisters* is all the more disconcerting for its factual credentials (Mullan drew, in part, on a previous documentary). The names of the Magdalene Sisters' charges are listed in the credits in the manner of a wartime Roll of Service.

Sons estranged from their fathers appear in *East is East* (Damien O'Donnell, 1999), *My Son the Fanatic* (Udayan Prasad, 1997), *Wonderland* (Michael Winterbottom, 1999) and *Bend It Like Beckham* (Gurinder Chadha, 2002). Here, as in Zadie Smith's hugely popular 2000 novel (and 2002 Channel Four TV series) *White Teeth*, differences between siblings and parents are prompted by the reactions of Asian-born Britons, or Britons of mixed race and culture, to their inheritance. In Shane Meadows' 1999 *A Room for Romeo Brass* and *Once Upon a Time in the Midlands*, *Eden Valley*, *Intimacy* (Patrice Chereau, 2000) and *The Full Monty*, sons are separated from their fathers by divorce. In Amber Films' *Eden Valley* (1994), Billy (Darren Bell) receives a suspended prison sentence for stealing drugs and leaves his mother and her boyfriend in Newcastle to live with his father (Brian Hogg) who breeds and trains horses for harness races in County Durham. At first, the father is as much a stranger to the son as the environment is strange. Hoggy discovers that his field is to be sold but makes a successful bid for it by bargaining with the fixer, Danker (Mike Elliott), who, in return, requires Billy to throw his first race. Billy fails to comply and Danker exacts his revenge by poisoning Billy's horse. But, in the course of the film, the relationship between father and son is strengthened.

Shot in black and white (sometimes in slow motion) in Nottingham, Shane Meadows' BBC-funded *Twenty Four Seven* (1997) evokes Reisz's *Saturday Night and Sunday Morning* (see Chapter 9). Whereas Arthur Seaton's life was marked by the drudgery of his job and his animus against his bosses, *Twenty Four Seven* is more concerned with the absence of gainful, let alone worthwhile employment. As for Arthur, there are rifts between sons and fathers cooped up in the same household. In spite of its retro references, *Twenty Four Seven* aimed at a contemporary audience with its eclectic soundtrack (including contributions from Johann Strauss, a Corsican choral work, Van Morrison, Paul Weller and The Charlatans). Lad mag *Maxim* endorsed it as 'Both a moving and Bloody Hilarious Film'. The story is told in flashback as Tim (Danny Nussbaum) reads the diary of Darcy (Bob Hoskins): 'Getting shit 24–7 . . . lads and people have lived the same way – they can't do anything singly to change it, that's why it stays the same'; 'If you've never had anything to believe in you're always going to be poor.' Darcy ('a casualty of the '80s – a forgotten 30 something') determines to set up a Boxing Club like they had when he was a boy. This is reminiscent of the well-intentioned 'herbivore' interventions depicted in Reisz's *We Are the Lambeth Boys* (1959) and John Fletcher's *The Saturday Men* (1962). Tim and his mates, Fag Ash (Mat Hand), Gadget (Justin Brady), Stuart (Carl Collins) and Benny (Johann Myers), join up, at first reluctantly, and Darcy endeavours to keep them to the straight and narrow path. Financial backing is volunteered by Ronnie Marsh (the local Napoleon – who tucks his hand like *that* into various coats and jackets). He also delivers the script's best one-liners: 'The money's laundered so much it's shrunk.' He has family problems of his own, his son Carl ('an Orang Utang – he's a serious monkey') bemoaning that Ronnie's trophy girlfriend is 'the third new mum this year'. Tim's father perpetually harangues him into getting a job (which does not exist) and often lashes out at him and his mother. Ironically, when it comes to an organised match, he insists that he won't allow Tim in the ring. But, ultimately, it is Darcy who needs the club and the discipline more than they do. At least the mates have each other and Tim's mum finally does the best thing for herself by leaving Tim's dad. Darcy is a lonely soul, vainly chatting up the girl in the local corner shop or taking his Auntie Iris dancing or out on a daytrip in his Robin Reliant. On the club's trip to Wales, he is isolated from the group to which he has attached himself. His efforts are recognised only when it is too late for him to appreciate it.

Children realise the ambitions of relatives, wittingly or unwittingly, in *Billy Elliot* (Stephen Daldry, 2000 – now resuscitated as a stage musical), *Bend It Like Beckham*, *Wondrous Oblivion* (Paul Morrison, 2004) and Mike Herman's 1998 adaptation of Jim Cartwright's 1992 stageplay *Little Voice*. Daldry had previously directed a short film, *Eight* (1998), in which Jonathan (Jack Langan-Evans), left alone with his mother (Gina McKee), imagines his father ('just a caretaker at a stinky school'), implicitly a victim of the Hillsborough disaster, to have been 'a train driver . . . a fireman . . . a pilot . . . before that, an astronaut'. Billy Elliot's father, Jackie (Gary Lewis), and older brother Tony (Jamie Draven) are out on strike in 1985. Against his initial prejudices and his political principles, but determined to hang on to his pride as a father, Jackie is even prepared to return to work to earn funds for Billy's audition at the Royal Ballet School in London. A raffle and a benefit is organised in the community and Jackie pawns his dead wife's jewellery. While the Miners' Union is eventually forced to agree terms, the hopes invested in Billy (Jamie Bell) are rewarded and personal ambition is fulfilled: the younger generation potentially achieves what 'might have been' (for nana in *Billy Elliot*) and what has been given up (by Jess Bhamra's father in *Bend It Like Beckham*) by going elsewhere. *Beckham* was one of a number of 'footie' films of the 1990s (including also David Evans' 1997 *Fever Pitch*, Roberto Bangura's 1997 *The Girl with Brains in her Feet* and Steve Barron's 2001 *Mike Bassett: England Manager*) – Parminder Nagra was voted a Football Personality of the Year in 2003. Gaz's young son, in *The Full Monty*, demonstrates solidarity with his dad by donating his post office savings to support the strip show performed by Gaz and his workmates. *Little Voice* (Jane Horrocks, on stage and screen) refuses to comply with her mother's plan to exploit her talent for commercial gain; indeed, the widowed Mari Hoff (Brenda Blethyn) loses out twofold when she discovers that the seedy London agent Ray Say (Michael Caine), 'the man with the Midas touch' against whom Shirley Bassey's song warns us, is using her merely as bait for the daughter and rates her as no catch at all. Little Voice is honouring the dreams of her dead father as does Gloria, the cornet player, in Herman's earlier *Brassed Off* (1996).

'To begin with', announces the voiceover, Jack Manfred (Clive Owen), in Mike Hodge's 2000 *Croupier* (for FilmFour, and sharing its scriptwriter, Paul Mayersberg, with Roeg's 1976 *The Man Who Fell to Earth* – see Chapter 10), has been educated at a public school in England, courtesy of his father's winnings. Manfred senior is not only a compulsive gambler but also an inveterate liar: calling from a payphone in a hotel in South Africa where he is working as a barman, he tells Jack that he is setting up a new company. Jack intends to strike out for himself as a writer. However, the job set-up for him at a London casino seems to promise potential material, in place of the football story or thug story suggested by his publisher ('plenty of sex, of course'): he can, at least, stick to what he knows. The story is then narrated by Jack from his presumed position 'above the world . . . the writer looking down . . . as a detached voyeur'. He dyes his hair and adopts a different persona – Jake. Because he knows all the tricks of the trade, cynically regarding the business as 'legal theft', he persuades himself he is in control, meanwhile affecting to despise his girlfriend's job as a store detective (which, while less glamorous, amounts to much the same thing) – Bella the bitch (Kate Hardie), former prostitute and fellow croupier, saves the day in a Mini Cooper. Ex-WPC Marion (Gina McKee) is also concerned that Jake's job as a croupier will threaten her relationship with Jack. Marion's fears that he will become implicated are proved valid as Jack loses Jake's plot and gets caught up in his father's larger game plan. 'His dad', he writes, 'was still dealing to his son from the bottom of the deck twenty seven years later and 8,000 miles away'; but, for once, he seems to have won.

The death of a relative provokes the re-examination of relationships, for siblings and friends, in *The Lawless Heart*, *Orphans* (Peter Mullan, 1997) and *Under the Skin* (1997). In *Secrets and Lies* (Mike Leigh, 1996), while one couple (Timothy Spall and Phyllis Logan) copes with their own unhappiness at not being able to conceive, a mother is reunited with the child (Marianne Jean-Baptiste) she long ago gave up for adoption. Hortense's search for her birth mother (Brenda Blethyn) is prompted by the death of her adoptive parents. *Orphans*, the first feature directed by actor Peter Mullan, uses black and surreal humour to demolish a number of jaded and politically correct stereotypes: Michael, the Scottish hard man (Douglas Henshall), is rendered ridiculous, dripping blood from a brawl for the film's duration then attempting a bogus claim for industrial compensation; his tediously virtuous older brother, the one-time altar boy Thomas (Gary Lewis), is equally the object of humour. When he is the only pall-bearer to arrive at the funeral, he offers to carry the coffin by himself: 'She ain't heavy – she's my mother,' he jokes inadvertently, in the manner of the song and subsequent Budweiser commercials. Meanwhile, disabled sister Sheila (Rosemarie Stevenson) argues rights of access to a wheelchair ramp and a baby is potential collateral damage in brother John's grudge-match. Men in cravats who try to chat up women in pubs by talking about *Jean de Florette* and *Manon des Sources* also receive their just comeuppance. But with their mother gone, Thomas decides to come to terms with the others and accepts their invitation to a curry (. . . if just for one mushroom pakora, perhaps . . .).

In *Some Voices* (Simon Cellan Jones, 2000), the catalyst is provided by the release of Ray (Daniel Craig) from a psychiatric hospital and the attempts of his brother Pete (David Morrisey) to manage his life outside the institution. Younger sister Iris (Samantha Morton) and older sister Rose (Claire Rushbrook), in *Under the Skin*, are obliged to discuss ancient jealousies and forge a new trust between themselves with the death of their mother (Rita Tushingham) – their father moved to Australia ten years ago. Iris confides her feelings in voiceover about her mother (remembering their happy times together in flashback), about Rose (they each think the other was their mum's favourite and argue over her wedding ring) and about Gary (Matthew Delamere), her self-absorbed boyfriend (while she wants to talk about trying to be a singer, he thinks that they talk enough already). Iris tries to stay close to her mother by dressing in her clothes. She tells Rose that she doesn't want mothering by her ('She still orders me about and tidies up') but, equally, wants Rose to hug her like a child. Iris leaves her job and Gary, and picks up a succession of casual attachments, none of whom provide the comfort she craves (she's repeatedly told that she has a good body). Massive Attack's 'I Believe in a One Love . . .' underscores the action. Her friends, Veronica (Christine Tremarco) and Eleanor (Clare Francis), dismiss her behaviour as sluttishness but, when she returns to Gary (he's the only one she can talk to), she finds that Veronica has moved in. Meanwhile, Gary cares more about who Iris is bedding, while Tom (whom she has bedded) has told her, 'It's not what you say it's what you do that counts.' Lonely, she tries to persuade Rose's husband Frank to let her sleep next to him – he knows that this is not a good idea. The spare room is full of toys awaiting Rose's baby, further reminding Iris of her status as a child and confirming Rose and Frank as grown-ups. But the reconciliation of the sisters is sealed by Iris being there for the birth (in the absence of Frank). Iris symbolically departs from her mother, throwing her ashes out to sea, and takes up singing.

In *Wonderland* and *Bridget Jones's Diary*, beleaguered parents deserve the support of grown-up children as much as it is given regardless. Both mum (Kika Markham) and dad (Jack Shepherd) (in the former) and, likewise, Gemma Jones and Jim Broadbent (in the latter – a couple I find more sympathetic than either Bridget and Daniel or Bridget and Mark) have their own troubles to bear, within and outside of their relationship with one another. In *Pure* (Gillies Mackinnon, 2002), a young son (Harry Eden) is responsible for 'parenting' and rehabilitating his widowed mother (Molly Parker), when she becomes addicted to heroin, betraying her supplier (and sometime lover) to the police; in *Sweet Sixteen*, a son's efforts to provide a better life for himself and his mother, newly released from prison, are (predictably, with Loach) thwarted. *Wonderland* covers three days in the life of a London family: the daughters, Nadia (Gina McKee), Molly (Molly Parker) and Debbie (Shirley Henderson), and their brother Darren (Enzo Cilenti). Nadia, like many characters in late 1990s films, works in a café (here in Soho) – compare, for instance, *Some Voices*, *The Lawless Heart* and the bar in *Intimacy*. The film presents itself with a sort of casualness (as if these could be any three days, denoted by intertitles, drawn at random); haphazard snatches of 'overheard' conversation, dialogue delivered with unexpurgated burps, hairdressers' clichés re. a tight perm dropping, information supplied which does not appear immediately functional to the narrative and so forth, busily recorded on a mixture of film stocks (this collage effect reproduced for Winterbottom's later *Twenty Four Hour Party People*), sometimes with the rough patina of 'amateur' video. However, in structure the film is classically contrived in terms of the disruption and restoration of an equilibrium in each of the three sisters' different stories. It neither begins nor ends arbitrarily, privileging Nadia's story and employing (as did David Hare's 1992 *Strapless* and Anthony Minghella's 1991 *Truly, Madly, Deeply*) the birth of a child as an easy means of culminating and supposedly resolving plot lines: Molly's absent husband returns, Debbie's lost son is safe and sound, love-sick Nadia may, after all, find romance on her doorstep rather than in newspaper listings and Darren, in London for the weekend, phones home to say that all is well.

Peace and harmony are not the natural state of family life in these films and nor is the survival of the family unit necessarily presented as a positive outcome. The family fails to serve as a stable social model. Those families which do pull through are often supported by friends and neighbours (as in *Wonderland*). The family of the 1990s prefers the friends it can choose.

New Communities

The fall of the Berlin Wall in 1989, the second Russian Revolution and wars in the Balkans, Africa and the Middle East in the 1990s resulted in the migrating of populations across and within an expanded Europe. While the loss of professionally qualified British-born subjects to overseas was termed a 'brain-drain', its converse, foreign-born subjects seeking employment in Britain, were widely disparaged as 'economic migrants'. After its opening in 1993, the policing of the Channel Tunnel became a contentious issue. The extent of desperation and its criminal exploitation was revealed by the arrival of Chinese bodies in a van load of tomatoes from a ferry in the summer of 2001. Immigrants and refugees were discussed in newspaper columns, exhibitions, television debates, 'undercover' investigations (BBC TV 2003), documentaries (such as Mark Isaac's *Calais*, screened at the Sheffield Festival in 2003 prior to transmission by BBC TV), gallery installations, television dramas and features. At the opening of *Blue* (1993), Derek Jarman recalls sitting in a café, served by young refugees from Bosnia.

In *Moonlighting* (1982), Jerzy Skolomowski presented a group of Polish builders sent by their boss to London to work on the house to which he intends to flee. It proved much cheaper to use illegally imported labour than to use British carpenters, plasterers, plumbers and electricians. Their foreman, Nowak (Jeremy Irons), the only English-speaker, withheld from them the news from home of the Solidarity uprisings and their military suppression by General Jaruzelski. Ironically, Nowak's control of his workmates' lives and their finite budget, his denial of information, his restriction of their personal freedoms, increasingly mimicked the state from which they had temporarily escaped. For Nowak, dealing with small-minded businessmen, unneighbourly neighbours and over-zealous store detectives proved no holiday at all. In the 1980s ITV series of Dick Clement and Ian Le Frenais' *Auf Wiedersehen, Pet*, a group of British workers were contracted to a project in Western Germany; in the subsequent recent series, they find themselves in a position to hire labour themselves and look to Eastern Europe for the most competitive tender. The Brummie Barry (Timothy Spall), now a successful businessman, secures the deal through his new Russian bride, her supposed 'brother' and his mafiosi accomplices. Both Skolomowski's film and the two series (billed as comedy but certainly worth taking seriously) are unusual in British film-making, I venture to suggest, for positioning Britain in a larger Europe and European market. Significantly enough, *Auf Wiedersehen, Pet* in 2001 (which also wittily aligned Antony Gormley's *Angel of the North* with the series' native Canadian participants) was pitched in the schedule against a remake/re-adaptation of the 1970s BBC costume drama series/1922 Galsworthy novel *The Forsyte Saga*: the present was set to compete with the past (albeit a suitably revamped view thereof) in the manner of Britain's split identity.[16]

In ITV's 2001 *Russian Bride*, Natasha Chemlavskaya (Lia Williams) finds her new life with a passionless English husband at best dull and at worst rendered unbearable by the dominating presence of his mother: effectively, she is kept as a domestic slave and seeks solace in an affair. In FilmFour's *Birthday Girl* (Jez Butterworth, 2001), a nondescript St Albans bank clerk, John (Ben Chaplin), having failed to do 'the girl next door thing' – there never was a girl next door – acquires Nadia (Nicole Kidman) through an internet dating agency. Meanwhile, he takes no notice of the interest shown in him by the girl who works at the next desk in the bank and Nadia wastes no time in reminding him of what he has been missing. Nadia's mafiosi accomplices, Alexei and Yuri (Vincent Cassell and Matthieu Kassovitz), arrive from Russia with vodka to celebrate her birthday, then take Nadia hostage in order to force John to rob his own bank. This he does, before realising that the threesome have pulled the same trick (in Switzerland, in Greece, wherever) on other dupes before. Furthermore, he realises that Alexei is Nadia's lover and that she is carrying his child. The hapless John (a latterday counterpart for Alec Guinness' bankclerk in *The Lavender Hill Mob*) decides to see through the adventure in which he has become embroiled. Alexei is alternately psychotic and maudlin; there are visual gags involving toy water pistols and verbal gags concerning giraffes. The scheming of the Russians is set against John's lack of guile: when Nadia reminds him that he could have gone to a prostitute instead of finding a woman on the internet he replies (flatly) that he did and accordingly gets slapped; when Nadia informs him that her real name is Sophia, John replies that his name is still John. As in Guy Ritchie's *Snatch*, Russians are the easy butt of humour: 'It's so cold we have to go to England to shag people to keep warm,' says Nadia, self-mockingly.

Calais documents Britons arriving in France intent upon buying cheap booze and fags. In the wake of the closure of the Sangatte refugee centre, it follows an affable Afghani, Ijaz, who is living and sleeping on the street between attempts to cross to Britain through the Channel Tunnel.[17] Ernesta is sent back to Lithuania and Paul (a Jamaican) is refused entry without a visa even though this is no longer a legal requirement. Waiting for a bus which never materialises, he observes wryly that he and all his antecedents have been born in a former British colony. The thoughts of various daytrippers on questions of immigration and asylum are recorded through the hatch of a chip stall. Some think Britain the best place in the world, while Steve (a Calais bar owner failing to attract business) swears that he and his French wife and children will never return: the end of the film finds them leaving for Spain in a camper van. Tulia (now seventy) and Leslie (now eighty-five) struggle to sell advertising services for French healthcare, banks and property agents to potential British customers. Dressed in floral, fuchsia or sunflower yellow kaftans with big hair and improbably painted eyebrows, Tulia is, at first, hard to take entirely seriously. But it emerges that she, too, has known exile and came to Britain as a refugee rescued by the Red Cross in the Second World War. The experience made her fearful of having children of her own.

Beautiful People plays the immigration card for laughs and sentiment. A number of storylines and protagonists are introduced at the outset: a Serb and a Croat (the film's running gag) fight on a London bus (the reasons for the fight being assumed rather than explained); a MP (Charles Kay), his wife and his parliamentary assistant quietly survey the newspapers and daughter Portia (Charlotte Coleman), a trainee doctor, leaves for work; Richard (Nicholas Farrell), a doctor, makes breakfast for his hyperactive sons, Tim and Tom, in the absence of the wife who has left him; his neighbour bemoans the failure of his son Griffin (Danny Nussbaum) and his mates to get jobs; Pero (Edin Dzandzanovic), also from former Yugoslavia, preens as he leaves his flat and encounters the doctor's wife in a café. The Serb, the Croat and Pero end up in the hospital where Richard and Portia work, along with Ismet and his wife Djamila (who is expecting a baby resulting from a rape by soldiers) and a Welsh Nationalist fire-bomber. Griffin, meanwhile, en route for an England match in Rotterdam, is separated from his mates and is loaded onto a UN aid flight to Bosnia. Here he encounters a BBC news reporter, Jerry (Gilbert Martin), whose daughter, coincidentally, attends the same school as Tom and Tim. Griffin returns with an injured child, nicknamed Lineker, redeems himself in the eyes of his parents by his accidental heroism and effects his friends' redemption in their show of compassion to the boy. Richard delivers Djamila's baby, Chaos, and a new family is provided for in the wreckage of his own. Portia's parents are won over to her new boyfriend by Pero's exoticism (his imperfect table manners are forgotten when he proves himself an accomplished pianist) and they are married with a gospel choir in attendance. In all this flurry of activity, causes and consequences are not pursued. As in *Welcome to Sarajevo* (Michael Winterbottom, 1997), hopes of salvation are totemically invested in children.

Winterbottom again casts a child as the central figure in *In This World*, following a boy and his grown-up cousin from Pakistan through Iran, Turkey, Italy and France. Here, he hides under a train and is taken through the tunnel to London. He, alone, survives the journey. The trafficking of people is condemned and the dangers of consigning a child's safety to criminals are clearly shown. But whether his life is any better as a waiter in London than in a camp in Pakistan remains to be established. The film presents the pain of leaving a familiar community, culture and landscape (all rendered photogenically attractive) rather than the joy of arrival at a distant destination.

In *Dirty Pretty Things*, Okwe (Chiwetel Ejiofor), a doctor, finds himself in London, afraid for his safety in Lagos, but what he wants most of all is to be able to return. He works as a minicab driver by day and as a hotel receptionist by night. The hotel manager, Señor Juan (Sergi Lopez), informs Okwe that people come to the hotel, at night, to do dirty things and that it is the job of the staff to make things pretty again in the morning. Okwe borrows the flat of a maid at the hotel, Senay (Audrey Tautou – fresh from international success in *Amélie*), to catch a few hours sleep between shifts. Juan uses his knowledge of Okwe's origins (he knows that he has arrived from Rotterdam illegally and that he is at odds with the Nigerian government) to attempt to blackmail him into co-operating with his own illicit nocturnal dealings. Senay, a Turk, is pursued by Immigration Enforcement officers for working illegally at the hotel and goes to work as a machinist in a sweatshop. Here the manager uses his knowledge of her status as leverage to exact sexual favours. Senay determines to accept Juan's conditions in exchange for a faked Italian passport, with prospects of fulfilling her fantasy life in America; Okwe makes his own conditions for a new passport which will enable him to go home to his daughter. Juliet (Sophie Okenedo), a prostitute (one of the 'unseen' who service the hotel by night), and Kwohi (Benedict Wong), a certified Chinese refugee who works unseen in a hospital crematorium, help Okwe to effect their escape. Juliet, the 'tart with a heart' of the piece, knowingly mocks her own character – 'What a pair, the virgin and the whore,' she says, comforting Senay. *Dirty Pretty Things* is concerned with the criminal exploitation of immigrants once they have arrived and the pursuit by law-enforcers of those who try to work rather than of those by whom they are illegally employed. Packed in the self-same polystyrene boxes, Señor Juan trades indiscriminately in human organs and in contraband French truffles. While Okwe refuses his offer of £3,000 to perform an operation (as Kwohi says, there is nothing so dangerous as a virtuous man), there are evidently others, less virtuous, more mercenary or more desperate who have accepted.

Documentary-maker Pawel Pawlikowski wrote and directed *Last Resort* as his first feature. Here, the officials required to enforce the immigration procedures appear as frustrated by

Margate is no Dreamland for Tania (Dina Korzen) and Artiom (Artiom Strelnikov), befriended by Alfie (Paddy Considine) in *Last Resort* (Pawel Pawlikowski, 2000)

the system as those to whom it applies. Tanya (Dina Korzen) arrives with her son Artiom (Artiom Strelnikov) thinking that they will be able to move in with her boyfriend, Mark. This plan falls through, but she cannot simply turn back: an asylum case could take as much as sixteen months to assess, a false claim could take six months to clear. They are taken to Stonehaven, where they are befriended by Alfie (Paddy Considine), who works in the local amusement arcade (Dreamland – as in the fairground of Lindsay Anderson's 1953 *O Dreamland*, its glory here fading into the background of the frame). Tania is told that she needs £300 to get out but cannot work without a work permit, although she is willing to produce illustrations as she used to. The vouchers she is given cannot be redeemed for cash and, as Artiom observes, 'There's no fish in the fish' they are served in the café they are obliged to use. The local children are adept at thieving and dealing their spoils at the camp. She gives blood (for cash) and is told that she could sell a kidney (an unfunny joke). When Tania and Artiom try to leave, they are obliged to return to the holding camp. Their rooms in a concrete housing block overlook more grey, concrete desolation. Tania is invited by Les and Frank to perform for internet sex but Artiom warns her that they are pimps and asks why she can't fall in love with Alfie. Alfie turns on Les and Frank and takes Tania and Artiom away in a boat. In a hostile environment, they are happiest by themselves as a surrogate family, cocooned below deck or huddled around a campfire on the beach. Tania confesses that she has made mistakes – all the women in her family have fallen in love with the wrong men. Alfie says that he was in a fight and went to prison for it – but then his father hit him, too. Tania determines to stop living in her dreams and to return to Russia, leaving the picture she brought with her as a parting present for Alfie.

The Short and the Long of It

In the 1990s, a number of production initiatives, competitions and festivals promoted the short film – increasingly attracting entries not made on film but shot and exhibited digitally. Seasons of shorts were successfully programmed in Manchester and Bristol, the BBC launched *The Talent* (a showcase for Lynne Ramsay's *Small Deaths* and *Gasman*) and *Short n Curlies* and FilmFour collaborated with Orange on a short film competition, while some cinemas showed selected shorts (some from the *In the Frame* contest) as an individual item, accompanying a better-known feature. With many slots in the schedules given over to lifestyle series and docu-drama, Sheffield continued stalwartly to support the documentary (both short and long). Bristol (home to Aardman) and Cardiff hosted animation festivals, with Aardman producing short and long plasticine animations of both *Creature Comforts* (*The Zoo* [1989] and *The Circus* [2003]) and series of adverts for PG Tips and for Power Electric (with the voice of Johnnie Morris from BBC TV's long-running *Animal Magic* [1962–83]) and *Wallace and Gromit* (with the voice of BBC TV's *Last of the Summer Wine*'s [1973–] Peter Sallis), moving from British to American production financing. *Belleville Rendezvous* (Canada/France, Sylvain Chomet, 2003) received funding from both BBC Bristol and BBC 4.

Directors moved from television to film (David Kane) and between film and television (Beeban Kidron's *Oranges Are Not the Only Fruit* for BBC TV in 1990, Coky Giedroyc's *William and Mary* for ITV in 2004, Stephen Frear's *The Deal* for Channel Four and Gillies McKinnon's 2004 *Gunpowder, Treason and Plot* for BBC 2). Michael Apted continued to work on the sequels to his lifelong documentary project *Seven Up* (Granada) alongside direction of the Bond movie, *The World is Not Enough* (1999), while, for Artangel, Mike Figgis directed the dramatic reconstruction of a key event in the 1984 miners' strike, *The Battle of Orgreave* (re-enacted in June 2001 and broadcast by Channel Four in 2002). *Bloody Sunday* (Paul Greengrass, 2000), controversially supported by the Film Council alongside Granada, was most widely viewed by British audiences in its broadcast on ITV. This benefited from the casting of ITV *Cold Feet* star James Nesbitt while, in the advertising breaks to *Cold Feet* (1998–2003) (and its repeats), actor Sean Pertwee (from *Cold Feet*) could be heard as the voice of Powergen and John Thomson (from *Cold Feet* and *The Fast Show* [1994–2000]) could be seen with Joely Richardson in a serial campaign for Lloyds TSB. The documentarist, Lucy Blakstad, moved from one-off series items (*The Lido* [1995] for BBC TV's *Modern Times*) to a series (*The Body* for Channel Four) to feature format (*Mostar*, screened at Sheffield and on TV) to advertisements for Johnson's Baby Lotion. Following the example of Hugh Hudson and

Ridley Scott (see Chapter 9), Shane Meadows moved between adverts and features. The former theatre director Jonathan Glazer directed a promo for Bristol band Massive Attack (*Karma Coma* in 1995) and the Guinness advert, *Surfer* (1999), before moving to features in Britain and America. Asif Kapadia's short student film *The Sheep Thief* (1997), shot in stunning locations in India, proved a calling-card for his feature-length, narratively and cinematographically epic *The Warrior* (2001), since released together on DVD. Christopher Nolan made *Doodlebug* in 1997 (shot in black and white) concerning a man persecuted by a scuttling creature in his room, who discovers the 'bug' to be a miniature version of himself, only to find (on the point of swatting him with a shoe) that he is himself the miniature version of a larger, paranoid self; *The Following* (1999), also shot in black and white (in the manner common to student films), is an uncommonly stylish tale of a would-be ingénu writer trapped by a wily upper-class English burglar and his moll. Nolan has since moved on to features in America, with *Memento* (2000) and the remade *Insomnia* (2002).

Christopher Morris has moved from radio comedy (BBC Radio 4's *The Day Today*) to television (Channel Four's *Brass Eye*) to direct a short film (*My Wrongs 8245-8249 & 117* [2002]), which cast a paranoid Paddy Considine opposite a talking hound. Derek Jarman's *Blue* was screened, televised and broadcast on radio in 1993. An ultramarine rectangle is both the backdrop and occasional subject matter of a commentary provided by John Quentin, Nigel Terry, Tilda Swinton and Jarman himself. A litany of the names of former lovers, past recollections and the sound of waves and water structure the soundtrack, while Jarman contemplates the metaphors and meanings which the colour carries: contemplating his own death (and the worst of the illness is the uncertainty) Jarman gazes into the blue yonder. Other directors have moved between different media in a different order of succession: while the British-designed computer game Lara Croft was sold to America as the idea for a feature film (*Tomb Raider*, Simon West, 2001), Guy Ritchie (following the pattern of *Life at the Top* [1965] and the tele-series *Man at the Top* [1970–2] – see Chapter 9) sold *Lock, Stock and Two Smoking Barrels* as a format for television before directing internet adverts for BMW. Other spin-offs and transferrals of format (such as *Kevin and Perry Go Large* and *Stella Street*) have proved less successful while *Johnny English*, featuring Rowan Atkinson in a role originating in a series of Barclaycard ads, proved hugely successful abroad.

Simon Beaufoy's transatlantic commercial success as writer of *The Full Monty* was not matched by his next projects, *Lucky Break* and *Among Giants,* and he subsequently chose to work on an interactive narrative and on the internet/cinema release *This is Not a Love Song* (Billie Eltringham, 2002), shot digitally and benefiting from Film Council support for new projection formats. Adopting the Sex Pistol John Lydon's song for its theme and its title, the story concerns the loyalty (even the need) of one friend for another: young Spike (Michael Colgan) is released from prison and collected by his older protector Heaton (Kenny Glennan). Together they make plans for a future together. They arrive at an isolated farm, in search of petrol, and Spike inadvertently kills the farmer's daughter. But Heaton stays with him. The surrounding landowners stalk the two men by day and night to an end which is bitter and vengeful; the grainy, frequently dark quality of the image here enhances the sense of pursuit and evasion.

Photographers Martin Parr (*UK Images*, for BBC TV, 1997) and Richard Billingham (*Fish Tank*, 1999) produced video renditions of recurrent subjects and preoccupations: the peculiarities of the British collectively at home and abroad; the peculiarity of one British family in a Birmingham high-rise. Introspective autobiography (or therapy) also featured in Tracey Emin's installation pieces in her 2001 show at White Cube 2, with a shed inverting the position of a child spying out onto her father in the garden and two children's chairs positioned before a confessional 'locked-off' screen discussion between Emin and her mother; Emin also confronted herself in dual roles either side of a door barred against a bailiff. Gillian Wearing, who similarly adopted the 'confessional' format and exhibited photographs alongside video as part of her *Drunks* project, sold *2 into 1* to Saatchi only to have it copied for an advertising campaign for Volkswagen managed by Saatchi's company (in which images of adults, speaking to camera, were voiced by children).[18] Mark Wallinger's perusal of the British tradition of sporting art has led him, via screenprints of jockeys' colours, the purchase of a race-horse and videos of greyhounds to *Cave* (2000): a slow-motion, four-screen installation in a darkened square space with the sound distorted and amplified to convey the 'inside-out' intimacy of a boxing ring.

While the tireless efforts of former Arts Council Officer for Films, David Curtis, were at last rewarded with a cycle of retrospective screenings of artists' work in the Tate Britain, contemporary British artists increasingly chose to work in film, video and digital media. The features director Atom Egoyan showed video installation work in the 2001 Venice Biennale and also exhibited material from his work on *Felicia's Journey* in the Hitchcock centenary tribute at MOMA, Oxford, in 1998. Isaac Julien, similarly, has worked between theatrical (*Young Soul Rebels*, 1991) and gallery screenings (*Vagabondia*, 2000). Channel Four's 2000 *Beckett on Film* season invited features directors (Anthony Minghella for *Play* and Neil Jordan for *Not I*) together with Damien Hirst for *Breath*. Meanwhile, artists Douglas Gordon, Steve McQueen and Sam Taylor-Wood drew inspiration from cinematic subjects and conventions. Taylor-Wood's show at the Hayward Gallery, London, included her 1999 seven-screen piece *Third Party* (shot on 16mm film) employing devices of eye-line match and spatial continuity between frames to construct a narrative enacted by familiar television and film personnel: Gina McKee, Marianne Faithfull, Ray Winstone and Adrian Dunbar; her 1996 piece, *Pent-Up*, positions the spectator between two sides of a shot-reverse shot scenario. The 1999 Kettle's Yard, Cambridge, exhibition *Physical Evidence* featured a number of responses from artists to kinetic photography and film, either as raw material (re-edited Muybridge, re-constructed Méliès), or as point of departure: in response to early films which recorded the removal of clothes in temporal sequence, Mark Dickinson's video *Untitled (Clothes)* (1995) pictures a man in a very confined space putting on layer upon layer of garments . . . for as long as the tape lasts. Tacita Dean (who has shown drawings and photographs alongside her film work) deliberately stages the mechanics of projection as part of the installation witnessed by the viewer: for instance, her *Delft Hydraulics* (1996), shot on 16mm, with the film looped as a Moebius strip and projected at waist height, and *Disappearance at Sea* (1996), in which the projector is raised and encased in glass, recalling the profile of an oilrig.

Andrew Kötting's feature-length *Gallivant* (1996) documents a 7,000-mile, ten-week trip in a camper van around the British coastline, recording the weather and geology; flora and fauna; industry, crops and livestock; accents and politics, pastimes, rituals and folklore of the mainland. It includes familiar landmarks, both natural (Beachy Head and Lulworth Cove) and man-made (Black-pool's illuminations, the Mumbles Pier, martello towers and Scotland's award-winning superloo). But, for Kötting, the expedition also fulfils a personal ambition, to bring together his ninety-year-old grandmother, Gladys, and his young disabled daughter, Eden, who is unlikely to survive into adulthood. They prove highly engaging companions. While Andrew grows an ill-advised beard and breaks an ankle, Eden learns to walk. Like Kötting's previous short films (the BBC/Arts Council funded *Hoi Polloi* [1990] and *Acumen* [1991]), *Gallivant* employs such techniques as accelerated speed, accentuated colour, overlaid sound (sometimes disconnected from the image track), inter-cut stills and archival footage; Kötting has since produced items for BBC Radio 4. Sometimes Eden provides the relevant commentary by signing to camera.

But, sadly, the exhibition of documentaries in general, short or long, has become all too rare. While Nick Broomfield secured cinema releases for *Kurt and Courtney* (made for BBC TV, 1998) and 1992 *Aileen Wuornos: The Selling of a Serial Killer* (revisited in 2003 with *Aileen: The Life and Death of a Serial Killer*), and Julien Temple screened *The Filth and the Fury* (2000), many others have been restricted to festival screenings and tours, or to the decreasing number of slots allocated in television schedules. Given Britain's longstanding reputation for non-fiction film and the inter-national resurgence of interest in documentary features, this is much to be regretted.

Ratcatcher (Lynne Ramsay, 1999)

Lynne Ramsay's first feature, *Ratcatcher*, was one of a clutch of films produced in Glasgow in recent years.[19] The Ken Loach trilogy, Peter Mullan's *Orphans* and John Byrne's *The Slab Boys* (from his own 1978 stageplay) all benefited from support from the local Film Fund. However, while in *Wilbur Wants to Kill Himself* (Denmark, Lone Scherfig, 2002) a young Glaswegian girl innocently asserts that 'bus' means the same in any language (to the embarrassment of her elders), Loach's *Sweet Sixteen* was deemed sufficiently regionally specific in its dialogue to require opening subtitles and *The Slab Boys* failed to secure distribution south of the border, *Ratcatcher* has been widely well received at home and abroad. While its story is set against the refuse workers' strike in 1978, the subject of the film (as with Ramsay's previous work, *Gasman*, *Small Deaths* and *Kill the Day* [1997]) concerns the relationships between characters and their relationships with their environment rather than the political causes or outcome of the strike itself. *Ratcatcher* sustains the short films' preoc-cupation with childhood. However, unlike other recent 'retro' films (such as *East is East*, *Anita and Me* [Metin Huseyin, 2002], *The Girl With Brains in Her Feet* and *Me Without You*), *Ratcatcher* does not conspicuously nor fondly accumulate period references in its costuming, settings and sound-track to position itself at a particular moment: Tom Jones sings 'What's New Pussycat?' (from the 1965 film) on television, alongside news reports of the ninth week of the strike, but beyond this, citations are minimal. Easy comparisons were made with Ken Loach's 'social realism' (especially his

1969 *Kes* – see Chapter 9) but Ramsay's work seems more ambiguous and her selection of images (their pace and their framing), colours and textures is as often significant as it is surreal.[20]

As the strike progresses, bags of rubbish pile up outside the housing block in which the Gillespie family lives. Litter strews the pavement and its gradual rotting marks the passage of time. It's a good game for the local children to beat the bags to make the rats run out and Anne-Marie, the younger daughter (Ramsay's niece, Lynne junior), sits on the bags eating her sandwich. At the opening of the film, one boy is pulled from the canal, dead, and the lingering stillness of his hand in the water preys on the thoughts of twelve-year-old James (William Eddie): he remembers the incident when he watches his mother's hand as she sleeps. When the hearse arrives for Ryan Quinn's funeral, the doors are blocked by yet more rubbish. Perpetually the Gillespie's flat is invaded by the noise of their neighbours. Mrs Quinn gives James the shiny new sandals which she had intended for her son but, partly in guilt, partly in embarrassment, James scuffs them with broken glass. James' mum (Mandy Matthews) and dad, George (Tommy Flanagan), think that it could easily have been him. The canal becomes polluted and when George later goes in to save young Kenny (an RSPCA supporter in the midst of an environmental cess pit), both he and Kenny (John Miller) are infected. Mice invade the tenements – James and Anne-Marie excitedly play with one in a trap (George flushes it down the loo), while Kenny tames one and calls it Snowball.

Anne-Marie (very much daddy's little girl) proclaims her father a hero and receives fifty pence from her mum's purse for saying so. She snitches on James when he inquisitively samples his dad's beer; in turn, James rejects the football boots with which George attempts to curry favour – they are too big and, he insists, he does not like football. Anne-Marie obligingly tells the rent-man that Mrs Gillespie is not in ('She's never in,' he replies, wearied and disbelieving) with mum in hiding in the background, whereas James lets the council people in (in the hope that it will hasten their removal to somewhere better). James' big sister is rehearsing for adulthood (using mum's cosmetics, presuming to tell James not to play with salt on the table) and doesn't want him sitting next to her on the bus cramping her style: but she too wonders when they are going to move to the promised new house. Possibly in a failed attempt to attract attention, possibly out of plain boredom, James tugs at mum's holed tights as she sleeps and tenderly tucks her toes in. The initial compelling image of the film (comparable in its seductiveness to the title sequence of Ramsay's later *Morvern Callar*) finds James wrapping and unwrapping himself in a curtain, simultaneously shroud and cocoon, bleached and sheer against the window.

James befriends Margaret-Anne (Leanne Mullen), two years his senior. With him she can still behave as partly a child, coaxingly inviting him to touch the cut on her knee (and covering his hand with hers) and splashing and throwing soap in a shared bath (intercut with George saving Kenny from the canal). Older boys rehearse their own manhood on Margaret (and she uses sex to bargain for her acceptance), while James (much to their amusement) is content undemandingly to lie with her, protectively covering her with his body. The allegiances between the children in the film shift as events present themselves: as one of the lads, James doesn't tell Margaret where to find the glasses which they have snatched from her but, picked on himself, then tries to retrieve them for her from the canal as a token of their new closeness. Poor Kenny, meanwhile, is readily perse-cuted for his simple guilelessness. James taunts Kenny (marking himself his superior) by pretend-ing that he's seen a perch biting in the disease-ridden water, but Kenny, equally, is happy to carry on fishing where no perch will ever be found. It's something to do and he won't be defeated. James bluntly tells him that Snowball (whom Kenny has attached to his birthday balloon and whom he imagines circling the moon and setting up home there with lots of baby Snowballs) is dead and that Kenny killed him. The giving and withholding of friendship is the only commodity with which Kenny can bargain: 'I'm not your pal any more,' he insists. Mum and dad, meanwhile, alternately fight and make up. Rarely are mum and dad and the children happy all together. Sometimes George uses his fists elsewhere, getting involved in a pub brawl where a wound inflicted is indi-cated by the raspberry sauce slowly dripping down an ice cream cone.

One day, for something to do, James takes the bus to the end of the line and finds a new house surrounded by cornfields. The house, as yet unfinished, is free from the clutter of the tene-ment and the city estate. James can move around it at leisure, alone and in silence. The house has a proper bathroom. This becomes his dream of escape, from the canal and the image of Ryan which continues to haunt him. Finally, we see George together with all his family and friends carry-ing their possessions through the rustling corn. Ramsay's treatment of childhood is gratifyingly unsentimental. However, unlike Loach, who rarely leaves one with room for optimism, Ramsay at least acknowledges a retrospective nostalgia for dreaming.

Notes

1. Julian Barnes, *England, England* (London: Jonathan Cape, 1998), pp. 83–5; see also J. B. Priestley, *English Journey* [1933] (London: Heron Books, 1949).
2. Anne Billson, 'Pity the Mister between the Sisters', *The Sunday Telegraph Review*, 24 January 1999, p. 11.
3. Re. Winterbottom's *9 Songs* and Emin's *Top Spot* (on which Winterbottom is credited as executive producer) see David Smith, 'Director Defends Rating for Explicit Film', *The Observer*, 24 October 2004, p. 12, and Luke Leitch, 'BBC Pays Emin', *Evening Standard*, 25 October 2002, p. 11.
4. What he actually said was 'I should try to interpose my own body'; for a reference to the tribunal, see David Garnett (ed.), *Carrington: Letters and Extracts from her Diaries* (Oxford: Oxford University Press, 1979), p. 69.
5. Although there were complaints in the press regarding the 'authenticity' of Rozema's adaptation, see Stephen Daniels and Denis Cosgrove, 'Spectacle and Text: Landscape and Metaphors in Cultural Geography', in James Duncan and David Ley (eds), *Place/Culture/Representation* (London: Routledge, 1993), pp. 67–73, for an appropriate discussion of the original; Bath's Museum of Costume *Jane Austen* exhibition (2004) discussed *Mansfield Park*'s deliberately contemporised frocks which accompanied Christopher Hobbs' walls stripped to the stonework and sparse upholstery.
6. For further discussion of the stylistic aspects of *Elizabeth*, see Amy Sargeant, 'Making and Selling Heritage Culture', in Justine Ashby and Andrew Higson (eds), *British Cinema: Past and Present* (London: Routledge, 2000), p. 312; for 'post-heritage', Claire Monk, 'The British Heritage-Film Debate Revisited', in Claire Monk and Amy Sargeant (eds), *British Historical Cinema* (London: Routledge, 2002), p. 194.
7. Robert Murphy, 'A Revenger's Tragedy', *British Crime Cinema* (London: Routledge, 1999), p. 132.

8. Quoted in Steve Chibnall, *Get Carter* (London: I. B. Tauris, 2003), p. 100.

9. For an account of Ronnie Kray's funeral and wake see Iain Sinclair, 'The Biggest Street Party Since the Death of Churchill', *Lights Out for the Territory* (London: Granta Books, 1997), pp. 32 and 68–88.

10. Andrew Spicer, *Typical Men: the Representation of Masculinity in Popular British Cinema* (London: I. B. Tauris, 2001), p. 128.

11. See Karen O'Reilly, *The British on the Costa del Sol* (London: Routledge, 2000), pp. 1–4; also *Secret History: Costa Del Crime*, Channel Four, 2003.

12. For further discussion of the Bridget Jones phenomenon and *Peter's Friends* see Amy Sargeant, 'Darcy, Mark Darcy and the Velveteen Rabbit', in Anna Antonini (ed.), *Film and its Multiples* (Udine: University of Udine Press, 2003), pp. 375–88.

13. Claire Monk elaborates on this aspect of *Trainspotting* in 'Men in the 90s', in Robert Murphy (ed.) *British Cinema of the 90s* (London: BFI, 2000), p. 162, and 'Underbelly UK', in Ashby and Higson, *British Cinema*, p. 285.

14. For example, 'Breaking News', *The Observer Magazine*, 17 August 2003, pp. 41–2, and 'This Much I Know', 27 June 2004, pp. 8–9.

15. Objections to *Twin Town*'s representation of Wales are indicated by Julia Hallam, 'Film, Class and National Identity', in Ashby and Higson, *British Cinema*, pp. 269–70.

16. Mark Leonard, author of the Demos report, claimed that 'renewing Britain's identity is not about shedding the past but finding a better fit between our heritage and our future' and found that six 'stories' fitted the declared criteria: 'Britain the "creative island" . . . Britain the "global hub" . . . Britain the "hybrid nation" . . . The nation of "buccaneering entrepreneurs" . . . Britain the "silent revolutionary" . . . The nation of fair play and support for the underdog': see *Views on Britain's Identity* (London: The Design Council, 1997), pp. 6–8.

17. Prior to the controversial closure of Sangatte, see, for instance, John Lichfield, 'Asylum-seekers Overpower Guards and Storm Tunnel', *The Independent*, 27 December 2001, p. 2.

18. Julian Stallabrass, *High Art Lite: British Art in the 1990s* (London: Verso, 1999), p. 200.

19. See Duncan Petrie, 'Economics and Aesthetics in the New Scottish Cinema', *twoninetwo* vol. 1, pp. 113–24, and James Hamilton, 'Northern Star', *Creation*, May 2000, p. 17.

20. Duncan Petrie, *Screening Scotland* (London: BFI, 2000), p. 217.

Conclusion

During the course of writing this book the systems of directing public funds and state support for British film production have changed: tax relief is now provided on the completion of projects rather than at the outset. This may further discourage small-scale, non-commercial or first-time producers (possibly a bad thing); it may discourage a repeat performance of *Sex Lives of the Potato Men* (possibly a good thing).

A continuing complaint against the vagaries of subsidy ('too little too late') has been, indeed, less its inadequacy than its inconsistency. Television contracts seemingly stepped into the breach as the climate harshened in the 1980s. Others have pleaded that distribution is as deserving of preferential treatment as production. British film commentary, meanwhile, has lurched between recurrent exaggerated claims of a renaissance (as in the 1940s and 1980s) and premature announcements of its demise (as in the 1920s).

However, such a complaint is not unique to cinema as a commercial and cultural product, nor unique to Britain. Since the 1920s, attempts have been made to pool European and other resources in order to counter American domination of the home and export market. Today, Ken Loach attracts financial support from France, while *Bend It Like Beckham* was co-funded in Germany. *Dirty Pretty Things* cast *Amélie*'s Audrey Tautou, while *Russian Bride* cast Vincent Cassell and Matthieu Kassovitz alongside Nicole Kidman (attempting to recoup production costs by an appeal to a French and international audience). Perhaps there is no harm in regarding film as a commodity akin to Rover cars, Rowntree chocolate or Brit Art, or a national football team, the swimming and rowing teams, providing that jobs are retained and national concerns continue to be represented in a national and international arena. This book has been largely interested in the prevailing and changing nature of such concerns, over three centuries.

Sometimes, producers and audiences have looked enviably across the Channel. France has continued to be vociferously and principally protective of native and francophone industries (notably in the GATT negotiations), especially when, on the home fronts, it seems to be losing the battle. In Paris, at least, plenty of independent cinemas appear to thrive alongside foreign-owned multiplexes, providing the punter with a wide range of choice: a quota of receipts (comparable to the Eady Levy of the 1950s, abolished in the 1980s) is reinvested in film production. A declining percentage of distribution and exhibition interests in Britain are British-owned and there is no automatic, statutory inducement to show British films on British screens (as there was in the 1930s).

Although cinema attendances have not fallen to the extent that they did in the 1950s nor to the extent predicted with the boom in video recorder sales in the 1980s, now, more than ever, films are as likely to be viewed initially on a good night in as a good night out. Richard Eyre's *Stage Beauty*, funded by BBC Films, has been broadcast by BBC television within months of its big screen debut. Sadly, with the exception of a very small number of specialist outlets, old films (usually the same old films repeated) are more likely to be viewed through purchase on video and DVD, or between adverts featuring Labradors and stairlifts, on daytime TV. Hiring a film is a bit like using a public library or downloading an e-book: there is little direct recompense for an author.

As in the 1930s, 1950s and 1960s, current new directors have often come to drama from documentary work – for instance, Pawel Pawlikowski (*Last Resort* and *Summer of Love*). Sadly, unlike the 1930s, documentaries now rarely receive big screen exhibition and the small screen opportunities, even with the advent of BBC 4, are dwindling. As in the 1930s, 1950s and 1960s, many have graduated from short films (sometimes adverts), such as Christopher Nolan and Jonathan Glazer. Lucy Blakstad has moved between television and film documentaries and adverts. While new projection formats have been publicly sponsored (as with the webcast *This is Not a Love Song*), other media have been projected in publicly or privately funded gallery spaces (Sam Taylor-Wood's Beckham video at the NPG; Tacita Dean's film *Boots* at RIBA).

Regardless of their site of exhibition, these works are simultaneously objects of commerce and of culture, essentially employing similar materials, and merit equal criticism. All too often, it seems to me, gallery work has been unduly revered as a consequence of its display when it deserves to be subjected to the same level of interrogation as any other projected or broadcast time-based medium. While film history is now appropriately turning its attention to cinema's antecedents, film criticism also needs to apply itself to cinema's other relations, even once or twice removed.

Over the course of three centuries, the sites of film-viewing, the institutions of cinema, the relation with other cinemas, the subjects of films and the substance of 'film' itself may have changed but many of the arguments, in a British context, remain the same. This is still British cinema, but not as we once knew it.

Select Bibliography

Aldgate, Anthony, *Censorship and the Permissive Society* (Oxford: Clarendon, 1995).

Aldgate, Anthony and Richards, Jeffrey, *Best of British* (London: I. B. Tauris, 2002).

Allsop, Kenneth, *The Angry Decade* (London: Peter Owen, 1958).

Amis, Kingsley, *Lucky Jim* [1954] (London: Victor Gollancz, 1996).

Amis, Kingsley, *Take a Girl Like You* (London: Victor Gollancz, 1960).

Amis, Martin, *Dead Babies* [1975] (Harmondsworth: Penguin, 2000).

Amis, Martin, *London Fields* (London: Jonathan Cape, 1989).

Archer, William, *Play Making* (London: Chapman and Hall, 1912).

Artley, Alexandra and Robinson, John Martin, *The New Georgian Handbook* (London: Ebury Press, 1985).

Ashby, Justine and Higson, Andrew (eds), *British Cinema: Past and Present* (London: Routledge, 2000).

Aubrey, Crispin and Chilton, Paul (eds), *Nineteen Eighty-four in 1984: Autonomy, Control and Communication* (London: Comedia, 1983).

Auty, Martin and Roddick, Nick (eds), *British Cinema Now* (London: BFI, 1985).

Balcon, Michael, *Michael Balcon Presents . . . A Lifetime of Films* (London: Hutchinson, 1969).

Bamford, Kenton, *Distorted Images: British National Identity and Film in the 1920s* (London: I. B. Tauris, 1999).

Barnes, John, *Pioneers of the British Film: The Beginnings of the Cinema in England 1894–1901*, vol. 1 (Exeter: Exeter University Press, 1998); vol. 2 (London: Bishopsgate Press, 1983); vol. 3 (London: Bishopsgate Press, 1983); vol. 5 (Exeter: Exeter University Press, 1997).

Barnes, Julian, *England, England* (London: Jonathan Cape, 1998).

Barr, Charles, *The English Hitchcock* (Moffat: Cameron and Hollis, 1999).

Barr, Charles, *Ealing Studios* (London: Studio Vista, 1993).

Barr, Charles (ed.), *All Our Yesterdays* (London: BFI, 1986).

Barry, Iris, *Let's Go to the Pictures* (London: Chatto and Windus, 1926).

Baynbridge, Beryl, *Sweet William* [1973] (Harmondsworth: Penguin, 1992).

Bennett, Alan, *Telling Tales* (London: BBC Worldwide, 2001).

Bennett, Arnold, *Lord Raingo* (London: Cassell, 1926).

Berghaus, Gunter, *Theatre and Film in Exile* (Oxford: Berg, 1989).

Berkoff, Steven, *The Collected Plays* (London: Faber and Faber, 1994).

Berry, Dave, *Wales and Cinema: the first hundred years* (Cardiff: University of Wales Press, 1994).

Berry, Dave and Horrocks, Simon (eds), *David Lloyd George: The Movie Mystery* (Cardiff: University of Wales Press, 1998).

Blades, James, *DrumRoll* (London: Faber and Faber, 1977).

Bliss, Arthur, *As I Remember* (London: Faber and Faber, 1970).

Bottomore, Stephen, *I Want to See this Annie Mattygraph* (Pordenone: Le Giornate del Cinema Muto, 1995).

Bourke, Joanna, *An Intimate History of Killing* (London: Granta, 2000).

Bourke, Joanna, *Dismembering the Male* (London: Reaktion Books, 1999).

Bowen, Elizabeth, *The Heat of the Day* [1949] (London: Jonathan Cape, 1964).

Boyd, William, *The New Confessions* (Harmondsworth: Penguin, 1988).

Bradbury, Malcolm, *The History Man* [1975] (London: Picador, 2000).

Braine, John, *Room at the Top* (London: Eyre & Spottiswoode, 1957).

Brandt, George, *British Television Drama in the 1980s* (Cambridge: Cambridge University Press, 1993).

Brandt, George (ed.), *British Television Drama* (Cambridge: Cambridge University Press, 1981).

Braybon, Gail, *Women Workers in the First World War* (London: Routledge, 1989).

Briggs, Asa, *The History of Broadcasting in the United Kingdom*, vol. II (London: Oxford University Press, 1965) and vol. III, 1970.

Brittain, Vera, *Testament of Youth* [1933] (London: Virago, 1978).

Brownlow, Kevin, *The War, the West and the Wilderness* (London: Secker and Warburg, 1979).

Brunel, Adrian, *Nice Work* (London: Forbes Robertson Ltd., 1949).

Buchan, John, *Greenmantle* [1916] (Oxford: Oxford University Press, 1993).

Buchan, John, *The Thirty-nine Steps* [1915] (London: Hodder and Stoughton, 1963).

Burke, Thomas, *East of Mansion House* (London: Cassell, 1928).

Burke, Thomas, *Limehouse Nights* [1916] (London: Grant Richards Ltd, 1917).

Burrows, Jon, *Legitimate Cinema: Theatre Stars in British Cinema, 1908–1918* (Exeter: Exeter University Press, 2003).

Burton, Alan, O'Sullivan, Tim and Wells, Paul (eds), *The Family Way: The Boulting Brothers and British Film Culture* (Trowbridge: Flicks Books, 2000).

Calder, Angus, *The People's War: Britain 1939–1945* (London: Pimlico, 1992).

Campbell, Beatrix, *The Iron Ladies: Why do Women Vote Tory?* (London: Virago, 1987).

Carey, John, *The Intellectuals and the Masses* (London: Faber and Faber, 1992).

Le Carré, John, *The Naïve and Sentimental Lover* (London: Pan Books, 1971).

Carrick, Edward, *Art and Design in the British Film* (London: Dennis Dobson, 1948).

Chanan, Michael, *The Dream that Kicks* (London: Routledge, 1996).

Chapman, James, *The British at War: Cinema, State and Propaganda 1939–1945* (London: I. B. Tauris, 1998).

Chibnall, Steve and Murphy, Robert (eds), *British Crime Cinema* (London: Routledge, 1999).

Churchill, Winston, *A History of the English-Speaking Peoples,* vol. III (London: Cassell, 1957).

Ciment, Michel, *Conversations with Losey* (London: Methuen, 1985).

Cook, Olive, *Movement in Two Dimensions* (London: Hutchinson, 1963).

Cook, Pam, *Fashioning the Nation* (London: BFI, 1996).

Corner, John and Harvey, Sylvia (eds), *Enterprise and Heritage: Crosscurrents of National Culture* (London: Routledge, 1991).

Courtenay, Tom, *Dear Tom: Letters from Home* (London: Black Swan, 2001).

Coward, Noël, *Noël Coward: Autobiography* (London: Methuen, 1986).

Cull, Nicholas J., *Selling War: The British Propaganda Campaign Against American 'Neutrality' in World War Two* (Oxford: Oxford University Press, 1995).

Curran, James and Porter, Vincent (eds), *British Cinema History* (London: Weidenfeld and Nicolson, 1983).

Curtis, David and Dusinberre, Deke, *A Perspective on English Avant-Garde Film* (London: The Arts Council of Great Britain, 1978).

Danischewsky, Monja, *White Russian: Red Face* (London: Victor Gollancz, 1966).

Dean, Basil, *Mind's Eye: an Autobiography* (London: Hutchinson, 1973).

Deighton, Len, *The Ipcress File* [1962] (London: Jonathan Cape, 1977).

Delafield, E. M., *The Provincial Lady* (London: Macmillan, 1947).

Dickinson, Margaret and Street, Sarah, *Cinema and State: the Film Industry and the Government 1927–84* (London: BFI, 1985).

Donnelly, Kevin, *Pop Music in British Cinema* (London: BFI, 2001).

Drabble, Margaret, *The Ice Age* (Harmondsworth: Penguin, 1978).

Drabble, Margaret, *The Millstone* [1965] (Harmondsworth: Penguin, 1968).

Drabble, Margaret, *A Summer Birdcage* [1963] (Harmondsworth: Penguin, 1967).

Durgnat, Raymond, *A Mirror for England* (London: Faber and Faber, 1970).

Dwoskin, Stephen, *Film Is . . .* (London: Peter Owen, 1975).

Dyer, Richard, *White* (London: Routledge, 1997).

Dyer, Richard, *Brief Encounter* (London: BFI, 1993).

Eberts, Jake and Ilott, Terry, *My Indecision is Final: the Rise and Fall of Goldcrest Films* (London: Faber and Faber,1990).

Edgar, George (ed.), *Careers for Men, Women and Children* (London: Caxton Publishing Co., 1911).

Eyles, Allen, *Odeon Cinemas* (London: BFI, 2001).

Eyles, Allen, *Gaumont British Cinemas* (London: BFI, 1996).

Fielding, Henry, *The History of Tom Jones* [1749] (Harmondsworth: Penguin, 1966).

Fleming, Ian, *From Russia With Love* [1957] (London: Jonathan Cape, 1972).

Fowles, John, *The Collector* [1963] (London: Pan Books, 1986).

Fowles, John, *Daniel Martin* (London: Jonathan Cape, 1977).

Frayn, Michael, *Spies* (London: Faber and Faber, 2002).

Friedman, Lester (ed.), *Fires Were Started: British Cinema and Thatcherism* (Minneapolis: University of Minnesota Press, 1993).

Frith, Simon, *Music for Pleasure: Essays in the Sociology of Pop* (New York: Routledge, 1988).

Fullerton, John (ed.), *Celebrating 1895: The Centenary of Cinema* (Sydney: John Libbey, 1998).

Furniss, Harry, *Our Lady Cinema* (Bristol: J. W. Arrowsmith Ltd, 1914).

Fussell, Paul, *The Great War and Modern Memory* (Oxford: Oxford University Press, 1975).

Geraghty, Christine, *British Cinema in the Fifties* (London: Routledge, 2000).

Gibbons, Stella, *Cold Comfort Farm* [1932] (Harmondsworth: Penguin, 1979).

Gidal, Peter, *Materialist Film* (London: Routledge, 1989).

Glancy, Mark, *When Hollywood Loved Britain* (Manchester: Manchester University Press, 1999).

Gledhill, Christine, *Reframing British Cinema 1918–1928: Between Restraint and Passion* (London: BFI, 2003).

Gledhill, Christine and Swanson, Gillian (eds), *Nationalising Femininity* (Manchester: Manchester University Press, 1996).

Glyn, Elinor, *Romantic Adventure* (London: Ivor Nicholson and Watson, 1936).

Golding, William, *Lord of the Flies* [1954] (London: Faber and Faber, 1988).

Gower, H. D., Stanley Jast, L. and Topley, W. W., *The Camera as Historian* (London: S. Low, Marston and Co. Ltd, 1916).

Graham, Ysenda Maxtone, *The Real Mrs Miniver* (London: John Murray, 2001).

Graves, Robert, *Goodbye to All That* (London: Jonathan Cape, 1929).

Greene, Graham, *The Ministry of Fear* [1943] (Harmondsworth: Penguin, 1985).

Greene, Graham, *Ways of Escape* (Harmondsworth: Penguin, 1981).

Greene, Graham, *The Third Man* [1950] (Harmondsworth: Penguin, 1977).

Greene, Graham, *A Sort of Life* (Harmondsworth: Penguin, 1974).

Greene, Graham, *Twenty-One Stories* (Harmondsworth: Penguin, 1973).

Greene, Graham, *The Pleasure Dome*, (ed.) John Russell Taylor (London: Secker and Warburg, 1972).

Greer, Germaine, *The Female Eunuch* (London: MacGibbon and Kee, 1970).

Grenfell, Joyce, *The Time of My Life* (London: Hodder and Stoughton, 1989).

Grenfell, Joyce, *Joyce Grenfell Requests the Pleasure* (London: Macmillan, 1976).

Guinness, Alec, *My Name Escapes Me* (Harmondsworth: Penguin, 1997).

Hall, Lesley A., *Sex, Gender and Social Change* (Basingstoke: Macmillan, 2000).

Hall, Stuart, Critcher, Charles, Jefferson, Tony, Clarke, John and Roberts, Brian, *Policing the Crisis: Mugging, the State and Law and Order* (London: Macmillan, 1978).

Hammerton, Jenny, *For Ladies Only?* (Hastings: The Projection Box, 2001).

Harding, Colin and Popple, Simon (eds), *In the Kingdom of the Shadows* (London: Cygnus Arts, 1996).

Harper, Sue, *Women in British Cinema: Mad, Bad and Dangerous to Know* (London: Continuum, 2000).

Harper, Sue and Porter, Vincent, *British Cinema of the 1950s: The Decline of Deference* (Oxford: Oxford University Press, 2003).

Hartley, L. P., *The Go-Between* [1953] (Harmondsworth: Penguin, 1958).

Hepworth, Cecil, *Came the Dawn: Memories of a Film Pioneer* (London: Phoenix House, 1951).

Herbert, Stephen, *A History of Pre-Cinema* (London: Routledge, 2000).

Herbert, Stephen and McKernan, Luke (eds), *Who's Who of Victorian Cinema* (London: BFI, 1996).

Higson, Andrew (ed.), *Young and Innocent? The Camera in Britian 1896–1930* (Exeter: Exeter University Press, 2002).

Higson, Andrew (ed.), *Dissolving Views: Key Writings on British Cinema* (London: Cassell, 1996).

Higson, Andrew, *Waving the Flag* (Oxford: Clarendon, 1995).

Higson, Andrew and Maltby, Richard (eds), *Film Europe, Film America* (Exeter: Exeter University Press, 1999).

Hill, John, *British Cinema in the 1980s* (Oxford: Clarendon, 1999).

Hill, John, *Sex, Class and Realism* (London: BFI, 1986).

Hoggart, Richard, *The Uses of Literacy* [1957] (London: Chatto and Windus, 1967).

Hornung, E. W., 'A Costume Piece', *The Collected Raffles* [1899] (London: Everyman, 1993).

Hunt, Leon, *British Low Culture: from Safari Suits to Sexploitation* (London: Routledge, 1998).

Hunter, I. Q. (ed.), *British Science Fiction Cinema* (London: Routledge, 1999).

Hurd, Geoff (ed.), *National Fictions: World War Two in British Films and Television* (London: BFI, 1984).

Hutchings, Peter, *Dracula* (London: I. B. Tauris, 2003).

Hutton, Will, *The State We're In* (London: Vintage, 1996).

Hynes, Samuel, *A War Imagined* (London: Pimlico, 1990).

Jackson, Lesley, *The New Look: Design in the Fifties* (London: Thames and Hudson, 1991).

James, P. D., 'An Unsuitable Job for a Woman' [1972], *The P. D. James Omnibus* (London: Faber and Faber, 1982).

Jarman, Derek, *Dancing Ledge* (London: Quartet Books, 1984).

Joll, James, *The Origins of the First World War* (Harlow: Longman, 1992).

Kaplan, E. Ann, *Women and Film: Both Sides of the Camera* (London: Methuen, 1983).

Kelly, Richard, *Alan Clarke* (London: Faber and Faber, 1998).

King, Alex, *Memorials of the Great War in Britain* (Oxford: Berg, 1998).

Kipling, Rudyard, *Traffics and Discoveries* [1904] (London: Macmillan, 1973).

Korda, Michael, *Charmed Lives: a Family Romance* (London: Allen Lane, 1980).

Kuhn, Annette, *An Everyday Magic: Cinema and Cultural Memory* (London: I. B. Tauris, 2002).

Kuhn, Michael, *One Hundred Films and a Funeral: Polygram Films: Birth, Betrothal, Burial* (London: Thorogood, 2002).

Lahr, John (ed.), *The Diaries of Kenneth Tynan* (London: Bloomsbury, 2001).

Lahr, John (ed.), *The Orton Diaries* (London: Methuen, 1987).

Laity, Paul (ed.), *Left Book Club Anthology* (London: Weidenfeld and Nicolson, 2001).

Lancaster, Osbert, *Progress at Pelvis Bay* (London: John Murray, 1936).

Lanchester, Elsa, *Elsa Lanchester Herself* (London: Michael Joseph, 1983).

Lant, Antonia, *Blackout: Reinventing Women for Wartime British Cinema* (Princeton: Princeton University Press, 1991).

Lassally, Walter, *Itinerant Cameraman* (London: John Murray, 1987).

Lawrence, D. H., *Sons and Lovers* [1913] (Harmondsworth: Penguin, 2000).

Lawrence, D. H., *The Lost Girl* [1920] (Harmondsworth: Penguin, 1977).

Lawrence, T. E., *The Mint* (London: Jonathan Cape, 1955).

Lehmann, Rosamund, *The Weather in the Streets* [1936] (London: Virago, 1981).

Lejeune, Caroline, *Chestnuts in her Lap* (London: Phoenix House, 1947).

Lejeune, Caroline, *Cinema* (London: Alexander Maclehose, 1931).

Light, Alison, *Forever England: Femininity, Literature and Conservatism Between the Wars* (London: Routledge, 1991).

Littlewood, Joan, *Joan's Book* (Basingstoke: Macmillan, 2000).

London, Kurt, *Film Music* (London: Faber and Faber, 1936).

Low, Rachael, *Film Making in 1930s Britain* (London: George Allen and Unwin, 1985).

Low, Rachael, *Documentary and Educational Films of the 1930s* (London: George Allen and Unwin, 1979).

Low, Rachael, *The History of the British Film, 1914–1918* (London: George Allen and Unwin, 1950).

Low, Rachael, *The History of the British Film, 1906–1914* (London: George Allen and Unwin, 1949).

MacInnes, Colin, *Absolute Beginners* [1959] (London: Allison and Busby, 1994).

MacInnes, Colin, *England Half English: A Polyphoto of the Fifties* (London: MacGibbon and Kee, 1961).

Manvell, Roger, *Film* (London: Penguin, 1944).

Marwick, Arthur, *British Society Since 1945* (London: Penguin, 2003).

Maschler, Tom, *Declaration* (London: MacGibbon and Kee, 1957).

Mathews, Tom Dewe, *Censored* (London: Chatto and Windus, 1994).

Matless, David, *Landscape and Englishness* (London: Reaktion, 1998).

McGillivray, David, *Doing Rude Things* (London: Sun Tavern Fields, 1992).

McKnight, George (ed.), *Ken Loach: Agent of Challenge and Defiance* (Trowbridge: Flicks Books, 1997).

Minney, R. J., *'Puffin' Asquith* (London: Leslie Frewin, 1973).

Monk, Claire and Sargeant, Amy (eds), *British Historical Cinema* (London: Routledge, 2002).

Montagu, Ivor, *The Youngest Son* (London: Lawrence and Wishart, 1970).

Moseley, Rachel, *Growing Up with Audrey Hepburn* (Manchester: Manchester University Press, 2002).

Moynihan, Michael (ed.), *People at War 1914–1918* (Newton Abbot: David and Charles, 1973).

Mullen, Pat, *Man of Aran* (London: Faber and Faber, 1934).

Murphy, Robert (ed.), *British Cinema of the 90s* (London: BFI, 2000).

Murphy, Robert, *Sixties British Cinema* (London: BFI, 1992).

Murphy, Robert, *Realism and Tinsel* (London: Routledge, 1989).

Neaverson, Bob, *The Beatles Movies* (London: Cassell, 1997).

Nicholson, Vivian and Smith, Stephen, *Spend, Spend, Spend* (London: Jonathan Cape, 1977).

Niven, David, *The Moon's a Balloon: Reminiscences by David Niven* (London: Hamish Hamilton, 1979).

O'Pray, Michael, *Avant-Garde Film* (Luton: John Libbey, 1996).

O'Reilly, Karen, *The British on the Costa del Sol* (London: Routledge, 2000).

Orwell, George, *The Lion and the Unicorn* [1941] (Harmondsworth: Penguin, 1982).

Osborne, John, *Damn You, England* (London: Faber and Faber, 1994).

Paris, Michael, *The First World War and Popular Cinema* (Edinburgh: Edinburgh University Press, 1999).

Pearson, George, *Flashback: an Autobiography of a British Film Maker* (London: George Allen and Unwin, 1957).

Perry, George, *Forever Ealing* (London: Pavilion Books, 1981).

Petrie, Duncan, *Screening Scotland* (London: BFI, 2000).

Ponting, Herbert, *The Great White South: or, With Scott in the Antarctic* (London: Duckworth, 1950).

Porter, Laraine and Burton, Alan (eds), *Scene-Stealing* (Trowbridge: Flicks Books, 2003).

Porter, Laraine and Burton, Alan (eds), *Crossing the Pond* (Trowbridge: Flicks Books, 2002).

Porter, Laraine and Burton, Alan (eds), *Pimple, Pranks and Pratfalls* (Trowbridge: Flicks Books, 2000).

Powell, Dilys, *Films Since 1939* (London: Longmans, Green and Co., 1947).

Powell, Michael, *A Life in Movies* (London: Heinemann, 1986).

Priestley, J. B., *The Good Companions* [1929] (London: Heinemann, 1974).

Priestley, J. B., *English Journey* [1933] (London: Heron Books, 1949).

Read, Herbert, *Art and Industry: the Principles of Industrial Design* (London: Faber and Faber, 1934).

Reade, Charles, *Peg Woffington* (London: Chatto and Windus, 1852).

Rees, A. L., *A History of Experimental Film and Video* (London: BFI, 1999).

Reeves, Nicholas, *Official British Film Propaganda* (London: Croom Helm and IWM, 1986).

Richards, Jeffrey (ed.), *The Unknown 1930s: an Alternative History of the British Cinema 1929–39* (London, I. B. Tauris, 1998).

Richards, Jeffrey, *The Age of the Dream Palace* (London: Routledge and Kegan Paul, 1984).

Richards, Jeffrey and Sheridan, Dorothy (eds), *Mass Observation at the Movies* (London: Routledge and Kegan Paul, 1987).

Rotha, Paul, *The Film Till Now* (London: Vision, 1951).

Rotha, Paul, *Celluloid: the Film Today* (London: Longmans, Green and Co., 1931).

Rowe, Marsha, *Spare Rib Reader* (Harmondsworth: Penguin, 1982).

Ryall, Tom, *Blackmail* (London: BFI, 1993).

Saki (H. H. Munro), *When William Came: a Story of London under the Hohenzollerns* [1913] (London: John Lane, 1926).

Samuel, Raphael, *Theatres of Memory* (London: Verso, 1994).

Sassoon, Siegfried, *Memoirs of an Infantry Officer* [1930] (London: Faber and Faber, 1995).

Shafer, Stephen C., *British Popular Films 1929–1939* (London: Routledge, 1997).

Shaw, Tony, *British Cinema and the Cold War* (London: I. B. Tauris, 2000).

Sillitoe, Alan, *Down from the Hill* (London: Granada, 1984).

Sinclair, Iain, *Lights Out for the Territory* (London: Granta Books, 1997).

Sissons, Michael and French, Philip (eds), *Age of Austerity* (London: Hodder and Stoughton, 1963).

Spicer, Andrew, *Typical Men: the Representation of Masculinity in Popular British Cinema* (London: I. B. Tauris, 2001).

Stallabrass, Julian, *High Art Lite: British Art in the 1990s* (London: Verso, 1999).

Stedman-Jones, Philip, *Metropolis: London* (London: Routledge, 1989).

Steer, Valentia, *Secrets of the Cinema* (London: C. Arthur Pearson, 1920).

Steer, Valentia, *The Romance of the Cinema* (London: C. Arthur Pearson, 1913).

Sutton, Dave, *A Chorus of Raspberries* (Exeter: Exeter University Press, 2000).

Sydney, Aurèle, *A Practical Course in Cinema Acting*, vol. 4 (London: Standard Art Book Co., 1920).

Sydney, Aurèle, *How to Act for the Kinema*, vol. 7 (London: FAS Publications, ca.1917).

Talbot, Frederick A., *Moving Pictures: How They are Made and Worked* (London: Heinemann, 1912).

Taylor, John, *A Dream of England* (Manchester: Manchester University Press, 1994).

Taylor, Philip M., *Munitions of the Mind* (Wellingborough: Patrick Stephens, 1990).

Thackeray, William, *The Memoirs of Barry Lyndon, Esq., Written by Himself* [1853] (London: Smith, Elder and

Co., 1890).

Toulmin, Vanessa, Popple, Simon and Russell, Patrick (eds), *The Lost World of Mitchell and Kenyon* (London: BFI, 2004).

Truffaut, François, *Hitchcock* [1966] (London: Secker and Warburg, 1968).

Tulloch, John, *Television Drama* (London: Routledge, 1990).

Ustinov, Peter, *Dear Me* (London: Heinemann, 1977).

Walker, Alexander, *Hollywood England: the British Film Industry in the Sixties* [1974] (London: Harrap, 1986).

Walker, Alexander, *National Heroes: British Cinema in the Seventies and Eighties* (London: Harrap, 1985).

Walker, John, *The Once and Future Film* (London: Methuen, 1985).

Warren, Low, *The Film Game* (London: T. Werner Laurie, 1937).

Watt, Harry, *Don't Look at the Camera* (London: Paul Elek, 1974).

Waugh, Evelyn, *Scoop* [1938] (Harmondsworth: Penguin, 2000).

Waugh, Evelyn, *Vile Bodies* [1930] (London: Eyre Methuen, 1986).

Waugh, Evelyn, *Put Out More Flags* [1942] (London: Chapman and Hall, 1959).

Waugh, Evelyn, *When the Going was Good* (London: Duckworth, 1946).

Wells, H. G., *The Time Machine* [1895] (London: J. M. Dent, 1992).

Wells, H. G., *The King Who Was a King* (London: Ernest Benn, 1929).

Wells, H. G., *Tono Bungay* [1909] (London: T. Fisher Unwin Ltd, 1925).

West, Rebecca, *The Essential Rebecca West* (Harmondsworth: Penguin, 1983).

Wilcox, Herbert, *Twenty-Five Thousand Sunsets* (London: Bodley Head, 1967).

Williams, Christopher (ed.), *Cinema: the Beginnings and the Future* (London: University of Westminster Press, 1996).

Williams, Michael, *Ivor Novello: Screen Idol* (London: BFI, 2003).

Williams, Raymond, *Culture and Society 1780–1850* [1958] (Harmondsworth: Penguin, 1982).

Williams, Raymond, *The Country and the City* (London: Chatto and Windus, 1973).

Wyndham, John, *The Day of the Triffids* [1951] (London: Penguin, 2000).

York, Peter, *Style Wars* (London: Sidgwick and Jackson, 1980).

Yorke, F. R. S., *The Modern House* (London: Architectural Press, 1934).

Young, Lola, *Fear of the Dark* (London: Routledge, 1996).

Index

Page numbers in **bold** indicate detailed analysis; those in *italic* denote illustrations; *n* = endnote.

List of Illustrations

Whilst considerable effort has been made to correctly identify the copyright holders, this has not been possible in all cases. We apologise for any apparent negligence and any omissions or corrections brought to our attention will be remedied in any future editions.

The Tempest, Clarendon Film Company; Mitchell and Kenyon Whitsuntide Catholic Procession, BFI; *A Visit to Peak Freans Biscuit Works*, BFI; *A Day in the Life of a Coalminer*, BFI; *Ultus: The Man from the Dead*, Gaumont Company; *Jane Shore*, Barker Motion Photography; *Tilly Works for a Living*, Hepworth Manufacturing Company; *Ultus and the Grey Lady*, Gaumont Company; *Dawn*, British and Dominions Film Corporation; *The Battle of the Somme*, British Topical Committee for War Films; *The Women's Land Army*, Broadwest Film Company; *The Battles of the Coronel and Falkland Islands*, British Instructional Films/Admiralty; *Piccadilly*, British International Pictures; *Bluebottles*, Angle Pictures; *The Sign of the Four*, Stoll Film Company; *Shooting Stars*, British Instructional Films; *Champagne*, British International Pictures; *Knight Without Armour*, London Film Productions; *First A Girl*, Gaumont-British Picture Corporation; *Evergreen*, Gaumont-British Picture Corporation; *Sunshine Susie*, Gainsborough Pictures; *The Stars Look Down*, Grafton Films; *The Life and Death of Colonel Blimp*, Archers Film Production; *Pastor Hall*, Charter Film Productions; *In Which We Serve*, Two Cities Films; *Millions Like Us*, Gainsborough Pictures; *A Diary for Timothy*, Crown Film Unit; *The Third Man*, London Film Productions; *Midshipman Easy*, Associated Talking Pictures; *Brief Encounter*, Cineguild/Independent Producers; *Night and the City*, Twentieth Century-Fox Productions; *Brighton Rock*, Associated British Picture Corporation; *Orders to Kill*, Lynx Productions/British Lion Film Corporation; *Look Back in Anger*, Woodfall Film Productions; *Together*, Harlequin Productions/BFI; *Expresso Bongo*, Conquest Productions; *Blind Date*, Independent Artists; *The Ipcress File*, Steven S.A./Lowndes Productions; *Billy Liar!*, © Anglo Amalgamated Film Distributors; *Blow-Up*, © Metro-Goldwyn-Mayer, Inc.; *Kes*, Woodfall Film Productions/Kestrel Films; *Lord of the Flies*, Allen-Hodgdon Productions/Two Arts; *Sebastiane*, © Disctac; *Up Pompeii*, Anglo-EMI/Associated London Films; *Sunday Bloody Sunday*, Vectia Films/Vic Films; *The Song of the Shirt*, Film and History Project/Royal College of Art/Polytechnic of Central London/Cinema Action/Greater London Arts Association/Arts Council of Great Britain/BFI; *The Long Good Friday*, Black Lion Films/Calendar Productions; *The Man Who Fell to Earth*, British Lion Film Corporation; *Paris by Night*, British Screen/Film Four International/Zenith Productions/Greenpoint Films/Cineplex Odeon Films; *A World Apart*, Working Title Films/Hippo Films/British Screen/Atlantic Entertainment Group/Channel Four; *Wetherby*, Greenpoint Films/Film Four International/Zenith Productions; *1984*, © Virgin Cinema Films; *A Zed and Two Noughts*, BFI/Artificial Eye Productions/Film Four International/Allarts Enterprises; *Rita, Sue and Bob Too*, © Channel Four Television Company; *Richard III*, First Look Pictures/Mayfair Entertainment International/British Screen; *This Year's Love*, Entertainment Film Distributors Ltd/Kismet Film Company/Scottish Arts Council Lottery Fund; *The Crying Game*, © Palace (Soldier's Wife) Ltd/© Nippon Film Development & Finance; *Felicia's Journey*, © Marquis Films/© Screenventures XLII Productions Limited; *Last Resort*, © BBC.

Queering
the Popular Pitch

Edited by Sheila Whiteley and Jennifer Rycenga

Routledge
Taylor & Francis Group
New York   London

Routledge is an imprint of the
Taylor & Francis Group, an informa business

Published in 2006 by
Routledge
Taylor & Francis Group
711 Third Avenue
New York, NY 10017

Published in Great Britain by
Routledge
Taylor & Francis Group
2 Park Square
Milton Park, Abingdon
Oxon OX14 4RN

International Standard Book Number-10: 0-415-97805-X (Softcover) 0-415-97804-1 (Hardcover)
International Standard Book Number-13: 978-0-415-97805-7 (Softcover) 978-0-415-97804-0 (Hardcover)
Library of Congress Card Number 2005030587

Library of Congress Cataloging-in-Publication Data

Queering the popular pitch / edited by Sheila Whiteley, Jennifer Rycenga.
    p. cm.
Includes bibliographical references and index.
ISBN 0-415-97804-1 (hb) -- ISBN 0-415-97805-X (pb) 1. Homosexuality and popular music. 2. Sex in music. 3. Gay musicians. 4. Gender identity in music. I. Whiteley, Sheila, 1941- II. Rycenga, Jennifer.III. Title.

ML3470.Q44 2006
781.64086'64--dc22
                                          2005030587

Taylor & Francis Group
is the Academic Division of Informa plc.

Visit the Taylor & Francis Web site at
http://www.taylorandfrancis.com

and the Routledge Web site at
http://www.routledge-ny.com

CONTENTS

EDITORS

Sheila Whiteley is the chair of popular music at the University of Salford, Greater Manchester, United Kingdom. She was general secretary (1999–2001) of the International Association for the Study of Popular Music and is now publications officer. She is a Reader for Routledge, Blackwell, and Ashgate. Her publications include *Too Much Too Young: Popular Music, Age, and Identity* (Routledge, 2005); *Women and Popular Music: Sexuality, Identity, and Subjectivity* (Routledge, 2000); *Sexing the Groove: Popular Music and Gender* (Routledge, 1998); and *The Space between the Notes: Rock and the Counter Culture* (Routledge, 1992). Shelia coedited (with Andy Bennett and Stan Hawkins) *Music, Space, and Place: Popular Music and Cultural Identity* (Ashgate, 2004) and has contributed chapters to *Remembering Woodstock* (Ashgate, 2004); *Every Sound There Is: The Beatles' Revolver and the Transformation of Rock and Roll* (Ashgate, 2003), which was awarded The Association for Recorded Sound Collections Award for Excellence in the category of Best Research in Rock, Rhythm and Blues, or Soul; and *Reading Pop: Approaches to Textual Analysis in Popular Music* (Oxford University Press, 2000).

Jennifer Rycenga is professor of comparative religious studies and coordinator of women's studies at San José State University in California. She teaches in the areas of American religious history, religion and music, gender and religion, and lesbian intellectual history. She coedited

Frontline Feminisms: Women, War, and Resistance with Marguerite Waller (Garland, 2001) and has written for *Repercussions: Critical and Alternative Viewpoints on Music and Scholarship, The Encyclopedia of Women and World Religion, The Garland Encyclopedia of World Music,* and *The Encyclopedia of Popular Music of the World.* Jennifer has contributed to *Progressive Rock Reconsidered* (Routledge, 2002); *God in the Details: American Religion in Popular Culture* (Routledge, 2001); *Keeping Score: Music, Disciplinarity, Culture* (University Press of Virginia, 1997); *Queering the Pitch: The New Lesbian and Gay Musicology* (Routledge, 1994); and *Adorno: A Critical Reader* (Blackwell, 2002). Currently, she is working on a cultural biography of Prudence Crandall, a nineteenth-century Abolitionist educator and feminist.

PREFACE

SHEILA WHITELEY

As a feminist musicologist with strong research interests in issues of identity and subjectivity in popular music, organizing a theme for the 2003 Biennial Conference for the International Association for the Study of Popular Music offered a rare opportunity to wrench queering from the doldrums of generalized gender debates and to foreground current issues—not the least of which are those concerning ethnicity and class. At the same time, the conference provided a special space to revisit *Queering the Pitch: The New Lesbian and Gay Musicology*,[1] to evaluate the significance of the original text and to update the debates with specific reference to popular music discourse.[2]

I was delighted, then, when Jennifer Rycenga agreed to be coeditor of the present volume, *Queering the Popular Pitch*. As a contributor to the original *Queering the Pitch* and a keynote speaker at the conference, her thoughtfulness and zest are evidenced in her contribution to the current volume, both as coeditor and in her chapter "Endless Caresses: Queer Exuberance in Large-Scale Form in Rock." It was also encouraging that the thirty or so papers presented in the conference's "Queering the Practice" stream demonstrated a palpable, continuing commitment to issues concerning sexuality and popular music. John Shepherd, for example, singled out Freya Jarman-Ivens's paper as one of the highlights of

the five-day conference in his closing address. Other (of many) exciting moments included Jason Lee Oakes's paper "Night of a Thousand Stevies," Vanessa Knights's paper "Tears and Screams: Performances of Pleasure and Pain in the Bolero," and Paul Attinello's paper "Closeness and Distance: Songs about AIDS," all included in this volume. Small wonder, then, that the conference became the catalyst for *Queering the Popular Pitch.*

We would especially like to thank Richard Carlin, our editor at Routledge, for his encouragement and unfailing sense of humor—a necessary quality in an editor, and one much appreciated. We also thank Katy Smith and Christian Muñoz of Routledge/Taylor & Francis, and Brian Bendlin, the freelance copyeditor of this book.

NOTES

1. Philip Brett, Gary C. Thomas, and Elizabeth Wood, eds., *Queering the Pitch: The New Gay and Lesbian Musicology* (New York: Routledge, 1994).
2. The full transcripts are included in the *GLSG Newsletter for the Gay and Lesbian Study Group of the American Musicological Society* 14, no. 1, Spring 2004.

INTRODUCTION

The significance of queering to contemporary popular music is reflected in the diversity of chapters contained in this book, which delve into issues concerning race and ethnicity, forgotten histories, the body in music, and the use of popular music in power politics. The chapters also forge alliances among academics and activists, scholars and listeners, with the aim of exploring the ways in which queering has challenged cultural, social, and musical structures, subverting the gendered heterosexual bias in popular music by invoking a different way of listening, a queer sensibility. Popular music, for these authors, is not a neatly squared-off discourse; rather, it can be considered as a social force that constructs heteronormativity *and* resistant queer sexualities, whether gay, lesbian, bisexual, transsexual, or transgender, and can thus claim to have played a significant, if often ambiguous role, in the shaping of queer identity and queer self-consciousness. In doing so, it has merged queer social relations with queer musical ones, thus demonstrating the transforming significance of musical discourses and the ways in which these are situated in historical time.

While the chapters herein engage with perspectives that date back to the 1930s, *Queering the Popular Pitch* is not a social history. Rather, it is a collection of essays by eighteen scholars who "read" the queer iconography implicit in a variety of art forms that include film musicals, videos, cabaret, Latin House music, poetry and, in some cases, cultural

personae. Not least, the essays reflect the importance of queering to the politics of popular music and the particular "pull" it exerts on both the individual and the collective imagination. This has largely depended on the queer audience being able to discern sympathetic attributes in periods when homosexuality remained for the most part legally and socially proscribed—for example, in prewar Germany, pre-1970s America and the United Kingdom, and pre-1988 Israel.[1] By using the term *queer*—as opposed to *lesbian and gay*—the authors show how same-sex desire can be foregrounded without designating which sex is desiring/being desired and, as such, a certain fluidity is achieved that refuses gender-based constructions. In short, *queer* becomes the taboo-breaker.

It is not our intention, here, to discuss the range of ways in which queering has been theorized. As readers are aware, the proliferation of undergraduate and postgraduate courses in queer studies has meant that students and academics often approach the field from one discipline (musicology, ethnomusicology, sociology, anthropology) while integrating insights from other fields and, as such, queer studies often straddle disciplines while breaking down barriers. This is evidenced in the range of articles, books, popular press articles, and websites referenced by our authors. As we are well aware, queering has a long history in cinema, literature, pulp fiction, and theatre. Popular music, in particular, contains both hidden histories and iconoclastic figures that have long attracted devoted audiences who sense something quite different from what the mainstream thinks is being projected. It would be misleading, then, to suggest that the chapters and the topics covered herein would be shaped by a single, inclusive theoretical approach. This, we believe, is this volume's real strength: it allows for both personal reflection and academic scrutiny of the ways in which sexual meanings are inscribed in different forms of cultural expression, and the ways in which cultural meanings are inscribed in the discourses and practices of popular music.

As such, popular music can be seen as a catalyst for different truths, for different interpretations that have worked to free the queer imaginary. it contributes to a more thoughtful understanding of identity, of "who I am," and hence the quality and meaning of human relationships, through providing more complex interpretations than the narratives might initially imply.

AN OVERVIEW OF THE BOOK

Queering the Popular Pitch has four parts. The first part, "Performing Lives, Hidden Histories," comprises five chapters that explore different contextualizations of gender, generation, community, race, and

sexuality. Starting with Judith Halberstam's "What's That Smell? Queer Temporalities and Subcultural Lives," the reader is confronted with the allure of subcultural life for the ladyman, the freak who wants to "rock with the tough girls." Her tour of dyke subcultures takes in riot dyke punk, drag kings, drag king boy-band parody groups, and slam poets in a groundbreaking chapter that critically evaluates subcultural theory and its failure to address queer subcultures. Notably, Halberstam's identification of "girl fan cultures, house drag cultures, and gay sex cultures" as lying at "the bottom of the pyramid of subcultures" underpins much of the raison d'être for *Queering the Popular Pitch* and its highlighting of "Hidden Histories."

Queer communities are also significant in Rachel Devitt's chapter, "Girl on Girl: Fat Femmes, Bio-Queens, and Redefining Drag." Addressing the interdependency of concepts of race and gender within the subversive sexuality of the cabarets, Devitt reflects on "the gender performance battlefield, long ridden with land mines of interpretation, appropriation, and identity." Her champions include such acts as the Queen Bees and other "girl on girl" drag artists like them who are new to the struggle, and how their entrance on to the field has been met with the requisite name-calling and hazing from the gender police. Like Halberstam, she notes the way in which conventional drag has become commodified and consumed ever more rapidly by the hegemonic mainstream (so as to produce and make realistic such an oxymoron as "conventional drag"), and why it is, in performances such as these, that we can find a new and newly radicalized performative voice in the gender underground. Devitt's investigation focuses on performers whose music is humorous and/or highly sexualized, and who rely on a particularly racialized image to generate subversion by employing musics that smack of overblown whiteness. This becomes both an acknowledgment and a problematizing of the role that whiteness has played in the construction of gender.

Jason Lee Oakes, in "Queering the Witch: Stevie Nicks and the Forging of Femininity at the Night of a Thousand Stevies," picks up the theme of performative gender play. Stevie Nicks has become an iconic figure for "dominant women, poets, gay men and lesbians, free-thinking heterosexuals, transvestites and transsexuals, fetish dressers, bisexuals and those who love them"—so the sign at the entrance to the club Jackie 60 claims. The annual Night of a Thousand Stevies (NOTS) has been celebrated in New York for the past thirteen years, with a serial procession of Nicks impersonators performing a single song, well into the morning hours. As Oakes argues, this event attempts to reconcile femininity and feminism—accounting for Stevie Nicks's contradictory reception. While her witchiness and hyperfemininity may confirm

gender stereotypes for more conservative listeners, from another perspective she serves as a model of female empowerment. The Stevie impersonators take advantage of Nicks's polysemous perversity, confirming their transgressive desires through multiple readings of her image, and queer "hearings" of her music.

Karen Tongson tackles similar issues, but takes us from the city to the suburbs, in "Tickle Me Emo: Lesbian Balladeering, Straight-Boy Emo, and the Politics of Affect." Tongson sees a vital connection between earnest lesbian music and emotional (emo), hetero, male, low-fi punk, largely through the latter's reliance on "emotionally raw incarnations of arrested development in [the] peripheral spaces" of American suburbia. In doing so, she explores modes of queer life and culture that are practiced beyond the parameters of gay urban ghettos, critiquing the typical "hardcore" male punk genealogy for emo to show how the call for emotional "authenticity" and political expressivity harkens back to the tenets of second-wave feminism.

Musical strategies for revealing and concealing gender and sexual identities are the concern of Anno Mungen's chapter "'Anders als die Anderen,' or, Queering the Song: Construction and Representation of Homosexuality in German Cabaret Song Recordings before 1933." This crucial time period, just before the rise of the Nazis, saw the growth of a queer culture in Germany. Being "different" was a condition that was mostly hidden, yet recorded songs show that the cabaret and its music reveal a performative gay (sub)culture. Three approaches are distinguished: queering by "dragging" the song—performing words originally meant for the opposite sex, thus indicating a sexual identity as *anders* (other), or gay; using certain vocal mannerisms such as a feminization of expression, shifting the emphasis from straight to gay; and through shared allusions in a song's content, as in the line, *Wir sind nun einmal anders als die anderen* (We are in fact other than the others).

The second part of the book, "Queering Boundaries," queers the oft-neglected histories of Latino and Israeli musics, starting with "Tears and Screams: Performances of Pleasure and Pain in the Bolero," in which Vanessa Knights explores the "suffering divas" and how specific features of the bolero genre allow for homoerotic readings. As she persuasively argues, audience identification creates a sense of belonging through an affective investment in the indeterminacy of the lyrics, the focus of the listener on the sensual singing voice, and the development of a style known as "feeling" that privileges the grain of the voice and dramatic performative strategies.

The sense of lyric indeterminacy identified by Knights emerges again in Gilad Padva's chapter "Hey Man, You're My Girlfriend!

Poetic Genderfuck and Queer Hebrew in Eran Zur's Performance of Yona Wallach's lyrics," which takes queering into Israeli territory and the problems inherent in a gender-identified language. With the focus on queer identity, Padva's discussion invites the reader to move to an alternative space, another delight, an "other" sex, providing a paradigmatic example of genderfuck in Zur's (male) performance of Wallach's (female) poems.

Mario Rey analyzes the career and sexual presentation of the Cuban singer Albita Rodríguez. The tensions between her transgressive declarations and the social conservatism of the Cuban exile community are studied in Rey's chapter "Albita Rodríguez: Sexuality, Imaging, and Gender Construction in the Music of Exile." He addresses the reception of Albita Rodríguez among disempowered Cuban groups, including young gay Cuban Americans, and her transcendence from lesbian iconicity to a broader symbol of exile subculture, expressing communal solidarity and nostalgia for prerevolutionary Cuba.

"Su Casa Es Mi Casa: Latin House, Sexuality, Place" explores the concept of "multidenties" and the cross-fertilization between House and Latin musics. Here Stephen Amico examines the ways in which the relationship of the homosexual to the "hometown" ("the site of one's introduction into one's initial culture") is fraught with complications. As hometown is a site of both humiliations and erasure, of an internally perceived or externally proscribed inability to become part of the social fabric, it has engendered a mass exodus to such major urban centers as New York City, a phenomenon he terms a "reverse diaspora," achieved through shared musical experiences.

The book's third part, "Too Close for Comfort," deals with musicians and musical moments that seem open to homoeroticism, yet also pull back from fully embracing the nonnormative. Sarah Kerton takes up the controversy surrounding the duo Tatu's dissemination by the media in "Too Much, Tatu Young: Queering Politics in the World of Tatu." Her analysis explores their debut album *200km/h in the Wrong Lane* and subsequent singles, and demonstrates how the press neutralized political agency by a reconstruction of the band through the constrictions of the male gaze. She also suggests that Tatu's refusal to confirm or deny their sexuality constitutes a queering of both the heteronormative values of the mainstream press, and the "homonormative" values perpetuated by the "majority minority" within the queer press.

Another celebrity's dance around sexual identity forms the topic of Emma Mayhew's chapter "'I Am Not in a Box of Any Description': Sinéad O'Connor's Queer Outing." O'Connor's claim to lesbian identity, and her later renegotiation of such a claim, provides an important case

study in queering. Arguing that O'Connor's "general queerness" has been evident from the beginning of her career, Mayhew explores how O'Connor's "self-outing" highlights the problem of representing a fluid and changing sexual identity.

Jeffrey Callen's chapter "Gender Crossings: A Neglected History in African American Music" revisits an almost two-decades-long revue, the Dukes of Rhythm, which features a female impersonator, Jean LaRue. As Callen observes, while everyone knew about female impersonators, the valorized history of African American popular music is largely silent on "the contributions of those who fell outside of, or refused to recognize, the gender boundaries."

A similar valorization of masculinity would make rap appear quite distant from the project of queering, but Freya Jarman-Ivens suggests that the masculinity of the genre elicits an intense homosociality, stresses linguistic skill, and otherwise makes for a presentation of masculinity that is not "straightforward and unproblematic." In her chapter "Queering Masculinities in Heterosexist Rap Music," Jarman-Ivens notes how Eminem's obsession with gay sex and his rhetorical strategies of self-abnegation imply that, perhaps, the projection of heteromasculinity by rappers is so overdone as to be self-parodic, and even in some cases to be functioning as a ruse.

Paul Attinello examines the phenomenon of songs about AIDS that are so oblique about the topic as to almost go unnoticed. In his chapter "Closeness and Distance: Songs about AIDS," Attinello examines songs by Tori Amos and James Taylor, and speculates that sympathy made gay men more acceptable to homophobic performers and audiences.

The fourth and final part of this volume, "Glamorous Excess," considers how the principle of queering can be theoretically supple in many situations. Jennifer Rycenga's "Endless Caresses: Queer Exuberance in Large-Scale Form in Rock" suggests that the hostility to musical experimentation in rock music stems from a masculinist normativity in formal matters. Drawing on two albums that have been more often derided than applauded—Yes's *Tales from Topographic Oceans* and PJ Harvey's *Is This Desire?*—she shows how large-scale forms, rather than being mere abstractions, instead can serve as a road into the immediacy of the music.

Sheila Whiteley explores "Popular Music and the Dynamics of Desire" through a conceptual framework based on (queering) fantasy. The ability to inhabit an imagined scenario that, in turn, produces what we understand as sexuality, signals both what is denied and what we would like to experience. Focusing on the 1970s and the paradox of legality (the passing of the U.K.'s Homosexual Reform Act, 1967) and

persecution (exemplified in the Jeremy Thorpe affair) she explores three linked case studies—those of Freddie Mercury, Patti Smith, and Rob Halford.

"Trans Glam: Gender Magic in the Film Musical" explores the potential diversity of audience response to film glamour, and its queer associations. Here Lloyd Whitesell adjusts the filmic focus from the gaze to the ear; from sex to gender; and from object to affect. Focusing on classical Hollywood from the 1930s to the 1950s Whitesell establishes codes of glamour in mainstream films of the period. He then moves to three subcultural films of the last ten years in which glam reemerges: *The Adventures of Priscilla, Queen of the Desert; Velvet Goldmine*; and *Hedwig and the Angry Inch*, noting how the films revisit and revise conventions of gender enhancement through queer consumption of mainstream images.

The collection concludes with Stan Hawkins's meditation "On Male Queering in Mainstream Pop." Hawkins considers how some male pop stars use queer cliché and innovative regendering in visual representations, commenting that the stars' "degree of acceptance is predicated on them *signifying* queer rather than 'being queer.'" Reflecting upon the spectacle of queering and the pursuit of pleasure, Hawkins focuses on the example of Justin Timberlake to leave us with questions for each reader's own speculations: "to what extent does the mainstream pop artist challenge the prejudices of homophobia by constructing his own unique homoerotic appeal?"

NOTE

1. (Male) homosexual acts were not legally sanctioned in Israel until 1988 (they were legally sanctioned by the British Mandate in Palestine, prior to the establishment of the State of Israel, in 1948). The age of consent is now 16 years old for hetero- and homosexuals (both lesbians and gays).

PART 1

Performing Lives, Hidden Histories

1

WHAT'S THAT SMELL?
Queer Temporalities and Subcultural Lives

JUDITH HALBERSTAM

QUEER TEMPORALITY

This chapter tracks the evolution and persistence of queer subcultural life and is drawn from a book-length study of the explosion of queer urban subcultures in the last decade in which my larger purpose is to examine how many queer communities experience and spend time in ways that are very different from their heterosexual counterparts. Queer uses of time and space develop in opposition to the institutions of family, heterosexuality, and reproduction, and queer subcultures develop as alternatives to kinship-based notions of community. In my work on subcultures I explore the stretched-out adolescences of queer culture makers and I posit an "epistemology of youth" that disrupts conventional accounts of subculture, youth culture, adulthood, race, class, and maturity.[1] While I do not wish to posit a complete or absolute opposition between the projects of subcultural involvement and reproduction, this chapter does produce a polemic within which subcultural lives are the radical alternative to gay and lesbian families. Queer kinship itself has a complex relation to reproduction, cultural production, and assimilation, and I do not mean to write off the possibility of resistant models of reproductive kinship; however, my emphasis on subcultural involvement is staged as an alternative life narrative. Queer subcultures produce

alternative temporalities, I will argue, by allowing their participants to believe that their futures can be imagined according to logics that lie outside of the conventional forward-moving narratives of birth, marriage, reproduction, and death.

An essay by Judith Butler in a volume dedicated to the work of Stuart Hall tackles the question of what kinds of agency can be read into forms of activity that tend to be associated with style. She asks, "[H]ow do we read the agency of the subject when its demand for cultural and psychic and political survival makes itself known as style?"[2] And, building on the work by Hall and others in the classic volume on subcultures *Resistance through Rituals*, Butler puts the concept of "ritual" into motion as a practice that can either reinforce *or* disrupt cultural norms. Liminal subjects—those who are excluded from "the norms that govern the recognizability of the human"—are sacrificed to maintain coherence within the category of the human, and for them, style is both the sign of their exclusion and the mode by which they survive nonetheless. The power of Butler's work, here and elsewhere, lies in her ability to show how much has been excluded, rejected, abjected in the formation of human community and what toll those exclusions take upon particular subjects.

Punk has always been the stylized and ritualized language of the rejected, the perverse, and the willfully artifical; as Poly Styrene of Xray Spex sings, "I am a poseur and I don't care!" Queer punk has surfaced in recent years as a potent critique of hetero- and homonormativity. Dyke punk in particular, by bands like Tribe 8 and The Haggard, inspires a reconsideration of the topic of subcultures in relation to queer cultural production and in opposition to notions of gay community. Subcultures provide a vital critique of the seemingly organic nature of "community," and they make visible the forms of unbelonging and disconnection that are necessary to the creation of community. At a time when "gay and lesbian community" is used as a rallying cry for fairly conservative social projects aimed at assimilating gays and lesbians into the mainstream of the life of the nation and family, queer subcultures preserve the critique of heteronormativity that was always implicit in queer life. *Community*, generally speaking, is the term used to describe seemingly natural forms of congregation. As Sarah Thornton comments in her introduction to *The Subcultures Reader*, "Community tends to suggest a more permanent population, often aligned to a neighborhood, of which family is the key constituent part. Kinship would seem to be one of the main building blocks of community."[3] Subcultures, however, suggest transient, extrafamilial and oppositional modes of affiliation. The idea of community, writes Jean-Luc Nancy, emerges out of the Christian ritual

of communion and expresses a sense of something that we once had that has now been lost, a connection that once was organic and life-giving that now is moribund and redundant. Nancy calls this the "lost community" and expresses suspicion about this "belated invention." He writes, "What this community has 'lost'—the immanence and the intimacy of a communion—is lost only in the sense that such a 'loss' is constitutive of 'community' itself."[4] Given, then, that quests for community are always nostalgic attempts to return to some fantasized moment of union and unity, the conservative embrace of "community" in all kinds of political projects is unmasked; this makes the reconsideration of subcultures all the more urgent.

THE BALLAD OF A LADYMAN

Sleater-Kinney's anthem "Ballad of a Ladyman" describes the allure of subcultural life for the ladyman, the freak who wants to "rock with the tough girls." The band layers Corin Tucker's shrill but tuneful vocals over the discordant and forceful guitar playing of Carrie Brownstein and the hard rhythm of Janet Weiss's percussion. This is a beat that takes no prisoners and makes no concessions to the "boys who are fearful of getting an earful." And while Sleater-Kinney are most often folded into histories of the "riot grrrl" phenomenon and girl punk, they must also be placed within a new wave of dyke subcultures. When taken separately, riot dyke bands, drag kings, and queer slam poets all seem to represent a queer edge in a larger cultural phenomenon. When considered together, they add up to a fierce and lively queer subculture that needs to be reckoned with on its own terms. This chapter tracks the significant differences between the ladymen who rock and roll and drag up and slam their way toward new queer futures and the punk rockers of an earlier generation of subcultural activity. My tour of dyke subcultures takes in riot dyke punk by bands like Sleater-Kinney, The Butchies, Le Tigre, Tribe 8, The Haggard, and Bitch and Animal; drag kings like Dred and drag king boy-band parody group Backdoor Boys; and slam poets like Alix Olson and StaceyAnn Chin. Queer subcultures are related to old school subcultures like punk, but they also carve out new territory for a consideration of the overlap of gender, generation, class, race, community, and sexuality in relation to minority cultural production.

I have long been interested in and part of various subcultural groups. As a young person I remember well the experience of finding punk rock in the middle of a typically horrible grammar school experience in England in the 1970s. I plunged into punk rock music, clothing, and

rebellion precisely because it gave me a language with which to reject not only the high cultural texts in the classroom but also the homophobia and sexism outside it. I tried singing in a punk band called Penny Black and the Stamps for a brief two-week period, thinking that my utter lack of musical ability would serve me well finally. But, alas, even punk divas scream in key and my rebel yells were not mellifluous enough to launch my singing career. Instead of singing, I collected records, went to shows, dyed my hair, and fashioned outfits from safety pins and bondage pants. And so I learned at an early age that even if you cannot be in the band, participation at multiple levels is what subculture offers. I found myself reminiscing over my punk past when I began researching drag king cultures for a collaborative project with photographer Del LaGrace Volcano. Through my new subcultural involvement I began to see some specific features of queer subculture as opposed to a larger historical subculture like punk rock.

After finishing my drag king book in 1999, I received calls every few months from TV stations wanting me to put them in touch with drag kings for talk shows and news shows. Most of these shows would invite the kings on to parade around with some drag queens in front of a studio audience. At the end of the show, the audience would vote on whether each king or queen was *really* a man or *really* a woman. A few of the kings managed to circumvent the either/or format and offer up a more complex gendered self; and so, Black drag king Dred took off her moustache to reveal a "woman's" face but then took off her wig to reveal a bald pate. The audience was confused and horrified by the spectacle of indeterminacy. Josh Gamson, in *Freaks Talk Back*, has written about the potential for talk shows to allow the "crazies" and "queers" to talk back, but most of the time when drag kings appeared in mass public venues, the host did all the talking.[5] Drag kings also made an appearance in HBO's *Sex and the City* and on MTV's *True Life*. On every occasion that drag kings appeared on "straight" TV they were deployed as an entertaining backdrop against which heterosexual desire was showcased and celebrated. As someone who has tirelessly promoted drag kings, as individual performers and as a subculture, I found the whole process of watching the mass culture's flirtation with drag kings depressing and disheartening; but it did clarify for me what my stakes might be in promoting them: after watching drag kings try to go prime time, I remain committed to archiving and celebrating and analyzing queer subcultures before they are dismissed by mass culture or before they simply disappear from lack of exposure or what we might call "subcultural fatigue"—namely, the phenomenon of burnout among subcultural producers.

As the talk show phenomenon vividly illustrates, mainstream culture within postmodernism should be defined as the process by which subcultures are *both* recognized and absorbed, mostly for the profit of large media conglomerates. In other words, when TV stations show an interest in a dyke subculture like drag kings, this is cause for both celebration and concern: on the one hand, the mainstream recognition and acknowledgment of a subculture has the potential to alter the contours of dominant culture (think here of the small inroads into popular notions of sex, gender, and race made by the regular presence of Black drag queen RuPaul on cable TV); but, on the other hand, most of the interest directed by mainstream media at subcultures is voyeuristic and predatory. The subculture might appear on TV eventually as an illustration of the strange and perverse, or else it will be summarily robbed of its salient features and subcultural form: drag, for example, will be lifted without its subcultural producers, drag queens or kings. In an essay that tracks the results of precisely this process, Marco Becquer and Jose Gatti examine the contradictory effects of the sudden visibility of Harlem drag balls and their drag practices. In their analysis of the co-optation of gay vogueing by Madonna's hit single "Vogue" and by Jennie Livingston's acclaimed independent film *Paris Is Burning*, Becquer and Gatti show how the counterhegemonic knowledge articulated in vogueing meets with "the violence of the universal." Becquer and Gatti write of Madonna's video and Livingston's film, "Both partake in the production of newness, a process which purports to keep us up-to-date as it continually adds on novelties to a relational system that absorbs them; both contain vogueing beneath the pluralist umbrella of hipness."[6] And so, while the queens in *Paris Is Burning* expressed a desire for precisely the kind of fame and fortune that did eventually accrue to vogueing, the fame went to director Jennie Livingston and the fortune went to Madonna. The subculture itself, the gay Black and Puerto Rican children of the houses of Chanel, Extravaganza, and LaBeija, disappeared back into the world of sex work, HIV, and queer glamour, and within five years of the release of *Paris Is Burning*, five of the queens in the film were dead.[7]

The mainstream absorption of vogueing highlights the uneven exchange between dominant culture scavengers and subcultural artists: subcultural artists often seek out mainstream attention for their performances and productions in the hopes of gaining financial assistance for future endeavors. Subcultural activity is, of course, rarely profitable, and always costly for the producers, and it can be very short-lived without the necessary cash infusions (in the words of Sleater-Kinney, "This music gig doesn't pay that good, but the fans are alright"). Some subcultural producers turn the subculture itself into a source of revenue and,

as Angela McRobbie comments, "Subcultures are often ways of creating job opportunities as more traditional careers disappear."[8] So while the subcultural producers hope for cash and a little exposure, the dominant culture scavengers are usually looking for a story and hoping for that brush with the "new" and the "hip" described so well by Becquer and Gatti. In my experiences working with drag kings, however, I found that while big media reached their "hipness quota" quickly with the addition of a few well-placed drag kings, in return, they almost never paid for drag king services; when they did pay, it was always a pittance. Obviously the payback for the subcultural participants cannot come in the form of material benefits; what seems more useful, then, in this exchange between mainstream attention and subcultural product, would be to use the encounter to force some kind of recognition upon audiences that what is appealing about mainstream culture may very well come from subcultures that they do not even know exist or that they have repudiated.

As George Lipsitz's work has shown in relation to ethnic minority cultures, cultural producers often function as organic intellectuals, in a Gramscian sense; as such, minority artists can produce what Lipsitz terms "a historical bloc" or a coalition of oppositional groups united around counterhegemonic ideas.[9] While in Antonio Gramsci's formulation, the organic intellectual undermines the role of the traditional intellectual who serves to legitimize and authorize elite political interests, in subcultures where academics might labor side by side with artists, the "historical bloc" can easily describe an alliance between the minority academic and the minority subcultural producer. Where such alliances exist, academics can play a big role in the construction of queer archives and queer memory, and, furthermore, queer academics can (and some *should*) participate in the ongoing project of recoding queer culture, interpreting it, and circulating a sense of its multiplicity and sophistication. The more intellectual records we have of queer culture the more we contribute to the project of claiming for the subculture the radical cultural work that otherwise merely gets absorbed into or claimed by mainstream media.

SUBCULTURES: THE QUEER DANCE MIX

Subcultures have been an important object of study for sociology and cultural studies since the 1920s. In about the 1980s, however, work on subcultures seemed to fall out of favor as scholars began to doubt the utility of the term itself and the descriptive potential of the binary opposition between *subculture* and dominant culture. While early

work on subcultures from the Chicago school assumed a relationship between subcultures and deviance or delinquency, later work from the Birmingham University Center for Contemporary Cultural Studies characterized subcultures as class-specific "youth formations."[10] One of the most influential texts on the subject, *Subcultures: The Meaning of Style* by Dick Hebdige, reads subcultures in terms of the way they challenged hegemony through style rather than simply through overt ideological articulations; Hebdige characterizes the recuperation of subcultural disorder in terms of either an economic conversion of the signs and symbols of the subculture into mass culture commodities or an ideological conversion of the subcultural participant into either complete otherness or complete spectacle.[11] Hebdige's work has been both widely celebrated and widely critiqued in the two decades since its original publication and obviously it cannot be applied in any simple way to contemporary subcultural scenes. And yet, it remains an important text for thinking about how to move beyond the contextualization of subcultures in terms of relations between youth and parent cultures and for its formulations of style and historicity.

Almost all of the early work on subcultures, including Hebdige's, has presumed the dominance of the male gender in subcultural activity and has studied youth groups as the liveliest producers of new cultural styles. The subcultures that I want to examine here are neither male nor necessarily young and they are less likely to be co-opted or absorbed back into dominant culture because they were never offered membership in dominant groups in the first place. Queer lesbian subcultures have rarely been discussed in the existing literature, and they offer today a new area of study for queer scholarship as well as exciting opportunities for collaborations between queer cultural producers and queer academics.

One of the reasons that theorists tend to look to subcultures for political mobilization has to do with the conflation of subculture and youth culture. In his essay "Posing . . . Threats, Striking . . . Poses: Youth, Surveillance, and Display," Hebdige, for example, understands youth subcultures to register a dissatisfaction and alienation from the parent culture, which is both "a declaration of independence . . . and a confirmation of the fact of Powerlessness."[12] Even though this reading provides us with a better understanding of how political protest might be registered in a youth subculture, it remains trapped in the oedipal framework that pits the subculture against parent culture.

Queer subcultures, unlike the male-dominated youth cultures that Dick Hebdige, Stuart Hall, and other members of the Birmingham school have written about, are not located in any easy relation to

so-called parent cultures: much of the Birmingham school work on subcultures indeed (and this is partly why it fell out of favor in the early 1990s) presumed an oedipalized structure within which rebel youths reject the world of their parents and create a netherworld within which to reshape and reform the legacies of an older generation. Economic, political, and social conflicts may be resolved in subcultural arenas, a ccording to these arguments, without really effecting any grand changes at the level of superstructure. Of course, such a theory of subcultures has long since been replaced by more nuanced understandings of the relations among class, youth, and mass media; indeed, in an essay on youth cultures, "Different, Youthful, Subjectivities: Towards a Cultural Sociology of Youth," Angela McRobbie comments, "There is certainly no longer a case to be made for the traditional argument that youth culture is produced somehow in conditions of working-class purity, and that such expressions are authentic and in the first instance at least uncontaminated by an avaricious commercial culture."[13] Yet while McRobbie goes on to rethink the relations between white youth and youth of color and the meaning of femininity in postmodern youth cultures, she still presumes a heterosexual framework. Queer subcultures illustrate vividly the limits of subcultural theories that omit consideration of sexuality and sexual styles: queer subcultures obviously cannot be placed only in relation to a parent culture. They tend to form in relation to place as much as in relation to a genre of cultural expression and, ultimately, they oppose not only the hegemony of dominant culture but also the mainstreaming of gay and lesbian culture. As Michael du Plessis and Kathleen Chapman report in an article about "queercore," for example, "queercore and homocore not only signaled their allegiances to post-punk subculture, but also positioned themselves as . . . distinct from lesbian and gay."[14] Furthermore, queer subcultures are not simply spin-offs from some distinct youth culture like punk; as we will see in relation to riot dykes, queer music subcultures may be as likely to draw upon women's music from the 1970s and early 1980s as from British punk circa 1977.

We need to alter our understandings of subcultures in several important ways in order to address the specificities of queer subcultures and queer subcultural sites. First, we need to rethink the relation between theorist and subcultural participant, recognizing that for many queers, the boundary between theorist and cultural producer might be slight or at least permeable. Second, most subcultural theories are created to describe and account for male heterosexual adolescent activity and they are adjusted only when female heterosexual adolescent activity comes into focus. New queer subcultural theory will have to account for nonheterosexual, non-exclusively male, nonwhite, and adolescent

subcultural production in all its specificity. Third, we need to theorize the concept of the archive and consider new models of queer memory and queer history capable of recording and tracing subterranean scenes, fly-by-night clubs, and fleeting trends; we need, in José Muñoz's words, "an archive of the ephemeral."[15] Finally, queer subcultures offer us an opportunity to redefine the binary of adolescence and adulthood that structures so many inquiries into subcultures. Precisely because many queers refuse and resist the heteronormative imperative of home and family, they also prolong the periods of their life devoted to subcultural participation. This challenge to the notion of the subculture as a youth formation could on the one hand expand the definition of subculture beyond its most banal significations of youth in crisis and on the other hand challenge our notion of adulthood as reproductive maturity. I want to now consider each one of these features of queer subcultural production in relation to specific lesbian subcultures.

QUEER SPACE/QUEER TIME

"Hot Topic": the Death of the Expert

First, let us consider the relations between subcultural producers and queer cultural theorists. Queer subcultures encourage blurred boundaries between archivists and producers, which is not to say that this is the only subcultural space within which the theorist and the cultural worker may be the same people.[16] Minority subcultures in general tend to be documented by former or current members of the subculture rather than by "adult" experts. Nonetheless, queer subcultures in particular are often marked by this lack of distinction between the archivist and the cultural worker; a good example of this blurring between producer and analyst would be Dr. Vaginal Creme Davis, a drag queen who enacts, documents, and theorizes an array of drag characters. Another would be Juanita Mohammed, Mother of the House of Mashood, a women's drag house in Manhattan. Mohammed keeps a history of the participation of women of color in the drag cultures even as she recruits new "children" to the House of Mashood. Mohammed also goes one step further and makes herself central to AIDS activism in relation to queers of color.

The queer archivist or theorist and the cultural workers may also coexist in the same friendship networks, and they may function as co-conspirators: a good example of this relation would be academic Tammy Rae Carland, who runs an independent record label, Mr. Lady, manages dyke punk band The Butchies, and teaches at the University of North Carolina. Finally, the academic and the cultural producer may

see themselves in a complementary relationship. Le Tigre, for example, a riot dyke band, have a song called "Hot Topic" in which they name the women, academics, filmmakers, musicians, and producers who have inspired them and whom they want to inspire. They sing:

> Carol Rama and Eleanor Antin
> Yoko Ono and Carole Schneeman
> You're getting old, that's what they'll say, but
> I don't give a damn, I'm listening anyway.

More typically, cultural theorists have looked to groups of which they are not necessarily a part, most often youth subcultures, for an encapsulated expression of the experiences of a subordinated class. The youth subculture then becomes the raw material for a developed theory of cultural resistance or the semiotics of style or some other discourse that now leaves the subculture behind. For a new generation of queer theorists, a generation moving on from the split between densely theoretical queer theory in a psychoanalytic mode on the one hand and strictly ethnographic queer research on the other, new queer cultural studies feed off of and back into subcultural production. The academic might be the archivist or a coarchivist or she might be a full-fledged participant in the subcultural scene that he or she writes about. But only rarely does the queer theorist stand wholly apart from the subculture examining it with an expert's gaze.

Wildcat Woman: Lesbian Punk and Slam Poetry

Second, queer subcultural theory should begin with those communities that never seem to surface in the commentaries on subcultures in general—namely, lesbian subcultures and subcultures of color. Cultural theory has created a hierarchy of subcultures that places English punk near the top and then arranges mods, rockers, metalheads, club kids, DJ culture, ravers, and rappers in some sort of descending order of importance. At the bottom of the pyramid of subcultures we will find girl fan cultures, house drag cultures, and gay sex cultures. Lesbian subcultures almost never appear at all: and so, even in the documentation on balls and drag cultures, women's involvement and relation to drag have been left out of theoretical accounts and subcultural histories. Recording the presence of lesbian subcultures can make a huge difference to the kinds of subcultural histories that get written, whether it is a history of drag that only focuses on gay men, a history of punk that only focuses on white boys, or a history of girl cultures that only focuses on heterosexual girls.

To give one example of the difference an awareness of lesbian subcultures can make, we can turn to early work in the 1970s on the participation of girls in punk subcultures. Theorists like Angela McRobbie, Jennie Garber, and others talked about the invisibility of female subcultures and the tendency of girls to participate in coed subcultures only as girlfriends or groupies. McRobbie and Garber concluded, "Girls' subcultures may have become invisible because the very term 'subculture' has acquired such strong masculine overtones."[17] In their essay, and even in more recent work on girls and subcultures, there tends to be little recognition that some girls, usually queer girls, may in fact involve themselves in subcultures precisely because of the "strong masculine overtones" associated with the activity. And so, a young queer girl interested in punk will not be put off by the masculinity of the subculture—she may as easily be seduced by it. In another essay written some twelve years later and collected in her book *Feminism and Youth Culture*, however, McRobbie articulates precisely the failed promise of subcultural membership for young girls: "Whereas men who 'play around' with femininity are nowadays credited with some degree of power to choose, gender experimentation, sexual ambiguity and homosexuality among girls are viewed differently." She then concludes that "the possibility of escaping oppressive aspects of adolescent heterosexuality in a youth culture . . . remains more or less unavailable to girls."[18] It is not until the 1990s that girls begin to find in subcultural life an escape hatch from heteronormativity and its regulations.

The work of Angela McRobbie over the years has served as a critique of the masculinism of early pronouncements on subcultures; but more than this, McRobbie has returned insistently to the topic of youth cultures and gender, race, and class. Indeed, McRobbie's opus by now stands as a rich, deep, and important theoretical archive on oppositional forms of culture making. In her collection of essays *Postmodernism and Popular Culture*, McRobbie models a form of intellectual practice that she calls "feminist postmodernism" and that allows her to "confront questions which otherwise remain unasked." In the process of engaging these otherwise unasked questions, she suggests, "we also find our academic practice and our politics undergoing some degree of transformation and change."[19] McRobbie's willingness to track the transformations in her own body of work and to trace changes in her own thinking about key topics provides an excellent model for cultural theory in an ever evolving and shifting field. In one key chapter, "Shut Up and Dance," McRobbie returns to the topic of femininity and subcultures and considers her position now as the mother of a daughter who attends raves. Commenting that we need to reorient our

analyses of youth culture given "shifts in gender relations" in the last decade, McRobbie examines the impact of feminism upon both mass media representations of femininity and gender norms circulated by and among young girls. She concludes that girls are now operating with more flexible gender norms and that "femininity is no longer the 'other' of feminism."[20]

McRobbie does not go on to study the punk femininities within dyke cultures, but if she did she would find a fabulous array of feminist and queer femme performances. Guitarists like Leslie Mah of Tribe 8 and vocalists like Kathleen Hanna of Le Tigre and Beth Ditto of The Gossip all articulate the explosive potential of a queer femininity that served as an undercurrent to much of the Riot Grrrl feminism and which is readable as radical style in queer punk. The recent explosion of dyke punk bands like Bitch and Animal, The Butchies, Le Tigre, The Need, The Haggard, and Tribe 8 also challenges the conventional understandings of punk as male-dominated and of queercore as a largely gay male phenomenon. This explosion also makes visible the queerness that energized the riot grrrl movement even as it was assiduously ignored by mainstream media. The hardcore styles of many of these bands remind us that punk in general, contrary to the usual accounts of the subculture, has always been a place for young girls to remake their genders. In her excellent book on women in punk, *Pretty in Punk: Girls' Gender Resistance in a Boys' Subculture*, Lauraine Leblanc tracks the relationship of girls to punk rock; while some girls involved themselves in the scene through their boyfriends, LeBlanc argues that some of the really tough girls involved in punk had to become "virtual boys" in order to earn the respect of their male counterparts. While the subculture remains resolutely heterosexual in form, Leblanc found that punk offered girls "strategies of resistance to gender norms."[21]

Lesbian punks are pretty much absent from Leblanc's otherwise excellent and thorough ethnographic study of punk girls; and this may have had as much to do with when she conducted her research as it has to do with the reluctance of the girls she studied to identify as queer. For as the wave of the riot grrrl crested and began to recede in the mid-1990s, many of the most interesting bands left standing were queer, female, and loud. Some of these bands, like Sleater-Kinney, retooled femininity and made punk femininity unreliable as a marker of heterosexuality. Sleater-Kinney modeled new femininities at the level of musical performance as much as at the level of style. For example, the band layers two very distinctive guitars over the drums, but they omit bass guitar. The bass can be read here as a "masculine" instrument in terms of its production of noise in the lower registers, but it can also be read as a stereotypically

"female" instrument given that many women in rock bands have been relegated to the role of bass player because lead guitarist was presumed to be a male role.[22] By using two guitars, Sleater-Kinney both undercut the notion of the "lead" and refuse the conventional arrangement of bass, guitar, and drums. Other bands, like The Haggard, a hard-core band from Portland, Oregon, produce a gender-bending sound by combining drum and guitar noise with a butch voice overlay. The singer, Emily, produces a guttural roar that is neither a male voice nor a female voice, and she spews her lyrics in an indecipherable growl. This butch voice shows no concern for intelligibility or virtuosity but it produces a raw and original sound while redefining the meaning of voice, singing, and lyric.

Just as the recognition of lesbian involvement in punk subcultures changes the way we understand both the punk phenomenon and the recent riot dyke music trend, so lesbian involvement in slam poetry forces commentators to rethink universalizing narratives about youth cultures. While slam poetry is a nationwide phenomenon, the emergence of highly talented lesbian slam poets has changed the nature of the slam event. Two performers in particular have garnered mainstream and local attention: white lesbian Alix Olson and Jamaican born StaceyAnn Chin. Olson was a member of the Nuyorican Slam Team that won the national championship in 1998. She was also the slam champion at the 1999 OutWrite writers' conference after a long and thrilling "slam off" between herself and Chin. Slam poetry is a form of competitive poetry in which poets perform three-minute poems for a panel of judges chosen from the audience; the judges rate the poems on a scale of 1 to 10, and the slammers move through preliminary rounds until they face off in the finals. This necessitates each poet often memorizing and performing up to ten poems a night. As popularized by the film *Slam*, the slam poetry contest can easily degenerate into a macho contest of speed and fury; but it is also an off-shoot of rap in terms of its rhythm and combination of spoken word with a beat. Slams therefore do attract poets of color in large numbers. Slam poetry appeals to queer youth and queer youth of color because of the very obvious connections to rap; in places like Oakland, California, spoken-word groups of color have been at the center of queer youth activity. Recently, queer poets of color like Sri Lankan slam poet D'Lo and the Jamaican Chin have made the slam a forum for very different messages about love, race, and poetry. In "Dykepoem," from her collection *Wildcat Woman*, Chin begins with the line, "I killed a man today," and tells of a young Black girl who fights off a rapist and justifies her sinful act saying, "I going to hell anyway / women who like

other women go there, you know." The poem closes with a vision of prison as

> *a place*
> *with only girl children inside*
> *that place ain't no hell*
> *sounds like heaven to me.*[23]

Chin is a superb performer, and she regularly slams at queer-people-of-color events all over New York City; she is as likely to appear in a nightclub as at a rally, at a conference as on the street. And while many of her poems are tough, sexy, and angry, she also infuses her work with a sense of irony and self-reflexivity. In "Don't Want to Slam," Chin writes,

> *I've decided*
> *I don't want to be*
> *a poet who just writes*
> *for the slam anymore.*

The slam, she goes on to say, is just a "staged revolution," a spectacle of word pimps selling lines and rhymes for a quick score of 10 from the judges. With breathtaking speed, the poem moves through a pointed critique of slamming and makes a call for poems that tell "true histories of me and you. . . ." But the last verse shows that the slam *is* true history, *is* revolution, and may just change the world by changing the *word*. By the end of the last line, we believe her:

> *I want to write*
> *I left my lover and*
> *now I want her back poems*
> *I miss Jamaica*
> *but now I'm never going back poems*
> *I know it's not a ten*
> *but it sends shivers down MY back poems*
> *poems that talk about life*
> *and love and laughter*
> *poems that reveal the flaws*
> *that make strikingly real people*
> *real poems*
> *poems that are so honest*
> *they slam.*[24]

Chin and Olson's slam poetry takes lesbian feminism and women of color feminism to a new stage and a new audience and makes poetry into the language of riot and change.

Shooting Stars: Queer Archives

Third, the nature of queer subcultural activity requires a nuanced theory of archives and archiving. Work on archives and archiving is well under way and can be found in the work of an eclectic group of queer cultural theorists including Lauren Berlant, Ann Cvetkovich, and José Muñoz. Ideally, an archive of queer subcultures would merge ethnographic interviews with performers and fans with research in the multiple archives that already exist online and in other unofficial sites. Queer zines, posters, guerilla art, and other temporary artifacts would make up some of the paper archives, and descriptions of shows, along with the self-understandings of cultural producers, would provide supplementary materials. But the notion of an archive has to extend beyond the image of a place to collect material or hold documents, and it has to become a floating signifier for the kinds of lives implied by the paper remnants of shows, clubs, events, and meetings. The archive is not simply a repository; it is also a theory of cultural relevance, a construction of collective memory, and a complex record of queer activity. For the archive to function it requires users, interpreters, and cultural historians to wade through the material and piece together the jigsaw puzzle of queer history in the making.

While some of the work of queer archiving certainly falls to academics, cultural producers also play a big role in constructing queer genealogies and memories; as we saw in Le Tigre's song "Hot Topic," the lyrics create an eclectic encyclopedia of queer cultural production through unlikely juxtapositions ("Gayatri Spivak and Angela Davis / Laurie Weeks and Dorothy Allison"), and they claim a new poetic logic: "Hot topic is the way that we rhyme." In other words, the historically situated theorists and filmmakers and musicians rhyme with each other's work—the rhyme is located in the function and not in the words. Similarly, while many lesbian punk bands do trace their influences back to male punk or classic rock, as we saw in the last section, contrary to what one may expect, they do not completely distance themselves from or counteridentify with 1970s and 1980s "women's music." In fact, some "dykecore" bands see themselves as very much a part of a tradition of loud and angry women. For example, on their CD *Are We Not Femme?* North Carolina–based band The Butchies perform a cover of feminist goddess Cris Williamson's classic song "Shooting Star." Williamson's soaring, emotion-laden song becomes

a tough, percussive anthem in the capable hands of The Butchies, who add drum rolls and screeching guitars to lift the song out of a woman-loving-woman groove and into a new era. On their liner notes, The Butchies thank Cris Williamson for "being radical and singing songs to girls before too many others were and for writing such a kickass song. . . ." If we compare the covers from The Butchies' CD and Cris Williamson's CD, it would be hard to detect the connections between the two. The Butchies' CD pays obvious homage to punk concept band Devo both in terms of its title (Devo's first album was called *Are We Not Men?*) and in terms of its iconography. The connection between The Butchies and Cris Williamson, however, runs much deeper than their relation to punk bands like Devo. The Butchies appear on the cover wearing short red leather miniskirts that recall the red plastic flower pot hats worn by Devo on the cover of *Are We Not Men?* Williamson, on the other hand, appears in dungarees and stands in what looks like Joshua Tree National Park. Her album title, *The Changer and the Changed*, references a modality of mutuality, organic transformation, and reciprocity. The song itself, in her hands, tells of "wonderful moments on the journey through my desert." She sings of "crossing the desert for you" and seeing a shooting star, which reminds her of her lover. The spectral image of the shooting star figures quite differently in The Butchies' version, where it takes on more of the qualities of a rocket than a galactic wonder. But The Butchies' cover version of Williamson's song has the tone of tribute, not parody; by making her song relevant for a new generation of listeners, The Butchies refuse the model of generational conflict and build a bridge between their raucous spirit of rebellion and the quieter, acoustic world of women's music from the 1970s and 1980s.

In an excellent essay on riot grrrls, feminism, and lesbian culture, Mary Celeste Kearney also points to the continuity rather than the break between women's music and the riot grrrl. But, she comments, links between earlier modes of lesbian feminism and contemporary riot grrrl productions are regularly ignored in favor of a history that makes the riot grrrl the female offspring of male-dominated punk. Like the new riot grrrl productions, women's music by Alix Dobkin, Cris Williamson, and others was produced on independent labels (like Olivia Records) and received only scant mainstream attention. The earlier music was made for, by, and about women and while much of it did consist of folk-influenced ballads, there was also a hard and angry subgenre that combined lyrics about man hating with loud guitar playing (Maxine Feldman's music, for example). As Kearney points out, however, the noncommercial practices of 1970s lesbian musicians have made them less easy to identify as major influences upon a new generation of "all-girl community," and so

while women's music is erased as a musical influence, so lesbianism is ignored as a social context for the riot grrrl. Kearney writes, "In spite of the coterminous emergence in the U.S. of riot grrrl and queercore bands like Tribe 8, Random Violet, The Mudwimmin, and Team Dresch, there have been relatively few links made by the mainstream press between lesbian feminism, queercore, and riot grrrl."[25]

Other lesbian punk or punk/folk bands see themselves both as heirs to an earlier generation of "pussy power" and as pioneers of new genres. Bitch and Animal, for example, authors of "The Pussy Manifesto," describe their CD *What's That Smell?* as "tit rock." In live performances, Bitch plays an electric violin and Animal plays an array of percussion. Their songs, like those of The Butchies, are themselves archival records of lesbian subculture. One song from *What's That Smell?* is called "Drag King Bar," and it posits the drag king bar as an alternative to a rather tired mainstream lesbian scene. With Animal picking out a "yee-haw" tune on the banjo, Bitch sings about a place where "all the boys were really girls and the fags whip out their pearls." Bitch tells of being picked up by one particularly bold king and the song ends in a rousing symphony of violin and drums. Bitch and Animal document and celebrate the emergence of a drag king scene in contemporary queer clubs, and they blend country-influenced folk with avant-garde percussion to do so. But their cover art and their manifestos hearken back to the era of women loving women in their embrace of the female body; at their website, furthermore, fans are encouraged to take up terms like *pussy* and *tits* with pride by brushing off the taint of patriarchal insult. Like The Butchies' decision to cover a Cris Williamson song, Bitch and Animal's pussy power reaches out to an earlier generation of women musicians refusing once and for all the oedipal imperative to overthrow the old and bring on the new. Recent women's music festivals like Ladyfest are also clear inheritors of a tradition of lesbian feminist music festivals, and they revive an earlier model of feminism for a new generation of "grrrls."

"I Want It That Way": A Time for Queers

Finally, queer subcultures afford us a perfect opportunity to depart from a normative model of youth cultures as stages on the way to adulthood; this allows us to map out different forms of adulthood, or the refusal of adulthood and new modes of deliberate deviance. Queers participate in subcultures for far longer than their heterosexual counterparts. At a time when heterosexual men and women are spending their weekends, their extra cash, and all their free time shuttling back and forth between the weddings of friends and family, urban queers tend to spend their leisure

time and money on subcultural involvement: this may take the form of intense weekend clubbing, playing in small music bands, going to drag balls, participating in slam poetry events, or seeing performances of one kind or another in cramped and poorly ventilated spaces. Just as homosexuality itself has been theorized by psychoanalysis as a stage of development, a phase that the adolescent will hopefully pass through quickly and painlessly, so subcultural involvement has been theorized as a life stage rather than a lifelong commitment. For queers the separation between youth and adulthood quite simply does not hold, and queer adolescence can extend far beyond one's twenties. I want to raise here the notion of "queer time"—a different mode of temporality that might arise out of an immersion in club cultures or queer sex cultures. While obviously heterosexual people also go to clubs and some involve themselves in sex cultures, queer urbanites—lacking the pacing and schedules that are inherent to family life and reproduction—might visit clubs and participate in sex cultures well into their forties or fifties on a regular basis.

At the same time that queers extend participation in subcultural activity long beyond their "youth," some queer subcultures also provide a critical lens through which to revisit seemingly heterosexual youth cultures. In new work on subcultures and gender/sexuality, generally speaking, there is the potential to explore the possibilities and the promise of rebellious youth genders. By focusing on the realization of tomboy desires or youthful femme aspirations in dyke punk bands and forms of queer fandom, we can see that pre-adult pre-identitarian girl roles offer a set of opportunities for theorizing gender, sexuality, race, and social rebellion precisely because they occupy the space of the "not yet," the not fully realized: these girl roles are not absolutely predictive of either heterosexual or lesbian adulthoods—rather, the desires and the play and the anguish they access allow us to theorize other relations to identity.

Gayle Wald's work on boy bands has also drawn attention to the homoerotic subtext in much of teen culture. Boy bands like the Backstreet Boys, Wald suggests, produce and manage anxieties about gay modes of gender performance. Boy bands perform what Wald calls "a girlish masculinity," and they channel the fantasy of perpetual youth referenced by the moniker *boy*, but they also play out socially acceptable forms of rebellion (*backstreet*, for example, conjures up images of working-class youth) that can be both expressed and neatly channeled into white, middle-class heteronormativity. The phenomenon of boy bands, for me, raises a number of questions not simply about the performance of masculinity but also about what Wald refers to as the threatening aspect of the "ecstatic responses that they elicit."[26] After all, while music

critics love to dismiss fandom as a passive "teenybopper" subculture, there is something all too powerful about a nearly hysterical audience of teen girls screaming and crying together; this activity may well have as much to say about the desire between the screamers as it says about their desire for the mythic "boys." Wald argues that the phenomenon of teenybopper fans and young boy bands creates a homophobic fear of both boy fandom and homoerotic dynamics on stage among the boy performers. The policing of male homosexuality, however, she continues, "creates opportunities for girls to engage in modes of consumption that have a markedly homoerotic component, although they are typically characterized in terms of (heterosexual) 'puppy love.'"[27] Again the notion of homoerotic bonding as a stage on the way to heterosexual maturity creates a context within which both subcultural activity and queer desire can be dismissed as temporary and nonserious. Wald's careful excavation of the sources of social scorn levied at teenyboppers and her contextualization of the boy band phenomenon within popular culture opens up new and important questions about youth cultures and femininity, and it makes possible a consideration of the queerness of even the most heterosexually inflected preadult activity.

I never invested much hope for queer alternatives in the performance of boy bands, I must admit, until I was present at the world premier of New York's drag king boy band, the Backdoor Boys. When the Backdoor Boys took the stage as A.J., Nick, Kevin, Howie, and Brian, I saw at last the butch potential of the boy band phenomenon. The queer audience screamed as each boy was introduced, picked their favorites, and began the ritual ecstatic fan worship that we associate with teenage girls but which seems to be fun at any age. The current between the stage and the packed house was electric. At least part of the appeal of the Backstreet Boys depends upon the production of seemingly safe and almost unreal masculinities: the boys croon about what they would do for their girls, about being there for them, buying them flowers, giving them gifts, doing everything that other boys supposedly won't do. The boys, in short, offer themselves as a safe alternative to the misogyny and mistreatment that many girls find and expect in adolescent relationships. Here, in a drag king context, the space of the alternative is taken back from the realm of popular culture and revealed as proper to the subcultural space. As the Backdoor Boys went into their version of the Backstreet Boys' "I Want It That Way" and began to act out the barely concealed homoerotic implication of the lyric, the queer crowd went wild; the source of pleasure for the queer fans had as much to do with the acting out of the song's homoerotic potential as with the sexual appeal of the drag kings. The Backdoor Boys performance of "I Want

It That Way" speaks to the purpose of what Wald calls "the deliberate sublimation of sexual explicitness" in the Backstreet Boys' lyrics and dance moves. The fans' desire and ecstasy can only be maintained by keeping at bay the erotic relations among the boys on the one hand and the potentially erotic relations among the screaming girls on the other. As the boys sing together, the girls scream together and the whole fragile edifice of heterosexuality could come tumbling down at any moment if the homosocial structures of desire are made explicit. The drag king impersonation of the faggy boy band, finally, recognizes the act as neither a performance of male heterosexuality nor a performance of gay masculinity; this is, rather, an intricate performance of butch masculinity—queer masculinity that presents itself to screaming girls as a safe alternative to heteromasculinities.

Finally, all of these representations of teen and youth genders offer us a space within which to think through the alternatives that young people create for themselves to the routine and tired options recycled by adult culture. When the Backstreet Boys croon "I want it that way" and the girls scream, we think for a moment that it does not have to be *this* way and that just maybe girl-and-boy partial identities can be carried forward into adulthood in terms of a politics of refusal—the refusal to grow up and enter the heteronormative adulthoods implied by these concepts of progress and maturity. The boy bands in particular allow us to think of boyhood, girlhood, and even tomboyhood and riot grrrl-hood not as stages to pass through but as pre-identities to carry forward, inhabit, and sustain.

CONCLUSION

In his powerful study of a disappearing sexual subculture in New York City's Times Square, queer pioneer Samuel Delaney describes queer subterranean worlds as "a complex of interlocking systems and subsystems."[28] The unimaginably precious meanings of these systems are of no consequence to the city planner who sees only ugliness and filth where Delaney sees a distillation of the promise of radical democracy. The porn theaters that Delaney visits and learns from offer him and other men, he claims, one of the last opportunities in urban America for "interclass contact and communication conducted in a mode of good will."[29] Counterpublics, as his book shows, are spaces created and altered by certain subcultures for their own uses. Since lesbians and women in general partake so little in public sex cultures, we, much more than gay men, need to develop and protect counter publics for subcultural uses. In the Bay Area—in San Francisco and Oakland in particular—there is a

long history of subcultural activity; counterpublics abound, new bands, spoken-word artists, and performers appear weekly at different shows in different venues. These counterpublics have survived the dot.com explosion and the latest recession, the yuppies and the businessmen; they have also survived (so far) the new patriotism of a post–9/11 culture and the new "homonormativity" of the recent lesbian baby boom. Let's return to Judith Butler's "Agencies of Style for a Liminal Subject" and another question she poses: "What sorts of style signal the crisis of survival?"[30] We can now answer that the crisis of survival is being played out nightly in a club near you. The radical styles crafted in queer punk bands, in slam poetry events, in drag king boy bands do not express some mythically pure form of agency or will; rather, they model other modes of being and becoming that scramble our understandings of place, time, development, action, and transformation. And for a more concrete example of how the "crisis of survival" may play out, we can go to the Bitch and Animal website, where Bitch and Animal present fans with a hard-hitting politics of transformation in their "Pussy Manifesto"; they counsel listeners as follows: "Wise, old, kick-up-shit chicks and chick lovers alike: Be not afraid to take up space! Manifest this Motherfuckers and let the Pussy rule!"[31]

NOTES

1. Thanks to Glen Mimura for the formulation of "an epistemology of youth."
2. Judith Butler, "Agencies of Style for a Liminal Subject," in *Without Guarantees: In Honour of Stuart Hall*, ed. Paul Gilroy, Lawrence Grossberg, and Angela McRobbie (London: Verso, 2000), 36.
3. Sarah Thornton, "General Introduction," in *The Subcultures Reader*, ed. Ken Gelder and Sarah Thornton (New York: Routledge, 1997), 2.
4. Jean-Luc Nancy, "The Inoperative Community," in *The Inoperative Community*, ed. Peter Connor, trans. Peter Connor, Lisa Garbus, Michael Holland, and Simona Sawhney (Minneapolis: University of Minnesota Press, 1991), 12.
5. Josh Gamson, *Freaks Talk Back: Tabloid Talk Shows and Sexual Nonconformity* (Chicago: University of Chicago Press, 1999).
6. Marcos Becquer and Jose Gatti, "Elements of Vogue," in *The Subcultures Reader*, ed. Ken Gelder and Sarah Thornton (New York: Routledge, 1997), 452.
7. For an article on the fate of the queens and children featured in *Paris Is Burning*, see Jesse Green, "Paris Has Burned," *New York Times*, April 18, 1993; sect. 9, p. 1. Green documents the deaths of Angie Extravaganza and Kim Pendarvis, among others. Drag queens are interviewed for the article, and Green reports on the anger that many in the ball world feel about

Jennie Livingston's film, reminding us that "the film's critical and financial success should not therefore be taken for the success of its subjects." While Jennie Livingston became a filmmaker as a consequence of the circulation of *Paris Is Burning*, the film's subjects continued to live in poverty.

8. Angela McRobbie, "Shut Up and Dance: Youth Culture and Changing Modes of Femininity," in *Postmodernism and Popular Culture* (London: Routledge, 1994), 162.

9. George Lipsitz, "Cruising Around the Historical Bloc: Postmodernism and Popular Music in East L.A.," in *The Subcultures Reader*, ed. Ken Gelder and Sarah Thornton (New York: Routledge, 1997), 357.

10. Stuart Hall and Tony Jefferson, eds., *Resistance through Rituals: Youth Subcultures in Post-War Britain* (1975; reprint, London: Routledge, 1993).

11. Dick Hebdige, *Subculture: The Meaning of Style* (New York and London: Methuen, 1979).

12. Dick Hebdige, "Posing . . . Threats, Striking . . . Poses: Youth, Surveillance, and Display," in *The Subcultures Reader*, ed. Ken Gelder and Sarah Thornton (New York and London: Routledge, 1997), 404.

13. Angela McRobbie, "Different, Youthful, Subjectivities: Towards a Cultural Sociology of Youth," in *Postmodernism and Popular Culture* (London and New York: Routledge, 1994), 179.

14. Michael Du Plessis and Kathleen Chapman, "Queercore: The Distinct Identities of Subculture," *College Literature* 24, no. 1 (1997): 45.

15. José Esteban Muñoz, "Ephemera as Evidence: Introductory Notes to Queer Acts," *Women and Performance: A Journal of Feminist Theory* 8, no. 2 (1996): 5–18.

16. Paul Gilroy, for example, was a DJ while working on Black expressive cultures; nowadays, many public intellectuals straddle the worlds of cultural production and theory. Josh Kun, for example, writes about "*rock en español*" and hosts a radio show. Patrick Johnson is a theorist of Black performance art, and he himself performs in a one-man show.

17. Angela McRobbie and Jennie Garber, "Girls and Subcultures," in *Resistance through Rituals: Youth Subcultures in Post-War Britain*, ed. Stuart Hall and Tony Jefferson (1975; reprint, London: Routledge, 1993), 114.

18. Angela McRobbie, "Settling Accounts with Subcultures: A Feminist Critique," in *Feminism and Youth Culture* (New York: Routledge, 2000), 36.

19. Angela McRobbie, "Introduction," in *Postmodernism and Popular Culture* (London: Routledge, 1994), 2.

20. McRobbie, "Shut Up and Dance," 173.

21. Lauraine Leblanc, *Pretty in Punk: Girls' Gender Resistance in a Boys' Subculture* (New Brunswick, N.J.: Rutgers University Press, 1998), 13.

22. For a great article on feminism and rock music see Gayle Wald, "Just a Girl? Rock Music, Feminism, and the Cultural Construction of Female Youth," *Signs* 23, no. 31 (2002): 585.

23. StaceyAnn Chin, "Dykepoem," in *Wildcat Woman: Poetry* (New York: self-published, 1998), 16–17.

24. StaceyAnn Chin, "Don't Want to Slam," in *Wildcat Woman*, 18.

25. Mary Celeste Kearney, "The Missing Link: Riot Grrrl, Feminism, Lesbian Culture," in *Sexing the Groove: Popular Music and Gender*, ed. Sheila Whiteley (London: Routledge, 1997), 222.

26. Gayle Wald, "I Want It That Way: Teenybopper Music and the Girling of Boy Bands," *Genders* 35 (2002): 1–39.

27. Ibid., 32.

28. Samuel Delany, *Times Square Red, Times Square Blue* (New York: New York University Press, 1999), xviii.

29. Ibid., 111.

30. Butler, "Agencies of Style," 36.

31. Bitch and Animal, "The Pussy Manifesto," available online at their website (http://www.bitchandanimal.com).

2

GIRL ON GIRL
Fat Femmes, Bio-Queens, and Redefining Drag

RACHEL DEVITT

With their backsides to the packed club, five performers stand at attention, hips cocked, their coiffed hair and expertly made-up faces the epitome of femininity, waiting for the walloping beats heard round the world of Kelis's 2004 hit song, "Milkshake." At the exact moment that ubiquitous, enigmatic chorus starts, the performers turn to the front and start gyrating their hips, tits out, rouged lips pursed, working the crowd with their best video booty girl moves as Kelis sasses, "My milkshake brings all the boys to the yard / And they're like, it's better than yours." There's one exception: these booty girls are Seattle's Queen Bees. They are queer women and gender queers who are predominantly feminine-identified. Their bodies run a curvalicious gamut from pixie-thin to "more cushion for the pushin'," and they erotically accentuate each inch of every sexy curve. They have labeled the gender performance work they do everything from "bio-queening" to "exploding femininity" to good old-fashioned drag queening. And just at this moment, as they finish their last stinging shimmy, they are about to be confronted by the reigning monarchs of drag and divadom.

Four conventional drag queens (boys dressed as girls) strut onstage, mirroring the Bees' rippled pop and thrust choreography and adding their own attitudinal moves. The two groups circle each other, each vying for dominance over the realm of queenly femininity, then retreat

Figure 2.1   The Queen Bees, 2004. Copyright Christopher Nelson 2004.

to either side of the stage. One Bee (Luscious Lollipop) and one queen (Aleksa Manila) face off in the center, their hands antagonistically clasped in the tried and true fight position of that most classic gang fight (the video for Michael Jackson's "Beat It," of course), then prepare to do battle with . . . a tube of lipstick and a makeup brush. The other performers follow suit, jabbing at, taunting, and, finally, almost teasing each other with various cosmetic weaponry until each gang has been

infiltrated by the other and it becomes difficult to discern a queen from a Bee. As the music fades out, all the performers on the now-integrated stage strike a seductive pose and point out at the audience, challenging them with Kelis's final words: "I can teach you / but I have to charge."

This is the gender performance battlefield, long ridden with land mines of interpretation, appropriation, and identity. In the hands of various scholars, drag has been both a kitschy, plucky attack on *and* a ruthlessly misogynistic reification of heterosexist gender norms. In the hands of TV shows like *Sex and the City* and movies like *To Wong Foo, Thanks for Everything, Julie Newmar*, drag and queer performance aesthetics have served as fabulous fodder for straight actors looking to round out their resumes with a skip down the yellow brick road. In other words, drag has been smacked up, flipped, *and* rubbed down by so many varying forces that it has virtually become old-hat even to my 83-year-old grandmother in rural Illinois.

Enter the femme drag queen or "bio-queen" (short for biological female who drag queens or performs a heightened femininity). She is at once campy and earnest, parodist and ecdysiast, all girl and then some, and she has an expertly manicured nail at the ready to rip drag up into something new, titillating, and meaningful once again. Using the Queen Bees as a case study, this chapter will address the kinds of performance femme drag queens do, the aesthetics they employ, and the contested community spaces in which they perform. The novel work these performers do to recontexualize and reclaim drag, pop, and the voluptuous variations on the femme body deserves an attempt at a scholarship, if not as sparklingly fabulous, just as spanking new.

FAUX, FEMME, BIO: IS IT DRAG?

Traditional notions of drag appear at first glance to be predicated on a sex-based performative cross accomplished through costume and mannerisms. Steven P. Schacht, in a recent article on queening, defines drag queens as "individuals with an acknowledged penis . . . that perform as women in front of an audience that all knows they are self-identified men, regardless of how compellingly female—'real'—they might otherwise appear."[1] In the chapter on kinging from her seminal work, *Female Masculinities*, Judith Halberstam describes a drag king as "a female (usually) who dresses up in recognizable male costume and performs theatrically in that costume."[2] Obviously, these rigidly sex-based notions of drag don't leave much room for "real girls" performing femininity.

That tricky little "(usually)" in Halberstam's definition, however, is what splinters the dichotomous drag seesaw into a billion little gender-queer pieces. Here, from the fragments of a tired, creaky structure that drag long ago grew too big for, the Queen Bees and artists like them have begun to build their hive.

Pinning the definition of drag so fixedly on a binary, sex-based concept of crossing not only belies the rich wealth of gender identities that inform contemporary gender performance and drag but also reifies the naturalness of that binary. Maybe not every female-to-male transsexual performer, for example, would consider the work he does as drag. But insisting that a masculine-identified butch lesbian who performs masculinity onstage and lives it offstage is a drag king, but that a femme dyke who performs a heightened femininity can't be a drag queen, serves only to reinscribe the rigid gender system that drag has always seemed poised to implode. If drag must entail a cross to the "opposite" of one's "true" identity, then that original, that biological sex-based identity becomes normalized and immobile, thus denying both the validity of the performer's self-identified gender and the power a drag performance has in questioning gender "realness."

Despite some of the rather limited definitions of drag offered, most scholarship on gender performance focuses more on the genre's ability to critique. Halberstam argues that drag kinging "exposes the structure of dominant masculinity by making it theatrical and by rehearsing the repertoire of roles and types on which such masculinity depends" (239). Judith Butler suggests that drag has the power to indicate that "'imitation' is at the heart of the *heterosexual* project and its gender binarisms, that drag is not a secondary imitation that presupposes a prior and original gender, but that hegemonic hetereosexuality is itself a constant and repeated effort to imitate its own idealizations."[3] Femme drag queening is actually in a unique position to out gender as performative because it does not depend on an assumed incongruity between "actual" and staged gender. If there is no hilarious disparity between miniskirt and penis and yet gender is still being performed and even parodied, then what becomes of the naturalized link between body/sex and gender?

The "Milkshake" piece calls into question the innate, natural originality of gender by staging femininity as something that is up for grabs among performers who represent a range of abject identities on which the gender binary depends to define normalcy against. Dueling with recognizable feminine markers (a tube of lipstick, a "killer rack"), each performer contends that she is the authentic woman, thus divorcing femininity from a particular body and exposing it as something that is

unstable, theatrical, imitable, and able to be owned by the queen who performs it best. The drag queens, who are not "real" girls, look the part: each model-thin queen, with her long, flowing hair, glamorously skimpy dress, and precariously high heels seems ready at any moment to table dance with Paris Hilton. The "real" girls, on the other hand, are queer women in form-fitting attire that emphasizes every juicy jiggle, love handle, and triple-D bosom (or utter lack thereof). Their shoeless feet and simple black clothing seem to toy with the very idea of naturalness, as if they have disposed of artifice, just as the queens have built it up, in order to highlight the ways in which their bodies conflict with and subvert the normalcy of femininity.

By staging this competition as a battle between two very "unnatural" groups of girls, the Queen Bees are also challenging the heterosexism and body policing of conventional gender. Further, by setting the skirmish to a pop song and imitating the sexy group choreography of hip-hop and pop videos, the performers are making a deliberate play for control and recontextualization of the kind of femininity mainstream pop culture instructs us is appropriate.

Each of these theatrical layers constitutes a deliberate performative move on hegemonic notions of gender. By playing femininity to the hilt and thus emphasizing its imitative nature, both the Queen Bees and the conventional queens employ the standard tactics of drag. And yet the telltale roots of gender binarism show themselves when the Queen Bees and others like them have gone searching for a name for the kind of performance they do. As Krista Smith (aka Kentucky Fried Woman), cofounder of the Queen Bees, has said in an interview, "The term *bio-queen* just seemed icky to me. Like, I no longer wanted to be called by a term that was related in any way, shape, or form to biological anything ... I know girls call themselves *faux queens* ... I really don't like that term because it's like, no—there's nothing fake about your queening, you know? ... I'm back to calling myself a drag queen. Because that's what I am. I mean, I really do believe that intentional gender performance is drag."[4]

The Queen Bees consider the bulk of the work they do to be drag queening. In order to maintain its subversive potential, drag must reorient and expand itself to continue to reflect the range of gender identities and performances, both onstage and off, that it encompasses.

GIRLIE ACTION: CAMP, EARNESTNESS, AND SUBVERTING GENDER NORMATIVITY

The Queen Bees' sting is packed with a penchant for exaggerated pop culture references, and their pieces drip with the kind of aesthetic

that has long been a strategy of drag queening—camp, which Richard Niles describes as a queer strategy for dealing with heteronormativity: "Objects can be appropriated from mainstream popular culture and then reinscribed in ways that allow them to be used as a means of communication and empowerment within gay and lesbian communities."[5] In other words, camp is a method by which the hegemony is queered, denaturalized, and, thus, subverted through overarticulation.

In a 2003 piece, Kentucky Fried Woman (Smith) worked with Seattle drag king Thirston W. Prescott (Sarah Johnston) to stage a reunion between (pop) star-crossed lovers Britney Spears and Justin Timberlake. During an excerpt from Timberlake's "Rock Your Body," Kentucky Fried Woman, her lusciously large frame draped in the naughty schoolgirl uniform made famous in Spears's "Hit Me Baby" video, lip-syncs the cooed female vocals ("Talk to me boy") with self-assured impertinence, while Thirston, looking every bit the part of Timberlake's chubby, baby-faced queer cousin, plaintively attempts to get her into bed ("Hurry up, cause you're taking too long"). The piece ends with them trading vocal parts, Kentucky Fried Woman menacingly mouthing Timberlake's final, aggressive lyrics ("Gotta have you naked by the end of this song") while gripping an astonished-looking Thirston by the collar.

This piece is already imbued with a simple, almost sketch-comedy-style camp, their over-the-top performances humorously exaggerating recognizable pop culture figures and narratives. Thirston takes Timberlake's cocky yet sensitive young pup persona to hilarious extremes, while Britney's jailbait cheekiness becomes almost dominatrix-like in the hands of Kentucky Fried Woman. Since they are performers, Spears and Timberlake are easy targets for exposing the artifice of gender. But by targeting the celebrities' love affair and the potentially real-life emotion behind their songs, Kentucky Fried Woman and Thirston are drawing attention to the link between the "authentic" and the performative in mainstream entertainment; in other words, they are revealing the ways in which pop culture informs and reproduces reality. By staging the storied reunification of a would-be pop culture Romeo with his Juliet (before she became Mrs. Federline and gave up stardom for domestic "bliss," that is) on fat, queer bodies, the performers have camped and thus critiqued the gender reality so quintessentially represented by pop stars, whether they are an "award-winning wife" or a post–boy band metrosexual dabbling in hip-hop pretense.

Camp, however, isn't the only tool at the disposal of femme drag queens to point out the flaws of the dominant gender paradigm. Many of the Queen Bees' performances are informed by a strategic earnestness that dances cheek-to-cheek with overstuffed irony to further queer

femininity. "Milkshake" is a funny piece because of the ways in which it pits various unconventional femininities against each other in an over-the-top battle for gender queendom. But it is also a seriously sexy performance that powerfully eroticizes those bodies that have been othered and desexualized by gender normativity. The Bees relocate sensuality in the soft rolls and sharp angles of their bodies, staking a corporeal claim for themselves within feminine sexuality. Gender—that seemingly stable piece of identity—is on the run, and the Queen Bees are in hot pursuit, going after it with the very markers by which femininity's innateness is defined and linked to specific, heterosexual bodies. By recasting themselves as the provocative booty girls but also insisting upon their right to ownership of every inch of feminine carnality the Queen Bees reproduce and reclaim normalized femininity on and for queer bodies, allowing them a uniquely critical vantage point that is both within and outside of hegemonic gender ideology.

The male/female binarism is predicated upon the idea that while the gender dichotomy itself is normative and authentic, masculinity (and, in particular, white hetero masculinity) is the original and femininity is the derivative other. By performing femininity, the Queen Bees are, in some ways, merely restating femininity's imitative tendencies within the original parameters of the gender binary. Halberstam suggests that drag kinging's reliance on an understated paring down of affect speaks to the ways in which "masculinity manifests itself as realism or as body" in mainstream gender (258). In this sense, kinging is able to critique the authenticity of masculinity by making its own lack of theatricality performative. On the other hand, femininity, according to Halberstam, "is often presented as simply costume" in the mainstream, and, thus, drag queens employ "outrageous artificiality" in order to further emphasize the performativity of femininity (258–59).

While Kentucky Fried Woman's Britney Spears is a great example of this technique, the strategy at work in "Milkshake" is something of a blend of the two performance styles Halberstam describes. The "outrageous artificiality" tactic is present in both the performance of the drag queens and the hyperbolic catfight between the queens and the Bees. But the Queen Bees, barefoot and in simple black clothing, are also making a move to naturalize a set of queer femininities that don't figure into the male/female, real/unreal dichotomy. By insisting, with their unadorned bodies, on a corporeality for this abject gender, the Queen Bees are once again making use of their "outsider within" standpoint in order to both legitimize the queer femininity they are performing and undermine the body/costume binarism of male and female. This stylistic earnestness, on its own and alongside camp, is a crucial performative strategy

for the Queen Bees' project of destabilizing and reclaiming femininity as something that they, queer bodies and all, can own and work tactically.

HOT AND STICKY SWEET: THE POLITICS OF FEMME EROTICISM AND DECENTERING MASCULINITY

In 2004, the Queen Bees en masse attended the sixth annual International Drag King Extravaganza (IDKE). This event, described on the official IDKE 6 website as "a three day conference which will draw together an international collection of people interested in celebrating the mutability and performance of gender, as well as the many aspects of drag king culture,"[6] culminates each year in a final exhibition of drag performance. The Queen Bees were featured in the 2004 showcase, performing a number to Def Leppard's "Pour Some Sugar on Me." For this piece, all twelve Bees came onstage in full "hair band" regalia—rocker T-shirts, ripped jeans, garish makeup, and, of course, monstrous, ratted hair—before stripping and drizzling each other with their own brand of the titular sugar (honey, of course).

The kind of drag the Queen Bees are doing in this performance could easily fit into Judith Halberstam's "femme pretender" genre of drag kinging,[7] in which a feminine performer dons masculine drag and, usually, "blows her cover by exposing her breasts or ripping off her suit in a parody of classic striptease" (249). Halberstam argues that this type of kinging is meant to stress the femininity of the performer, who stages "the failure of her own masculinity as a convincing spectacle" that results in a "consolidation of femininity rather than a disruption of dominant masculinity." She criticizes this performance style for offering a "reassurance that female masculinity is just an act and will not carry over into everyday life" and, thus, restabilizing the gender binary (249–50).

Given the history of this particular song and, especially, within the context of the IDKE, however, I believe the "Pour Some Sugar on Me" piece is actually making a bold strategic move on hegemonic masculinity (even as it is duly queered by all the means Halberstam delineates in *Female Masculinities* elsewhere at the IDKE), against (both queer and hetero-) sexism, and for femme visibility. The IDKE showcase, while noncompetitive, is cast by a selective process, with one of the qualifying factors being that each act in the showcase is encouraged to feature "centralized drag king content," according to the IDKE's mission statement. According to Smith, who has attended four IDKEs, "There's a rule for the showcase, and that is, the main person in the number *has* to be masculine." Since Smith began attending the conference, performing femininity there for three years with Santa Barbara drag king troupe the

Disposable Boy Toys and in 2004 with the Queen Bees, she and other dyke drag queens have worked to create a space for the performance of femininity at the IDKE. Through discussion groups, conference feedback, and, in 2000, a piece of writing ("The Bio-Queen Manifesto"), Smith and other femme performers have criticized the IDKE's showcase restrictions on several levels.[8]

The authors of "The Bio-Queen Manifesto" contend that this policy belies the presence of femme performers at the conference and reinforces the limited and often sexist ways in which femmes are represented in performances structured around the privileging of masculinity. Describing the content of the manifesto, Smith says, "Basically, it was kind of like, we *are* present here. Last night we counted how many people we'd seen the night before performing, how many women there were. And, you know, we're in your numbers. It's just that we're your sex objects or we're your mothers or we're your evil, bad girlfriend that you're going to leave or whatever."

While Smith recognizes and respects the potential counterargument that the IDKE is meant to be a celebratory space for the art of drag kinging, she contends that dividing the dyke drag world into feminine and masculine camps would only serve to further marginalize a community with an extremely limited number of resources at its disposal. I would also argue that such a move would work to stabilize restrictive divisions of male and female. Finally, regardless of how unlikely or even inappropriate a drag kinging conference may seem as a forum for drag queening, the IDKE itself has already set the precedent for including femininity in its showcased performances. As Smith notes, "[W]e're in your numbers." The Queen Bees are not plotting a hostile takeover of a precarious performance space. Rather, they are attempting to reevaluate and remedy the ways in which femininity is already portrayed at the IDKE in order to both replace sex objects and ruthless femme fatales with strong subjects, to curtail the potential for sexism, which is damaging to both feminine and masculine performers, and to gain ground within a dyke community that is vital and personally significant for them.

The "Pour Some Sugar on Me" number was, at least at the IDKE, a clever tactic on the part of the Queen Bees to get around the masculinity prerequisite for the showcase. And rather than an exercise in exposing the "failure of [their] own masculinity," the Bees' strip from "cock-rock" drag to unequivocally girlish figures was meant to point out the flaws in privileging masculinity at the expense of queer femininity, serving as a potent reminder, for conference attendees and organizers, of the femininity on which masculinity and performances of it depend. By embodying and then exposing the soft, feminine underbelly of the very

masculinity that restricts their participation in the showcase, and by re-creating the femme props of some drag king acts as powerful queens, the Queen Bees are flipping—or at least, flipping off—the power structure of the IDKE and the dyke drag world.

Beyond the IDKE, however, the "Pour Some Sugar on Me" piece pokes dominant masculinity in a few more sore spots. This song can be easily categorized as lite- or pop-metal, a 1980s genre remembered fondly for the predilection of the bands within it to dabble in drag. Pop-metal bands like Poison and Twisted Sister, drawing on careful notes taken during glam rock's beauty school in the late 1970s, lipsticked the übermasculinity of hard rock with an exaggerated femininity, performing live shows and appearing on album covers in a kind of hetero drag with full feminine makeup and overly coiffed manes of long hair. This kind of "pink-face" minstrelsy was designed to incite the kiddies and provoke their parents,[9] while the bands made sure to remind everyone which team they played for by penning head-banging odes to cherry pie girls who make grown men cry and waxing statutory for scorching hot, scantily clad schoolteachers in their videos.

In their version of a metal makeout session, however, the Queen Bees reclaim metal's hetero gender bending, queerly embodying it once again as a subversive performance strategy. They play the cocksure, sticky sweet rock god and his sugar-dispersing conquest, granting agency to the object of rock's lascivious gaze by channeling and challenging the power of rock 'n' roll masculinity.

A final critical strategy can be found in the unabashed femme sex play of "Pour Some Sugar on Me" and other Queen Bees' pieces. Smith notes that "one of the things that we always love is showing sexual interactions with each other, trying to reclaim femme-on-femme sexuality from, you know, what it is, which is basically for straight male viewers." The Queen Bees steal the girl-on-girl fantasy back from leering hetero masculinity, re-creating it as a powerful femme eroticism that belongs only to them.

This move also outs stereotypes of lesbian sexuality (a butch-femme mimicry of heterosexuality, a lipstick lesbian girlie show meant for hetero male pleasure) as the hegemonic fictions that they are. While a rich critique can certainly be found in the erotic play between lesbian masculinity and femininity, the Queen Bees are making sure that the queer femme is given the same legitimate subjecthood as the dyke butch. The "Pour Some Sugar on Me" piece makes a demand for a strong, independent feminine sexuality that directly combats the ways in which Smith and others feel that femmes have often been portrayed as mere sexual props in the IDKE's theater of masculinity.

The questions raised by the Queen Bees and other femme performers have resulted in a gradual political shift at the IDKE. Discussion at the conference has increasingly addressed the need to reevaluate the dyke drag space to make room for theatrical femininity. Smith reports that a large number of performances—including some by renowned drag kings—at the IDKE 6 centralized queening, and the emphasis of the conference's theme, "gendeRevolution," on the "ever evolving definitions of drag" represents a considerable shift from the event's original, drag king-focused mission statement.

CONCLUSION: "DRIPPING WITH HONEY AND PACKING A STING"

Femme drag queens are throwing a gender-queer block party that provides an opportunity not only for critiquing tired, outdated structures of gender identity and performance, but also for building alliances among queer performers that have the capability to undermine some of the authority of the heterosexist gender paradigm.[10] The Queen Bees' performances rip a ten-inch stiletto through the restrictions placed on them by mainstream homophobia and queer sexism, while their work as a collective builds a support network that buoys performers and audiences against counterattacks from the gender hegemony. The feisty, high-femme divas they play are just as likely to spank your ass as kick it, but their sexy sass is abuzz with an accessibility that is meant to recontexualize, resexualize, and celebrate queer feminine bodies of all shapes and sizes.

The kind of work that femme drag queens are doing has yet to be seriously considered in academic scholarship. This new kind of drag queen, while she shares a certain family history with conventional drag queens, manages to circumvent many of the critiques leveled at male-to-female queening, including that genre's reliance on humorous incongruity (which depends heavily on the audience's assumption that there is a "real" boy under that fabulous wig) and the alleged potential for misogyny in its parody, simply because it is performed by biological women. Performing and parodying the gender they are assumed to have allows femme drag queens to critique the connection between biology or body and gender or performance in ways not available to conventional drag queens. At the same time, although they certainly dip into the conventional queen's campy makeup case, the earnestness that infuses performances by the Queen Bees and other drag queens also speaks to a different project, namely the resexualizing and reempowering of bodies

that are hegemonically inappropriate and queer in myriad ways, ranging from sexuality to body size or shape.

As we have seen, femme drag queening also often shares community and performance spaces with female masculinity and drag kinging, but the scholarship on drag kinging does little to address either the performance of femininity or the ways in which femininity and masculinity intersect and overlap within drag king spaces. Femme drag queening must ultimately be approached for what it is—an entirely new species of drag deserving an equally fresh, distinct scholarship. Taking the Queen Bees as a locally and stylistically specific example, this chapter is intended to move toward a theory or theories of femme drag queening. Armed with a drag queen's attitude and the self-confident sexuality of a striptease artist (and thus positioning themselves within a lineage of performative femininity tracing back through drag to classic burlesque), performance artists like the Queen Bees are repopulating drag with strong femme subjects who know their way around a pair of heels and a roll of nipple tape and aren't a bit shy about using them as radical outsider art that is aimed at revolution.

NOTES

1. Steven P. Schacht, "Four Renditions of Doing Female Drag: Feminine Appearing Conceptual Variations on a Masculine Theme," *Gendered Sexualities* 6 (2002): 159.

2. Judith Halberstam, *Female Masculinity* (Durham, N.C.: Duke University Press, 1998), 232; hereafter, page numbers cited parenthetically within the text.

3. Judith Butler, *Bodies That Matter: On the Discursive Limits of "Sex"* (New York: Routledge, 1993), 125; emphasis in the original.

4. "Bio-queen" is short for a "biological female who performs femininity" (Krista Smith, interview with the author, September 18, 2004). Earlier in this interview, Smith said that she didn't have a word for the kind of performance she was doing until a friend of hers, returning from a trip to New York City, told her, "I saw girls doing what you're doing and they called themselves *bio-queens!*"

5. Richard Niles, "Wigs, Laughter, and Subversion: Charles Busch and Strategies of Drag Performance," *Journal of Homosexuality* 46, nos. 3–4 (2004): 42.

6. International Drag King Extravaganza, "What's It All About?" (2004); available on the IDKE website (http://idkechicago.com/oldidke/home1.html).

7. Halberstam's "femme pretender" was originally part of a taxonomy of styles she found in the 1995–1996 drag king contests at New York's Hershe Bar. While her examples seem to be specific to the performers at that club,

the taxonomy is part of a broader claim she is making about drag kinging in general.

8. Jessica Eva Humphrey, Stephanie Merton, Krista Smith, and Tristan Taeramino, "The Bio-Queen Manifesto" (presented at the International Drag King Extravaganza [IDKE], Columbus, O.H., 2001).

9. Credit for this term, "pink-faced minstrelsy," which to my knowledge has heretofore not been mentioned in a published work, must be given to Matthew Toland of Western Illinois University.

10. "Dripping with Honey and Packing a Sting" is a quote from the Queen Bees' website (http://www.queenbees.org).

3

QUEERING THE WITCH
Stevie Nicks and the Forging of Femininity at the Night of a Thousand Stevies

JASON LEE OAKES

I'm from a huge, close-knit Italian working-class family. Music was always a very strong presence in my life growing up. My sisters introduced me to Janis Joplin, Jackson Browne, Jimmy Buffet, and it was my mother who introduced me to Stevie Nicks. She liked the song "Leather and Lace" and got the album for Christmas. Well, as soon as I saw it I was like, "Wow!" The hair, the boots, and Stevie's music. Like one of those sirens on the rock—she sang, I followed, and never left her enchanted island. . . . I had never performed in drag before, although every Halloween I would inevitably come up with some sort of female costume—usually a gypsy or witch, and once I was Donna Summer. But around four years ago I saw my first drag show with some friends of mine in it. So I asked if I could be a part of the next show, and I was welcomed by my big sisters with warm, open arms. They knew how much I loved Stevie Nicks and Janis Joplin, so that's what I did. No one had ever really done such rock icons before, so it was something new.
—Salvatore Mauro III, aka BellaDonna

I was born and raised in Houston, Texas. My mom worked in real estate until her death in 1993, and my dad is a financial advisor type. They divorced when I was about ten and I lived with my mom until I went to college. She and I were really tight. . . . I remember my aunt had the "Rumours" 8-track in her car when I was a kid. [Nicks's] music is simple but deep. Her lyrics are truly poetic. I love all the witchy imagery—I am a Faerie, after all. Her image is beautiful and fierce and she doesn't seem to rely on a stylist or anyone to tell her what's "cool." . . . I bought a $200 piano at a thrift store while I was in Los Angeles. "Rhiannon" was one of the first songs I figured out how to play. Before long I had learned "Dreams," "Gold Dust Woman," "Sara," and some others. I would play and sing them to myself, sometimes until I cried. That helped me deal with the breakup I was going through. And when friends would come over, I would play for them and try to get them singing along—especially to "Dreams." Now I hear that song as a spell or hymn I've taught, or reminded, to other members of my tribe.

—**Michael Meagher, aka Michael Glamour Goblin**

I was in the seventh or eighth grade in Jersey, and a girlfriend of mine had a very nice voice and loved to sing. And every day after school—she had really cool swings in her backyard—we'd always be out there singing. We'd sing all the way home, we'd sing on the swings, we'd sing everywhere we went. One day she came to school and she's like, "Liz, you've gotta hear this lady's voice, you sound just like her!" I'm like, "Yeah, sure." She said it was Fleetwood Mac with some new girl, Stevie Nicks. That day after school she played "Landslide" and I'm like, "Who's that woman with my voice?" She had the album cover and then I saw her picture and I was like, "Oh my God, isn't she pretty?" I wished I was pretty like that. I just thought she was gorgeous, and I didn't even fit that image. . . . Later I moved to Texas and did hair and cosmetology and got married. I've always been very much into that—when I'm at home I'm strictly a sweats girl and barefoot and all that—but out and about and even at work I love frilly and dainty things and the whole "Leather and Lace" thing.

—**Lizzie Davis**

Stevie Nicks is the dream of what every young woman wants to be. She is the dance, of budding femininity, before it gets killed by the frost. She is the poet in our hearts who speaks for us. Stevie Nicks is sunlace and paper flowers. She is the expression of youthful

femininity through the power of a woman. Stevie is the aura
of Juliette, the myth of Rhiannon, the mystical gypsy. She is
the dichotomy of strength in the masculinity of her names,
combined with the softness of long flowing hair; a deep, mellow
voice, with twirling, wispy hemlines, she is the blended gender
we can relate to. She is leather and lace. She is the fire, when she
walks into a room. Stevie Nicks is the expression of the female
spirit through booming amplifiers!
      —Barbara Bruner, "Amplified Femininity"

Why do the above fans—with diverse backgrounds and interests—identify with Stevie Nicks so strongly? Nicks is known as one of the three
singer/songwriters in the band Fleetwood Mac (whose 1977 album
Rumours broke all previous records for album sales) and for her successful solo career throughout the 1980s. In the statements above, Nicks
is described as a "one of those sirens on the rock," "beautiful and fierce,"
an embodiment of "amplified femininity" linked with adjectives like
"frilly," "dainty," and "witchy" (though not without certain dichotomies).
The fans quoted above were introduced to Nicks's music by their sisters,
mothers, aunts, and girlfriends, and thus Nicks functions as a reminder
of female bonds for these avid listeners.

    For Salvatore Mauro, Nicks was the medium through which he first
took on a female gender role in drag performance. For Michael Meagher,
Nicks was a catalyst to his eventual membership in the Radical Faeries,
a loosely organized group of gay men who practice a form of paganism or nature worship—often with the veneration of a goddess figure.[1]
For Lizzie Davis, a biological woman who seemingly wouldn't have to
"learn" how to be woman, Nicks has served as a model of femininity no
less than for the others. While it's dangerous to overgeneralize based on
these three people, fans and critics have consistently positioned Nicks as
an embodiment of normative femininity. It's not unusual to read sweeping statements, for instance, claiming that Nicks was "the first woman to
find a *feminine* way to rock,"[2] or that "with her unique ability to convey
both power and vulnerability . . . [Nicks] writes songs that elevate the
feminine to a sacred place."[3]

    But why choose Stevie Nicks to represent femininity? While
Nicks's femininity has been established discursively, it is at the same
time highly performative. Nicks is known for wearing frilly clothing—
long, flowing dresses made of chiffon, lace, or velvet—and for rampant
accessorizing with scarves and shawls; in her stage movements she is
strongly influenced by her ballet training. Also, Nicks usually appears
on stage playing a tambourine. With its circular figure and supportive

musical role, the tambourine has been coded in rock music as feminine, played by female backup singers and others with a low musical status, and opposed to the phallic, musically foregrounded electric guitar. Nicks, however, has reclaimed the disparaged instrument, famously customizing her tambourines and featuring the instrument on album covers and promotional artwork. Finally, Nicks is inextricably linked to one of the most long-standing and highly suggestive symbols of femininity, the witch. Given her black-clad, big-hatted, shawls-and-flowing-frock visual presence, and with lyrics that often dwell on mysticism, inscrutable women, and primordial nature imagery, it is perhaps no surprise that Nicks has often been rumored to be a witch. Throughout her career, Nicks herself has toyed with the image, naming her published company Welsh Witch Music and speaking in interviews about her belief in magic and mysticism.

Given Nicks's strong association with markers of conventional femininity—and her heavy rotation on album-oriented-rock (AOR) radio stations mostly dominated by so-called cock rock (e.g., Led Zeppelin, Aerosmith) and masculinized "rock chicks" (e.g., Joan Jett, Ann and Nancy Wilson of the band Heart)—one is led to wonder why a sizable contingent of her fans appear to take a highly unconventional approach to gender and sexuality. During the 1990s a spate of Nicks tribute events began popping up in various urban locales across the United States, most of which were rooted in gay and drag subcultures. So why is it that Stevie Nicks, as a heterosexual representative of conventional femininity, has been taken up as a "queer" icon? How is Nicks's femininity "forged," and why do drag queens and other gender benders often amplify Nicks's most hyperfeminine qualities? What can this linkage tell us more generally about linkages between gender and sexuality, in terms of how they are mutually defined and imagined?

To address these questions, I will focus on one particular case study. The Night of a Thousand Stevies (NOTS, for short) takes place in New York City. An annual gathering first held in 1991, Nicks fans and Nicks "impressionists" pay tribute by collectively reenacting and reimagining her music and image. NOTS is the flagship Stevie Nicks queer tribute event, serving as a model for subsequent tributes such as the Wild Heart Affair in San Francisco and the Blue Lamp Tour based in Atlanta. And so it is to NOTS that I now turn.

THE NIGHT

The club Mother sits at the far end of Fourteenth Street near the Hudson River in New York City's Meatpacking District.[4] A red velvet rope blocks

the entrance, and a black-clad, dark-headed woman sits outside. Her name is Kitty Boots and she is tonight's "doormanatrix."[5] A sign is affixed to the entrance: "Jackie 60 is a club for dominant women, poets, gay men and lesbians, free-thinking heterosexuals, transvestites and transsexuals, fetish dressers, bisexuals, and those who love them. If you have a problem with this please don't come in.—The Management." Passing through a short entryway one finds a cramped, dimly lit room decorated with a cluster of plastic white doves that hang from the ceiling.[6] Inside, men and women mill about wearing chiffon, velvet, and lace, and many are carrying tambourines decorated with ribbons and baby's breath. Even though dozens of people in the crowd are dressed like Stevie Nicks, they look less like duplicates of Nicks than variations on a Nicksensian theme—male and female, big and small, spitting images and distant doppelgangers.

As the preshow entertainment, two female "Stevies" dance on the proscenium stage. The dancers are introduced as Dolly and Eliza Domination.[7] Their lacy black dresses are accessorized with crochet shawls, thigh-high leather boots, and beribboned tambourines. The two Stevies move seductively to a recording of Nicks's pulsating "I Can't Wait." Eliza strikes the curtseying, arms-extended pose pictured on a Nicks record sleeve (for the song "Stop Dragging My Heart Around"), while Dolly Domination wears a crocheted headpiece from another record cover (for the song "Edge of Seventeen").[8] Every so often the dancers clutch their customized tambourines and twirl in circles, spinning with their arms extended; at other times they create a surreal vision of Stevie Nicks seducing herself, kissing each other and miming other sexual acts.

Next up on the stage is a woman, or perhaps a drag queen, introduced as Empress Chi Chi Valenti.[9] With no microphone in hand, she lip-synchs Nicks's career-defining song about the Welsh witch, "Rhiannon," as she circles around the stage making elaborate hand gestures. During an instrumental break, Valenti takes a lacy black veil, drapes it around her shoulders and twirls ecstatically in a circle. This move becomes a leitmotif through the evening—"the Twirl" is executed so that Valenti's long platinum blond hair whips dramatically around her head, further accented by the flowing veil trailing one beat behind.[10] When the song ends, Valenti takes the microphone stand, with ribbons and baby's breath attached, and welcomes the crowd: "You know how much the night is about Stevie lovers, Stevie dreamers from all over the country and the world, to come in, to perform for you . . . the Gypsies that remain."[11]

The remainder of NOTS is organized as a procession of Nicks impersonators, otherwise known as "Stevies," each of whom performs

a single song before being replaced by the next Stevie (hereafter "Stevie" or "Stevies" will refer to impressionists, while "Nicks" will refer to Stevie Nicks herself). Among the roughly two dozen Stevies are the aforementioned BellaDonna, Michael Glamour Goblin, and Lizzie Davis, as well as a performer from Queens, New York, who goes by the name Nicole Nicks. With her striking, straight blond hair contrasted by a flowing, black diaphanous gown, Nicole takes the stage with her back to the audience. Arms extended, she stretches a fringed shawl across her shoulders like a set of wings. As the introductory vamp draws to a close, she turns to face the audience, and with her eyes fixed in an inward stare she begins to sing.

Nicole's performance is accompanied by a recording of Nicks performing live, singing a medley of "Outside the Rain" and "Dreams." Although Nicks's voice is heard over the sound system, Nicole's microphone is live and her voice emerges in the sound mix literally singing along. At times the two voices are intertwined so seamlessly that it is difficult to distinguish one from the other. While singing, Nicole deftly impersonates many of Nicks's familiar stage gestures and vocal patterns. She shakes the microphone stand frenetically back and forth, mimicking Nicks's voice as it reaches suddenly into a higher register, ending in a brief melismatic flourish. Those nearest the stage reach out to touch Nicole on stage as if in thrall to a real rock star. Nicole moves toward the audience and grasps their open hands one by one, accepting one young man's offering of a tambourine that she shakes in time. After Nicole sings the first verse and chorus of "Dreams," the curtain is drawn closed in a moment of confusion, and the prerecorded portion of the sound mix cuts out. The audience, most of whom obviously know the song by heart, fills in the silence, continuing to sing the lyrics a cappella. The sound person then deftly incorporates this into the performance as the curtain reopens, bringing the sound mix up, and then down, and then up and down from one line to the next. A layered, call-and-response pattern is created with the original recording, with vocal parts traded back and forth among the recorded Stevie Nicks, the performer Nicole Nicks, and the audience. As the song ends, the audience sings the final chorus unaccompanied, and then erupts in a deafening chorus of cheers and clapping, blending seamlessly with the applause on the soundtrack.

QUEERING STEVIE

Following from the above scene, NOTS is structured as a dialogue, a call-and-response between mass-mediated culture and people's everyday lives. This dialogue is structured through multiple overlaps and layerings, and

through all of the ambiguities that are created in their wake. Multiplicity is foregrounded in the name of the event itself—Night of a *Thousand Stevies*—and over the course of the night the Stevies' various impressions build layer upon layer in a cumulative and at times conflicting dialogue. Combining sincere tribute (Nicks is referred to simply as "the goddess") with broad satire (her once-notorious cocaine habit is a frequent target), an ambiguous stance is taken that combines the earnestness of a serious fan with a camp aesthetic of exaggeration and parody.

Multiple overlaps destabilize the standard distinction usually drawn between star and fan, performer and audience. In the earlier example, is Nicole the "star" or a representative of the other fans in the audience? Is the audience reacting more to Nicole herself or to the "Nicks aura" she evokes? Ambiguity is also created between what is "live" and "mediated." Some Stevies sing to a karaoke-style backing, others lip-synch, others sing along with Nicks's records, and a few even perform with live musicians. In the above example, Nicole Nicks uses a recording from a live Stevie Nicks concert, meaning that one has to go back *four levels* to get back to what the song started as—a live enactment of a sound recording of a live performance of a song that started as a studio recording. Acoustically, NOTS is structured through multiple layerings and overlapping. In the performance space a densely textured web of sounds is woven together—an enveloping mix of music, crowd noise, and rattling tambourines can at times make it hard to tell if certain sounds are coming from the performer, the recording, or the audience. All in all, then, established boundaries are subverted on multiple fronts—straddling usually strict divisions between star and fan, live and mediated, production and consumption, and fantasy and reality—but, one may ask, to what ends?

A clue may be provided if one approaches NOTS as a queer event, that is, an event where the above ambiguities overlap and intermingle with the realm of gender and sexuality. As in these other arenas, multiplicity and categorical subversion are par for the course when it comes to gender at NOTS. The Stevies themselves range from straight women and men to cross-dressers, transgenders, and others who defy simple categorization. Often it is not clear whether a given performer is biologically male or female, performing in drag, is oriented gay or straight, or somewhere in between. As Chi Chi Valenti, the emcee and creator of NOTS, puts it, "We have gender benders of all persuasions, and sometimes you have to go back through *four levels* to get back to what they were born as."[12] Even the biologically female Stevies—such as Valenti herself—are sometimes mistaken for female impersonators. With performances strongly influenced by the drag queen Stevies who founded

NOTS, women effectively take on the role of *female* female imperson-ators—that is, women impersonating men who impersonate women. With this pervasive layering of genders, many of the Stevies aren't eas-ily mapped onto a two-dimensional grid of male/female or straight/gay. Through this lack of fit, and through the adoption of interstitial sexuali-ties and genders, these and other binary distinctions are broken down or, in other words, *queered*.

The word *queer* in this context is not a synonym for "gay and les-bian"; to the contrary, queerness is less a category of sexuality than an approach to sexuality that may be shared by homosexuals, bisexuals, transgenders, and even heterosexuals who feel a lack of fit within es-tablished sexual frameworks. Moving another level out, many queer theorists argue that queerness should be deployed "beyond the realms of sexuality and sexual identity," where a queer critique is "a means of traversing and creatively transforming conceptual boundaries."[13] Acting as a critique of prevailing cultural categories, queerness can be used to challenge identities that are usually broken down according to strict bi-naries of straight/gay, masculine/feminine, and other dualisms. Thus, in queer theory an effort is made to challenge "the differences and silences that have been suppressed by the homo-hetero binary," and to "unpack the monolithic identities 'lesbian' and 'gay,' including the intricate ways lesbian and gay sexualities are inflected by heterosexuality, race, gender, and ethnicity."[14] As will be demonstrated below, these interrelationships among sexuality, gender, race, class, and other factors certainly come into play in the history of NOTS as a queer event.

THE QUEER-FEMININE NEXUS

According to regular attendees, much of the audience at NOTS—described by Michael Meagher as a motley collection of "freaks, geeks, fags, and hags"[15] —does not fit comfortably either in straight culture or in dominant gay subcultures centered in New York's Chelsea and West Village neighborhoods. In its early years NOTS was born directly out of queer culture in New York City. The first NOTS was held as one of a series of regular theme parties known as Jackie 60. Hosted at a club called Mother, the party was established in 1990 by Chi Chi Valenti and her partner Johnny Dynell in the then-seedy Meatpacking District. Dynell says the parties were geared toward breaking down divisions between gay, drag, and women's clubs.[16] Attracting an unusual assortment of downtown hipsters and less-well-heeled outsiders, Jackie 60 brought together individuals from the underground club scene and the drag/transgendered scene, as well as the occasional meat market employee.

At the same time it is a "queer" event, NOTS also grew out of an explicitly articulated feminine/feminist agenda. The Jackie 60 parties were organized as a series of rotating tributes dedicated to icons, predominantly female, including Dusty Springfield, Bettie Page, Patti Smith, and, of course, Stevie Nicks (and held, notably, at a club called Mother).[17] Valenti maintains that NOTS and the other Jackie 60 events were produced with the goal of communicating a "female-dominant aesthetic."[18] Initially, she conceived the Jackie 60 parties as a sort of female counterpart to the uptown, Harlem voguing scene, where black gay men competed, impersonating social types (e.g., businessman, supermodel) through stylized dress and dance movements.[19] Through their cultural poaching, the competitors exposed naturalized social and gender categories as highly performative, effectively forging identities to which they were otherwise restricted access.

Likewise, feminine identities are forged at NOTS, where the verb *to forge* is doubly inflected, referring both to forgery, the act of creating a convincing fake, and to the forging, or making, of a unique entity. Taking these definitions together one could say that, through masquerade, gender is made for real. Valenti describes men and women alike as performing in drag, meaning that women too must work to perform femininity. Thus, by exposing the artifice and effort that goes into constructing a feminine identity, the socially negotiated category of femininity is queered at the very same time that it is valorized.

At NOTS, queerness is explicitly gendered. Feminist scholars have long noted that the masculine/feminine dyad is operative in other binaries, with masculinity linked to the default side, and the feminine marked as the "other" (i.e., the "queer"). At NOTS, one could argue that gender is embedded in the many other binary constructions that are highlighted through their subversion. With performers occupying a middle ground between male and female, live and mediated, production and consumption, and identities marked by the dichotomy of stability/ fluidity, femininity is commonly aligned with the second semiotic axes listed above—that is, women as mediated, as consumers, as unstable and mutable. Whereas NOTS is queer in its destabilization of gender-related and other binary categorizations, the irony is that this destabilization itself may be culturally coded in gendered terms. *Queer*, after all, suggests another binary distinction, presumably, between queer and nonqueer; and queerness, with its basis in highly mediated and mutable identities, can itself be marked as a feminine subject position. Significantly, this mutability—which underpins the linkage made between femininity and queerness—takes on a special significance in the music of Stevie Nicks, especially in "queer hearings" of her music at an event such as NOTS.

THE MYSTICAL RHIANNON: FEMININITY
AND QUEER HEARINGS

How are feminine-queer linkages made through Nicks's music? To explore this question, I will perform a brief analysis of Stevie Nicks's song "Rhiannon," the Fleetwood Mac hit that firmly established her popular image and musical style. "Rhiannon" is based on the legend of the Welsh witch of the same name. Appearing to a traveling lord as a bewitching woman dressed in gold, she escapes his horseman riding on a magical white mare. Both the legend and the song follow the venerable theme of the ideal yet unattainable woman, in Nicks's words "a mystical woman who finds it very hard to be tied down in any kind of way."[20] Like many of Nicks's songs, the lyrics of "Rhiannon" focus on a mysterious, capricious female protagonist.[21]

Notably, the images of women contained in the lyrics—mutable, whimsical, unstable, tied to nature and to mystical forces, idealized yet safely removed from everyday existence—could just as easily have come from a song by Led Zeppelin or Jimi Hendrix, but they are placed in a quite different musical setting (the significance of which will be discussed shortly). The trope of the mystical maiden, the earth mother, and the like is heard in many "classic rock" songs from the late 1960s and 1970s, promoting a vision of "women [who] are etherealized within a dreamlike and unreal world, detached from reality, defined by the male as a fantasy escape from reality."[22] It's a trope that harks back to the literary heroines of nineteenth-century Europe, who themselves referred nostalgically back to an imagined medieval and Renaissance society full of Ophelia-like tragic beauties. Why then, at NOTS and other queer-based Nicks tributes, would performers and audience choose to reinforce what Sheila Whiteley calls "repressive representations"? Is it possible for women, queers, or other marginalized subjects to reposition these patriarchal myths and their portrayal of femininity, and could male-associated fantasies serve instead as a basis for female empowerment?

Rather than looking solely to Nicks's lyrics for answers—a common myopia in popular music analysis—musical analysis is also needed for the unique insights it might provide. In fact, I would argue that the feminine-associated traits of "Rhiannon"—and the potential *queerness* of the protagonist's desire not to be pinned down—are communicated most clearly of all in the musical structure. The entire song, except for a brief bridge section, is based around a circular chordal movement that alternates between A minor and F major, meaning that it's difficult to find an unambiguous cadence point. If one hears the opening chord of A minor as the tonic, then almost the entire song rotates between

this chord and a deceptive cadence that never resolves. Meanwhile, the lead guitar and vocal outline the main melody, but in a heterophonic relationship where they seem to chase each other up and down the circuitous melody—moving repeatedly up and down along the same trajectory—and never matching up in perfect unison. Accented words such as *rings*, *bell*, and *love* are transformed into two-syllable words, beginning on one pitch and then sliding a semitone or whole tone up or down, and the accented syllables are positioned as sixteenth- or eight-note pickups that anticipate the downbeats on two and four, never landing directly on the beat. The vocal melody of Rhiannon is filled with a constant stream of nonchord tones including suspensions, anticipations, passing tones, and neighboring tones. These melodies are not provided with a sense of resolution, as they never conclude on the root of the chord, thus giving the impression of an unsettled Nicks/Rhiannon who is unwilling to be pinned down tonally, melodically, or otherwise. Likewise, Nicks's vocal articulation is also indefinite; when she lands on a sustained syllable, the note is usually held with a wide, raspy vibrato that circumnavigates the central pitch, a vocal quality that is exaggerated by many of the Stevies at NOTS (as are the twisty, melismatic passages that Nicks frequently inserts into her live performances). Much like the Stevie "Twirl" and the feminine-associated tambourine, Nicks's vibrato and her melodies work in perpetual motion around a seemingly fixed point of arrival that is never reached.

These musical and kinesthetic qualities—whether labeled as circuitous, oblique, mutable, undifferentiated, oceanic, and so forth—are typically gendered as feminine, as qualities that stand in stark contrast to the "tonal narratives of the masculine canon since the seventeenth century . . . organized teleologically with the illusion of unitary identity promised at the end of each piece."[23] The nonteleological, "feminine" quality of Nicks's music, however, is open to widely varying interpretations. To some listeners Nicks's music might come off as indecisive or "flaky," consistent with negative stereotypes of femininity. Others, however, may hear Nicks's musical indeterminacy as a form of resistance, as Nicks rarely sings anything "straight." Furthermore, this may be interpreted as having particular connotations when it comes to gender and sexuality, especially given the gendered subject matter of many of her songs, and the prominence of gender and sexuality in the discourses around Nicks. So, while none of the above musical techniques may be remarkable taken on their own and are certainly not unique to Nicks, their accretion and the Stevies' audible identification with them—foregrounding and even heightening the shaky vibrato and melodic circuitousness—open up a space for potential queer hearings of her music.

QUEERING THE WITCH

Given Nicks's image and songs like "Rhiannon," a well-known piece of pop music folklore has it that Nicks is actually a witch. At NOTS, the witch mythology is constantly played up with references to Nicks as "the enchantress" and exhortations to "worship the goddess." For centuries the image of the witch has provided an index of societal attitudes toward femininity, projecting an image of the feminine as "other" writ large. With their ability to control forces of nature, witches are mediators of the natural sphere, just as women's bodies have been thought to mediate nature through menstruation and pregnancy. The mystical powers witches possess to cast spells are correlated to women's assumed ability to manipulate men, using sexual wiles to control and consume them. Witches are portrayed as cackling, hysterical, generally unstable women who have the ability to shape-shift. Likewise, women have been stereotypically depicted as less consistent than men, emotionally erratic, and physically transformable through natural and unnatural means (e.g., pregnancy, makeup).

The above markers of witchiness paint a picture of femininity unbounded, rooted largely in a fear of female sexuality that overflows strict boundaries. Recently, however, female-centric spiritual movements have reclaimed the word *witch*, viewing it as a stereotype that can be turned on those who use it pejoratively.[24] In the reclaimed version, formerly negative qualities shift to being viewed as positive. Derogatory representations of the effeminate subject—as hysterical, seductive, and capricious—are viewed through a new lens as sensitive, sensuous, and adaptable. While many earlier feminists fought patriarchy by trying to gain access to institutions and identity markers linked with masculinity, spiritual feminists take the opposite tact, subverting patriarchy by exaggerating and even camping up femininity.[25] In this way, there is an attempt to reconcile femininity and feminism, just as one finds at NOTS.

In representations of femininity, even those meant to be pejorative, queer subjects find a model for identities that are established upon a certain built-in instability (read: flexibility, adaptability). While Nicks's witchiness and hyperfemininity may confirm gender stereotypes for more conservative listeners, from another perspective Nicks serves as a model of female—and, more specifically, feminine—empowerment. At NOTS, the Stevie impersonators take advantage of Nicks's malleability, confirming their transgressive desires through queer hearings of her music. Femininity is thus engaged as a construct to be applied strategically, with music as a pathway for queering sexual and gender boundaries that may otherwise be difficult or even dangerous to breach.

NOTES

1. This promotion of femininity also comes across in the group's use of the word *Faerie*, a deliberate play on words in that *fairy* is now most common as a disparaging term for a homosexual or (especially) an overly feminine man of any sexual persuasion.

2. Jim Farber, "Lacing up Again: Stevie Nicks, Solitary Romantic, Has a New Album," *New York Daily News*, May 6, 2001, emphasis added. It is worth noting here the assumed contrast between femininity and the genre of rock.

3. Steffie Nelson, "Stevie Nicks: Gold Dust Woman Returns," April 2001, available online from VH1's website (http://www.vh1.com/news/features/stevienicks/). Despite keeping a low profile through most of the 1990s, Nicks has been cited by contemporary female artists, from Tori Amos to Sheryl Crow to Courtney Love, for inspiring a belief that they as women could make it as rock stars.

4. Although written in the present tense, the following description is based on the 1999 NOTS. This was the last year the event was held at Mother before it closed. Since 2000 NOTS has been staged at various venues around New York City. For an explanation of the club's closing, see its website (http://www.mothernyc.com/mothersend/index.html).

5. For more on Kitty Boots, see the House of Domination website (http://www.houseofdomination.org/members/kitty/kitt.html).

6. This is an allusion to the lyric "Just like the white winged dove / sings a song" from the Nicks song "Edge of Seventeen" on the Stevie Nicks album *Bella Donna* (1981).

7. See the House of Domination website (http://www. houseofdomination.org/).

8. These record sleeve images can be found at the official Stevie Nicks website (http://www.nicksfix.com/stopdraglarge.jpg and http://www.nicksfix.com/edge17.jpg).

9. For more on Chi Chi Valenti, see the Mother website (http://www.mothernyc.com/empress/).

10. The In Her Own Words website (http://www.inherownwords.com/rhiannon.htm) has a video-clip illustration of the twirl.

11. This is a reference to Nicks's song "Gypsy," on the Fleetwood Mac album *Mirage* (1982): "To the gypsy that remains / faces freedom with a little fear / I have no fear, I have only love."

12. Alba Clemente, "The Little Nightclub That Could," *Interview*, December 1999, p. 31.

13. Phillip Brian Harper, Anne McClintock, José Esteban Muñoz, and Trish Rosen, "Queer Transexions of Race, Nation, and Gender: An Introduction," *Social Text* 52–53 (1997): 1.

14. Rosemary Hennessy, "Incorporating Queer Theory on the Left," in *Marxism in the Postmodern Age*, ed. Antonio Callari, Stephen Cullenberg, and Carole Beweiner (New York: Guilford, 1994), 266.

15. "Straight" people (especially women) who are drawn to queer culture are sometimes known as "fag hags."

16. Johnny Dynell, "Live from Jackie 60," in *Sampling the City: The Portable Lower East Side*, ed. Kurt Hollander (New York: New York State Council on the Arts, 1994), 65–66.

17. For more on Jackie 60, see the Mother website (http://www.mothernyc. com/jackie/60.html).

18. Althea Loveless, "Chi Chi Valenti: Biography of a New York Nightclub Empress," April 2002, available at the Mother website (http://www. mothernyc.com/empress/chibio1.html).

19. In 1988 Valenti authored a *Details* cover story on voguing—before Jennie Livingston's hit documentary *Paris Is Burning* and Madonna's chart-topping "Vogue"—that helped popularize the dance and music culture.

20. Stevie Nicks, radio interview by Jim Ladd, KMET, Los Angeles, 1976.

21. Consult the amazingly comprehensive official Stevie Nicks website (http:// www.nicksfix.com/) for lyrics and other song information.

22. Sheila Whiteley, "Repressive Representations: Patriarchy and Femininities in Rock Music of the Counterculture," in *Mapping the Beat: Popular Music and Contemporary Theory*, ed. Thomas Swiss, John Sloop, and Andrew Herman (Malden, Mass.: Blackwell, 1998), 163.

23. Susan McClary, *Feminine Endings: Music, Gender, and Sexuality* (Minneapolis: University of Minnesota Press, 1991), 155.

24. Cynthia Eller, *Living in the Lap of the Goddess: The Feminist Spirituality Movement in America* (New York: Crossroad, 1993).

25. There are earlier precedents, however, such as the group WITCH (Women's International Terrorist Conspiracy from Hell), formed in 1968.

4

TICKLE ME EMO
Lesbian Balladeering, Straight-Boy Emo, and the Politics of Affect

KAREN TONGSON

During her solo set at the 2002 San Francisco Queer Arts festival, Kaia Wilson, the lead singer of the dyke punk trio The Butchies, broke into an unplugged rendition of a few bars of Celine Dion's megaballad, "My Heart Will Go On." This incursion of pop schmaltz into the subcultural setting was, predictably enough, met with more than a few chuckles and the appropriate ironic posturing by the audience. Yet something in Wilson's earnest delivery of the tune (and the sense that she kept wanting to play it despite the audience's studied hipster aversion to the piece) suggested that the interlude was more of an homage than an urban crowd at a dyke punk show was comfortable with. Her performance was also part of an "intergenerational" night of music: she shared the bill with the iconic butch folkie Ferron as part of the festival's attempt to bring both young and "mature" artists and fans together. In this setting, Wilson's earnest acoustic tribute to sappy love songs did more than evoke VH1 images of an artificially windblown Dion spasmodically belting a weeper. Wilson echoed a musical affect from another era and a "prelapserian" musical market—a more sentimental and, for some, a retrospectively embarrassing era of lesbian and "womyn's music" from the 1970s and 80s.

This chapter explores modes of queer affect by revisiting earnest lesbian music as an influence on—as well as coeval manifestation of—the spatially marked music niche known as emo (short for "emotional"): hetero, male, low-fi punk originating in unlikely places like the suburbs of Washington, D.C., Florida, and southern California. To that end, I will offer a more impressionistic chapter that provokes rather than answers a series of questions about the suburbs, sentimentality, teen narcissism, and gender and sexuality—about both emo's and queer culture's reliance on emotionally raw incarnations of arrested development in peripheral spaces. What can we learn about sexuality and space when we consider the intimate and distinctly noncosmopolitan vibe that inflects both straight-boy emo and lesbian balladeering? How does nonurban space inform and justify the production of sentimental musical forms? Does emo potentially owe something to queer music—lesbian folk and folk rock balladeering in particular—that has also dabbled earnestly with romantic sentimentality? How is race sublimated by the fetishization of affect in these spatially and stylistically marked musicalities? And can queer studies engage productively with such a white, suburban, boy-driven pop phenomenon like emo in order to imagine other musical forms that account for the effects of suburban and rural feelings on a queer imaginary often preoccupied with gay urban meccas?

It seems only appropriate that popular culture's iconic emo boy these days isn't even a musician, but the primetime pinup character Seth Cohen (played by the doe-eyed Adam Brody) on the Fox TV network's teen soap opera smash *The O.C.* Seth—especially after he managed to seduce a hottie Newport Beach girlfriend named Summer—is certainly more than several times removed from the emocore front men of yore, like Guy Picciotto of Rites of Spring and Blake Schwartzenbach of Jawbreaker. As a well-to-do suburban wit with the dough to plop on Munsingwear Penguin revival gear, Seth is not at all (or at least not anymore) one of the profoundly heart-scarred boys glorified on "orthodox" emo websites, a virtual last stand by emo connoisseurs desperately defending the genealogical integrity of a musical form widely considered to be the spawn of when "punk" and "indie rock" mated somewhere in a suburban basement during the mid-1980s. Many emo fans are loath to provide a precise definition of the term lest it sully the "purity" of what the music and the movement should stand for, and codify the concept for consumption as well as ridicule (both of which have occurred several times over at various moments throughout the late 1980s, 1990s, and the first years of this century).

Among the most thorough and thoughtful genealogies for emo is a website by the talented young photographer (and presumably an emo fan

himself) Andy Radin.[1] Rock critic Andy Greenwald, author of the controversial but thus far definitive trade book on emo, *Nothing Feels Good: Punk Rock, Teenagers, and Emo,* invokes an emo origin myth that dates and locates the emergence of the movement in "1984 (or thereabouts), in suburban Washington, D.C. (or thereabouts)."[2] As the story goes, bands like the Rites of Spring and Embrace, fronted by charismatic lead-singers like Guy Picciotto and former Minor Threat frontman Ian MacKaye, respectively, forged a new sound that married the tonal urgency of punk with melodic indie pop as they explored profound, confessional subject matter marked vocally by occasional moans, whimpers, and emotive displays of breathiness. As Radin remarks, "Singer Guy Picciotto keeps an out-of-breath punk style most of the time . . . [although] his voice breaks down at climactic moments into a throaty, gravelly, passionate moan," while "MacKaye's vocals retain his trademark bold enunciation, with only occasional sparks of emotive delivery."[3]

While most connoisseurs and critics of emo agree on the music's founding moments and forms, the term *emo* has taken on a life of its own, to refer to a much broader movement of "bands that weren't punk" as well as "fashion trends" and "sad-eyed kids in the back of class" (Greenwald, 2). If emo is so diffuse, so ephemeral, so easily applicable to a range of affects, styles, and personalities, how is it possible to pin the term down in order to imagine it in concert with queer forms of music? As Greenwald insightfully suggests, "Emo isn't a genre. . . . What the term does signify is a particular relationship between a fan and a band" that can register "sentiments particularly relevant in an increasingly corporate, suburban and diffuse culture such as ours. Emo is a specific sort of teenage longing, a romantic and ultimately self-centered need to understand the bigness of the world in relation to *you*" (4–5; emphasis in the original). As we shall see in subsequent sections of this chapter, the notion of music and style forming an "emotional" if not explicitly politicized movement intersects with certain elements of lesbian collectivity and a communal imaginary burdened with traumas of the everyday, or "to use less clinical terms, feeling bad" as queer theorist Ann Cvetkovich phrases it.[4] Cvetkovich argues for a theoretical nuanced appreciation of the so-called lesser traumas of "girls like me feeling bad," traumas that do not "appear sufficiently catastrophic because [they don't] produce dead bodies or even, necessarily, damaged ones.[5]" Strikingly, Cvetkovich's narrative frame for her profound book—which tackles a range of sexual and political traumas like abuse, incest, and the AIDS crisis—is framed in part by the Michigan Womyn's Music Festival and the inspirational musical archives of dyke bands like Le Tigre and Tribe 8. As we shall see, however, as much as emo shares in a *queer feminist* project that dignifies

affect and confronts structures of repression in a "home" that functions as a synecdoche for the disaffected nation, queer and feminist influences remain problematically unacknowledged.

"WHERE THE BOYS AREN'T"

This subtitle isn't just a cheeky play on Connie Francis's hit, but a tribute to Jessica Hopper's brilliant rant, "Emo: Where the Girls Aren't." Hopper explains that as America "settled into the armchair comfort of the Clinton era" and as "mixtapes across America became soiled with torrential anthems of hopeful boy hearts masted to sleeves," she became increasingly alienated from the emo and punk scenes.[6] She hopes to encourage the swooning "front row girls" at emo shows to rediscover the radicalized possibilities of punk and reenter its leagues as producers— as musicians and performers rather than as consumers, or, in Hopper's scalding words, "muses at best. Cum rags or invisible at worst."[7] While Hopper envisions emo narcissism as a target for feminist critique, I would like to propose a more twisted version of how emo and feminism (primarily of the second wave variety) are actually strange bedfellows. Emo has benefited from and ultimately exploited a second-wave feminist emphasis on emotional earnestness, and has implicitly put into octave-chord practice the idea that the "personal is political" in the musical staging of its own critique of suburban repression and alienation. My efforts to make visible the intersections among feminism and emo are not meant to disavow the political content in much of the women's music that arose in concert with earlier waves of feminism. Rather, by presenting this mutant genealogy, I hope to make something of a queer methodological intervention in how we interpret pop music and popularized subcultures. By thinking about feminist and queer political and aesthetic influences on emo, we can crawl out of the rut of a masturbatory, "boy-centric" musical critique that dwells like a needle in a broken groove on points about "better" incarnations of this or that kind of music produced by a bunch of musical forefathers—or at least cooler older brothers—who really *were* groundbreaking, and not derivative tools slicked up by the major labels. If anything, this chapter offers a critical addendum to Hopper's deliciously caustic rant about the music itself, a way for women and queer critics to intervene in phallic showdowns over music trivia by creating ruptures in the seamless narratives of male musicianship, its rise, progress, and decline. It is not my aim, in other words, to create the definitive timeline for emo or to wax nostalgic about how bands like Jawbreaker, the Promise Ring, Sunny Day Real Estate, or Texas is the Reason, among others, are not properly commemorated,

let alone *known*, by latter-day emophiles who have cribbed their style from *Seventeen* magazine and amassed their record collections exclusively from the Vagrant and Drive-Thru record labels' catalogs.[8]

While emo has certainly benefited from feminist work that made it possible for feelings to get due respect, there is little hard or even circumstantial evidence to suggest that emo bands even realize what effect women's music or feminist politics of the earlier or post–Lilith Fair varieties have had on their own—although the Promise Ring did admit to being Sarah Maclachlan fans in a late-1990s *Spin* magazine interview (Greenwald, 119). And this lack of realization about affective musical genres that exist beyond an individual boy's heteronormative heartrending experiences is part of emo's problem. Some newer bands are hard-pressed to name their male punk and emo predecessors, let alone women's music artists like Ferron, Chris Willamson, or even more recent female and dyke punk predecessors and contemporaries like Bikini Kill, The Butchies, Team Dresch, or Tribe 8, who in certain instances share a similar project of exploring emotional despair and spatial alienation. One can more easily trace emo's heart-on-the-sleeve heroics to various strains of male, European romanticism from the late-eighteenth-century's "spasmodic poets" on through to the late nineteenth century. Greenwald makes several gestures to this "Keats and Yeats are on your side" genealogy by drawing comparisons between Guy Picciotto's "Rites of Spring" lyrics and the poetry of Paul Rimbaud (Greenwald, 13). While I certainly want to acknowledge this aspect of emo's cultural pedigree and poetic ethos—one focused on the exceptionalism of the boy who dares to share his heart in all of its acne-scarred glory—I think it's crucial to insist, if somewhat forcibly, upon emo's unacknowledged debt to a wave of feminism that brought attention to the suburbanite's emotional plight.

Emo shares with feminism a scathing view of suburban isolation and the roles demanded by the family structure so intertwined with the spatial layout of the suburbs and the suburban home. For the women and wives of mid-twentieth-century subdivisions, the duty to manage the home and home-life assumed the character of having to put on a happy face, regardless of the affective torrents (inner or outer) that threatened to rend "the family" asunder (see any Julianne Moore flick circa 2002). As literary critic Catherine Jurca writes about suburban despair, "Middle-class women feel bad insofar as their status limits their aspirations, while with men, the satisfaction of aspirations deadens into discontent."[9] For the boys, especially adolescent ones, the most woeful suburban predicament is not having anything to do. Thus, any experiences—even nonexperiences like missed encounters and unrequited

love—assume a heightened urgency. A thematic trademark of emo is the social snub, or the relationship that never was. Though firmly ensconced in white middle-class privilege, emo luxuriates in suffering—in playground or homeroom martyrdom where exclusion is not based on gender, race, class, or sexuality but on the finer, elusive points of teen signification: the clothes, the looks, the hair. While both second-wave feminist and emo representations of emotional estrangement owe something to the topography of the suburbs and the concept of the middle-class home, in the end there are crucial differences between desperately seeking out "A Room of One's Own," and having the adolescent privilege to mope, Brian Wilson–style, "In My Room."

The shift to the emotional and personal in feminism articulated an experience not explicitly engaged with adolescence—an awkwardness that from an emo standpoint inevitably matures into the expression (often literary) of middle-class male ennui about having to take on suburban dad "responsibilities" as a bread-winner for the kids and the ball and chain.[10] Indeed, this is part of what emo struggles to opt out of with its solipsistic insistence on the lovelorn "me" that is loathe to become anaesthetized to all feelings when it has to assume the compulsory obligations of paternal male adulthood. Feminists, on the other hand, envisioned "getting personal" (in the words of Nancy K. Miller) as a way of maturing out of, rather than wallowing in, the repressed emotionalism and spatial claustrophobia of the suburbs.

Thus far, my comparison between emo and feminism has presumed the heteronormativity of the suburban context. Earlier I invoked the TV character Seth Cohen on *The O.C.* to discuss the emergence of suburban ennui as a highly legitimized form of creative inspiration. *The O.C.* and its emo bandwagoning taps into the cultural zeitgeist of a "generation of disaffected kids on the outskirts of the country's cultural capitals seething with resentment and untapped energy" (Greenwald, 9). Yet suburban isolation and spatial alienation is not only fodder for brooding white boys who barely play guitar; or for their mothers struggling to keep a household intact as an ideal representation; or even for their fathers who wrote and continue to write prize-winning novels on the same subject. Suburban and rural ennui is also an affect that has fueled queer forms of subcultural, as well as pop cultural, expression.

The really striking links between emo and feminism are made legible in the transition to a lesbian aesthetics of affect that was also generated in peripheral spaces. The butch lesbian folk musician Ferron once replied with the following quip to someone who asked her what it was like to live in an artist's colony: "Artist's colony? I just thought I lived in the suburbs."[11] For artists like Ferron, feminism's ethics of emotionality

was politically revised when the act of love—of choosing to love someone of the same sex—assumed a political urgency, especially in spaces away from the urban gay ghettos of major metropolitan areas like New York and San Francisco.[12] Yet Ferron, despite her quip about the suburbs and some of her references to kitschy pop objects like "Care Bears" in songs like "Alice Says Yes," is not the most exemplary dyke figure to link with emo. When Ferron inhabited her butchness in her music she also welcomed the care-giving paternalism that emo eschews as part of her queer gender politics. Ferron is nevertheless one among many dyke artists who paved the way for a wounded lesbian balladeering about breakups that resonates musically and lyrically with what we now call emo.

From bottles to be consumed, kissed, cuddled, to mementos of lost lovers like letters and pictures, both genres of music commemorate mundane, everyday objects while they grasp at emotional profundity. One marvels, for example, at the resonances among some of the songs composed by latter-day emo poster boy Chris Carrabba of Dashboard Confessional, and Emily Saliers's lesbian breakup ballads for the iconic Indigo Girls. One of the most beloved tracks from Carrabba's early Dashboard album *The Swiss Army Romance* is "Living in Your Letters," which employs the same tropes of correspondence and haunting as Saliers's signature ballad "Ghost" from the Indigo Girls' *Rites of Passage* album. Carrabba sings mournfully that "I'm living in your letters / Breathe deeply from this envelope it smells like you / And I can't be without that scent." Saliers's "Ghost," meanwhile, also broods over "a letter on the desktop that I drug [*sic*] out of the drawer." Both imagine the quiet if profound trauma of an everyday life without their respective love objects but surrounded by the mementos, scents, and sensations of what once was. Saliers writes, "There's not enough room in this world for my pain," while Carrabba is "poring over photographs" as a means of conjuring the beloved's presence.

Although the lyrics in this instance share striking similarities, musically Amy Ray's contributions to the Indigo Girls come closer to what we might think of as Dashboard-era emo. Ray is the self-professed punk-influenced half of the duo, whereas Saliers is the "softer," more folk-inspired songwriter. Ray's pounding, rhythmically driven, and less noodly guitar work—which, incidentally, dabbles every now and then with the signature emo octave chord—is closer to what we hear in early Dashboard. In fact, the rhythmic guitar chords of "Living in Your Letters" are evocative of the Ray-penned "Strange Fire," an earlier song in the Indigo Girls' oeuvre. Likewise, Ray's vocal style is more gut-wrenching—she summons forth a belty, alto voice from the chest and occasionally

improvises stream-of-consciousness rants at live performances to offset and complement Saliers's sometimes wispier, pensive, mezzosoprano voice from the head. Ray's improvised stream-of-consciousness rants— or as fans on the Indigo Girls' Internet message board refer to them, her "SOCs"—are comparable to early displays of emocore improvisation taken up later by the likes of Carrabba during emotive interludes in live performances of the Dashboard favorite "Hands Down." Yet despite these resonances, there are significant differences to be gleaned between Carrabba, the manchild from Boca Raton, Florida (an emo elder, since he's in his thirties and most of the latter-day crop of emo bands are the same age as their teen fans), and the Indigo Girls from Georgia. I chose to bring them together, however, because I wanted to create a very obvious and explicit connection between the tropes of sentimentality adopted very earnestly from feminism via the Indigo Girls, and emo in its most contemporary, popularized MTV sense. Other similarities between the Indigo Girls and Dashboard Confessional abound—the least of which are the full-throated fan sing-alongs at both groups' shows, their reliance on a fervent grassroots and Internet fan network, and their oblique entry via punk and punk venues onto the music scene (the Indigo Girls debuted on the national scene at the venerable punk club CBGB in New York City).

I remarked earlier that second-wave feminism inhabits "feelings" as an expression of the yearning for growth, whereas emo shirks and shivers in fear of development as it revels in "the self-conscious romanticism and high-stakes emotional desperation of the years between high school and whatever comes next" (Greenwald, 43). I should clarify, however, that this trajectory of development in feminism does not necessarily carry over into politicized queer incarnations of affect and time. In fact, among the resonances shared by emo and dyke punk is the self-conscious opting-out of normative time. What Judith Halberstam depicts as a "queer temporality" is precisely the kind of high-pitched, truncated temporality tapped into by Chris Carrabba and his emo brethren, as well as dyke punk artists from spatial peripheries. The emo ethos loathes a responsible suburban future from the vantage point of a miserable suburban present. Queer time, according to Halberstam, also deviates from the normative time that unfolds in the suburban context—life's narrative arc of marrying, buying a house, having babies, and the like.[13] Time is what inevitably separates bands like the Indigo Girls and Dashboard Confessional. The lesbian-identified Indigo Girls are not necessarily purveyors of the kind of queer time or politics Halberstam describes in her account of subcultural formations and postmodern geographies. The Indigo Girls have been advocates of gay marriage—of opening up the dream of suburban

stability to gay men and lesbians. Especially in their later work, in Saliers's songs in particular, the Indigo Girls revel in the simple pleasures of longtime companionship in such celebratory ditties as "The Power of Two." There is an orthodoxy to the Indigo Girls' relationship to second-wave feminism—and some of their neoliberal political causes attest to that. Their high-stakes emotionalism, then, acquires the structure of nostalgia, of memory, whereas emo of the Dashboard variety perpetually reinhabits the painful moment as it reopens "This Old Wound" (the title of one of Carrabba's most self-obsessed, self-lacerating pieces), never allowing it to heal.

CONCLUSIONS ON QUEER TIME AND SPACE

When I first conceptualized this chapter, I imagined more resonances between emo and its true contemporary (both conspiratorial as well as adversarial) dyke punk. The melodic dyke punk of bands like The Butchies or Team Dresch is also born of peripheral spaces and a profound relationship to feminism in its many waves. The Butchies, and lead-singer Kaia Wilson in particular, are not afraid to tap into their own everyday emotionalism about breakups, unrequited longing, and spatial ennui. Unlike their emo counterparts, however, The Butchies are staunchly self-conscious about the musical genealogy that makes such emotional contemplation possible—and their driving punk covers of early women's music numbers like Chris Williamson's "Shooting Star" attest to this sense of political as well as musical history. The Butchies commemorate feminism both subtly and explicitly in their own take on space, sexuality, and love, yet they also underscore some of the limitations of its narcissistic tenets and heteronormative affects.

One of the most salient issues that emerged when I began looking at the links between emo and second-wave feminism is that the emotionalism espoused in both fails to account for race in any significant way, precisely because both engage with an *ideal* of suburbanism even as they strive to critique it. In their suburban imaginaries, the wounded self becomes the focal point of analysis and contemplation—and this self is presumed to be white, privileged, and heterosexual. Even though both feminism and emo ultimately became collective movements in their own right, the starting point for these movements is the alienation that comes with privilege rather than a striving toward affiliation with others who share the same plight. They focus on the individual's exemplarity—or rather, on the individual's failure to be exemplary in a space that demands the vigilant policing of whiteness and heterosexuality. There have been, of course, racialized accounts and critiques of the suburbs,

but rarely have they taken musical form. The work of media artist Lynne Chan, for example, parodies the narcissism and self-obsession of pop stars who emerge "out of nowhere," while taking a jibe at the fan fervency of movements like emo in her faux fan-site for JJ Chinois, a "rock star" from Bakersfield, California via the Central Valley wasteland of Coalinga, California.[14] The performance collective Butchlalis de Panochtitlan (BdP), based in the greater Los Angeles area, also explore the suburban playscapes of southern California for queers of color who have inhabited or continue to inhabit what author Sandra Tsing-Loh has dubbed "lesser Los Angeles," such as the satellite city of Bell Gardens. BdP also uses their performances to take on the angst and leisure habits of suburban social subcultures, invoking the Latino/a queer encounter with punk-inspired "dirty white grrls" at riot grrl gatherings in Pomona during the early and mid-1990s, while staging skits about the philosophy of love and butch-of-color mentorship in casual community settings like interleague softball games. It is only a matter of time before these experiences become transposed into a musical language and musical performance. There are rich soundscapes for both JJ Chinois's and the BdP's performance projects, more often than not a combination of 1980s and '90s dance music that saturated the suburban airwaves, combined with the melodic early indie rock of that era, most notably music by the Smiths, who had a significant cult following among the Latino teens of southern California.[15]

In the spirit of JJ Chinois's and the BdP's more sanguine take on coming from nowhere spaces, and experimenting with historical incarnations of lesbianism, I would like to conclude with a glimpse at a band that has managed to take the burden of earnest lesbian music to another level. The queer quartet Lesbians on Ecstasy takes the dyke anthems throatily belted by Melissa Etheridge, k.d. lang, and yes, even the Indigo Girls and turns them into punky-electroclash dance covers. Though at first listen Lesbians on Ecstasy (LOE) appear to be producing a twisted parody of the earnest dyke music that has come before them, they very staunchly insist on the importance of being earnest. LOE has chosen to overcome the traumas of the everyday with a kind of collective musical experimentation that does not obsess upon the wounds of the self but turns wounded music into something that might literally move others who connect with the lyrical content of the songs—move them to dance. LOE member Fruity Frankie puts it this way: "We want to reach lesbians who don't normally listen to dance music . . . but we also want to introduce political content to dance music." Fellow LOE member Bernie Bankrupt adds, "That's what's so great about a lot of lesbian music. It doesn't shy away from strong political messages."[16] Perhaps the answer

to Jessica Hopper's call for women to take back punk rock from the heterosexual male narcissism exemplified by emo lies in LOE's twisted, politicized take on tribute rock. Just maybe—in the words of Anita O'Day—it's time to "face the music and dance."

NOTES

1. See Andy Radin, "What the Heck *is* Emo Anyway?" (http://www.fourfa. com/).
2. Andy Greenwald, *Nothing Feels Good: Punk Rock, Teenagers, and Emo* (New York: St. Martin's, 2003), 1; hereafter, page numbers are cited parenthetically in the text.
3. Andy Radin, "History" (www.fourfa.com/history.htm).
4. Ann Cvetkovich, *An Archive of Feelings: Trauma, Sexuality, and Lesbian Public Cultures* (Durham, N.C.: Duke University Press, 2003), 2.
5. Ibid., 3.
6. Jessica Hopper, "Emo: Where the Girls Aren't," in *Da Capo Best Music Writing 2004*, ed. Mickey Hart (Cambridge, Mass.: Da Capo, 2004), 123.
7. Ibid., 124.
8. In fall 2002, an issue of *Seventeen* magazine featured a photo spread and fashion guide titled "Am I Emo?" The project of Vagrant Records and its founder Rich Egan is best described in Greenwald, *Nothing Feels Good*, 74: "Rich Egan's punk rock was a third way in the underground music scene. Too smart for mainstream, too lame for the subculture. Egan was one of the earliest examples of the suburban punk fan to which his label now caters, finding a new definition of punk in the rejection of the rigid orthodoxies of self-proclaimed punk."
9. Catherine Jurca, *White Diaspora: The Suburb and the Twentieth-Century American Novel* (Princeton, N.J.: Princeton University Press, 2001), 59.
10. Ibid., 11.
11. Ferron made these remarks at the San Francisco Queer Arts Festival in 2002.
12. What has long been common lore about the different spatial circumstances of gay men and lesbians—that gay men live in hip neighborhoods in cities, while lesbians generally have to traverse some bridge, tunnel, or undesirable stretch of freeway to participate in urban life—has recently been affirmed by the data in *The Gay and Lesbian Atlas* (as problematically framed some of the data is, since it is culled from the 2000 U.S. Census Bureau, which only accounted for same-sex couples). As the authors note, "Same sex male and female couples share only five states (California, Washington, Arizona, Massachusetts, and Vermont) among their respective top 10 states . . . and the difference in location patterns is even more apparent at the county level, where only San Francisco County appears in the top 10 counties for both male and female couples." They thus conclude, "Lesbian couples are less

urban than their gay male counterparts, as the top 10 counties for lesbian couples are much less urbanized than the top 10 counties for gay men. While 57 percent of gay male couples live in central counties of metropolitan areas with a population of more than 1 million, only 50 percent of lesbian couples live in these counties. Conversely, 28 percent of lesbian couples live in areas with populations between 250,000 and one million, while only 25 percent of gay male couples reside in these areas." See Gary J. Gates and Jason Ost, *The Gay and Lesbian Atlas* (Washington, D.C.: Urban Institute Press, 2004), 28.

13. Judith Halberstam, *In a Queer Time and Place* (New York: New York University Press, 2005), 5.

14. Among the most accessible of Chan's JJ Chinois art and performance projects is her website (http://www.jjchinois.com).

15. Iain Aitch has written an article for the *Guardian* about the Smiths' lead singer Morrissey's Latino fan base in Los Angeles, as well the documentary film on this phenomenon by William E. Jones. See Aitch, "Mad about Morrissey," *Guardian* (London), March 25, 2005.

16. "Dykes can Dance! The gals of Lesbians on Ecstasy deliver the goods," interview by John Custodio. Available online at the *Montreal Mirror* website (http://www.montrealmirror.com/ARCHIVES/2003/073103/diverscite_6.html).

5

"ANDERS ALS DIE ANDEREN,"
OR QUEERING THE SONG

Construction and Representation of Homosexuality
in German Cabaret Song Recordings before 1933

ANNO MUNGEN

INTRODUCTION: MUSICAL PERFORMANCE
AND GENDER IDENTITY

This chapter is devoted to the analysis of musical performance, which is not only based on aural experience but also refers to the visual, and in many cases is related to corporal representation reflecting gender identities.[1] Musical-theatrical performance, with its aural and visual aspects, offers diverse opportunities to play with gender identities and fulfill gendered dreams. As with the genre of opera, which was also constructed as a space for gender crossing (where men could perform as women and women as men), there is thus an implied opposition to the "real" world that is largely ruled by the politics of definition and separation.

Another space for the development of gender diversity came about at a time that was in fact politically less conservative and restricted. Germany in the 1920s offered a great deal of liberalism, creating opportunities for different approaches to gender other than a simple dichotomy of the sexes. Artistic space for gender crossing was created within the popular music culture. This was especially true for the German cabaret

song, or *Schlager*,[2] which revealed—in broader terms—a political significance, specifically toward sexual liberalism. Within the context of queer identities and the 1920s German Schlager, the issue of separation is reflected in a famous line used both as a title for a film as well as for a well-known song: the "Lila Lied" or "Purple Song." This title—"Anders als die Anderen" ("Being Other than the Others")—refers to social differentiation, expressing that a person or group of people can feel different from another group (the mainstream), reflecting on the social arrangement and the order of life.

Being "queer" can be exposed in public performance on one level using visual strategies of crossing gender identity through drag.[3] On a second level—as will be seen—it is expressed by specific musical means in order to represent "otherness" by what could be called *queering the song*. The fascination for drag on both levels is based on a feeling of uncertainty on the observer's side. What one sees and/or hears is not what the performer seems to be.[4]

Image in (musical) performance refers not simply to a pictorial representation of somebody (or something), but also to the question of identity. Here the music helps the performer/singer to create an image of herself by visual and aural means. Although aspects of gender and the visual are directly linked, I have organized this chapter in a specific way to concentrate on a medium that basically works without images but still reveals identity issues through a specific image: the record. As a nonvisual medium, the record creates images in the mind (based on experienced, live, or mediatized audiovisual performances on film).[5] After exploring the historical situation in Germany in the 1920s in the first section, I will discuss both live performance and film as media of reference for "pure" audio. I will take into account the visuality of the performance within the concept of cross-dressing as well as the aural representation in the audiovisual in the second section. I will argue in the third section that despite the fact that the recording concentrates on the aural and therefore can be described as restricted, the record seems to go further in representing a queer identity in two respects, beyond the "full-size" live performance and film. First, while the dresses on men and the suits on women function more as an "outer skin" and reflect the crossing of gender on a more superficial level, the voice not only comes—literally—from inside but is also based on the use of breath, being closer to human existence. Second, gramophone recordings open up different spaces for new live acts, both through the lack of visuality and—sometimes—the lack of lyrics.

BEING QUEER AND THE QUEST
FOR IDENTITY IN 1920s GERMANY

The relationship between sexual identity and the performative is given a particular value in the queer world. Queer people develop a sense of theatricality in everyday life in order to hide (if they have/had to) their sexual identity.[6] It is suggested that these circumstances have helped to create a specific fascination in the queer world for the performative not only within the theater itself but also in everyday life.

The German cabaret song, the Schlager, indicates this affinity in many ways.[7] In the 1920s the Schlager, with its witty lyrics, was a popular medium reflecting on the political and cultural situation of the Weimar Republic in a very general sense. Schlager were performed and heard not only in performance but were also spread through the media of modernity—the radio (Schär, 46), the gramophone (Schär, 43), and the movies (Schär, 51). Although the songs in many cases revealed erotic contexts,[8] gay performers—as the recordings show—usually did not come up with their own lyrics or music but mostly performed "straight" songs in their own manner, re-creating the existing music and situating it in a new performative context.[9] The recordings of these songs reflect the model of the straight world creating gay identities through artistic expression.

A famous exception to this is the "Lila Lied," which specifically refers to a gay context in both the lyrics and the music.[10] The song has all the qualities of a real Schlager. The tune is easy to sing and to memorize, offering a hymnlike tone appropriate to the function of the song within the community. The marching rhythm and the melody suggest the character of a national anthem, establishing a mood of unity. While the verses are composed in a minor key, the refrain shifts to a major key. This symbolic expression of change from suppression to hope could be understood by everybody.[11]

Berlin after World War I can serve as an example of how the transition from hiding sexual desire to acting out sexual identity in semipublic or public spaces (bars, theaters, and cabarets) started to play out. German society in the large cities of these years can be considered one of the most liberal in history.[12] During the 1920s, Berlin's bar scene and associated subculture was enormous, and included many venues frequented by homosexual women and men. Almost one hundred clubs and dance venues offered socializing and entertainment for different classes and different gender mixes: for either lesbians and gay men separately, for lesbians and gay men together, and also for gay and straight

people together. The glamorous and sophisticated bars and dance halls in the wealthy western part of the city at Kufürstendamm became fashionable both with the gay and the nongay crowd (Schär, 213).

Despite the fact that there were many venues for different classes within the gay subculture there was also a tendency toward mixing up the classes. There is a report of a men's bar called Mariencasino, where young men in drag and in sailor's outfits danced with students and bank accountants, as well as with older wealthy men, to the "Lila Lied" (Schär, 208). The fact that everybody danced to the same song created a sense of equality. The unifying tune, as well as the lyrics of the song and the feel of being the same—at least in one respect—helped to overcome social barriers. Being "other" in the first place meant being separated from the rest of (straight) society, be it rich or poor. But being other also created its own peer references, supported by the fact that everybody danced to this music. This example supports Christian Schär's assumption that Schlager music and dance in the 1920s played an important part in the process of defining social and sexual identities (Schär, 205). Male and female homosexuals of the 1920s created their own (sub)culture because they were dependant on these tools of self-expression. More than entertainment, the shared song fostered an urge to support and create one's self-confidence through the performative. The emancipation of gays and lesbians was expressed through music and dance and was fed by these means at the same time.

THE WOMAN'S DRESS

This chapter deals with historical performance analysis through a consideration of three levels: the live performance, performance on film, and—most important—performance on gramophone records. The main distinction between the first, second, and third levels is the difference between live and mediatized performance.[13] Live performance, with its audiovisual aspects, cannot be kept on records as a whole experience. Only particular aspects of stage performances can be re-created with the help of certain sources (as descriptions, photographs, etc. are presented in packaging). Compared to this, everyday performance is even more difficult to speak about.[14] Cabaret song is a particularly interesting example of the relationship of stage to everyday performance, and therefore also on the shift from public to private. The semiprivate situation of performance in some bars opens up a very private dimension, like that of music and dance at home, where two people might re-create the bar experience.

But even live performance on stage is—as I said before—difficult to reconstruct. The source material in newspapers and magazines is restricted,

especially as it relates to music, voice, and sound. An article on a locally well-known female impersonator of the 1920s in Cologne by the name of Tilla concentrates on the gender confusion the person creates, neglecting the actual performances he/she delivered.[15] The writer of the daily newspaper *Rheinische Zeitung* describes *her* dress and accessories and is fascinated with *his* male features: the muscular arms, the beer drinking, and so on. The fact that Tilla sang was of much less concern for the writer, who only mentions that she delivered the song in an "earthy" (*derb*) style.[16] Although we don't learn a lot about Tilla's actual performance, the description of her physical appearance indicates a good deal of male features. This is proved by a photograph of Tilla, released in the magazine *Die Freundin* in 1927.[17] Dressing generally creates specific relationships among body, gender, and identity. The fashion of the 1920s introduced a new style of women's dress, which was shorter and looser and favored a more casual male-looking haircut—the so-called *Bubikopf*.[18] For anybody (woman or man) wearing women's clothes this meant a new freedom and openness: fashion got looser, but the contact while dancing got tighter and offered new options, making erotic acts between partners possible (Schär, 136). In the context of dance music recordings I will be coming back to this aspect later. Women's fashion after 1920 offered women, as Schär suggests, a new self-consciousness in sexual terms. If this was true for women, it was also the case for men in drag—by wearing women's clothing, they could escape the body restrictions imposed by men's more (up)tight fashions of the time. Cross-dressing also demonstrated a high level of self-confidence in itself. Cross-dressing men like Tilla still lived in a basically homophobic society, but were brave enough to dress up as women.

While discussions of Tilla's performance rely on material published in print media, a famous example of woman-to-man cross-dressing in German movie history reveals musical aspects of this phenomenon. Although Reinhold Schünzel's comedy *Viktor und Viktoria* was completed while the Nazis were in power in the fall of 1933 and first released in December of the same year, it was still created with the cultural openness of the Weimar era.[19] Tilla's example, where cross-dressing serves equally to highlight such male characteristics as muscular arms and heavy drinking, seems almost simplistic when compared to the case of "gender trouble" reflected in *Viktor und Viktoria*. The movie's main character, Susanne Lohr (played by Renate Müller), is looking for a job and ends up playing a man who acts on stage as a woman.[20] At the beginning of the film, she is a woman who needs (out of circumstance rather than desire) to turn into a man, whose profession is then to be a woman on stage. That's how she becomes "*der* Viktoria," as she is called

in the movie, combining her second female name with the male article. The story takes place in Berlin, but leads the successful Viktoria very quickly to the Savoy Theatre in London.

The following five situations within the movie are of interest in moving toward a construction of gender through voice and body in performance:

1. The scene in a men's wardrobe of a Berlin theater, where Susanne, alias Viktor, is going to have her first appearance as Viktoria, exposes the movie's main female character as playing a man offstage. While other male artists are getting undressed and redressed with their costumes for their acts, Viktor puts on her wig and becomes Viktoria. This all happens with no dialogue and basically in silence. Music is heard only from the background, indicating that other cabaret acts are already going on.

2. Susanne's first stage appearance with a Spanish act and song, "Komm doch ein bißchen mit nach Madrid" ("Do you wanna take a ride to Madrid with me," with lyrics by Bruno Balz[21]) presents her as a woman (Susanne) who plays a man (Viktor) acting as a woman (Viktoria). She delivers the song in a high-pitched operatic tessitura, establishing no reference to any male characteristics. The musical (double) drag on a realistic level seems to make little sense if we consider that a man would be unlikely to have that perfection in imitating a women's voice. At the end of the performance Susanne uncovers her "true" identity as a man by taking off the wig. The short haircut underneath and the Spanish costume she is wearing highlights her broad naked shoulders and gives the impression of being a man.

3. Susanne, at her first London appearance, performs the same act. She not only sings the song in English but also in a different style, making the gender crossing of the song more plausible. She starts off in a low speaking voice and slowly shifts into a singing manner, still remaining in her low register. After a dance interlude, her style of singing changes again. Now, indecisively, it shifts a few times between high and low pitch. After the act is finished, she again takes off her wig, to a surprised audience.

4. After her big success we find Susanne in her hotel room together with Viktor (Susanne's friend who manages her). Susanne is getting dressed to go out, wearing a male evening outfit. Walking along, the two start singing a duet, "An einen Tag im Frühling."[22] In this scene she sings in a high-pitched woman's voice, which

makes sense because she is shown as a private character without audience in this scene: both know she is a woman. When she reaches the restaurant, Viktor, the young male and glorious star, gets all the attention, especially from the female crowd.

5. In the final scene of the movie, it is now the real Viktor presenting the Spanish act at the Savoy. Viktor himself is Viktoria, wearing the same Spanish women's dress as Susanne before, and performs the song in German. Susanne's serious singing and dancing act becomes much more of a slapstick number as the "real" man-to-woman travesty takes on the quality of a parody of a drag show. Viktor uses his low register and only sometimes switches to a higher pitch, giving his performance a more flamboyant touch.

Since the lyrics of the Spanish song are not gendered (i.e., they do not focus on either female or male), they can be sung by either a man or a woman. The movie is built around the performance of this particular song, which is delivered in full three times, indicating the variety of options in gender construction. The treatment of Susanne's singing within the whole movie is not consistent—being "natural" on the one hand, but also imitating male characteristics. This fits perfectly with the woman-to-man-to-woman confusion. Susanne consistently sings with a high female voice and it is only in the London performance that she comes up with a more masculine sound. Although the treatment of the voice is part of the performance in the movie, visuality remains the important tool to indicate the gender switches within this movie. We need to *see* in order to understand.

THE MAN'S VOICE

The new medium of radio was sometimes criticized in general terms for its programs, as expressed in an article by Hermann von Wedderkop, who considered nothing else to be as dull as the popular-entertainment music programs on the radio. In his opinion all other musical genres were more interesting, be they classical (Ludwig van Beethoven, Johannes Brahms, or Franz Schubert) or—as he put it—"der gesang der tunten" ("the songs of the queens"; Schär, 47). This brief hint of gay cabaret performance on radio suggests that the topic in question was not only treated as a discrete musical genre; it was also part of an actual discourse. The performances and recordings in question were, in fact, played on radio and found an appreciative audience. If music performance represents and constructs sexual identity, it is important to realize that not only a selected audience

received the message. Rather, given radio's status as a medium of public, social and musical construction (Schär, 54),[23] it can be surmised that homosexuality was not completely censored or relegated to the private domain.

With its portable apparatus—the gramophone—music on recordings re-created the public medium of radio as private, especially if we consider the fact that the record only became a mass medium form of entertainment relatively late, and at the same time as the radio. The gramophone player made it possible to set up musical performances in various contexts and environments: in a bar, in a private setting at home, or even at a picnic on the lawn in the country. Yet, while bands and piano players usually furnished the bars with dance music, gramophones were mostly used in private contexts and brought modern dance music to the homes (Schär, 48, 127).

Queer contexts in recordings of the 1920s can be found most often through the fact that men sang songs that were originally written for a women performer, and women sang songs that were supposed to be for men. My interest lies not so much in the phenomenon as such, but rather the way the performers delivered their songs. More specifically, I will look at recordings of the time,[24] considering the fact that sound recordings compared to live performance and films are based on reduction. In all cases they lacked visual images, and in many cases the lyrics of the verses were banned on the recordings. Given these restrictions, I am concerned primarily with the strategies used by queer performers in creating new/alternative meanings. Consider how queering a song was preeminently a question of performance: one strategy refers to the question of vocal performance as seen with the example of *Viktor und Viktoria*. Since the visuals of performance are missing in the examples to be discussed here, the voice itself gains a higher significance. Yet the reduction, I want to argue, enriches the experience.

Claire Waldorff, performing "Ach wie ich die Lena liebe" from 1920 (*Schwule Lieder*, disc 2, track 15), sings in a low voice without using her head register. With the often repeated "Ha! Ha! Ha!" and its descending three-note motif, Waldorff forces her voice into an extreme low register, implying a male vocal gesture. Another song performed by Waldorff, "Hannelore" from 1929 (*Schwule Lieder*, disc 2, track 18), portrays a woman appearing both in men's clothing and in the new female fashion with the characteristic Bubikopf.[25] The performer takes the position of an observer peeking on Hannelore while she walks through Berlin. Although the vocal line is set higher than in the example discussed above, Waldorff does not use her head register. Her interpretation creates a particular image and recalls the sound of a teenage Berliner newspaper

kid, a *Zeitungsjunge* selling on the street. Both recordings are examples of what could be called—in analogy to cross-dressing—"cross-singing," offering different ideas of masculinity. The first can be considered a parody of a "real" (butch) man, while the second one plays with a boyish and androgynous appeal.

Recordings by male performers provide similar observations concerning the diverse approaches to the musical construction of gender through cross-singing. It is interesting to note that most performers generally keep their voice in a regular register, not implying, as Waldorff does, a switch of gender. Yet, the recordings of the mostly tenor voices offer a great deal of variety on how to handle the given gender switch through the lyrics. This variety is not surprising if we take into account that German cabaret singing of the 1920s was largely characterized by witty language and in live performances through gestures, movements, and the actual acting. Some of the recordings just keep the usual—for those days—light and sometime nasal quality of a regular tenor's voice. Others insert head-register singing at particular moments to introduce flamboyant aspects to the performance. One example is Paul O'Montis's recording of "Was hast Du für Gefühle, Moritz" ("What Are Your Feelings, Moritz?") from 1927 (*Schwule Lieder*, disc 1, track 5) where, especially in the second refrain, he increasingly uses the high register. Moritz, a guy who can't decide who to love and what to be, is sexually attracted to both men and women.

The vocal representations of queering in a famous Schlager of the period, "Am Sonntag will mein Süßer mit mir segeln gehen" (*Schwule Lieder*, disc 2, track 11) is, unlike the other examples cited, not just based on the strategy of cross-singing.[26] The three given verses in this recording by Theo Lucas offer different perspectives on the same plot: Two lovers are planning to go sailing over the weekend. Each verse presents a different situation and another main character who, in all three cases, answers, "On Sunday my [male] sweetheart wants to go sailing with me"[27]—the first line of the song's refrain. The first verse narrates the story of a secretary telling her boss that she wants to spend the weekend on the boat with her lover (and not with him). Although Lucas in this 1929 recording takes over the part of the secretary, he basically delivers this first refrain in a neutral manner, using his regular tenor voice. The second verse introduces Minna, one Professor Krause's daughter, who explains—in a Berlin accent—to her mother that she has no time over the weekend. Again, Lucas does not introduce any kind of feminization to his voice, although once more he sings the part of a woman. In fact, the opposite seems to be the case: the slightly rough-sounding Berlin accent gives this verse a relatively tough or

butch color. The third verse, compared to the second, includes softer singing, establishing a contrast by using high-pitched notes in the head register, especially on the main beat of the bar. This verse tells the story of a woman coming to the famous Eldorado Bar in Berlin (a place mainly frequented by gay men and where Lucas himself performed as a singer).[28] The woman asks a man to go out with her, and Lucas, now slipping into the role of the man, gives—and this is the punch line of the whole song—the now well-known answer that he is not available because he is going out on that boat trip with his (*male*) sweetheart. The voice not only transports the listener into the atmosphere of queer and camp in the bar, but also implies the man is smiling at the woman (which, of course, we don't see): how could she have missed the fact that he was not interested in her in the first place? It also implies the self-confidence I was discussing earlier. From our perspective, the flamboyant (*tuntige*) expression in this third verse (and in other of these recordings) might be associated today with negative images of camp. The qualification of camp as a mannerism has shifted historically. In the 1920s it had a modern and even avant-garde appeal. The fact that some (supposedly) straight radio listener expressed his favor for the "gesang der tunten" broadcast across the whole of Germany reflects the fascination for this idiom.

Second, popular music heard on radio and records in general sometimes creates a need to see and even—as will be shown now—to act;[29] listening to music becomes a performance in itself.[30] Many recordings of these 1920s songs are dominated by instrumental playing, and only the refrain of the song was performed with voice, a phenomenon called *Refraingesang*.[31] While banning the verse lyrics relates and contributes toward the tendency of reduction observed in the examples above, it is interesting to see how these reductions opened up different interpretations, options, and functionalities of the music. In effect, the song with no lyrics in the verses can be interpreted as a stimulus for something else. The lack of visuality and lyrics relate to the fact that the recordings of Schlager music of the 1920s mainly had the function to be danced to as the contemporary term *Gramophon-Tanzplatte* ("Gramophone Dance Record"; Schär, 42) suggests.

The recorded singer's performance within the refrain was, however, not simply an invitation to dance; it was also an invitation to act out the song. Many songs used metaphors of erotic allusion, as the song "Heinrich, wo greifst du denn hin?" ("Heinrich, where are *you* going?" or "Heinrich, what are *you* doing?") recorded by Heinrich Koppel in 1929 (*Schwule Lieder*, disc 2, track 2) suggests. The recording starts out with a section executed by the orchestra, which can be recognized as

the first "verse." The refrain sung by Koppel is delivered in a flamboyant manner. His soft tenor's voice highlights the name "Heinrich" by switching to the head register. One might assume that Koppel's Heinrich actually did reach out for him, which makes him change the voice at that point. The refrain is followed by an orchestral interlude—the second "verse"—and the recording finishes with one more refrain. If we take the given situation of the Gramophon-Tanzplatte of two men dancing, maybe one dressed up as a woman (think of Tilla's picture), one might imagine that the couple after listening to the first refrain takes over the roles as the lyrics suggest: one is the singer, and one is Heinrich. Time for "acting" while moving their bodies to the music is offered during the orchestral interlude. The dancers don't need the full lyrics and its story for their dance, because they create their own story, and the missing lyrics become an enrichment to the dancers. They/we only hear what they/we fill up with their/our own images and acts.

CONCLUSION

Compared to other modes of performances discussed above, audio recordings reveal different functionalities and offer new options.[32] The songs, revealing erotic contexts, offered an opportunity for the dancers to act out the music. Their eroticism invites the dancer-listeners, the "new performers," to act "it" out, to experience the song physically with each other. Therefore, two levels of music performance can be distinguished in this case—one as mediatized, the other one as live represented by the dancers. The first performer is the actual singer of the song (relating to the concept of performance on stage), and the second performer is the dancer-listener re-creating that performance as a non-stage act and everyday performance.

The relationship between live performance and mediatized performance is complicated and also relates to the specifics of the actual historical status in media discourse. In the 1920s the reflection of life in media, and media in life, gave *queering the song* a public space. At the same time, publicity and feedback also gave reasons for a queer identity in semiprivate and very private situations in bars and at home. In purely audio representations of the queer, the singing compared to the lyrics, the treatment of the voice, and the gestured expression of singing can all become indicators of specific gender identities and crossings.

The phenomenon discussed is captured here by the term *cross-singing*, in which the voice touches the specificity of gender. If we do not know what the person wears, the effect of difference, which is intrinsic for drag, can only be achieved musically. Being "other among

others" through the acts of performances finally gains a physical quality that could be exhibited in dance venues as a social reality. What the hymn-like song "Anders als die Andern" expressed in a more political (public) way is taken in these performances to a physical (private) level. As such, the restriction of the medium is also its richness. Most of the recordings—especially those in *Viktor und Viktoria*—show the variety rather than constructing a new, complete, and consistent gender. In the case of audio recordings, flamboyant aspects contextualize the verbal parody. Queering the song in the 1920s—as the examples here show—did not just create a new "straight" perspective on gay identities; the transformed songs meant something else, something different, something *queer*, in order to be "Anders als die Andern."

NOTES

1. Simon Frith, *Performing Rites: On the Value of Popular Music* (Cambridge, Mass.: Harvard University Press, 1996), 211; Anno Mungen, "The Music Is the Message: The Day Jimi Hendrix Burned His Guitar: Film, Musical Instrument, and Performance as Music Media," in *Popular Music and Film*, ed. Ian Inglis (London: Wallflower, 2003), 60–76; Anno Mungen, "Von Jeanne d'Arc zu den 'Memoiren einer Sängerin' Geschlechterwechsel im Rollenrepertoire Wilhelmine Schröder-Devrients," in *Bühnenklänge: Festschrift für Sieghart Döhring zum 65. Geburtstag*, ed. Thomas Betzwieser, Daniel Brandenburg, Raimer Framke, Arnold Jacobshagen, Marion Linhardt, Stephanie Schroedter, and Thomas Steiert (Munich: Ricordi, 2005), 59–72.
2. The term *Schlager* does not really translate properly into English. The closest translation seems to be "pop song," which does not include the specific musical characteristics implied by the German term.
3. Elizabeth Ashburn, "Drag Shows: Drag Kings and Female Impersonators" (87) and Andres Mario Zervignon, "Drag Shows: Drag Queens and Female Impersonators" (90), in *The Queer Encyclopedia of Music, Dance, and Musical Theater*, ed. Claude J. Summers (San Francisco: Cleis, 2004).
4. Judith Butler, *Gender Trouble: Feminism and the Subversion of Identity*, 2nd ed. (New York: Routledge, 1999), 175.
5. "Mediatized" was introduced by Philip Auslander, *Liveness: Performance in a Mediatized Culture* (London: Routledge, 1999), 5–6.
6. Bud Coleman, "Cabarets and Revues," in *The Queer Encyclopedia of Music, Dance, and Musical Theater*, ed. Claude J. Summers (San Francisco: Cleis, 2004), 39.
7. Christian Schär, *Der Schlager und seine Tänze im Deutschland der 20er Jahre: Sozialgeschichtliche Aspekte zum Wandel in der Musik- und Tanzkultur*

während der Weimarer Republik (Zürich: Chronos Verlag, 1991), 35; hereafter, page numbers cited parenthetically in the text.

8. Volker Kühn, *Hoppla, wir beben: Kabarett einer gewissen Republik 1918–1933* (Weinheim, Germany: Quadriga, 1988), 147.

9. Ralf Jörg Raber, "'Wir . . . sind, wie wir sind!' Homosexualität auf Schallplatte 1900–1936," *Invertito: Jahrbuch für die Geschichte der Homosexualitäten* 5 (2003): 47.

10. The song can be heard on *Schwule Lieder, Perlen der Kleinkunst: Historische & Lesbische Aufnahmen 1908–1933*, disc 1, track 2, Membran International 221324-311/A-B, 2003. This set of recordings was used for this chapter; songs are hereafter cited parenthetically in the text.

11. The full text of the lyrics can be read in Ruth Margarethe Roellig, *Berlins lesbische Frauen* (1928; reprint with French translation, Paris: Cahiers Gai-Kitsch-Camp, 1992, 46–49).

12. See Schwules Museum, ed., *Goodbye to Berlin! 100 Jahre Schwulenbewegung: Eine Ausstellung des Schulen Museums und der Akademie der Künste* (Berlin: Verlag rosa Winkel, 1997), 123–28.

13. Auslander, 5–6.

14. Frith, *Performing Rites*, 204.

15. Although Berlin was the center of gay and lesbian life, it must be pointed out that other big cities in the 1920s, such as Cologne, also had vibrant cultural and subcultural scenes.

16. This article from May 5, 1926, is reproduced in Centrum Schwule Geschichte, ed., *Himmel und Hölle: 100 Jahre Schwul in Köln* (Cologne: Selbstverlag, 2003), 29.

17. *Die Freundin* was a magazine for lesbians, where one could find many personal ads and advertisements for woman impersonators. The image discussed here is reproduced in Centrum Schule Geschichte, ed., *Himmel und Hölle*, 30.

18. Heike Schader, "Konstruktionen weiblicher Homosexualität in Zeitschriften homosexueller Frauen in den 1920er Jahren," *Invertito* 2 (2000): 16ff.

19. Rick Thompson, "He and She: Weimar Screwballwerk," *Senses of Cinema: An Online Journal Devoted to the Serious and Eclectic Discussion of Cinema* 22 (2002) (online at http://www.sensesofcinema.com/contents/cteq/02/22/viktor.html). There was great interest in the Weimar years in the topic of cross-dressing, as can be seen in movies like *Amor am Steuer* (1921); *Der Himmel auf Erden* (1927), with Reinhold Schünzel in a female part; *Donna Juana* (1927) with Elisabeth Bergner in the title role; and *Die—oder keine* (1932). The 1982 Blake Edwards remake (*Victor, Victoria*, with Julie Andrews and James Garner) is based on the story of the German original.

20. For a more detailed summary of *Viktor und Viktoria*, see Thompson, "He and She."

21. Bruno Balz also wrote the lyrics for an explicit gay Schlager in 1924, "Bubi, lass uns Freunde sein"; see Raber, "'Wir . . . sind, wie wir sind!,'" 64.

22. The operetta-like movie as an early representative of the sound era offers intriguing musical solutions. What is unusual is that Franz Doelle's score for *Viktor und Viktoria* integrates a mix of realistic sound, spoken regular dialogue, rhymed spoken dialogue, rhymed sung dialogue in a recitative manner, singing within regular situations (as in the case of this duet), and singing in stage situations, and also includes scenes without any other sound or dialogue that are fully accompanied by diagetic music, picking up on the tradition of the silent movie era. The German cinema of the early 1930s was extremely creative, with solutions and suggestions for the new medium of the "talkies." The regret of losing the "good old silent movies"—with their highly differentiated culture of music—combined with a fascination for operetta stimulated, in the first years of the new medium, many different approaches to sound in film; see Thompson, "He and She."

23. Raber, "'Wir . . . sind, wie wir sind!,'" 39, sees the record more as an indicator of changes in society.

24. In addition to *Schwule Lieder* (see note 9, above), the following list of CDs gives an overview of new releases of the recordings discussed here. See *Wir sind wie wir sind! Homosexualität auf Schallplatte, Teil 1; Aufnahmen 1900–1936*, Bear Family, BCD 16055AS; *Die schwule Plattenkiste: Vom Hirschfeldlied zum Lila Lied. Schwules und Lesbisches in historischen Aufnahmen* (Edition Berliner Musenkinder, 05183); *Es ist ja ganz gleich, wen wir lieben: Lieder vom anderen Ufer 1926–1942*, Mister Phono.

25. Raber, "'Wir . . . sind, wie wir sind!,'" 49.

26. Raber "'Wir . . . sind, wie wir sind!,'" 51, points out that the third verse used in this recording was not usually found in the printed version of the song.

27. In German, the distinction between male and female is made with this noun; "Liebster" is male.

28. Raber, "'Wir . . . sind, wie wir sind!,'" 52.

29. Auslander, *Liveness*, 73ff.

30. Frith, *Performing Rites*, 203.

31. Raber, "'Wir . . . sind, wie wir sind!,'" 62 and n. 60, argues that this practice derives from the fact that the entertainment industry was dominated by male singers, while only particular big female stars recorded the songs. With the special practice of Refraingesang, according to Raber, it did not matter if the song was sung by a man or a woman. Yet the gender crossing within the song remains a fact. Raber himself earlier points out that the flamboyant and the queer had the quality of avant-garde. Therefore it could be argued that the recordings also reflected on this aspect.

32. Auslander, *Liveness*, 73.

PART 2

Queering Boundaries

6

TEARS AND SCREAMS
Performances of Pleasure and Pain in the Bolero

VANESSA KNIGHTS

Over the course of its long history the bolero has shifted from the relatively private (or semipublic) performance of the serenade with simple guitar accompaniment in nineteenth-century Western Cuba to the public stage and wider audience of theatres, radio, the recording industry, film, and eventually television.[1] The sonic requirements of the new performance arenas and early recording techniques influenced the change in instrumentation, with the use of piano, orchestras, and big bands, which paradoxically served to place increased emphasis on the vocality of the performer, who became the focal point for audience identification. As the bolero was internationalized the original rhythmic hegemony of the *cinquillo cubano* (five notes' value: long–short–long–short–long) was lost and melodies increasingly followed the prosody of the lyrics. With the advent of electrical recording, more sensitive condenser microphones, and improved amplification techniques in the 1920s, the singer's voice and timbre of instruments such as the violin were more closely identified in the production of an apparently intimate sound.

The voice in the bolero may be yearning and seductive, offering promises of eternal love and images of the ideal other to the emotionally involved listener. Indeed, the bolero is commonly conceived of as a discourse privileging unrestrained romanticism or sentimentality, and love in its multiple variations is the predominant theme of the bolero.[2]

However, it is important to note that many boleros deal with the flip side of what might be deemed romantic love: deception, disillusionment, jealousy, abandonment, and betrayal. Through a study of a corpus of 635 boleros, María del Carmen de la Peza Casares notes that 80 percent of the songs studied focus on negative aspects of relationships.[3] According to the Puerto Rican critic Iris Zavala, the bolero speaks the language of desire, of its absence and presence, of illusion and disillusionment and is therefore not so much about love or pleasure but about a desire that by definition is impossible to realize: the pursuit of the unattainable other.[4] It would thus seem to express modern theories of desire in its tension between absence and desire for presence. As Manuel Delgado Ruiz notes, "Es como si inopinadamente, los Lara, Domínguez, Machín, etcétera, hubieran intuido, en clave músico-sentimental, las actuales teorías del deseo" (It's as if unexpectedly, Lara, Domínguez, Machín, etc., had intuited, in an emotional-musical code, current theories of desire).[5] This psychoanalytic interpretation of the bolero is further explored by Karen Poe, who examines it as an attempt to erase difference and transgress the limits of the ego through an analysis of the discourse of the bolero, the grain or erotic texture of the voice and the closeness of dance, in relation to the oneiric world of impossible dreams and a return to the space of Julia Kristeva's maternal semiotic.[6]

Following on from Poe's analysis of the depiction of femininity as the repressed "other" or Freudian "dark enigma" in bolero lyrics, many critics have interpreted the bolero as a conservative genre in terms of gender politics.[7] In other words, the desire being articulated is resolutely male and heterosexual. However, as I have argued elsewhere, the bolero is far from being an exclusively male-produced discourse.[8] In addition to numerous female performers, there were many famous women composers of boleros such as the Mexicans María Grever and Consuelo Velázquez, and the Cubans Isolina Carrillo and Marta Valdés, to name but a few.[9] Frances Aparicio engages in a more nuanced reading of the bolero that attempts to take into account the ambivalences inherent in the genre with regard to gender.[10] She draws on two Puerto Rican texts: Iris Zavala's essay "De héroes y heroinas en lo imaginario social: El discurso amoroso del bolero" ("Of Heroes and Heroines in the Social Imaginary: The Amorous Discourse of the Bolero") and Luis Rafael Sánchez's "fabulation," *La importancia de llamarse Daniel Santos* (*The Importance of Being Daniel Santos*).[11] Along with Zavala and Poe, Aparicio traces the development of bolero lyrics from the Western traditions of courtly love and romanticism through the *modernista* imagery of poets such as Rubén Darío, in which women are mythified as almost divine figures, eternal and unattainable seductresses, objects of

male unrequited longing or unconsummated love.[12] In contrast to this idealization, many lyrics feature a rather decadent femme fatale drawn from the nineteenth-century romantic tradition of poems dedicated to "fallen" women. While this would seem to fall into the typical dichotomy of woman as angel or whore, the latter is often celebrated rather than denigrated. Prostitutes and relationships outside the legal confines of marriage were particularly immortalized in the boleros of the prolific (and iconic) Mexican composer Agustín Lara, who began his career as a pianist in brothels and cabarets of ill repute. In these boleros the motifs of absence, separation, and abandonment are central, and Aparicio suggests that they are a reaction to the increased access of women to public spaces as Latin America became increasingly industrialized and urbanized through the course of the twentieth century. In contrast to these narratives of loss, Aparicio argues that women composers and singers break with social norms in boleros that often take up this motif of separation to voice women's desire for an alternative, independent path in life in which the emphasis is on mobility and freedom of movement, clearly subverting the gendered binary division of masculine activity and feminine passivity.[13] However, Aparicio's reading of the libidinal economy inscribed in the bolero begins by examining songs in which the power differential between men and women is articulated through a discourse of male sexual domination. The synechdochal representation of women through fragmented eroticized body parts—particularly the eyes, lips, mouth, and hands—would again seem to take up a long-standing poetic tradition, harking back to the troubadours, in which women are portrayed as fetishized objects of male desire and fantasy. Indeed, in a later analysis she asserts that in bolero lyrics women are inscribed in the sentimental discourse of patriarchal society as the object of male desire and unrequited love, physically absent and emotionally distant.[14] That notwithstanding, in an inversion of traditional male-female relationships in a patriarchal context, the male in the bolero is frequently presented as suffering and vulnerable, victimized by the female.[15] Aparicio cites "Usted" ("You"), by the Mexican composer Gabriel Ruiz, as an example of a bolero inculpating women as the source of men's problems. It begins with the lines "Usted es la culpable / de todas mis angustias" (You are responsible / for all my anxieties).[16] However, as these accusations serve to reveal male dependency on women's love and presence, the woman in "Usted" is constructed as the man's hope and ultimately his life.

Aparicio draws on Zavala's analyses of the discursive ambiguity of the bolero, which focus on the gender fluidity of the central signifiers or semiotic shifters, *yo* (I) and *tú/usted* (you). The majority of boleros

are not addressed to a specific named, and therefore gendered, subject. Furthermore, many bolero lyrics make no explicit reference to gender whatsoever, allowing for multiple meanings that shift through performance depending on who is singing, who is listening, and whether the listener identifies with the singing subject or the addressee (or both), thereby facilitating hetero- and homoerotic identifications, queer/straight positionings, and hetero- and homosocial bonding.[17] For example, "Tú me acostumbraste" ("You Got Me Used To"), by Frank Domínguez, includes no gendered adjectives and has been recorded by such diverse artists as Elena Burke, René Cabel, Lucho Gatica, and Olga Guillot without requiring any morphological transformation. In its oblique references to "esas cosas" (those things) or "un mundo raro" (a strange world) it opens up possibilities for a new semantics of the homoerotic articulation of desire.[18] In a fascinating article about melodrama and nostalgia, the Puerto Rican critic Eliseo Colón Zayas discusses a number of bolero recordings in which the heteronormative binary divisions of gender and sexuality are clearly broken down through forms of vocative address, combinations of male and female voices, and audience/singer cross-identifications.[19] A fluid space is created for diverse subjectivities to be expressed, thus queering the normative, heteropatriarchal constructions of gender and sexuality.

The indeterminacy of bolero lyrics also allows the relatively easy regendering of lyrics; for example, "Usted" (discussed earlier) has been performed by the American singer Eydie Gorme and simply transformed into "Usted es *el* culpable."[20] A space is opened up through the ambivalent gender politics of the discourse of the bolero for a strong female voice that may be accusatory or passionate, and erotically transgressive. For example, the lyrics of Mexican composer Consuelo Velázquez's "Bésame mucho" ("Kiss Me a Lot"), premiered by Chela Campos in 1941, openly express sexual desire through a repeated series of imperative exhortations that suggest more than a modest kiss on the mouth. Furthermore, the bolero provides a discourse of affective self-disclosure in both the public and private realms as romantic music is not just used as a background sound for courtship in Latin America. As Deborah Pacini Hernández notes, it may be used actively as a surrogate voice that articulates emotion and negotiates relationships through such acts as dedicating a song on the radio, giving someone a record, or serenading a loved one.[21] While the bolero can contest patriarchal categories of gender by subverting the binary of masculine activity and feminine passivity, thereby allowing women to express openly sexual desire, passion, and anger (traditionally masculine qualities), its conventions also provide a sanctioned musical space within which men

can cathartically express their emotions and sensitivity (traditionally feminine attributes): big boys can—and do—cry.

René Campos argues that the masculine voice expresses both passion and vulnerability through the bittersweet lyrics of the bolero and vocal techniques such as *portamento*, the lengthening of syllables at the end of a phrase.[22] However, this technique is by no means exclusive to male singers. It is a feature of the *filin* ("feeling") style made famous by female singers such as the Cubans Elena Burke and Olga Guillot. Filin, as its name suggests, is an explicitly emotional or expressive style of singing achieved through various techniques.[23] It can be characterized not only by features of composition and vocal technique that can be traced back to the influence of U.S. jazz and race records in Cuba in the 1930s and 1940s—for example, the use of impressionistic or jazz-inflected harmonies and the varying of tempo and stress—but also by its gestural performance style incorporating silences and pauses for dramatic effect.[24] Through the explicit emphasis on deliberate performance, filin provides a queer cultural space in which gender identities and sexual roles can be destabilized.

In the case of male bolero singers, it is interesting to note that the blurring of traditional gender attributes that occurs within the lyrics and the performance onstage on the whole does not necessarily seem to compromise the perceived masculinity of the singers offstage or affect their popularity. The "Inquieto Anacobero" (Devil that never stands still) Daniel Santos, also known as the "Ace of Hearts" or the "Charming Voice," was a legendary Don Juan figure (in)famous for drinking to excess, brawling, and getting arrested. As captured in the iconography of his record covers, his image is that of the hard-drinking, smoking man frequenting cantinas and listening to boleros on the jukebox (the Victrola, or *vellonera*). His position as a crooner of romantic songs, such as "Dos gardenias" ("Two Gardenias")—which was composed by a woman, Isolina Carrillo, in 1947—did not interfere with his status as iconic "protomacho" par excellence.[25] A perhaps more obviously "romantic" heartthrob is the brilliantine-haired Lucho Gatica, who with his suave image was allegedly the dream man of thousands of female admirers. However, his clear dominion of high registers could be described as feminine according to traditional categorizations of vocal gender. While on the one hand Gatica is identified as the heterosexual, attractive *galán* (heartthrob), as José Quiroga notes, the "Gentleman of Song" is a potential border crosser with whom a homosexual audience has also identified.[26] Even more fascinating is the process by which an openly effeminate performer like Juan Gabriel, whose closeted homosexuality has been described as a *secreto a voces* (open secret), has

gained the affections of the Mexican public in a society perhaps more noted for its overt homophobia and machismo.[27]

However, on the whole, the bolero performers who have become queer Hispanic icons are women whose lives are integral to their artistic aura, such as La Lupe and Chavela Vargas. These are female divas, as defined by Alberto Mira in his dictionary of Hispanic gay and lesbian culture. He notes, "Quizá la clave que define a la diva es el modo en que habita su propio mito, el modo en que su vida supura en sus creaciones." (Perhaps the key to defining the diva [as opposed to the star] is the way in which she inhabits her own myth, the way in which her life oozes through her creations.)[28] Similarly, for José Quiroga, La Lupe is a queer idol or fallen diva precisely because of the taboo elements of her broken life of "rumor, innuendo and myth."[29] The fascination these wounded divas exact from gay audiences is complex, and the identification is not necessarily on the level of gender or sexuality. It may be accounted for by many factors, including identification with the marginal and vulnerable combined with a survivalist aesthetics of strength (pace Gloria Gaynor), with resilience in the face of emotional suffering and intense pain, with risqué eroticism and excess, with the semiotics of glamour. In his analysis of Judy Garland, a key icon for the Anglophone lesbian, gay, bisexual, transgender, and queer community, Richard Dyer suggests that it is the combination of suffering and survival that produces a particular register of intensely authentic feeling or emotional intensity.[30] In the words of Quiroga, "La Lupe stands for the raw instead of the cooked, for not being afraid to make a scene and scream and shout."[31]

La Lupe was born Guadalupe Victoria Yoli Raimond on December 23, 1936, in the *barrio popular* (working-class neighborhood) of San Pedrito in Santiago de Cuba.[32] From an early age she showed a natural talent for music and, influenced by the performances of the filin star Olga Guillot, declared that she wanted to be an artiste. Her nickname "La Yiyiyi" stems from the interjections that characterized her exuberant, youthful performances. However, her father (a worker for Bacardi Rum) was quite strict and insisted on her acquiring an education. She duly graduated as a schoolteacher in Havana in 1958 and, following her father's instructions, proceeded to marry that same year. She married a musician, Eulogio "Yoyo" Reyes and with another singer, Tina, they formed the Tropicuba Trío. Once she was liberated from her father, La Lupe's nonconformist and rebellious character began to manifest itself more clearly. She was not content to share center stage and frequently ignored Yoyo's direction in her performances. Professional and personal differences (Yoyo's affair with Tina) led to the breakup of both the marriage and the group in 1960. This blurring of La Lupe's private and public life was to mark her career.

She began to perform solo in a small nightclub, La Red (which still exists in Havana), and soon had an enthusiastic crowd of fans who packed the tiny locale, applauding wildly at the end of each number. La Lupe was a cultural phenomenon, reputedly admired by artists as diverse as Guillermo Cabrera Infante, Ernest Hemingway, Pablo Picasso, and Jean-Paul Sartre. Her uninhibited stage show was marked by her transgressive performative style, which was excessive in both vocal technique and bodily display and highly erotically suggestive, breaking with social norms of decorum and passivity for women in Cuba in the 1950s. Her flamboyance called attention to the artifice of presumed natural gender roles through its acting out of images of excess, marked by an excessive intensity of emotion and feeling. Indeed, La Lupe frequently stated in interviews that feeling is the essence of life. There is a sustained tension between this confessional authenticity or sincere feeling and her radically aggressive performativity. In a June 2000 interview I conducted with Jesús Madruga, journalist and presenter for Radio Cadena Habana, he stated that for him La Lupe stood out because of her performances rather than her voice (in contrast with other Cuban singers who were her contemporaries such as Celia Cruz, Freddy, or Olga Guillot). That is not to deny her tremendous vocal range and sense of phrasing. Yet while her voice has a particular timbre and vibrato all of its own, a strident raw quality described by Quiroga as "like tin foil, like shattered glass, like nails on a blackboard,"[33] La Lupe sang with more than her throat. She sang with her whole body. She would scream, laugh wildly, cry, swear at the audience, bite, pinch and scratch herself, hit her pianist Homero with her shoes, lift her skirts, tear her clothes, pull her hair, stamp her feet, throw her beads and false eyelashes at the crowd, bang her head against the scenery and fall to the ground.

Sitting on men or women in the audience and moaning and groaning in imitation of orgasm, La Lupe publicly flaunted her sexuality. According to Cuban commentators, she wore strong makeup and revealing clothes associated more conventionally with *putas* (tramps, whores). However, her act was not exclusively characterized by excessive bodily display. In one of her key numbers, "No me quieras así" ("Don't Love Me that Way") by Facundo Rivero, she denied the audience visual access to her face, physically controlling the spectacle by facing the wall, hence the song's nickname "La pared" ("The Wall"). La Lupe has been described by Cuban novelist and playwright Humberto Arenal as the most outrageous female performer in Cuba at that time, breaking with social norms of decorum and passivity for women in her explosively dynamic performances. Her flamboyance called attention to the artifice of presumed natural gender roles through its acting out of images of excess, and her

success in 1960, recognized by the awarding of a gold disc for popularity by RCA Victor, is perhaps an indication of the heady atmosphere
and tensions following the revolutionary triumph of 1959. However, La
Lupe was not popular with all sectors of the public and music press. Her
first LP, released in 1961 on Discuba, was titled *Con el diablo en el cuerpo*
(*With the Devil Inside*), and indeed that is how some commentators described her: dionysiac, scandalous, eccentric, mad, hysterical, feverish,
in the throes of a seizure, flailing, flagellating, convulsive, in a trance.
These terms, conventionally associated with feminine emotion and irra-
tionality, are also used by her fans when praising her.[34] She is allied with
the transgressive figures of the gorgon, witch, madwoman, or prostitute.
While her radical, aggressive style was well suited to the marginal space
of La Red, it did not translate to the mainstream medium of television,
as a disastrous experience in 1961 would show. She was dismissed as being in bad taste, vulgar, and even grotesque for her sexual abandon. The
identification of her vocality with a violent, belligerent female sexuality,
both sadistic and masochistic, provoked both desire and fear in that it
seemed out of control. Both were characterized as primal and torrential; her rhythm qualified as savage. As Leslie Dunn and Nancy Jones
have noted in their study of embodied female vocality, "Whether it is
celebrated, eroticized, demonized, ridiculed or denigrated, [the female
voice] is always stigmatized, ideologically 'marked' and construed as a
'problem' for the (male) social critic or auditor who demands concern
if not control."[35]

The reasons for La Lupe's departure from Cuba in January 1962 differ in accounts given inside and outside of Cuba. Cuban cultural commentators, such as Arenal and Raúl Martínez Rodríguez, point out that
1961 was not a very successful year for La Lupe. She lost her job in La
Red due to personal differences with the owner and there is a hint of
scandals of a personal nature. In interviews La Lupe claimed that she
was summoned to the radio station CMQ and ordered out of the country (after a personal intervention by Fidel Castro) because "lupismo"
was setting a bad example in the new moral climate of austerity being
promoted by the revolutionary ideologues.

What is certain is that an Italian entrepreneur took her to Mexico,
and from there she went on to Miami and New York City. She began performing at the cabaret La Barraca, and was offered a contract by Mongo
Santamaría recording Afro-Cuban inflected jazz with renowned musicians such as Chocolate Armenteros. However, her definitive rise to success in the United States came when Tito Puente invited her to sing with
his orchestra. Their collaboration was to be a commercial and critical
success. La Lupe was singled out in 1965 and 1966 as the most important

singer in the Latino press, which dubbed her the "Queen of Latin Soul." Prior to La Lupe joining the orchestra, Puente had been playing traditional Cuban rhythms. La Lupe helped provide a bridge from the big band sound to the brasher/harsher sound of the Latino barrio that would become known as salsa; her modulations and the grain of her voice gave the band a more up-to-date sound.[36] However, the relationship was not to last. Puente, like Yoyo before him, complained about La Lupe's informality and lack of discipline and fired her in 1968 (ironically, the year she was crowned "Queen of Salsa"). Puente was also worried about her public image due to La Lupe's open practice of the Afro-Cuban religion Santeria, which was to be in part responsible for La Lupe's decline in fortune both publicly, where it was ill received by U.S. audiences, and privately, as she was later to blame it for a long chain of personal disasters. In 1971 she paid $15,000 for a pair of "saints," Changó and Ochún. That year her husband Willy García was diagnosed with schizophrenia and over the following four years she lost all her money and home trying to help him overcome the illness, to no avail.

Despite these personal setbacks, La Lupe's career was not finished just yet. She toured Venezuela to popular acclaim and, back in New York, recorded a number of boleros by the Puerto Rican composer Catalino "Tite" Curet Alonso: "La tirana" ("The Tyrant"), "Carcajada" ("Roar of Laughter"), and "Puro teatro" ("Pure Theater"). These are some of her most famous numbers, embodying the notion of defiant suffering and retribution. "La tirana" openly contests negative constructions of the feminine by sarcastically deconstructing a subjective male point of view in which the woman is set up as the villain of the piece:

Según tu punto de vista
yo soy la mala
vampiresa en tu novela
la gran tirana
[According to your point of view
I'm the wicked one
the vampire in your novel
the great tyrant]

The irony evident in these opening lines pervades the song and is reinforced musically by the crescendo that accompanies the final stanza, affirming the woman's victory, which is socially sanctioned:

Si dice la misma gente
el día en que te dejé
fui yo quien salí ganando

[As everyone else says
the day I left you
I came out the winner]

"Puro teatro" is also accusatory in tone: the wronged woman has been deceived by her lover's pretense, which is described as "drama," "theatre," "a role," and "play acting." His very way of being is performance, but his performative strategy is used deliberately to mislead in a well-rehearsed simulacra of love. In La Lupe's hit rendition of "Puro teatro" she interjects a spoken line from "La tirana": "Y acuerdáte que según tu punto de vista yo soy la mala" (Remember, according to you I'm the wicked one). She thus emphasizes her awareness of—and draws the listener's attention to—the performative tactics at play in both songs. Most commentators note that to fully appreciate La Lupe you had to see her live because of her particular talent for improvising and the variations she introduced into songs whose nonnarrative format allowed for the interchanging of verses. Indeed, La Lupe's trademark interjections of "ahi na má," in which she controls the progress of the song, and the excessive cry of "yiyiyi" are central to the signifying process. To borrow from Roland Barthes's analysis of the grain of the voice via Julia Kristeva, the geno-song or materiality of the voice is as crucial as the pheno-song or communicative element in constructing meaning from the listening experience.[37] Utterances whose meanings are not wholly determined by linguistic content—in other words, the bodily, sonorous element of vocality—are crucial to understanding La Lupe's performances.

Over the course of 1977 La Lupe gave a number of electrifying performances. On January 30 she played the Bronx's Puerto Rico Theatre, backed by Machito. Introduced as the "Queen of Latin Soul," she came onstage dressed in a long white gown and tiara. On June 8 she played Madison Square Garden. According to the description given by Peter Hamill in the *Daily News* of June 20, 1977, "She pulled out all the stops: moaning, making a chattering sound with her voice, her right hand kneading her breast, whipping the dress around her, tearing at her hair, the sound orgasmic and huge as the band moved to the end and the song stopped and she was gone."[38] Indeed, she was soon to vanish from the scene. La Lupe's wild woman act was before its time and she was increasingly marginalized by the salsa mainstream. Her 1977 album *One of a Kind* received relatively little promotion or airplay. Her personal misfortunes were also to continue: her apartment was destroyed in a fire and she fractured two vertebrae in a domestic accident leaving her in a wheelchair. La Lupe was forced to rely on social security and begging for food stamps. While in the hospital in 1986 she met an evangelist and

joined the temple of Jorge Rascke, who she claims gave her the ability to walk and dance freely through divine intervention. Her last years were spent as an active Christian and she released an LP of hymns, *La samaritana* (*The Samaritan*). She died of a heart attack on February 28, 1992. On the whole, obituaries and other articles published after her death focused on her religious conversion and the series of personal tragedies that befell her rather than her impact on Afro-Hispanic music.

La Lupe deserves recognition as a foundational figure not only for female listeners but also for Latino/a queer audiences and performers due to her radical performativity in the 1950s and 1960s.[39] In *Listening to Salsa* (a gender-inflected study of the genre), Frances Aparicio argues that La Lupe has been subjected to a masculinist silencing in the historiography of salsa because of her transgressively erotic articulation of a different female subjectivity.[40] She is consistently constructed as a singer in relation to men—Curet Alonso, Tito Puente, and Yoyo. Aparicio instead suggests that the key to analyzing La Lupe is in her subversive performative style. In addition to the songs by Alonso that I have already discussed here, Aparicio picks out two tracks from the 1977 LP *One of a Kind*: "Canta bajo" ("Sing Bass") and "La dueña del cantar" ("The Mistress of Song"). According to Aparicio, the first number openly articulates erotic desire in vocal and physical dialogues with the double bass, which La Lupe exhorts to sing while caressing it and placing her fingers inside it. Moans and kisses add to the overall effect. In "La dueña del cantar" La Lupe asserts her right to be recognized as a central figure in the development of salsa despite her insertion into the Fania record label's "family." Her voice is echoed by the chorus as they repeat "dueña del cantar," symbolically reaffirming the right of female voices to be heard.

Another female voice censured for her openly sexual stance in the 1960s was Chavela Vargas, by contrast, an overtly lesbian performer.[41] Vargas's origins are a matter of controversy. She was born in 1919 in either Mexico or Costa Rica. What is certain is that her success came in Mexico in the 1950s with her impassioned performances in a number of genres including the bolero and *canción ranchera* (which fuse together in the *bolero ranchero*). She "lesbianized" lyrics originally alluding to heterosexual masculine subjects of desire, and identified with a masculinized eroticism—grabbing her crotch in performances of her signature song "La macorina" and posing caressing a guitar (traditionally sexualized as the body of a woman)—and the macho culture of smoking and drinking, reputedly making her way through 45,000 liters of tequila over the years. She originally wore her hair scraped back in a ponytail, then later cropped, and typically dressed in a Mexican *jorongo* or Peruvian

ruana (ponchos, respectively), trousers, and indigenous *huaraches* (flat sandals). In the iconography of her album covers, her body is not sexualized through overt display, but covered up.[42] Lesbian fans identify with Chavela or Chabela (a more colloquial spelling) as a *macha*, or butch. In 1960s Mexico the aura of scandal surrounding her sexuality, violent temperament (she was nicknamed *pistolas*—pistols—for allegedly firing at her audience), and heavy drinking led to her being blacklisted, and by the early 1970s she was performing in gay-friendly locales only, such as El Hábito in Coyoacán.

It was only in the 1990s that Vargas was definitively reclaimed as a queer icon—and brought to the attention of a much wider audience— after being brought to Spain by Manuel Arroyo and her recuperation in the films of the highly successful Spanish director Pedro Almodóvar. Vargas was featured in the soundtracks of *Kika* (1993), *La flor de mi secreto* (*The Flower of My Secret*, 1995), and *Carne trémula* (*Live Flesh*, 1997).[43] In 1993 at the age of 74 she toured Spain to great acclaim. Indeed, the tour became known as *el chavelazo*.[44] Given the Catholic church's stance on homosexuality, Yvonne Yarbro-Bejarano notes with interest the religious imagery used to describe Vargas in the Spanish press: *La Jornada* described Almodóvar as the priest of "chavelismo," and the Madrid newspaper *ABC* stated "blessed are they who got tickets for the show."[45] In the Madrid show in 1993 Chavela bantered with Almodóvar from the stage, joking that they would marry and have lots of "Pedritos." He wryly remarked that she was capable of performing miracles—in reference to both her advanced age and their respective sexualities. Almodóvar has also referred to Chavela as the ultimate martyr: "Nadie, excepto Cristo sabe abrir los brazos como Chavela Vargas" (Nobody except Christ knows how to open their arms like Chavela Vargas).[46] This imagery seems clearly sacrilegious when linked to other statements made by Almodóvar, such as, "esa mujer canta de donde le sale el coño" (that woman sings out of her cunt).[47] Like La Lupe, Chavela's voice transcends the lyrics being sung to communicate emotion and eroticism through the body. In her variance of tempo and stress according to her emotional state during performances, her vocal performance could be characterized as of the filin style (being slightly before or after the beat).[48] Like La Lupe, whose visceral voice breaks and drags, the materiality of Chavela's voice transcends the lyrics being sung to communicate emotion and eroticism through the body. There are passionate breaks in register, marked contrasts of tempo and volume, and a whole gamut of (guttural) sounds is employed including sighs, moans, groans, grunts, laughter, and cries.[49]

The aim of this brief analysis of two key female performers has meant to demonstrate how the potentially conservative gendered discourse of romantic genres such as the Latin American bolero can simultaneously provide the opportunity for resistance to structures of domination and queering of the heterosexual matrix. The power of the music is enhanced by its direct appeal to the listener, creating a sense of belonging through affective investment. Transgressive performances of erotic pleasure and emotional pain invoke authenticity of feeling as male and female voices and bodies provide a potentially empowering site for a range of listeners identifying with the multiple positions held open in the semiotic excess of the bolero song form. To fully understand this phenomenon, bolero scholars need to follow in the footsteps of Sheila Whiteley in *Sexing the Groove* in order to engage in an analysis that goes beyond lyrics and musical features to closely examine performance style (including costume) and the materiality of the voices/bodies of the bolero.[50]

NOTES

I wish to acknowledge the support of a British Academy Small Grant and University of Newcastle Arts and Humanities Research Fund Internal Fellowship for my research into the bolero. Many thanks are due also to colleagues for their feedback on earlier versions of this paper, presented at seminars at the Centre for Gender and Women's Studies, University of Newcastle upon Tyne; the Institute of Popular Music, University of Liverpool; and the 2001 United Kingdom and Ireland conference of the International Association for the Study of Popular Music (IASPM) in Surrey and 2003 IASPM conference in Montreal. Particular thanks are due to Ian Biddle, Freya Jarman-Ivens, Marion Leonard, Chris Perriam, Jason Toynbee, and Jacqueline Warwick for supplying copies of papers and references.

1. As technology has developed, so have the dissemination networks of the bolero, with many classic/canonical artists now available for download in digital formats such as mp3.

2. René A. Campos, "The Poetics of the Bolero in the Novels of Manuel Puig," *World Literature Today* 65, no. 4 (1991): 637.

3. María del Carmen de la Peza Casares, *El bolero y la educación sentimental en México* (Mexico City: Universidad Autónoma Metropolitana-Xochimilco, 2001), 70.

4. Iris Zavala, *El bolero: Historia de un amor* (Madrid: Alianza, 1991). Other definitions talk about the promise of pleasure (see Tony Evora, "Boleros con sabor," *Cambio 16*, 28.6 [1993]: i); illusion as substance (see Rafael Castillo Zapata, *Fenomenología del bolero* [Caracas: Monte Avila 1991], 91); the bitter aftertaste of pain that accompanies passion (see Manuel Domínguez,

"Bolero: Golpe bajo al corazón," *Cambio 16*, 19.4 [1993]: 80); and a romantic lament comprised of melancholy, frustration, and solitude (see Roberto
Saladrigas, "Con la vana ilusión de un bolero," *La Vanguardia* [Barcelona],
December 15, 1983). Its simultaneous expression of dichotomies forms the
basis of both Castillo Zapata's and Zavala's book-length studies.

5. Delgado Ruiz is referring to various male composers/singers of boleros; see
Manuel Delgado Ruiz, "La reconquista del cuerpo: ideologías sexuales" in *La
sexualidad en la sociedad contemporánea: Lecturas antropológicas*, ed. Manuel
Delgado Ruiz and José Antonio Nieto (Madrid: Universidad Nacional de
Educación a Distancia-Fundación Universidad Empresa, 1991), 95.

6. See Karen Poe, *Boleros* (Heredia, Costa Rica: Editorial de la Universidad
Nacional, 1996).

7. See Campos, "The Poetics of the Bolero"; Alonso Aristizabal, "La América
del bolero y el tango," *Cahiers du Monde Hispanique et Luso-Brésilie*, 48
(1987): 145–48; and Carlos Monsiváis, *Mexican Postcards*, trans. John
Kraniauskas (London: Verso, 1997).

8. This chapter draws on my previous discussion as to how the bolero trans-
gresses the heterosexual matrix of gender relations and sexuality; see
Vanessa Knights, "Transgressive Pleasures: The Latin American Bolero,"
in *Cultura Popular: Studies in Spanish and Latin American Popular Culture*,
ed. Shelley Godsland and Anne M. White (Oxford: Peter Lang, 2002), 209–
28; these ideas are further developed in relation to the theorization of camp
and queer and the early films of Pedro Almodóvar in a Spanish context in
Vanessa Knights, "Queer Pleasures: The Bolero, Camp and Almodóvar," in
Changing Tunes: The Use of Pre-Existing Music in Film, ed. Phil Powrie and
Robynn Stillwell (Aldershot, England: Ashgate, 2006), 91–104.

9. See Rubén Caravaca, *313 Boleros por ejemplo.* (Madrid: Ediciones Guía de
Música, 1995), chap. 11.

10. See Frances R. Aparicio, *Listening to Salsa: Gender, Latin Popular Music, and
Puerto Rican Cultures* (Hanover, N.H.: Wesleyan University Press, 1998).

11. Iris Zavala, "De héroes y heroinas en lo imaginario social: El discurso amoroso del bolero," *Casa de las Américas* 30, no. 179 (1990): 123–29; and Luis
Rafael Sánchez, *La importancia de llamarse Daniel Santos* (Mexico City:
DianabcdefghijkLiteraria, 1989). The term *fabulation* is taken from the introductory section of Sánchez's extraordinary hybrid text (16).

12. Aparicio, *Listening to Salsa*, 125–28.

13. Ibid., 130–32.

14. Frances R. Aparicio, "La Lupe, La India, and Celia: Toward a Feminist
Genealogy of Salsa," in *Situating Salsa: Global Markets and Local Meaning
in Latin Popular Music*, ed. Lisa Waxer (New York: Routledge, 2000), 137.

15. Campos, "The Poetics of the Bolero," 638.

16. Aparicio, *Listening to Salsa*, 154. All bolero lyrics cited herein are from
Caravaca, *313 Boleros*.

17. As Simon Frith notes with reference to popular song and sexuality, the play of identity and address may allow the listener to be both subject and object regardless of gender; see Frith, "Afterthoughts," in *On Record: Rock, Pop, and the Written Word*, ed. Simon Frith and Andrew Goodwin (London: Routledge, 1990), 423.
18. Zavala, *El bolero*, 76–78.
19. Eliseo Colón Zayas, "Desmayo de una lágrima: Nostalgia, simulacra y melodrama desde el bolero," *Cuadernos del Lazarillo: Revista Literaria Cultural* 7 (1995): 30–34. See also Pamela Robertson, *Guilty Pleasures: Feminist Camp from Mae West to Madonna* (London: I. B. Tauris, 1996); and Stephen Maddison, *Fags, Hags, and Queer Sisters: Gender Dissent and the Heterosocial Bonds in Gay Culture* (London: Macmillan, 2000) on identification across normative boundaries of gender and sexuality.
20. The distinction is in the gender: the original lyric's *la* implies a woman, whereas Gorme's *el* implies a man.
21. Deborah Pacini Hernández, *Bachata: A Social History of a Dominican Popular Music* (Philadelphia: Temple University Press, 1995), 192.
22. Campos, "The Poetics of the Bolero," 638.
23. Jaime Rico Salazar, *Cien años de boleros*, Bogota: Panamericana, 2000), 73.
24. On the interchange of recordings between black U.S. marines and Cuban musicians, see Luis Antonio Bigott, *Historia del bolero cubano 1883–1950* (Caracas: Ediciones los Heraldos Negros, 1993), 216–21, in which he cites Dandy Crawford and Maxine Sullivan as particularly influential singers. Sarah Vaughan is also commonly cited by Cuban critics. For the Cuban musicologist Natalio Galán, filin demonstrates a camp sensibility, particularly associated with the highly dramatic, gestural performances of certain popular female singers; see Galán, *Cuba y sus sones* (Valencia: Pre-textos/ Música, 1983), 296–99.
25. In contrast on the perceived threat to masculinity of the early crooners of the 1920s and 1930s in Hollywood, see Allison McCracken, "Real Men Don't Sing Ballads: The Radio Crooner in Hollywood 1929–1933," in *Soundtrack Available: Essays on Film and Popular Music*, ed. Pamela Robertson Wojcik and Arthur Knights (Durham, N.C.: Duke University Press, 2001), 105–33.
26. José Quiroga, *Tropics of Desire: Interventions from Queer Latino America* (New York: New York University Press, 2000), 161.
27. I am grateful to Rodrigo Laguarda for a copy of "Vamos al Noa Noa: de homosexualidad, secretos a voces y ambivalencias en la música de Juan Gabriel," paper presented at the Fourth Conference of the Latin American branch of the International Association for the Study of Popular Music, Mexico City, April 2–6, 2002.
28. Alberto Mira, "Divas," in *Para entendernos: Diccionario de la cultura homosexual, gay y lésbica* (Barcelona: Ediciones de la Tempestad, 1999), 235.

29. José Quiroga, "The Devil in the Flesh," *San Juan Star*, January 22, 1995.

30. Richard Dyer, *Heavenly Bodies: Film Stars and Society* (London: British Film Institute, 1986), 147–49; see also Lloyd Whitesell, "Trans Glam: Gender Magic in the Film Musical," chapter 17, this book.

31. Quiroga, "The Devil in the Flesh."

32. Thanks are due to Cristóbal Díaz Ayala of Fundación Musicalia (San Juan), Raúl Martínez Rodríguez of the Cuban Music Museum (Havana), and Agustiné Vélez of the Puerto Rican Record Collectors Association for providing press clippings on La Lupe from their archives.

33. Quiroga, *Tropics of Desire*, 166.

34. These descriptive terms have been drawn from the archives of articles/ press clippings on La Lupe mentioned above.

35. Leslie Dunn and Nancy Jones, "Introduction," in *Embodied Voices: Representing Female Vocality in Western Culture*, ed. Leslie Dunn and Nancy Jones (Cambridge: Cambridge University Press, 1994), 9.

36. See César Miguel Rondón, *El libro de la salsa: Crónica de la música del Caribe urbano* (Caracas: Editorial Arte, 1980), 46–47.

37. See Roland Barthes, "The Grain of the Voice," in *Image, Music, Text*, trans. Stephen Heath (London: Fontana, 1977), 179–189.

38. Peter Hamill, quoted in Max Salazar, "Remembering La Lupe," *Latin Beat*, May 2000, p. 27.

39. Aparicio, "La Lupe, La India, and Celia," 147. Since the 1990s a number of stage shows and documentaries based on La Lupe's life and work have premiered in Puerto Rico and New York. Aparicio analyzes her influence on the recordings and performances of a new generation of salsa singers such as Yolanda Duke and La India.

40. Aparicio, *Listening to Salsa*, 177–83; see also Vernon Boggs, "Latin Ladies and Afro-Hispanic Music: On the Periphery but Not Forgotten," in *Salsiology: Afro-Cuban Music and the Evolution of Salsa in New York City*, ed. Vernon Boggs (New York: Greenwood Press, 1992), 109–119, on marginalization of women in histories of Afro-Hispanic music.

41. See Alberto Mira, "Chavela Vargas," in *Para entendernos*, 720–721; Yvonne Yarbro-Bejarano, "Cruzando fronteras con Chabela [sic] Vargas: Homenaje de una chicana," in *Sexo y sexualidades en América Latina*, ed. Daniel Balderston and Donna J. Guy (Buenos Aires: Paidós, 1998), 69–82; and Chavela Vargas, *Y si quieres saber de mi pasado* (Madrid: Aguilar, 2002).

42. See Yarbro-Bejarano, "Cruzando fronteras," 74–76, for a detailed discussion of four of Vargas's album covers.

43. La Lupe's voice also featured in Almodóvar's 1988 film, *Mujeres al borde de un ataque de nervios* (*Women on the Verge of a Nervous Breakdown*).

44. The suffix *-azo* in Spanish is an augmentative that can be rendered as "Chavela's triumph" or, more colloquially, "Chavelamania."

45. Yarbro-Bejarano, "Cruzando fronteras," 72. In October 2000 Vargas received the Gran Cruz de la Orden de Isabel la Católica from the Spanish government for her services to Hispanic culture.
46. Mariano del Mazo, "Canción desesperada," *Clarín*, September 9, 1999.
47. Yarbro-Bejarano, "Cruzando fronteras," 81.
48. The subsequent difficulty of accompanying Vargas is noted by the guitarist Manuel Guarneros in an interview with the Uruguayan internet radio station Espectador; see Chavela Vargas with Manuel Guarneros and Oscar Ramos, "Cantar es como celebrar un rito sobre todo con el jorongo puesto," interview by Diego Barnabe, available online from Espectador (http//:www.espectador.com/text/clt03142.htm).
49. Yarbro-Bejarano, "Cruzando fronteras," 81.
50. See Sheila Whiteley, *Sexing the Groove: Popular Music and Gender* (London: Routledge, 1997).

7

HEY, MAN, YOU'RE MY GIRLFRIEND!
Poetic Genderfuck and Queer Hebrew in Eran Zur's Performance of Yona Wallach's Lyrics

GILAD PADVA

On the blue-shaded cover of his album *You Are My Girlfriend* (the *You* refers here to a man, as we will see below),[1] the Israeli pop star Eran Zur sits on the edge of a double bed in a dark blue sweatshirt, his head turned sideways, his eyes closed. His position is innocent and sensual, exhausted and passionate. The bed is turned down for sleep, but it is empty. No female or male partner is waiting in bed for this handsome performer. In a queer way, he is alone. The mysterious male girlfriend is absent. It would appear that there is to be no sex tonight.

Eran Zur, one of the most prestigious Israeli pop stars, usually composes his own sophisticated, polysemic, and ironic lyrics. He has many devoted fans, both straight and gay, who not only like his musical talent, intelligent writing, and sensual baritone, but also appreciate his good looks. He was born in 1965 in Qiriat Bialik, a small town near Haifa, in northern Israel; his mother was a kindergarten teacher and his father a schoolteacher, who died when Zur was 15 years old. "My childhood was over," he recalls.[2] As a teenager, his favorite pop groups were Pink Floyd and Genesis, and he was an avid fan of the American filmmaker and gay icon John Waters.

Zur was not conscripted into the Israeli army, and at the age of twenty he moved to Tel Aviv, where he studied at the Rimon School of Jazz and Contemporary Music and became a member of a pop band called Tattoo, which released an album in 1988. He then founded a new band, Carmella-Gross-Wagner (named after some of his Tel Aviv neighbors), which released an album, *Perakh Shahor* (*Black Flower*), in 1991. After spending some time in New York, he returned to Tel Aviv, and the band released its second album, *I'ver Bé'Lev Yam* (*Blind in the Middle of the Sea*) in 1995. His album *Atta Khaverah Sheli* (*You Are My Girlfriend*) was recorded in 1997, and since then he has released another album, *Takhlit Ba'Tahtit* (*A Purpose at the Bottom*), as well as a collection of his hit songs, *Parparei Ta'a'tu'a* (*Delusive Butterflies*), in 2001. Zur has been married to his wife Avital for several years, and in October 2001 their child Liam was born.

Although Eran Zur is straight, his sexuality, as reflected in some of his own lyrics, is apparently enigmatic, and the local gay community swiftly appropriated some of his songs. His hit song "Ratoov ve'Kham" ("Wet and Hot") is an explicit homoerotic interpretation of all-male intimacy between ultravirile football players.[3] Zur was inspired by a picture he saw in an Israeli sports magazine of football players kissing and hugging each other in the locker room. He identified a significant contrast between the expected homophobia of these straight players and their actual all-male interaction.[4]

His "queerest" album, however, is *You Are My Girlfriend*, which is an homage to the late woman writer Yona Wallach (1944–1985), one of the most influential and provocative Israeli poets. Wallach's texts often involve split identities, delirium and madness, blurred erotic borderlines, poetic genderfuck (subverted *and* melted gender identities), explicit queer imageries, and implicit political criticism. This chapter focuses on how Zur interprets and elaborates Wallach's transsexual patterns and semiotics in his performance of her transgressive lyrics and liminal world.

SEXUAL LANGUAGE AND QUEER MANEUVERS

Sheila Whiteley has suggested that musicological investigation requires fresh analytical explorations of the ways in which musical discourses work in tandem with lyrics, performance styles, gendered identities, and consumer positions. She notes that the emphasis on self-invention implicit in the performing styles of artists such as Mick Jagger, the Pet Shop Boys, and Madonna opened up new critiques on sexuality in the 1980s and 1990s.[5] Because Hebrew is a gendered grammatical language, sexual

positioning and queer maneuvers are both more complicated and more explicit than in English. In the title of the album *You Are My Girlfriend* the word *You* (*Atta* in Hebrew) clearly refers to a man, not a woman (if referring to a woman, it would be *Att*). Hence, the speaker's girlfriend is a man, not a woman. This Hebrew title is thus immediately perceived as queered.

In her poem "Hebrew Is a Sex-Maniac," Wallach notes that in English, there is no difference between *you* female and *you* male, and there is no need to think before one relates to a sex. By contrast, she defines Hebrew as a sex maniac.[6] Zafrira Lidovsky-Cohen notes that grammatical structures—artificially and arbitrarily imposed on language—imperiously imprison their speakers in a world predetermined by them. Wallach's main contribution to modern Hebrew poetics is her creative use of the language—particularly her ingenious ability to flex it for her highly subjective expression, thus deconstructing its predetermined grammatical structures.[7]

Yona Wallach was born in 1944 in Qiriat Ono, a small town near Tel Aviv. Her father died in the War of Independence in 1948, when she was only four years old. She started to write poems when she was eight, and her first book was published when she was nineteen. She died of aggressive breast cancer in 1985, at the age of forty-one. Wallach was charismatic, colorful, and flamboyant. She was involved in various scandals, most notably the one that followed the publication of her 1982 poem "Tephillin" ("Phylacteries"), in which she eroticizes a traditional Jewish artifact made of leather, representing it with an explicit sadomasochistic vocabulary. After a conservative right-wing female politician called her "a beast in heat," Wallach agreed to be photographed with a nude male model behind her, demonstrating the religious ritual of Tephillin. In 1967 she joined an avant-garde group of young poets in Tel Aviv who promoted modern and down-to-earth Hebrew poetry. She published her poems in major literary magazines. Many of them were set to music and performed, including those on the important 1991 album *Batzir Tov* (*A Good Vintage*) by Ilan Virtzberg and Shimon Gelbetz. She also published several books. Notably, she exposed her private life to the Israeli media, including her intimate relationships, her LSD trips, her experience in a mental hospital (including electroshock therapy), and her struggle with the malignant disease that would kill her.

Although most of Wallach's intimate relationships were with men, her biographer, the Israeli journalist Igal Sarna, presents her at times in transgressive, almost transgendered terms, as a beautiful woman who used to wear boys' clothes; he even analogizes her to Virginia Wolf's fictional character Orlando, who changes sexual identities, experiencing

everything. At bohemian parties in Tel Aviv in the late 1960s, when sex between men was still illegal in Israel (this law was rescinded by the Knesset only in March 1988),[8] there was a rumor about Wallach's attraction to women.[9] Her biographer notes her arrival at a party organized by a gay male friend. Unexpectedly, hundreds of people attended this party: "Some of them were pale after so many years in the closet" (Sarna, 101). After the guests left, the host remained on the floor, a sleepy boy in his arms, and Wallach, who was drunk, sat on a mattress, embracing a girl she had met that evening. At about that time, Wallach also met a romantic and restrained girl who was attracted to women, death, astrology, and stars. Later, a love triangle developed, when Yona met the astrologist's friend, the petite, dark, and beautiful daughter of an Israeli art collector (Sarna, 103).

In many of the poems performed on Eran Zur's album, Wallach explicitly refers to a female lover. Simon Frith argues that three levels of performance are involved: the persona created in interpreting the particular song; the image of the performer as performer (the "star"); and the actual individual physically present before us. As he notes, a performer can move between these, as it were, commenting on them; moreover, they can seem to slide together or move apart.[10] In her poem "k'shé'Batti Lakahat Otta Me'Ha'A'nanim" ("When I Came to Take Her Away from the Clouds"), written in the 1960s, Wallach is writing about a female subject (the Hebrew word *otta* clearly refers to a female person) whom she has picked up from the clouds. When the speaker arrives, the woman is ready and adorned, a cuckoo is calling and a barn owl ardently caresses her ears.[11] While taking the woman from the clouds can be interpreted as guiding her out of a drug-induced hallucination, the verb *take* can also be read as an erotic, sexual connotation. When recording this poem as a song, Zur decided that a young woman singer, Rona Keinan, would perform these lyrics. Zur himself joins her only later in this song, and both the female and the male voices appear to be actually yearning for the same female subject.

Significantly (and surrealistically), Wallach mentions in this poem a male character, Pink Julian, who left the poet and her female lover a twisting cobweb. She adds that she already knew that her lover would fall, but she tries over and over again to rescue her, while Pink Julian has spun red cellophane with a red ribbon around the speaker. Dorit Zilberman notes that Julian is an unknown and strange figure, and thus, he makes this poem vague.[12] The queer imagery in this poem, however, includes all-female intimacy, the color pink, an erotic twisting cobweb, and even a red ribbon, which only later, in the early 1990s, would become a symbol of solidarity with the struggle against AIDS.

In the performance of these lyrics, the female voice represents Julian as a possible mentor for the female couple, while the male voice perceives Julian as a sensual being, who might join him *and* his female friend to create a passionate love triangle.

Another song on this album that celebrates all-female intimacy is "Sham Yesh" ("There, There Are") performed by Zur's colleague and close friend Corinne Allal. This leading Israeli singer and musician officially came out to her audience four years later, in 2001. This song articulates an imaginary, erotic place where there are storms and lightning, shining silver, movement, waves, singing, many lovers, celestial bodies, roses, and people making love.[13] Wallach notes that on the other side of this utopia, however, people are silent, hidden, and do not flow—expressions that closeted queers, whether gay, lesbian, or transgendered, can identify with.[14] Allal recorded this song for Zur's album only a short while after she released her own album *k'she'Zeh Ammok* (*When It's Deep*), which included some explicit same-sex love songs. These songs, and Allal's sexual identity, have been ignored by the Israeli press, despite the fact that her lesbianism has been an "open secret" among journalists, musicians, and the many straight and lesbian fans who have identified with her messages.[15]

A PHALLIC WOMAN IN EROTIC STRAWBERRY FIELDS

An interesting gender blending is manifested in Zur's recording of Wallach's poem "Tutim" ("Strawberries"). The song describes a spectacular sexual encounter with a woman who is wearing a black dress printed with strawberries and a black brimmed hat decorated with strawberries. This woman, who wears no underwear, offers him strawberries. Then, like a marionette, she is lifted by strings, and positioned precisely on his cock.[16] Although Zur's performance represents this situation as a *heterosexual* encounter, Wallach had originally referred in these lyrics to a female lover, even using the strawberry as a sensual image: a red, shiny, rounded, and saucy fruit that could be associated with intimate female organs, including the clitoris and its delights.

Remarkably, Wallach describes herself in "Strawberries" as a person with a cock. According to the queer vocabulary of these lyrics, this person is unlikely to be genetically male but s/he might be a transgender, transsexual, or, rather, a genetic (straight or lesbian) woman with a dildo that symbolizes phallic power. Judith Butler notes that the phallus belongs to no body part, but is fundamentally transferable and is the very principle of erotogenic transferability. Moreover, it is through this transfer, understood as a substitution of the psychical for the physical,

that body parts become phenomenologically accessible at all. "Here we might understand the pain/pleasure nexus that conditions erotogenicity," she adds, "as partially constituted by the very idealization of anatomy designated by the phallus."[17]

Furthermore, sexuality and gender are interrelated but are still distinctive cultural constructions, and sexuality, in particular, must be thought of as irreducible to gender. Therefore, June L. Reich supports the theory of genderfuck, which deconstructs the psychoanalytic concept of difference without subscribing to any heterosexist or anatomical truths about the relations of sex to gender (e.g., the binarisms: male = masculine, female = feminine, masculine = aggressive, feminine = passive). Instead, genderfuck structures meaning in a symbol-performance matrix that crosses through sex and gender and destabilizes the boundaries of our recognition of sex, gender, and sexual practice.[18]

A paradigmatic example of this strategy of genderfuck is Zur's (male) performance of Wallach's (female) poems "k'shé'Tavvo'" ("When You Come") and "k'shé'Tavvo Lishkav I'tti Kmo Shoffet" ("When You Come to Sleep with Me as a Judge").[19] These two poems describe a brutal sadomasochistic sexual encounter between the female speaker and her male lover; Zur, however, performs these lyrics in their original Hebrew gendered grammar. In "When You Come" he requests another *man* to wear a policeman's uniform, treat him like a juvenile delinquent, torture him, and force secrets from him. He promises that he won't be a man; rather, he'll confess, break down, sing, and turn everybody in. Then the male counterpart should spit on the speaker, kick his stomach, break his teeth, and take him out by ambulance toward the future, toward tomorrow. Thus, for Wallach, "victimization"—that is, the pain and suffering of enslavement—is quintessentially the royal path to salvation and redemption.[20] In Zur's performance of "When You'll Come to Sleep with Me as a Judge" the male addressee is even required to take him standing up, and to impale him until he no longer knows where he is. He notes that these are games only his partner knows how to play. Otherwise, he'll not remember that it was him and wouldn't know who his partner is. He asks his partner to make him know. This sort of sadomasochistic maneuver imitates but also rescripts, dramatizes, theatricalizes, and parodies powerful institutions and power relationships in modern society (e.g., police, prison, court) that affect people's lives and fantasies; in sadomasochistic relationships, as contrasted to reality, roles can be easily shifted.[21]

In particular, Zur's entreaty to another man—not a woman—in his performance of these two "straight" poems is highly homoerotic. In referring to a male addressee, he may be positing himself in an imagined

masochistic role in spectacular gay bondage/discipline/sadomasochism scenes that provoke anxiety not only in the straight sexual imagination but are also considered controversial within the gay community itself.[22] Hereby, Zur proves his courage in daring to take the role of the apparently masochistic, unprivileged, passive, impaled, and tortured counterpart in these powerful erotic games that integrate pain and pleasure in a dissident, transgressive, and often condemned unconventional sexual practice of queer sadomasochism.

ANDROGYNOUS BOYFRIENDS AND VIRGINAL GIRLFRIENDS

The most paradigmatic expression of Wallach's politics of disruption, deconstruction of gender and sexual boundaries, and criticism of the traditional erotic spheres of pleasure is her poem "Atta Khaverah Sheli" ("You Are My Girlfriend") from the 1980s, also performed on Zur's album of the same name. In this poem, Wallach refers to a man, who lives with his girlfriend, as the poet's girlfriend. Wallach speculates that his girlfriend is actually a lesbian who prefers men, and that he is a gay man who prefers women. She suggests that this combination can be maintained because one's mind is more important that one's physique, which she blatantly describes as fake balls that hide a passionate pussy or, alternatively, a pussy hiding balls.[23]

After these extravagant androgynous articulations, in which biological sex organs masquerade as other biological sex organs, Wallach tells the addressee that she can hear his ruined voice, which is smoked, burnt, and cynical, and that she recognizes from the angle of his insult the particular voice of the gay man who is expecting her to give him everything (Wallach, in *Moffa'*, 63). She then apologizes for considering him a man, and even crucifies herself immediately for this mistake, and compliments her addressee as her sweet girlfriend with balls and a boy's body, who is the first girlfriend from whom she understands how a girl's mind works (64). The poet challenges the concept of "sexual essence," and finally she imagines a sort of sexless body with no pussy or cock between the legs. She fantasizes about a soul without a body, a soul that is moving around the house, and she even wonders about adopting an impossible identity, albeit one who is suspicious enough (64).

Chris Straayer notes that we patrol gender expressly because our claim to "normality" (that is, conventional humanness) has been made to rely on it—to not be one's "true" sex is a crime against the law of pure differences. Straayer, however, understands gender and gender formation to be more flexible than the paradigm that sexual binarism

produces, and also to be continually influenced by social experience.[24] Jay Proser points out that *transgender* describes a gender, not a sexual identity. Transgender thus came into being as a specific gender category: one that distinguished subjects from those whose cross-gendered identity was occasional; from those for whom it entailed changing sex; and from those for whom it was a function of their gay sexuality. *Transgender*, however, also functions now as a catchall term that includes, along with transgenderists, those subjects for whom it was originally invented to distinguish them from: transvestites, transsexuals, and drag queens, in addition to butches, drag kings, bull dykes, androgynes, and intersexuals—indeed any form of what has been dubbed a "gender outlaw."[25]

Following the idea that gender identity is instituted in repetitive acts, Moe Meyer suggests that queer performance is not expressive of social identity but is, rather, the reverse—the identity is self-reflexively constituted by the performances themselves. Moreover, Meyer notes that whether one subscribes to an essentialist or constructionist theory of gay and lesbian identity, it comes down to the fact that, at some time, the actor must *do* something in order to produce the social visibility by which the identity is manifested.[26]

Wallach's radical politics of genderfuck become even more complex and polysemic in Zur's performance of "You Are My Girlfriend." In his sensual baritone voice, this male artist inverts the female poet's articulations of androgynous bodies and multisexual fantasies. Considering the rigid Hebrew distinction between references to male and female addressees, the performance of this poem by a genetic male—whether a gay- or straight-identified artist—amplifies, inverts, and traverses the already transgressive lyrics. For example, when Zur sings about a man who is his girlfriend and has a girl's mind, which makes him a girl-girl (Wallach, in *Moffa'*, 62), it is immediately interpreted as an explicit homoerotic statement, even if later the speaker identifies himself as female. Wallach—represented/mediated by Zur—recalls that sweet kid who told her with great appreciation, that she is a girl-boy, or, conversely, a boy-girl, because from the beginning, the woman's value is reduced (Wallach, in *Moffa'*, 62). As Wallach had already claimed in the 1960s, women's liberation and gay liberation would arrive together (Sarna, 180).

Accordingly, this poem *and* song represent the situation of those who do not fit into the distinction between masculine and feminine but still try to fabricate normality according to the dominant social criterion. This pretense results in a totally empty life without contents (Wallach, in *Moffa'*, 62). Furthermore, Wallach describes in this poem society's violence toward those transgressive subjectivities whose essences are different, and

how they are silent, silenced, and censored (62). Lilly Rattok notes that Wallach emphasizes the lack of effective linguistic ways in Hebrew to describe different sexualities in order to condemn the dictatorship of the dominant culture that avoided legitimization of sexual alternatives.[27]

Zur, on his album, proceeds to amplify Wallach's politics of genderfuck and erotic disruption. His and his colleagues' performances of Wallach's lyrics follow her radical revision of heteronormative categorizations and classifications. One of the most significant tracks on the album is "Shir Kdam-Shnatti (Sex Akher)" ("Pre-Somnolence Poem [Different Sex]."[28] Wallach appears to be masquerading here as a bunch of chauvinistic straight men who yearn for another sex because they are tired of their wives and their virginal girlfriends, and they can satisfy themselves only through pictures that prove that there *is* another, different sex.[29]

Further, the apparently patriarchal speakers say that if there is another sex in another world, if new women who "know how" do exist, they should free the tired speakers' mind (Wallach, in *Collected Poems*, 79). The phrase about women who know how is complicated here, because in Hebrew, *lada'at* means not only "to know how" or "to be aware of," but also has a biblical sense for a man: to have intercourse with a woman, to "know" her body. The phrase "women who know how" can thus also be read in its subversive meaning as a reference to imagined women who have phallic potentiality, even if they do not have—or do not wish for—a cock or a dildo.

Significantly, Zur sings this song in a duet with Dana International, who represented Israel and won the Eurovision Song Contest in 1998 (a year after Zur's album was released) with her hit song "Diva." Dana International is well known in the Israeli public sphere as a male-to-female transsexual who is attracted to men, and who identifies herself as a person who has had both hormonal treatments and a sex-change operation. Thus, when she performs this yearning for refreshing, sexy *women* in her sensual voice, the allegedly chauvinist demand manifested in this song is not reconfirmed but instead subverted and highly parodied; patriarchy is mocked or, rather, genderfucked.

As Amalia Ziv notes, Dana International does not only "pass" the test of femininity successfully, but is even identified with paradigmatic female stardom. Yet she never tries to conceal her past. Rather, she has established her public persona upon an ethos of openness and sincerity. She also continues to perceive and represent herself as an integral part of the Israeli gay community, and she is even its advocate. This stance of belonging and commitment is expressed in her relationships with both the local gay community and Israeli straight society.[30]

SPECTACULAR BODIES AND GAY MELANCHOLIA

Zur's album ends with Yona Wallach's reading aloud of her poem "Mett Ba' Aretz" ("Dead in the Land"). In this stirring poem and performance, Wallach mourns a beloved boyfriend after she has found his beautiful body in her blossoming garden, located in a pastoral landscape. She describes how she bent over the spectacular white body of her poor beloved, and his blood was like a most beautiful circle. She remembers his heart and his neck that she has loved (Wallach, in *Collected Poems,* 101). It is left unknown whether this beloved man has died from a disease or has been shot. Wallach finds it difficult to mourn her male lover. She writes that she could lament, sing, freeze. She refers to her dead lover and tells him that no songs are in her blood, and adds that this land has not endowed songs for the particular dead man in her garden but to another dead man (101).

Although the speaker in this poem does not frame a gender, she appears to be identified with the female poet while the dead person is explicitly articulated as male. Thus, the poem supposedly refers to a male-female relationship. Nevertheless, queer readers can also identify with its spectacular visions of Eros and Thanatos, and the difficulty of expressing feelings of pain, anguish, and agony after having lost a loved one. Butler refers to the absence of cultural conventions for avowing the loss of homosexual love. She notes that it is this absence that produces a culture of heterosexual melancholy, one that can be read in the hyperbolic identifications by which mundane heterosexual masculinity and femininity confirm themselves. What is most apparently performed as gender is the sign and symptom of a pervasive disavowal.[31]

Moreover, Butler notes that it is precisely to counter a pervasive cultural risk of gay melancholia that there has been an insistent publication and politicization of grief over those who have died from AIDS; the Names Project quilt is exemplary, ritualizing and repeating the name itself as a way of publicly avowing the boundless loss. Insofar as grief remains unspeakable, rage over the loss can redouble by virtue of remaining unavowed, and if that very rage is publicly proscribed, the melancholic effects of such a proscription can achieve suicidal proportions. According to Butler, the emergence of collective institutions for grieving are thus crucial to survival, to the reassembling of community, the reworking of kinship, and the reweaving of sustaining relations. And insofar as they involve the publicization and dramatization of death, they call to be read as life-affirming rejoinders to the dire psychic consequences of a grieving process culturally thwarted and proscribed.[32]

After Wallach finds it difficult to mourn her dead lover, after she has noted that there are no songs left in her blood because the land had endowed them to *another* dead (Wallach, in *Collected Poems,* 101), she finally finds the strength and courage to express her own mourning over the loss of her beloved one. At the end of her poem, she does acknowledge, cry for, and praise her own beautiful dead. She notes that the expected is that she is going to see past received conventions. She considers beauty as only conditional, like a flash of horror (101). After Wallach's performance of her poem is finished, Zur and Eli Avramov's quiet keyboard melody that had accompanied her reading turns into stirring rock music, with bass and drums and repetitive samples of Wallach's psychedelic phrases about changing colors; the entire composition sounds like a unique and original requiem to this most unique and original late poet, who had tragically forecast her own death. She refers to her dead lover, stressing that no songs are in her blood, adding that this land had endowed songs for another dead.

EROTIC FLEXIBILITY AND POETIC GENDERFUCK

Queer identification with the musical album *You Are My Girlfriend*, with its sophisticated manipulations of Hebrew (a gender grammatical language that "frames" both the speaker's gender and sexuality), means more than just an appropriation and queering of Yona Wallach's poems and Eran Zur's performances—a straight female writer's works performed by a straight male musician. As reflected in its title, this album *is* a queer musical statement, a disruption of constituted sexualities and identification. This politics of erotic flexibility is celebrated not only in Wallach's lyrics and in the transgressive performances of Zur, Allal, Keinan, and Dana International, but is also embraced and celebrated by a devoted queer audience that identifies itself with this liberating musical practice.

On the back cover of Zur's music album, a double bed with pale blue pillows and bedspread is turned down for sleeping, but the performer himself is absent. The room looks empty. The night-light is turned off. One of the most intimate spaces in the artist's private sphere is fully exposed here in its most melancholic moments. There are no sexual maneuvers, no erotic identity games, no sensual masquerade, no passion; no heavenly bodies are making love between these sheets. It is probably the artist's decision to leave his bedroom. For some devoted listeners, this can also be interpreted as a musical invitation to move to another space, another phase, another erotic zone, another experience, another delight, an "other" sex.

NOTES

The author is grateful to Naomi Paz from Tel Aviv University for her advice and insights in exploring Wallach's (queer) Hebrew to English speakers. The author is thankful to Professor Sheila Whiteley and Professor Jennifer Rycenga for their encouragement and support.

1. Eran Zur, *Atta Khaverah Shelli* (You Are My Girlfriend), NMC Music, NMC 20296-2, 1997; all songs discussed herein are from this CD unless otherwise noted.
2. See Eran Zur's Internet website (http://www.eranzur.com).
3. Eran Zur, "Ratoov ve'Kham" (Wet and Hot), on *Parparei Ta'a'tu'a* (Delusive Butterflies), NMC Music, NMC 20570-2, 2001.
4. This explanation appears in a pamphlet enclosed in Zur, *Parparei Ta'a'tu'a*, p. 7.
5. Sheila Whiteley, "Introduction," in *Sexing the Groove: Popular Music and Gender*, ed. Sheila Whiteley (London: Routledge, 1997), xvi.
6. Yona Wallach, "Hebrew Is a Sex Maniac," in *Moffa'* (Appearance) (Tel Aviv: Ha'Kibbutz Ha'Meuhad, 1985), 10; hereafter, page numbers for poems from this volume will be cited parenthetically in the text. Translated in Zafrira Lidovsky-Cohen, *"Loosen the Fetters of Thy Tongue, Woman": The Poetry and Poetics of Yona Wallach* (Cincinnati, Ohio: Hebrew Union College Press, 2003), 186.
7. Zafrira Lidovsky-Cohen, "Back from Oblivion: The Nature of 'Word' in Yona Wallach's Poetry," *Hebrew Studies* 41 (2000): 99–117.
8. Amit Kama, "From Terra Incognita to Terra Firma: The Logbook of the Voyage of Gay Men's Community into the Israeli Public Sphere," *Journal of Homosexuality* 38, no. 4 (2000): 143.
9. Igal Sarna, *Yona Wallach* (Tel Aviv: Keter, 1993), 101; hereafter, page numbers will be cited parenthetically in the text.
10. Simon Frith, *Performing Rites: On the Value of Popular Music* (Cambridge, Mass.: Harvard University Press, 1996), 159.
11. Yona Wallach, "k'shé'Batti Lakahat Otta Me'Ha'A'nanim" (When I Came to Take Her Away from the Clouds), in *Shirra* (Collected Poems) (Tel Aviv: Siman Kriah/Mif'alim Universitayim Le'Hotza'ah La'Or, 1976), 14.
12. Dorit Zilberman, *Ivrit He Saffa Mitrakhetzet: 6 Prakim al Shirat Yona Wallach* (*Essays on the Poetry of Yona Wallach*) (Tel Aviv: Yaron Golan, 1993), 55.
13. Wallach, "Sham Yesh" (There, There Are), in *Collected Poems*, 127; hereafter, page numbers for poems from this volume will be cited parenthetically in the text. Translated in Lidovsky-Cohen, *Loosen the Fetters*, 100.
14. Lidovsky-Cohen, *Loosen the Fetters*, 102, notes that for Wallach, "there is life" only in a supernal realm of living devoid of literal thinking—that is to say, a dreamlike or imaginary mode of existence, or else in a world without social and religious taboos.

15. Gilad Padva, "'When It's Deep—You Know It': Sexuality, Liminality, and Hebrew in Corinne Allal's Pop Songs," *Women and Language* 26, no. 2 (2003): 9–14.

16. Yona Wallach, "Tutim" (Strawberries), in *Or Peré* (Wild Light), ed. by D. Green (Jerusalem: Eyhut/Design Engineering, 1990), 52–53.

17. Judith Butler, *Bodies That Matter: On the Discursive Limits of "Sex"* (New York: Routledge, 1993), 62.

18. June L. Reich, "Genderfuck: The Law of the Dildo," in *Camp: Queer Aesthetic and the Performing Subject: A Reader*, ed. Fabio Cleto (Edinburgh: Edinburgh University Press, 1999), 255.

19. Yona Wallach, "k'shé'Tavvo'" (When You Come) in *Wild Light*, 54–55; translated in Lidovsky-Cohen, *Loosen the Fetters,* 147. Yona Wallach, "k'shé'Tavvo Lishkav I'tti Kmo Shoffet" (When You Come to Sleep with Me as a Judge), in *Wild Light*, 56–57; translated in Lidovsky-Cohen, *Loosen the Fetters,* 150–51.

20. Lidovsky-Cohen *Loosen the Fetters*, 149.

21. Anne McClintock, "Maid to Order: Commercial S/M and Gender Power" in *Dirty Looks: Women, Pornography, Power*, ed. Pamela Church Gibson and Roma Gibson (London: British Film Institute, 1993), 207–31.

22. Lynda Hart and Joshua Dale, "Sadomasochism," in *Lesbian and Gay Studies: A Critical Introduction*, ed. Andy Medhurst and Sally R. Munt (London: Cassell, 1997), 341–55.

23. Yona Wallach, "Atta Khaverah Sheli" (You Are My Girlfriend), in *Appearance*, 63; translated for this chapter by Gilad Padva.

24. Chris Straayer, "Transgender Mirrors: Queering Sexual Difference," in *Between the Sheets, in the Streets: Queer, Lesbian, Gay Documentary*, ed. Chris Holmund and Cynthia Fuchs (Minneapolis: University of Minnesota Press, 1997), 216, 221.

25. Jay Proser, "Transgender," in *Lesbian and Gay Studies: A Critical Introduction*, ed. Andy Medhurst and Sally R. Munt (London: Cassell, 1997), 310.

26. Moe Meyer, "Introduction: Reclaiming the Discourse of Camp," in *The Politics and Poetics of Camp*, ed. Moe Meyer (London: Routledge, 1994), 1.

27. Lilly Rattok, *Mal'akh Ha'Esh* (Angel of Fire: The Poetry of Yona Wallach) (Tel Aviv: Ha'Kibbutz Ha'Meuchad, 1997), 114–15.

28. Yona Wallach "Shir Kdam-Shnatti (Sex Akher)," in *Collected Poems*, 79; translated in Lidovsky-Cohen, *Loosen the Fetters*, 66–67, more accurately as "Presleep Poem."

29. *Akher* means "other," "another," "different," "varying."

30. Amalia Ziv, "Dana International," in *Fifty to Forty-Eight: Critical Monuments in the History of the State of Israel*, a special issue of *Teoria ve'Bikoret*, ed. A. Ofir (Jerusalem: Van Leer Institute, 1999), 401.

31. Butler, *Bodies That Matter*, 236)

32. Ibid.

8

ALBITA RODRÍGUEZ
Sexuality, Imaging, and Gender Construction in the Music of Exile

MARIO REY

"I am woman!" announces Albita—dressed in a *guayabera* with cuff links,[1] tailored men's suit, and two-toned shoes—"with all five letters of the word."[2] During the same performance, she offers an audience member a glimpse of her flexed bicep. These exchanges and contradictions— "transgressive" images of male drag coupled with sudden affirmations of femaleness—reveals the complexity of gender. Émigré singer-composer-performer Alba Rodríguez, commonly known as Albita, who in 1993 landed in the storm and stress of political exile in "heteropolitan" Miami, emerged as the maximal musical exponent of the Cuban diaspora. Her gripping style and intoxicating performances have galvanized the live music scene, while her recordings have garnered multiple Grammy Awards and nominations, securing her position as one of the leading Latina voices of the new millennium.

What has distinguished Albita from other expatriate artists is her arresting visual image, manner of interpretation, and husky contralto voice. Her trademark masculine performance style and androgynous stage persona sharply contrast with the swanky feminized aesthetic cultivated for the Hispanic market. Albita's music performances, while undoubtedly promoting communal and national identity, are noteworthy for the politics of gender that they articulate. The use of musical codes that

have been claimed as symbols of Cubanness, and of a broader Pan-Latino consciousness, make her performative transgressions all the more daring. These contraventions subvert established prescriptions regarding dress, comportment, vocality, production, control, and any number of ideologies associated with the social condition of being female. However, the most compelling aspect of Albita's media persona is the deployment of sexuality to define and transgress boundaries as a form of counter-hegemonic resistance, carving out a queer space and rendering a Latina lesbian aesthetic. Although she displays no overt homosexual performative gestures, Albita challenges social stereotypes through the articulation of a non-conformist gender identity. Characterized by chameleonic transformations, she perpetuates a combination of social identities—female, Cuban, rural, émigré, queer—and mediates the often contradictory meanings connected with these social categories. Music, among all cultural practices, constitutes a privileged site for the representation and negotiation of these various classes of identity. As a refugee artist intersecting multiple identity categories, Albita's reception among disempowered groups has facilitated her transcendence from lesbian iconicity to a broader emblem of diasporic culture. Moreover, the physicality of her performances and constructions of femininity are diametrically pitted against the hypersexualized images of woman promoted by the Latin recording industry. These discordances afford the exploration of how concepts of gender representation in music are modified by the female appropriation of characteristically male performance techniques.

Albita's performances and appropriation of traditional music genres are ostensibly narrative strategies for reinterpreting the past through the "staging of nostalgia" for a diasporic community. They are, in fact, gendered discourses signifying sites where asymmetrical power relationships are played out. Recognizing sexual/gender identity as a discursive, bodily performance that can contest society's gender structure—historically subjugating women as inferior subjects of patriarchy—prompts an analysis of Albita's musical codes in relation to Hispanic immigrant culture.[3] Accordingly, this chapter examines how sexuality and gender affect and are affected by musical production, focusing on Albita's musical performance not solely from its implication in the double narrative of gender and ethnicity, but as a broader study in the aesthetics of transgression in Latino exile culture. Of particular interest are the ways in which these performance narratives reflect the dialectic of erotic and national discourses, destabilizing the privileged discursive gender positioning in Cuban dance music. A contextualization of Albita begins the discussion, defining the social framework that facilitated the development, promotion, and maintenance of the performing persona.

As Albita unquestionably privileges the performative over the textual, this chapter subsequently assesses how the double narratives are articulated both extratextually (via visual imaging, drumming practice, and dance) and intratextually (through the focal repertoire and the oppositional content of the song lyrics).

THE SOUNDSCAPE OF CULTURAL MEMORY

To contextualize the Albita phenomenon, one must first unravel the conundrum of Cuban Miami, a mystifying, bicultural society endeavoring to mythologize the homeland and to revive a hallowed past through its collective historical memory. But the grief of cultural displacement breeds a corrosive nostalgia—the nostalgia of exile, a longing derived from memorial historicity that is both alienating and solidarizing. These contradictions nonetheless engender creative acts.[4] For the diasporic community, music making constitutes a site of historical recovery. Dance and musical performance constitute primary vehicles through which the cultural archive of the Cuban diaspora is re-created and preserved, allaying, if only temporarily, the immigrants' greatest fear—the irrevocably fading imagination. These activities serve as cultural acts of opposition, mediating between assimilation and resistance, between an impaired present and the past imperfect. Only in the smoke-filled clubs of Hispanic Miami, where all things immigrant are regarded with suspicion, do politics and prejudice surrender to the rhythms and secret language of Afro-Cuban drumming. Given this context of cultural retention, Albita landed on a perfectly suited, musical niche as a purveyor of the traditional, pre-revolutionary music that was even staler in Cuba than it was in Miami. She became an instant ambassador of Cubanness, a symbol of a paradisiacal preterit suddenly made relevant.

Certainly, the function she fulfills in the diasporic reconstruction of Cubanness has afforded her the kind of recognition that eluded her in her homeland, where foreign music dominates the youth culture. Reportedly Fidel Castro's favorite musical performer, her disillusionment with the revolution and disdain for musicians who continue to cooperate with the socialist system bolstered her standing among the diasporic fan base. The fact that Albita was also astute enough to address those subjectivities that straddled the hyphen (e.g., Cuban-Americans) further broadened her appeal. As a woman of multiple categories herself, she has become an empowering agent by courting the historicity of those permanently hyphenated identities, as well as those distinctly subculturated with hyphen after hyphen (e.g., gay-Cuban-Americas, urban-lesbian-Latinas, yucas [young-urban-Cuban-Americans]).

CONSTRUCTING THE PERFORMATIVE PERSONA

Albita provides a fascinating case study as a social agent responsible for constructing her stage persona and developing her own strong visual identity, attesting to the volitional aspect of gender appropriation. She has unflinchingly downplayed the feminine attributes, and rendered an androgynous image to an upwardly mobile Latino market accustomed to women emulating the traditional ideals of feminine propriety. As an androgynous figure in the very heart of macho Miami, her interpretations of basic love songs can suggest parody. While Cuban society does not stigmatize the morality of a woman pursuing a career in musical performance, it is comparatively rigid in its gender role norms. For the female performer, a moral tension emerges from the incongruity between the society's emphasis on demure public behavior and its penchant to offer up the female body as spectacle.

The eroticizing of Latina femininity is centered on the appearance and (hetero)sexuality of the performing body—a discursive site regarding the social meaning of masculine women. In performance, the body is invariably accentuated with provocative dress codes.[5] However, Albita fashions an identity not only out of clothes, but also out of an array of gender role signifiers. Characterized by close-cropped, slicked-back hair, angular boyish features, and dapper tailored suits, Albita has appeared in some of the world's top fashion magazines. The use of "masculine" markers in an ambiguously sexed stage persona challenges a culture that marginalizes non-conforming women. In the liberation of the self, she subverts the patriarchal iconography of female sexuality. Her unapologetic self-representation, imprinted in a dapper, butch sensibility that eschews the "Latin look," has generated image descriptions remarkably consistent across the media: "androgynous," "gender-bending," "mannish." By assuming a male character in female-to-male drag, she suggests a regulatory fiction that defines gender identity as a variable, fluid performance, dislocating the boundaries imposed by patriarchal codes.[6]

Albita appears to relish the fact that her image encourages conflicting readings. Rather than deflect society's gaze, she exhibits a performative stance similar to the male transvestite's self-positioning as masked object of the gaze. To be sure, Albita's disposition is informed by the hostile social response to gender dissonance experienced in her homeland, where the gender structure and regulation of heterosexist subordination is markedly rigid. Despite some conciliatory gestures toward homosexuals, the Cuban Revolution has a history (both recent and long standing) of suppressing gay voices.[7] Consequently, in a country where

the eradication of gender oppression and homophobia was more smoke than substance, the appropriation of a lesbian voice was simply not an option. However, the experience of exile is transformational in myriad ways. Subsequent to her defection, Albita developed a performative persona that, while transgressive of heteronormativity in a culture not entirely comfortable with gender dissonance, nonetheless answers a need among a diverse audience.

GIRLS WITH DRUMS

In addition to her visual appearance, one of the most arresting features of Albita is her degree of performativity. Musical roles and repertoire are generally defined between the sexes in Cuban society. While sound production does not inherently possess male or female qualities, the gendering of music is a historically constructed mechanism of the broader system of asymmetrical power. As such, women's participation in Cuban popular music has, until recently, been limited to the role of the vocalist rather than instrumentalist. This positioning is consistent with the gendered division of labor in many cultures (i.e., male—instrumental performer; female—singer/dancer). Moreover, women who have challenged the conventions of salsa as instrumentalists have tended to be keyboardists. As certain sound instruments in most human societies are considered gender appropriate and connote sexual stereotypes,[8] Cuban colonialist gestures deem the flute, violin, and piano as traditionally "feminine," while masculinizing the guitar, trumpet, and drum. In this regard, the composition of Albita's band has been extremely atypical in that women execute the singing, guitar playing, and some of the percussion and horn parts. Albita herself has challenged the patriarchal standards as a guitarist, drummer, and purportedly, one of the few female tres players in the world.[9]

Certainly, the most subversive of these practices is her drumming. A mythic signifier encapsulating larger cultural meanings, the drum connotes phallic power among many cultures, which contributes to colonialist censorship of female drumming. Albita's drum performance not only invalidates rigid gender roles, but also becomes an important symbol of liberation, and an iconic embodiment of power. More transgressive still is her staged performance of ritual batá aberíkula (unconsecrated) drumming, which is historically forbidden for women, homosexuals, and effeminate men.[10] Albita, nevertheless, performs toques with unquestionable authority.[11]

Referencing a sacred world, Albita embodies an ideal performance of masculinity encoded in ritual batá drumming. As the practice of this

codified drum language constitutes a metaphor of sexual dominance, her secularization of *oriché* drumming creates a liminal site beyond the realm of religious ritual in which to subvert the established social-sexual order. Whatever the effect on her audience, the transgressive performance is fraught with multiple statements. These performative intentions include challenging the politics of exclusion, interrogating the institutions that support these male-biased exclusionary discourses, reversing gender roles as a means of empowerment, affirming Cuban roots as staged folklore, denouncing racial denigration, and evoking the (prerevolutionary) past through ancestral reverence in Santería possession practice.[12] Thus, her performances of Santería drumming may function as a micropolitical act in the Foucauldian sense, reacting against the hegemony of several interrelated systems of power.

DANCING WITHOUT A PARTNER

Given the importance and historical connection between music and dance in Cuban society, the role of embodiment in creating a phenomenological space for performing Cubanness and Latinidad is essential for Albita—a self-described *sonero*.[13] Performatively engaging her body—a site of contestation for women—she transforms dancing into a subliminal and subversive space. During an evening performance, the spectator is lured and challenged by the free expression of her sexuality as she executes a grinding movement to the rhythms with an on-the-beat isolation of the hip in a back-and-forth rocking motion. Her kinesthetically constructed strutting, shimmying, and flaunting of the hip movement presents the performing body in the rhythmical articulation of *cubanidad*. The swaying of the hips is an embodied practice that imbues the Latina queer body with a sense of history and community. Decolonizing the body through the act of dancing, Albita negotiates both Latina and queer discourses. Her movement is not only a directed performance of queer identity, but also the corporalization of lesbian Latinidad.

The most choreographed segment of her concerts has been the immensely popular percussive *baile de la chancleta* (dance of wooden flip-flops), a type of Cuban clogging. Although women traditionally perform the dance, Albita subverts this gender bias by involving male band members, transforming them into colonized, exotic objects. While intended to showcase national terpsichorean creativity, the choice is unusual given that Cuban social dances favor coupled rather than independent dancing. This preference for the embrace underscores the curious absence of a dance partner in her video for the song "Que

Manera de Quererte" ("What a Way to Want You"). Albita dispenses with the courtship of salsa dancing, where the men exact their relative dominance over women, opting to dance about an empty chair—a stand-in for a gendered partner. Singing in direct address and avoiding the cross-gendered embrace, she is rendered the wallflower—dancing without a partner. The absence becomes a presence discursively only through evocation in the queer voice of the singing subject. That is, through homoerotic rewriting, the absence becomes woman. While Albita has no cause to conceal her sexual orientation, she makes neither a performative statement in support of her sexuality nor an act of heteronormativity. Rather, she creates liberatory musical images through the monology of her companionless dance. Moreover, in the live performance, which is the defining mode of the Albita myth, she asserts a Foucauldian privileging of the body as sensual object for her own self-fulfillment and artistic self-creation.

REGENDERING THE REPERTOIRE: SON AS METAPHOR, SALSA AS SIGNIFIER, AND DOUBLE-NARRATIVES

Albita's performances enunciate a double-edged narrative of sexuality and nostalgia. Through her focal repertoire, she targets the culture of nostalgic consumerism. The use of the *son* and other homeland music as a tool for cultural reaffirmation arguably acts to strengthen internal social cohesion while attenuating what Arjun Appadurai calls the "nostalgia of exile."[14] Concomitantly, the significance of sexuality and gendered discourse emerges in both the choice of musical forms and the songs' narratives. The central genres of son and salsa (particularly *salsa erótica*) reflect male-dominated domains virulent with machismo, where women have been vastly underrepresented in the areas of musical production, composition, and arranging. For the Cuban-American community, the son constitutes a metaphor for an irretrievable past, an opportunity to symbolically reexperience their relationship with the idealized homeland and the loved ones left behind. As the leading exponent of the genre, Albita freely navigates between the feminized creature that is *son hembra*, and the aggressive tendencies of the *son macho*.[15] However, the music genre with which her name is closely identified is the *son renovado* (alternative son), situated in a gray zone between son and salsa.

Hispanic immigrants in the United States engage salsa as a locus for cultural reaffirmation and contestation. Deployed as a marker of ethnic identity, salsa reflects postmodern preoccupations with cultural displacement, intergender relations, the delimiting of freedom, and the marginality of the working class. The masculinist centrality of salsa in

Latino urban culture systematically privileges the male utterance with misogynist textualizations of women, rendering mute the equitable representation of the female voice. Recent discourses on the sexing of musical genres assert the decisive control that men exert over the production, presentation, and marketing of salsa.[16] Moreover, the politics of record production have ostracized Latinas from the mainstream. Female artists have been predominantly relegated to the sphere of *salsa romántica*, where they could renegotiate the pejorative constructs and hypersexualized images of women common to heavy salsa. For Albita, however, exposing the artificial boundaries erected by the phallocentric culture of the transnational salsa market, and the legitimization of the female voice, are paramount. They provide the impetus to navigate against the depoliticized discursive streams of salsa romántica toward the more transgressive, liberatory language of salsa erótica, with its explicit revelations of female desire historically sublimated in salsa. Appropriating this masculinist music as both performer and composer, Albita destabilizes the privileged discursive gender positioning, and subverts the (hetero)sexual politics of salsa. Regendering salsa and inverting the object of sexism, she in fact becomes the acting subject, contesting the priapic narratives of Latino culture.

Reading the songs as literary texts reveals the recurring themes of sexual possession and the exile's preoccupation with national identity. These motifs are articulated independently or as double narratives, where the discourses of unfulfilled desire, queer identity, and Cubanness intersect.[17] The treatment of these discourses is demonstrated in the following examples from her patriotic and erotic texts. Instances of the latter are gleaned from woman- and lesbian-identified songs, respectively.

Her hit single "Que culpa tengo yo?" ("Why Am I to Blame?") from the CD *No se parece a nada* (*Unlike Anything Else*, 1995) is noteworthy among the pieces targeting the diasporic national imagination. Inscribed in the collective unconscious of *el exilio* (the exilic community), the song is immediately recognized as a kind of Cuban-American anthem in its invocation of cultural belonging and validation of nationhood. Sentimental and panegyrical, the text asks the rhetorical question, "De donde soy?" (From where am I?), followed by the focal, nonrhetorical question, "Que culpa tengo you de haber nacido en Cuba?" (Why am I to blame for being born in Cuba?). Musical intertexts referencing a classic Cuban son and conga, and the obliquely articulated desire for the Latina body through the synecdoche of the *caderas* (hips), imbue the lyrics. However, the anaphoric structure of the refrain, formed by the reiterative use of the song's title, proposes two levels of reading. Repetition of the phrase "Why am I to blame?" on the queer dance floor operates on a second discursive

level, as in the disclaimer "I'm sorry, but what choice did I have?" which is neither truly apologetic nor supplicatory. Rather, the singing voice simultaneously rejects the guilt for having been born in a country from which so many of its citizens have fled, and the opprobrium for a love regarded as shameful. Despite the homosexual undertones, the song's nationalistic function masks the politics of sexuality. What distinguishes Albita's writing is the particular tenor of the discourse of nationhood. Rarely does she adopt the mournful mode of exilic Miami, grieving the increasingly abstract concept of a prerevolutionary Cuba. Rather, she imparts optimism for the nascent relations of Cuban Americans with the present Cuba, and the imaging of an island nation "after Castro" with an affective culture more tolerant of both political and sexual differences.

In the more sexually charged songs, Albita enunciates male-inflected lyrics with embedded erotic metaphors, which become suggestive of both homosexual and heterosexual desire. Occasionally presented from a woman's point of view, or conceivably a queer perspective, the texts are invariably articulated in the confessional tone of the first-person voice. Sensual imagery suffuses "Deseo de mujer" ("A Woman's Desire") from the CD *Albita llegó* (*Albita Has Arrived*, 2004), as the singing voice percolates with female sexual desire, propositioning the eroticized object with promises to "cabalgar desnuda / provocar tus manos hacer el amor" (straddle naked / provoke your hands to make love to me), and pleas to "piérdete en mi piel / dame de beber deseos de mujer" (abandon yourself in my flesh / have me drink a woman's desire). A more hesitant, faltering form of love is suggested in "Quien le prohibe" ("Who Forbids," from *No se parece a nada*), imploring "no me prohibas ir de viaje por los rincones de tu cuerpo" (don't forbid me to journey through the corners of your body), and comparing her lovemaking to the "viento" (wind) that cannot be obstructed from rustling the palm fronds.

Other sexually infused texts ambiguously speak to different sexual orientations. "Que manera de quererte" ("What a Way to Want You," from *No se parece a nada*) proposes alternate ways of loving decidedly outside the mainstream, challenging the listener to assume, if only temporarily, the perspective of gay or straight otherness. Albita asks, "Donde podré vivir sino en tu sexo?" (Where could I live if not in your sex?). Although the authorship confounds the discernment of gender ideology, the listener nonetheless infers the gender of the desired object and the manner of "sex" implied by the singing voice.

The negotiation of a lesbian existence in exile is addressed in several of Albita's song texts. In "Mírame, Rózame, Ámame" ("Look at Me, Brush against Me, Love Me"), from the album *Dicen Que . . .* (*They Say . . .*, 1996), the lyrics suggest a furtive love relegated to the shadows, with

requests such as "Yo quiero que tu me beses/pero no quiero testigos" (I want you to kiss me / but I don't want witnesses), and "Esta noche si tu puedes mírame entre la gente / mírame sin que lo noten / rózame a escondidas" (Tonight, if you can, look at me through the crowd / look at me without their noticing / brush against me surreptitiously). Resigning herself to society's homophobic anxieties in "Aunque no entiendan" ("Even if They Don't Understand") from the CD *Hecho a mano* (*Handmade*, 2002), she states "Voy a ti . . . y soy feliz / aunque no entiendan" (I go to you . . . and I am happy / even if they don't understand).

Undoubtedly, Albita's strongest indictment of the marginalized status of gay men and lesbians is articulated in "Solo porque vivo" ("Solely Because I Live," from *No se parece a nada*). The singing voice denounces the stigmatization, cultural repression, and homophobia experienced as a lesbian, suffering through "traición" (treason), "incompresión" (incomprehension), and "injuria" (insult), "solo porque vivo / solo porque soy" (solely because I live / solely because I am). However, a more liberatory tone is raised against the condemnations of a hypocritical society in "Me da la gana" ("I Feel Like It," from *Albita Llegó*). The subject responds to the various strategies employed by those who "siembran sus dudas y odios / y en nombre de Dios condenan . . . y solo les digo: / me da la gana!" (plant their doubts and hatred / and condemn in the name of God . . . I only say to them: / I feel like it!). The defiant response, which serves as the song's title, is performed with the potential for becoming an empowering refrain for the queer autonomous subject.

In contrast, Albita promotes the strategy of indifference to social censuring in "Andan diciendo por ahí" ("They Say," from *Hecho a mano*, 2002), stating "me resbala / como el jabón sobre la piel / las cosas malas terminan por el huequito del baño" (water off a duck's back / like soap across the skin / bad things finish down the shower drain). The repetition of *jitanjáforas*—onomatopoeic nonsense syllables (e.g., *ble, bla, bururu, barara*)—represents the frivolous language of rumor and malicious gossip, the nature of which is never directly stated in the text.

Through the dialectic of erotic and national discourse in Cuban dance music, these song texts are transgressive in that they expose the artificial boundaries erected by heteronomativity. Characterized by ambiguous language, the texts are consciously ungendered in their multiple levels of discourse, and do not clearly present a female subject. Constructions of queer identity are made intratextually through oblique references, and extratextually via public awareness of the sexual politics of the singing voice. While the songs are generally interpreted as narrative of the singer-songwriter's life experiences, Albita has remained elusive and unusually guarded concerning the details of her personal

life, which are not played up in music or promotion. However, homo-eroticism as subtext should not be construed as sublimated expression. It may signify, rather, the necessary compromise that womyn authors must make in order to facilitate the consumption and soften the impact of gender politics on the etic listener. While Albita's songs are not necessarily lesbian-targeted works, homoerotic readings of the texts are not paralogical given her status as the first Latina lesbian voice. Also, the texts do not necessarily define *a priori* what function they may serve. The promise of double readings, or multilayered interpretive possibilities, surfaces as the listeners construct meaning out of a text in different ways, according to their individual needs and experiences. This reading of an alternate discourse is akin to the rewriting that gay men and lesbians engage in when consuming music. The commercial success of Albita's brand of gender and sexuality in musical narrative suggests considerable concessions in the prevailing attitudes toward women in a patriarchal system, where male control and discourses nonetheless continue to dominate.

QUEER ICONICITY AND PERFORMATIVITY

In the intercultural confluence that is Albita's audience, the performance represents a complex interweaving of different desires—namely, to (1) enhance the appreciation for Cuban expressive modes among non-Latino tourists; (2) evoke nostalgia among Cuban Americans; (3) provide a rallying point for solidarity and the affirmation of a pan-Latino identity among Hispanics; (4) empower women and challenge hetero-sexist subordination; and (5) articulate the liberatory struggles engaging the queer subjectivities. Thus, the performative narratives are complex, polyvocal communications for constituting identities. However, it is in the interpretation of dance music that the queer links are strongly established. These performances dramatize a queer narrative of longing that is culturally configured to be, among other things, relatively ambiguous to heterosexuals. Through the metaphoric vehicle of unfulfilled desire and the cultural practice of nostalgia, Albita obliquely targets the queer subjectivities, inviting them to reconcile their pasts, and take charge of certain sociosexual processes. Her integrative imaging of Cubanness and queerness, and its very contradiction given the exile community's relative discomfort with homo culture, has made her music an important site for gay performativity and resistance.

The queer act of dancing in a gay club articulates a privileged site that provides access to the mechanisms for self-representation. The meaning of improvised social dancing produced in queer club culture

represents more than a metaphor for sexual mobility, but a process of contestation where minoritarian subjects negotiate the emergence of community. This is particularly true for Latino queers engaged in the subcultural collectivity of dance. The club provides an emancipating cultural place for Latina lesbians, whose Hispanic identities are aurally transmitted through rhythm and historically embodied in the act of dancing. Here, they can claim their space in the social realm, decolonizing the body with libidinal drives, and shifting the power dynamics, however transient, to the dance floor.

Because of its cultural symbolism as the international musical marker of Latinidad, salsa has been appropriated among Hispanic lesbians. However, salsa—a profoundly heterosexual articulation—is promptly queered, and reconfigured under a different cultural autonomy. Through reinterpretive listening practices, this masculinist idiom is reinscribed with liberatory meaning. Particularly favored is Albita's salsa erótica, forging a lesbian *salsera* identity negotiated through the ambivalent positioning of the Cuban queer and the salsa diva in club space. Her role in queer club culture is centered on both the lack of role models for lesbian youth in America and on the symbolic preference for the salsa aesthetic, with its defiant polyrhythmic and subversive *clave* pattern. Hence, she answers the iconic needs of the lesbian Latina. As a salsera parodizing masculinity, she has become a paragon of queer performativity. More significantly, Albita queers Latinidad. She has become an idol for lesbian audiences who are creating particular meanings through the consumption of her music. Her salsa erótica has become an emblem for the formerly "invisible" Latina lesbian identity. Concurrently, her curious brand of patriotism strikes a chord with Cuban American lesbians who, by and large, have been more politically concerned with the poetics of Cubanness than queerness. Consequently, the political resignification of Albita's music, and the reconfiguration of queer cultural forms as centered on specifically Cuban musical histories, promotes local gay community solidarity. Furthermore, they provided a forum for the negotiation of this historicized locality against hegemonic configurations of gayness.

FORGING FEMININITY

Perhaps the most unsettling aspect of Albita's meteoric career is the series of image transformations.[18] Gone now are her trademark androgynous visage, the tailored suits, and the two-toned shoes. Albita has emerged reinvented, with ample cleavage, platinum hair, and the full imaging of Latina femininity. Her subsequent revelation of femininity draws a host of questions including the reconfiguring of lesbian "other" as promotional

strategy, and the commercial pandering to the male gaze. The cover of the album *Dicen Que . . . (They Say . . .*, 1996) reflects the problems of the visualization of the diva's body in media representation. The images capitulate to the self-eroticizing impulse and the fetishization of the female body, hypersexualizing through garish, provocative costuming such as a tight bustier to accentuate the breasts and hourglass figure. Newly packaged as an icon of hyperfemininity, Albita now has an image that suggests a rather prurient come-on to potential consumers. While it may be argued that her image transformation suggests another instance of the internalization of patriarchal codes, it nonetheless conceals other interpretive possibilities, as the public implicitly addressed is not so much male as it is female. For instance, the strategy of reappropriation, of symbolically regaining control of the body, foreshadows Albita's taking control of her recordings via a self-produced, independent label (Angel's Dawn). However, the femininity that Albita claims is more associated with female impersonation in its excess, suggesting reversal of drag: woman as man as woman. As a self-conscious caricature burlesquing femininity, she is a hyperbolic over-characterization that in its very exaggeration neutralizes the objectification of the female body. Her challenge to social stereotypes through parody is blatantly counter-hegemonic. But like a Cuban chameleon, the image reshifts. The androgyne and the *puta* (loose woman) have receded, replaced by comfortably flowing, smart pantsuits, almost anti-aesthetic in their nondescriptness. But transformation can be understood as a process of self-empowerment as much as a matter of image-marketing, and despite her deconstruction of gender, Albita never decontextualizes herself from her Cuban, postrevolutionary identity.

CONCLUSIONS

Attesting to the ambiguity and mutability of identity, Albita's performativity and continual reinvention of her stage persona as a series of conflicting images reflects the multiple roles that she models for women. In her exploration of these diverse images through the use of masquerade and parody, she disrupts various stereotypical codes of gender and sexuality. Both regressive and progressive, these conflicted constructions also suggest the use of the performing body as a site of gender dialogism, of oppositionality and resistance challenging heterosexist subordination.

As a performative chameleon, Albita channels the oppositional binaries of masculine/feminine, cultural "other"/insider, past/present, and sublimated object/controlling object. Her performances are thus multiple meaningful events, the most salient of which is the double

discourse of political and sexual dissidence. In this narrative, the theme of escape is articulated, of fleeing from the social constructs circumscribing one's biological gender as well as from socialist oppression. Occupying multiple sites of meaning that evoke different configurations of the self, Albita summons divergent readings among various subcultural groups. As her music is culturally, sexually, and socially grounded, Albita is at the intersection of multiple social categories. Her various representations of "otherness" deliberately dislocate cultural and gender boundaries. Most significantly, through the poetics of performing gender, she has redefined Cuban national identity and affirmed a lesbian existence in exile, contesting a hegemonic structure in both the social and musical domains.

NOTES

1. The *guayabera* is the traditional Cuban man's shirt.
2. "Yo soy una mujer, con las cinco letras de la palabra!" she announced, during a performance at the Yuca nightclub, Miami Beach, April 2001.
3. Ellen Koskoff, "An Introduction to Women, Music, and Culture," in *Women and Music in Cross-Cultural Perspective,* ed. Ellen Koskoff (Westport, Conn.: Greenwood, 1987), 10.
4. Jean Starobinski, "The Idea of Nostalgia," *Diogenes* 54 (1966): 101.
5. Albita recounts an incident in which the management of Havana's Tropicana nightclub, in a failed attempt to feminize her image, suggested that she wear "lentejuelas y algunas plumas" (sequins and some feathers). "Si me ponía lentejuelas, me mataban a piedra!" (Had I worn sequins, they would have stoned me to death!) she said, referring to her fans' unequivocal embrace of her anti-aestheticism. Interview with the author, 1997.
6. Judith Butler, *Gender Trouble: Feminism and Subversion of Identity* (New York: Routledge, 1990), 25.
7. One example was the institutionalization of homosexuals, dissidents, and other "deviants" into the Unidad Militar de Ayuda a la Producción (Military Units to Aid Production), a series of agrarian labor camps for ideological rehabilitation.
8. See Lucy Green, *The Sexual Politics of Music: Discourse, Musical Meaning, and Education* (Cambridge: Cambridge University Press, 1997); and John Sheperd, "Music and Male Hegemony," in *Music as Social Text* (Cambridge: Polity, 1987), 151–72.
9. A *tres* is a Cuban guitarlike chordophone with three pairs of strings.
10. The sacred *batá* drumming ensemble consists of three hourglass-shaped drums that play a repertoire of interlocking melody-rhythms for the *orichás* (predominantly Yoruban deities). According to Steven Cornelius, the batá represents "a divine womb fertilized by the phallic driving of the

drummer's hands"; see Stephen Cornelius "Personalizing Public Symbols Through Music Ritual: Santería's Presentation to Aña," *Latin American Music Review* 16:1 (1995): 27. Consequently, the disempowering of the instrument through menses and the imbalance of gender energies are among reasons proffered for this gender-biased restriction in batá drumming.

11. The *toques* are batá ritual pieces whereby communion with the divine is activated.
12. Santería is an Afro-Cuban religion syncretizing Spanish Catholicism with West African pantheons.
13. *Sonero* is a Cuban term that, in addition to signifying a player of the son music, refers to an all-around entertainer who can sing and dance.
14. As the preeminent musical expression of Cuba, the son functions as an identity emblem. Although historically associated with the working underclass, the genre's negotiation of binary opposites (e.g., Hispanic/African, dominant/subaltern, rural/urban) satisfied the aesthetic preferences of listeners across racial boundaries and social strata. In effect, the music functioned as a metaphoric expression of Cuban cultural heterogeneity. See Arjun Appadurai, *Modernity at Large* (Minneapolis: University of Minnesota Press, 1996), 165.
15. The son is stylistically dichotomized into two gendered subtypes defined by rhythmic, instrumental, and functional factors—the *son macho* (male), and *son hembra* (female). The son hembra is predominantly performed for listening, while the greater rhythmic complexity, percussiveness, and brass augmenting the musical backing on the son macho suggests music designed for dancing. According to Oscar Bombillo, tres player for group Son Picante in Havana, Cuba, "the former invites the listener while the latter forces you to dance." Personal communication with the author, 1996.
16. See Frances R. Aparicio, *Listening to Salsa: Gender, Latin Popular Music, and Puerto Rican Cultures* (Hanover, N.H.: Wesleyan University Press, 1998), and Lise Waxer, "Las Caleñas Son Como Las Flores: The Rise of All-Women Salsa Bands in Cali, Colombia," *Ethnomusicology* 42:2 (2001): 228–261.
17. Gustavo Pérez-Firmat observes that many Cuban-American love songs characteristically exploit the language of love to impart political frustrations, wherein the motif of longing for a past lover is used as a metaphor for the lost island; see Pérez-Firmat, *Life on the Hyphen: The Cuban-American Way* (Austin: University of Texas Press, 1994).
18. The title of this section, "Forging Femininity," is an allusion to Robert Walser's proposition of "forging masculinity," concerning the performance of identity in heavy metal rock; see Robert Walser, *Running with the Devil: Power, Gender, and Madness in Heavy Metal Music* (Hanover, N.H.: University Press of New England, 1993).

9

SU CASA ES MI CASA
Latin House, Sexuality, Place

STEPHEN AMICO

As for me, I have changed my first name, my religion, and my address, and I profess political views and a sexual orientation that are at odds with those held dear by most Cuban-Americans. My English is even more fluent than my Spanish, thought I still speak both with a telltale accent (and a lisp!). My lover, most of my friends, and my economic, social, and cultural life are largely non-Hispanic, and I cannot visit Calle Ocho these days without realizing that I do not belong there anymore. . . . As an openly gay man, I can never be reconciled with Little Havana, as it is personified by my relatives and by other Cubans and Cuban-Americans with whom I come in contact.

—Jesse G. Monteagudo, "Miami, Florida"

The "hometown,"[1] the site of one's introduction into one's initial culture, into the machinations of the social, the familial, serves not only as the site for cultural instruction through praxis but additionally (and perhaps more profoundly) as a locus for the cognitive and affective production of one's subjective place. Although in an ever-increasingly mobile society the hometown may be but a transitory locus, the originary site doubtless leaves its imprimatur on all subsequent productions of place for those who have ventured beyond its parameters; indeed, despite his

disjunction from Little Havana, Monteagudo notes that he is "[s]till
. . . Cuban by birth, descent and upbringing" and that "Calle Ocho will
always be a street of memories that, with the flight of time, becomes
increasingly better. Growing up in Little Havana has made me what I
am today."[2]

This reconciliation with the past, however, is effectuated through
the palliative light of the historical and, in fact, highlights the ambivalence with which many homosexual men and women view what may be
for heterosexuals a relatively unproblematic sphere of social induction
and comity. I do not want to suggest that adherence to the mores of
the sexual majority obliterates any sort of problematic enculturation, or
guarantees an uncomplicated, effortless interface with the social. I do,
however, wish to emphasize that the relationship of the homosexual to
the hometown is often wrought with complications; it may be the site of
both humiliations and erasure, of anathemization and contumely, of an
internally perceived or externally proscribed inability to become part of
the social fabric—all of which are contributory to many homosexuals'
decisions to escape the hometown in search of a location in which a
more salubrious place may be effectuated. Following James Clifford's
suggestion to reconceptualize diaspora (noting, for example, that
"[d]ecentered, lateral connections may be as important as those formed
around a teleology of origin/return"[3]), we must also, in the context of
the experiences of many homosexual men and women, consider variables of movement and *direction*: specifically, the idea of a *reverse diaspora*, the movement of people not radiating out from a fixed origin but,
rather, from disparate and diffuse locations into those (few) that may
be perceived as not only less inimical to but, in fact, supportive of their
(sexual) selves, a movement more centripetal than centrifugal. These
resulting "gay meccas"—generally major urban centers—thus become
the new sites in which a formation of place occurs, a place that encompasses and is partially predicated upon that variable which had previously been obliterated: homosexuality.[4]

"Place" itself, however, is not an unproblematic concept in relation
to the reverse-diasporic homosexual, a generic positionality into which
one effortlessly fits by dint of sexual attractions. While the concepts of
a "gay community" and "gay (male) culture" are frequently encountered
in all manner of media, they are often replete with *de facto* connotations
of white and the middle class, steroids and Fire Island, nipple rings and
Cher—even, in fact, "American."[5] While the idea of a unified and univocal
community may be used for utilitarian, often political, reasons,[6] actual
experience, as well as historical and contemporary accounts,[7] seem to
gainsay this rather simplified model; the presentation of mass-media

images notwithstanding, the "gay community" is obviously neither exclusively white nor (upper) middle class.[8] In this chapter, focusing on New York City, I will examine how such movement, from one place to another, engenders the production of a new sense of place, one composed of numerous, sometimes conflicting variables, incorporating both that which may be "there upon arrival" and that which is "brought," and how music (specifically, Latin house) contributes to its production among certain gay Latino men.[9] Moreover, I will also illuminate some musical syncretisms that may have become occluded in order to illustrate the ways in which complex identities impact upon musical, social, and cultural production.[10] Although the stereotyped "public face" of the "gay community" may be monochromatic, its variegated soundtrack, the product of its true heterogeneity, at least gives lie to this image; the music, in this regard, queers any simplistic notion of a homogenized gay community or culture.

The bulk of fieldwork for this chapter was undertaken in the early 2000s, a time during which not only had Latin house become extremely popular, but also Latino artists such as Christina Aguilera, Marc Anthony, Jennifer Lopez, Ricky Martin, and Carlos Santana had achieved major mainstream successes.[11] In addition to speaking with several patrons of the club La Nueva Escuelita (to be discussed below), I was also fortunate enough to have spoken with DJ/producer/engineer/performer/writer Norty Cotto, one of the most well-known and fecund artists on the house music scene, and Aldo Marin, co-owner of Cutting Records (a major Latin record label in New York City), both of whose comments are included in the text. I should note that I am using the term *Latino* here to indicate men from numerous geographic backgrounds; in actuality, the scene at Escuelita comprises mainly men of Puerto Rican, Cuban, and Dominican descent, including those of "mixed" (e.g., Latino/African American) heritage; likewise, the genre of Latin house draws largely upon the musics of these locations.

Although Latin house has, according to Marin, "only recently been seen [by the major labels] as a distinct genre," he also noted that it has been around since at least the late 1980s, adding that "it's already lasted a lot longer than anyone thought it would."[12] Marin cited some of the earliest manifestations of the genre as including Bad Boy Orchestra's "Arroz con Pollo" (which he described as "freestyle beats mixed with Latin beats"[13]), and Wepaman's "Esa Loca." Another source concurs with Marin's time line,[14] placing the genesis in the second half of the 1980s, at which time "some of the pioneers of house music of Latin American descent gave birth to this genre by releasing house records in Spanish" (such as Spanish versions of the songs "Can't Get Enough," and

"Payback Is a Bitch" by the American Puerto Rican singer Liz Torres[15]).
The 1990s witnessed the emergence of both new labels and artists (including Nervous Records and the Strictly Rhythm label, and producer/writer/DJ Armand van Helden), and, by the mid-1990s, both Cutting Records (with artists such as Sancocho, 2 in a Room, and Fulanito) and Norty Cotto had risen to preeminence in the field.

The "Latin" component of the genre will be discussed shortly, and despite the generic appellation, its function as an identificatory locus for some gay Latinos is probably comprehensible. House music, however, in the past decade or so, has become a constituent of the urban soundscape, entering the arena of mass-commodification, and perhaps slaking off some of its subcultural (homosexual) connotations in the process. Cotto, for example, described house to me as an inherently "open" genre, transcending boundaries of race, sexuality, and gender.[16] Still, house is, in historical perspective, popular consciousness, and actual practice, an appurtenance of some segments of the "gay (male) community," a "de facto soundtrack of the queer nation,"[17] and a genre often viewed with homophobic antipathy even among aficionados of African American music styles in general.[18] This relationship of house to gay audiences is further sedimented through its stylistic and sociohistorical relationship to disco, another genre largely related to homosexual men; as Marin told me, "house *is* disco." Latin house is, however, by no means listened to/produced for/purchased by an *exclusively* homosexual audience;[19] according to Cotto, its audience, while mostly Latin, is neither wholly homosexual nor heterosexual. Additionally, its various creators and promulgators—writers, producers, performers, DJs, and the like—generally self-present as heterosexual.

The wide range of Latin music styles included under the broad rubric of Latin house is evident in the numerous compilations such as the *Latin House Party* series (mixed by Cotto) or *The House of Cutting* (mixed by Steve "Chip-Chop" Gonzalez and Lord G), among others. For example, *merengue* samples and rhythms are used in both Armand van Helden's "Entre Mi Casa" and Sancocho's "Tumba la Casa" or "Alcen Las Manos,"[20] the latter of which is described in the Cutting Records catalog as "merenhouse." *Montuno*-like sections of call and response, evocative of both Cuban *son* and salsa, are evident in Reel to Reel's "Mueve la Cadera" (which also features a salsa-like harmonic ostinato of tonic-dominant [I–V]), Bad Boy Orchestra's "El Loco," and samples of (assumed) salsa or son recordings (which appear in That Cuban Guy's "Buscando Ildo" or Bad Boy Orchestra's "Bomba Remix"). Additionally, instances of either manifest or implied 2-3 or 3-2 *clave* patterns abound (La Cubanita's "Locame," Lesson One's "Vamos a Gozar," El Aficiao's "Presente,"

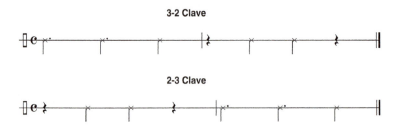

Figure 9.1 Clave rhythms.

and, appropriately enough, Isaac Santiago's "La Clave"[21]), including an unmistakable rumba clave (DJ Lucho's "El Pito") (see Figure 9.1).

The clave pattern, found in such genres as son and salsa, is itself particularly useful in illuminating both a musical and a social locus for the syncretism of Latin and house musics, as innumerable tracks of the latter make use of a clave that is either fully realized or incomplete (my terms). For example, Shine's "Stimulating and Exciting" features a sample of a woman screaming, the pattern of which is an unmistakable 3-2 clave (see Figure 9.2), while in Everything But the Girl's "Missing" a synthesizer appearing throughout the song makes use of an incomplete clave pattern, outlining in the chorus a harmonic progression of i–VI–VII–iv (see Figure 9.3).

The syncopation of the clave, combined with the steady four-on-the-floor thud of the kick—that is, an accented hit on each beat of a 4/4 measure, typical of house—forms a particularly seductive groove, one that fairly compels dancing or bodily movement of some sort. The connections go beyond formal analysis, however, reflecting the movements of and relationships among actual musicians. For example, the rhythmic transcription of "Missing" is from the version remixed for club play by Todd Terry, an artist who "more than any other producer . . . defined New York house during the 1980s."[22] However, it is also important to note that Terry had been active in the world of Latin music, working with "Little" Louie Vega and Kenny "Dope" Gonzalez, both of whom had been prolific in the Latin music field, and from whom Terry later appropriated the "Masters at Work" moniker.[23] A similar intersection of the house and Latin music scenes can be witnessed in the connection between John "Jellybean" Benitez and Madonna (whose "Vogue" features an unmistakable incomplete clave rhythm in the piano accompaniment); Benitez was not only instrumental in presenting Madonna's earliest recordings to a wide audience (via his position as a club DJ, at such locations as New York City's Danceteria), but also coproduced

Figure 9.2 Shine, "Stimulating and Exciting."

Figure 9.3 Everything But the Girl, "Missing," Todd Terry remix.

her first, eponymous album, which was instrumental in advancing her career. As founder of HOLA (Home of Latino Artists) Recordings in 1995, Benitez has also fostered the careers of many aspiring Latino musicians, although this is only one facet of a career that has crossed into several musical genres from pop to freestyle to hip-hop.

The same sort of genre-crossing is true of Cotto's work. With an impressive roster of credits in numerous genres—a DJ with international engagements, writer (2nd Tribe's "Que Te Gusta," Bad Boy Orchestra's "Todo Puerto Rico," Sancocho's "Alcen Las Manos," and others), producer (Sancocho, Bad Boy Orchestra, the hip-hop group KRS-One), engineer (Soul II Soul, KRS-One, the Sugarcubes), and remixer (including four

years with house "legend" Tony Humphries)—Cotto characterizes himself with humor, in reference to his peripatetic nature, as "a mess."[24] His deep investment in the music, one that enables him to effectively communicate with his audiences, encompasses not only his desire to project a Latino identity, but also a more general, freely defined musical identity. "Giving voice to the Latin experience—that's always at the forefront," he notes. "I've always represented for the race, I was on the radio here in New York City, on a Spanish radio station, representing for the Latinos . . . but more than anything, I want to represent the *music*—and I just *love* house music. That's why I try to do a bit of everything . . . the vibe, just the whole groove [draws me]."

Postmodern theory has invoked the image of the "schizophrenic" as illustrative of identity in a global and increasingly rapidly dislocating and dislocated society, but this assessment seems to me, while theoretically necessary, to be sometimes more sensationalistic or tabloid-esque than representative. While Enlightenment-based concepts of a unified, unproblematic identity have been replaced by the idea of the decentered subject, it is still important not to eschew the idea that, for many, the belief in a "stable" identity functions within their own discourses of self-presentation; if we value such "bottom-up" discourses on a par with (though not displacing) those of the "top-down" variety, they cannot be dismissed *tout court*. This is particularly important in addressing the issue of race (vis-à-vis sexuality); as Samir Dayal notes, "[W]hile . . . queering is a useful counter to simplistic identity politics, for many minorities it remains an imperative to assert an ethnic identity grounded in material specificity in the everyday and the local—an identity that is firmly historicized . . . there is some suspicion of 'performativity' as a liberal, elitist, or Euro-centric construct."[25]

In Lisa Lowe's tripartite scheme, immigrant identities are seen as concurrently heterogeneous ("[indicating] the existence of differences and differential relationships within a bounded category"), hybrid (" [referring] to the formation of cultural objects and practices that are produced by the histories of uneven and unsynthetic power relations"), and multiple ("designating the ways in which subjects located within social relations are determined by the contradictions of capitalism, patriarchy and race relations with . . . particular contradictions surfacing in relation to the material conditions of a specific historical moment").[26] This conceptualization is useful in that it acknowledges the manifold components of identity without recourse to a vocabulary of either pathology or simple essentialism. It is just such *multidentitied* agents (author's neologism) who, as shown, contribute to musical syncretization.

There are, of course, numerous similar examples of such musical cross-fertilization via multidentitied artists,[27] and the dynamic must be seen as one of reciprocity; if Latin elements emigrate into other genres of music, then the reverse is true as well. For example, Cotto noted a predilection for underground house styles, and these are readily apparent in many of his Latin house projects; also, the use of augmented fourths and Phrygian seconds, as well as an aesthetic of fragmentation, typical of the progressive/hard house style, show up in the Latin house track "El Loco," performed by Bad Boy Orchestra, and written and produced by Cotto. The occurrence of clave in house is thus neither a serendipitous nor accidental instance of syncretism, to my mind; rather, it is the outcome of multidirectional influences among genres that do not exist in isolation. Here, syncretism itself is viewed not as an abstract process whereby amorphous musical "forms" intersect and produce new progeny via alchemy, but, as one carried out by actual, living, multidentitied musicians interacting with other forms and agents.[28] Furthermore, the bidirectionality of musical influence suggests a parallel with the social; as Benigno Sánchez-Eppler and Cindy Patton note, the "diasporic queer" is both transformed and transformer in his engagement with the new place, one that must be thought of as provisional and malleable rather than given.[29]

***

On a late Thursday night (or, more precisely, an early Friday morning[30]), the line on West Thirty-Ninth Street in Manhattan is snaking around the corner from its origin midway down the block, a queue of approximately 150 men (largely Latino, African American, or "Blatino") assembled in the unseasonably cold weather, each waiting patiently to enter La Nueva Escuelita.[31] Moving at a speed so slow as to render incremental advances toward the entrance almost imperceptible (save, in retrospect: "I was back there twenty minutes ago"), it is the thud of the kick, barely perceptible from outside the entrance, which reconfirms that our wait in the chill air is, in fact, finite.

Once inside, the thud-thud-thud-thud is entirely overwhelming, the sonic envelopment seeming to highlight the closeness of the space—the low ceilings, the packed bodies, the almost viscous air (moisture seemingly its lone, constitutional element). The floor is packed with men moving to the house-house-house-house-beat-beat-beat-beat,[32] the bar two deep, the go-go boys undulating on slightly raised platforms, although still within easy reach of those who wish to show approbation via a bill placed (with an often lingering and exploratory hand) inside the dancer's scant covering. Over the loudspeakers, Kevin Aviance's

voice ("I am the master / you are the servant / and the rhythm is my bitch"), four on the floor, clave. At one point in the evening, the music, almost surreptitiously, segues into a Latin set—the house beat remits, salsa emerges. Men are dancing with men, some continuing the solo generic club dancing, a few paired off (man and man or, less frequently, man and woman) and dancing as couples, holding one another loosely (in Spanish, *parajes enlazadas*), as is typical when dancing to salsa. Salsa becomes merengue and, for a while, the four on the floor returns—the saxophones "hit" only on the beats (or simply on the downbeat), and a sampled piano ostinato of tonic/dominant is superimposed.

There is an abrupt break, the cessation of the music accompanied by the appearance of channels of light emanating from two sweeping follow spots positioned at the far end of the dance floor. Dance music is replaced by an RKO/MGM-esque trumpet fanfare; the dancers on the floor stay where they are and lower themselves, en masse; dance floor becomes ass floor. An announcer's voice is heard, a vampy riff begins, and, from behind the glittering curtain, a glamorous woman appears, lip-synching to the recorded female singer's voice. One by one, three equally concupiscent women appear, each taking a solo verse and all joining in on the chorus of "Trouble": "I'm evil, my middle name is misery / I'm evil, so don't you mess around with me." These "gender illusionists,"[33] all of them "women of color"—Karen Covergirl ("six feet, four inches of goddess"), Lorena St. Cartier, Cherry Pie ("our Asian goddess"), and Victoria Lace—come together for the final chorus, "selling" the song via bodily gestures and facial inflections, the crowd applauding, howling, in support.

On this occasion, the opening number is followed by the emergence of the ultraglamorous (and ample) Miss Angel Sheridan, the emcee of the evening's show, meticulously lip-synching to a live version of Bette Midler's "When a Man Loves a Woman," replete with Midler's onstage banter. On another evening, Miss Sheridan emerged in a leafy, lime-green cape, which, as the music kicked in to Gloria Estefan's "Conga," she shed, revealing a matching, sequined unitard. Finally, to a female vocalist's rendition of "La Bamba," Miss Sheridan shook everything she had, the choreography turning her into a wildly gesticulating, dervish-like juggernaut. After her impressive workout, Miss Sheridan, panting, repeated into the microphone (to much laughter), "I'm too big for this! I'm too big!"

After her various opening numbers, she will generally "work" the audience; a combination of comic abuse (directed at both them and herself) and fondness,[34] interacting with the assembled, culling her material from those before her, as well as from current events. For example, upon

noticing several young men with bleached hair and visible dark roots one evening: "Word, you look just like a Dominican woman! Honey, there ain't a drop of peroxide left in the Bronx." And regarding both her Cuban roots, and the then media saturation of the Elian Gonzalez saga: "Send that muthafucka home [cheers from the audience]. I'm tired of that bitch interrupting *All My Children* . . . Nobody gave me all this attention when I came here . . . When I swam over from Cuba, I was wearing a black and white bathing suit. I washed up on the beach, and everyone shouted, 'roll it back, roll it back!' And I said, 'Get your hands off me, you Orca motherfuckers!' "

Following Miss Sheridan's "monologue," the various solo performers take to the stage, one at a time, each lip-synching (and often dancing) to standards, show tunes, or dance/house tracks, some of which allude to the strength of women (e.g., Victoria Lace's performance of Jennifer Holliday's "A Woman's Got the Power"; this particular number ending with Miss Lace caterwauling through the audience, her blond hair whipping about).[35] Others will, in fact, impersonate or "channel" known divas (e.g., preternaturally evocative performances of Dionne Warwick and Whitney Houston by Victoria Lace and Tyra Allure, respectively). And although Miss Sheridan's caustic humor may seem rather vicious at times, she introduces each of the performers with warmth, alluding to the "familial" connection ("Ladies and gentlemen, your diva and my daughter, Miss Karen Covergirl!"),[36] and importuning that the audience show "love" to them.

The show completed, the lights again dim, and the dance music resumes, the DJ (often Steve "Chip-Chop" Gonzalez) now spinning a set featuring hip-hop (to which many of the people will sing/rap along) and reggae/dub (Mad Cobra, for example), this leading to pop/soul/old-skool hits by such artists as Santana, The Jackson 5, Soul II Soul, or McFadden and Whitefield. Following this set, the music segues back into Latin/tribal house, pop-diva hits, or occasionally trance, on one occasion effectuated by a cessation of all sound except for the kick drum repeating a *tresillo* rhythm (Figure 9.4).

This "set," occurring at approximately 3:00 A.M., coincides with the "hottest" part of the evening—the dance floor is particularly crowded, the people spilling over onto the area surrounding it, the house beat unremitting, the heat (literally) rising. Tracks such as "Pasilda" by Afro Medusa (featuring both a clave and a salsa-like piano riff) or Negrocan's "Cada Vez" (with a montuno-like call-and-response section) may be heard, as well as the decidedly non-Latin "Castles in the Sky" by Ian Van Dahl. On one evening, the song that seemed to occupy the peak moment was Whitney Houston's "I Learned From the Best"; on another, that position was occupied by Vanessa Mitchell's "This Joy." On yet another

Figure 9.4 Tresillo rhythm.

occasion, the crowd was whipped into a joyful frenzy with the playing of Santería chants mixed over a house beat, several people singing along with them (a common occurrence).

Throughout the evening both English and Spanish can be heard—in Angel Sheridan's dialogue, among the guests, and in the vocals of the tracks. The use of language (that is, Spanish) as a marker of ethnicity is certainly important, and there are Latin house tracks that may indeed feature Spanish language as the only specific Latin attribute (i.e., 68 Beats' "Tribal Anthem," which, absent the Spanish vocal, is extremely stylistically similar to the tribal mix of their track "Music to My Ears"). Some, however—for example, Victor Calderone's "Give It Up/Price of Love," featured on a Latin house compilation—lack even this trait; the only "Latin" aspect may, in fact, be a foregrounding of the rhythm tracks and a concomitant backgrounding of harmonic and/or melodic (including vocal) material. Cotto has noted that in some cases "the main Latin aspects of the tracks are kind of fading away, and it's gotten more tribal-y and percussive—not necessarily [specifically] clave-wise, but more percussive, like drums, almost African-ish."

Indeed, the genre of tribal house, extremely popular in New York City since at least the 1990s (both at clubs and via compilations on disc),[37] as well as, for example, some of Armand Van Helden's work (e.g., "Rumba," "The Witch Doktor," and "Zulu," the latter two of which feature rhythm tracks that might be considered generically "African-ish") may be seen as comporting with the aesthetic adumbrated by Cotto; it is clear that both tribal and Latin house—via such artists as Van Helden—have contributed to each other's stylistic development. But, Cotto suggested another reason for the importance of the vocal aside from "ethnic marking"—specifically, the ability of the song to attract listeners and, concomitantly, to garner radio play. Absent vocals, radio play is unlikely, in his opinion ("you can't sing a sample hook over and over . . . [you] don't hook onto them on the radio"); absent radio play, selling to a wide audience is difficult; ultimately, in his opinion, without the wide base of support for the genre via radio play, Latin house would be increasingly de-Latinized.

This brings me to the idea of musical affect and its importance in the production of place. Lawrence Grossberg, in his discussion of youth cultures and postmodern American culture, sees the "affective alliances" of the 1960s as engendered largely through a relation to rock music, noting that "it is music which founds place . . . [and] which

affectively locates [people] in the world by constructing the rhythms of their stopping and going."[38] While a certain romanticism permeates segments of the text, it nonetheless necessarily foregrounds that which often underlies the intricate machinations of self- and social formation (that is, the affective), and furthermore theoretically engages the discourses of music's importance so often encountered when speaking with the nonacademic or nonmusician/nontheorist: music, for many, is profoundly influential.[39] It is clear that there are numerous variables at play in bringing about an "affective alliance" at La Nueva Escuelita, in the context of a place (both physical and imagined) defined in large part by music: the drag show (a symbol widely understood as gay both within and outside "gaydom"), with constant references, musical and otherwise, to Cuban, Dominican, or Puerto Rican cultures; the social history of La Escuelita itself, of which many may be cognizant, or in which many may have been involved; the connection with or simply the visual presence of familiar people and faces on a weekly basis; and the heightening of experience through prolonged and intense bodily movement (and, for some, various stimulants), surrounded by other moving bodies. All of these things—and certainly others—contribute to the production of an affective state both subjectively and intersubjectively, and a production of place that includes not only the actual, physical site, but, equally as important, the placing of oneself into a social and aesthetic formation. To be "at" La Escuelita is to be someone who goes to La Escuelita, who shares the experience of being in that place, who carries those experiences, those images, those visceral excitements with him—accompanied by the actual sounds or sonic memories of the music. I want, however, to end by returning to voices, preceded by a brief overview of Silvan Tomkins's work on affect.

According to Tomkins, the affect system is the primary motivational force in humans, and one that is extremely ductile (as distinct from and in comparison to the drive system) in terms of—among other things—variables of time, intensity, density, and object.[40] The organism, through an (often unsuccessful) process of trial and error, seeks to maximize positive affective states and, conversely, minimize negative ones. One such positive state to be maximized is "enjoyment–joy," which can be effectuated/experienced through numerous modalities—communication/communion, recognition of familiar objects, and identification, among others. Although there is clearly a biological basis to his theory, Tomkins insists there is no "correct" object of affect, nor any "correct" modality. For example, what is important is not "the breast" and the feeding situation *per se*, the connection of which "has functioned essentially as an unconscious symbol in the minds of many investigators, each of

whom has probably attributed to it his own private dream," but rather "the magic of the breast and the oral stage . . . [as] a symbol of the most intimate communion." And while many of these affective states can be related to infantile experience, Tomkins is also clear that arousal of such "claustral and pre-verbal complexes," rather than indicative of a regressive pathology, are "perennial and human."[41]

The voices at La Escuelita—voices in Spanish, of gayness—produced overwhelmingly by people of color (male, female, transgender), often singing in the "mother tongue," each suggesting a human face (a most "potent" stimulus for the affect of enjoyment, per Tomkins[42]), serve then not only as superficial "ethnic markers" but as sites of enjoyment-joy on numerous levels: as loci for identification (with she who, like me, is beautiful, powerful, talented, sexual), recognition ("knowing" the person/performer, knowing a song, the latter of which may even engender positive affect via a sense of mastery—knowing a song not only "lexically," but its rich semiotic cache as well) and/or communication/ communion (singing along with the songs, with others singing along with them, displaying myself as "affected" by the experience to the other bodies around me).[43] Such affective states are further intensified by the sensuous, physical properties of sound itself, the audible and the highly amplified moving of the air, the tactile, literal waves on the skin, on the surface, or penetrating, vibrating of the membranes of the eardrums, vibrating the gut.[44]

This is not to retreat into a comforting romance of an ahistorical, autonomous human body, one outside of or immune to a production through discourse, technologies, or ideologies, and one that may indeed be a site for ever-stronger relationships between the haptic and erotic, the cyborgian and the orgasmic. But the body and its sentience should not be obliterated in an attempt to vanquish the affect of "fear–terror" (Tomkins's term) of suspected immutability. Tomkins himself reminds us that "[m]an is neither as free as he feels nor as bound as he fears."[45] Accepting that the human body still exists at this point in time, and that it is implicated in the production and experiencing of affective states does not imply a vanquishing of the cultural by the biological; to the contrary, attention to the conduits of the musically affective open up a wide variety of queer possibilities related to putatively fixed raced, sexed, or gendered bodies. The very syncretic nature of the music at La Escuelita (referring both to specific genres, such as Latin house, as well as an evening's entire musical offering); the shuttling back and forth from English to Spanish; the centrality of the gender illusionists; the opportunity for the (biological) male's identification with the (biological) female, via voice, sound, discourse—all of these obviate the possibility of

imagining neat, antipodal relationships (here/there, native/immigrant, man/woman) based upon corporeality, suggesting instead the requisiteness of the indeterminate, the recalcitrant, the queer. It is useful to note here Eric Hirsch's schematization of space and place, wherein the space (the "background," the "way we might be") becomes, in the course of one's relocation, the place (the "foreground," the "way we are now"), place and space interacting dialectically not only synchronically, but diachronically as well.[46] It is the dynamic relation between these two points that must be highlighted, as the resituation does not eradicate the past; the push/pull of place/space are in flux, shifting back and forth as the subject feels himself now "here," now "there"; likewise, other supposed polar opposites interact in a mutually constitutive and intimately enmeshed fashion, informed by both "nature" and "culture."

Eve Kosofsky Sedgwick and Adam Franck, in their introduction to *Shame and Its Sisters: A Silvan Tomkins Reader*, suggest that in postmodern theory "[t]he distance of any account [of human beings or cultures] from a biological basis is assumed to correlate near-precisely with its potential for doing justice to difference . . . to contingency, to performative force, and to the possibility of change."[47] My account, which does not deny the bodily affects of music, however, also affirms the malleability and multiplicity of identity and place, as well as that of both the musics and musical discourses impacting such constructions. Overemphasis on those variables assumed to be most salient (i.e., Latino/homosexual) or insistence on a strict metonymic relationship between genre and subject(s) (group A listens to/makes/is identified with music X) obviously misses the point. In the same way that creative music makers such as Norty Cotto constantly "experiment" through their involvement in music, so do people in their process of the production of place, interacting with and incorporating a myriad of musical and social variables into the ever-mutable end product that is, in fact, never an ending, but only a conditional "hometown" itself.

NOTES

For their insights, assistance and generosity, many thanks are due to Elizabeth Binford, Norty Cotto, Robin Harris, Ellie Hisama, Peter Manuel, Aldo Marin, Evan Rapport, and the "Escuelitites" who endured my questions; any errors contained herein, however, are mine. Additional and heartfelt thanks to Francesca and Salvatore for everything.

1. Jesse G. Monteagudo, "Miami, Florida," in *Hometowns: Gay Men Write about Where They Belong*, ed. John Preston (New York: E. P. Dutton, 1991),

11–20. The book is a collection of essays, by gay men, all of which deal with the authors' relationships to and memories of their geographical "roots."

2. Ibid., 19–20.

3. James Clifford, "Diasporas," *Cultural Anthropology* 9, no. 3 (1994): 306. On the reconceptualization of diaspora, see also Rogers Brubaker, "The 'Diaspora' Diaspora," *Ethnic and Racial Studies* 29, no. 1 (2005): 1–19.

4. On the construction of the geographic "gay space" (or "gay ghettos"), see Robert Bailey, "Sexual Identity and Urban Space: Economic Structure and Political Action," in *Sexual Identity, Queer Politics,* ed. Mark Blasius (Princeton, N.J.: Princeton University Press, 2001); Benjamin Forest, "West Hollywood as Symbol: The Significance of Place in the Construction of a Gay Identity," *Environment and Planning D, Society and Space* 13, no. 2 (1995): 133–57; and Michael Sibalis, "Urban Space and Homosexuality: The Example of the Marais Paris 'Gay Ghetto'," *Urban Studies* 41, no. 9 (2004): 1739–58.

5. See Dennis Altman, *The Homosexualization of America, The Americanization of the Homosexual* (New York: St. Martin's, 1982).

6. See Mary Bernstein, "Celebration and Suppression: The Strategic Uses of Identity by the Lesbian and Gay Movement," *American Journal of Sociology* 103, no. 3 (1997): 531–65; and Ralph R. Smith and Russel R. Windes, "Identity in Political Context: Lesbian/Gay Representation in the Public Sphere," *Journal of Homosexuality* 37, no. 2 (1999): 25–45. This is not to suggest that "unity" does not confer real benefits upon those who see it as an actuality—for example, creation of a positive identity and a positive self-perception; cf. Deborrah E. S. Frable, Camille Wortman, and Jill Joseph, "Predicting Self-Esteem, Well-Being, and Distress in a Cohort of Gay Men: The Importance of Cultural Stigma, Personal Visibility, Community Networks and Positive Identity," *Journal of Personality* 65, no. 3 (1997): 599–624.

7. See, for example, Elizabeth Lapovsky Kennedy and Madeline Davis, *Boots of Leather, Slippers of Gold: The History of a Lesbian Community* (New York: Routledge, 1993), a historical ethnography of a highly fragmented "lesbian community" in Buffalo, New York, during the period of the 1930s through the 1950s. See also Martin Duberman, *Stonewall* (New York: Dutton, 1993); Charles Kaiser, *The Gay Metropolis, 1940–1996* (Boston: Houghton Mifflin, 1997); and Steven Seidman, "Identity and Politics in a 'Postmodern' Gay Culture: Some Historical and Conceptual Notes," in *Fear of a Queer Planet: Queer Politics and Social Theory*, ed. Michael Warner (Minneapolis: University of Minnesota Press, 1993) for accounts of the divisiveness in early attempts to form a gay (political/social) "community." On the heterogeneity of contemporary queer identity and experience, see Arnaldo Cruz-Malavé and Martin F. Manalansan IV, "Introduction: Dissident Sexualities/Alternative Globalisms," in *Queer Globalizations: Citizenship and the Afterlife of Colonialism,* ed. Arnaldo Cruz-Malavé and

Martin F. Manalansan IV (New York: New York University Press, 2002), 1–10.

8. This is, apparently, also the case outside the United States, where a homogenized racial/class picture seems to obtain in presentations of the "gay community." For a discussion of the situation in Australia, see Gerard Sullivan and Peter A. Jackson, "Introduction: Ethnic Minorities and the Lesbian and Gay Community," *Journal of Homosexuality* 36, nos. 3–4 (1999): 1–29; the authors also find a "prevalence of white males as sex symbols in advertisements and movies, and the extreme under-representation of anyone but white men in gay culture" (5). And while gay men of color are certainly not absent from the visual discourse in the United States, their visibility is often tied to images of hypermasculinity (and hypersexuality, or greater sexual prowess), and may serve more as fantasy fodder than three-dimensional representations (or the "default" representation of white). On this, see also Steven P. Kurtz, "Butterflies under Cover: Cuban and Puerto Rican Gay Masculinities in Miami," *Journal of Men's Studies* 7, no. 3 (1999): 371–90, which finds that in Miami, Florida, "Latin men's status actually benefits from the *macho* mystique they often wield in the imaginations of Anglo men" (383). For a very useful discussion of the historical roots of the phenomenon of "whitening" see Tracy D. Morgan, "Pages of Whiteness: Race, Physique Magazines, and the Emergence of Public Gay Culture," in *Queer Studies: A Lesbian, Gay, Bisexual, and Transgender Anthology*, ed. Brett Beemyn and Mickey Elliason (New York: New York University Press, 1996), 281–97. On African Americans and gay culture see also Essex Hemphill, ed., *Brother to Brother: New Writing by Black Gay Men* (Boston: Alyson, 1991); and Dwight A. McBride, *Why I Hate Abercrombie and Fitch: Essays on Race and Sexuality* (New York: New York University Press, 2005).

9. Of course, some men may eschew either or both variables—gay and/or Latin (or other race)—in the process of constructing identity (and place) due to a perceived or insurmountable dissonance between the two. On this, see J. L. King, *On the Down Low: A Journey Into the Lives of "Straight" Black Men Who Sleep with Men* (New York: Broadway, 2004); and Sullivan and Jackson, "Introduction."

10. On the numerous syncretisms (or "creolizations") that have contributed to the formation of various "Latin" musics, especially in the Caribbean, see Peter Manuel, *Caribbean Currents: Caribbean Music from Rumba to Reggae* (Philadelphia: Temple University Press, 1995), especially chaps. 1–5; see also John Storm Roberts, *The Latin Tinge: The Impact of Latin American Music on the United States*, 2nd ed. (New York: Oxford University Press, 1999).

11. Writing in the popular press, Brook Larmer, with contributions from Veronica Chambers, Ana Figueroa, Pat Wingert, and Julie Weingarten ("Latino America," *Newsweek* 134, no. 2, July 12, 1999), found that "[h]ip

Anglos on both coasts are dancing salsa, learning Spanish and dabbling in Nuevo Latino cuisine." They note, however, that the influence was not confined to popular culture, but impacted politics and demographics as well.

12. Aldo Marin, interview by the author, May 2, 2000, New York City.

13. Freestyle, the original mainstay of the Cutting label (which fostered such popular artists as Sa-Fire), was one of the earlier genres to afford opportunities to Latino musicians. Although a few people with whom I spoke related it stylistically to house, there are also many dissimilarities; for example, house's reliance upon the four-on-the-floor beat contrasts with freestyle's rhythmic armature, one highly dependent upon backbeat and drum-kit patterns. Additionally, freestyle often makes use of a song format, whereas house—although song format is not unknown—is often much more highly narratively fractured.

14. Information herein comes from the website The Home of Latin House (http://members.tripod.com/maliverno).

15. Regarding Torres's songs, Marin noted that he considered them more representative of the Chicago house style, rather than that of Latin house.

16. Cotto did, however, note that underground house is, in fact, largely associated with a "gay crowd . . . only because they appreciate music *more*," in his estimation, and are thus more attuned to the musical "sophistication" found in this specific subgenre. Norty Cotto, interview by the author, May 2, 2000, New York City. All Cotto quotes in this chapter are from this interview.

17. Will Hermes, "Hip House Hooray! Blowing Up but not Going Pop with New York's Screwiest DJ Savior," *Spin*, July 2000, p. 147.

18. See David Lubich's website (http://www.jahsonic.com/DavidLubich).

19. The cover art of certain releases (i.e., Cutting Records' *Latin House Party*, Vol. 4), replete with scantily clad women (a commonplace visual in Latin music recordings), suggests marketing for a predominantly heterosexual audience. On the use of such images, see Frances R. Aparicio, *Listening to Salsa: Gender, Latin Popular Music, and Puerto Rican Cultures* (Hanover, N.H.: Wesleyan University Press, 1998).

20. "Tumba la Casa" is probably a play on the familiar Cuban *comparsa* tune "Tumba la Caña" (Knock Down the Cane).

21. On another compilation, the same track is noted as performed by Los Rumberos. Cotto attributed this to either a mistake or to the fact the Santiago may, in fact, *be* Los Rumberos. This latter instance illustrates a common occurrence in Latin house (and dance musics in general) whereby many artists are ensembles of studio musicians and/or producers who operate under various (often ever-changing) monikers. For example, techno superstar Juan Atkins produced work, at various times during his career, under the names Cybotron, Model 500, and Infiniti, among others.

For an overview of *clave* in both Cuban and Dominican musics, see Peter Manuel, *Popular Musics of the Non-Western World: An Introductory Survey* (New York: Oxford University Press, 1988).

22. John Bush, "Todd Terry," *All Music Guide* (http://www.allmusic.com/cg/amg.dll?p=amg&sql=11:wsuk6j8h7190~T1).

23. Terry, like other house artists, used a number of "aliases" for his productions (Black Riot's "A Day in the Life," Gypsymen's "Hear the Music," Royal House's "Can You Party?," etc.), which, as noted above, is a common occurrence.

24. In a similar vein, DJ/producer/writer Armand van Helden (a Latino, despite his Dutch name), included himself as part of "a race of people ... [that] can't be classified." From http://streetsound.pseudo.com/zine/nuschool/armand.html, which is currently inactive.

25. Samir Dayal, "By Way of an Afterward," in *Postcolonial, Queer: Theoretical Intersections*, ed. John C. Hawley (Albany: State University of New York Press, 2001), 307. On identity politics, see also Jeffrey Escoffier, *American Homo: Community and Perversity* (Berkeley and Los Angeles: University of California Press, 1998); Robert Reid-Pharr, "Introduction," in *Black Gay Men: Essays* (New York: New York University Press, 2001), 1–17; and Seidman, "Identity and Politics in a 'Postmodern' Gay Culture."

26. Lisa Lowe, *Immigrant Acts: On Asian American Cultural Politics* (Durham, N.C.: Duke University Press, 1996), 67. Whether or not an "immigrant" identity is one that we might associate with gay men or lesbians is certainly questionable. However, I do find the specifics of Lowe's scheme to be entirely compatible with a reading of minority identity and, insofar as the term *minority* functions as a descriptor (theoretical reappraisals notwithstanding) of the nonheterosexual, entirely compatible with the gay or lesbian person. Additionally, as many gay Latinos in New York are, in fact, immigrants, the application of Lowe's concepts is certainly apropos.

27. For example, on the Latin influence on early hip-hop, see Juan Flores, "Recapturing History: The Puerto Rican Roots of Hip Hop Culture," in *Island Sounds in the Global City*, ed. Ray Allen and Lois Wilcken (New York: New York Folklore Society, 1998), 61–73.

28. I am not asserting (nor am I foreclosing upon the possibility) that there are (always) *conscious* intents to inject Latin musics into non-Latin musics; it is, I suppose, entirely possible that the instances of clave I have noted in house have no relation whatsoever to clave used in son or salsa. Additionally, it is not uncommon to find clave-like patterns in the guitar riffs of, for example, 1950s rockabilly artists. However, the sheer number of Latinos involved in dance musics in general would make it at the very least plausible to assume a connection between rhythms found in house and rhythms found in Latin American/Caribbean musics, perhaps similar to positing a connection between the rhythms of Caribbean musics and jazz.

See Christopher Washburne, "The Clave of Jazz: A Caribbean Contribution to the Rhythmic Foundation of an African-American Music," *Black Music Research Journal* 17, no. 1 (1997): 59–80. The connection can be further implied through house's connection to disco, the latter of which made much use of Latin percussion and rhythms (e.g., Vicki Sue Robinson's "Turn the Beat Around," the Michael Zager Band's "Let's All Chant," and Ralph MacDonald's "Calypso Breakdown," to name but a very few).

29. Benigno Sánchez-Eppler and Cindy Patton, "Introduction: With a Passport Out of Eden," in *Queer Diasporas*, ed. Cindy Patton and Benigno Sánchez-Eppler (Durham, N.C.: Duke University Press, 2000), 6. See also Elizabeth Grosz, "Bodies—Cities," in *Places through the Body*, ed. Heidi J. Nast and Steve Pile (London: Routledge, 1998) on the mutually constitutive nature of bodies and cities.

30. Although the club opens at 10:00 P.M., it generally starts "happening" only past midnight. The exception to this is the late afternoon/early evening Sunday "tea dance."

31. The name *La Nueva Escuelita* is indicative of the fact that there was an earlier incarnation of Escuelita, located a few blocks from its present site. As one person told me, the appellation stemmed from the club's location in the basement of a language school, and the use of diminutives by Puerto Ricans when giving directions—the club was, thus, the place under the "little language school" (*escuelita*). This person also stated that the original manifestation of the club was an integral part of the neighborhood and featured communal tables at which communal drinking would occur. This drinking style is no longer present at La Nueva Escuelita, which has a typical bar and several café tables where small groups of patrons may sit either before or during the nightly drag show.

32. Although a few women are seen at La Escuelita, the clientele on most evenings is generally overwhelmingly male, including numerous transgender/transvestite individuals. Greater numbers of women are often present for the club's Her/She Bar on "Freaky Fridays."

33. In my conversations with people at La Escuelita, the term *gender illusionist* was often used instead of *drag queen*, although the latter was not uncommon.

34. This dichotomization—the ample, verbally combative and humorous emcee versus the beautiful and glamorous "showgirls"—is often a staple of drag shows. For a historical, ethnographic account of drag bars in the late 1960s, see Esther Newton, *Mother Camp: Female Impersonators in America* (Chicago: University of Chicago Press, 1979).

35. The presentation of the diva/woman as powerful is also evident in advertising materials for the club. For example, one postcard features several of La Escuelita's gender illusionists arranged in a phalanx in New York's Time's Square, under the title "Diva Rough Necks."

36. Jennie Livingston's 1991 documentary *Paris Is Burning* examines the "houses" of participants in Harlem's "drag balls," illuminating the dynamic of family that obtains among members of these groups.

37. Although the use of the word *tribal* is certainly related to the mania for the exotic that one finds in many dance music circles, an additional implication might, indeed, be related to the production of place, a dynamic also prevalent in the often (highly) segmented world of dance music and dance music venues. In this regard, on the concept of "tribes," see also Michel Maffesoli, *The Time of the Tribes: The Decline of Individualism in Mass Society,* trans. Don Smith (London: Sage, 1996).

38. Lawrence Grossberg, *We Gotta Get Out of This Place: Popular Conservatism and Postmodern Culture* (New York: Routledge, 1992), 154; Grossberg's views echo, to an extent, those of Jacques Attali (see Attali, *Noise,* trans. Brian Massumi, Manchester, England: Manchester University Press, 1985).

39. On the production of place via music, see also Sara Cohen, "Sounding Out the City: Music and the Sensuous Production of Place," in *The Place of Music,* ed. Andrew Leyshon, David Matless, and George Revill (New York: Guilford, 1998). Grossberg's work, it should be noted, lacks a discussion of the actual machinations or specific functioning of affect. For a more intensive (and biologically based) view, see Joseph P. Forgas, ed., *Handbook of Affect and Social Cognition* (Mahwah, N.J.: Lawrence Erlbaum, 2001); and Eve Kosofsky Sedgwick and Adam Frank, ed., *Shame and Its Sisters: A Silvan Tomkins Reader* (Durham, N.C.: Duke University Press, 1995). For a discussion of music's role in defining time and place among Mexican immigrants, see Cathy Ragland, "Mexican Deejays and the Transnational Space of Youth Dances in New York and New Jersey," *Ethnomusicology* 47, no. 3 (2003): 338–53.

40. See Silvan Tomkins, "What Are Affects?," in *Shame and Its Sisters,* 33–74.

41. Tomkins, "Enjoyment–Joy," in *Shame and Its Sisters,* 88, 89.

42. Ibid., 82.

43. On the voice in music see, among others, Roland Barthes, *Image Music Text,* ed. and trans. Stephen Heath (London: HarperCollins, 1977); and Simon Frith, "The Body Electric," *Critical Quarterly* 37, no. 2 (1995): 1–10.

44. Cotto seems to concur with the investment that many gay men make in music. In his opinion, gay audiences are "the greatest crowds to play *for.*" Of course, this investment may take the form of disapprobation toward a (perhaps) "untalented" DJ. According to Cotto, "They're critical . . . if you [can't mix] . . . they *know.* They'll boo you." Indeed, the affective investment of people in Escuelita was often quite manifest; for example, one evening as the lights were coming up (at around 4:30 P.M.), a sweaty, beaming, and handsome twenty-something ran to the space in front of the DJ booth,

fresh from the dance floor, and with a massive smile emblazoned across his face shouted, "I love you, Chip-Chop!"

45. Tomkins, "What Are Affects?," in *Shame and Its Sisters*, 33.
46. Eric Hirsch, "Introduction—Landscape: Between Place and Space," in *The Anthropology of Landscape: Perspectives on Place and Space,* ed. Eric Hirsch and Michael O'Hanlon (Oxford: Clarendon, 1995), 1–30. Arjun Appadurai has called for a rethinking of the term *landscape* in the postmodern, global society, proposing "an elementary framework for exploring such disjunctures [between economy, culture and politics] [by] look[ing] at the relationship between five dimensions (or '-scapes') of global cultural flow." See Appadurai, "Disjuncture and Difference in the Global Cultural Economy," *Theory, Culture, and Society* 7 (1990): 295–310. This conceptualization is undoubtedly useful in the analysis of phenomena that may transcend geographic contiguity; regarding homosexuality, one might make use of the term *ideo-bioscape*, the unwieldy and inelegant hyphenation utilized in an attempt to mollify either side of the social constructivist/essentialist debate.
47. Eve Kosofsky Sedgwick and Adam Frank, "Shame in the Cybernetic Fold: Reading Silvan Tomkins," in *Shame and Its Sisters*, 1.

PART 3

Too Close for Comfort

10

TOO MUCH, TATU YOUNG
Queering Politics in the World of Tatu

SARAH KERTON

In 1999, Britney Spears became an overnight sensation, appearing in the video for her first single, "Hit Me Baby (One More Time)," as a playful schoolgirl, complete with miniskirt, pigtails, and sexualized dancing. In 2003, it seemed Russian girl band Tatu went one better. Dressed in matching school uniforms, the band kissed and fondled their way through the video for their debut English-language single, "All the Things She Said." Whereas Spears's presentation passed relatively unnoted, Tatu attracted intense media attention for the visualization of their ode to teenage lesbian infatuation. Daytime TV hosts Richard Madeley and Judy Finnegan denounced them as "sick, paedophilic entertainment" and called for the song to be banned. Upon the lead-up to the 2003 *Eurovision Song Contest* television show, rumors that the girls would kiss while performing Russia's entry, "Ne Ver, Ne Bojsia," led to a huge media frenzy.[1] Due to the vast amount of pop acts presenting highly sexualized representations of women, it seems that what set Tatu apart for intense scrutiny was their presentation of a lesbian relationship, portrayed not only within their music video—where various otherwise taboo subject positions are culturally accepted as artifice—but constructed as part of their lived existence.

Tatu comprises two teenage vocalists, Yulia Volkova and Lena Katina. Classically trained musicians, they each made their musical

debut in the Russian choral group Neposedi. Katina was allegedly expelled in 2000 for "lewd behavior" with Volkova "mysteriously" leaving the group some time later (according to Neposedi's producer Elena Pinzhoyan, they actually left because "we do not keep children over 14"). Both girls successfully auditioned later that year for a new project named Taty, an abbreviation for "Ta Lyubit Ty," which roughly translates as "This girl loves that girl." Within two years, Taty sold 850,000 legal copies and four million bootlegs of their debut Russian language album, *200 Po Vstriechnoy*, signing a deal with Universal Records to release in Europe and the United States. The album was partly rerecorded in English with producer Trevor Horn and released worldwide throughout 2003, with Horn subsequently renaming the band Tatu for their British launch.[2]

Following on from a pop tradition of boy/girl groups established throughout the 1990s through such British acts as Take That and the Spice Girls, and American counterparts *N Sync and Destiny's Child, it is unsurprising that the European and subsequently American record industry were keen to promote Tatu in the Western world. While the sweet unthreatening asexual boy group format promoted by Westlife and Boyzone was seemingly floundering in the pop market, it was the "girl power" lineage established by the Spice Girls and championed by such acts as Girls Aloud and the laddish, loutish subject positions of pop-garage act Blazin' Squad that received maximum media coverage, airplay, and subsequently single sales in the chart market. Combined with the cultural phenomenon of "gal pal"-ism, Madonna's flirting with bisexuality, and the press interest in high-profile lesbian figures like Ellen DeGeneres and k. d. lang, it remained only a matter of time before pop produced an act that reflected the cultural commodities of the time—highly sexualized, empowered, queer, and female.

Through their constructs and discourse, Tatu represent alternative femininities, queering both the norms of femininity evident in mainstream society and that found within the imposed femininity of popular music discourse—in both the traditional arena of masculine performance and representation, and the representation of gender through female pop artists. The concept of one "femininity" within popular music is a troublesome one, yet through articles and interviews with the band, it is evident that they are aware of the supposed characteristics of "woman" that include "appropriate" modes of physical and verbal address—from sonic qualities such as pitch, vocal range, and musical accompaniment, dress code and physical performance boundaries, to avoidance of taboos including swearing, social commentary, and certain topics of discussion within interview.

These themes are explored throughout their debut album,[3] *200km/h in the Wrong Lane*, with the band situated at odds with their parents ("All the Things She Said"), society ("Not Gonna Get Us"), and eventually each other ("Stars"). Translated from the Russian, *200 Po Vstriechnoy*, a title that conveys concepts of unity, exploration, and excitement, the English title situates the band in an altered subject position for a Western audience, signifying a moral defiance and conjuring imagery of being dangerously out of control while hurtling at high speeds—directly against the law, social code, and convention. Retaining the European *km/h* in defiance of the Anglo-American *mph*, despite translating the title into English, firmly ingrains the "exotic" within. This representation of the confrontational reflects the altered positioning of Tatu within a Western framework. Constructions of "otherness" supposedly inherent within a Third World context are obviously problematic, overplaying the differences between cultures while ignoring similarities and assimilations, yet it is from this observation of disparity that the Western perception of Tatu arises. While the appropriation of "exotic" modes of address within Western acts is constructed as a social acceptance of non-Western ways of being, those recognized as wholly "other" to Western discourse are still universalized within the cultural constructions seen as "natural" to their ethnicity, and knowledge of this is evident in the fluid genre and subject positioning adopted by Tatu as an attempt to challenge these "cultural norms."

Musically, Tatu juxtapose the sonic qualities of euphoric European trance pop and Russian folk melodies with a riff-based, hard-hitting edge more fitting of male "nu-metal" stars Marilyn Manson and Linkin Park. Their first single, "All the Things She Said," was released in Britain in January 2003, accompanied by a bombardment of media attention. The lyrics reflect defiance, strong personal independence, and an exploration of youthful sexuality; the two central characters not only battle but assert their right to be in love: "I'm feeling for her what she's feeling for me."

The song is rooted in E minor, with two basic chordal structures:

1. Cadd9 | G/B | Em7 | G
2. Em7 |Em7 | D | D | G | G | Bm | Bm

This is underpinned by the D note acting as a pedal. The harmonic and structural approach of the track is evocative of folk composition, using chord changes and voicings idiomatic of a European folk tradition. However, the instrumentation combines elements of electronic dance music, utilizing samplers and drum machines, juxtaposed against "live"

distorted guitars reminiscent of 1990s American rock, and underpinned by driving unrelenting rhythmical structures more commonly associated with the 1970s punk movement.

The track begins with an eight-bar synthesizer introduction; a short drum fill launching straight into the double voiced chorus, based around chord structure 1. The dense textural framework of this initial introduction/chorus provides a contrast to the sparse spatial arrangement of the first verse (chord structure 2), as all other melodic instruments drop out, leaving a synthesized bass defining the harmonic movement. Pitched sonar samples, combined with an underlying cavernous reverb effect on the singular whispered vocal, suggest solitude and loneliness, enhanced by the minor tonality of the phrase. The first-person narrative of the verse phrases places the listener in a framework of voyeurism. The listener begins the piece as an intruder, observing the situation without being directly involved. Initially, the first two lines seem ambiguous. Who is the protagonist "asking for help" from? This is answered in the following two lines: the use of "being with you" situating a silent other within the narrative and reflecting an epiphany of sorts. The second verse stanza is voiced by another female, placing the lyric as conversation, with the two central characters seemingly locked in discussion about the state of their relationship. Both characters are positively questioning the situation they have found themselves in, reflective of the first stages of love.

The line, "Nobody else so we can be free," situates Yulia and Lena at odds with society. It is the others around them who restrict them, and escape to a solitary place containing only each other would release them from this containment. The whispered vocal delivery, combined with the spatial arrangement underpinning this, gives a sense of intimacy, secrecy, and conspiracy, further driven by the racing quality of the shuffled four-on-the-floor kit. The drum break between the verse and chorus provides a moment of reflection and suspense, as distorted guitars enter high within the mix, and both vocals enter in unison.

The chorus serves as a reflection, with the pronouns moving from the personal "you and I" to "she and I." Any ambiguity of gender is now replaced with certainty that this is two women singing about—and to—one another. Where the "question and question" phrases of the verse place the two vocalists within the same mind-set, the double voicing on the chorus serves to reinforce the sentiments shared by the protagonists. Through a timbral buildup into the chorus, the passage is instilled with a sense of aggression and unity, reinforced by the solid rhythm section and repetition of the beginning phrase. The chanted unison vocal line imbues a hypnotic quality to the vocal text, the repeated lyric and phrase shape adding to an overall feel of obsession and determination.

The listener is now allowed into the space that they were once intruding on, with the use of the nonpersonal implicit. The uncomfortable timbre of the vocal delivery of "this is not enough" with the second answering repetition raised in pitch and distorted, further underscores the indignation of the characters. "This is not enough," states Yulia—to be confirmed, more directly and forcefully, by Lena's mirroring passage.

The juxtaposition of these two passages, with Lena's strained and distorted repetition transcending the "naturalized" register transcribed by normative popular practice, effectively represents a subversion of prescribed gender roles so vigorously upheld within mass culture. As discussed by Wayne Koestenbaum, "Register represents a zone of opportunity or of prohibition,"[4] in which the vocalist can disturb the socioculturally created stables of gender. While popular music certainly lacks the voice manuals of opera, this "sonic cross-dressing" challenges the normal vocal modes for female singers, from Mariah Carey's vocal acrobatics to Dido's comfortable, limited-range terraced lines, placing Tatu outside of the binary synthesis of register. While previous attempts to negotiate this have involved the use of screaming and growling as mimicry of aggressive male expression,[5] the use of an aggressive, confrontational address in a naturally distorted, pushed chest voice, more comfortably handled in the lower head range, combined with the content of the lyric, leave the listener with no anchor of mimicry or parody, and the readiness to transcend the "natural" rules and limits of vocal performance represents a threat to vocal characterization, and thus queers the set limits of desire and performance placed upon female musicians.

This subversion is also reflected within the structural movement within the track, as the expected movement from the "first" chorus into a second verse section established by the implicit ABA form is withheld by a climactic solo section also queered in its instrumentation. The use of distorted guitars within the chorus section, alongside cultural coding, suggests electric guitar as the "primary" accompanying instrument of the piece, and thus privileged with the role of soloist. Instead, an artificial-sounding synthesized waveform voices a decorated version of the verse motif, idiomatic of a popular string arrangement (see figure 10.1).

The use of a distinctly electronic sound source instead of violins or a synthesized string effect furthermore roots the sense of alienation and difference implicit throughout the track; the stepped movement of

Figure 10.1

the vocal line followed by the repetition of the arpeggio figure create a feeling of containment and an attempt to "escape" the limits set by both the limiting vocal stanza and conversely those suppressing the protagonists themselves. Ultimately, this attempt serves as nothing more than a reflection upon the tense situation, as the promised resolution of the rising instrumental line cuts back to a sparse, singular voiced second verse.

The final verse stands out as reflective of cultural situations specific to Russia itself. The bridge section, with its reflective, "Yes, I've lost my mind," seemingly comments upon the practice of committing young lesbian women to mental asylums. As Anne Buetikofer has noted, "When a lesbian love relationship was reported to the authorities by the parents or another legal guardian, the former could see to it that a psychiatric problem was diagnosed, usually a disorder of personality. The young women (most of them 15 to 19 years old) were then held in a psychiatric clinic for three months. They would then receive a mind-bending drug treatment before being forced to register with a local psychiatrist as mentally ill."[6] By articulating the challenge through the parental, the agency of the girls is effectively muted, their judgment reliant upon the responses and attitudes of their elders.

The accompanying video continues to explore the themes of love, defiance, and escape raised within the text of the song. The scene of the video is one fixed location, placing Tatu, clad in identical school uniforms, apart from a varied crowd of onlookers, separated by a high iron fence. The synthesized rain effect and thunderclap opening of both the video and the album track—accompanied by images of rain, snow, and the spectators' umbrellas, protecting them from the rain—creates a sense of pathetic fallacy further enhanced by the green and blue color hues across the scenes. The overall focus throughout the video is upon the physical interaction of the girls themselves, the camera placed upon the other side of the fence to Tatu, situating the viewer among the gathered onlookers.[7] While the interaction of the rain-soaked girls is focused upon each other—oblivious to the camera and the effects of the weather—short interspersed shots of the varied crowd appearing and gathering, returning the camera's gaze, imbue a voyeuristic element also contained within the lyrical narrative, insinuating that it is, in fact, the girls who are "caged." Throughout the buildup to the first chorus, Yulia and Lena caress each other, the camera closing up to shots of Lena's hair being stroked by Yulia, suggesting an offscreen kiss. The suggestion of partial sexual fulfillment disrupted abruptly with interspersed crowd scenes further pushes for a resolution not yet satisfied within shots and mirrored by the vocalized "this is not enough."

The reflective instrumental verse section that follows then provides this resolution, with lingering shots of the girls kissing, caressing, and holding each other. Though the implied sexual interaction is now realized, shots are cut between wide-angled scenes of the girls, seated separately, holding their heads, pulling at the barriers and screaming. The pleasurable viewing, parodic of heterosexual "lesbian" pornographic fantasy is withheld and distorted by images of the girls in emotional pain, trapped and contained behind the fence, which in turn holds back the mixed gendered/raced/aged crowd, reflective of mass society. While reflective of the treatment of young lesbian girls in mental asylums, this also serves to place the band within the exotic, eroticized separate from the crowd, representative of the "mainstream," and thus disrupting the normative readings that could be made.

The video ends with shots of the sky, clouds dispersing, and the sun coming out, dramatized through the inclusion of red and yellow hues into the video's coloring. The smiling girls hold hands and skip along the fence, revealing an end to the "containing" wall as they run off into the distance, "crossing the line" voiced within the lyric. This realigns and distorts our initial readings of the situation, with a dawning realization that it is actually the crowd who is caged.

Several contradicting and fluid readings can be taken from the video, reflective of Tatu's social positioning. Initially, the viewer believes the girls to be trapped, both physically and emotionally, under the gaze of the voyeuristic. Through the moment of epiphany made visible in the last scene, the interaction of the girls behind the fence can be read as a knowing manipulation of the positioning offered to the viewer. By blurring the boundaries between the reality and fantasy of the acted scenes, and realigning the initial readings delivered, Tatu problematize interpretations that can be made of the band. Are they pandering to normative male fantasies of "lesbian" interaction by consciously providing a "staged show" of their sexuality, or are they challenging the subject positions placed upon lesbian women, defiantly flaunting their sexuality in public, constructing beneath a gaze that is seen as universal and inescapable, before making a mockery of this construct by escaping to an unknown "other" place? Yulia provides some insight into Tatu's own interpretation of their stance, stating that "we appeared in our school uniforms, caged behind bars and fences. Behind the bars, we were declaring our love to the world, in front of the stunned eyes of passers by. Some people had actually rather badly reacted, screaming scandal and provocative intentions."[8]

In an interview with Irish tabloid the *Sunday Tribune*, Marie Mullholland, editor of *Gay Community News*, was asked to discuss the

response to Tatu from the lesbian community. Mullholland defines the young lesbian as iconoclastically driven, "because being a lesbian, especially when you're young, is about going against the stereotype." She considers Kelly Osbourne and Pink as strong positive constructions of femininity for lesbian women, "because they're independent and doing their own thing," despite their conformation to the patriarchal notions of "women in rock." Tatu are dismissed as mere images for the male gaze, due to "the rain soaked shirts and that sort of thing."[9]

Larry Gross argues that images of minorities are created by the majority, for the majority. He states that the reasons for misleading imagery within the media stem from a lack of control over means of production, positing that the "ultimate expression of independence" for a minority group is to become the creator of one's own images.[10] While this argument certainly reflects the problems facing the dominant's construction of the minority, it also addresses issues created by the proactive voices within the minority.

As Barbara Smith asserts, "The image of the lesbian and gay movement that predominates is one that is the glitziest, and the most media driven, and the most affluent, and the whitest, and the most male." The privileging of the conservative mainstream white gay man as the homosexual "other" that most closely resembles the dominant normative, raises his voice to that of the "majority minority," setting him apart as the creator of his own images and in turn constructing new power relations within the "gay movement."[11] Mullholland's commentary upon Tatu cannot speak for the "lesbian community" as a whole, but reflects the "majority minority" of the lesbian movement. Although representative of the "minority voice," the active standpoint within lesbian-focused publications is still reliant upon conventions of a lived gay culture. By virtue of its separatist stance, the subject position of such magazines is generally reflective of a radical feminist second-wave outlook, tempered somewhat by the third wave "postfeminist" movement, while remaining mostly representative of women who actively participate in localized gay communities. While providing a physical presence for lesbians within the vast array of media representations, the journalist takes on the role of an "authentic social commentator," constructing an individual response that is taken as a universally lesbian viewpoint. By constructing Tatu as deriving solely "from the majority, for the majority," the lesbian media distance themselves from any messages contradictory to their own that Tatu may uphold, preferring to construct them within a heteronormative framework. Tatu effectively disrupt not only the mainstream's comprehension of what it means to be "lesbian," but also the homonormative constructs. By denying Tatu an empowered voice within such

magazines, the "lesbian media" operate in much the same way as the assumed "straight" mainstream, denying any democracy of gender. As such, I would argue that the minority gay press is not queered at all, but representative of Steven Seidman's normalized gay person who "is presented as fully human, as the psychological and moral equal of the heterosexual. . . . However, the normal gay also serves as a narrow social norm. This figure is associated with specific personal and social behaviours."[12] As Judith Butler states in an interview with Berlin's *Lolapress*, "Queer is not being lesbian. Queer is not being gay. It is an argument against lesbian specificity: that if I am a lesbian I have to desire in a certain way. Or if I am a gay I have to desire in a certain way. Queer is an argument against certain normativity, what a proper lesbian or gay identity is."[13]

Since the release of "All the Things She Said," debates surrounding Tatu's visual characterization and social narratives have increasingly dominated the mainstream British press. Reactions have been registered across the spectrum, from characterizing Tatu as "a saucy combination of knee-socks and Sapphic love"[14] or "a couple of Russian teenagers who claim to be lesbian lovers"[15] to interpretations of them as the media savvy saviors of confused teenage girls: "whatever their motives, they've captured the anguish of young Sapphic love remarkably well and the fact that it has endeared them to the [heterosexual] teenage market is little short of miraculous."[16]

The vast majority of media responses to Tatu share a narrow focus upon their portrayed sexuality, frequently dismissed as manufactured for the sole purpose of male titillation. These constructions are often negative, seeking to "out" both Yulia and Lena, Tatu's teenage singers, as straight, providing past boyfriends as evidence of their conformation to heteronormative society,[17] or otherwise presenting them as hypersexualized, their interest in other women predatory and out of control.[18] Even within "positive" constructions, such as Jemima Lewis's article (see note 15), their sexuality is still something viewed first and foremost as a marketing tool, with little consideration into any sociological reasoning behind their gender construction and none whatsoever toward their musical validity.[17] The immediacy with which their sexuality has been dismissed, accepted as created, and their music subsequently scorned, trivialized, and demonized as a springboard to launch an act "specifically designed to tap into the paedophile market,"[19] provides particular insight problems confronted when women, especially teenage "girls," explore their sexuality. As Lena comments, "Parents have to understand we don't give a fuck. We are talking to teenagers about them, about us. We love each other, and we don't give a fuck."

Tatu employ a fixed ironic use of stereotypical feminine imagery through their appropriation of school uniform, at once parodying and confronting patriarchal fantasies of childhood sexuality and vulnerability. Tatu expose the hypocritical nature of a society in which hysteria over pedophilia has become a front-page issue, yet teenage girls are increasingly encouraged to mimic the dress, behavior, and sexual personas of adults; as psychologist Francis Black has noted, "Put a 40-year-old in a vamped-up school uniform and she's saucily sexy, do it at 25 and she's looking hot. At 16 the same outfit is perfectly legal, but six months earlier, fertile and blooming into womanhood, and you're delving into the realms of perversion. . . . At 15 a girl has most of the attributes which will make her desirable as a woman, but to recognize her sexuality as taboo—who wouldn't be confused?"[20]

The school uniform has been employed in the gendered construction of several pop artists. The symbolism of the schoolgirl as a sexualized being calls into play definitions of developing womanhood, the "bad girl" of her patriarchal defined femininity, and taboos associated with the use of childhood modes of dress. The excitement of this sexuality resides within the other, a danger and difference outside of the cozy constraints of everyday lived existence. Britney Spears is contained completely within the representational register she calls up, is based on, and subsequently displaces and redefines. Her use of school uniform is an acceptable taboo—challenging, but ultimately a safe submission to the normative desires of postcapitalist America. While the characters of the Spice Girls, Pink, Kelly Osbourne, and "pop's appointed rebels" automatically inhabit "a heterosexual utopia in which young girls learn to be independent enough to be adventurous but not so independent that they challenge white, middle-class social order,"[21] Tatu destabilize this subject positioning through their manipulation of gender, defiant positioning, and social challenge. Indeed, while the band itself completely exceeds the logic of this normative representation, Yulia and Lena still manage to be constructed firmly within it. By seemingly conforming to masculine desire, the band queers a surface representation of mass heteronormative appeal with deeper subplots of alienation, oppression, betrayal, rejection, and confusion. Simultaneously, their use of the school uniform provides the viewer with mental clues as to their social placement, and its associations with childlikeness and teenage rebellion. Tatu construct themselves as a band of teenagers, for teenagers.

This subject positioning is demonstrated within "Show Me Love." The first two lines, sung by Yulia, tackle the fragility of youth, questioning the subject position the addressed—here Lena—has been placed in, with Lena's response making a metaphor of their relationship, comparing their fragile situation to a "game of pick up sticks"—a popular children's

game particularly in Russia—incongruously juxtaposed against the use of the word "fucking," a subversion of acceptable modes of childhood speech.

This challenge to forms of authority, situating "them" as outside to the intimate secret world the girls share, is a common rite of passage for young women, flirting with concepts of their own sexuality and learning of their self-eroticism: "There will be nothing quite as exciting as this love between girls ever again," notes Naomi Wolf. "This love has codes and repression, innocence and distant expression, all intensified by the secrecy of the feelings involved, and the knowledge of the world's disapproval 'if they only knew.'"[22]

Tatu say of their album, "The main message is basically to very simply say that if you are gay or lesbian, that's fine and it's nothing to be worried about. It's completely normal!"[23] Complicit in their portrayal of lesbian love, both Lena and Yulia are degree students, studying psychology and music, respectively. While the media depict both girls as innocently manipulated by their svengali-type manager, evidence of their intellectual pursuits outside of Tatu suggests an awareness of the social implications of their actions. Scenes broadcast throughout the Russian television series documenting the making of their second album, combined with their ultimate decision to part from manager Ivan Shapovalov, also seem to support the girls' own agency. Both remain seemingly vague and noncommital in an interview regarding their supposed sexuality, aware of and questioning the media interpretations of their gendered performance. Nevertheless, they engaged in a debate on Russian television with a priest about the role of lesbianism in Russian society, the priest condemning them to "eternal damnation." These are not the actions of the "bubblegum" pop movement they are identified with, and they are certainly not the actions of Pink, who while personally identifying as bisexual has only had public relationships with men. Ultimately, does Tatu's "lived" sexuality matter, or is it their understanding and comprehension of their gender performance, whether true to their "actual" selves or not, that is enough to make valid social commentary?

By expressing overt sexuality through their album and music videos, Tatu expose the barriers and challenge the restraints placed upon female physical expression. By negotiating the space between "lived" sexual identity and the constructed "norms" of socialization, it is suggested that Tatu occupy a queered social space, challenging the heavily pressured gender ideals present in popular music by deconstructing the expectations, conventions, and examples of female sexualities presented in the mainstream.

Their greatest strength lies in this subversion and realignment of Western values, challenging and questioning the gendered positioning placed upon female performers in popular music practice. As such, Tatu undermine and challenge both heterosexist and homosexist assumptions about lesbianism with representations of a lesbian love at odds with both worlds' constructions of teenage discovery. As homosexuals themselves have queered terms such as *homo, faggot, dyke*, and *queer*, so Tatu queer the conventions of the girl band. The techniques, systems, and structures that were once used against us, now belong to us. Tatu may well not be gay, but they are certainly queer. By encapsulating both the wants and the fears of the zeitgeist simultaneously, Tatu create a challenge to hypocrisy that is impossible to ignore—their use of youthful (homo)sexuality both excites and reviles a media obsessed with female flesh and front-page scandal. As such, it matters not whether Yulia and Lena have a physical relationship, nor if they continue to do so. Tatu show us that we are caught up in a process of labeling and boundaries, even within the so-called queer community. Tatu offer no clear-cut distinctions, nor do they rally to the "lesbian" label, but, situated as complete outsiders both in the context of their album and their reception from the media, they continue with their defiant stance and make insightful commentary, most notably on their album track "Stars," where they sing, "Like the night we camouflage denial."

NOTES

1. While the *Eurovision Song Contest* is contextualized as family viewing through its Saturday night broadcast slot and surrounding marketing, it has nevertheless attracted a significant gay audience, evidenced through the creation of "gay icons" from such entrants as Abba; Brotherhood of Man and Gina G; Israel's transsexual entry, Dana International; and the droll/camp commentary of Terry Wogan.

2. Horn is famous for his work with Bronski Beat, Frankie Goes to Hollywood, and the Pet Shop Boys, exponents of the 1980s queerpop scene. He has also produced tracks for artists as diverse as Tori Amos, Eddi Reader, and Yes.

3. While this paper focuses on their first album, their second release, *Dangerous and Moving* (2005) continues with the themes discussed here, including the song "Loves Me Not," which explores the protagonist's bisexuality.

4. Wayne Koestenbaum, "Queering the Pitch: A Posy of Definitions and Impersonations," in *Queering the Pitch: the New Gay and Lesbian Musicology*, ed. Philip Brett, Gary Thomas, and Elizabeth Woods (New York: Routledge, 1994), 1–5.

5. Instances can be found within (but not exclusive to) the Portland riot grrrl scene and various "queercore" acts.

6. Anne Buetikofer, "Homosexuality in Russia," *Die* 9 (1998): 6–8.

7. This camera technique is often used by news crews during riots, situating the camera from the police's point of view, observing the "dysfunctional."

8. Tatu interview at the Tribumove website (http://www.tribumove.com/accueil2/index.htm).

9. Marie Mullholland, quoted in Anna Carey, "Love That Dares to Speak Its Name," *Sunday Tribune*, February 16, 2003 (online at http://www.web.lex-is-nexis.com/executive/print?dd_Jobtype=spew&_m=a79293e5e947c5).

10. Larry Gross, "Minorities, Majorities, and the Media," in *Media, Ritual, and Identity*, ed. Tamar Liebes and James Curran (London: Routledge, 1998), 87–102.

11. Barbara Smith, "Where Has Gay Liberation Gone? An Interview with Barbara Smith," in *Homo Economics: Capitalism, Community, and Lesbian and Gay Life*, ed. Amy Gluckman and Betsy Reed (London: Routledge, 1997), 195–207.

12. Steven Seidman, *Beyond the Closet: The Transformation of Gay and Lesbian Life* (New York and London: Routledge, 2002), 13–14.

13. Judith Butler, "The Desire for Philosophy," *Lolapress* 2 (2001) (online at http://www.lolapress.org/elec2/artenglish/butl_e.htm).

14. Fiona Sturges, "Sex and the Singles Chart," *Independent*, February 7, 2003 (available at http://www.findarticles.com/p/articles/mi_qn4158/is_20030207/ai_n12677751).

15. Jemima Lewis, "Sing the Praises of Tatu, the Teenage Lesbians," *Independent*, February 10, 2003.

16. Ibid.

17. Yvonne Holmes, "Tatu Much," Gay.com, January 9, 2003 (online at http://uk.gay.com/printit/1604).

18. John Dingwall, "The Tatu Prowler," Daily Record, May 24, 2003 (online at http://www.dailyrecord.co.uk/news/page.cfm?method=full&objectid=12992150).

19. Iain S. Bruce, "Too Much, tATu Young," *Sunday Herald*, February 2, 2003 (online at http://www.sundayherald.com/31089).

20. Francis Black, quoted in Bruce, "Too Much, tATu Young."

21. Michelle Gibson and Deborah T. Meem, "The Case of the Lovely Lesbian: Mabel Maney's Queering of Nancy Drew," *Studies in Popular Culture* 19, no. 3 (1997): 23–36.

22. Naomi Wolf, *Promiscuities: A Sexual History of Female Desire* (London: Chatto and Windus, 1997), 34.

23. Tatu interview at Tribumove (http://www.tribumove.com/accueil2/index.htm).

11

"I AM NOT IN A BOX OF ANY DESCRIPTION"
Sinéad O'Connor's Queer Outing

EMMA MAYHEW

Queer is a complex and multidimensional term that has long had a place in the fashion and celebrity world of popular music.[1] Playing with sexual mores and norms has been one way of signaling rebellion in rock and pop from Little Richard and David Bowie to Annie Lennox. Although many "queer" rock stars turn out to be conventionally heterosexual in their personal lives, a queer aesthetic or sensibility has often been a hallmark of an artistic and transgressive identity in rock. Thus a queer/artistic nexus has existed in rock that has not necessarily been associated with the personal sexual practice of the subject, but rather has been about challenging the normal common sense understanding of gender—aligned, unproblematically, with a biological and anatomically defined sex. This is done by invoking a different way of listening, a queer sensibility, which does and can exist alongside a heterosexual reading.

One element of this queer sensibility is the theme of indeterminacy that challenges the dichotomous labels of male/female and feminine/masculine in relation to sexual identity. As Warren Hedges has noted, "To say that someone is 'queer' indicates an indeterminacy or indecipherability about their sexuality and gender, a sense that they cannot be categorized without a careful contextual examination and, perhaps, a whole new rubric" (Hedges 1996).

In the analysis of Sinéad O'Connor's public career that follows, the term *queer* is understood as a descriptor focused on behaviors, images, and biographical episodes defined to be outside the gendered and sexual norms of the mainstream. However, in analyzing the queer subject in popular music we also need to consider the media production of celebrity, and how the tension between straight and queer helps produce ideas of uniqueness and individuality, as well as opening up opportunities for the ridicule of celebrity figures by audiences and the media. It is argued in this chapter that the fascination the media have had with Sinéad O'Connor as a famous—or infamous—female figure in popular culture has been partly to do with her queerness as a gendered, sexual, and musical celebrity identity. O'Connor has, from the beginning, confused audiences and the media with her mixture of outspokenness and vulnerability, including a visual image that has made her a significant target for media interest. However, in 2000, O'Connor intensified this representational tendency by briefly coming out as a lesbian, adding the layer of a lived personal sexual identity to a queerness that had already been established through a career of challenging the normalcy of mainstream society. Controversy erupted when—no sooner had the media declared her lesbian credentials— O'Connor backed away from her previous quoted statements. In examining the queering of O'Connor through these "coming out" events, and by putting them into context within her whole public career, this chapter analyzes the way O'Connor's celebrity encompasses queer meanings. These queer readings position her through several—often competing—identities including the manipulative celebrity, the creative and respected individualist, and the ridiculous public figure. These last two positions represent a dynamic of respect/ridicule which in the context of O'Connor's coming out also involves "another dynamic; that of queer/ normative invocation and recuperation" (Rahman 2004).

IN AND OUT

In 2000 O'Connor made several statements, in different press interviews and profiles, that suggested that she identified with a lesbian sexuality. In an interview for the U.S. lesbian magazine *Curve* the following exchange between the interviewer and O'Connor was published.

Why do you think lesbians are so drawn to you and to your music?
Um, I think they see themselves in me.

Because you're outspoken? Non-traditional in your appearance?
Yeah, and because I'm—what's the right way to put it? [Pause].
I think I am very like them. I would say that I'm a lesbian.

Although I haven't been very open about that and throughout most of my life I've gone out with blokes because I haven't necessarily been terribly comfortable about being a lesbian. But I actually am a lesbian.

You are a lesbian?
Yeah. So the thing is, I think that's probably why they would see themselves in me, because they could see something in me that perhaps I hadn't actually necessarily acknowledged in myself. (Anderson-Minshall 2000)

Besides this "confession," O'Connor had also written a letter to *Hot Press* stating, "I am a lesbian, I haven't been comfortable with that fact until recently. I have striven to be straight and to hide myself. I love men, but I prefer sex with women" (*USA Today* 2000). However, shortly after these comments the editors of the Irish *Sunday Independent* asked her to elaborate on her sexual status. O'Connor then wrote a letter to John Chambers, an editor, explaining that her previous comments had been honest but "slightly confused" answers to personal questions that had made her uncomfortable. She explained that her answers had been influenced by her loyalty to an ex-female lover. In this letter she stated, "Of perhaps thirty people I have been with since eleven years of age, two have been women, the rest men. I am rarely attracted to women but loved making love with the women I loved. . . . I believe it was overcompensating of me to declare myself a lesbian. It wasn't a publicity stunt. I was trying to make someone else feel better. And have subsequently caused pain for myself" (*USA Today* 2000).

However, there were several other explanations that O'Connor herself put forward, that made it difficult for commentators and audiences to determine a fixed narrative behind her statements. In an interview with the *Advocate* two years later O'Connor suggested that in fact she was misquoted, that "this woman reporter asked why did I think lesbians liked me so much or why was I so popular with lesbians, and I said it was probably because they thought I was one of them, meaning that I don't believe in gay or straight and I don't believe love is conditional. But obviously the reporter ran with it and the paper hyped it, because it probably sold a lot of issues, and, really, I was quite happy for them to do that" (Che 2002).

Although such explanations were a withdrawal from an unequivocal lesbian identity, they did not negate the continuing possibility of O'Connor's sexuality being outside the norm. In many press interviews there has been a refusal on the part of O'Connor to clear up any ambiguity about her sexual identity, which had been fueled by her comments.

Asked in the *Advocate* interview as to whether she thought herself bisexual, she stated, "I suppose some people are confused, but like I said, I don't think there really is such a thing as gay or straight. That's where I stand" (Che 2002).

The story of O'Connor's self-outing is not only queer in its representation of sexual identity but is also shaped by a tension that can be detected in most media representations of celebrity, a tension of both respect and ridicule (Rahman 2004). For O'Connor, the respect/ridicule dynamic has been strongly present throughout her career, although it has more obviously made an appearance at times of controversial events, such as her contradictory coming out. Throughout O'Connor's career, media accounts offer up respect and awe for her singing voice, her courage in speaking out and being an alternative role model for women in popular music. On the other hand she is represented as a target of ridicule, often through her shaved-headed image, as well as her opinions. This has been especially prominent when her music has attempted to assert a political message. One such example is the song "Famine," which lyrically suggested, controversially, that the potato famine in nineteenth-century Ireland had been caused by English imperialism, through its exportation of all other food sources out of Ireland. Such political statements have often been ridiculed as laughable; as one commentator observed, "Sinéad can write and sing songs which, in the hands of others, would lead only to a kind of nausea-inducing mawkishness. She has the ability to take lazy sentimentality and trite philosophizing, and transform it into something that is actually moving. Well, except for that rap about the Irish potato famine on *Universal Mother* which still has me in hysterics" (Shanahan 2000).

Sinéad O'Connor's concern about her own media treatment, especially in relation to her characterization as preposterous or laughable, has often sparked a counteroffensive by her through letters to editors and public statements taken out in prominent newspapers. In fact, she has been one of the most vocal celebrities who have directly and consistently maintained a public dialogue with the media—particularly commentators in Ireland—about their representations of her and other celebrity figures. These exchanges, although not obviously clearly linked to overt questions of alternative sexuality, nevertheless point to a queer sensibility. Her clashes with the media over their representations of her invite a queer identification in that they focus on the issue of identity and difference. Furthermore, this media conflict between O'Connor and the media can be read as a struggle against dominant institutions that seek to normalize and/or explain those outside its boundaries. O'Connor, in this context, represents a strong but alternative voice who seeks to

disrupt this process by claiming the right to speak as well as express her pain at her treatment.

For example, in 2004 O'Connor took out a full-page advertisement in a national newspaper asking to be left alone after her declaration of retirement earlier that year. This was in response to articles that detailed her call for an Irish "national delousing day" as another one of O'Connor's misguided attempts to insert herself into the Irish public life. In this public plea O'Connor continually referred to the ridicule that she felt the media had directed at her throughout her career, claiming that it had become a nation pastime to treat her "like a crazy bitch." "To me, this issue is not about me," she wrote, "but about the freedom God gave all of us, in fact the DUTY we have, to be ourselves. And we all have the right to be who we are, without being ridiculed and abused every time we set foot out the door to go to work" (O'Brien 2004).

An important theme that arises here and is present throughout the media's production of celebrity concerns the separation of, and tension between, the "real" self and its media representations. This tension is significant in opening up the possibility of reading O'Connor as a queer subject, especially given her own statements regarding questions about her sexuality. O'Connor's claims of being punished for being herself, and her clashes with the media concerning issues of representation, point to a queer sensibility that challenges the normal heterosexual roles and norms. Although the focus of her criticism of the media has not specifically addressed the oppression of sexual normativity, it has often been in the context of criticizing the effects of dominant mainstream discourses on gender and sexual behavior. Her comments regarding her own sexual abuse, her contradictory sexual identity, her support of abortion in Ireland, as well as her expression of her own personal religious beliefs have pushed the boundaries of acceptable celebrity causes and behavior. Further on in the aforementioned letter she related her outsider status to her rejection of traditional femininity, writing, "I don't think there can be any person male or female from this country who has been as consistently lashed as I have been and always am no matter what I set out to do. And what have I done to deserve these lashings? I have not behaved the way a woman is supposed to behave" (O'Brien 2004).

However, at the time of her comments regarding her lesbianism, attempts were made to normalize O'Connor through several strategies. For instance, her inability to sustain a believable consistent identity, as either straight or gay, provided the opportunity for some to suggest that O'Connor's claim to queerness was superficial and publicity seeking. O'Connor's sexual transgressions could then be seen as an intentional manipulation of image to gain alternative currency and media attention.

This reading was strengthened as O'Connor's statements coincided with the release of her new album *Faith and Courage*. As one journalist stated at the time, "Her recent claim (made after this interview took place) that she does consider herself a lesbian, coming as it did on the heels of *Faith and Courage*'s release, smacked of calculation, though what it was intended to achieve, if anything, remains unclear" (Randall 2000).

This interpretation of O'Connor as seeking publicity was buttressed by a career of previous "media stunts" and a personal life that included, at the time, a marriage and two children. This kind of attitude is reflected in comments by Ray Senior, editor of *ShowbizIreland*, who writes, "People perceive her to be a naïve and innocent person with very strong views, but she is extremely astute and she has pulled off one media stunt after another and managed to keep an interest on a global basis" (Najafi 2003). Her inauthenticity as a lesbian and bisexual was further evidenced when later that year she married her second husband. Through highlighting such personal "facts" her sexuality could be normalized despite the other comments O'Connor had made about previous relationships with women and her ambiguous statements about claiming a heterosexual identity. Her heterosexuality could be emphasized through highlighting a fixed and binary separation between her real self (who was married and a mother) and her hyperreal celebrity self (who took advantage of the media to promote herself). Such descriptions in the press provide what Mohmin Rahman describes as an "encoded red carpet" out of queerness through a reemphasis of heterosexual credentials (Rahman 2004).

Another way of dealing with O'Connor's inconsistencies as a sexual subject is to see her through the tropes of romantic creativity. The eccentricity and deviance of the artistic subject are therein credited as the ultimate markers of an authentic and personal expression. Many writers have noted the compatibility in values promoted by both rock and romanticism. Robert Pattison notes, "The artistic virtues of rock and romanticism are originality, primal order, energy, honesty, and integrity" (1987, 188). Similarly, Wil Greckel suggests that the musical eras of romanticism and rock have very similar characteristics underlying their seeming musical differences. These parallel characteristics include, for example, the expression of intense emotion and the expression of rebellion against traditional social and moral constraints (Greckel 1979, 177–78). Romanticism also maintains a hierarchical superiority for creativity that has been carried over into the pop/rock dichotomy and has helped continue to construct rock as a discourse, including one that represents authentic creativity as opposed to commercial interests.

For instance, O'Connor's musical artistic subjectivity is often positioned outside the mainstream music industry and is represented

through a long tradition of the artist as the skilled, unique, individual creator of her art. In particular, her musical vocal skill and the seemingly biographical directness of her performances construct her as an authentic voice within a discourse of rock that values immediacy, rawness, and emotional authenticity. Her first album, *The Lion and the Cobra*, and its angry vocal delivery represented to many a voice that was taking risks. Her voice, while being able to express a conventionally fragile and beautiful femininity, could also take on a loudness and directness that was often interpreted as a sign of her individuality. One reviewer described the songs as representing "a strong, stubborn individuality—a willingness to go out on a limb and shout when she gets there" (Pareles 1988).

Yet, sometimes it is the representation of her voice, through this discourse of creativity, that attempts to override O'Connor's queerness and render it secondary. In fact, her voice has become a way in which the media attempt to normalize or contain her identity within patriarchal and heterosexual boundaries. As one critic commented, "Sinéad O'Connor has been a Pope-baiting rebel, a fierce advocate for victims of child abuse, a Catholic priest, and now, a lesbian. . . . Through it all she has sung with a voice of an angel" (Hicklin 2000). Thus, although her extramusical public presence may be challenging, her voice is a normalizing factor, re-creating an authentic femininity that the media can emphasize, despite her other differences.

These representations of O'Connor's voice capture a tension in her vocal styles, "the use of two distinctive voices: a more private, confessional, restrained and intimate voice, and a harsher, declamatory, more public and often nasal voice that frequently slides into a snarl or shout" (Negus 1997, 181). Even though these two styles may seem opposed in various ways, both voices have been represented by critics and media commentators as signifiers of her ultimate creativity and emotional authenticity. As discussed above, O'Connor's "feminine," "sweet" voice is hailed for its delicacy and openness while her loud and strident vocality is aligned with a protest tradition and the prestige of punk, folk, and rock.

It is not only her voice that helps to construct O'Connor as unique and emotionally authentic. Her lower record sales and popularity since her 1990 hit ("Nothing Compares 2 U") provide a career narrative that suggests that O'Connor has been pursuing a creative path, rather than one focused on commercial success. At around the same time as the *Curve* interview appeared, O'Connor parted ways with the record label she was signed to; as she has explained, "It was a pretty mutual desire to part ways. I wanted to be out of the mainstream so I could have my

creative freedom again because, understandably, if a label pumps loads of money into an artist, they want you to make records that make a lot of money back. But I don't really want to make those kinds of records now. . . ." (Che 2002).

The press and O'Connor mobilize this discourse, which sets up a dichotomy between creativity and commercialism, to reinforce her status as a musical artist. O'Connor is quoted in one interview how her rise to worldwide fame through the single "Nothing Compares 2 U" was an accident and something that did not reflect a personal interest in fame: "I'm not a charts or mainstream artist. I accidentally slipped in there and decided to cause a bit of trouble while I was there" (CTV 2000). These kinds of "personal" explanations of her motivation in producing music strengthen her position as an authentic artist, uninterested in the commercial profit or sales, as well as rejecting fame and any expected behavior it might attract.

The relationship between these authentic discourses of artistic authenticity and the story of O'Connor's queering is important in understanding the way some parts of the media have made sense of the contradictions and inconsistencies of O'Connor's "private" identity. The above representations of O'Connor as artistically authentic, both at the time of her statements in 2000 and since, have been an attempt to deflect and paradoxically normalize O'Connor's statements and "unstable" personal identity. By doing so it provides a way of explaining her behavior as an outcome of her creativity and artistic talent rather than a conscious attempt to manipulate the media.

Whatever the reality of O'Connor's sexual relationships, and the attempts to normalize and contain the contradictions and inconsistencies, she has obviously had a career that has a queer identification for some of her audience. Her authentic creative credentials discussed above and the queerness that such a reading allows need to be understood alongside what might be called a queer aesthetic. This queer aesthetic can be detected in her visual image, as well as the musical styles and lyrical themes explored in her music.

For the modern celebrity, the visual representation of an image or set of images is essential to the promotion of salable commodities. Also, much academic analysis of popular culture has concentrated on the postmodern turn in celebrity identity and its emphasis on the surface images of media culture. For example, Madonna has been analyzed as a celebrity who has wholly embraced the aesthetics of a postmodern, fluid, and decentered identity through her multiple self-images, which, for many, highlights her queerness. Notes Reena Mistry, "Madonna's notorious image changes demonstrate what Butler referred to as the

'fluidity of identity.' As part of these periodic style changes, Madonna dramatizes the discontinuity of sex, gender and desire, particularly in 'Justify My Love,' 'Truth or Dare,' and 'Sex'" (Mistry 2000).

Although O'Connor's visual image has had a continuity in relation to her hairstyle, which the media have had a clear obsession with over the years, she has also, like Madonna, played with the conventional and comfortable heteronormative images. For example, her androgynous image can be read as a way of avoiding traditional heterosexual presentation of herself as sexually available to a male gaze. In fact, her shaved head has been her most enduring and recognizable feature and has provided an almost continuous visual identity for media comments (see Negus 1997, 186). However, more important, it represents O'Connor's queerness, a queerness seemingly self-imposed and confusing to a normalized understanding of gender roles, feminine beauty, and female celebrity.

As the term *queer* has many meanings, so too has the image of the shaved female head. In fact the hairstyle has a number of meaningful associations, which all seem applicable to a reading of O'Connor as outside the mainstream. It carries with it masculine associations representing aggression and negation of any feminine interest in aesthetic beauty. In this sense the shaved head is a symbol of a masculine utilitarian approach to image. However, the shaved head also can signify punishment, and in various historical epochs it has been particularly used against women to strip them, against their wills, of their femininity. In more recent history, the image has been linked with lesbian identity and second-wave feminism, which, in some forms, rejected what it identified as patriarchal definitions of feminine beauty. In fact, feminism has long been used in the language of popular culture as a euphemism for lesbianism, and the seeming rejection by O'Connor of traditional notions of feminine beauty has helped construct her queer credentials. For example, in a quote from the article in the lesbian magazine *Curve*, which broke Sinead O'Connor's lesbian confessions, O'Connor's androgynous image is linked to a queer sensibility through its attraction to lesbian fans: "She thumbed her nose at conventional notions of female beauty and brazenly spoke her mind . . . and lesbians couldn't get enough of her" (Anderson-Minshall 2000).

Beyond this visual signage of the queer outsider, O'Connor's musical performances have also helped fuel speculation of her possible sexual deviations from the norm. In 2000, not only did she court controversy by claiming a lesbian identity, but she also performed her single "No Man's Woman" on the *Rosie O'Donnell Show*, "making the tune something of a lesbian anthem" (Najafi 2003). This performance added to the queer readings of a song that already, lyrically,

could be read as a challenge to heterosexual relationship norms with the chorus exclaiming "I haven't traveled this far to become / No man's woman." This challenge to heterosexual norms is made more complex and less straightforward through the verses' lyrics, which suggests that O'Connor is talking about her love for a man whom she names as a spirit, evoking a possible God figure as the source of her love. This love is compared to an earthly relationship with a man who can fake his love, causing her pain and misery. This interest in the spiritual realm is a strong theme in O'Connor's music, which, as we will see, is open to a queer reading.

However, her musical output had already had both feminist and queer associations before her claims of being a lesbian. Her greatest popular hit, "Nothing Compares 2 U," was a song written by another queer icon (Prince), with lyrics containing a subtle but nevertheless queer tension between a recognizable female and male point-of-view. For instance, one of the key themes of the lyrics involves trying to forget the pain of a broken heart by finding comfort in other physical relationships, traditionally a masculine point of view in popular music. There are also other signals of the indeterminacy of the sexual identity and desire when Sinéad sings to a protagonist whom she names as "mama." Although this could possibly be interpreted as a reference to her own mother, this seems rather unlikely when the lyrics of the song are directed at her lover who is the "you" of the dramatic dialogue of the song. However, the musical and visual delivery of a song, as well as its general success, tend to overshadow any obvious disruptions to the heterosexual norm. Certainly the accompanying video, with O'Connor famously crying at the dramatic last chorus, may have overwhelmed any niggling doubts about the song's gendered meanings.

Such latent queer readings of O'Connor's work have grown stronger and more intentional through the years, especially since her media outing of 2000. For instance, on her 2002 album *Sean-Nos Nua*, O'Connor performs a version of the traditionally male-sung song "Peggy Gordon." The queer meaning this performance evokes, far from being secondary to the objective of producing a cover album of traditional Irish songs, was intentionally sung to emphasize a reading of lesbian love. In the liner notes to the album O'Connor writes, "It is usually sung by men in Ireland but I like it as a song sung by a female. I first heard it from a woman who was singing it as an expression of mourning for the loss of her female lover. I fell in love with the song as an expression of homosexual love, which often is not allowed voice itself in Ireland. It is a whisper of a song, which to me expresses the sheer fragility of homosexual love in a world that teaches, against God, that love is conditional."

O'Connor's queer aesthetic can also be established through her musical tastes and wide-ranging interest in alternative, marginalized, and seemingly mundane musical genres. Her musical career and collaboration with other artists have covered reggae, dub, hip-hop, country, Irish folk, rap, and Tin Pan Alley. In fact, she has often mixed these musical elements in new and surprising ways, for example, being one of the first musical performers to produce a Celtic/hip-hop sound. However, early in her career punk was often the most prominent descriptor of both her style and music. O'Connor's roots in the Dublin punk scene of the early 1980s were present in her first album *The Lion and the Cobra* (O'Brien 1995, 389) and especially read into her vocal performance. Her appearance also situated her within a punk aesthetic, especially with her shaved head and its associations with aggressive skinhead street culture. It could be argued that her association with queerness starts here, and it is no coincidence that queer politics and a punk style have long been associated. As Judith Halberstam states in her discussion of the queer punk movement, "Punk has always been the stylized and ritualized language of the rejected" (chapter 1, this volume).

O'Connor's punk associations not only link her with the politics of queer; they also emerged in their late 1970s incarnations as liberation, of sorts, for women from the very rigid feminine stereotypes. The music itself was often unconcerned with the usual pop and rock themes of feminized romance and male sexual conquest. Certainly, O'Connor's position as protester and rebel has parts of its roots in a punk aesthetic and has extended to her appeal as a queer icon. For example, her outsider status, represented in the use of the label "punk individualist," is articulated as part of a queer aesthetic in the profile in the *Advocate*: "O'Connor's gay and lesbian fans have remained loyal to and interested in one of the true punk individualists" (Che, 2002). It also added to her reputation as outspoken and somehow dangerous as a woman in the public eye. O'Conner has stated, "People judge books by their covers and build up an image of me based on their narrow-mindedness. If they think a certain way about a woman with a shaved head, bomber jacket and boots, that's their problem" (O'Brien 1995, 387).

Not only did her shaved head predispose a reading of her as a punk; it also has become over the years associated with O'Connor's religiosity, with its links with a religious monasticism. In her musical texts and associated explanations of her motivations to perform and record, spirituality and religious belief have become overwhelming themes in her public career. However, for O'Connor, this spirituality is not the straightforward traditional Christianity, drawing on a set of white Christian signs, but has the eclecticism of an alternative

religious language. For instance, her interest and identification with Rastafarianism, a specifically black Jamaican style of Christian faith, illustrate how she can be read as eccentric in her approach to religion. The language and influence of Rastarfarianism is recognizable in songs such as "Fire on Babylon," which uses the metaphor of Babylon, in particular spiritual retribution and redemption, to explore the theme and the emotions of the abused child. Although Babylon has an obvious place in white Catholicism and Protestantism, it has been a central symbol in the black West Indian experience of being taken from Africa into slavery and made to live in a foreign land. These connections are strengthened through the Rastafarian symbolism featured on several of her albums' artwork, along with the album *Faith and Courage* being dedicated "to all Rastafari people, with many thanks for their great faith, courage, and above all, inspiration."

O'Connor has also drawn on an eclectic paganism and New Age mysticism to reintroduce the idea of the goddess as a way of reclaiming a feminine god, outside the gendered moralizing double standards of the church. In fact, her album *Universal Mother* explores these themes, with the liner notes containing a vow of undertaking to the goddess, "The Charge of the Goddess," a text that apparently survives from ancient times through certain pagan sects. Part of this text provides images that strengthen a queer reading and identification with her audience:

> *She says,*
> *Whenever ye have need of anything, once*
> *in the month, and better to be when the moon is full,*
> *then shall ye assemble in some secret place; to*
> *These I shall teach things that are yet unknown*
> *And ye shall be free from all slavery*

O'Connor's use of alternative religious metaphors and images in her music and her celebrity packaging have helped her make connections between her outsider status, with her use of the heretical spiritual subject, and a marginalized queer identity. For instance, her ordination as a priest through her involvement in the Catholic Tridentine order and her announcement that she was changing her name to Mother Bernadette were moves that went beyond the normal rock celebrity dabbling with alternative spirituality. Like her declaration as a lesbian, her ordination and subsequent claims to want to practice as a priest were met with both ridicule and bafflement as it seemed to be yet another contradictory position, especially for a woman who had made strong criticisms of the Catholic Church in the past. As one critic has commented, "Having fought the church for many years, O'Connor recently became a part

of it. She is now a priest, she says, ordained into the Latter Day Latin Tridentine movement—a strange choice given that the Tridentines are ultra conservative" (Herrick 2000).

Her religious and spiritual interests, inserted within the popular music form, signal an obvious queer element in O'Connor's star text, bringing the "private" world of religious belief into the public secular world. Her religiosity has become part of her infamous eccentricity and oddity, as well as part of a general criticism of her inappropriateness as a public figure, most famously in her ripping up of a picture of the Pope on *Saturday Night Live* in the early 1990s. Her interests in both criticizing Catholic Christianity and promoting a spirituality, especially in the extratextual realm of political protests, have become a strong focus through which to queer O'Connor, built up over many years of "out of bounds" behavior. By providing a language that acknowledges difference, even her use of a language of redemption and healing— let alone her stubborn maintenance of unorthodox beliefs in spite of opposition—can fit a queer aesthetic.

CONCLUSION

On O'Connor's 2003 album *She Who Dwells. . .* there is a live version of the song "Thank You for Hearing Me." In this version she includes the lyrical line "Thank you for queering me." This lyrical line is part of a long list of "thank you" statements within the song that we can imagine are addressed to a possible number of protagonists in the singer's life, including her audience, the media, and other individual personal relationships. The choice of these lyrics is one example, of many, of the way O'Connor has had a queer dialogue with the media and her audience. This queering of herself, both inside and outside the musical text, represents the celebration of difference, but also a humanist struggle to be oneself. The queerness of O'Connor does not in fact lie solely with her revelations of her sexuality, or with her image, but in a challenge to a division between the private and public, especially in her transgression of acceptable media celebrity behavior. The confusing representations of Sinéad O'Connor as neither lesbian nor straight in 2000 strengthened O'Connor's already queer status as an eccentric and alternative celebrity, as well as provoking media ridicule. This media criticism understood O'Connor as intentionally positioning herself as superficially queer, for media attention and shock value. This reading was seen as credible in light of previous contradictory and seemingly inappropriate behavior, which had put O'Connor in the media spotlight. It also was validated through O'Connor's personal biographical facts of high-profile

heterosexual relationships, motherhood, and marriage. Yet O'Connor's whole public career can also be understood through a tradition of the artist as outsider who, while exasperating the cultural and art critics of the day, is nevertheless given the artistic license and freedom to pursue taboo subjects and behave outside the norm. Her position as rebel and provocateur is thus tolerated through a romantic construction of the artist. In O'Connor's case her inappropriate behavior, including her refusal to be either gay or straight, is allowed through a focus on the skill and emotional authenticity of her voice. However, O'Connor is never completely normalized through these strategies of containment as she continues to baffle categorization through her musical texts and in her engagements with the media.

NOTE

1. The quote "I am not in a box of any description" comes from a public state-ment released by Sinéad O'Connor in 2000, in the wake of the controversy surrounding her comments suggesting she identified with being a lesbian, explaining her understanding of her own sexuality.

REFERENCES

Anderson-Minshall, Diane (2000). "Sinéad O'Connor Is No Man's Woman." *Curve* 5, no. 5 (available at http://www.curvemag.com/Detalied/169.html).

CTV Television (2000). "An Interview with Sinéad O'Connor" (transcript avail-able at http://www.members.tripod.com/dcebe/fac_int0608.htm).

Che, Cathay (2002, November 26). "Straight Talk." *Advocate* (available at http://www.advocate.com/html/stories/877/877_sinead.asp).

Greckel, Wil (1979). "Rock and Nineteenth-Century Romanticism: Social and Cultural Parallels." *Journal of Musicology* 3: 177–202.

Halberstam, Judith (2006). "What's That Smell?: Queer Temporalities and Subcultural Lives" (chap. 1, this volume).

Hedges, Warren (1996). "Howells's 'Wretched Fetishes': Character, Realism, and Other Modern Instances." *Texas Studies in Literature and Language* 38, no. 1 (available at http://www.sou.edu/English/IDTC/Terms/terms.htm).

Herrick, Stefan (2000, July 22). "Mother of Mercy." *Evening Post* (Wellington), p. 26.

Hicklin, Aaron (2000, August). "Mother Courage," *DIVA Magazine* (posted August 12, 2000 to jitr@postmodern.com).

Mistry, Reena (2000). "Madonna and 'Gender Trouble'" (available at http://www.theory.org.uk/madonna.htm).

Najafi, Yusef (2003, October 31). "Stepping out of the Spotlight." *Washington Blade* (available at http://www.washblade.com).

Negus, Keith (1997). "Sinéad O'Connor—Musical Mother." In *Sexing the Grove: Popular Music and Gender*, ed. Sheila Whiteley. London: Routledge.

O'Brien, Lucy (1995). *She Bop: The Definitive History of Women in Rock, Pop and Soul*. London: Penguin.

O'Brien, Paul (2004, September 24). "Sinéad's Extraordinary Step to Be Left Alone." *Irish Examiner* (available at http://www.cnn.com/SHOWBIZ/Music/09/24/ireland.oconnor.ap/index.html).

Pareles, Jon (1988, January 31). "On a Limb Shouting." *New York Times* (available from http://www.members.tripod.com/dcebe/tlatc01.txt).

Rahman, Mohmin (2004). "Is Straight the New Queer? David Beckham and the Dialectics of Celebrity." *M/C Journal* 7, no. 5 (available at http://journal.media-culture.org.au/0411/15-rahman.php).

Randell, Mac (2000, July 8). "Soul Stirrer." *Launch* (available at http://music.yahoo.com/read/interview/12048471).

Pattison, Robert (1987). *The Triumph of Vulgarity*. Oxford: Oxford University Press.

Shanahan, B. (2000, July 2). "Sinéad O'Connor." *Sunday Telegraph* (Sydney).

USA Today (2000, June 26). "Sinéad O'Connor Throws Another Curve," p. 2.

12

GENDER CROSSINGS
A Neglected History in African American Music

JEFFREY CALLEN

I had a female impersonator for years named Jean LaRue. I didn't tell you about that. She was out of Oakland. I don't know if she is living or dead. She was with me for years. Name was Jean LaRue.

—Clarence "Little Red" Tenpenny, interview with the author, August 14, 1998

Clarence "Little Red" Tenpenny was a fixture of the African American music scene in the East Bay area of Northern California for almost two decades (late 1940s–mid 1960s).[1] His revue, the Dukes of Rhythm, performed regularly in local nightclubs and at dances held by African American fraternal organizations. For about five years, the Dukes of Rhythm featured Jean LaRue, a singer whose specialty was slow numbers—torch songs and jazz ballads. Little Red and I spoke at length several times about his musical career and Jean LaRue's name came up early in our conversations. However, Little Red failed to mention that Jean LaRue was a female impersonator.[2] When Little Red did mention it, it was as an interesting, but not important, piece of information that he had forgotten to include. I was surprised that a blues revue had a female impersonator as a vocalist and I immediately assumed that the performance options for female impersonators had been limited. Little Red

assured me that had not been the case. Jean LaRue was a popular local entertainer and often made his own deals with club owners. Little Red also said that Jean LaRue was not the only female impersonator he had used; he was just the best. My confusion heightened when I asked Little Red about other female impersonators who sang blues, and he mentioned Willie Mae "Big Momma" Thornton alongside another female impersonator who had sung for his revue. Big Momma Thornton, a well-known female performer of the Urban Blues from the 1940s to the late 1960s, had regularly appeared on- and offstage in male attire, but I had never considered her as someone who crossed gender lines.

What I learned from my conversations with Little Red ran contrary to the histories of African American popular music that I had read. Until recently, histories of African American popular music have assumed the primacy of male contributions. The history of African American music has been effectively "gendered," constructed as a male realm with maleness assigned a narrow range of meaning. These histories have created and relied upon two central male images—the jazz innovator and the bluesman—which have become archetypal figures in the popular imagination. The development of both jazz and blues are sketched as histories of innovation by great men that mirror the history that was constructed of European art music. The contributions of women (the necessary "other" to any definition of maleness) have received some, often grudging, recognition.[3] However, the contributions of those who fell outside of, or refused to recognize, the gender boundaries are largely ignored. This chapter examines the history of two groups of performers who clearly disrupt the gender boundaries of these histories—female and male impersonators—and the reasons for the exclusion of these voices.

FEMALE IMPERSONATION IN AMERICAN ENTERTAINMENT

Mainstream Traditions

The primary forms of gender crossing in American entertainment prior to the early twentieth century were the parodied and realistic portrayals of females by male performers that occurred in a variety of settings—commonly referred to as female impersonation. Female impersonators performed in "legitimate" theaters, bars and cabarets, and, most significantly, minstrel shows. The roots of female impersonation in the United States are in the English theatrical tradition, which barred female performers from the stage until the seventeenth century. Women replaced men in the English theater in the seventeenth century but female impersonation made a comeback in the early nineteenth century in a new

setting, the English music hall.[4] It then quickly crossed the Atlantic and became a widely used feature of "comic travesty" in American theaters. A new form of popular entertainment, the minstrel show, soon became the primary training ground for American female impersonators. White minstrel show performers regularly posed as "plantation yellow girls" and "plantation princesses." These characters presented images that played on the popular imagination of the time: the highly sexual, sassy but subjugated (and therefore available) "mulatto" slave girl and the imperial (and imperious) but delicate, and somewhat foolish, daughter of the slave owner. Female impersonators soon became stars and, in the period immediately following the Civil War, were the highest paid minstrel show performers. The most famous female impersonator of the day, Francis Leon, was so convincing that many refused to believe he was a man (Bullough and Bullough, 233–34).

Near the end of the nineteenth century, two new forms of entertainment developed from the disappearing minstrel show tradition: vaudeville and burlesque. Vaudeville and burlesque each appealed to different audiences and featured two distinct styles of female impersonation.[5] Vaudeville developed from those minstrel shows that, since the Civil War, had catered to a largely female audience from the growing White middle class. Vaudeville impersonators deemphasized the minstrel show's raunchy humor and lampooning of women and offered instead a celebration of femaleness and cultural norms in which impersonators strove for realistic portrayals of "ladies of fashion." This respectable style of female impersonation was one of the most popular forms of theatrical entertainment of the early twentieth century (Hamilton, 235). Its most famous practitioner, Julian Eltinge, developed a national following and debuted on Broadway in 1903 (Bullough and Bullough, 24).

Burlesque, which developed out of those minstrel shows that had appealed to working-class, largely male audiences, maintained the minstrel show's raunchy humor and lampooning of cultural norms. Female impersonators working in burlesque did not strive for artful illusions; their goal was comedy. The typical woman they portrayed was a brassy tart drawn from working-class street culture (Hamilton, 144–45). Many burlesque comics also included female impersonations in their acts and several became national celebrities. The most popular, Bert Savoy, built a national reputation and appeared in a number of early talking movies (Bullough and Bullough, 234). Savoy's character, a brassy, smart-mouthed, red-haired dame, is considered the prototype for Mae West's stage persona.[6] For some commentators, the burlesque style of female impersonation was the most visible manifestation of a style of female impersonation practiced in working-class concert saloons since the late

nineteenth century (Hamilton, 144). Historian Marybeth Hamilton describes the thrill these female impersonators (commonly know as "fairy impersonators") offered their audiences as a feeling that they were not watching a performance at all. The fairy impersonator, "[l]ike the burlesque dancer whose raunchy presence suggested an offstage identity as a prostitute . . . blurred the boundary between stage life and street life and displayed his authentic self—as a 'third sexer,' and 'invert' who straddled the gender divide" (Hamilton, 145).

For New York critics, the "sexual underworld" of the fairy impersonator was a realm that was in clear contrast to the world of respectable theatrical female impersonation (Hamilton 141–44). In 1928, Mae West's play *Pleasure Man*, which offered a behind-the-scenes look at the performers in a "drag show," created a public outrage in New York by portraying them as homosexuals. Critics accused West of "single-handedly perverting female impersonation, of fabricating a connection between the sexual underworld and the world of the theatrical female impersonator" (Hamilton, 144). George Chauncey, in his impressive historical work *Gay New York*, describes the working-class bars in which fairy impersonators worked in New York City. Centered in Irish, Italian, and African American neighborhoods, their clientele was both "gay" and "straight" but usually segregated along ethnic lines.[7] However, terms such as *gay* and *straight* or *homosexual* and *heterosexual* had little meaning up until the 1930s (Chauncey, 3).

The idea of the *homosexual* as a distinct form of personal identity is a modern construction. Doctors first used the term in the 1880s and it did not originally refer to a person who felt erotic desire for a member of the same sex but to someone who possessed the mental state of the other gender.[8] By 1920, doctors had redefined numerous behaviors, previously considered immoral or odd, as "sexual perversions." These included cross-dressing (given the label *transvestitism* in 1910); doing the work of the other gender; playing the games of the other gender; drinking the drinks of the other gender; and, performing the sexual acts of the other gender, including feeling erotic desire for members of the same sex (Katz, 145–46). However, these distinctions did not become dominant in popular opinion until the late 1930s (Chauncey, 21). During the first part of the early twentieth century, the most important popular distinction made regarding sexual behavior was between "normal" (procreative) sex and "abnormal" (nonprocreative) sex (Katz, 169). The primary gender/sexual division of men was between "fairies" and "real men," a distinction based not on sexual behavior or erotic desire but on the gender persona and status individuals assumed in their daily life (Chauncey, 28). Additional categories that defined male "homosexual"

behavior further complicated matters. Both real men and fairies could be "queer" (erotically interested in other men), and real men could be "trade" (willing to accept the social and sexual advances of a queer; Chauncey, 16, 21). In the Black community, *faggot* and *sissy* were more commonly used terms than *fairy* or *queer* (Chauncey, 249–50).

Fairies (or sissies) communicated their identity through their manner of dress and behavior. Different codings applied in public and private settings. Style of dress signaling that a man was a fairy could range from a "bit of flash" to outrageous male clothing (such as green suits or suede shoes) to full drag (Chauncey, 51–52). Fairies could also announce their identity by taking a woman's name, and some who became full-time entertainers or prostitutes permanently left their birth name behind. Many fairies chose campy, flamboyant names such as Queen Mary or Cleopatra; others chose names that highlighted a personal characteristic or played on their birth names. Among fairy impersonators, the names of well-known female entertainers were especially popular. Gloria Swanson was probably the most popular drag persona of the 1920s and the stage name of the most famous African American female impersonator of the 1930s (Chauncey, 51). The common popular perception in the early twentieth century was that fairies were "virtual women" or a "third sex."[9] However, the homosexual-heterosexual binarism that governs contemporary thought was already making steady inroads among the middle class, where it would be widely accepted by the end of the 1930s. Among the working class, the distinction between fairies and "normal men" would remain the dominant image well into the 1950s (Chauncey, 48). This was despite the emergence of "homosexuality" as a marker of personal identity for a growing number of individuals in urban areas.[10]

Little information is available on female (or male) impersonation by African American entertainers—and there is virtually none for the period before the 1920s. One of the few sources of information is Chauncey's *Gay New York*, a history of gay life in New York City from 1890 to 1940. During the 1920s and 1930s, Harlem was one of the two important centers of gay life in New York City and an important center of African American culture and entertainment.[11] Through the lens of Harlem during the 1920s and 1930s, we can get a view into the neglected history of Black female impersonators and their female counterparts who assumed male personas in their performances.

African American Female and Male Impersonators

During the 1920s and 1930s, Harlem was the largest African American community in the United States and considered the unofficial capital

of Black America. During the 1920s, the era of the famous Harlem Renaissance,[12] Harlem was a center of music, literature, and art, and a major entertainment district for Black and White audiences. Its music scene included a large number of "sissy" (gay) and "bulldagger" (lesbian) entertainers who worked in a variety of venues.[13] The 1920s and 1930s were also periods of gay "chic" in New York City. Historian Ned Miller writes that in Harlem, license mixed with sexual ambiguity: sexual identities were fluid and those who had same-sex relationships rarely defined themselves as homosexuals.[14] Gay and straight Whites frequented Harlem's nightclubs, speakeasies, and house parties in order to experience a taste of the "exotic." Local entrepreneurs openly catered to this market and the featured entertainment included explicit sexual acts. The most famous was the "daisy chain," a "sex circus" (commemorated in compositions by Fats Waller and Count Basie) that presented a variety of sexual acts and featured an enormous transvestite named "Clarenz" (Garber, 232).

The gay subculture, which had been established in Harlem in the early part of the century, expanded dramatically during the 1920s and 1930s (Garber, 318–19; Chauncey, 25). Drag queens were regularly seen in Harlem's streets and clubs. Although the queens risked arrest by the Irish policemen who patrolled the neighborhood, neighborhood residents showed them a high degree of tolerance. Chauncey reports that, as in many working-class neighborhoods, gay men were integrated into Harlem's working-class culture (25). Ned Miller presents a slightly different picture of gay life in Harlem. He writes that the community tolerated gay men and that gay men stressed their identity as Black men over their identity as gay men. Miller asserts that even with the sexual experimentation of the 1920s and 1930s, there was an emphasis on heterosexual marriage, even for gay men and lesbians (Miller 154, 156).

During this period, the blues was the preferred musical style among working-class African Americans, and blues songs frequently depicted the place of gay men and women in Black working-class culture (Chauncey, 250).[15] Many popular female blues singers of the day were openly lesbian or bisexual and, along with songs about separations from loved ones, petty employers, and abusive husbands, they sang about sissies and bulldaggers (Chauncey, 251). Ma Rainey was one of the major blues stars of the 1920s and her sexual involvement with women was common knowledge among her audience. The advertisement for her song "Prove It on Me Blues" displayed a drawing of Rainey on a street corner in a man's hat, jacket, and tie attempting to seduce two women.[16] In another song, Ma Rainey complains about her husband leaving her for a "sissy man" named Miss Kate, and several male blues singers

recorded the song "Sissy Man Blues," which demands, "If you can't bring me a woman, bring me a sissy man." These records, particularly Rainey's, were widely marketed in Black working-class communities. These songs did not celebrate sissies and bulldaggers and, in fact, often ridiculed them, but the songs "recognized them as part of Black working-class culture."[17]

An "aura of sexual ambivalence" similar to that expressed in the blues characterized Harlem nightlife (Miller, 150). Gay and straight audiences freely mixed in nightclubs, cabarets, house parties, and speakeasies. Male and female impersonation was at its peak as nightclub entertainment and a large number of Black female and male impersonators became prominent entertainers (Chauncey, 252). The female impersonator Gloria Swanson came to Harlem in 1930 after winning a number of prizes at drag balls in Chicago, where he also ran his own nightclub. As the hostess of a popular Harlem club, he sang bawdy parodies of popular songs and was described as "so perfect a woman that frequently clients came and left never suspecting his true sex." Gangsters, hoodlums, pimps, and entertainers regaled Swanson with presents (Chauncey, 251). Other prominent female impersonators included Phil Black, Frankie "Half Pint" Jaxon, and George Hanna, who all openly used homosexual themes in their acts (Garber, 325).

Male impersonator Gladys Bentley became a legendary figure in Harlem, as famous for her attire and girlfriends as for her singing (Chauncey, 252). A striking figure—a three-hundred-pound piano player and singer, dressed in white tails and a top hat—Bentley was celebrated for her ability to improvise obscene lyrics over popular melodies (Garber, 324). In the late 1930s, Bentley toned down her lyrics to the merely risqué and headed a "pansy chorus line" composed of female impersonators (Chauncey, 253). Another prominent male impersonator was the comic Jackie "Moms" Mabley who performed with a chorus line of female impersonators (Garber, 331).

The single most important social event of the year for female impersonators in Harlem (and throughout New York City[18]) was the annual Hamilton Lodge Ball, a drag ball organized by Lodge Number 710 of the Grand United Order of Odd Fellows of Harlem. The ball began in 1869 and no one is sure when it became a female impersonator event but, by the late 1920s, everyone in Harlem knew it as the Faggots' Ball. Participants, Black and White, came from throughout the city and from up and down the Atlantic seaboard. As Abram Hill, a writer working for the Federal Writers' Project, described the 1939 ball, "There were corn fed 'pansies' from the deep South breaking traditional folds by mixing irrespective of race. There were sophisticated 'things' from Park Avenue

and Broadway. There were the big black strapping 'darlings' from the heart of Harlem. . . . The ball was a melting pot, different, exotic and unorthodox but acceptable" (Chauncey, 261).

Black and White drag queens mixed at the Harlem drag balls across racial lines but never forgot them (Chauncey, 263). The drag ball was a fixture among African Americans in a number of other cities in the East and Midwest, including Baltimore and Chicago, and Black communities typically greeted the balls with a measure of ambivalence. Black newspapers, though frequently disparaging in their coverage, reported on the balls and included photographs and drawings of the participants (Chauncey, 257–63). Descriptions, such as the following by Abram Hill of the 1939 Hamilton Lodge Ball, offer insight into the preferred visual images of Black female impersonators:

> The balls became a site for the projection and inversion of racial as well as gender identities. Significantly, though, white drag queens were not prepared to reverse their racial identity. Many accounts refer to African-American queens appearing as white celebrities, but none refer to whites appearing as well-known black women. As one black observer noted, "The vogue was to develop a 'personality' like some outstanding women," but the only women he listed, Jean Harlow, Gloria Swanson, Mae West, and Greta Garbo, were white. (Chauncey, 263)

The Depression put an end to the boom in Harlem. By the end of the 1930s, most of the entertainment venues closed and many entertainers left town. However, a few clubs remained in business. "Moms" Mabley continued performing with a chorus of female impersonators at the Ubangi Club and female impersonator Phil Black inaugurated a new drag ball in 1945 that continued for several decades. Another national event that signaled a change in the cultural climate also contributed to the decline of male and female impersonation. The passage of the 1933 Hollywood Motion Picture Professional Code, which banned all performances of "sexual perversion," put an end to female and male impersonation in the mainstream theatrical tradition.[19]

The 1940s—GI Impersonators

One of the arenas in which female impersonation flourished during the 1940s was the military. GI female impersonators often entertained their fellow GIs when no female performers were available. Paradoxically, this occurred during World War II when the military introduced "the concept of the homosexual" into its policies and procedures and homosexuality became grounds for discharge.[20] In practice, the military tended to place

identifiably (or suspected) gay men into stereotypical homosexual jobs as clerks, medics, chaplain's assistants—and female impersonators. This experience helped create the strengthened sense of a gay community that emerged during the 1940s (Miller, 233–34).

The "Pansy" Scare of the 1950s

The history of Black female and male impersonators comes to an abrupt halt in the early 1950s. The Red Scare, the anticommunist hysteria of the 1950s, is well remembered. Less well remembered is the antigay hysteria that also became endemic. There were widespread firings when government agencies, including the FBI and the postal services, began monitoring the activities of men they suspected of being gay (Miller, 259). This political climate affected not only the public perception of gay people but also the day-to-day circumstances of gay men's lives. Phil Black continued his drag balls in New York City, and Jean LaRue and undoubtedly other female (and male) impersonators continued performing, but there does not appear to have been the level of activity that had characterized earlier decades. The almost twenty-year gap before Black female impersonators were again widely seen coincides with the emergence of the gay liberation movement in the 1970s. The tradition of Black male impersonators seemed to disappear with the changing social mores.[21] Comic "Moms" Mabley, no longer cross-dressing or risqué, became a regular entertainer on numerous television variety shows. "Big Momma" Thornton continued to perform in male attire, but it is doubtful if any of the mostly White fans who were discovering her for the first time during the blues revival of 1960s thought of her as a male impersonator.

CONCLUSION

Gender-crossing performance—male and female impersonation—was a significant form of entertainment in the United States from the mid-1800s up until World War II, but it has been largely written out of histories of popular music. Black female and male impersonators do not even merit a footnote in the histories of American popular music. The conclusion of this chapter examines some of the social and cultural factors that created the exclusion of these performers from their proper place in the history of American music.

Voices command attention relative to the degree that they control some form of power—moral, economic, cultural, political. Female and male impersonators and other individuals who disrupt gender roles remain a marginalized group with only limited access to moral, economic, cultural,

and political capital. This includes reduced access to the process of history writing. Female and male impersonators are among those who challenge fundamental assumptions of Western culture regarding the nature of gender. This challenge is countered not only by the commonsense perceptions of everyday life, but also by the traditional precepts of Western scientific and academic scholarship. As Marcia Herndon has commented, "European and Euro-American middle class values permeate academic discourse," and have formed the assumptions with which scholars approach gender issues. Herndon notes the fallacy of these assumptions: other numbers and kinds of gender roles exist in cultures throughout the world.[22] Within the last few decades, scholars have uncovered the fallacy of the standard assumptions regarding the nature of gender even when looking at our own culture.[23] Within the realm of science, the imposition of rigid gender boundaries is a relatively recent phenomenon. The institutionalization of medical definitions of sexuality and gender, which began in the late nineteenth century, created a clear binary opposition of straight ("healthy" sexuality) and gay ("unhealthy" sexuality). This institutionalization was not complete until the end of World War II. Gayness was redefined as "deviance" that could be corrected, and the scientific definitions of gender roles became widely accepted as a natural fact.[24] The 1933 Hollywood Motion Picture Code, which banned sexual "perversion" from movie screens, the definition by the U.S. military during World War II of the homosexual as unsuitable for service, and the 1950s climate of antigay hysteria helped persuade and coerce people to accept a reformation of social mores regarding gender roles.

Within the African American community, the longstanding tension between the Black aristocracy and the Black working class extended to views of music, popular culture, and proper social behavior. During the pre–World War II era, the Black upper class wanted to use music as a tool for "uplifting the race." However, the Black upper class considered secular popular music, such as blues and jazz, crass and reinforcing of stereotypes Whites held of Blacks. The music that they felt could uplift the race was "cultured" music, particularly music from the European classical tradition.[25] The ambitions of Black aristocrats to be assimilated into White society were tied to the belief that Whites were inclined to judge their "race" by its worst elements.[26] Many members of the pre–World War II civil rights movement,[27] as well as the civil rights movement of the 1950s (Miller 361–62), shared this belief. The reinstitutionalization of male authority in the home after the disruption of the war years was a factor in downplaying the role of female civil rights leaders, as well as the closeting of several prominent gay civil rights leaders.

The Black church has played a significant role in policing gender boundaries. For well-understood historical reasons, Black churches have taken upon themselves the dual role of advocate for the rights of the community and arbiter of moral standards. The moral standards espoused by Black churches created an idealized version of African American life that places "nontraditional" gender roles and sexual behavior outside the realm of acceptable morality. The slowness with which many Black churches responded to the AIDS crisis is but one recent example of the effect of not only their exclusion of gay life as moral behavior but also their failure to acknowledge its existence and the contributions of gay African Americans to Black culture. The Black Nationalist movement of the 1960s also promoted conservative images of African American gender relationships based on an idealized version of a mythical African past. Some Black Nationalist leaders went so far as to declare that homosexuality was equivalent to a betrayal of the race, and some feminists have accused Black Nationalists of increasing the level of homophobia in the Black community.[28] In opposition to racist portrayals of Black people as hypersexual, many Black Nationalists strove to present an image of respectability that did not include gay men and lesbians, and certainly did not include transvestites or transsexuals.[29]

The often subtle shaping of the choices made by individual scholars can also lead to the exclusion of marginalized voices. When I encountered the "discovery" that led to my consideration of these issues, I was intrigued, but hesitated to follow up on my curiosity. It was outside the realm of my objectives, which I had discussed at length with community members before beginning my research. Additionally, I had assured local residents that I was respectful of their community and their history, and my intuition told me that this was not an avenue of investigation they would appreciate. After unsuccessfully trying to find Jean LaRue, I—rightly or wrongly—backed away from the subject. In balancing what I felt was important, I found that I did not want to do anything that might cause distress to the people who were helping me with my research.

History is by nature a contested space, and the stories recorded inevitably reflect the ideologies of their times. However, with the passage of time, the opportunity can be lost to document groups and individuals whose stories are omitted. The stories of the female classic blues singers of the 1920s and 1930s were largely neglected in blues histories until the 1980s. However, their commercial success made it impossible to ignore them completely and provided materials that scholars could consider and reexamine. The stories of Black female and male impersonators do not have that advantage. There is little record of their work. The primary

resources that remain are the recollections of the few individuals who remember and are willing to talk. With the passage of time, these individuals will no longer be with us and a part of the history of American popular music will be lost.

NOTES

1. I interviewed Little Red as part of my master's degree research on the role the blues played in forming a local sense of identity for residents of North Richmond, California; see Jeffrey Callen, "Musical Community: The 'Blues Scene' in North Richmond, California," M.A.Thesis: University of California–Santa Barbara, 2001. In a few short years during the 1940s, North Richmond was transformed from a sparsely populated, predominantly White community into a densely populated, predominantly Black community with a thriving nightclub district.

2. The proper use of pronouns for this chapter is an unsolvable problem. I have chosen to base my choice of pronouns upon the birth sex of the individual, which allows me to escape the arduous task of determining which gender persona each individual chose to embody in his or her offstage life.

3. See, for example, Angela Davis, *Blues Legacies and Black Feminism* (New York: Vintage, 1991); and Peter Antelyes, "Red Hot Mamas: Bessie Smith, Sophie Tucker, and the Ethnic Maternal Voice in American Popular Song," in *Embodied Voices: Representing Female Vocality in Western Culture*, ed. Leslie C. Dunn and Nancy A. Jones (Cambridge: Cambridge University Press, 1994), 212–30.

4. Vern L. Bullough and Bonnie Bullough, *Cross Dressing, Sex, and Gender* (Philadelphia: University of Pennsylvania Press, 1993), 232; hereafter, page numbers for this volume will be cited parenthetically in the text.

5. Marybeth Hamilton, *When I'm Bad, I'm Better: Mae West, Sex, and American Entertainment* (Berkeley and Los Angeles: University of California Press, 1995), 144–45; hereafter, page numbers for this volume will be cited parenthetically in the text.

6. George Eells, *Mae West: A Biography* (New York: William Morrow, 1982), 35.

7. George Chauncey, *Gay New York: Gender Urban Culture and the Making of the Gay Male World 1890–1940* (New York: Basic. 1994), 72–79; hereafter, page numbers for this volume will be cited parenthetically in the text; Hamilton, *When I'm Bad, I'm Better*, 65–66.

8. Jonathan N. Katz, *Gay/Lesbian Almanac* (New York: Harper & Row, 1983), 137, 147; hereafter, page numbers for this volume will be cited parenthetically in the text.

9. This distinction is similar to that made by recent scholars who have studied gender roles. See Gilbert Herdt, "Introduction," in *Third Sex, Third*

Gender: Beyond Sexual Dimorphism in Culture and History, ed. Gilbert Herdt (New York: Zone, 1994); and Sabrina Petra Ramet, "Gender Reversals and Gender Cultures: An Introduction," in *Gender Reversals and Gender Cultures: Anthropological and Historical Perspectives*, ed. Sabrina Petra Ramet (London: Routledge, 1996), 1–21.

10. See Hamilton, *When I'm Bad, I'm Better*, 94, where it is noted that historian John D'Emilio ties the development of these communities to social changes that created a separation between sexual desire and procreation and between "personal life" and work life.

11. The other important center of gay life in New York was Greenwich Village, a largely White neighborhood.

12. A number of gay artists and patrons (both Black and White) were prominent in the Harlem Renaissance, but they generally had little involvement with popular entertainment; see Samuel A. Floyd, Jr., "Music in the Harlem Renaissance: An Overview," in *Black Music in the Harlem Renaissance*, ed. Samuel A. Floyd (Westport, Conn.: Greenwood, 1990), 4–9.

13. Eric Garber, "A Spectacle In Color: The Lesbian and Gay Subculture of Jazz Age Harlem," in *Hidden From History: Reclaiming the Gay and Lesbian Past*, ed. Martin Duberman, Martha Vicinus, and George Chauncey, Jr. (New York: New American Library, 1989), 318–19; hereafter, page numbers for this volume will be cited parenthetically in the text.

14. Neil Miller, *Out of the Past: Gay and Lesbian History from 1869 to the Present* (New York: Vintage, 1995), 148, 150; hereafter, page numbers for this volume will be cited parenthetically in the text.

15. See also Davis, *Blues Legacies and Black Feminism*.

16. Judith Halberstam, "Mackdaddy, Superfly, Rapper: Gender, Race, and Masculinity in the Drag King Scene," *Social Text* 52–53 (1997): 113.

17. Chauncey, *Gay New York*, 251; see also Hazel Carby, "It Jus' Be's Dat Way Sometime: The Sexual Politics of Women's Blues," in *Keeping Time: Readings in Jazz History*, ed. Robert Walser (New York: Oxford University Press, 1999), 351–65.

18. In New York City, they were also a fixture within the White gay community; see Chauncey, *Gay New York*, 263.

19. Halberstram, "Mackdaddy, Superfly, Rapper," 113.

20. In the past, sodomy (not mere identification as homosexual) had been a crime that could result in years in prison and/or discharge; see Miller, *Out of the Past*, 231.

21. One exception was African American male impersonator Storme DeLaverie, who performed from the 1940s until the 1960s; see Halberstam, "Mackdaddy, Superfly, Rapper," 114.

22. Marcia Herndon, "Biology and Culture: Music, Gender, Power, and Ambiguity," in *Music Gender, and Culture*, ed. Marcia Herndon and Susanne Ziegler (Berlin: Florian Noetzel Verlag Wilhelmshaven, 1990), 12.

23. Judith Lorber, "Embattled Terrain. Gender and Sexuality. Revisioning Gender," in *Revisioning Gender*, ed. Myra Marx Ferree, Judith Lorber, and Beth B. Hess (Thousand Oaks, Calif.: Sage, 1999), 416–48; see also Herdt, "Introduction."

24. Miller, *Out of the Past*, 249. Miller also notes that the American Psychological Association removed homosexuality from its list of psychiatric disorders in the 1970s (256).

25. Lawrence Schenbeck, "Music, Gender, and 'Uplift' in the Chicago Defender, 1927–1936," *Musical Quarterly* 81, no. 3 (1997): 349.

26. Ibid., 350.

27. Joy James, *Transcending the Talented Tenth: Black Leaders and American Intellectuals* (New York: Routledge, 1997), 16–24.

28. E. F. White, "Africa on My Mind: Gender, Counter Discourse, and African-American Nationalism," *Journal of Women's History* 2, no. 1 (1990): 81–82. Black lesbian poet and commentator Cheryl Clarke asserts that the homophobic sentiments and postures of Black nationalist and leftist male intellectuals during the 1960s and '70s helped institutionalize homophobia in the Black community; see Clarke, "The Failure to Transform: Homophobia in the Black Community," in *Home Girls: A Black Feminist Anthology*, ed. Barbara Smith (New York: Kitchen Table, 1983), 197–208. Clarke makes the further point that homophobia weakened the political potential of the Black community and placed limits on "a natural part of all human beings, namely the bisexual potential in us all" (207).

29. White, "Africa on My Mind," 75.

13

QUEER(ING) MASCULINITIES IN HETEROSEXIST RAP MUSIC

FREYA JARMAN-IVENS

Thanks to acts such as NWA, The Geto Boys, Tupac Shakur, D12, and 50 Cent, rap music has come to be perceived as a violent, aggressive, misogynist, and male-dominated genre. In accordance with the generalized exscription of women from a great deal of music history,[1] women tend to appear in forms of hip-hop culture as marginal figures.[2] The elimination of women from the rap arena is effected on several levels. Lyrical content interacts with visual imagery, including, but not limited to, the music video. All-male spaces are constructed visually by way of the "crew." Groups of disenfranchised young men work to enact an almost excessive display of masculinity, not only through the actual exclusion of women from their space but also through physical actions such as grabbing their genitals or keeping their hands close to the pelvic area, and swaggering boastfully. When women are granted entry to this all-male space they are often objectified and fetishized in a way that constructs the space as male dominated and heterosexual. Eminem, for example, displays blatant objectification combined with misogyny, portraying various women as blow-up dolls: Christina Aguilera in the video for "The Real Slim Shady" and his ex-wife Kim onstage.[3] Rap music has become particularly notorious for its lyrical content, which is seen as typified by violence, homophobia, misogyny, and, again, the objectification of women. The Bloodhound Gang, for example, deploy

a kind of toilet humor that commonly includes references to women's genitals as odious, recalling perhaps the *vagina dentata*. The fetishization of particular female body parts is also a factor, reducing the implicated female character to a set of disembodied components.[4] Such responses to female sexuality and physicality are founded upon an exaggerated notion of disgust that borders on the comic, being almost a parody of itself. It may well be that comedy is deployed as a distancing strategy by the group, such that the offensive potential is somewhat lessened by an implicit caveat emptor: "It's just a joke." More overtly, Eminem concludes a tirade of misogynist violence with the line, "I'm just playin' ladies—you know I love you."[5]

Gangsta rap as a style is typically less concerned with distancing itself from the violence contained within its lyrics; on the contrary, since its emergence in the late 1980s, its exponents have courted the surrounding controversy. James Haskins summarizes, "Gangsta rap is harsh, hard-hitting, brutal, bloody and usually obscene . . . its lyrics deal with guns, gang wars, treacherous females, drugs, alcohol and going against . . . the police."[6] Although a significant subtext of gangsta rap is a black reaction against oppression by white authority (typically embodied by the police),[7] running parallel to this is the domination of women by "hypermasculine" men. A content analysis of the representation of violence against women in rap music between 1987 and 1993 reveals that 22 percent of gangsta rap songs contained violent and misogynist lyrics,[8] and that the content and frequency of such references have increased significantly with the emergence of artists such as Eminem.[9] Examples thus abound of misogynist lyrics, in which women are referred to as "bitches," "sluts," "whores," and "hoes," and otherwise generally demeaned, objectified, and subjected to apparently gratuitous violence. Rappers' masculinity is, notably, also constructed as unquestionably heterosexual, perceptible through a mixture of homophobic lyrics and the insistence of heterosexual activity between the rapper(s) and women—even if they appear simultaneously disgusted by or aggressive toward those women. In the case of Eminem, homosexuality merges with pedophilia, and both are amalgamated in the concentrated scapegoat form of his regular character Ken Kaniff.

Gangsta rap and its descendants have become gothic expressions of violent and obscene imagery, a great deal of which represents hypermasculinity through misogyny and homophobia, thereby supporting the stereotype of the (hetero)sexist male rapper.[10] There are, however, already certain incongruities to confront before determining rap as a genre to display a uniform and unquestionable masculinity. First, the exclusion of women to create a homosocial arena mobilizes discourses surrounding

the slippage between homosociality and homosexuality. Eve Kosofsky Sedgwick describes a continuum of male bonds, with homosociality on the one hand and homosexuality on the other, and crucially, this continuum is "radically disrupted";[11] it does not contain the potential for slippage between social and sexual that is integral to, say, Adrienne Rich's formation of a "lesbian continuum."[12] Within the male system of relations described by Sedgwick, the exchange of women between men forms homosocial bonds, while simultaneously serving to assuage fears of homosexuality. Thus, I am not suggesting here that all rap crews contain an element of the homosexual, or that rap crews are gay, or even verge on it. Rather, if the exchange of women ensures heterosexuality, we should undoubtedly examine the ways in which women are exchanged within such groups of men, since such exchange goes some way also to defining their masculinity. When women are objectified and fetishized—reduced to body parts—they become ideally packaged for exchange as cultural capital. Yet, if they are demeaned and rejected with disgust, as is also often the case, we should certainly query these men's desire for the women by whom they are apparently repulsed.

LANGUAGE AND THE MALE

The very centrality of lyrics to rap's identity as a genre may—or may not—also mark it as being well suited to male dominance, since language has culturally located meanings in terms of gender. As Mary Key notes, there is something of a myth of male superiority when it comes to the usage of language, implying that men are typically held to be more skilled in the realization of language's potential, both writing and speaking more fluently and eloquently, and possessing (and using) a wider vocabulary than women, who are charged with an emotional emphasis in their uses of language.[13] This notion is indeed in opposition to a great deal of evidence—academic and anecdotal—that young boys actually develop their language somewhat behind their female counterparts.[14] In later years, the study of language at school (be it a first language, literature, or a foreign language), as well as those subjects that demand essay-writing skills, tend to be female-dominated: where there is a choice as to whether or not to take a subject, the sex division is notable in the classroom demographics; where there is little or no choice, the division might be traced through exam results.[15] The question should therefore be raised as to how to reconcile these apparent contradictions: from the beginning to the end of childhood, boys are either behind their female peers in linguistic ability, or disinterested in the study of a "female" subject. There may in fact be very little to corroborate the myth

of male linguistic superiority. Similarly, despite the analogous myth that women's use of language is excessive and frivolous, "There has not been one study which provides evidence that women talk more than men."[16] The assumptions maintain their cultural hegemony nonetheless, and this is a highly relevant point given the male- and language-dominated nature of rap as a genre.

It seems also that different styles of writing have variously gendered meanings. According to Lorri Nielsen, there is an expectation in educational settings to write in one of three modes: expository (telling), transactional (doing), and argumentative.[17] In the face of this institutional bias, creative and poetic writing modes are marginalized.[18] Nielsen's studies suggest that "women and girls opted for lyric forms of communication (expressive, personal) over rationalist discourse."[19] Poetic and lyrical forms of writing may thus offer radical alternatives to rationalist forms of language, associated in their rationality and by virtue of their institutionally endorsed cultural superiority with patriarchy. This has particular implications for rap, inasmuch as the lyrics tend to be extremely personal. Many genres of popular music prize some version of "authenticity," often constructed in part through debates concerning song lyrics. The lyrics put forward by rappers are intensely personal, and visibly so, and often claimed by the artists as "true" self-expression. Thus, artists often name themselves and their "crew," and may use their own identity as the central feature of a song.[20] Moreover, this presumption of authenticity, and of agency, is extended into more complex descriptions of acts that the rapper claims to have seen or done. The emphasis on the particular and specific, and indeed the specifically unusual, in rap's lyrics is to be contrasted with a greater tendency toward the general in other popular music genres. While we would expect artists in teen-oriented pop or easy listening genres to appear "genuine" in performance, the content of such lyrics can very easily be transported into the lives of many listeners, and that is their aim.[21] By contrast, many of rap's lyrics are not personally claimable by any listener. What is central to rap's lyrics is a fluctuation between the general and the specific. Thus, in "The Real Slim Shady," Eminem moves from talking about his relationship with the music press and other artists to generalized sentiments that may easily be adopted by the audience. Moreover, this song is one of several that focus on Eminem's audience, and their emulation of him. The chorus in particular encapsulates the dual function of rap's lyrics. Although the chorus hears Eminem declaring himself to be the "real" Slim Shady, the idea of Slim Shady is expanded here to become a notion, a particular kind of person. Eminem then overtly calls

to the listeners to participate in the chorus, thus allowing them also to be "real" Slim Shadys.

The cultural importance of linguistic skill is also an important factor. The significance of this is that linguistic ability has been prized since the very roots of rap music.[22] As Dale Spender notes, in contemporary Anglophone cultures, "To be inferior when it comes to language is frequently to be discounted."[23] Not only this, but the inappropriate or inaccurate use of language—or the lack of language at all—is very often associated with neurological or psychiatric disorder.[24] The manifestation of language has long been an apparent indicator of a subject's state of mental health. The subject might not speak at all, withdrawing from communication altogether, might insist on talking primarily to himself, or might express himself inappropriately in some way. In the late 1830s, on his release from the asylums where he had been contained for being "religiously insane," Englishman John Perceval wrote, "To halloo, to bawl, to romp, to play the fool, are in ordinary life, signs of irregularity."[25] Moreover, it must be noted that if madness is associated with an unusual relation with language, it has also historically been associated with women. The nineteenth century saw the trope of the madwoman enjoying particular cultural relevance, as medicine and psychiatry proposed scientific foundations for the already longstanding presumption that mental disorder and effeminacy were mutually implicit.[26] The paradoxes of gender and language are these: men are characterized as possessing superior linguistic skill, while women are represented as chatterboxes and hysterics; and it is mostly male writers and poets who have taken their place in the literary canon, while girls and young women seem to display greater aptitude for the study of literature and greater enthusiasm for personal expression by way of poetry and journals. Rap as a genre depends heavily on linguistic skill—both in the writing and in the speaking—but is this a validation of the myth of male superiority of language, or does it problematize the male expression of masculinity in the genre?

In fact, even the linguistic content of certain rap artists is not as unproblematically male dominant as the stereotype would have us believe. While boasts of sexual prowess are prevalent, a kind of masochism also abounds.[27] Furthermore, in a kind of accordance with the generic approval of personal texts, many lyrics penned by Eminem, in particular, speak of personal difficulties throughout his life. Thus, in "Kim,"[28] while the overriding image is of Eminem slitting his wife's throat, the rapper also describes in painful detail the rejection he feels she has dealt him. The anguish in Eminem's voice is central to the song. The overall effect is

of a man split between his desire for his wife and his desire to destroy her, and the tension between those desires clearly affects his mental state in the course of the song. David Stubbs describes the song as "a repugnant, yet blood-raw and gripping performance, draining for all concerned," in which Eminem is "clearly as much tormented as tormentor, confused and crumbling inside. . . . At times he's pathetic, cripplingly insecure."[29] While it may seem to undermine the male supremacy that rap's lyrics tend to endorse, male masochism is also a strategy by which superior masculinity has been constructed. Discussing films such as *Raging Bull* (1980, dir. Martin Scorsese) and the *Rocky* series,[30] Judith Halberstam argues that "masochism is built into male masculinity, and the most macho of spectacles is the battered male body, a bloody hunk of ruined flesh, stumbling out of the corner for yet another round. The winner is always the one who has been beaten to a pulp but remains standing long enough to deliver the knockout punch."[31]

A similar tactic is deployed in the film *8 Mile* (2002, dir. Curtis Hanson), which starred Eminem as Jimmy "Rabbit" Smith in a semiautobiographical role and has tellingly been described as "the rap *Rocky*."[32] In the climactic scene, Rabbit competes in a freestyling rap contest ("battle") against his nemesis Papa Doc. Given their already antagonistic history, Rabbit is duly concerned about some of the subjects that Doc may use against him in the battle. Rabbit is given the first turn, however, and soon launches into a self-deprecating rant that he uses as a springboard from which to insult Doc and destroy his credentials. In the final seconds, a cappella, Rabbit proclaims, "I'm a piece of fuckin' white trash and I say it proudly / . . . / [*throwing the mic to Doc*] Here, tell these people something they don't know about me." Because Rabbit has subjected himself to all the humiliation possible, Doc no longer has any tools to use against him and is forced to surrender. In this masochistic moment, a subtle twist on the boxing film trope, the "macho spectacle" here is the male ego battered by his own words.

LANGUAGE AND/AS PATRIARCHAL STRUCTURE

In psychoanalytic terms, the issues surrounding the uses of language are deeply embedded in the human psychic makeup, with language figured as part of a fundamentally patriarchal structure: the symbolic realm, which incorporates law, culture, and religion. It is upon entry to the symbolic that the subject acquires language, inasmuch as language is a structure of symbols, the relation between signifiers and signifieds.[33] At any rate, entry into the symbolic involves the separation of the child subject from his mother. Toril Moi writes, "In the Oedipal crisis

the father splits up the dyadic unity between mother and child and forbids the child further access to the mother and the mother's body."[34] Consequently, although female subjects must in some way negotiate entry into the symbolic order, their fundamental exclusion from it is also implicit. In terms of language as symbolic system, as message, we have already seen how masculinity is constructed as heterosexual male dominance through violent misogyny and homophobia. Clearly, this is a highly problematic and potentially offensive expression of masculinity, but it is what might be seen as the logical extreme of a continuum of masculinity. Yet language also has functions that operate apart from this. The idea of language as sound *outside* of its communicative dimension recalls what Roland Barthes calls "geno-song." In contrast to "pheno-song," which refers to "everything in the performance which is in the service of communication," the geno-song is not concerned with communication and representation, functioning instead as a playful signifier with no culturally recognized signified.[35] Certainly, there are issues raised by Barthes's model: the dualistic construction of pheno-song versus geno-song is arguably idealistic and is founded upon an unhelpful dualism, for Barthes presents geno-processes as extracultural, and whether anything can exist entirely outside of culture is debatable.[36] "Grain" and geno-song are necessarily *constructed* as extracultural by Barthes who, in turn, is necessarily located *within* culture. What may be most useful to take from the model is not necessarily a pair of discrete and opposing characteristics in order to categorize sonic objects, but the fact that a great number of sonic experiences have some kind of meaning or effect apart from the linguistic message they carry. Thus, we might think of certain vocal actions not as *un*assimilated, but *under*assimilated. Popular music is littered with this kind of action: it is not that a voice has or does not have a geno-song, but that geno- or pheno-processes are variable in terms of their visibility (audibility) and perhaps relevance. In rap music, the vocal interest very often emerges not simply from the linguistic content, but from the rhythmic work achieved by the vocal line. At the same time, the content itself is frequently obscured by the intensity of rhyme and alliteration, and the rhythmic pace.

One outstanding example of this can be heard in Eminem's "Remember Me?"[37] The rhythmic stability is already undermined by the beginning of the first verse. The first four bars set up a rhythmic pattern that is repeated unerringly throughout the track. The primary instrumental action, as with much rap music, is generated by drum and bass parts, which throb in unison rhythm: ‖: ♩ ♩♪ ♪ ♩ | ♩ ♪ ♪♪ ♪ ♪ :‖

The snare accentuates each crotchet off-beat, while the hi-hat sounds on each quaver (apart from those sounded by the snare). In the third bar

of each four-bar set, however, the snare fails to hit on beat two, placing the aural focus onto the drum and bass. The bass drum and hi-hat fill the gap left by the snare by sounding together on that second beat: ♩♩ ♩♩♪♪ instead of ♩♩♪♪♪ . This four-bar phrase is repeated, and bars 9–12 introduce the vocals, which form the chorus. Bars 13 and 14, however, are two bars of vocal rest, while the rhythmic pattern continues, shifting the instrumental and vocal parts out of synch with each other. Once the verses commence, the disruptive bar—previously the third of each four-bar set—is now the first of each set. In the first instances of this four-bar phrase, the omission of the snare drum and the additional bass drum hit combined to disrupt the rhythmic continuity, giving an impression that the downbeat may have shifted to the second beat of the bar. The fact that this point of interest occurred on the second beat of the third bar (in a four-bar phrase) means that it occupied an even more irregular position in the pattern. The ensuing two bars of rest in the drums (bars 13–14), however, have the effect of shifting this rhythmic pattern by two bars, such that the anomalous bar now occurs in bar 1 of each four-bar phrase. With this comes further rhythmic instability, since the deviation is harder to gloss over aurally.

The most striking section of cross-rhythms comes in the second verse, rapped by Sticky Fingaz. In one section, starting "Better come better," the vocal rhythm tends toward a compound triple time, pushing against the predominating $\frac{4}{4}$ pulse. This rhythmic contrast works not only in terms of a juxtaposition between triple and double time, but more noticeably in that the implicit triple-time bar-lines cut across those demarcated in $\frac{4}{4}$, because the $\frac{6}{8}$ tempo runs at approximately ♩ = 122 bpm, while the $\frac{4}{4}$ tempo is more like ♩. = 90 bpm. After "Evidence? / Nope, never leave a shred-o," the vocal line starts to move back to a $\frac{4}{4}$ pulse with quaver rhythm, although a ghost of the cross-rhythms is to be found in "shred-o," just as the words "let her" had preceded the section. Rhythmic stability is not fully restored until the later line, "My mom's got raped," because from "Evidence?" until that point, the four beats of each bar cut across the beginning and end of each line of the lyric. Over four $\frac{4}{4}$ bars, eleven $\frac{6}{8}$ bars are implied, and although there are anchor points of synchronicity where $\frac{4}{4}$ and $\frac{6}{8}$ coincide, the quavers of $\frac{6}{8}$ rarely generate a traditional 3 vs. 2 syncopation.

These tensions between words and music might be viewed as a gendered conflict, if we were to read in the long-standing terms of music as feminine, concerned with senses, and of language as masculine, a rational structure.[38] But this would surely be to oversimplify the gendered work occurring in passages such as this. What is more significant is that

the speed of Sticky Fingaz's rapping, the intensity of his rhymes, and the ways in which they are juxtaposed with the prevailing $\frac{4}{4}$ pulse, all combine to render the message nearly incomprehensible. What we hear at this point is not the words as message, but the words as sounds, very much the geno-song of which Barthes writes. If language (as communication) is inherently a patriarchal structure, as Jacques Lacan and others suggest, then geno-song is, in a sense, operating outside of that, thus presenting a potential threat to the supremacy of the sign and patriarchy. Furthermore, sections where geno-song prevails force the listener to hear the voice as *object*, beyond the voice as *carrier of meaning*. In Lacan's graph of desire (see Figure 13.1),[39] the object-voice is an offshoot: it is that which is left over after meaning has been extracted and is positioned in the graph as subsidiary to the "normal" process of developing subjectivity—the vector from $ to I(A).

The example of "Remember Me?" is not unusual. There are many moments in rap music where words become incomprehensible, already undermining the patriarchal structure of communicative language by evading meaning, and where geno-song has a significant presence.[40] To consider rap in these terms opens up something of an irony: that in the demonstration of their linguistic skills, which purports to confer patriarchal approval upon them, and in the delivery of misogynist and/or homophobic lyrics, male (gangsta) rap artists invoke a mode of utterance that works precisely *against* the hypermasculine, male-centric world in which they profess to operate.

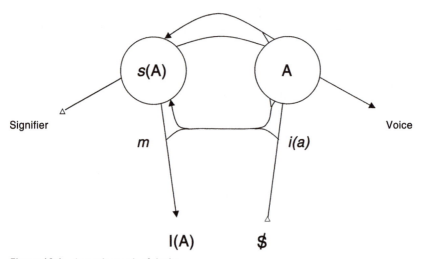

Figure 13.1   Lacan's graph of desire.

MUSICAL DETAIL AND THE CONSTRUCTION
OF MASCULINITY

Apart from the ways in which the voice in rap becomes intertwined with the specifically musical details, there are also important ways in which musical factors serve to undermine the ostensible hypermasculinity constructed by rap's lyrics and visual imagery; a great deal of this has to do with the tendency in rap toward cyclic motifs. Although much popular music relies heavily on repetition of musical material, at different levels,[41] it seems that rap has an interesting relationship with its tendency toward repetition. Typically, a few small musical units are strategically repeated and layered over the course of a track, with an effect of musical simplicity generated through an emphasis on cyclic patterns. Susan McClary has famously noted the development in Western art music, beginning with seventeenth-century opera, of a "musical semiotics of gender: a set of conventions for constructing 'masculinity' or 'femininity' in music."[42] McClary's book rests on this foundation, and taken as a whole it argues that teleological movement and musical gestures concerned with unproblematic closure have historically been associated with masculinity, while cyclic movement, repetitive gestures, and unrelenting undulations have been associated with the feminine. There are many points at which McClary seeks to move outside of the stereotypes that perpetuate (and are perpetuated by) these codes.[43] Similarly, I do not wish to reproduce the problematic conceptions of gender on which the "musical semiotics" is based. Rather, my point here is that the associations described by McClary persist in contemporary understandings of gender and musical representation. At the same time, it would be contentious to suggest that the majority of popular music listeners knowingly deploy this kind of cultural association in their listening. That said, the connotations of certain musical gestures are undoubtedly, if subconsciously, gendered. The ebbs and flows of a lush, romantic string section, and the persistent, uncompromising beat of a heavy metal drummer each have gendered associations deriving from their use in classical musics, and are surely both deployed and received with varying levels of "knowingness."

As a basic example, Eminem's "My Name Is" operates well outside of the teleologically masculine model.[44] Four main motifs dominate the instrumental action in varying combinations:

1. electric piano, semiquaver-based: rising from third to root note of each chord; semitonal semiquaver upbeat giving blues-scale feel; fourth bar leading back to first bar

2. bass: first beat of each bar with semiquaver upbeat; root of each chord
3. sustained organ/synthesizer: root and third of each chord played in sixths
4. sine wave/synthesizer: root and fifth tones of each chord played in crotchets

Motif 2, being the bass line, persists throughout, even at the beginning of the third verse, where the drums cease, such that the bass is the only support for Eminem's voice. Each motif is a variation on the harmonic progression that constitutes the song: I-II-IV-♭III (F-G-B♭-A♭), with each chord. While there are a significant number of rap tracks that emphasize a tonic-dominant harmonic relation,[45] "My Name Is" is far from unique in its refusal of the dominant. As a consequence, the relentlessly cyclic motifs combine with an avoidance of the traditionally "strong" (read: masculine, in the musical semiotic system) perfect cadence, which typically signifies closure, to generate a sequence that is repeatable ad infinitum. If we were to accept the "musical semiotics" that McClary describes, this harmonic behavior could be seen to work against the traditional musical representation of masculinity. The refusal of Western notions of musical tension and release, historically achieved through the tonic-dominant relationship, almost certainly has to do with the African American inflections not only in popular music generally, but especially in rap music, which, as a genre, maintains a particularly strong association with African American identity. Thus, a number of tracks whose harmonic relations work outside of the tonic-dominant relation also reveals a black musical history through jazz or reggae inflected gestures and riffs resting on blues scales (such as motif 1 listed above).[46] The perceptibility of the harmonically troubled gender expression by a nonanalyzing listener is questionable. The refusal of the tonic is not to be presumed as a consciously recognizable factor, but the harmonic foundation of this track undoubtedly resists the kind of tension and release found in some other tracks. The overall effect of layering the motifs above is one of constant repetition with subtle variation. The harmonies and layering combine with other musical factors (such as tempo and orchestration) to give a laid-back, docile air to the track that would not generally be associated with overt masculinity.

There are occasions on which the cyclical tendency serves also to undermine the rhythmic stability of the song, which, in the model described by McClary (although not necessarily endorsed by her), could also be taken as a threat to hegemonic masculinities. We have already seen how "Remember Me?" rests on a shaky rhythmic foundation,

which is further destabilized by Sticky Fingaz's rapping. In D12's "Purple Pills," a single synthesizer motif—already cyclic and repetitive by its own nature—is repeated throughout verses and chorus, but its persistence highlights a rhythmic shift mobilized by the vocalists.[47] The original motif, which opens the song and recurs throughout the verses, makes use of an initial crotchet anacrusis and an imitative, descending pattern played in quavers, with a repeated quaver upbeat.

♩|♩ ♪ᵧ ⁊ ᵧ ♪|: ♫ ♩ ♪ᵧ ⁊ ᵧ ♪:|

At bar 5 of the song (0:10), D12 first sing the chorus, and the anacrusis of their line coincides with the downbeat of the original motif. Thus, the crotchet that was originally an upbeat becomes the first beat of the bar.

Although over the course of the song the pattern is ultimately maintained in its original formation, the vocal elision of the end of each verse into the upbeat of the chorus has the effect of disrupting the rhythmic continuity. This is particularly obvious with the first vocal entry, especially because the rapped verses then proceed to realign the vocal and instrumental meter. If it were not for the persistence of the synthesizer motif, the subtle change of rhythmic emphasis might not be nearly as noticeable. I do not intend here to propose a simple equation between normative masculinity and rhythmic stability. However, it is quite clear that examples such as this display a tendency to subvert dominant musical structures, and that this is achieved through cyclic motifs and intense repetition. On a generalized level, the subtle shifts of rhythmic emphasis give moments of an almost limping nature, arguably causing doubts about the "perfect masculinity" of those articulating this message. In the semiotic scheme outlined by McClary, such musical behavior would serve to undermine the construction of the kind of masculinity at stake in these songs.

IS IT QUEER?

Thus far this chapter has explained ways in which traditional constructions of masculinity are subtly problematized in rap music, and how part of the problematic nature of traditional masculinity in the genre has to do with musical details. Two key questions thus arise. First, is there anything *queer* (in any sense of that word) about the masculinity presented in rap, albeit conveyed through various problematizing vehicles? And second, have the musical problematics I have depicted not rested entirely on an essentialist semiotics of music? (McClary

herself makes it clear that the semiotic system she describes only serves to represent a particular formation of masculinity, by way of a few specific, essentialist codes.) As an initial response to this, it might be suggested that the cyclic musical tendencies displayed in rap serve to represent not "the feminine," but an aggressive, stubborn, unrelenting, almost bullying kind of masculine expression. While I plead guilty to the charge of using an essentialist system, I also suggest that this very same system still operates with remarkable currency in the current musical context. Therefore, I would argue that the musical means by which rap's notorious lyrics and attitude are put forward are both central and, crucially, problematizing factors for consideration. It is only on accepting momentarily the relevance of this semiotics as a system—even as we dispute the accuracy or relevance of the presumptions on which it is based—that we can accept that representations of masculinity are rendered in any way queer in rap music.

I am not suggesting that we presume any kind of overtly homosexual activity by or between rap artists simply because they operate in exclusively male spaces and confirm their heterosexuality to a point verging on excess, while simultaneously deriding women and rebuffing their genitals. Rather, it is my contention that some sense of these troublesome factors emerges alongside the problematic musical construction of masculinity in the genre. According to the system McClary describes, the musical details do little to reassure the listener of the rapper's unquestionably normative masculinity (which includes his position as heterosexual). Thus, it is the conglomeration of all of these factors that renders unstable any construction of masculinity in the genre. The male body and ego become, in many ways, so hypernormatively masculine that they spill over into the grotesque. And, in the raucous display of such masculinity—verbal and visual display—rap artists descend into an extravagant display verging on the positively camp: certainly, the male body and ego as "to be looked at," and in many cases deriding itself, is not a symbol of robust heteronormative masculinity. In this way, *queer* is not to be understood here as a direct denotation of self-aware homosexuality; rather, as Niall Richardson summarizes, it is used to describe "mismatches or incoherencies between sex, gender, and sexuality."[48] The paradox of overdetermined surface message and underlying means of representation, even (or especially) in the face of manifest misogyny and homophobia, may well give cause to respond to rap: methinks the rapper doth protest too much.

This is certainly the response of gay activist Peter Tatchell to Eminem, who writes, "For someone who says he hates fags, Eminem is totally obsessed with gay sex. Almost every track on his *Marshall Mathers* album [2000] has a reference to homosexuality, much of it

dwelling on oral and anal sex. . . . If he loathes homosexuality, why does he keep rapping about it all the time? . . . Eighty percent of aggressively homophobic men are self-loathing, repressed homosexuals, according to Prof. Henry Adams of the University of Georgia."[49] Tatchell also cites Eminem's image as evidence for his suggestions: "His short-cropped, bleached blonde hair, earrings, tattoos, and white vests are typical gay club fashion. It would be easy to mistake him for a gay man." Although Tatchell concedes that Eminem may well be an "exception to the general rule," his overall argument is sound: that the lyrics of Eminem in particular—and heterosexist rap in general—seem like a "desperate attempt to prove . . . masculinity and heterosexuality." It is surely in the combination of lyrics, music, and image that the "queer" in straight rap comes to the surface. The lyrics work counterproductively, being so extreme as to make a listener suspect over-defensiveness (although this response surely only materializes in listeners who are already suspicious in some way). The musical details may also have a surface effect of anger, aggression, and hostility, thereby portraying a stereotypically masculine position. Yet within the semiotic system described by McClary, certain musical gestures also serve to challenge the construction of an unproblematic and "conventional" masculinity. Furthermore, the image of rap artists, as Tatchell argues, in many ways resembles gay male style.[50]

Eminem is not the only example. On the cover of two of his albums, 50 Cent at first seems to appear in an unashamedly dominant-male pose, his well-built muscular form placed centrally and drawing the viewer's gaze toward him. The most recent album, *The Massacre*, shows a more well-defined form than the earlier *Get Rich or Die Tryin'*, but both display an unequivocally powerful physique that is undoubtedly intended to assure the viewer of his male, masculine, phallic power.[51] Yet this erect, phallic male body quickly sees its identity as such destabilized. First, in both examples, 50 Cent's body is quite obviously "to be looked at." In an attempt to deflect the potential for anxiety provoked by the male body on display, the male body is typically pictured as categorically heterosexual (by way of a token, complementary female body), or as *doing* something: "it's feminine to be on display."[52] This is the case also (especially?) in competitive male bodybuilding: photographic representations of the male bodybuilder either see the male body "draped with a female model" or "straining against a heavy weight or else flaunting his strength through the flexed muscle."[53] The display of 50 Cent's body is not deflected in either of these ways: he appears at first glance to be relaxed, although the image "still promises activity by the way the body is posed . . . standing taut ready for action."[54] Yet the fact of being poised and

ready does not entirely defuse the danger of being inert at that moment, and 50 Cent's body is distinctly on display. Superimposed over this, both album covers in some way rupture his body. *Get Rich* simulates a piece of glass splintering around a central hole (presumably from a gunshot) that is focused on 50 Cent's sternum, where hangs a crucifix.[55] In a similar move, *Massacre* sees his already obviously muscular frame accentuated by sketch lines, outlining the major lines of muscle definition. At several points, these sketch lines continue beyond the body's own frame, taking it outside of itself, and adding further semiotic burden to an already heavily laden site. In a sense, these rupturings perform a similar kind of work to the women or weights seen in bodybuilding photographs, acting as a veil that must be negotiated before the male body can be seen, and thereby defusing the male body's position as displayed and objectified. Arguably, they also have a contradictory effect, of drawing attention specifically to the display of muscularity, especially in the case of the defining lines on the *Massacre* cover. This is to be expected, of course, as "muscularity is a key term in appraising men's bodies."[56] The muscularity on 50 Cent's CD covers is especially notable, however, since his body tips over into being "on display," while this display is almost certainly for a primarily male audience. His muscular hardness may well incite discourses of phallic power: despite being worked for, muscle is constructed culturally as "the *sign* of power—natural . . . phallic."[57] At the same time, his feminized position as "on display," his consumption by a male gaze, and his muscularity combine to mobilize counterdis-courses of homoeroticism.

What seems to be at work in images such as these—and heterosexist rap as a genre overall—is a layering of discursive structures, each struggling for some kind of hegemony. While the black man has historically been economically and politically subordinated in white Western societies, he may still enjoy a culturally and historically contingent hegemonic gendered position: the apex of rap masculinity is arguably embodied by the straight black man. As Dyer observes, "Images of male power are always and necessarily inflected with other aspects of power in society."[58] The rapper 50 Cent appears on one level as a powerful man; he is also a powerful *black* man. His blackness in this context serves to confer authority upon him as a rapper, while also implicitly confirming his heterosexuality. Perhaps it is as a defense against his whiteness in a black-dominated genre that informs Eminem's extreme homophobia: while Ice Cube asserts, "True niggaz ain't gay" (1991), there is no equivalent presumption for the white man.[59] With the black man figured as the "embodiment of bestial, violent, penis-as-weapon hypermasculine assertion,"[60] the white man potentially emerges

as impotent, castrated, and effeminate. Eminem's disproportionate declarations of heterosexuality might be taken as an alignment of himself with his (supposedly) unquestionably heterosexual black colleagues. It is interesting, then, that Eminem's body contrasts so radically with 50 Cent's. Where 50 Cent's is the consummate erect, muscular, phallic body, Eminem's oscillates between erect and positively flaccid. In between classic rap gestures designed to signify phallic power (extending his arms, and thereby expanding his bodily space, holding his crotch, or the metonymically associated pulling up of his trouser leg), there are frequent moments when he displays a loose, flexible, floppy body, frequently squatting on the floor with an underlying effect of the antiphallic.[61]

The layers of meaning in the construction of gendered and sexualized identity through rap music are intricate. An apparently straightforward message of heterosexist male supremacy is quickly complicated by moments of self-deprecation, raising the ugly specter of the withered fin-de-siècle male masochist,[62] and by the rapper's verbosity, which in turn invokes images of the hysteric. The extreme nature of rap's assertions of heterosexuality may serve—not as intended—to question why these messages are so violently asserted, and one presumption is that it is an over-zealous defense against repressed homosexuality. Supporting this now fragile message is a brittle musical structure, which at times gives an effect of belligerence and aggressive persistence—bullying, even—but which can also be seen as harmonically and rhythmically troubled and cyclic. These two levels—words and music—become particularly intertwined in rap, by its definition as a genre. The effect of this is that the already hysterical heterosexuality becomes even more frantic in its expression, with the message eventually subsumed by linguistic dexterity, which takes us back to the problems of the language-based expression of this supposedly unquestionable brand of masculinity. All of these factors are then embodied by men whose images may be intended to be as normative and categorically heterosexual as their messages are. Yet the result is equally contradictory, since extreme heterosexual masculinity blends smoothly into gay style, and the bonding of multiple such men blurs the gaps between the homosocial and the homosexual (particularly since the exchange of women between these men is also problematic). Without doubt, there is a great deal more work to be done here with regard to the relationships among race, class, gender, sexuality, and sex as they are played out in heterosexist rap music. It is quite clear, however, that the idea of a straightforward and unproblematic masculinity in the genre is indeed only an idea—an always-already lost gender formation that the genre tries in vain to (re)construct, enacting a kind

of gender nostalgia. This applies not only to the masculinity constructed in rap music but, as Judith Butler argues, it is a thoroughgoing facet of hegemonic gender formations.[63] Yet rap, as we have seen, (unwittingly) deploys several strategies to bring this to the foreground. What is left in place of this lost gender is an uncanny construction where the primary signifiers point the casual observer in one direction, while underlying contradictions are also apparent, mismatching gender, sex, and sexuality, and allowing them to oscillate: homosexual or otherwise, such a construction of masculinity is indeed decidedly queer.

NOTES

1. Several works have been published precisely in response to this imbalance. See Gillian G. Gaar, *She's a Rebel: The History of Women in Rock & Roll* (London: Blandford, 1993) and Lucy O'Brien, *She-Bop: The Definitive History of Women in Rock, Pop and Soul* (London: Penguin, 1995).
2. Nancy Guevara, "Women Writin' Rappin' Breakin'," in *Droppin' Science: Critical Essays on Rap Music and Hip Hop Culture*, ed. William E. Perkins (Philadelphia: Temple University Press, 1996), 51.
3. Eminem, "The Real Slim Shady," *The Marshall Mathers LP* (Aftermath/ Interscope 490761-2), 2000. Note also the Experience Music Project Grand Opening, June 23, 2000, when Eminem held a blow-up doll's face to his pelvis, simulating oral sex. During the *Up In Smoke* tour (2000), he kicked a blow-up doll representing ex-wife Kim around the stage.
4. For examples, see the Bloodhound Gang, "You're Pretty When I'm Drunk," *Use Your Fingers* (Sony Music Entertainment 4807032), 1995; "Kiss Me Where It Smells Funny," *One Fierce Beer Coaster* (Geffen 425124-2), 1996; and "Three Point One Four," *Hooray For Boobies* (Geffen 490455-2), 2000.
5. Eminem, "Kill You," *The Marshall Mathers LP* (Aftermath/Interscope 490761-2), 2000. Compare this with his closing statement in "White America," *The Eminem Show* (Interscope 4932902), 2002.
6. James Haskins, *The Story of Hip-Hop: From Africa to America, Sugarhill to Eminem* (London: Penguin, 2000), 76.
7. NWA's song "Fuck Tha Police," *Straight Outta Compton* (Ruthless/Priority CDL-57112), 1989, presents this perspective.
8. Edward Armstrong, "Gangsta Misogyny: A Content Analysis of the Portrayals of Violence against Women in Rap Music, 1987–1993," *Journal of Criminal Justice and Popular Culture* 8, no. 2 (2001): 99. Armstrong himself notes that this is based on a "both/and" approach: "only" 22 percent contain *both* violence *and* misogyny. It would be reasonable to presume that the percentage of songs that contain only misogyny may well be higher than 22 percent.
9. Ibid., 104–5.

10. This stereotype and its logical analogy in the form of the "feminist female rapper" have counterexamples to disprove the generalization, just as they have examples to support them. See Gaar, *She's a Rebel*, 424, and Tricia Rose, *Black Noise: Rap Music and Black Culture in Contemporary America* (Middletown, Conn.: Wesleyan University Press, 1994), 147, for a sense of the tensions between the sexes in rap.

11. Eve Kosofsky Sedgwick, *Between Men: English Literature and Male Homosocial Desire* (New York: Columbia University Press, 1985), 2.

12. Adrienne Rich, "Compulsory Heterosexuality and Lesbian Existence," in *Adrienne Rich's Poetry and Prose: Poems, Prose, Reviews, and Criticism*, ed. B. C. Gelpi and A. Gelpi (New York: W. W. Norton, 1993), 217.

13. Mary R. Key, *Male/Female Language, with a Comprehensive Bibliography* (Metuchen, N.J.: Scarecrow, 1975), 15.

14. Eleanor Maccoby, "Sex Differences in Intellectual Functioning," in *The Development of Sex Differences*, ed. Eleanor Maccoby (London: Tavistock, 1966), 26.

15. See *Statistics of Education: Public Examinations GCSE/GNVQ and GCE/ AGNVQ in England 2000* (London: HMS Stationery Office, 2001), 38–39, 90–92.

16. Dale Spender, *Man-Made Language*, 2nd ed. (London: Routledge and Kegan Paul, 1985), 41. This myth has as long a cultural history as that of male superiority; see, for example, Michèle Cohen, *Fashioning Masculinity: National Identity and Language in the Eighteenth Century* (London: Routledge, 1996), 32–33, on the anxieties surrounding "talkativeness" and gender in eighteenth-century England.

17. Lorri Nielsen, "Writing and Possibility: Embracing Lyricism in Women's Writing and Poetry" (unpublished essay), 4.

18. Lyrical writing modes are taken here to denote any "fairly short poem expressing the personal mood, feeling, or meditation of a speaker," and to include but not be limited to the words of a song; see Nielsen, "Writing and Possibility," 2.

19. Ibid., 5.

20. Rose, *Black Noise*, 86–87.

21. Donald Horton, "The Dialogue of Courtship in Popular Song," in *On Record: Rock, Pop, and the Written Word*, ed. Simon Frith and Andrew Goodwin (London: Routledge, 1990), 25.

22. Haskins, *The Story of Hip-Hop*, 13.

23. Spender, *Man-Made Language*, 10.

24. See *Baillière's Encyclopaedic Dictionary of Nursing and Health Care* (London: Baillière Tindall, 1989), 68.

25. John Perceval, quoted in *The Faber Book of Madness*, ed. Roy Porter (London: Faber and Faber, 2003), 23.

26. See Elaine Showalter, *Sexual Anarchy: Gender and Culture at the Fin de Siècle* (London: Virago, 1996); see also Lisa Appignanesi and John Forrester, *Freud's Women* (London: Virago, 1992), 398–99, and P. W. Martin, *Mad Women in Romantic Writing* (Brighton, England: Harvester, 1987), esp. 18–19, 36–40.

27. For boasts of sexual prowess, see D12, "Nasty Mind," *Devil's Night* (Interscope 490897), 2001; Ice Cube, "Dirty Mack," *The Predator* (Priority 57185), 1992; Too Much Trouble, "Best Little Whorehouse in Texas," *Player's Choice* (Rap-a-Lot/Priority 4992-57186-4), 1993. For masochistic moments, see Eminem, "Criminal" and "The Kids," *The Marshall Mathers LP* (Aftermath/Interscope Records 490761-2), 2000.

28. Eminem, "Kim," *The Marshall Mathers LP.*

29. David Stubbs, *Eminem—Cleaning Out My Closet: The Story behind Every Song* (London: Carlton, 2003), 74.

30. *Rocky* (1976, dir. John G. Avildsen); *Rocky II* (1979, dir. Sylvester Stallone); *Rocky III* (1982, dir. Sylvester Stallone); *Rocky IV* (1985, dir. Sylvester Stallone); *Rocky V* (1990, dir. John G. Avildsen).

31. Judith Halberstam, *Female Masculinity* (Durham, N.C.: Duke University Press, 1998), 275.

32. Colin Kennedy, "Review of *8-Mile,*" *Empire* 278 (February 2003): 42.

33. For how language also incorporates the imaginary, see Dylan Evans, *An Introductory Dictionary of Lacanian Psychoanalysis* (London: Routledge, 1996), 98.

34. Toril Moi, *Sexual/Textual Politics* (London: Routledge, 1985), 99.

35. Roland Barthes, *Image, Music, Text*, trans. Stephen Heath (New York: Hill and Wang, 1977), 295.

36. I use the term *geno-process* (and the analogous *pheno-process*) to denote a broader range of functions than either Julia Kristeva's "texts" or Barthes's "songs," both of which are specific to their respective objects of study. The idea of *process*, for me, suggests an action or moment in the mode of *geno-* or *pheno-*, in the Kristevan/Barthesian sense, but without particularizing these notions.

37. Eminem, "Remember Me?," *The Marshall Mathers LP.*

38. This division is played out in a great deal of R&B music, where a male artist's rapping in the verses is complemented by a female artist singing the chorus.

39. For his development of the graph, see Jacques Lacan, *Écrits: A Selection*, trans. Alan Sheridan (London: Routledge, 1989). For explanations of the graph and the terms used, see Evans, *An Introductory Dictionary.*

40. Examples can be heard in 2Pac, "Something Wicked," and "Tha' Lunatic," *2Pacalypse Now* (Interscope 41633), 1991; Bloodhound Gang, "Shut Up," *One Fierce Beer Coaster*; D12, "American Psycho," *Devil's Night*; and Eminem, "My 1st Single," *Encore* (Aftermath/Interscope 986488-4), 2004.

41. The specter of Theodor Adorno's pessimism is clearly looming here. It is worth noting that, as a rule of thumb, popular music indeed tends toward repetition without significant variation or development. By comparison, Western art music privileges development and varied repetition of motifs, even when it also depends on repetition in both the musical foreground and at a large-scale structural level.

42. Susan McClary, *Feminine Endings: Music, Gender, and Sexuality* (Minneapolis: University of Minnesota Press, 1991), 7.

43. See, for example, McClary, *Feminine Endings*, 10.

44. Eminem, "My Name Is," *The Slim Shady LP* (Aftermath/Interscope 490287-2), 1999.

45. A few examples include: Tha Alkaholiks, "Hip Hop Drunkies" (released as single) (RCA RCA64881CD), 1997; D12, "Nasty Mind" and "Ain't Nuttin' but Music," *Devil's Night*; Eminem, "Criminal" and "I'm Back" *The Marshall Mathers LP*; KRS-One, "MCs Act Like They Don't Know" (released as single) (Jive JIVECD384), 1996; and Snoop Doggy Dogg, "Who Am I (What's My Name)" (released as single) (Simply Vinyl S12DJ154), 2004.

46. For examples of rap referencing black musical history, see 2Pac, "Tha' Lunatic," *2Pacalypse Now*; The Fugees, "Nappy Heads" and "Temple," *Blunted on Reality* (Columbia 4747139), 1996; and Ice Cube, "No Vaseline," *Death Certificate* (EMI 543 3412), 2003. Eminem's whiteness must not go unacknowledged. Although there is not the space to deal with the layering of racial identities here, it would certainly be interesting to see how his solo work negotiates its black musical heritage through musical gestures such as those mentioned.

47. D12, "Purple Pills," *Devil's Night*.

48. Niall Richardson, "The Queer Activity of Extreme Male Bodybuilding: Gender Dissidence, Auto-Eroticism and Hysteria," *Social Semiotics* 14, no. 1 (2004): 50. Richardson takes his own use of the term *queer* from Annamarie Jagose, *Queer Theory* (Melbourne: Melbourne University Press, 1996).

49. Peter Tatchell, "Is Eminem Queer?," 2004 (available at www.petertatchell.net/popmusic/iseminemqueer.htm).

50. This same sarcastic suspicion of the supremely homophobic also seems to have informed the writing of the Pet Shop Boys, "The Night I Fell In Love," *Release* (Parlophone 5385982), 2002, which tells the story of a schoolboy who falls for, and has a one-night stand with, a gay rapper who is never referred to by name but clearly intended to represent Eminem.

51. 50 Cent, *Get Rich or Die Tryin'* (Interscope 4935642), 2003, and *The Massacre* (Interscope 9880667), 2005.

52. Susan Bordo, *The Male Body: A New Look at Men in Public and Private* (New York: Farrar, Straus and Giroux, 1999), 173.

53. Richardson, "The Queer Activity of Extreme Male Bodybuilding," 52.

54. Richard Dyer, "Don't Look Now: The Male Pin-Up," in *The Sexual Subject: A Screen Reader in Sexuality*, ed. Mandy Merck (London: Routledge, 1992), 270.

55. This effect only appears on the American release cover; the U.K. cover shows 50 Cent in the same pose, but not layered beneath the shattered glass. The reason for this is not clear, but may well have to do with the violence implicit in the American version.

56. Dyer, "Don't Look Now," 273.

57. Ibid., 273.

58. Ibid., 270–71.

59. Ice Cube, "Horny Lil' Devil," *Death Certificate* (Priority 57155), 1991.

60. bell hooks, *We Real Cool: Black Men and Masculinity* (London: Routledge, 2004), 79.

61. See the videos by Eminem for "The Real Slim Shady" and "My Name Is," *E*, dir. Phillip Atwell and Dr. Dre (Aftermath/Interscope 0608199), 2000; and *All Access Europe* (Interscope 49332192002b), 2002.

62. Suzanne Stewart, *Sublime Surrender: Male Masochism at the Fin de Siècle* (Ithaca, New York: Cornell University Press, 1998).

63. Judith Butler, *Bodies That Matter: On the Discursive Limits of "Sex"* (London: Routledge, 1993), 125.

14

CLOSENESS AND DISTANCE
Songs about AIDS

PAUL ATTINELLO

The most atrociously appropriate, viciously ironic of cultural crises in the West: sex and death bound together as Isolde never could have dreamed, all of it sharply complicated by dichotomies of gay versus straight, using versus clean, sexual freedom versus celibacy, caring for invalids or fleeing from them—women or men, black or white, healthy suburbanites confronted by wasted urban ghosts. Spanning the distance from Europe to Africa, from Washington to Bangkok, from the gated community to the gay ghetto, from the hand to the knee, from one pair of lips to the next, it exploded in 1981: suddenly there was GRID, Gay-Related Immunodeficiency Disease, and panic spread in the gay communities of the Castro and Christopher Streets. The first plays in 1983, and novels, stories, and films throughout the years since, grew into what is now a vast collection of narrative responses to AIDS. The visual arts jumped in to establish an antimodernist beachhead of slogans and visceral self-expression, fueled by rage and a race against the clock.

Musical works began to appear more slowly, but there were many by the late 1980s—benefits; protest songs; the musicals *March of the Falsettos* and *Zero Positive*; a prestigiously publicized symphony by John Corigliano, the new Lieder of the AIDS Song Quilt; a slew of works commissioned by various gay men's choruses; and a rude punk song titled "Rimmin' at the Baths."

Since this research concerns cultural products, perception and experience are vastly more important than concrete facts. Although statistical curves of infection, mortality, and treatment in different locations have changed variously over the past twenty-five years, the broad perception in the urban West of an inescapable crisis of illness and death was probably at its sharpest peak in 1987–88. The ensuing years saw some softening of this eschatological view, as treatments were found to fend off various opportunistic infections. The biggest change came in 1996 with the appearance of protease inhibitors; since that year, life expectancy and general prognosis have immensely improved, as long as patients can get the newer medications. Of course, the pills don't work for everyone and, more significantly, many people all over the world have no access to them; but Western journalists and intellectuals have tended to treat the crisis as less threatening than before—even as if, for practical purposes, the crisis is over. This means that the sense that this might be the end of the world—banging shutters on empty buildings in gay neighborhoods, gutters filled with corpses in Bangkok, camps surrounded by barbed wire, masked policemen, closed borders, quarantines—has receded from the public imagination, as have the atomic bomb scenarios of the Cold War.

As a result of this retreat from the apocalyptic to the mundane, people do not seem as compelled to make art about AIDS these days as they did between 1983 and 1996. That period saw the creation of a great deal of AIDS-related work—manifold novels and memoirs, with their detailed, tragic personal narratives; various approaches to theater, emphasizing the confrontative, the didactic, or the fantastic; poetry, much of it narrative, and more immediate than one might expect; and, of course, a vast array of visual artworks, including installations of many kinds. All of these are linked to the rise of political art during the 1980s in America, as discussed by Wendy Steiner.[1] In fact, I would suggest that the public reaction to AIDS was an important part of that increasingly political nature of American art, as it was also a central reason for the move toward greatly increased media expression of tolerance and empathy aimed at a wide range of medical conditions and social problems. It also seems plausible that AIDS was a significant source of the boom in New Age musics and softer, more impressionistic musical styles, as linked to the expansion of the realm of "healing" music.

However, there does seem to have been less of a musical response to AIDS than from the other arts; it also seems that music, across all its genres, is frequently more oblique and cautious in its presentation of strongly charged material such as political slogans or medical terms. A typical example is Burt Bacharach and Carole Bayer Sager's "That's What Friends Are For,"[2] a benevolent pop ballad designed for the typical Hollywood star benefit. This song is exceptionally careful not to mention anything specific

to AIDS, instead broadcasting a generic message of support that could fit practically any situation. In fact, years ago when I was a member of the Gay Men's Chorus of Los Angeles and we were singing backup to the songwriters as the climax of a benefit for AIDS Project Los Angeles, I realized only during the dress rehearsal that the song was specifically written to support people with AIDS—this despite the overwhelming presence of AIDS in my social circles in the mid-1980s. Of course, many songs and reinterpretations designed for benefit performances tend to avoid specifics; this makes sense, as their purpose is to generate the kind of uncontroversial empathy that encourages people to give money.

Reasons why all the genres of music seem less political than comparable production in the other arts would certainly include commercially actuated censorship in the music industry, or obedience to the norms of social reserve in the classical sphere. Increasingly, however, I think a more generous explanation can be found—that music often works better as an expression of feeling states than it does as a vehicle for establishing a political stance, or documenting a contemporary situation. I do not, of course, intend for such an explanation to apply to all music—in the long-standing ethnomusicological argument over the existence of music universals, I am firmly on the side of the nays, and in any case there are always musical works and activities operating outside the boundaries of the merely typical. However, we do have a lot of ingrained musical habits in the West, many of them linked to sentiment and the creation of feelings—after all, the love song is a more central trope for music than the romance novel is for literature. Therefore, though the typical construction of music related to AIDS often reflects a certain social or political timidity, I suggest that might be because it is intended to convey more private or more fragile feelings than the shouting of slogans would allow.

My own research has tended to focus on musical works written in response to the crisis, thus bypassing, for instance, repertories by musicians who have died, or reinterpretations and modified stagings of preexisting musical works. I have also tended to concern myself with works that are commercially available—as a result, most of the more than two hundred recordings and scores I have collected were produced in North America, with smaller numbers from Western Europe, Australia, and South Africa. Certainly, there is music about AIDS outside the urban West; however, a useful consideration of, for instance, protest songs in Brazil or educational jingles in Thailand is better served through fieldwork by scholars who know the culture and speak the language. Partly because of this Western bias, most of my materials also refer in some way to the gay subculture; it should come as no surprise that, of the various groups who have been most affected by

HIV in the West, the middle-class white gay male community includes many of those with the best access to, and interest in, the creation and commercial distribution of artistic products.

The pieces I have collected cover most of the major genres on sale in record stores—classical, avant-garde, pop vocalists and groups, musicals, and film scores. It is interesting to note that each genre tends to present tropes and ideas that are fairly consistent within that genre, but there is much less similarity among the genres—for instance, classical lieder are frequently pastiches of a rather self-dramatizing, late-nineteenth-century tragic manner, but the musicals (with the partial exception of the most famous example, *Rent*) suggest the overwhelmingly sincere soft-rock style of the mid-1970s. Punk songs are charged with despairing rage or savage abuse, while hip-hop tends to focus on much more reasonable, even didactic, approaches to the education of the Black community. Such similarities and contrasts can be seen as a simple confirmation of social construction theory; they also suggest where channels of communication among musical communities exist in the late twentieth and early twenty-first centuries. They also make division into generic and cultural groupings useful, as it is frequently possible to discuss gestures typical to a whole genre—aside from the exceptions, of course, which then become especially interesting. In popular songs, for instance, both the typical approaches and their exceptions reveal surprising, even culturally symptomatic, tropes.

POPULAR SONGS AND AIDS

Most popular songs about AIDS can be divided into three categories by performer. First, groups often produce surprisingly aggressive political statements; it seems that performing in a group context opens up a more public and automatically more confrontational position. Second, soloists who keep themselves separate from the Top 40, including a wide range of "alternative" artists, together with what one might call grassroots performers (i.e., performers with small repertories and no real link to the music industry), often create songs based on various unexpected emotional revelations.

Third, the most public arena—and the one I will introduce here—includes solos by a variety of well-known songwriters and vocalists; Madonna, Boy George, Janet Jackson, Elton John, Reba McEntire, Lou Reed, Linda Ronstadt, Sandie Shaw, Tori Amos, and James Taylor are all members of this group. Most of the songs in this category establish an intimate space of mourning, memory, or dialogue between two people who know each other well. The content is practically always about the singer remembering someone who has died; even in Elton John's "The Last Song," where the

singer's fictional identity is that of a dying son (and is possibly intended to suggest the famous, and notably heterosexual, Ryan White), the text is carefully constructed so that it would be difficult to mistake the singer for the song's protagonist. All of these songs seem designed to generate a consensus of sympathy in the listener, subtly but effectively establishing an atmosphere of supportive empathy and helping construct a broad shift toward increased tolerance in the late 1980s and early 1990s.

A song that can be taken as both typical and at the same time unusually direct is Madonna's double elegy "In This Life" from the album *Erotica*.[3] The slow pacing, the expression of loss and resentment, and the generalized declarations of tolerance are threaded through two personal memories and questioning choruses. These all come into sharper focus for the last verse, in part, because of the delivery: Madonna drops into spoken voice, suggesting the blunt and unavoidable reality of the situation behind the song, and conveying a grief and anger that can only find outlet in a broad complaint about an uncaring society. This remains one of the most publicly assertive songs by a major pop star; unlike Janet Jackson's touring performances of "Together Again,"[4] Madonna's performances of this song never seem to elide its serious and political intent. However, despite the relative strength of the feelings expressed, the song operates completely by implication rather than direct, unmistakable reference. Like most of the songs by major pop stars, it would be easy for this one to pass without comment in the normal stream of hits on any radio station.

I would like to look briefly at two songs by Tori Amos and James Taylor that are somewhat outside this mold. What is unusual in these two songs is not that they are more confrontative than the others: on the contrary, they are heavily coded in abstruse metaphors that make the implied meanings nearly incomprehensible, even on repeated hearing. They are interesting, however, because the dense coding draws the listener's attention more than the rather anodyne texts of the other "star" songs: it would be difficult to mistake either of these two for a typical love song. The coding seems to cover up a certain discomfort: unlike Madonna, Janet Jackson, Elton John, and others, these are not vocalists evidently expressing solidarity with the gay members of their performing or professional entourages. Amos and Taylor are instead distinctly uncomfortable with the objects of discussion—gay men with AIDS—as their images are constructed in each song.

AT THREE IN THE MORNING, WITH BOTH PEDALS DOWN

Many of Tori Amos's songs involve a defiant attempt to overcome the social limitations imposed on women, combined with a resulting rage

aimed at men, both as individuals and as representatives of their gender. In this song, ("Not the Red Baron"), however, she forgives men—though in a roundabout manner. Her poetic techniques include tangles of images and intentionally mixed metaphors that suggest complex emotional states. These strategies are not common on her first two albums; the early song "China," which refers to cracked plates on the table and the Great Wall in a continuous, mildly surreal rhetoric, provides hints of how her lyrics would grow. With her third album, *Boys for Pele*, tangled images become more important as the musical textures become more unusual; the mysterious "Not the Red Baron" presents an obscurely connected set of referents held together by a sensual, resonant piano texture that suggests reflection, melancholy, even grieving.[5]

This texture, a shimmering, ringing repetition of notes that recalls a trope of piano writing familiar since Chopin, suggests both a plodding, sad inevitability and a rich atmosphere of meditation, not unlike the experience of playing the piano, alone in a large room, at three in the morning, with both pedals down. This creates a space of sensual but isolated reflection, a self-created version of the womblike envelope of sound, as posited by David Schwarz in his discussion of John Adams's textures.[6] I also considered the difference between how the song was perceived by the "naive" listener, as opposed to someone who had searched out interviews and discussion of the meaning of various details. I will elide all that and simply note the following.

The opening lines by the audio engineers, spoken through microphone connections that suggest radio communications, are transformed for the purpose of the metaphor into simulacra for the voices of pilots in airplanes; Amos interrupts them with oblique questions, but we cannot hear the answers. With the appearance of her singing voice, which displays a breathy, elaborately ornamented, private complexity, we shift from overhearing to listening. The content is not, however, clear; the lyrics do not follow a continuous narrative, but seem to repeatedly traverse the same oblique territory in a series of partially erased gestures. Each verse starts with repeated negatives; the first verse says this is *not* a song about the Red Baron, that is, not a comic situation with a final frame that shows a doghouse covered with bullet holes but safely returned to earth. Amos's breaking up of this familiar trope brings the dead metaphor back to life, and the cliché of "going down in flames" becomes once again pathetic. The second verse uses the same pattern, but different negatives; this is *not* about someone called Judy G.—Judy Garland, of course. The dead star is used as a referent for a melancholy narcissism, where the person grieving is more interested in displaying his or her

emotions than in really grieving—a stance Amos will not allow herself without an ironic, negating distance.

It is clear that in this bizarrely quiet, introverted interlude to an already complex album, men are being treated in a way that is unusual for the singer. In an interview, she explained the emotional turn that is implied here: "Then . . . we move into a whole other moment. 'Not the Red Baron' is the moment of compassion for all the men on the record. It's where I could see their planes crashing, I could see that they have a side too. And if their planes would crash I started to gain compassion for their side of it."[7]

But these men that she's talking about, that the song goes on and on about—who *are* they? Pilot and Snoopy imagery, all denied; devils with halos and beautiful capes, their burdens, and their heels pointed; Judy Garland and Jean—Jean Harlow, I think—both obvious gay icons, cited in the second verse as definite contrasts to the world of Snoopy and his doghouse. The screen going down in flames suggests the collapse of a world of movies, perhaps of artifice and camp spectacle; the flames of hell may be heaven here. The key for all of this is, of course, the red ribbons of the last lines—these men are gay, and they have AIDS. The entire chain of negatives and overlapping, surreal images suddenly comes into focus, and it becomes clear that the message is one of a detached, undramatic empathy with men who are not only not threatening—because, being gay, they cannot be cast in the rapist roles common in Amos's early songs—but dying. This song also isn't a reaction to a personal connection or relationship; Amos isn't writing about "anyone I really know," just about those who happen to be going down in flames. All that distance and detachment is, however, belied by the shimmering beauty of the piano and the throaty, gasping vocal intonations—despite its apparent coolness, the grief that this song evokes seems stronger than it would if the song were more dramatic, more spectacular. Standing by the grave, the one who says little, in a low voice, may be more deeply wounded than the one who yells, cries, and flails her arms.

A SEPARATE HEAVEN

An equally complex example that covers related territory is James Taylor's strangely titled "Never Die Young," from the 1988 album of the same name.[8] Although the continuity of the verbal images is simpler, and the song follows a clear narrative path, the lyrics are again almost surreal—that is, images appear in sequence rather than being knotted up together, but they don't really clarify into any familiar story. The rising bass includes

a chromatic note—a sharp fourth of the relative minor—that it passes through, always briefly; this cues the listener that something is going on, that the warm, fuzzy surface of the song is not its real story.

Again, I'll elide the song's coded nature; it is difficult to make any sense of it without thinking of various apparently unrelated images in groups. The key is not given at the end, as in Amos's song, but is found by following a trail of clues, especially those that identify those being talked about and those talking. *We* are looking at *them*; and they are true love, they are never alone, they seem to be a little too sweet and a little too tight—and as for the song's "we," we couldn't stand to think "they" might make it and wouldn't touch them with the proverbial ten-foot pole. Considering Taylor's own social position—the easy-going country boy who moved to the shimmering flamboyance of Beverly Hills—it all becomes clear: this is the straight man, seeing himself as part of the world of the "normal," looking at those who aren't normal, and who are characterized by both romance and effeminacy. Taylor is trying to see himself, or more accurately his former attitudes, from some external, more objective viewpoint, at least as much as he can manage it—acknowledging his own distaste while recognizing something intimate and frankly rather sweet about those others who bother him so much. As in the Amos song, they—unavoidably, gay men— lose their threatening quality when they are themselves threatened: if they have their backs against a wall, Taylor suddenly experiences sympathy and even a wish to help, even a willingness to hold their frail, dying bodies. This reflects a crucial shift in American culture in the later 1980s and early 1990s, where gay men were suddenly regarded as objects of pity rather than threat; although we might all wish this had been less traumatically achieved, there's no doubt that pathos did a great deal of cultural work that pride and self-assertion couldn't quite manage.

It would be useful to consider the skeleton structure and harmony of the song. The general form is not unusual, and each quatrain is similar, but they go in different directions, suggesting a changing and slightly unexpected narrative:

	Introduction into Cycling Vamp*	
Verse 1	A	
Verse 2	A´	
Verse 3	B	Ending in V
Verse 4	A	
Verse 5	A´	
Verse 6	Chorus	Ending in I
Verse 7	A	

Verse 8	A´	Ending in I
Verse 9**	Chorus with coda	
	and cycling vamp	
	Repeated final lines	Combined I + V

The song opens with a vamp that cycles repeatedly through a set of functionally suspended harmonies.
**Lyrics not included in CD booklet.*

Essentially, we go through the same material three times, but each time with a very different musical ending, outlining the song's story of a change in heart. The last of those endings, a combination of chorus, coda, and cross-rhythmic cycling vamp, takes us in an ecstatic, harmonically circling rise to heaven—a transcendent heaven where the difference between the singer and those scary gay men becomes unimportant, and in fact they become "our golden ones," almost like the magical beings of shaman and berdache folklore. Other details include the acknowledgment that "other hearts were broken" (which might suggest the entire late-1980s argument of AIDS receiving so much attention while, for instance, breast cancer research remained underfunded) and balloons (which likely refer to the practice of releasing balloons at memorial services in the late 1980s, a ritual of letting go of the spirits of the dead).

Ultimately, this song intends to create an atmosphere of affection and support, but I can't help but react with a certain discomfort: if the "golden ones" are going to another land under another sky, doesn't that suggest not only that they are going to heaven, but that they might be going to a *separate* heaven—perhaps not the one that the "we" of the song will be going to? Some of my discomfort comes from a suspicion of *which* heaven I, and other gay men, will be allowed to enter—does it resemble the Limbo of Dante's strictly circumscribed world, or is it more a sort of dog heaven? If such uncomfortable questions can be deferred until after death, back here on earth we face other kinds of separation. This song works hard to transform distaste into a qualified tolerance, creating a world where those who die will arise to a place where they are free from harm; but they will also, and not at all incidentally, be isolated from the living.

CONCLUSION

Both of these songs chart journeys of awareness, replacing anger or revulsion with tolerance and even love, and giving listeners room to experience and pass through their own discomforts. Incidentally, they are useful in classrooms for that reason—students who have been pretending to be comfortable with a gay lecturer or a queer topic seem

more relaxed at the end of the discussion of these songs, as though any confusion they might have been feeling is now out in the open, and can thus be more easily surmounted.

My own reaction is ambiguous: I am of course grateful for the increase in sympathy and tolerance but can't help noting that it comes with a price—it's easier to accept dead people than living ones. It seems that heaven isn't only a wonderful place, it's also a way of getting moved out of the way, isolated from the social spaces of what journalists used to call the "general population." I suppose we should be glad of whatever we can get: people are complicated, prejudices are tangled, and no cultural change happens to an entire population at once, or to the same degree. Perhaps, in the case of these two songs, it's better to note the honesty and self-criticism implied, without expecting the instantaneous transformation of attitudes. Ultimately, though, all of these songs tend to cover up the conflict that was going on, that *is still* going on; and, as in war and politics, looking closely at the cover-up is what reveals the conflict. A bit too often, it seems that sympathy for the person with AIDS comes with an articulated separation—fear and distaste aren't really banished, but only silenced. And, as we all should have learned by now, silence = death.

NOTES

This chapter introduces my projected work on music about AIDS. This version is based on presentations at colloquia, classes, and conferences since 1997, including the 2003 conference of the International Association for the Study of Popular Music; I am grateful for comments received from many listeners and colleagues, only a few of which are implemented in this version. Due to the usual problems with reproduction rights, this version does not include my transcriptions or the lyrics; I suggest the reader read the lyrics on one of the many Internet sites devoted to them.

1. See Wendy Steiner, *The Scandal of Pleasure* (Chicago: University of Chicago Press, 1995), chap. 1.
2. Burt Bacharach and Carole Bayer Sager, "That's What Friends Are For," performed by Dionne Warwick, Elton John, Gladys Knight, and Stevie Wonder, *Dionne Warwick: Greatest Hits 1979–1990* (Arista ARCD-8540), 1990.
3. Madonna, "In This Life," *Erotica* (Maverick/Sire 9 45031-2), 1992.
4. Compare the DVD performances of Janet Jackson, "Together Again," *The Velvet Rope Tour: Live in Concert* (Image ID5518ERDVD), 1998, with Madonna, "In This Life," *The Girlie Show: Live Down Under* (Warner Reprise Video 2-38391), 1993.
5. Tori Amos, "Not the Red Baron," *Boys for Pele* (Atlantic 892862-2), 1996.

6. See David Schwarz, *Listening Subjects* (Durham, N.C.: Duke University Press, 1997), chap. 1.
7. Tori Amos, "A Bottle of Red: Tori Amos, Tea, and Sympathy with Sandra A. Garcia," *B-Side*, May–June 1996.
8. James Taylor, "Never Die Young," *Never Die Young* (Columbia CK 40851), 1988.

PART 4

Glamorous Excess

15

ENDLESS CARESSES
Queer Exuberance in Large-Scale Form in Rock

JENNIFER RYCENGA

Critiques of formalism, organicism, and the preeminence given to musical form have been central to feminist and queer musicology. From Theodor Adorno through to the work of Susan McClary, Ruth Solie, and many others, Western art music's emphasis on formal analysis has been seen as upholding dualisms, distancing music from physicality, and serving ideologies that seek to control and contain affect.[1] Consider, for instance, this articulation of ideal form, from a well-known pedant of the early twentieth century, Percy Goetschius, in which he stresses the need for rational clarity: "A musical composition . . . in which *Order* prevails, in which all the factors are chosen and treated in close keeping with their logical bearing upon each other and upon the whole; in which, in a word, there is *no disorder* of thought or technique—is music with *Form* [i.e., *good* form]."[2] Not only is Goetschius's obsession with order patent, but, in the best idealist tradition, he adds ontologizing capital letters for "Order" and "Form," giving them a status approaching Platonic ideas. Furthermore, by implication, "Order" and "Form" are allied with the "natural" and the "normal," for Goetschius writes, one page previous, that "[d]isorder, constitutes a condition which is regarded with abhorrence and dread by every rational mind.[3]"

The forms music students are taught—from sonata form to A–B–A song form to pallavi–anupallavi–charanam—effectively operate as

hegemonies. The authority of the form reaches widely, but is upheld through an already-negotiated consent rather than by overt policing. In fact, these forms behave reproductively; they tell us that a certain musical train of events is predictable, that it resembles its parent with but small variations. These variations between parents and children can be charming or annoying: Franz Joseph Haydn seems to have created winsome formal offspring, each with his or her own quirks, while the band Def Lepperd removed all the grace in favor of unmitigated power in the forms it received from its über father, Led Zeppelin. The principle of reproducibility means that once listeners know, and have internalized, the template of a form, the (alleged) pleasure in formal listening arises from measuring the music against an abstract and absent model. With both a kind of compulsory reproductive mandate, and an imperative for abstraction, it is little wonder that feminist and queer musicologists have been concerned about the aridity and antisomatic bias of formal listening.

But is form always so orderly? Is form always an abstraction? Does form always dictate musical function? Examining my own experience (an oft-used feminist methodology), I'll admit I've always enjoyed unusual, unique forms. It began early, when the piece that most shaped my adolescent decision to pursue the study of music was Ludwig van Beethoven's *Grosse Fugue*. From my first listening at age twelve, I found the flow of events themselves to be exhilarating. What I repeatedly discovered, from that time forward, was that form had its pleasures, and that those pleasures were both intellectual *and* physical. Describing form as masculine, antisomatic, functional, or intellectual reinscribes a body/mind split, and denies my own visceral response. As McClary puts it, not only is the form/content distinction a false dualism, but "the entire complex" of form/content "is content—social, historically contingent content."[4]

Using two starkly contrasting artists and works—PJ Harvey's album *Is This Desire?* and "The Ancient" from Yes's much-maligned *Tales from Topographic Oceans*[5]—this chapter explores how form has multiple functions, and how (queerly) it can become embodied. Once reproduction and predictability are no longer considered normative or requisite, a more sensuous and exuberant approach to form can materialize. Physical immanence, in which form is not an external control on the music, but instead leads reflexively into sonic experience, manifests in the examples herein described. Furthermore, the responses generated against these works—often voiced as disdain for experimental form—were as historically contextual as the artists' works. Opposition to the normative and breaking down false naturalisms are constituent hallmarks of queering.

Yes and PJ Harvey can be seen as "queering" form to such an extent that they are perceived as not able to "rock 'n' roll."

The two works under consideration here have been dismissed more often than embraced by rock critics. *Is This Desire?* consists of twelve songs—all in standard song form—that together form a meditation, and a complex weaving, on the album's title question. *Tales from Topographic Oceans,* widely cited as one of the most pretentious albums of all time, is a four-movement work of well over an hour, exploring, through a connotative technique that many find amorphous, an indisputable utopia.[6] Whatever the virtues of these albums—and I believe they are many—they do not contain the artists' best "songs." The rock press savaged them precisely because these albums create a formal sensous engagement, where the pleasure in listening emerges from immersion.

The metaphor of immersion suggests a mode of physical interaction with these forms. Conventions, predictability, and other linear expectations usually constitute the markers of form. By contrast, these albums enmesh us in their sense of time, connectivity, and timbre. They nudge us forward and backward, to other songs, sounds, images, moments, and structures. Immersion in them, like immersion in lovemaking, is a *repeated* pleasure because one is not trying to solve a puzzle or map real-time experience onto a Platonic timeless ideal. The pleasure is repeatable because these albums prefer contact to closure, creating relation rather than certitude.

The two albums achieve this through contrasting means. Yes's output of the mid-1970s extended ideas of rock composition in ways that evoked art music without mimicking it.[7] The resulting dilemma: they managed to aggravate rock critics—who scorned complexities of form as something for longhairs and eggheads—and yet the band also flew under the radar of art music theorists, uninterested in the perceived crudities of popular music. Falling between that rock and the other hard place bruised the band enough that, by the end of the 1970s, they abandoned more experimental long forms for traditional song styles.[8] But in their heyday, Yes collectively groped toward fashioning a new approach to form in rock music, one that would maintain traditional structural markers (such as distinct sections, strategies of transition, motivic elaborations, repetition, etc.) without ever rigidifying form into a definitive template. Or, by rendering a multivalent sense of form into an audible part of the physical pleasure and participation in these pieces, they effectively queered the concept of form in rock music, much to the scorn of a rock press set on policing rock's virility.

By contrast, PJ Harvey's *Is This Desire?* represents an anomaly in her own work, an album that drew less critical acclaim than her previous

efforts (especially *Dry* and *To Bring You My Love*). The simply stated title question hovers over the entire album and within each of the twelve songs, evoking a charged range of desires. The songs are individual distillations of that moment in desire when something truly terrifying and/or truly exhilarating is about to happen—and one cannot be certain whether it will be the terror, the joy, or both. Each of these moments is embedded in a narrative fragment—each song a torn-off page from a lost story—so that the flash of desire is personalized and immediate. Such directness is a hallmark of Harvey's style; however, unlike her previous albums, the address here is not in the first person, but rather through third-person vignettes. These fragmentary narratives hint at—even beg for—interconnection; there are clear external indications of lyrical and musical parallels, and tendrils of relational possibility hover around the whole album, creating a prismatic, morphing sense of form. Obvious as it is that the songs belong together, the questions of how and why grow and shift rather than resolve, driving repeated listenings.

SONIC IMMANENCE AND FORM

Immanence is a feature of pantheistic and panentheistic religious systems, which perceive the sacred as indwelling, pervading, and inherent in reality. In immanent religious systems, all things—material and immaterial, visible and invisible—have the potential of being conceived as sacred. Therefore, practitioners of immanent religions (most indigenous religions, pre-Christian European religions, New England Transcendentalism, Shinto, some types of Hinduism and Daoism) tend to look *toward* the material world rather than turn away from it. It is interesting to note that immanent religious systems have been markedly less hostile to homosexuality than the transcendent traditions; in some significant cases they have even prominently incorporated same-sex and transgendered peoples in rituals and myths, as well as according them special spiritual status. (This pattern has been recognized by most feminist scholars of religion, as well as lesbian and gay thinkers such as Paula Gunn Allen, Gloria Anzaldzúa, Edward Carpenter, Randy Connor, and Harry Hay.[10]) In previous work on both Yes and PJ Harvey I have outlined ways in which they incorporate immanence in their music, lyrically, sonically, and somatically.[11]

Jon Anderson, the lead singer and lyricist of Yes (as well as being one of the more prominent composers in the band), has all the earmarks of an immanentalist. This was made manifest in his sun-worshipping theology, particularly on *Tales from Topographic Oceans,* whose four movements were intended as a cosmological map, albeit a map without

rigid boundaries: as its oceanic title implies, the album is rather fluid. Anderson's lyrics—always more connotative and evocative than denotative or narrative—carried the additional burden of a self-imposed epic scope on *Tales*. His words still point back into the musical phenomena in which they participate, rather than forming a set of references external to the sound; their lack of narrative cohesion leaves even dedicated fans unsure of what any given song is about, other than the music itself.

The third movement of *Tales from Topographic Oceans* is titled "The Ancient." It carries explicit pagan references, as Anderson intones names of the sun in fourteen different languages. The play of form and immanence is especially prominent in this section (6:00 to 8:23), although similar instances can be found across the piece (one of the features of immanent systems is a reflexivity of whole and part). The movement features the guitar playing of Steve Howe, whose virtuosity consists not only of the usual technical prowess, but a vast timbral range as well. His sense of phrasing, especially concerning the attack characteristic of notes, is fecund.

Noteworthy motivic elements across the movement include the use of a jagged major seventh interval, in an isolated, sharply accented pattern (the pattern sometimes occurs with an interval other than a seventh, and has various gestural effects throughout the movement). This contrasts with a much subtler interweaving of intervals of fifths and fourths, often with the guitar's enunciation of them seeming to appear without any audible attack. More traditionally melodic sections include a march theme and a fully contained, harmonically simple song in A–B–A–B–Coda form near the end of the movement.

The "key" to understanding this movement structurally is to not hear form as an external key, or as any single known structure. The section featuring the sun-name chants is clearly, definitively, concerned with formal markers. But architectonics and abstractions from the musical moment are not its function. Form does not clarify this music; it adds another layer of complexity. Here is a breakdown of this section:

6:00 end of previous section with accented upbeat
6:06 transition melody on B♭ minor
6:12 "caressing" melody on B♭ minor
6:20 first four sun names on A
6:25 "caressing" melody
6:33 second three sun names on A
6:38 march melody initially in G
7:01 jagged melody of fifths and sevenths around D, in 7/4 time, repeated eight times
7:28 "caressing" melody

7:36 third set of four sun names
7:41 "caressing" melody
7:49 final set of three sun names
7:53 march melody initially in G
8:22 end of section with accented upbeat
8:23 abrupt shift into new section

If form concerns the hierarchic relation of sections to each other, there are problems here. The most important text of the movement—Anderson's priestly intoning of the names of the deity—goes by in a flash, and with less contour melodically than the average chant, although compensated for somewhat by rhythmic unpredictability. In fact, the melody that I have designated as "caressing" because of its rhythmic flexibility on reiteration, appears to have greater importance by virtue of its placement; Anderson's clipped utterances form a contrast to the more vocal articulation of the melody by the multitracked guitar. Despite frequent motivic echoes, this important melody does not reappear in the piece. The rather striking 7/4 melody, repeated eight times, is likewise making its only full appearance in the movement, at the center of this crucial section; its sixteenth/eighth combination is echoed cadentially by Howe near the beginning of the movement (1:17) and then in a polymetric sequence (at 8:59) the bass line reappears. The march theme, which had had an earlier iteration in an earnest, blocky manner (4:31, 5:20), here has been softened by triplet rhythms, whose consonances quickly give way to more troubled harmonic waters. In other words, in a structurally and lyrically important two minutes, there is a profusion of moments, with wide *latitude* in their treatment, their relative importance, and their echoing through the rest of the composition. Every formal marker leads the listener back into the music for its location, meaning, and echoing; no sequence of events gives the "key" to unlock the piece's secret: the form is about listening pleasure, not about interpretive closure or external control. That is, I think, as close as one can get to a definition of immanent form—and a *queering* of form that eschews narrow notions of formal function.

It was exactly this kind of compositional construction—in which formal markers are everywhere, but the form as an abstract external entity remains inscrutable—that annoyed rock critics. Samples of their bile (some of these writers were Yes boosters, like Chris Welch):

The endless changes of direction . . . meant there was little *human* expression.[12]

a fragmented masterpiece. . . . *cohesion is lost* . . . to the gods of drab self-indulgence.[13]

there was *little, if any, clear cut structuring* in the music. . . . Yes had only the foggiest notion of where they were going while recording it, despite the two months they'd spent rehearsing. . . . *Topographic* was largely ad lib.[14]

too long . . . psychedelic doodling . . . *barren*, if cleverly executed . . . the music of *Tales* leaves the listener grappling for some perspective.[15]

In these and similar reviews, formal complexity was read as confusion, and, at the time, that was unanimous; Anderson admitted, "We haven't had one good review [of *Tales*]."[16]

Academics and fans have provided some positive feedback, attempting to vindicate the vision and, at least, the attempt at formal complexity. But, interestingly, many analysts try to force these long pieces into some classical form; sonata form is a favorite, but in the case of "The Ancient," one writer tried to turn it into a classic third movement by declaring it a scherzo and trio![17] More prudently, Bill Martin notes that this movement is "the most experimental and avant garde" but "could also be criticized for meandering a bit too much." He then adds, however, that meandering seems to be the point.[18]

More germane to the queering of form, note how the critical dismissal of these works relies on terms synonymous with "meandering" and "self-indulgent." The lack of clear linear trajectories marks the form as not merely different, but *too different*. The resulting condemnation implies that they have deviated too far from the norm, and are not providing usable—meaning generative—models.

PJ Harvey also meanders in *Is This Desire?*, but the meandering is different. None of the songs, individually, deviates from standard song form. No matter how innovative the sounds, the vocal tessitura, or the lyrics, the songs are all unproblematically cast into verse-chorus, or repeated verse, structure. We are in a different world from that of Yes, where the appearance of an easily parsed song form is an anomaly. Instead, Harvey's play comes in the album form itself. Neither the composer, nor the singer, nor the songs, are telling us for certain if—and how—they (as constituent elements) relate to one another. This tentativeness somehow only underlines their undeniable entanglement.

The album invokes the form known as a song cycle—a very queer genre indeed. The song cycle is architectonically amorphous, a feeling rather than a brute formal fact. Reinvented every time one is composed, the song cycle becomes a repository of allusions both internal and external. Unified by mood, song cycles start from and stubbornly retain

subjectivity: each cycle has its unique inner logic. To the extent that the song cycle as a form produces other song cycles, it looks like queer self-fashioning rather than heterosexual reproduction.[19]

The album consists of twelve songs; convincing threads can be found among songs organized in arch form, arched pairs, pairs, trios, and halves. Timbral similarities can be uncovered in less symmetrical patterns, as well as orchestration, tempo, and vocal style choices. Narration and character voice are quite persuasive in building connections between songs. As mentioned previously, these songs evoke a range of desires—thwarted, unrequited, about to be consummated, abusive, and gentle, to name a few. Some are obviously heterosexual, some are more easily read as same-sex, but such concerns are secondary to the mood of immanent desire and imminent danger. Many of the songs name an individual, or change from third- to first-person narration. The album opens with the haunting "Angeline," in which the opening line is a declaration of her name: the first gambit in a gallery of female voices Harvey will take up across the album, whose names thus become legion.

Angeline is joined by one (or maybe two) Catherine(s), Leah, Elise, Joy, and Dawn, as well as some nameless others. Each song concerns specific individuals, in very specific situations. For instance, "My Beautiful Leah" inhabits the voice of the lover who is pursuing—perhaps stalking—Leah, in conversation with a man the narrator thinks might have seen her. The narrator ventriloquizes the absent Leah. This kind of double-narrative remove is common on the album: Harvey singing a character's voice, who then quotes a silent/absent other. It comes to the fore most notably, in the trio of songs 7, 8, and 9, which have the most same-sex innuendo; perhaps Harvey enjoys the connotative space of the closet—for herself, her characters, or both. For instance, the song "Joy" concerns a very inaptly named woman, suffering amid a complex commentary on U2's "Red Hill Town" and its male bonding, and the Beatles' "I Want You (She's So Heavy)" with its unspecified and potentially risky desire.[20] Harvey describes Joy's situation: thirty years old, unmarried, and eager to leave the "red hills" but unable to do so, because of an undefined "condition." But this last line is then repeated in the first person, in Joy's voice, with no marked change in intonation or vocal style. As her spiritual nihilism is noted, Joy looks to the gendered possibilities with similarly allegorically named characters: she flirts with Hope! Of course, she rejects this, and, as in the Beatles' song, the end of the piece must come like a sudden jolt, as if torn off the tape recorder, rather than leading to any resolution.

It would be difficult not to connect Joy to the other declared unwed figure, the Catherine of the third song, who builds a temple to worship her own image. Likewise, Angeline had anticipated untold joy back at the album's beginning. Do Catherine and Joy know each other? Do Angeline and Joy meet? Why are they on the same album? Are they, therefore, in the same universe? Thematic connections can be easily discovered: walking (songs 1, 2, 4, 8, 10, 12), the road (1, 6, 10), prayer (2, 5, 8), spiritual nihilism (3, 9), the devil (1, 8, 10), dawn (2, 7, 8, 12), wind (3, 6, 8), washing (3, 10), and birds (8, 10).

Harvey's meditation on desire is filled with characters who slip and slide, as though they came from a short story written in a dream state. The salient characteristic of the album's form is never letting us know, definitively, whether to interpret this as an intentional cycle, whether to assume palpable connections as intentional connections. This form functions as desire functions—as a delectable longing. The music remains elusive, like holding rushing water in the hand—something remains, but certainty slips through the fingers. This form invites a listener to repeatedly embrace this amorphous structure. In other words, the form of this album—a mesh between songs so tantalizingly referential yet nowhere certainly so—is a physical pleasure (for this listener, at least). Like sex, listening becomes a repeated act, not in hopes of solving a riddle, creating order, or achieving closure, but for the contact that forms connections.

Critical reception of the album was mixed, though even the most positive reviews failed to note the interrelations of the song. But the negative reviews implied, as with Yes, that Harvey's preference for open-ended connotation in form was meandering. The encyclopedist Dave Thomas seemed dismayed that "*Desire* remains so mysterious it doesn't even answer its own title's question."[21] Bill Wyman, writing in *Salon,* was far more savage; his review is titled "Is This Desire, or Just Bad Performance Art?"[22] Saying this album was "posturing," he laments the "internal drabness" of the songs, writing, "They don't sound alike, but the feel of each one is dismayingly unchanging, with verses and choruses left behind in service of each song's droning sameness. You remember the tracks not as songs or as about something, but by their most noticeable musical bit of foofaraw. . . . Sound is all that these songs are about: They all start up and then sort of drift off or just stop. . . . I say it's spinach and I say the hell with it."

Spinach can be good for you, of course—but not if a steady diet of meat and potatoes is necessary to reinforce the heterosexual credentials of rock form.

EXUBERANT FORM

These two contrasting examples suggest that a queering of form can have somatic dimensions, while eschewing the idea of form as template, which makes of form something more or less mechanical, and renders the organic equivalent to the predictable. But that's not how nature works in forms. Throughout history, much homophobia and heterosexism has centered on privileging reproduction as *the* function of sexuality. This poses obvious dangers for same-sex sexualities, which can be condemned as useless or even counterproductive by social authorities. One of the standard techniques for denouncing same-sex lovers is to argue that homosexuality is a crime against nature, and that animals do not engage in such perversions of natural function. But in his monumental *Biological Exuberance*, Bruce Bagemihl has forever disproven the notion of a heteronormative animal world. Culling the scientific literature (and reading past its homophobia), Bagemihl shows that "the 'birds and the bees,' literally, are queer" as "the diversity of animal homosexuality reveals itself down to the very last detail."[23] Bagemihl argues persuasively that reproduction is not the only function of sexuality—it is one of many. He suggests that a queer approach to biology will jettison some of our elementary (or, should I say, secondary) knowledge. "Contrary to what we have been taught in high school, reproduction is not the ultimate 'purpose' or inevitable outcome of biology," he notes. "It is simply one consequence of a much larger pattern of energy 'expenditure'. … Earth's profusion simply will not be 'contained' within procreation: it wells up and spills over and beyond this. . . . The equation of life turns on both prodigious fecundity and fruitless prodigality" (255).

Instead of seeing same-sex activity as biologically useless, anomalous, or in need of being explained away, Bagemihl embraces Georges Battaile's concept of placing "excess and exuberance" rather than scarcity or function, as the "primary driving forces of biological systems" (252–53). Finally, in addition to noting the correlation between acceptance of same-sex expression and indigenous cultures, Bagemihl's description of "biological exuberance" rings with an immanent tone: "Every individual, every behavior . . . has a part to play. Its role is not *in* the tapestry of life, but *as* the tapestry of life: its existence is its 'function.' Biological diversity is *intrinsically* valuable, and homosexuality/transgender is one reflection of that diversity" (252, emphasis in the original).

As countless lesbians and feminists have pointed out, Bagemihl notes the scientific puzzlement and embarrassment surrounding the clitoris. "The clitoris poses serious challenges to conventional biological theories. Its only 'function' appears to be sexual pleasure, and the notion

of pleasure in animals, particularly as it relates to the phenomenon of female orgasm, is a difficult one for biologists to come to terms with" (210). Since no "mechanistic 'explanation' is available for the female orgasm," scientists search (almost desperately) for some reproductive role for the clitoris, "rather than seeing it as something inherently valuable that requires no further 'justification'" (211).

Transposing Bagemihl's theses into theories of musical form, what would be the result of queerly reconceiving organicism? What would it mean for musical theorizing if organicism no longer implied only order, predictability, regularity, or (metaphors of) reproduction? What if the organic was seen as extravagant, luxuriant, inelegant, even clitoral? What if pleasure itself was understood as organic, as an intrinsically valuable function of musical form and content? Would that change how we listen, change the equation of intellect and affect, so that they are no longer seen as separate components, but as unified aspects embodied in the same listener?

The heart of Bataille's theory of exuberance, as presented by Bagemihl, is the excess of solar energy given to all life forms, "'the super-abundance of biochemical energy' freely given . . . by the sun" (253), such that "exuberance is the *source* and *essence* of life, from which all other patterns flow" (255, emphasis in the original). It may be merely coincidence that Yes's "The Ancient" is among the most explicit sun-worshipping compositions of the twentieth century, and two of *Is This Desire?*'s most passionate and positive moments occur in the presence of characters named "Dawn." But there are deeper connections at the level of religious immanence and exuberant form. The form of "The Ancient" is *in* time rather than being *about* time. It is for wallowing in, moment to moment, rather than ticking off formal markers like passing railroad stations. The only constant, musically, is Steve Howe's guitar playing—electric and acoustic, melodic, harmonic, and noisy, accented and floating—but always alive and moving, "the serpent which drags its tail over all" things, as Martin describes it with that resolutely pagan symbol.[24] Enlivened by excess, the guitar embodies temporality by enacting the form of the piece through its timbre and activity. PJ Harvey, likewise, uses her voice as the continuity between all her characters, drawing an excessive number of potential connections, moving the listener backward and forward in time across the album. Both the first and last songs raise the question of death, but marginalize it in favor of ongoing desire. In both pieces examined, excess queers the form, merging the boundaries between content and form, making of form a somatic temporal experience. Metaphors of nature and organicism can be complex, philosophically immanent, and downright queer, and they do not have to be antisomatic or dualistic.

After all, only an excessive exuberance, a profligate, irregular, queer sense of form, enabled queers to survive and flourish. Or (to paraphrase Jon Anderson) our connections are fluid, changing, not tied into societal forms, so that our links occur in "endless caresses" for freedom.[25]

NOTES

1. See Theodor W. Adorno, *Quasi una Fantasia*, trans. Rodney Livingstone (London: Verso, 1992); Theodor W. Adorno, *Philosophy of Modern Music*, trans. Anne Mitchell and Wesley Blomster (New York: Seabury, 1980); Susan McClary, *Feminine Endings: Music, Gender, and Sexuality* (Minneapolis: University of Minnesota Press, 1991); Susan McClary, *Conventional Wisdom: The Content of Musical Form* (Berkeley and Los Angeles: University of California Press, 2000); and Ruth Solie, ed., *Music and Difference: Gender and Sexuality in Music Scholarship* (Berkeley and Los Angeles: University of California Press, 1993).
2. Percy Goetschius, *Lessons in Music Form: A Manual of Analysis of All the Structural Factors and Designs Employed in Musical Composition* (Boston: Oliver Ditson, 1904), 2; capitalization in original, emphasis added. Goetschius (1853–1943) taught at the New England Conservatory of Music and the predecessor to the Juilliard School. Composer Howard Hanson was one of his pupils.
3. Ibid., 1.
4. McClary, *Conventional Wisdom*, 7.
5. PJ Harvey, *Is This Desire?* (Island 314-524-563-2), 1998); Yes, *Tales from Topographic Oceans* (Atlantic SD 2-908), 1973.
6. To give but a single citation for the claim that *Tales from Topographic Oceans* is pretentious would be, itself, pretentious; let me recommend putting the words *topographic* and *pretentious* into any Internet search engine—they will call up over a thousand entries!
7. John Covach, "Progressive Rock, 'Close to the Edge', and the Boundaries of Style," in *Understanding Rock: Essays in Musical Analysis*, ed. John Covach and Graeme M. Boone (New York: Oxford University Press, 1997).
8. In the late 1990s, Yes did return to large-scale new compositions, but those pieces fall outside the purview of this article. For interested listeners, the most successful of these later pieces ("Be the One" and "That, That Is") can be found on *Keys to Ascension* (CMC International 86208-2), 1996.
9. PJ Harvey, *Dry* (Too Pure/Indigo 555001), 1992; PJ Harvey, *To Bring You My Love* (Island 524085), 1995.
10. For a good starting point on some of these gay and lesbian theorists, see Randy Conner, David Hatfield Sparks, and Mariya Sparks, *Cassell's Encyclopedia of Queer Myth, Symbol, and Spirit: Gay, Lesbian, Bisexual, and Transgender Lore* (London: Cassell, 1997).

11. Jennifer Rycenga, "Sisterhood: A Loving Lesbian Ear Listens to Progressive Heterosexual Women's Rock Music," in *Keeping Score: Music, Disciplinarity, Culture,* ed. David Schwarz, Lawrence Siegel, and Anahid Kassabian (Charlottesville: University Press of Virginia, 1997), 204–228; Jennifer Rycenga, *Is This Desire?* (review), the *Gay/Lesbian Study Group* [American Musicological Association] *Newsletter* 10, no. 1 (2000): 8–10; Jennifer Rycenga, "Tales of Change within the Sound: Form, Lyrics, and Philosophy in the Music of Yes," in *Progressive Rock Reconsidered,* ed. Kevin Holm-Hudson (New York: Routledge, 2001), 143–66.

12. Chris Welch, "Caught in the Act: *Tales* Concert Review," *Melody Maker,* December 1, 1973, p. 64; emphasis added.

13. Chris Welch, "Yes—Adrift on the Oceans: record review of Yes's *Tales from Topographic Oceans,*" *Melody Maker,* December 1, 1973, p. 64; emphasis added.

14. Dan Hedges, *Yes: The Authorized Biography* (London: Sidgwick and Jackson, 1981), 89; emphasis added.

15. Gordon Fletcher, "Psychedelic Doodles: Record Review of Yes's *Tales from Topographic Oceans,*" *Rolling Stone,* March 28, 1974, p. 49; emphasis added.

16. Chris Welch, "Yes Weather the Storm," *Melody Maker,* December 15, 1973, p. 9.

17. Thomas J. Mosbø, *Yes, But What Does It Mean? Exploring the Music of Yes* (Milton, Wisc.: Wyndstar, 1994).

18. Bill Martin, *The Music of Yes: Structure and Vision in Progressive Rock* (Chicago: Open Court, 1996), 151–52.

19. Not even the most resolutely heteronormative of song cycles, Robert Schuman's *Frauenliebe und Leben (A Woman's Life and Love),* op. 42, was able to impose predictability upon the song cycle as a form!

20. U2, "Red Hill Town," *The Joshua Tree* (Island 90581-2), 1987; The Beatles, "I Want You (She's So Heavy)," *Abbey Road* (Apple SO-383), 1969.

21. Dave Thompson, *Alternative Rock* (San Francisco: Miller Freeman, 2000), 412.

22. Bill Wyman, "Is This Desire, or Just Bad Performance Art?" *Salon,* September 30, 1998 (available at http://archive.salon.com/ent/music/feature/1998/09/30feature.html).

23. Bruce Bagemihl, *Biological Exuberance: Animal Homosexuality and Natural Diversity* (New York: St. Martin's, 1999), 9, 30; hereafter, page numbers will be cited parenthetically in the text.

24. Martin, *The Music of Yes,* 152.

25. Yes, *Tales.*

16

POPULAR MUSIC AND THE
DYNAMICS OF DESIRE

SHEILA WHITELEY

Desire: to long for; to wish for; to regret the loss of; earnest longing or wish; prayer or request; the object of desire, lust.
—Chambers Dictionary

Although it is somewhat of a tired cliché to observe that popular
music lays a particular emphasis on the body beautiful, its historical
engagement with the sexually provocative has provided a particular
forum for exploring and questioning gendered identity. Elvis Presley's
simulated pole-dancing in *Jailhouse Rock* (1957, dir. Richard Thorpe),
for example, provides a graphic insight into why he transcended mere
identification with the performer's public image. As the character
Clarence (Christian Slater) muses in the 1993 film *True Romance* (dir.
Tony Scott), "Man, Elvis looked good. Yeah, I ain't no fag, but Elvis, he
was prettier than most women, most women." He continues, "I always
said if I had to fuck a guy—*had* to if my life depended on it—I'd fuck
Elvis. . . . Well, when he was alive, not now."[1] Similar observations could
be made about Marc Bolan, David Bowie, Mick Jagger, and the larger-
than-life stars of heavy metal—not least such bands as Kiss, Mötley
Crüe, and Poison. While it would be easy to suggest that identification
relates strongly to their androgynous images, it is nevertheless evident
that they also provide multiple possibilities of what it means to be

male in our culture—one image may be used by gay men, another by heterosexual men. For women, they can equally provoke both desire and/or identification. As fantasy figures they bring with them a whole range of possibilities and, notably, the potential to queer the heterosexual bias of popular music.

This, then, is the premise that underlies my discussion of popular music, queering and, more specifically, the fantasies that relate to erotic desire. As Katherine Liepe-Levinson observes in her book *Strip Show*, "Sexual desire in Western culture is, in fact, rarely represented through signifiers of the 'normal.' Unlike sexual relations which can be regulated by the state through institutions such as marriage, sexual desire is often taken to be something beyond social organization or rational control. That is one reason why erotic arousal is so frequently experienced, theorized and portrayed as being downright 'dangerous' as well."[2]

Liepe-Levinson's identification of the danger inherent in erotic desire is an underlying premise that informs my discussion of queering popular music. The realization that the world is made up of less-than-total satisfaction and an always present feeling of absence—that there are social "laws" that govern and prohibit total self-expression, especially those concerning sexuality and sexual difference—are parts of the common sense of everyday life. Daydreams, fantasy, and the desire for the unobtainable—whether expressed as simply a wish for or, more strongly, as an object of lust—are part of an "imaginary scene in which the subject is a protagonist."[3] Theorized by Jacques Lacan, and others following Sigmund Freud, as a primal experience of absence, the developing child becomes aware that "the world is not simply my pleasure experience," but rather is constituted by both the presence and absence of pleasure. Biological need (the sucking of a mother's breast) is countered by a longing for pleasure for pleasure's sake (sucking for the sake of sucking) and "from this moment on, the child begins to learn to tend toward those acts which reduce tension and maximize the seeking of pleasure, a tendency Freud calls the 'pleasure principle.'"[4]

The drive for unity and pure pleasure (as experienced by the pre-oedipal child) and its displacement by desire as a site of prohibition is significant. Socialization involves an acceptance of a preexisting system of roles and rules and, as such, drives are repressed; the longing for full satisfaction and plenitude remains in the unconscious, however, re-emerging as fantasy. Theorized as the promise of "full satisfaction and total meaning in a world marked by separation, absence, and traumatic disruption,"[5] fantasies provide a way to negotiate prohibited desires without fear of social reprisal. They are, in effect, a safe way out of potentially disruptive situations.

The relationship between desire and sexual arousal—more specifically, why it happens—is explored by Elizabeth Cowie. Teasing out the relationship between denotation (such as a biological response to a nude body) and connotation (the mise en scene and implied narrative), Cowie concludes that sexual desire, for both men and women, is created by connotation—a system of signification that is, in fact, fantasy. The emergence of desire, and hence our biological response, is thus bound up in our ability to fantasize, to inhabit an imagined scenario that, in turn, "produces what we understand as sexuality."[6] It is here that popular music provides a specific insight into the ways in which fantasy—whether through watching a live performance, or in the intimacy of listening to music in the private space of the bedroom—can signal both what is denied and what we would like to experience. It is also suggested that fantasy, as a setting for desire, provides a particular space for the performer herself, allowing access to otherwise prohibited thoughts and acts via the subversion of performance codes associated with particular musical genres. In effect, the performance of popular music can construct both heteronormative and resistant queer sexualities. My first case study, of the song "Bohemian Rhapsody" by the band Queen, explores the relationships among reality, fantasy, and desire and the ways in which they provide a particular insight into gay identity in the mid-1970s.

Characteristic of many glam rock acts, Queen lead singer Freddie Mercury's camp theatrics stood in sharp contrast to the vigorous heterosexuality of traditional rock. The use of Zandra Rhodes silks, nail varnish, and makeup all contributed to a sense of "otherness," but Fleet Street's obsession with sexuality—"Who do you sleep with Freddie?" and his bantering response, "Girls, boys, and cats"—kept his performances salacious but his private life at arm's length. While this is, as they say, no big revelation, it is salutary to remember why Janis Joplin kept her bisexuality hidden from the public gaze,[7] and why Dusty Springfield fled to Los Angeles to escape the scrutiny of an always zealous press.[8] The U.K.'s Homosexual Reform Act (1967) may have seemed a step in the right direction, but the current climate was unforgiving of outed homosexuals and lesbians alike. The tremors surrounding Jeremy Thorpe, former leader of the British Liberal Party, shook the walls of the establishment in 1975. Accused of having a homosexual relationship with Norman Scott, who claimed to have been threatened by Thorpe after the end of their affair, he was subsequently one of four defendants in a court case, but was acquitted of attempted murder. The ensuing scandal ruined his Parliamentary career, and the animosity and hysteria directed at him by the media was a timely reminder that it was better to stay in the closet.

The paradox of legality/persecution is reflected in "Bohemian Rhapsody," a signature track from Queen's 1975 album *A Night at the Opera* that provides an intriguing insight into Mercury's private life at the time; the song's three separate acts reflect three separate turmoils— all, it seems, underpinned by Catholic guilt.[9] The title draws strongly on contemporary rock ideology, the emphasis on creativity legitimizing the individualism of the *bohemian* artists' world, with *rhapsody* affirm- ing the romantic ideals of art rock,[10] as an epic narrative related to the heroic, with ecstatic or emotional overtones. Like all good stories, the opening starts with a sense of tension and enigma.

The multitracked voices are unusually situated at the opening of the piece, the rhythm following the natural inflection of the words, the block chords and lack of foreground melody creating an underlying ambiguity—who is speaking, who is the promised epic hero? This sense of uncertainty is heightened by the harmonic change from B♭ (6) to C7 in bars 1 and 2; the boundaries between "the real life" and "fantasy" are marked by instability, and "caught in a landslide," the octave unison at the end of bar 3, propels the listener into the next phrase. Here "no escape from reality" provides a clue to the underlying turmoil, but the piano arpeggios in bars 5–6 and the stabilizing effect of the harmonic progression, anchored this time by the root of the chords, shift the mode of address: "Open your eyes."

The introduction of the central character is marked by a restate- ment of the rhythmic motif in its realigned position in the lead vocal and piano. Underpinned by the vocal harmonies there is a sense of pa- thos that is interrupted by a chromatic movement in the first inversion block chords of the voices and piano (bars 10–11, "Easy come, easy go") before the confessional of "Mama, just killed a man."

Here, the effected warmth of the vocal and the underlying arpeg- gios on piano suggest an intimate scenario. It is both confessional and affirmative of the nurturant and life-giving force of the feminine and the need for absolution. The emotional quality is given a particular reso- nance in bars 21–24. Framed by a lingering "Mama," the melody opens out, the vocal rising to a falsetto register only to fall dramatically down- ward at the end of bar 23. Underpinned by chromatic movement in the bass, there is an underlying mood of desperation ("If I'm not back again tomorrow"), which is opened out in bars 25–31 as the melodic phrases fragment, "carry on . . . as if nothing really matters."

The year 1975 was somewhat of a turning point in Freddie Mercury's personal life. He had been living with Mary Austin, manager for the London boutique Biba, for seven years, but had just embarked on his first gay love affair with David Minns. Aware of the constant surveillance by Fleet

Street, Mary accompanied him when dining out with his new boyfriend. It was apparently a very romantic affair, one that lasted until 1978, but the tugs between security (Mary), escape (David), and an acknowledgment of Mercury's sexuality are there. The confessional of "Bohemian Rhapsody" and its intimate address to "Mama" provide an initial insight into Mercury's emotional state at the time: living with Mary ("Mama"), wanting to break away ("Mama mia, let me go" in bars 88–89). Bars 80–85, in particular, provide an emotional setting for the dialectic interplay between the masculine and feminine voices. The heavy timbres of the lower voices, underpinned by the phallic backbeat of the drums and tonic pedal, traditionally connote the masculine ("We will not let you go") while the shrill, higher voices in first inversion chords imply the feminine "other" ("Let me go").[11] They signal entrapment and the plea for release.

The heightened sense of urgency seems to resonate with Mercury's inner turmoil, leaving the security of Mary Austin (who, in fact, remained a close friend throughout his life), coming to terms with gay life ("Easy come, easy go"), and living with a man ("So you think you can stone me and spit in my eye"). Mary was, however, more perceptive than the song implies. At the time, Freddie had asked her if she thought he was bisexual. Her reply—"I don't think you're bisexual. I think you're gay"[12]—provides an insight into their relationship and her continuing support. Even so, the "just gotta get out" supplies a metaphor for desperation as it moves toward the climax, the guitar supported by an aggressive drumbeat, before the emergence of the piano at bar 120. The return to the opening tempo thus suggests a release of tension, the outbursts are over and the final "Nothing really matters to me," where the voice is cradled by light piano arpeggios, suggests both resignation (minor tonalities) and a new sense of freedom in the wide vocal span.[13]

"Bohemian Rhapsody" dominated the 1975 U.K. Christmas charts and remained at number 1 for nine weeks, its popularity reinforced by an elaborate and highly innovative video production. While Queen's popularity can be related to the ascendancy of glam and glitter in the early to mid-1970s, it is apparent that the flirtation with androgyny and bisexuality that characterized many of its prominent performers (not least David Bowie and Gary Glitter) was not accompanied by an acceptance of gay sexuality by the general public. As mentioned previously, the tremors surrounding the "outing" of Jeremy Thorpe were already shaking the walls of the establishment in 1975, and the animosity and hysteria directed at him by the media provoke comparison with Oscar Wilde, who had been found guilty of homosexual offenses and sentenced to two years' imprisonment with hard labor in 1895. Both were

at odds with society; both subverted the "wholesome, manly, simple ideals of English life;"[14] both relate to the "outsider"—the "misfit" repressed and oppressed because of nonconforming individuality and sexuality. "Bohemian Rhapsody" thus provides a particular insight into the tensions surrounding gay identity in 1970s Britain, and Mercury's performance can be interpreted as challenging social, cultural, and musical structures in its invocation of gay male desire. In effect, its operatic camp revealed the "queer" imaginary that underpinned Queen's musical output, the "innuendo" that was not fully acknowledged until 1991 when Mercury confirmed publicly that he had AIDS.[15] He died from bronchial pneumonia a day later (November 24), and "Bohemian Rhapsody" was rereleased on December 9, with royalties from sales being donated to an HIV and AIDS charity, the Terence Higgins Trust.

My second case study, Patti Smith's live 1976 performance of "Land" on the BBC-TV music show *The Old Grey Whistle Test*,[16] is also concerned with historical contextualization and how particular public figures function as icons for their queer audience. Unlike the version of "Land" that appears on her 1975 album *Horses,* which moves straight into the narrative of the heroin addict Johnny, in this live performance Smith initially confronts the camera with a measured four-line recitation interspersed with a muttered "Jah lives":

Mr. Death
Oscar Wilde
Mr. Thorpe
The time is now, the time is now

This dedication provides a specific contextualization for the "outsider," linking Johnny (the heroin addict antihero of "Land") to others who have experienced both condemnation and alienation by a judgmental society, dedicated to upholding the status quo of so-called normality. While the underlying sentiments remain (the acoustic play on words, "sea/seize possibilities"), there is a more pronounced sense of immediacy, "Have no fear . . . if you are male, choose other than female."

The preface to "Land" is thus given a sense of contemporary action, "There's a possibility in taking more than one possibility" as if saying, "You must take responsibility for holding the key to freedom." It is, then, no accident that the end of this live performance segues into the opening chords of "Hey Joe" (Smith's first single, from 1974[17]) with its sustained reference to urban terrorist Patty Hearst. This confirms, once again, Smith's identification with the rebels and outsiders who have shaped her powerful rock poetry and her conflation of the cultural with the historical that marks this performance as topical, moving between

the real and the unreal. The cry to God, to Jah, and the direct address to "Mr. Thorpe" within a song that deals primarily with the outsider in its focus on heroin is both demanding and challenging. Allied to Smith's own androgynous appearance, which contradicts the norms of femininity, the live performance of "Land" embodies a fierce sense of defiance, an example of punk at its most powerful in its identification with the marginalized and repressed.

It is relevant, here, to return briefly to the formative influences on Patti Smith, her identification with the poetic communities of Greenwich Village and the New York Pop art scene of the 1960s. As an epicenter for the thriving poetic communities of the 1950s, Greenwich Village had attracted a bohemian culture centered on existential values, nihilism, jazz, poetry, drugs, and literature. Popularized by the Beat writers Gregory Corso, Allen Ginsberg, Jack Kerouac, and Gary Snyder and influenced by such French intelligentsia as Simone de Beauvoir and Jean-Paul Sartre and renegades of high culture Louis-Ferdinand Celine, Arthur Rimbaud, and William Butler Yeats, the Beat philosophy of anarchy and individualism was also reflected in the curious figure of Andy Warhol,[18] the most prominent figure of the New York Pop art scene. His mass-produced and recurring visual images are now recognized as symbolic of 1960s gay culture: the silkscreen prints of Elvis Presley and Troy Donahue (1962–1964); the New York World's Fair mural *Thirteen Most Wanted Men* (1964); the films *Sleep* (1963), *Blow-Job* (1963), *My Hustler* (1965), *Lonesome Cowboys* (1967), and *Flesh* (1968).[19] More specifically, Warhol's endless promotion of camp taste and drag culture at the Factory,[20] and his personal involvement with the Velvet Underground (Warhol designed the infamous peel-off banana screen-print for the *Velvet Underground and Nico* album sleeve, 1967) provided a crucial context for the band's uncompromising insights into urban culture, sexuality, and voyeurism that, in turn, were to influence Patti Smith's album, *Horses*. Produced by John Cale of the Velvet Underground, the album invoked the influence of Smith's 1960s heroes Bob Dylan, Jim Morrison, the Rolling Stones, and, in particular, the Velvet Underground's fascination with contemporary street culture and its antagonism toward middle-class values. Warhol's Factory also provided a refuge for drag queens who are celebrated in *The Philosophy of Andy Warhol* (1975), thus providing a crucial link with the June 27, 1969, police raid on the Stonewall Inn gay bar on Christopher Street in Greenwich Village and the subsequent riots that were the flashpoint of the American gay liberation movement of the 1970s.[21]

The significance of personal freedom and identity politics were central to Smith's stand against the establishment, not least in her tracks "Gloria," "Redondo Beach," and "Break It Up," her various self-projections

as lesbian, androgyne, martyr, priestess, and female God and, of course, her rallying cry to "Mr. Thorpe." Her other major influence at the time was her part-time boyfriend Robert Mapplethorpe, whose later photographs and images provide obsessive insights into the sexual imagery of the gay leather scene and sadomasochistic sex, as well as the contemporary icons William Burroughs, Marianne Faithful, Debbie Harry, Iggy Pop, and Andy Warhol. In essence, Mapplethorpe's work explores sexual ambiguities; his flowers, for example, "with their drooping or thrusting penile leaves complement the concentrated postures of Mapplethorpe's men,"[22] while his photographic images of Patti Smith (with whom he lived for a while) have a sexual ambiguity that challenges the onlooker, exacting a complex emotional reaction.

What is evident from my brief survey is that the New York scene of the 1960s and 1970s provided an environment that fostered individualism, and that this included a determination to confront the persecution of the gay community. It also included a play on gendered identity—whether this was concerned with Mapplethorpe's array of images and discourses *about* sexuality, or the queering inherent in the performance art of Warhol's Factory and Exploding Plastic Inevitable. Smith's adoption of the black and white insignia of Bohemian dress codes (white T-shirt and black leather trousers) thus incorporates a range of meanings, the most culturally prominent of which pivots on gender. Her clothes, her stance, her attitude served as outward marks of difference that were both fluid and curiously asexual. What was at stake in this experience of the dualism of gender and sexuality was the possibility of distancing the feminine through an assumed persona that denaturalized sexual difference. Given that Smith's only female hero, Joan of Arc, was herself a desexed martyr, her self-styled sexual ambiguity is not too surprising. As a woman conventionally defined by her body, her appearance masked her femininity; but rather than constituting a denial of her identity it became instead an assertion of her autonomy—a strong, sexy woman challenging both the confines of gender and the entrenched attitudes of the establishment. It is thus not surprising that she should frame her live performance of "Land" with a challenge to the normative status quo, queering the original song with her provocative call to "Oscar Wilde" and "Mr. Thorpe." As a woman committed to defending the outsider, she clearly recognized the depths to which social prejudice undermined the effectiveness of the 1967 Sexual Offences Act, and her public performance identified her as spokeswoman for the many who continued to stay closeted in isolation, fear, and repression. Patti Smith's continuing commitment to queer politics is evidenced in her tribute to William Burroughs at the June 2005 Meltdown Festival. Reading from

Burroughs's *The Wild Boys* and climaxing with his moving, retrospective introduction to *Queer*, she ended on her knees, bellowing disjointed phrases with a spaced-out, shamanistic intensity Burroughs would undoubtedly have approved of.

My final case study remains within the rock genre—this time, the hypermasculinity of heavy metal and the problems inherent in gay identity. More specifically, I want to examine Robert Walser's premise that "Heavy metal, like all culture, can be read as an index of attempts to survive the present and imagine something better in the future; it is one among many coherent but richly conflicted records of people's struggles to make sense of the contradictions they have inherited, the tensions that drive and limit their lives."[23] While Walser's observation relates to the diversity of heavy metal music—from its Birmingham roots in Black Sabbath through to the extremes of thrash, speed, and death metal—the genre's principal impact remains one of power, whether associated with the overdriven amplification and effects of the guitar, the distortion and detuning (which gives the instrument a heavier, fatter sound), the aural effect of power chords, or the virtuosity and expressive virility (from the Latin, *virilis-vir*, man, robustly masculine, sexually potent) of the performers. The concept of power is also evidenced in the social practices (which can involve, for example, displays of combat on the dance floor or in the moshpit) and the shared cultural meanings and experiences that unite the performer and the fan. In essence, metal is about men being manly, and while Walser relates this to the codes of misogyny, excription, and the fraternalistic culture of bands and fans, problems arise when connecting the sweaty gods to their often androgynous images—the long hair, mascara, spandex, and leather. While this does not suppose that the singer, lead guitarist, or, indeed, the bands as a whole are necessarily androgynous (as having the characteristics of both male and female as suggested by the image of, for example, Marilyn Manson) nor an implied femininity (as in the glam and glitter of bands such as Kiss and Bon Jovi), it does suggest a performative image that attracts the scopophilic gaze—often to the crotch and heightened by the phallic thrusts of guitar and microphone stand. The normative associations of metal would imply, however, that the emphasis on the body and the deliberate isolation of the crotch, buttocks, and widespread legs relates more to the codes of "manliness" as evidenced by David Lee Roth's flamboyant image and performance style—sporting trousers with the backside cut out (or "bare ass," as his fans prefer)—with the emphasis shifting to the more macho association of "kiss my —" and its sense of dismissal rather than a camp sensibility. Roth's wild partying and escapades (he was rumored to have taken out paternity insurance in the event that one of his

sexual conquests did not go as planned) confirmed his reception by fans as embodying a brash, cocky, sexual machismo: he was "all man" and for metal fans, man = heterosexual.

Returning, then, to my original quote from Walser ("the contradictions they have inherited, the tensions that drive and limit their lives") there is clearly a tension between the displays of masculinity inherent in metal (whereby the body is foregrounded as an object of desire) and being gay (in an ostensibly heterosexually inscribed genre). As Walser notes, while gay heavy metal fans may have read heavy metal videos as erotic fantasies, straight fans resisted the homoerotic implications and identified only with the power and freedom depicted.[24] Either way, it seems, the emphasis lies on the reception by the fans and not the sexuality of the performer who, it seems, is destined to remain resolutely straight.

At this point, I would like to return briefly to the implications of the Stonewall Rebellion and how the "toughness" of the riot was reflected in the butch image that was to influence both Freddie Mercury of Queen and later Rob Halford of the metal band Judas Priest. The leather wear and the mustache (aptly dubbed the "flavor saver") were, as Thor P. P. Arnold (Mercury's lover at the time) aptly commented, an overt body language, "screaming out for steaming man sex,"[25] and were quickly adopted by Mercury and by Halford (although the latter without the mustache). Black leather jackets; heavy studded leather belts; chains, thongs, and straps; heavy boots; and black leather jeans or chaps that exposed the flesh eroticized the body, drawing into association both bikers and sadomasochism.

It would appear, then, that Judas Priest's adoption of leather as the band's hallmark was no accident.[26] As Kurt Loder observed, Halford was "unique in the annals of heavy metal, not so much for his searing vocals as for his black-leather-and-bondage image, which appears to have been lifted straight out of Kenneth Anger's classic rough trade film, *Scorpio Rising*."[27] The video for the song "Hell Bent For Leather" (1978) took the image to its extreme, with Halford roaring onstage on a Harley Davidson. Key songs like "Living after Midnight" (1979), "Breaking the Law" (1979) "You've Got Another Thing Comin'" (1980), "Eat Me Alive" (1984), and "Ram It Down" (1988) were performed with straight faces but with carefully choreographed movements, the guitarists overemphasizing the moshing gestures of their fans with synchronized swishy hair movements. While the connotations may have been ignored by the straight audience, the fact that Rob Halford did not come out as gay until the early 1990s does suggest that he was fully aware of the homophobia associated with the metal scene and its implications if he were to be formally "outed."[28] Clearly, the queering of metal by Halford can be

interpreted as simply an ironic gesture—an exaggeration of metal's hy-permasculinity—and T-shirts with logos such as "I've been whipped by Rob Halford" can be taken as either an acknowledgment of the leather and sadomasocism connotations or as part of the underlying humor inherent in the metal scene. For gay fans, however, Halford's excessive fixation on leather and his well-developed sense of innuendo meant that the closet doors of the metal scene were a little less closed, and that the implied fraternalism associated with the genre was susceptible to very different readings from queer audiences. Thus, while the male body in metal culture is marked as a source of (male) heterosexual pleasure and strength, as a cultural "sex possessor," it is also marked as a source of the fan's own (male) sexual pleasure and strength—and this is where fantasy and identification can resonate with queer sensibility.

It is also apparent that rock has been subject to queering from the onset, whether overtly in the camp persona of Little Richard, the posturings of Elvis Presley, as mentioned in my opening paragraphs, or in the Red Hot Chili Peppers' pastiche on their *Abbey Road EP* (1988), where they appeared naked on the record's sleeve, walking across the famous street with their genitalia covered only by socks. While attempts to queer the Beatles are still regarded as somewhat outrageous, Anne Shillingworth's analysis of the Beatles' films shows how a seemingly asexual male homosociality was underscored by the deployment of a queer camp coding (particularly on the part of John Lennon) due largely to the crafting of their public image by their closeted gay manager, Brian Epstein.[29] Similar points can be raised with reference to the Rolling Stones, not least in such tracks as "Cocksucker Blues" (1979) and "Brian, Dear Brian" (unreleased). John Travolta arguably took the queering of rock codes one step further with his Elvis-infused performance in the movie *Grease* (1978, dir. Randal Kleiser), descending from the ceiling on a car engine, dressed in leather, and surrounded by his crew—who owe more than a little to the choreographing of the film *Gentlemen Prefer Blondes* (1953, dir. Howard Hawks), where the male lifeguards engage in a display of physical jerks under the powerful gaze of Dorothy (Jane Russell). The fixation on the male body is taken one step further in *Saturday Night Fever* (1977, dir. John Badham), where John Travolta's "hips, groin, and buttocks [become] the mesmerizing center of attraction," especially when he appears in sexy form-fitting briefs. As Susan Bordo observes, "His routine anticipates a future of sexual encounters that, in turn, set in motion for the spectators a vision of countless other cycles of undressings and re-dressings. Depending on the inclinations and imagination of the spectator, these images and narratives may be endlessly replayed and adapted, used as tinder

for what is still conventionally thought of as real sexual experience or sexual relations," straight or gay. "Travolta's carefully choreographed performance also foregrounds the fact that he is at risk for legal and social sanctions if his penis takes 'phallic' shape,"[30] but that, I suggest, is where fantasy really exerts its power.

As Patricia Juliana Smith writes, artists "evoke a response of affection identification, and admiration from a devoted queer or audience [due to the] presence in each of characteristics that were, in their time, implicitly or explicitly contrary to societal or cultural ideals and sexual mores in a manner resonant with queer sensibility."[31] It is this sense of resonance, allied to fantasy and desire, that has informed my discussion of Freddie Mercury, Patti Smith, and Rob Halford herein, and why I have chosen to focus primarily on the 1970s—a period when fantasy was arguably preferable to the continuing problems associated with gay identity within the real and unforgiving world of popular music.

NOTES

1. Tony Scott, dir., *True Romance* (film), cited in David Sanjek, "Can a Fujiama Mama Be the Female Elvis? The Wild, Wild Women of Rockabilly," in *Sexing the Groove: Popular Music and Gender*, ed. Sheila Whiteley (London: Routledge, 1997), 137–38.

2. Katherine Liepe-Levinson, *Strip Show: Performances of Gender and Desire* (London: Routledge, 2002), 183–84.

3. Jean Laplanche and Jean-Betrand Pontalis, "Fantasy and the Origins of Sexuality," in *Formations of Fantasy*, ed. Victor Burgin, James Donland, and Cora Kaplan (New York: Methuen, 1986), 66–67.

4. Stephen Hinerman, "'I'll Be Here with You': Fans, Fantasy and the Figure of Elvis," in *Adoring Audience: Fan Culture and Popular Media*, ed. Lisa A. Lewis (London: Routledge, 1992), 111.

5. Ibid., 114.

6. Elizabeth Cowie, "Pornography and Fantasy: Psychoanalytic Perspectives," in *Sex Exposed: Sexuality and the Pornography Debate*, ed. Lynne Segal and Mary McIntosh (New Brunswick, N.J.: Rutgers University Press, 1993), 135–36.

7. Joplin never openly acknowledged her bisexuality. It is possible that the risks were too great for a high-profile female performer. As Gayle S. Rubin points out, "A single act of consensual but illicit sex, such as placing one's lips upon the genitalia of an enthusiastic partner, is punished in many states with more severity than rape, battery, or murder. Each such genital kiss, each lewd caress, is a separate crime"; see Rubin, "Thinking Sex," in *The Lesbian and Gay Studies Reader,* ed. Henry Abelove, Michele A. Barale, and David Halperin (New York: Routledge 1994), 19. See also Sheila Whiteley,

Women and Popular Music: Sexuality, Identity, and Subjectivity (London: Routledge, 2000), 51–61.

8. As Stacey D'Erasmo has noted, Springfield's public personae raised "that essentially queer question: do you want to be her or have her?" See D'Erasmo, "Beginning with Dusty," *Village Voice* 29 (August 1995): 67. Patricia Juliana Smith notes that Springfield created a decidedly queer persona while achieving popular success in a trendy milieu in which lesbianism, lacking the criminal status and thus the glamour of male homosexuality, remained invisible and unfashionable. Utilizing the tactics of camp, she adopted more visible (and modish) marginalized identities by "becoming" a gay man in drag (or, conversely, a *female* female impersonator) visually and a black woman vocally. In this manner she pushed accepted notions of femininity to absurd extremes. See Smith, "'You Don't Have to Say You Love Me': The Camp Masquerades of Dusty Springfield," in *The Queer Sixties*, ed. Patricia Juliana Smith (New York: Routledge, 1999), xviii.

9. My discussion here is informed by North One (prod. for Channel 5 Television), *Freddie's Loves*, July 14, 2004.

10. The rhapsody was first introduced by the Bohemian composer Johann Wenzel Tomaschek in 1803.

11. In the song, the lyric "Bismallah!" (In the name of Allah) was more widely heard by Queen's fans as "Miss Miller!"

12. North One, *Freddie's Loves*, July 14, 2004.

13. For her musical analysis of "Bohemian Rhapsody," I am indebted to Holly Marland, "The Five Codes and the Philosophy of S/Z," (unpublished essay, University of Salford, 1997), which has both informed and supported my discussion herein.

14. Jonathan Dollimore, "Different Desires: Subjectivity and Transgression in Wilde and Gide," in *The Lesbian and Gay Studies Reader*, ed. Henry Abelove, Michele A. Barale, and David Halperin (New York: Routledge 1993), 635.

15. "Innuendo" (1991) gave Queen their third U.K. number 1 hit, and the album of the same name also topped the British charts.

16. For those unfamiliar with "Land," see Sheila Whiteley, *Women and Popular Music: Sexuality, Identity, and Subjectivity* (London: Routledge, 2000), 95–107; and Sheila Whiteley, "Patti Smith: The Old Grey Whistle Test, BBC-2 TV, May 11, 1976," in *Popular Music and Performance*, ed. Ian Inglis (Aldershot, England: Ashgate, 2006), of which this discussion is a part.

17. The release of "Hey Joe" was funded by Smith's "soul twin," Robert Mapplethorpe.

18. As Kelly Cresap, "New York School's 'Out': Andy Warhol Presents Dumb and Dumber," in *The Queer Sixties*, ed. Patricia Juliana Smith (New York: Routledge, 1999), 43, notes, "The naïf-trickster persona fashioned by Andy Warhol provides a crucial paradigm of 1960s queer visibility. Andy was audaciously swish by the standards of the time, and yet his public demeanor

suggests that naivete was perhaps a more favored 'orientation' for him than homosexuality."

19. Ibid., 52.

20. The Factory was the name given by Andy Warhol to his studio, offices, and production space, the home of his multimedia "freak show." The Velvet Underground—Lou Reed (guitar, vocals), John Cale (bass viola), Sterling Morrison (guitar), Maureen Tucker (drums), and Nico (vocals)—was part of Warhol's touring "total environment" show, the Exploding Plastic Inevitable. The Factory also provided a safe harbor for drag queens, and he can thus be seen, according to Cresap, "New York School's 'Out,'" 52, as "enabling . . . the history of drag liberation and of the Stonewall Rebellion itself."

21. In the United States, prohibitions against homosexual activities were a matter of state and local, rather than national, law. As such, no national legal reform (as in the United Kingdom) was possible.

22. Alan Hollinghurst, *Robert Mapplethorpe 1970–1983*, exhibition catalog (London: Institute of Contemporary Arts, 1983), 17.

23. Robert Walser, *Running with the Devil: Power, Gender, and Madness in Heavy Metal Music* (Hanover, N.H.: University Press of New England, 1993), 171.

24. Walser, *Running with the Devil*, 115–16.

25. North One, *Freddie's Loves*, July 14, 2004.

26. As Halford has commented, "The metal scene back then didn't have a definitive look, it was just whatever you put on your back. So I just went for the leather look. And having a compulsive-obsessive personality, when I go for something I just go for it, blow it all out of proportion. So I went to Mr. S in London, the local S&M shop, and went mental putting on 20 pounds of leather with whips and chains"; see Steffan Chirazi, "Q & A with Rob Halford," *The San Francisco Chronicle*, April 19, 1998, p. 44.

27. Kurt Loder, "Judas Priest: Evangelists of Heavy Metal," *Rolling Stone*, September 18, 1980, p. 14.

28. Neither Freddy Mercury nor Rob Halford came out until the early 1990s—some twenty years after their initial debuts.

29. See Anne Shillingworth, "'Give Us a Kiss': Queer Codes, Male Partnering and the Beatles," in *The Queer Sixties*, ed. Patricia Juliana Smith (New York: Routledge, 1999), 127–46.

30. Susan Bordo, *The Male Body: A New Look at Men in Public and Private* (New York: Farrar, Straus and Giroux, 1999), 170.

31. Patricia Juliana Smith, "You Don't Have to Say You Love Me," xv.

17

TRANS GLAM
Gender Magic in the Film Musical

LLOYD WHITESELL

In the recent film *School of Rock* (2003, dir. Richard Linklater), a hopeful but deluded guitarist posing as a substitute teacher molds his captive schoolchildren into a rock band. Assigning tasks according to perceived abilities, he puts costume design into the hands of Billy, a scrawny, prim, lisping Liza Minnelli fan, whom he nicknames Fancypants. The first idea Fancypants comes up with is a throwback to 1970s glam rock. Two band members model body-hugging outfits in gaudy colors. This idea gets vetoed—as too dazzling? too unisex?—in favor of a tamer, 1980s-inspired concept. But Billy never doubts his own talent for design. When asked before the climactic show whether "beautification" is under control, he snaps, "Are you kidding?" This character is a pint-sized version of the popular stereotype linking gay men and beautification. In musical film, such an association goes back to the very first backstage musical, *The Broadway Melody* (1929, dir. Harry Beaumont). The costume designer in this case is a swishy walk-on character who highlights the queer male labor behind the sumptuous feminine garments. In a brief appearance he admonishes the showgirls not to ruin his hats, whose extravagant brims won't fit through the dressing room door.

These films follow the doctrine of the "queer eye," representing gay men as custodians of the glamour of the theater. Several questions arise regarding this archetype: What meaning does it hold for queers with

lesser talents in the visual department? What about the queer *ear*—how important is the story's musical setting? What does music have to do with the glamorous image? And to whom is this beautifying labor addressed? Like many queer viewers, I'm unsatisfied by universal, monophonic interpretations, tired of having my own perspective left out of the picture; but I'm also wary of doing something similar myself, making an exclusive link between minority authors and minority spectators. I'm less interested in this chapter in identifying a distinct subcultural tradition than in probing the mystery of people coming together in a mass audience. What is going on in all our different minds? How do we make connections across particularities of identity? How do the purveyors of sex appeal and bodily style pitch their ideas to all sorts, each with their own experience of gender and sexual subjecthood?

Thus, in pondering film glamour and its queer associations, I'd like to adjust the focus from the gaze to the ear (i.e., from the visual to the sonorous field of meaning); from sex to gender (from the stable position of sexual identity to the choreography of gender effects); and from object to affect (from material spectacle to the intense emotional relations experienced by participants and observers). As my examples will show, the pursuit of beauty involves strong feelings—for the stars, of course, but even for their support staff, whose creative labor resembles a kind of alchemical experimentation with the precious and volatile attributes of gender, isolated from their living cultures. My search will be guided by the intersecting coordinates of music, aesthetics, gender, and feeling. Much of my discussion will focus on Hollywood from the 1930s to 1950s in order to establish the codes of glamour in mainstream films of the period; in the final section, I will explore how such codes have been reworked in subcultural films of recent years.

To be precise about terminology: according to *Merriam-Webster's Collegiate Dictionary*, *glamour* denotes "an exciting, often illusory or romantic attractiveness." It refers to an image as well as an emotional attitude. In storytelling and stagecraft, anything can be glamorized—a life of crime, a struggle with disability, a crude cabin on the frontier, a state-of-the-art forensic lab. Characters or settings that are gritty or tedious in reality can be made attractive through an enhanced presentational style—the play of shadow on a gangster's hard face, the sheen of rain on his tailored suit, the languid insinuations of jazz curling in from the street. An unpleasant situation can also be made attractive through an intensification of sentiment—think of Scarlett O'Hara starving in the ruins of Tara, raising her fist in a defiant silhouette; or the favorite melodramatic scene of terminal illness, the moment of death carefully stage-managed in soft beds, swelling orchestras, and shining halos of

self-sacrifice. Such technologies of aesthetic and sentimental enhancement are what Hollywood traffics in. In this sense glamour is pervasive
in the entertainment industry, and music forms a crucial component.
But my focus is less on glamour as a technique than as a subject in its
own right, a quality represented as inhering in a character or setting. In
this sense, glamour is mainly an aesthetic category, evoking emotions
of envy, excitement, or desirous identification. Socioeconomic factors
determine the resources one can count on in its pursuit, but class does
not automatically confer or withhold glamour. The disco in *Saturday
Night Fever* (1977, dir. John Badham) is one example of a working-class
setting for glam hopefuls.

Predictably, in mainstream cinema the codes of glamour are different for men and women. The visual presentation of men in general is
less showy. Glamour more likely attaches to what men do rather than
how they look. For instance, the action/adventure hero from Tarzan
to Indiana Jones has a look that is predominantly casual and athletic.
Nevertheless, certain male character types are granted a special aesthetic flair, two of the most important being the Prince Charming type and
the outlaw. A Prince Charming evinces the untouchable mystique of the
aristocracy. Immaculately turned out, he cuts a dashing figure in society.
He can embody a high-toned romantic ideal, as in the Disney fairy tales,
or the more worldly magnetism of the playboy. The full-blown outlaw
allows for a more unbuttoned presentation. Douglas Fairbanks, the silent film star, mined this type in an influential series of action pictures
from 1920 to 1926, introducing in quick succession a band of iconic cut-
purses and swashbucklers: Zorro the bandit, in sleek black satin, mask,
and kerchief (*The Mark of Zorro*, 1920, dir. Fred Niblo); D'Artagnan the
musketeer in velvet, high-cuffed boots, and flowing hair (*The Three
Musketeers*, 1921, dir. Fred Niblo); Robin Hood in rustic leather, mail,
and skirt (*Robin Hood*, 1922, dir. Allan Dwan); the thief of Bagdad [*sic*],
in bronze makeup, headband, and fringed harem pants (*The Thief of
Bagdad*, 1924, dir. Raoul Walsh); and the black pirate (*The Black Pirate*,
1926, dir. Albert Parker), predecessor to Johnny Depp's campy pirate
(*The Pirates of the Caribbean*, 2003, dir. Gore Verbinski). Still, outlaw
fashion is kept within limits and safely paired with athletic vigor. To get
a sense of the limits of male display one need only consider Rudolph
Valentino, Fairbanks's contemporary, whose prettiness and objectified,
extravagantly decorative style were viewed by male spectators with suspicion as signs of gender failure.[1]

A much wider range of glamour types is available for women. There
is a freer abandonment to pleasurable display, and a greater exploration
of glamorous excess. On the other hand, female glamour is generally

treated as more passive and intrinsic. Two ubiquitous archetypes are the princess and the bride. The radiant princess is well known from fairy-tale settings: Snow White among the dwarves, Glinda among the Munchkins. Her cousin in more realistic narratives is the society lady, draped in jewels, privilege, and haute couture. Often her royal status, like Cinderella's, must be won or disclosed, and forms the focus of an aspirational narrative. The musical genre from *A Star is Born* to *My Fair Lady* is crammed with such tales of discovery and transformation. The visual styles of princess and bride are highly congruent, and in fact the two types often merge; thus in another Cinderella story, *The Sound of Music* (1965, dir. Robert Wise), Sister Maria becomes Maria von Trapp, achieving her highest peak of glamour during her wedding at the cathedral. Princess and bride are essentially decorative roles, expressing a glorified femininity. They tend to validate one's nature and position, rather than one's accomplishment or skill—unless we speak of one's skill at being a girl.

Another important type, given the setting of professional entertainment, is the showgirl. Embodying glorified femininity for a paycheck, she aspires to stardom, material prosperity, or access to high society. The showgirl can be further categorized according to two presentational styles: the energetic hoofer and the immobile mannequin. In general, the less vigor in her routine—the closer she is to posing—the purer the glamour. Think of Marilyn Monroe's famous gold-digging number, "Diamonds Are a Girl's Best Friend," from *Gentlemen Prefer Blondes* (1953, dir. Howard Hawks), in which she doesn't dance so much as walk, flirt, allow herself to be carried, and arrange herself in poses shading from glamour to burlesque. Not surprisingly, the showgirl's wardrobe freely borrows the iconography of princess and bride.

I'd like to consider a few examples of high-end glamour, the kind made possible when a whole dream factory goes to work. The goal is an idealized beauty, through cosmetic enhancement as well as the special framing of a woman's body. Often she is literally placed on a raised platform. This can happen as if accidentally, as in the fairy tale genre with its castle towers and balconies. In an early scene from *The Merry Widow* (1934, dir. Ernst Lubitsch), Jeanette MacDonald, as Madame Sonia of Marshovia, is discovered in her boudoir, perfectly posed. Her unfastened hair and ruffled negligee soften the outlines of her form. Hearing the music of the peasants, Sonia steps out onto her balcony. She responds in a voice marked as elite by its refinement, consistency, and control. As the number ends she climbs into an ethereal vocal register, supported by the anonymous chorus. Sonically and scenically she is accentuated and elevated above the crowd.

In backstage mode, no artifice is spared in the search for new ways to place women on a pedestal. Showgirls are lifted on globes, pillars, and skyscrapers, stacked on fountains, hung from chandeliers, and fixed to the wall in decorative patterns. In an early scene from *Broadway Melody* there is a Trojan number titled "Love Boat" in which the exalted chorines represent fantasy figureheads. Just before curtain, one faints and falls from her perch, offering an indirect comment on the precariousness of the gender ideal. This provides an opening for Queenie, the ingénue, to be elevated from hoofer to mannequin. We are shown her excitement and jittery nerves at the birth of her new career. The elite voice of a Trojan Prince Charming, backed by male chorus, is trained on the women like an acoustic spotlight (see Figure 17.1). Opulent in timbre and harmony, the music imparts a heavenward lift through harp flourishes and vocals that walk an operatic tightrope.

The fictional producer in this film, Francis Zanfield, is a barely concealed reference to Florenz Ziegfeld and his Broadway revues. Running from 1907 to 1931, the Ziegfeld Follies were enormously successful showcases of female pulchritude, designed to "glorify the American Girl."[2] Lavish in scale and megalomaniac in showmanship, Ziegfeld and his productions inspired a series of film dramatizations through the 1930s

Figure 17.1 "Love Boat" (*Broadway Melody*, 1929, dir. Harry Beaumont): Queenie gets her chance. Courtesy of M6M/Photofest © M6M.

and 1940s. The 1936 biopic *The Great Ziegfeld* (dir. Robert Z. Leonard) features a showstopping centrepiece display of Ziegfeld style at its most "cinematacular." The stage accommodates a vast rotating platform conveying a procession of human tableaus. As curtains lift we become gradually aware of a gargantuan pillar, wreathed by a spiral staircase. The theme of the number is musical beauty, spinning off from the Irving Berlin tune, "A Pretty Girl is Like a Melody." After a tuxedoed tenor sings his tribute, the listener is swept through a fanciful architectonic pileup of familiar classical tunes, alluding to a range of historical moments and national settings. Thus a divertimento by Antonín Dvořák gives way to the japonism of Giacomo Puccini's *Madame Butterfly*, Franz Liszt's Romantic *Liebestraum* is overtaken by a Viennese waltz, and the histrionics of Ruggiero Leoncavallo's *Pagliacci* are capped by George Gershwin's *Rhapsody in Blue*. The musical arrangement is mammoth in its duration, draped in aural swags and filigree, and hauled aloft by glowing clouds of strings and voices. There is a modernist updating of glam in the Gershwin segment, with its snappy, brassy, streamlined palette. Yet the dancers, in their abstract, reflective catsuits, are mere acolytes, slinky kinetic accessories to the befrocked but stationary girl at the top of the stairs (see Figure 17.2).

We can clarify the glamour codes deployed in this scene by comparing it to a tragic miscalculation. The movie *Cover Girl* (1944, dir. Charles Vidor) contains a suitably Ziegfeldian production in which a series of magazine beauties leads up to a fabulous Rita Hayworth, elevated and etherealized. She descends gracefully from her perch down a curvilinear rampway. So far, so dreamy. Unfortunately, when she lands among the chorus boys she switches gears with a clunk, working way too hard in an athletic dance routine. Even worse, the director has her run all the way back up the ramp, racing to reach the top by the close of the number.

In contrast, Ziegfeld placed emphasis on elegance and poise. Choreography for his A-list showgirls was ritualized into the famous Ziegfeld Walk, in parade across the stage or down a staircase. Beautiful bodies in decorous movement were further enhanced by upscale couture: sensuous to the touch, dazzling to the eye, or fantastic and impractical in construction. My next examples come from *Ziegfeld Girl* (1941, dir. Robert Z. Leonard), which is interesting not only for its spectacle but also for its trifocal narrative. The stories of three hopefuls are woven together—the gold-digger, the trouper, and the slummer. Each plays out a distinct affective relation toward gender performance and the glamour ideal. Hedy Lamarr takes most naturally to the high-class role; significantly, her character is European and associated with classical music. In the end, she finds personal fulfillment through submission

Figure 17.2 "A Pretty Girl is Like a Melody" (*The Great Ziegfeld*, 1936, dir. Robert Z. Leonard): The top of the stairs. Courtesy of M6M/Photofest © M6M.

to her husband, a concert violinist. Having viewed her showgirl job all along as silly, merely a way to make ends meet, she gives it up when her husband launches his own career. Judy Garland's character, born in a trunk, is bent on success. But her talents are as a dancer-singer, not a high-end beauty; when she is shoehorned into the mannequin role, it fits awkwardly. An important aspect of Garland's star image, in this film and beyond, is her aura of the gender oddball, falling short of ideal girlhood (Richard Dyer analyzes this quality as an aspect of

Garland's appeal to gay men).[3] She serves up a subjectivity born from self-conscious misalignment, in famous lyrical asides such as "But Not for Me," "The Man That Got Away," or in this film, "I'm Always Chasing Rainbows." But the rest of the time, she is busy embodying that other character trait essential to the musical: unquenchable energy.

Lana Turner, however, playing the classic gold-digger, has the most intense relation to glamour. Three archetypal scenes capture the melodramatic arc of her career. We are first introduced to her in the uniform of an elevator operator; hers is a lowly job but one that allows her to rub shoulders with the nabobs. She overflows with ambitious dreams of discovery. Later, at her peak, she is visited in her Park Avenue nest by her old neighborhood boyfriend, who scorns her materialism and kept situation. In an attempt to convince him of her elevated status and sense of arrival, she casts one of her fur coats to the floor and walks on it. Eventually, a lapse into alcoholism costs her her job. At the moment of her greatest disgrace, she steals into the theater to recall the days of glory. Finding herself alone and unseen on a grand staircase, she indulges in a few steps of the trademark Ziegfeld Walk, only to collapse in her final illness. What are Turner's qualifications for becoming a Ziegfeld girl, for "winning her Z," as the film's backstage lingo goes? Beauty, of course, but also a certain intangible quality, an ability to assume the mantle of glorification. This quality is expressed in the simple act of walking stylishly down the stairs. A performance so minimalistic indicates the elusive nature of the skill involved, her grasp of what we might call gender magic. In trying to define this quality, I have mentioned certain modes of heightened representation by which a girl is made to seem extraordinary. As the tenor sings in one of the film's most lavish numbers, "You stepped out of a dream, you are too wonderful to be what you seem."

The specialness of glamour can be distinguished from two other tonalities of visual/aural style important in the musical genre: the ordinary and the burlesque. The ordinary is crucial to the so-called folk musical, set in homey locales such as Oklahoma, St. Louis, or New York's West Side. It's also crucial to many fairy-tale musicals that involve a passage from an ordinary to a fantasy world. Thus characters like Maria of Salzburg or Dorothy of Kansas are presented as common, just like you and me (only more so). This makes their brush with mirrored ballrooms and ruby slippers all the more exciting. The interaction of ordinary and glam (what I'll call O-style and Z-style) can be an important source of narrative tensions. Judy Garland's career was charged through and through by a sense of desirous, unpredictable transitivity between O and Z.[4] Thus, in *A Star is Born* (1954, dir. George Cukor), the lackluster Esther Blodgett is laboriously polished up to become Mrs. Norman

Maine. In *Summer Stock* (1950, dir. Charles Walters), farmer Judy schlumps around in workaday attire for the bulk of the movie, until her astonishing appearance in the number "Get Happy," swanky and leggy in a daring high-concept tuxedo. Garland is also especially intriguing in that her access to glam can be conveyed through sound alone. Ever versatile in her vocal persona, she can come off as perky, brassy, torchy. But in certain sentimental songs she unveils a voice of incredible suavity and polish. Dorothy in the barnyard in *The Wizard of Oz* (1939, dir. Victor Fleming), in pigtails and gingham, is just like you and me—until she opens her lips, and we are saturated in specialness: a voice that shimmers, leaps, and settles with perfect poise and sophistication, whose rich tone and ecstatic fluidity already transport us to that other, more glorious world.

On another axis, the etherealized rhetoric of glam is distinguished from the carnality of burlesque. Burlesque is also a showgirl tradition, but here the appeal to the flesh is more direct, not as obliged to tropes of aesthetic refinement. To this category belongs Marlene Dietrich's lumpen nightclub singer in *Blue Angel* (1930, dir. Josef von Sternberg), taunting her audience with disregard for any niceties. Also counting as burlesque would be the bump-and-grind circuit in *Gypsy* (1962, dir. Mervyn LeRoy), the shabby chic Kit Kat Klub in Bob Fosse's *Cabaret* (1972), and the leering, eye-flashing revelry of Frank N. Furter in *The Rocky Horror Picture Show* (1975, dir. Jim Sharman). It's not that burlesque doesn't have its own code of beautification—it just falls on the side of the vulgar, the seedy, or the brazen. This is a tonality that celebrates base desires, and thus is more tolerant of aesthetic degradation—what Sally Bowles in Cabaret would call "divine decadence."

Burlesque has its music, which plays to the low and fleshly, just as glam plays to the sublimated and elevated. Returning to the key of Z, I'd like to examine its constituent affects. For now let's put aside the emotional narrative conceived in relation to glamour—that is, the longing to be someone special, or the shame of falling from the pinnacle. Focusing on the state of grace itself, we can identify two primary affects in its expression, having to do, respectively, with well-being and self-worth. For a visual example of the first, one can refer to the numerous glamour portraits of stars from Rita Hayworth to Marilyn Monroe in which the subject radiates a self-generated pleasure, as if musing, "How unbelievably wonderful it is to be me." Such ecstasy can shade toward physical abandon, as appropriate to a bombshell type, or toward spiritual exhilaration, for a more wholesome image. For the second effect, think of the regal demeanor common to stars like Gloria Swanson or Greta Garbo, who suggest condescension: "One could never *hope* to be me." Marlene

Dietrich, in top hat and tails, with her sexual arrogance and faraway looks, is another expert in imperiousness. These two states—euphoria and hauteur, elevated well-being and elevated self-worth—provide the basic affective palette for glam expression. Returning to Lana Turner and her colleagues in their ritual of the glorified girl (see Figure 17.3): what is their smiling, elegant performance but an expression of euphoria and hauteur in perfect balance? The two affects have their musical correlates. Euphoria translates into a kind of sensuous pleasure that is

Figure 17.3 "You Stepped Out of a Dream" (*Ziegfeld Girl*, 1941, dir. Robert Z. Leonard): Lana Turner does the Ziegfeld Walk. Courtesy of M6M/Photofest © M6M.

lavish in timbre and harmony, and giddy in its reach. Hauteur translates into burnished surfaces, smooth modulations, and consistency in flow. Composers and arrangers use musical dimensions of range, mass, and sonority to suggest pleasurable affective fullness, tempering this with a tone of decorum and refinement.

Such extravagant glam representations waned after the eclipse of the studio era. This is partly due to economic factors, but there are also ideological impulses behind the shift in style. The rise of the counter-culture in the 1950s through the 1970s fueled an awareness of independent and dissenting voices, thus helping to discredit the authority of a social consensus, which the industrialized, big-bucks, middle-class-targeted Hollywood product under discussion can be said to epitomize. Furthermore, countercultural discourse fostered a critique of the ideological underpinnings of social-aesthetic forms. Thus it became more possible to see how glorified cinematic images were tied to a restrictive parsing of gender roles, with woman as passive, decorative, and objectified. According to this line of argument, dominant aesthetic styles serve to naturalize a stable, hierarchic boy/girl binary. Yet despite the validity of the argument, in such a starkly reduced form it doesn't account for the complexity of the "golden age" movies' mass appeal. Even the endless showgirls are never represented as mere wallpaper or eye candy—they are also hard workers, hopeful subjects, fast-talking wise-acres, celebrated performers, and trustees of cultural value. Nor does the oppressive binary argument take into account the diversity of audience response, then and now. For some spectators—perhaps some of our best friends—the enjoyment of an aesthetic bodily style is not anchored in a specific gender; put another way, gender magic is commutable across the binary.

In fact, my discussion has been guided all along by the proposition that mainstream Hollywood images freely invite queer consumption. Of course, nominal narrative safeguards are in place to maintain the appearance of alignment with prevailing concepts of gender. But the storylines are hardly strong enough to contain all that is going on in the affective and aesthetic realms. For any spectator so inclined, there is plenty to suggest a counterideological pleasure. By focusing on the gender ideal as a matter of aesthetics, mainstream musicals propound a view whereby femininity, say, is not an innate quality granted to all women but instead a special effect available to anyone with the proper skill and accessories. Moreover, the staged musical numbers, in their sheer excess, permissive indulgence in fantasy, and temporary suspension of the social and moral demands of the narrative, create a space where the experience of glamour takes on a life of its own, tentatively

floating free of real systems of gender attribution. They project a gender magic characterized by experimentation and bravura rather than adherence to essential facts or prescribed categories.

To recount evidence of the subcultural reception of such images at the time of their release is not my project here. Instead, I turn to three recent films in which glam reemerges: *The Adventures of Priscilla, Queen of the Desert* (1994, dir. Stephan Elliott), *Velvet Goldmine* (1998, dir. Todd Haynes), and *Hedwig and the Angry Inch* (2001, dir. John Cameron Mitchell). All three are backstage musicals, geared toward a niche audience whose marginality encompasses the gay, transvestite and/or transgender, off-Broadway, artsy, glam rock, punk, and Abba-fan communities. Due to their subcultural purview, the films are not as beholden to stable gender binaries or heteronarrative goals. Thus, glamour appears to different effect in the new context, even as familiar theatrical formulas are brought into play. In their various ways, the films revisit and revise conventions of gender enhancement, providing artifactual examples of the queer reclamation of mainstream images. Rather than offer extended readings of the individual films, I will identify common aspects crucial to their projection of a queer perspective on gender and aesthetics.

The conventions themselves are quite recognizable: heightened staging, accentuated costume, abstracted bodily style—even the basic expressive palette. *Priscilla* opens with an updated expression of euphoria in a solo performed by Mitzi (Hugo Weaving) on the runway in a drag club, lip-synched to the breathy, sugary tune "I've Never Been to Me": "I've been to paradise, but I've never been to me." Later, Felicia (Guy Pearce) performs camp hauteur, installed on a makeshift throne atop the bus, clad in silver garb with a regal train of impossible length, channeling Giuseppe Verdi's *Traviata* in a coloratura soprano. Cinderella narratives also figure prominently, but survive in battered, disillusioned form. The bride at the end of *Priscilla* is middle-aged, acid-tongued Bernadette (Terence Stamp), tentatively settling down with her tagalong mechanic. In *Hedwig*, the sex reassignment of the title character (John Cameron Mitchell) is botched, she is repatriated to a trailer park by a husband who leaves her, and her performing career is eclipsed by a protégé who makes off with her intellectual property. *Goldmine* has the most incoherent, time-dislocated narrative of the three films, but it also plays with hopeful yet troubled arcs of man-on-man love, big-time careers, Bowiesque star image, and gender bricolage.

Several factors work together to create a new ethos for glam conventions. The first is DIY (do it yourself). No makeover factory is in place to sweep up the queer starlet on her way to the heights. The pursuit of

glamour is of necessity a personal project. Fancypants, in other words, is no longer an employee behind the scenes in service of a chorus line; now he/she is busy designing his/her own show. In this self-mounted project he/she has to make do with limited resources, augmented with a great deal of imagination. Such low-budget creativity is evident in the white trash setting of *Hedwig,* where laundry lines stand in as drop curtains, with 8-tracks and flip wigs providing the longed-for aesthetic boost. *Priscilla* also deals in the DIY of the small traveling show, with its secondhand bus, portable chrome-highlighted cassette players, and frocks made out of flip-flops. But the alchemy is stronger here, as out of that bus are pulled fantastic Seussian creations in extruded plastic and aerodynamically engineered lamé.

Second, the self-staging outside the dictates of bourgeois custom allows for a greater amount of mix-and-match (or, as *Hedwig* has it, "cut-and-paste"). The Priscillarians combine styles of O, Z, and burlesque in their "Groove Thing" number in the outback bar, with their "kinderwhore" attire—pigtails, glitter, and hot pants. Affects are mixed as well: the familiar palette of the decorous and ethereal is notably alloyed with anger in all three films. Bernadette must come to Felicia's rescue with a well-placed punch; her ass kicking and verbal aggression are always balanced by the re-aestheticizing gesture of sweeping her hair back into place. In *Goldmine,* rock star Curt Wild (Ewan MacGregor) is introduced in an antic stage number during which he oils his bare chest, sprinkles himself with glitter dust, drops his trousers, and treats the audience to the double finger. Hedwig, with her angry inch, continues the exploration of thrash dance styles, audience provocation, and fuck-you chic. And of course, gender signs are casually assembled, decorative hair and appliqués negligent in their disguise of masculine body bulk. Gender enhancement here is a matter distinct from realness, textural finish, or semiotic integrity.

Third, the films espouse a ghetto or cult dynamic of aesthetic value. The entire glam enterprise is clearly represented as adopting a socially discredited vocabulary. *Hedwig,* for instance, deliberately adheres to discarded fashions: Sophia Loren glasses, beehive hairdos, vinyl, fringe, and tube tops. In musical terms, the Z-tonality, with its slick, decorative, sublimated aesthetic (typified in the 1930s by the sweet big-band sound) has suffered deposal by the classic rock regime with its values of rough emotion, defiance, and sexual power. Thus, bringing glam into the rock musical creates an incoherence of conventions difficult to puzzle out. Abandoned codes of musical enhancement mix uneasily with the reigning aesthetic of crudeness and aggression. Of the three films, *Priscilla* embraces Z-style most wholeheartedly, defiantly bringing a

big-city excess of beautification to the outback where it has no use value. It recycles 1970s recordings, rummaging through disco and pop for treasures to be preserved in the modern wasteland. The old byword of unquenchable dance vitality is renovated in the anthem "I Will Survive" (embellished with didgeridoos and aboriginal chanting). The old dream of discovery and glorification is revitalized in the showstopper "Finally It Happened to Me," with its breathtaking progression of costumes from desert lizards to Marie-Antoinette-as-Sydney skyline.

The conventional images of glam specialness are handled in these films so as to appeal to those falling outside the system. Near the end of *Goldmine*, the ingénu (Christian Bale) and the rock idol climb to the roof, wish upon a star, and are scattered with fairy dust. Their lovemaking is overseen, in a fantasy sequence, by rocker Brian Slade (Jonathan Rhys Meyers) in full glitter regalia, doing a version of the glam walk along a decrepit theater balcony. The erstwhile codes of feminine enhancement—elevation, sparkle, fanciful costume, elegance, bodily abstraction, personal aspiration, musical luster—are now applied to the casual romantic union of two men, portrayed as nonconformists in terms of music, gender, and sexuality. Meanwhile the sequence implicitly pays homage to the moviegoing experience of a previous era by invoking the dreamlike backdrop of a sumptuous but derelict theatre. Gender magic in these films is explicitly disarticulated from stable categories of identity expression. Now it inheres in larger-than-life characters who are no longer girls or boys. Gender-queer euphoria is captured in Hedwig's upbeat "Wig in a Box" number. After a series of stunning personal setbacks involving her gender transition, Hedwig picks herself up from abject depression by fixating on the talismanic power of hair enhancement ("Suddenly I'm Miss Farrah Fawcett from TV"). The number builds to a raucous finale in which the wall of the trailer hinges outward to become a spotlit stage, and Hedwig's entire costume becomes a fantastic extension of her long blonde wighair. Gender-queer hauteur is embodied in the aristocratic bearing and scrambled somatic style of Jack Fairy, the presiding genius of *Goldmine*. In the film's final number, Jack appears onstage as if by magic in a brilliant black gown topped with extravagant plumage and fully cut away at the chest, to sing a loving farewell to glam ("I was moved by your screen dream"). These nouveau-glamorous characters, beyond the pale of bygone Hollywood in their embodied expression, nevertheless acknowledge an emotional debt to the old screen dreams. Their stories show queer people constructing uncommon self-images from mainstream representation. As Hedwig might say, it's what we have to work with.

NOTES

A version of this paper was presented for the Lesbian and Gay Lectureship at Bowdoin College, and for the Seminar in Sexuality Studies at Concordia University, Montreal. I want to thank James McCalla for the original invitation to undertake this research.

1. Miriam Hansen, *Babel and Babylon: Spectatorship in American Silent Film* (Cambridge, Mass.: Harvard University Press, 1991), 259–64.

2. Linda Mizejewski, *Ziegfeld Girl: Image and Icon in Culture and Cinema* (Durham, N.C.: Duke University Press, 1999), 2.

3. Richard Dyer, *Heavenly Bodies: Film Stars and Society* (New York: St. Martin's, 1986), 165–77.

4. See Dyer, *Heavenly Bodies*, 156–58, on her "ordinariness."

18

ON MALE QUEERING IN MAINSTREAM POP

STAN HAWKINS

There is no shortage of gossip surrounding pop celebrities on the Internet, where sites dealing with stories of sexual orientation never fail to draw in surfers. Nothing seems to spark off more enthusiasm than the presumptuousness surrounding categorizations of sexuality. What does this tell us about the contested areas of queerness at the beginning of the twenty-first century? And how might we continue to critique the hegemonic links between gender, sex, and sexuality? Using these two questions as pivot points, this chapter seeks to consider masculinity within a queer context by underlining the strategy of queering and its exploitative rendering in pop culture. My argument begins with the idea that male queering in pop culture seeks entry into mainstream culture through acceptance as much as resistance. Many of the issues taken up will build on my earlier studies,[1] which have considered how identity politics form useful points of departure for working out how the performance can entice us into new spaces for social and cultural assimilation. Let us say that the differences reified by being queer are there because we still cling to some belief that there are tangible variations in gender representation and that these matter significantly. Given this, we need to remember that masculinity belongs to no single gender, sexuality, race, or discipline. There are therefore valid reasons for considering how homosocial bonds and desires operate and structure all aspects of culture.[2]

On first glance, it might seem that queer identities in mainstream pop culture have broken through the idea of sexual deviations and gender roles. The unmistakable images of lesbian and gay representation and queer signs are ubiquitous in many performative spaces, where such displays of otherness often represent a norm that is perceived more as performance than as a connection to sexual preferences. Just over fifteen years ago, to describe a person as "queer" was a blatant term of abuse. Mark Norris Lance and Alessandra Tanesini refer to how being queer, in the old usage, was about being excluded and reviled for not being "proper." By contrast, nowadays the term *queer* is commonly employed "to endorse that exclusion and to turn the evaluation on its head" by considering difference as a challenge to all that is considered as proper.[3] Despite the range of difficulties encountered in queer theory,[4] not least in its tendency to "de-ghettoize" gay and lesbian studies, scholarship in this field has escalated and has been important for aesthetic criticism and deconstructing gender behavior in music. As a consequence, numerous scholars have linked their discussions of queerness to concerns of authenticity, positionality, corporeality, and representation.[5]

Since the 1950s, the connections between pop music and art-based institutions have defined the marketplace. As a result, advertising corporations have steadily embraced images that purposefully inscribe gendered identity as ambiguous and ambivalent. Indeed, the art school traditions that paved the way for a strong alliance between British pop and commercial enterprise contributed significantly to the aestheticization of masculinity. By the 1980s the emergence of the male pop artist was contextualized by representations of a more sensitive, less macho type. For the first time, mainstream culture shifted the focus onto the male by encouraging men to view themselves as objects of desire. Suddenly it seemed as if traditional male representations had dissolved into the style-conscious, groomed young male figure that surfaced in the marketplace. Images of men through the 1980s and into the 1990s signified a subtle blend of the soft and hard: a chiseled muscularity framed by beautiful clothes, makeup, and flawless complexion. Research studies into the reordering of consumption in British society in the 1980s have identified the effect of this on the expansion of social identities available for young men. For instance, Frank Mort has explained how the cultural landscape of Britain in the 1980s and '90s was shaped by the competitive dynamics of the market in ways never experienced before. At the level of popular politics, there is little doubt that Thatcherite market politics were mirrored in the new rituals of shopping and the display of personal goods for men. As Mort notes, the 1980s witnessed a period when the "commercial address to men provided a way into posing a number of broader questions

about contemporary changes to masculinity."⁶ While the relationship of young men to traditionally feminine roles of shopping, taking care of one's appearance, and style journalism had its origins in earlier decades, there was, however, an intensification of this in the 1980s and '90s. What ensued during these decades was an escalation in the plurality of masculinities. We know that by the late 1980s the fashion palette alone for male consumers was extensive. Evident in men's magazines, tabloids, and music videos, a greater variety of looks and poses had become available. Contrary to the poor-faced, stony images of American fashion models of the time, the British counterparts were feeding irony as one of their main selling points, which generated a diverse spectrum of styles. Changes in representations of the British male were encapsulated in two of the most popular magazines of the 1980s, *The Face* and *Arena*. Mort describes the significance of their effect, noting, "For the editorial team at *The Face* pluralism was also part of their overall understanding of contemporary sensibility. This combination of factors worked to produce *The Face* and *Arena* as polysemic texts about masculinity. Taken together, the two magazines suggested a flurry of discourse around the subjectivity of younger men, with little movement towards stabilisation.... what the style magazines appeared to offer was a seemingly endless variety of choices."⁷

All this had a strong bearing on the homosocial gaze that was directly influenced by what was happening in British pop music. Hence, the last two decades of the twentieth century consisted of a mix of representations, from androgynous boys to New Romantics and boy bands, all of which marketed a new brand of masculinity. Above all, a greater emphasis fell on narcissistic display that challenged traditional norms of virility and toughness. Indeed, the rhetoric of the marketplace seemed to reject conventional masculinity by distancing itself from heteronormativity. But this reshaping-through-style coterie was subtle and, arguably, deceptive and did not necessarily signify a direct rejection of patriarchy; on the contrary, it was as if the whole project was an elaborate extension of modernization.

In the wake of these developments and what preceded them was a spectacular expansion in male representations that introduced into the British pop scene personalities who could be labeled as queer. Among those who stood out during this period were artists such as Marc Almond, David Bowie, Boy George, Jarvis Cocker, Elton John, George Michael, Morrissey, Jimmy Somerville, and queer bands like Bronski Beat, the Communards, Culture Club, Depeche Mode, Frankie Goes to Hollywood, the Pet Shop Boys, and Soft Cell. Mainly to their advantage, these groups played on queerness, articulating the ambivalence of their

sexual orientation, thus highlighting a more ambiguous masculinity. Indeed, their distinctly camp mannerisms not only served to accentuate an opposition to gendered stereotypes, but also threw down the gauntlet for a new generation of pop stars born in the 1970s and '80s. Being a pop artist came to require a symbolized disruption of gender and sex norms. Hence, a steady process of destabilization has been detectable in the countless gender-bending spectacles where the emphasis on "being different" functioned on many fronts, where what was "in" and trend-setting wrangled with rigid inscriptions of fixed male identity.

Today it is often the case that when mainstream artists appropriate gender-ambivalent coding, their degree of acceptance is predicated on them *signifying* as queer rather than *being* queer. In this sense, queering knowingly spells out a form of appropriation where the practice of appearance swiftly substitutes that of self-representation. From this one might say that signifying queerness has very little to do with being conscious of queer politics. This might explain why queer performances can quickly undermine the subversive side of gender politics,[8] something that has its parallels in race, ethnicity, and class. Indeed, signifying as queer is a lot more about maintaining tensions than resolving them. Indisputably, the aim of androgynous and homosexual display in the music industry has been part of a spectacularization of gender play that mocks sets of conventions, but at a price!

Inevitably, interpreting queerness in popular music through performance raises numerous issues that are political. Furthermore, queer performativity exposes the arbitrariness of gender and its social construction. The "self" creates the "other" when queering is constructed in order to define straightness. In most pop forms of the late twentieth century, performance is predicated upon a form of visual display in which the focus falls primarily on gender and sexuality. Accordingly, it is the body that inscribes politics of representation. Put differently, the aestheticization of the body is part of politicizing style and expression. This implies that politics configure narratives that, in turn, allegorize libidinal positions of desire. Following on from this, representations of queerness, androgyny, and gayness in pop are inextricably linked to the technical and stylistic properties of sound that lock into music composition.[9]

Entering this debate from another angle, I want to suggest that queering makes expressive a space between sex and sexuality, for queer culture is urban, bold, and postmodern while at the same time it can be sexually transgressive. Significantly, strategies of queering set up a range of expectancies that feed off pleasure and sexual identification. What better example of this than the New York group Scissor Sisters, who register many of the changes and developments in recent pop history. Of

all the groups around at the time of this writing, they are the most camp in their mode of expression and, not surprisingly, more popular in the United Kingdom than in the United States.[10] Packaged as camp, Scissor Sisters' iconography and sound carry heavy symbolic connotations, not least because of the group's mix of openly gay and straight members.[11] As a group, Scissor Sisters neither fix nor deny gender identification. Instead, they tease out their act by a strategy of genderfuck that helps deconstruct concepts of difference at the same time it destabilizes the boundaries of heterosexist control. Overall, their fluidity of gender display is articulated by them pandering to a queer gaze that is encoded as much by their sound as their visual spectacle.

Historically, Scissor Sisters owe their success to MTV and its televisual platform for addressing a culture of shifting gazes and enunciating a host of different desires. Originally established for promoting pop songs and pop artists, the importance of MTV is indisputable. From a gay perspective, Steven Drukman has insisted on MTV's "gay draw" to videos that expose identities as fictional and inauthentic. Drukman points out how through the dreamlike experience of viewing MTV, "'reality' and 'appearance' are thrown into question."[12] To this I would add that the pop spectacle is predicated as much on musical codes of expression as visual displays. Accepting that the fetishization of bodies in pop videos produces meanings, we need to ask how pop performances encode meanings that can be read as queer. At this point, I am keen to argue that the packaging of desire in music videos does more than produce pleasure and states of gratification. It externalizes the idea of spectacle in terms of the discipline it imposes on different gendered bodies. In brief, music videos provide us with an apparatus for considering the objectification of men and women in specific social and cultural frames. What constitutes the viewer's desires and notions of "reality" varies considerably from one person to the next, which is influenced by how we respond to individual biography, not least when it is scripted through queering. In other words, identification with pop artists feeds off biographical details and not least gossip. Take Justin Timberlake, former member of boy band *NSYNC, ex-boyfriend of Britney Spears, and a rich male celebrity who is always featured alongside "beautiful" girls. His performances, as I read them, are personal narratives on masculinity and queering. At any rate, his producers are well aware that his sexual availability to a wide audience is conditional on record sales and survival. Yet the story does not end here. In shaping a sound that is queer, and genderless, Timberlake plays out his roles between fantasy and reality, where the pleasure principle lies in searching for the clues to who the real star is through video performances.

In contrast to Timberlake, another male artist who likes queering is Robbie Williams. His approach to this is quite different due to his nationality, culture, gender, space, and place. In 1995, the British press based their construction of the "Robbie phenomenon" around the popularized notion of lads misbehaving. Depictions of him were in stark contrast to the camp sensibility of Take That, where he was matched against the other members in color-coordinated costumes, making the group a success with gay audiences. More than any of the other band members, Williams was a prime target of gay rumors. In the summer of 1995, his departure from Take That was accompanied by heavy drinking bouts, tagging along with the notorious group Oasis, and drugging himself numb while partying. One decade later, Williams's rise to success could be best described as meteoric. In his chirpy cheeky manner, he succeeded in captivating a wide audience and, in the process, pushed up his currency as a gay icon. This is borne out in the November 2004 issue of Britain's most popular gay magazine, *Attitude*, where the editors invited the pop star back for what had become their monthly, legendary feature, "How Gay Are You?"—this time featuring Williams grinning like a Cheshire cat on the front page, tattoos well defined on a toned, shirtless torso. The selling caption was: "World Exclusive Interview: How Gay is Robbie Williams?" Reveling in stories and anecdotes concerning his sexual transgression, promiscuity, breakups, and rehabilitation, the interviewer had very little trouble in getting Williams to say what he wanted. The conclusion of this seven-page interview with glossy photos (one of them nude) was that the United Kingdom's "biggest pop star is a bona fide gay boy." This carried a qualifier in the next sentence that this is in a "kinda . . . in a ridiculous, pointless, SO post modern, gay magazine kind of way. Hurrah. Now bow Robbie and we'll dub you."[13] Perhaps most significant, Williams's responses to the gay press demonstrated a queer masquerade at work.

The declaration by *Attitude* that Williams is gay is fabulously convoluted by insinuations that he is also straight. (Yeah, well, right on!) While the claim that he is *gay* rather than *queer* plays little role in this case: both terms operate as equivalent mechanisms of seduction. Working out how this masquerade functions can shed light on how queering "dehomosexualizes" and denies any gay undercurrent because masquerading is all about constant change and deviation. As Chris Holmlund explains, masquerades "change according to who is looking, how, why, at whom." Holmlund's study of masculinity as a multiple masquerade acknowledges the role of masquerade in the doubling and hyping of masculinity in film. He writes, "If we are to assess how they (masquerades) are linked to power, and to resistance, we must think about how they function, and unravel the ways they are interconnected. We need,

in other words, to distinguish dressing up (embellishment) from putting on (parody, critique), from stepping out (affirmation, contestation)."[14]

Certainly, Williams's masquerade embraces all these elements. Indeed, the hyperspectacle of his toned body in the period of his album *Escapology*—as visible in interviews, live concerts, videos, and award ceremonies—demonstrates how tenuous "putting on" heterosexuality could be. Not surprisingly, homophobic reactions to Williams are quite common. As homophobia and homoeroticism are intertwined through stereotypes (read: queer and British), class (read: working-class Northerner), and race (read: white), Williams's hyping of masculinity through masquerade is not unproblematic. Indeed, pop acts are nostalgic where the gestures of the star fall into a lineage with which society is familiarized. Williams's homage to gay icons is well known. Lest we forget, his first single was a George Michael cover of the song "Freedom '90," a disaster in terms of record sales, but a most symbolic launch for his second single, "Old Before I Die," from his first solo album *Life Thru a Lens* (1997), which turned him into a pop star. Notably on this track, he asks the question, "Am I straight or gay?" In an unbridled ride through glam rock to alternative soft rock to dance, this album draws heavily on Oasis and other Britpop stars as Williams's camp style is epitomized by the aggressive burnout of songs like "Ego a Go Go" and "South of the Border." This is in contrast to his soft, mellow crooning on "Angels" and "Lazy Days," which displays an ability to exaggerate and oversentimentalize everything he sings about in the most endearing and cheeky manner. In all his songs, his identity comes over as a white, heterosexual lad misbehaving and having a good laugh, which must be reassuring for a wider public. Yet on another level his image is fluid, queer, and homoerotic in culturally obvious ways; British fans have little trouble in empathizing with how he, in Holmlund's terms, "dresses up," "puts on," and "steps out." Moreover, his roguish masquerade is constructed around a tough and sexy brand of masculinity that is exaggerated on and off various stages.[15]

Indeed, the import of the "bad lad" into mainstream pop culture—through queering and fooling about—is not new, and has a long literary and cinematic association in the form of other rebellious males who have queered, such as Marlon Brando, James Dean, and River Phoenix. All through rock and pop history rebels and angry young men have paved the way forward for brothers in arms.[16] And in Simon Reynolds's and Joy Press's description of the typical rock artist, "penetration, self-aggrandizement, violation, acceleration and death-wish are conflated in a single existential THRUST"[17]—an apt description for Williams's outpouring of emotional excess.

As evident in the *Attitude* article, there can be little doubt that the employment of interchangeable terms such as *gay*, *straight*, or *queer* can be contentious. The difficulties of such a positioning have entered scholarly debates on queer theory since the 1990s,[18] a period marked by groups of people shifting their self-descriptions from *gay* to *queer*—a political act that rejects a minority mode of toleration for a more thorough form of resistance. What the term *queer* designates today is far from unified or adequate in any generalized way. Rather, it gets into trouble each time it is employed. Let us dwell on this matter for a while.

For all intents and purposes, queer theory has attempted to bring to the surface a number of epistemological issues that are seldom addressed. According to Alan Petersen, men's studies, in their response to feminism, have been characterized by an essentialization of identity that has cast men as victims of social and political orders. In such scholarship sexuality is hardly dealt with, while those who do not fall into the categories of white, European, or heterosexual are often excluded. As Petersen indicates, it is a conventional modernist conceptual approach that emphasizes the self as unitary and presocial, the result of which is that "cultural assumptions about men, their desires and their identities remain unexamined."[19] Petersen argues that the challenges posed by queer theorists help draw attention to the implicit heterosexist biases of the disciplines of sociology and psychoanalysis, which have produced and "normalized" knowledge about the masculine. Above all, the study undertaken by Petersen reveals the queering of sexual identity by emphasizing the arbitrariness of conventional sexual taxonomy. In this regard, he demonstrates how the notion of a "natural" sexual orientation is problematic and difficult to sustain. Thus, denaturalizing the "natural" becomes part of not only understanding queering, but also reconceptualizing male identity. Indeed, queerness needs to be theorized beyond gender and also considered as part of a wider political debate.

To return to Justin Timberlake, his queerness—modeled on African American artists, such as Michael Jackson, Little Richard, and Prince— lies more in his sound than the spectacle of his act. On his debut album *Justified* (2002) his highly punctuated, falsetto phrases are delivered in a slick, quirky, and camped-up manner, where the emphasis is placed on being playful. Certainly, the Neptunes' production, which dominates *Justified*, contributes to the album's success, with a stylish feel that is more romantic than that found in most modern R & B recordings. As the prototype white boy next door who appropriates black culture, Timberlake is sophisticated and cunning. While any intention of appearing queer is probably inadvertent, he certainly comes across this way. Indeed, his musicality feeds off a sense of queerness that is artificial and contrived

at the same time it is fun. Almost effortlessly, his agile, well-trained body adapts easily to dancing and performing live. Like Williams, Timberlake has a vast fan base and accesses boy fans as much as girls. When it comes to his videos, his propensity for queering is realized through the organization of a homosocial gaze, which serves as a reminder that the circumstances that determine historical periods always promote one fantasy of masculinity over the other. Further, the erotics of his look as much as his sound function as a phantasmatic free play on the fixity of masculinity. Another way of saying this is that his masculinity is positioned within a buoyant cultural context in which a profound aesthetic investment in the body takes place. Take his second hit single, "Cry Me a River," from *Justified*: there is a moment when Timberlake tells a girl that she must have him "confused" with some other guy and that he is not like the rest of them. In the video of this song, directed by Francis Lawrence, any suggestion of sexual ambivalence through Timberlake's feminization or dance routines is avoided by his juxtapositioning to beautiful women. Much the same strategy of positioning is found in the video for his song "Senorita." Closer inspection of both these videos reveals a personal narrative that profiles the showbiz male, who is successful with women, in a space where masculinity exists in a desirable form that is as accessible for boys and girls.

Clearly, Timberlake cushions his identity in different ways from the generation that precedes him. It is as if queering can stretch him one notch further. Certainly, the sexual appeal of Timberlake's queering is different from Williams's, although both artists' acts involve complex processes of dominance and compliance through their inscriptions of "metrosexuality."[20] For instance, the almost obligatory inclusion of beautiful women permits their queer performativity, which is executed differently from predecessors such as Elton John, George Michael, Morrissey, the Pet Shop Boys, and Prince. But only up to a point can queering succeed as a useful mechanism for poking fun at the restrictive roles of sexual identification. In the pop world, queering is constituted by the calculated strategies that determine its results: high record sales, popularity, and control. Hence, queer masculinity differentiates itself through an oppositional relation to the genders it desires and does not desire. And during this process, queerness is naturalized and rationalized on heterosexual terms.

Let's go back to the band Scissor Sisters. It only took Jason Sellards (aka Jake Shears) and his college buddie, Scott Hoffman (aka Babydaddy) a few ideas on a Roland D-50 synthesizer to start something going. Originally named Dead Lesbian and the Fibrillating Scissor Sisters, they changed their name to a shortened version for their first

performance. Having met vocalist Ana Lynch (Ana Matronic), hostess of a decadent cabaret night at the Cock nightclub in New York's East Village, they went on to make their debut live appearance at the club in late 2001. These three were soon joined by guitarist Derek Gruen (Del Marquis) and drummer Patrick Seacvor (Paddy Boom) to complete the quintet Scissor Sisters. Soon a contract with Polydor, based on the production of a spate of demos, led to a year's work on their first album, *Scissor Sisters*, which was released in 2004 to enormous critical acclaim. Clearly inspired by artists such as the Bee Gees, Frankie Goes to Hollywood, Giorgio Moroder, the Pet Shop Boys, Roxy Music, the Smiths, and even fellow New Yorkers Blondie, Scissor Sisters charged in from a queer angle. Well aware of the prejudice that encircles the music industry, they produced an album that set out to challenge countless norms in rock music through elements that drew from burlesque and drag shows. Having succeeded in New York, Scissor Sisters delighted British and European audiences when they toured in early 2004. From their name (slang for a lesbian sex act) to their image to their sound, it is as if these four boys and a girl set out to show what it was to be queer in 2004.

Flaunting an unabashed brand of camp, their style is sassy, flashy, sexy, and naughty, with song titles, such as "Take Your Mama Out," "Comfortably Numb" (a completely revamped version of an earlier Pink Floyd song), "Filthy/Gorgeous," and "Tits on the Radio." Take the video of "Filthy/Gorgeous," for example, which reveals the group in the most decadent and debauched party nights imaginable, with band members being spanked, exposed to a variety of sex toys, and being ridden by a sex-starved midget. Scandalous in its narrative, this video is a narration of a song that questions our way of judging people on first glance and goes about breaking through barriers. Mostly, it is their brazen ability to cross over any style possible and still remain camp that signifies Scissor Sisters' queerness. Music this queer can only be matched by memorable live performances and videos, which might explain why it did not take long for Scissor Sisters to whip up a frenzy wherever they toured—well, with the exception of Middle America, of course.

From what has been said so far it might just seem a tad bit obvious that pop is a perfect field for investigating queering. One way of understanding how this works is through music's role as a socializing agent. Hence, the performing out of music gains its currency by communicating something to all of us about our own identities. Indeed, music provides a valuable field for the project of acknowledging the celebration of queer performativity. It would be, however, somewhat reductive to claim that pop stars who play out their queerness continually

challenge and disrupt heterosexual norms of sex and desire. Whether we are talking of Scissor Sisters, Timberlake, or Williams, the reading of their performances as queer always remains a matter of interpretation, and as such it takes little time to pry open the closet door and perceive the binarisms that enforce one another. My position is that we need a broad framework to continue asking questions about mainstream pop icons and, moreover, to call to attention the vagaries of performance within a space that consists of competing discourses; for music contains no inherent essence, and, as Gary C. Thomas has remarked, it has no "determinate subject matter and is available for use by anyone for any purpose."[21] Yet this is not to say that queer spaces are not controllable or policed. On the contrary, it is a sober reminder that more than ten years after Thomas's essay on George Frideric Handel's sexuality appeared, the control of the feminine and spaces occupied by homosexuality still reflect an ongoing crisis in gender politics, where queering is threatening and demonstrative of a type of vulnerability that provokes at the same time it destabilizes. To put this differently, the suspicions inherited from a patriarchal legacy are as discernible today as in almost every other period before now. If anything, the contemporary postmodern space is easier controlled in spaces where queering becomes acceptable as long as it is maintained and dependent on patriarchal control.

As noted earlier, the intricate relationship between queerness and masculinity raises questions concerned with the plurality of signification. When pop stars borrow from queer chic, their self-identification with gender ambivalence can be interpreted as nothing more than gender tourism. This is a claim that has been waged against Madonna as much as Prince for many years. For queerness can quickly become a strategy in pop music of postmodern intent without any form of political resistance. At any rate, the queer aesthetics that result from this provide a powerful mechanism for the further heterosexualization of the music industry. No better is this apparent than in the homoerotic component of spectatorship. In pop videos, as much as in popular cinema, the disavowal of the explicit homoerotic takes place through a process of queering, which raises the issue of narcissism and the mission of the not-so-new man.

Taking up this issue, Paul Burston has claimed that the manipulation of homoerotic imagery during the 1980s was largely due to the increased availability of nude male images in advertising.[22] Historically, this signaled a break with a tradition whereby women had been denied erotic images of the male and the social power to scrutinize. In contrast to gay men's access to the homoerotic and pornographic, the limited exposure of the male body in mainstream cinema is significant.[23] In her focus on this matter and

the heterosexual female gaze, Suzanne Moore has argued how the codes and conventions of gay porn have created new and different spaces for women as active spectators of homoeroticism. Moore fittingly unravels the construction of gendered subjectivity from a feminist perspective by questioning how we might "unmake the processes which we feel are oppressive."[24] Her suggestion challenges the ideologies that tell us that men and women are "naturally" different. Taking on board Moore's critique for a moment, it is useful to understand the paradox of male spectatorship and male objectification especially in the case of numerous mainstream artists who queer around. On this note, it would seem that the transference of intimacy between male fans and their pop heroes is powerfully unstated on many levels. Yet displays of sexual ambiguity are carefully regulated, and the erotic potential of any male performance is determined as much by a voyeuristic positioning of the spectator as by the performer himself. Williams, as much as Timberlake, is depicted in his videos as deriving autoerotic pleasure from the attention afforded him. Yet, constantly faced with the threat of homoeroticism or the gay gaze, these artists have no option other than to control the queer and homosocial gaze on their terms by extending their erotic interest and claiming pleasure. Thus, playing safe becomes a prerequisite for such strategies, as they want to communicate that they are "straight queer" through their self-centered sense of autoeroticism, which is anchored in their relationship to women on- and offscreen. In other words, in contrast to Scissor Sisters, their queerness is inscribed through them being recognized as "really" straight. As queer identification is never fixed, homoerotic representations dissolve the distinction between passive object and active subject.[25] The point here is that there is no guarantee of stability in these representations as mainstream male pop stars highlight the social constructedness and vulnerability of masculinity. Exploiting the boundaries of sexuality established by heteronormativity, they set up a range of contradictions that constitute new patterns of behavior that nevertheless construct an account of sexuality that is reducible to gender.

At this point I want to concentrate on the idea of a discursive construction of queering, a performing out of masculinity, which is not necessarily the same as the sexual desire that it is connected to. Indeed, queering in pop culture puts into question a range of strategies used for marketing music. The implications for this are that queering remains a tough site of contest. Queering parodies male domination by seeking empathy, and this is dealt with through humorous intent, the type of which we have become accustomed to in interviews, documentaries, videos, and live performances. Indeed, the function of humor in a queer

context is primarily to reduce anxiety, which often takes place through the jokey pleasures of gender identification. Up to a point, such strategies enable men to appear different and lay bare the constructed nature of conventional masculinity. Ostensibly, then, queerness challenges traditional behavior while also reinforcing it. More succinctly, the provocative tactics of many pop celebrities of the late twentieth century have been to undermine the security of heteronormativity. In Williams's case, his machismo, characterized by a muscular mesomorphic body, goes a long way in symbolizing an ideal that is connected to acceptable cultural views on masculinity and the role of the male as strong, aggressive, and efficacious. However, a tendency by him and other mainstream pop stars to appropriate gay culture and seek adoration from gay men can be perceived as problematic in that such a strategy defines a reaction that cashes in on privilege. This begs the question, to what extent does the mainstream pop artist challenge the prejudices of homophobia by constructing his own unique homoerotic appeal? Far from being a strategy of assimilation, then, queering is a sign of being different, or an expression of pleasure that is designed to appeal and titillate.

Let us say that the pop performer claims a particular type of space with territorial aggression: "This is my turf, plentifully bought by my immense popularity, so back off!" And it is in the domain of male homoeroticism that the potentially reactionary responses to queer texts surface. This would imply that when it comes to queer reception it is not necessarily "nonstraightness" that circumscribes liberation. As I hope to have suggested, there are valid reasons for understanding the complexities of queering. Shifting meanings of queering move in and out in ways that underline the polymorphous states of human difference, and, moreover, emphasize the imaginary identities that rely on structures of symbolic order. Behind what is queer is the indefinable, with all the inflections and nuances you choose to afford it. Finally, that queering can be a matter of enjoyment and pleasure beyond the bounds of pain and violation is clearly bound up with rhetorical devices that will never constitute an authentic identity. Rather, queering constructs a structural order that is conditional on the imperative of representations and the ongoing ordering of homophobic oppression.

NOTES

1. See Stan Hawkins, "Perspectives in Popular Musicology: Music, Lennox, and Meaning in 1990s Pop," *Popular Music* 15, no. 1 (1996): 17–36; Stan Hawkins, "I'll Never Be an Angel: Stories of Deception in Madonna's

Music," *Critical Musicology Journal* online (1997); Stan Hawkins, *Settling the Pop Score: Pop Texts and Identity Politics* (Aldershot, England: Ashgate, 2002); and Sheila Whiteley, Andy Bennett, and Stan Hawkins, eds., *Music, Space, and Place: Popular Music and Cultural Identity* (Aldershot, England: Ashgate, 2004).

2. Eve Kosofsky Sedgwick, *Between Men: English Literature and Male Homosocial Desire* (New York: Columbia University Press, 1986). Sedgwick implies that through relations of social and economic exchange there are varying degrees of homosociality in all men. When it comes to the homosocial bonds that operate between and within women, Sedgwick emphasizes that social and economic control gives way to an identification of being on the "other side" of the gender divide.

3. Mark Norris Lance and Alessandra Tanesini, "Identity Judgements, Queer Politics," in *Queer Theory*, ed. Iain Morland and Anabelle Willox (Basingstoke, England: Palgrave Macmillan, 2005), 171–86.

4. There are many examples of incidents in which queer theorists have skimmed over the history and writings of gay liberation and the politics that have paved the way forward for gay and lesbians since the 1970s. This is a critique taken up by scholars such as Dennis Altman, among others.

5. See, for example, Calvin Thomas, ed., *Straight with a Twist: Queer Theory and the Subject of Heterosexuality* (Urbana: University of Illinois Press, 2000); and Iain Morland and Anabelle Willox, eds., *Queer Theory* (Basingstoke, England: Palgrave Macmillan, 2005).

6. Frank Mort, *Cultures of Consumption: Masculinities and Social Space in Late-Twentieth-Century Britain* (London: Routledge, 1997), 10.

7. Ibid., 45.

8. Many studies have taken up this important issue. For example, research into Madonna's appropriation of queerness, homosexuality, and androgyny have been addressed by a range of scholars including bell hooks, Susan McClary, Pamela Robertson, and Sheila Whiteley.

9. In the first chapter of Hawkins, *Settling the Pop Score*, 9–12, I take up a discussion of musical codes and their compositional design by advocating an approach that is concerned with how codes attach arbitrarily to the discourses that construct them.

10. Scissor Sisters frontman Jakes Shears has informed the British press on various occasions that the reason the band has not been successful in their native America is because of the conservative values of Middle America. Shears is one of three gay members of the hit band, which include bassist Babydaddy and guitarist Del Marquis.

11. In recognizing the difficulty in employing the term *camp* in conjunction with *queer*, it is an important part of my argument to explore how these two terms interlock at the same time they blur the distinction with gayness. I have explored the effect of this in my study of Madonna's construction of

campness through performativity. See Stan Hawkins, "On Performativity and Production in Madonna's Music," in *Music, Space, and Place: Popular Music and Cultural Identity*, ed. Sheila Whiteley, Andy Bennett, and Stan Hawkins (Aldershot, England: Ashgate, 2004), 180–90.

12. Steve Drukman, "The Gay Gaze, or Why I Want My MTV," in *A Queer Romance: Lesbians, Gay Men, and Popular Culture*, ed. Paul Burston and Colin Richardson (London: Routledge, 1995), 88.

13. Paul Flynn with Matthew Todd, "How Gay are You? Robbie Williams," *Attitude*, November 2004, p. 46.

14. Chris Holmlund, "Masculinity as Multiple Masquerade: The 'Mature' Stallone and the Stallone Clone," in *Screening the Male: Exploring Masculinities in Hollywood Cinema*, ed. Steve Cohan and Ina Rae Hark (London: Routledge, 1993), 213–29.

15. At the beginning of 2005, Williams's appearance on *Little Britain*, a popular British television show, revealed the artist in drag. Sporting a pink dress with large fake breasts and a curly wig, Williams was reputed to say that he felt that he had discovered his real self. During the sketch, he was persuaded to dress up as a woman and later pranced down the street shouting, "I'm a lady!"

16. For example, groups such as the the Doors, Guns N' Roses, Nirvana, the Rolling Stones, the Sex Pistols, and the Stranglers epitomize these types of men.

17. Simon Reynolds and Joy Press, *The Sex Revolts: Gender, Rebellion, and Rock 'n' Roll* (Cambridge, Mass.: Harvard University Press, 1995), 117.

18. See, for example, Alan Petersen, "'Queering' Sexual Identity," in *Unmasking the Masculine: "Men" and "Identity" in a Skeptical Age* (London: Sage, 1998), 96–119. Petersen argues that a central problematic in queer theory involves the question of "nonstraightness." As this includes so many categories, there is a need to question what happens to the sexual minorities and marginalized groups who seek protection within well-defined political communities.

19. Petersen, "'Queering' Sexual Identity," 113.

20. British author Mark Simpson has been credited by the *New York Times* as coming up with the term *metrosexual* when it first appeared in an article for the *Independent* in 1994. Originally used by Simpson, satirically, to point out a new generation of men who were in touch with their feminine sides, regardless of their sexuality, the term is now in standard use. Football star David Beckham has certainly played his part in the popularization of the metrosexual in mainstream culture all around the world. See Simpson, *Sex Terror: Erotic Misadventures in Pop Culture* (Binghamton, N.Y.: Harrington Park Press, 2002), for a collection of parodic essays that addresses the rise of the meterosexual who is always in easy reach of the metropolis and whose existence depends on hairdressers, gyms, clubs, and top clothing-design shops. And if one imagines that this only pertains to the major world

capitals, take a visit to Oslo, where ever since the mid-1990s the majority of young men from the affluent west side of the city have jumped onto the bandwagon of metrosexuality. This is mainly attributable to the profound influence of British popular culture on Norway—especially through pop music and football.

21. Gary C. Thomas, "Was George Frideric Handel Gay?" in *Queering the Pitch: The New Gay and Lesbian Musicology*, ed. Philip Brett, Elizabeth Wood, and Gary C. Thomas (London: Routledge, 1994), 187.

22. See Paul Burston, "Just a Gigolo? Narcissism, Nellyism, and the 'New Man' Theme," in *A Queer Romance: Lesbians, Gay Men, and Popular Culture*, ed. Paul Burston and Colin Richardson (London: Routledge, 1995), 111–22.

23. Yvonne Tasker takes up numerous debates around the posturing of male bodies and their different inscriptions in Hollywood cinema; see Tasker, *Spectacular Bodies: Gender, Genre, and the Action Cinema* (London: Routledge, 1993).

24. Suzanne Moore, "Getting a Bit of the Other—the Pimps of Postmodernism," in *Male Order: Unwrapping Masculinity*, ed. Rowena Chapman and Jonathan Rutherford (London: Lawrence and Wishart, 1988), 170.

25. Kobena Mercer, "Skin Head Sex Thing: Racial Difference and the Homoerotic Imaginary," in *How Do I Look? Queer Film and Video*, ed. Bad Object-Choices (Seattle: Bay Press, 1991), 182.

CONTRIBUTORS

Stephen Amico is a Ph.D. candidate in the ethnomusicology program at the Graduate Center of the City University of New York (CUNY). Having recently completed sixteen months of fieldwork in St. Petersburg and Moscow, he is presently writing his doctoral dissertation, which will focus on the connections between gay men and popular music in Russia. He has been an adjunct faculty member within the CUNY system, where he is currently a writing fellow, and has published articles in *Popular Music* and *Men and Masculinities: A Social, Cultural, and Historical Encyclopedia*, as well as having presented papers at various local and international conferences. His research interests include (homo)sexuality, affect, and psychoanalysis.

Paul Attinello is a lecturer in the International Centre for Music Studies at the University of Newcastle upon Tyne, United Kingdom; he has also taught at the University of Hong Kong and University of California–Los Angeles. His 1997 dissertation analyzed the aesthetic implications of European avant-garde vocal music in the 1960s. He has published in the *Journal of Musicological Research, Musik-Konzepte, Musica/Realtá*, the revised *New Grove*, and several collections. He coedited the first three volumes of the newsletter of the Gay and Lesbian Study Group of the American Musicological Society and contributed to *Queering the Pitch: The New Lesbian and Gay Musicology* (Routledge, 1994). Current

projects include a monograph on music about AIDS, a coedited book on *Buffy the Vampire Slayer*, and books on Meredith Monk and Gerhard Stäbler.

Jeffrey Callen received his Ph.D. in 2006 in ethnomusicology from the University of California–Los Angeles, where he was a teaching fellow from 2003 to 2004. His dissertation (*French Fries in the Tagine: Re-Imaging Moroccan Popular Music*) examined alternative trends in Moroccan popular music. In 2002, he was awarded a Fulbright-Hayes fellowship to research popular music in Morocco. He received his B.A. from the University of California–Berkeley and his M.A. in music from the University of California–Santa Barbara. His master's thesis (*Musical Community: The "Blues Scene" in North Richmond, California*, 2001) examined how the presence and eventual loss of the blues scene in North Richmond affected community life. Jeffrey has contributed to *Performance and Popular Music: History, Place, and Time* (Ashgate, 2006) and *Pacific Review of Ethnomusicology* 9(1): 1999.

Rachel Devitt is currently working on her Ph.D. in ethnomusicology at the University of Washington, Seattle, where she studies pop music and drag in North America and pop music and diaspora in Southeast Asia. She has presented her work at the annual meetings of the Society for Ethnomusicology, the International Association of the Study for Popular Music, and the Experience Music Project Pop Conference. She teaches classes in American popular and folk musics at the university and has held a research internship at Seattle's Experience Music Project pop music museum. Rachel also works as a music critic, and her writing has appeared in publications such as the *Seattle Times*, the *Seattle Weekly*, the *Village Voice*, and the *Washington Blade*.

Stan Hawkins is professor of musicology at Oslo University, Norway. He coedited (with Sheila Whiteley and Andy Bennett) and contributed a chapter to *Music, Space, and Place: Popular Music and Cultural Identity* (Ashgate, 2004) and is the author of *Settling the Pop Score: Pop Texts and Identity Politics* (Ashgate, 2002). He has contributed chapters to *Madonna's Drowned Worlds* (Ashgate, 2004); *Analyzing Pop* (Cambridge University Press, 2003); *Reading Pop: Approaches to Textual Analysis* (Oxford University Press, 2000); and *Sexing the Groove: Popular Music and Gender* (Routledge, 1998). He is the current editor of two major journals, *Popular Musicology Online* and the Norwegian journal of research, *Studia Musicologica Norvegica*.

Judith Halberstam is professor of English at the University of Southern California, Los Angeles. She teaches courses in cultural studies, gender studies, film theory, and queer studies. She is the author of *Female Masculinity* (Duke University Press, 1998) and *Skin Shows: Gothic Horror and the Technology of Monsters* (Duke University Press, 1995); she co-authored *The Drag King Book* (Serpent's Tail, 1999) with Del LaGrace Volcano and coedited *Posthuman Bodies* (Indiana University Press, 1995) with Ira Livingston. Judith has just completed a book called *In A Queer Time and Place: Transgender Bodies, Subcultural Lives* (New York University Press, 2005).

Freya Jarman-Ivens is a lecturer in popular music at Liverpool University, United Kingdom, and has recently completed her doctoral thesis, which explores ways in which identity and authenticity are fragmented and problematized in late twentieth-century popular music, especially through use of the voice. Her research interests include queer theory and performativity, psychoanalytic theory, and technology and musical production. Freya's favored musical material for analysis ranges from easy listening to alternative rock and hip-hop. She is the coeditor (with Santiago Fouz-Hernández) of *Madonna's Drowned Worlds* (Ashgate, 2004), a collection of new essays on Madonna's subcultural transformations, and is also working on a volume of new articles on masculinities and popular music. Freya has also contributed to the Proceedings of the 13th Biennial International Association for the Study of Popular Music (IASPM) International Conference, 2005 (Rome, forthcoming) and *Popular Musicology Online* (forthcoming).

Sarah Kerton is currently undertaking her Ph.D on the constructions of youth sexualities in popular music at the University of Salford, Greater Manchester, United Kingdom. She teaches popular musicology at the university and is also a research fellow on a European Social Fund (ESF) project, Making Waves, which enables women's participation within the digital creative industries. Sarah has contributed papers to the United Kingdom and Ireland 2004 International Association for the Study of Popular Music (IASPM) conference and Hetero Factory (Norrköping, Sweden, 2006). She is also heavily involved in the Manchester band scene and fronts a queer cabaret band, The Dick Ban Dykes.

Vanessa Knights is a senior lecturer in the School of Modern Languages at the University of Newcastle upon Tyne, United Kingdom. She began working at the university in 1995 as a lecturer in Hispanic studies after completing her Ph.D. at the University of Cambridge, United Kingdom,

on the work of contemporary Spanish author Rosa Montero. She is on the management committee of the Centre for Gender Studies at the University of Newcastle upon Tyne and has guest lectured on gender studies at the Universidad de Chile and Pontificia Universidad Católica de Santiago de Chile. She has coauthored *A New History of Spanish Writing, 1939 to the 1990s*, published a monograph on Montero, contributed chapters to *Contemporary Latin American Cultural Studies* (Arnold, 2003) and *Cultural Popular: Studies in Spanish and Latin American Popular Culture* (Peter Lang, 2002), and written diverse articles on Spanish feminism, women writers, fantasy and science fiction, and the bolero. Vanessa is currently researching constructions of identity (individual, collective, national, and transnational) in the bolero in Cuba, Mexico, and Puerto Rico for a book, and coediting volumes on popular music and national identity, the bolero in literature, and music in the television series *Buffy the Vampire Slayer* (with Paul Attinello).

Emma Mayhew completed her Ph.D. thesis (*The Representation of Women in Popular Music: The Feminist, Feminine, and Musical Subject*) at the University of Wollongong, Australia. She also has taught cultural studies, gender studies, and sociology at the university and currently works for the Federal Department of Communications, Information Technology, and the Arts. Her research interests include the music press, fan cultures, and the representation of the singer's voice in popular culture. She contributed a chapter to *Music, Space, and Place: Popular Music and Cultural Identity* (Ashgate, 2004).

Anno Mungen is professor of musicology at the University of Bonn, Germany. He received his Ph.D. from Technische Universität, Berlin, in 1995 with a dissertation on Gaspare Spontini and the contemporary German opera (Tutzing: Schneider, 1997). He studied the flute at Staatliche Hochschule für Musik in Duisburg, Germany, as well as musicology (with Carl Dahlhaus and others) and art history at Technische Universität, Berlin. From 1995 until 2002 he was the academic director of research projects and assistant professor in the music department at Mainz University. His postdoctoral thesis (*An Archaeology of Film Music: Panoramas, Dioramas, and Tableaux Vivants in Multimedia Performances in the 19th and Early 20th Centuries*, Remscheid: Gardez Verlag, 2006) dealt with the simultaneous fusion of sound and image, which involved a one-year research scholarship in the United States. Teaching experiences include classes at Hanns Eisler Hochschule, Berlin; Johannes Gutenberg Universität, Mainz; and Universität Bayreuth.

Jason Lee Oakes received his Ph.D. in ethnomusicology from Columbia University, New York, where his thesis was entitled *Losers, Punks, and Queers (and Elvii too): Identification and "Identity" at New York Music Tribute Events*. Specializing in urban studies and popular musics, he is now a professor at Manhattan College. His most recent publication is "Pop Music, Racial Imagination, and the Sounds of Cheese: Notes on Loser's Lounge," in *Bad Music: The Music We Love To Hate*, edited by C. Washburne and M. Derno (Routledge, 2004). He has also contributed reviews to the *Yearbook for Traditional Music* and presented papers at international conferences held by the Society for Ethnomusicology and the International Association for the Study of Popular Music (IASPM).

Gilad Padva is a doctoral student at the Shirley and Leslie Porter School of Cultural Studies and the department of film and television at Tel Aviv University, Israel. His thesis focuses on mainstream and alternative visualization of sexuality and desire in American and British cinema and television in the 1990s and early 2000s. He has published articles about queer aspects of popular culture, pop music, and gender studies in the *International Journal of Sexuality and Gender Studies, Sexualities, Women & Language, Feminist Media Studies,* the *Journal of Communication and Critical/Cultural Studies,* the *Journal of Communication Inquiry, Cinema Journal,* and *Film Criticism,* and wrote entries for several international encyclopedias. Gilad has also presented many papers at international academic conferences in the United Kingdom, United States, Korea, Spain, and Israel.

Mario Rey is associate professor of ethnomusicology at the East Carolina University (ECU) School of Music. He specializes in traditional, vernacular, and art musics of Latin America and the Caribbean. Current research projects involve issues of bimusicality, musical acculturation, and immigrant identities. He has published numerous articles in professional journals and is the director of Zamba Yawar, ECU Afro-Andean Ensemble. Mario teaches world music, ethnomusicology, music theory, and non-Western instruments (quena, quenacho, zampoña, charango, and guitarrón) and is an active member and Past President of the Society for Ethnomusicology Southeast and Caribbean (SEMSEC) chapter. He is also a member of the College Music Society, International Association for the Study of Popular Music (IASPM) Latinoamérica, and the Society for Music Theory. He was the recipient of the 2003–2004 Board of Governors Distinguished Professor for Outstanding Teaching Award.

Karen Tongson is assistant professor of English and gender studies at the University of Southern California, Los Angeles. She previously held a University of California President's Postdoctoral Fellowship in Literature at the University of California–San Diego and a Humanities Research Institute Residential Research Fellowship on "Queer Locations: Race, Space and Sexuality" at the University of California–Irvine. She received her Ph.D. in English from the University of California–Berkeley in 2003 for a project on the literary history of identity politics, entitled "Ethical Excess: Stylizing Difference in Victorian Critical Prose from Carlyle to Wilde." Her next major research project focuses on an emergent queer-of-color suburban imaginary in popular culture, literature, and the media arts. She has published essays on a range of topics from Thomas Moore's *Irish Melodies* to dyke film maker and provocateur, Lynne Chan's *JJ Chinois* projects. Karen is currently guest-editing a special issue for the journal *Nineteenth-Century Literature* on "Lesbian Aesthetics, Aestheticizing Lesbianism." She has contributed to *GLQ: A Journal of Lesbian and Gay Studies* 10: 2004; *The Idea of Music in Victorian Fiction* (Ashgate, 2003); *Repercussions: Critical and Alternative Viewpoints on Music and Scholarship* 9(1): Fall 2001; and *American Indian Culture and Research Journal (AICRJ)* 20(4): 1996.

Lloyd Whitesell is assistant professor at McGill University, Montréal, Quebec, Canada. He was awarded the Philip Brett Award, given by the Gay and Lesbian Study Group of the American Musicological Society, for *Queer Episodes in Music and Modern Identity*, coedited with Sophie Fuller (University of Illinois Press, 2002). Lloyd has also published articles in the *Journal of the American Musicological Society, Popular Music, American Music,* and *Women and Music.* He is currently working on a book manuscript, *The Music of Joni Mitchell* (Oxford University Press).

INDEX